EFFECTIVE GROUP DISCUSSION
Theory and Practice

TWELFTH EDITION

EFFECTIVE GROUP DISCUSSION

Theory and Practice

GLORIA J. GALANES
Missouri State University

KATHERINE ADAMS
California State University at Fresno

Boston   Burr Ridge, IL   Dubuque, IA   Madison, WI   New York
San Francisco   St. Louis   Bangkok   Bogotá   Caracas   Kuala Lumpur
Lisbon   London   Madrid   Mexico City   Milan   Montreal   New Delhi
Santiago   Seoul   Singapore   Sydney   Taipei   Toronto

Higher Education

EFFECTIVE GROUP DISCUSSION: THEORY AND PRACTICE
Published by McGraw-Hill, a business unit of The McGraw-Hill Companies, Inc., 1221 Avenue of the Americas, New York, NY, 10020. Copyright © 2007, 2004, 2001, 1998, 1995, 1992, 1989, 1986, 1982, 1978, 1974, 1967 by The McGraw-Hill Companies, Inc. All rights reserved. No part of this publication may be reproduced or distributed in any form or by any means, or stored in a database or retrieval system, without the prior written consent of The McGraw-Hill Companies, Inc., including, but not limited to, in any network or other electronic storage or transmission, or broadcast for distance learning. Some ancillaries, including electronic and print components, may not be available to customers outside the United States.

This book is printed on acid-free paper.

1 2 3 4 5 6 7 8 9 0 WCT/WCT 0 9 8 7 6

ISBN-13: 978-0-07-313523-6
ISBN-10:   0-07-313523-2

Vice President and Editor-in-Chief: *Emily Barrosse*
Publisher: *Phillip A. Butcher*
Sponsoring Editor: *Suzanne S. Earth*
Senior Developmental Editor: *Jennie Katsaros*
Senior Marketing Manager: *Leslie Oberhuber*
Managing Editor: *Jean Dal Porto*
Project Manager: *Meghan Durko*
Art Director: *Jeanne Schreiber*
Designer: *Marianna Kinigakis*

Cover and Interior Design: *Ellen Pettengell*
Photo Research Coordinator: *Natalia C. Peschiera*
Cover Credit: © *Walter Hodges/Photodisc/Getty Images*
Media Project Manager: *Stacy Bentz*
Media Producer: *Nancy Garcia*
Production Supervisor: *Jason I. Huls*
Composition: *10/12 Garamond, by Techbooks*
Printing: *45# New Era Matte, Quebecor World*

Photo Credits: Page 1: © Stuart Pearce/age fotostock; 13: © Jose Luis Pelaez, Inc./Corbis; 47: © Stephen St. John/National Geographic Image Collection; 62: © Stuart Pearce/age fotostock; 63: © Syracuse Newspapers/The Image Works; 107: © Digital Vision/Getty Images; 113: © Purestock; 141: © Digital Vision/Getty Images; 167: © Marty Heitner/The Image Works; 201: © Michael Pole/Corbis; 246: © Michael Newman/PhotoEdit; 281: © Javier Larrea/age fotostock; All chapter opener images: © Walter Hodges/Photodisc/Getty Images

Library of Congress Cataloging-in-Publication Data

Galanes, Gloria J.
    Effective group discussion: theory and practice / Gloria J. Galanes, Katherine Adams,
with John K. Brilhart.—12th ed.
        p. cm.
    Includes index.
    ISBN-13: 978-0-07-313523-6 (softcover : alk. paper)
    ISBN-10: 0-07-313523-2 (softcover : alk. paper)
    1. Small groups. 2. Communication in small groups. 3. Group problem solving.
4. Discussion. I. Adams, Katherine H., 1954- II. Brilhart, John K. III. Brilhart, John K.
Effective group discussion. IV. Title.
HM736.B75 2007
302.3'4—dc22

                                                             2006041863

The Internet addresses listed in the text were accurate at the time of publication. The inclusion of a Web site does not indicate an endorsement by the authors or McGraw-Hill, and McGraw-Hill does not guarantee the accuracy of the information presented at these sites.

www.mhhe.com

Brief Contents

Contents

PART III

Group Observation and Evaluation Tools   167

PART IV

Small Group throughput Processes   201

Preface

The 12th edition represents a substantial revision and reorganization of the material. In order to prepare for this revision, we met, via telephone, with a focus group of users and nonusers of this text and listened carefully to what they told us. This edition incorporates many of their suggestions, along with ideas we ourselves have been developing over the last few years. Our primary goal remains the same: to help students become more effective small group members and leaders by giving them the research-based tools—both in terms of theoretical understandings and practical suggestions—for effective participation in groups. We have also focused on another primary goal: to help instructors present the material in a way that is logical and accessible for how they teach the course. When students complete their study of small groups, we hope they will know how to use the information and tools we present and understand why one group is satisfying and another feels like torture. Most important of all, we hope they will understand what they can *do* about it.

Effective Group Discussion focuses on secondary groups, such as work groups, committees, task forces, self-directed work teams, and other small groups with tasks to complete. The text is written for academically prepared beginning students of small group communication and is likely to be most useful to upper-division students who can appreciate the extensive research base that grounds the narrative. Increasingly, students who use *Effective Group Discussion* have taken a previous introductory course in communication. For this reason, we have streamlined our discussion about the foundations of human communicating. The text also serves well as a reference source for advanced communication students, consultants, or group leaders.

Overview

Generally, the chapters move the discussion from systems inputs to throughput processes to outcomes. The text is designed so that instructors have the flexibility to skim or skip chapters or cover them in a different order. For instance, we offer a section that covers basic communication theory for students without a previous course in communication, but this section can be skimmed quickly if it reviews materials that students already know.

Part I presents an overview of small group and human communication theory. Chapter 1 introduces several ideas developed in subsequent chapters:

the importance of small groups in our lives, types of groups, what constitutes ethical behavior, and why members should become participant-observers in their groups. Chapters 2 and 3 present the basics of communication theory that serve as the foundation for studying small groups. Students who have already had an introductory course in communication may skim these chapters quickly to review previously learned material. In Chapter 4, we present systems theory as the organizing framework used throughout the text.

Part II begins the discussion of group developing by focusing on the members, the main small group inputs. Chapter 5 introduces the importance of diversity and the contribution that members' cultures and co-cultures make to that diversity. Chapter 6 discusses how member characteristics contribute to the roles that members play in groups.

Part III, Observing and Evaluating Groups, presents tools for assessing and improving small groups. Many instructors told us they would prefer to have this information presented earlier in the semester so that students can use the observation tools as they are learning the concepts. Even so, it will be easy to present this chapter at the end of the course if that fits the instructor's organizational preference.

Part IV focuses on the development of the group as an entity by presenting information about a variety of throughput processes. Chapter 8 consolidates logically the information about norms, fantasy themes, and cohesiveness; and Chapter 9 presents conceptual information about the leadership and leadership development.

Part V discusses the importance of having appropriate decision-making and problem-solving processes to improve the quality of group outputs. To make these processes more effective, groups must use the most up-to-date and relevant material they can find, which is the topic of the Internal Appendix that initiates this discussion of decision making and problem solving. Rather than talking about each process separately, we continue to devote two chapters to these processes, but have integrated discussion of both processes. Chapter 10 focuses on the first three steps of the problem-solving process: problem description and analysis, generation of solutions, and evaluation of those solutions. Chapter 11 concludes the discussion of problem solving and decision making by looking at the emergence of consensus and what can go wrong in the problem-solving process, solution implementation, and the use of technology to assist problem solving and decision making. Chapter 12 focuses on how conflict, if managed well, can improve group decisions. Chapter 13 provides guidelines for designated group leaders; it can serve as a useful primer for leaders because it pulls together much of the information discussed throughout the text.

Many groups must make public presentations based on their work, which is the topic of the appendix. Basic information about public speaking is discussed, but the appendix also focuses on how groups can organize group presentations of their work so that the presentation is seamless and smooth.

Changes

This 12th edition of *Effective Group Discussion* is substantially reorganized to fit the way many instructors have told us they prefer to teach.

- We have retained our research base, have consolidated conceptual information where possible, removed material and examples that seemed redundant or out-of-date (*Consider This* boxes and *Quotes* from small group leaders), and added current theoretical information.
- We have integrated each chapter's opening case more thoroughly with the information presented throughout the chapter.
- Instead of presenting small group techniques in one chapter, we have integrated these techniques throughout the text so that students can more readily link the concepts to the techniques.
- We have continued to develop our discussion of technological issues and have enhanced our discussion of diversity and linked cultural and co-cultural differences more closely to that discussion.
- We believe that problem solving and decision making are intertwined; discussing each process individually artificially separates them. Thus, we have reorganized our discussion into two chapters that talk about both processes as they occur simultaneously during a group's discussions.
- We have reorganized our discussion of member characteristics, included additional information about attitudes and behaviors relevant to small groups, and linked these member characteristics explicitly to the development of member roles.
- We have incorporated more tools and assessments that students can use throughout the course.
- We have replaced the overall chapter summary at the end of each chapter with several recap boxes placed throughout the chapter. We have removed the end-of-chapter exercises that most instructors told us they did not use.
- As always, we have updated this edition with the most current research available.

Features

Case Studies: Each chapter begins with a case study illustrating that chapter's main points. These are real-life stories designed to help students retain key concepts and understand how that chapter's information is relevant to the real world. We have linked these case studies more explicitly to information presented throughout the chapter.

Recap Boxes: We have placed Recap boxes—internal summaries—throughout each chapter. These replace the end-of-chapter summaries and, we believe, will be more effective because they provide logical "breathing places" for students to review what they have learned.

Emphasis on Diversity: The importance of diversity and intercultural communication cannot be overemphasized! In addition to a chapter devoted to this topic, relevant information about diversity is distributed throughout the text.

Learning Aids: Each chapter includes *learning objectives* and *margin key terms,* which are boldface in the text. The end of chapter material includes *Questions for Review* and a *bibliography* that provides additional reading material. The *Glossary* at the end of the text provides definitions of all key terms.

Online Learning Center at **www.mhhe.com/galanes12** provides online activities for students that supplement the topics in the chapter. An icon at the end of each chapter guides students to relevant tools and activities, including interactive quizzes, and glossary flashcards.

Resources for Instructors

Instructor's Resource CD-ROM with the *Instructor's Manual* and *Testbank:* The manual provides sample syllabi, sample lecture notes, additional exercises, writing assignments, "writing to learn" assignments, suggestions for relevant videos and films that illustrate chapter contents, and a test bank of objective and essay questions to help the instructor.

Videos: Two videos are available with the text. *Communicating Effectively in Small Groups* offers four scenarios that lend themselves to extended analysis. Each scenario focuses on a specific small group topic: leadership, conflict, effective problem solving, and ineffective problem solving. *Communicating in Groups: Short Takes* provides 24 short scenes, each depicting a specific concept discussed in the text.

Web site: The Online Learning Center at **www.mmhe.com/galanes12** provides the instructor's manual, PowerPoint slides, and up-to-date weblinks.

Gloria J. Galanes
Katherine Adams

Acknowledgments

We would like to thank all of the instructors and students who have used *Effective Group Discussion*. We welcome your written reactions to its content and composition. You can send your comments to us via the Department of Communication, Missouri State University, Springfield, Missouri; or the Department of Communication, California State University, Fresno, California.

May all your groups be enjoyable and satisfying!

Numerous people contributed to this book; we can name only a few. First, we acknowledge our debt to instructors and writers Freed Bales, Ernest Bormann, Elton S. Carter, B. Aubrey Fisher, Larry Frey, Kenneth Hance, Randy Hirokawa, Sidney J. Parnes, J. Donald Phillips, M. Scott Poole, Marvin Shaw, Victor Wall, and W. Woodford Zimmerman.

Finally, we want to acknowledge the vision and contributions of Jack Brilhart, who wrote the first version of this text in the late 1960s as one monograph in a communication series. For many years, Jack has shared his expertise, his passion for understanding and working with small groups, and his vast experience working with a variety of groups. We enjoyed working with him and appreciated his generosity. Jack died last year. We will greatly miss him.

The following instructors were exceptionally helpful in supplying thoughtful, carefully considered suggestions:

Bruce G. Bryski
Buffalo State College

W. Paul Buczko
Chaffey College

Christy C. Coker
University of North Carolina, Charlotte

Dennis S. Gouran
Pennsylvania State University

Sandy H. Hanson
University of North Carolina, Charlotte

Emily J. Langan
Wheaton College

The Foundations of Communicating in Groups

The four chapters in Part I provide introductory information to focus your study of small group communication. Chapter 1 introduces important terms and concepts used throughout the text. Chapter 2 lays the groundwork for understanding the communicative dynamics of small group interaction. Chapter 3 continues with fundamental ideas about verbal and nonverbal behavior in small groups. Chapter 4 presents systems theory as a framework for studying and understanding small groups.

The Small Groups in Everyone's Life

CENTRAL MESSAGE

If you want to succeed in modern organizational and social life, you must understand how to be a productive member of a group.

STUDY OBJECTIVES

As a result of studying Chapter 1 you should be able to:

1. Explain why you need to understand small group communication and to participate productively in small group discussions.
2. Use correctly the terms presented in this chapter, particularly *group*, *small group*, *small group discussion*, and *ethics*.
3. Describe the difference between various primary and secondary groups.
4. Describe the five ethical principles most relevant to small group communication.
5. Consciously and intentionally become a participant-observer during group discussions.

In the Grimm fairy tale *The Bremen Town Musicians,* an old donkey, grown too frail for hard labor in the fields, knows his days are numbered.[1] He sets off for Bremen to become a town musician. Along the way, he meets a decrepit dog, too old to hunt, that has run away from the master who plans to kill him. Donkey and Dog soon encounter an ancient cat, escaped from the mistress who plans to drown her because she has become too slow to catch mice. Presently, the three are joined by Rooster, who has discovered his mistress's plan to offer him up as Sunday lunch. On their way to Bremen, the four friends spy a brightly lit cottage in the distance. Hoping the owner will offer them food and shelter for the night, Donkey peeks in the window. He sees robbers getting ready to enjoy a tasty feast. The animals devise a plan to frighten the robbers away. Donkey places his forelegs on the window, Dog stands on his back, Cat climbs on Dog, and Rooster perches on Cat's head. Donkey brays, Dog barks, Cat meows, and Rooster crows. The terrified robbers scatter, leaving the feast for the four friends to devour. Later, with the lights out and the animals sleepy, one robber returns to investigate. His candle makes Cat's eyes look like live coals, which he tries to light. Cat shrieks and claws him. Running away, the robber trips on Dog, who bites him, and stumbles on Donkey, who kicks him. Rooster, aroused by the noise, crows "Cock-a-doodle-doo." The thoroughly petrified robber explains to his cronies that a witch has claimed the cottage. The witch scratched him, a man stabbed him, a monster beat him, and a judge condemned him. The robbers abandon the cottage for good. The four friends decide to forgo becoming musicians in Bremen—they will live happily ever after in the cottage instead.

This fable makes an important point about real-life groups. One person—or animal—alone does not have all the talent, skill, or ideas to accomplish a complex task. But by working together, individuals in a group can achieve far more than individuals working alone. If your project is at all complex, you need others to help carry it out. A small group can help ensure your chances of success.

Small groups, whether the context is education, business and industry, health care, social services, religion, family life, politics, or government work, are the basic building blocks of our society and are themselves smaller models of the interactive processes operating in the society as a whole.[2] We agree with Lawrence Frey, a leading scholar of small group communication, who believes that the small group is *the* most important social formation:

> Every segment of our society—from the largest multinational organization to the political workings of federal, state, city, and local governments to the smallest community action group to friendship groups to the nuclear and extended family—relies on groups to make important decisions, socialize members, satisfy needs, and the like.[3]

We spend a tremendous amount of our time in formal and informal groups. For example, Cole reported that executives spent an average of half their time in business meetings,[4] and Lawren noted that there are an estimated 20 million meetings each day in the United States.[5] When you add to this the amount of time people spend in groups unconnected with work, you begin to understand how pervasive groups are in modern society. Moreover, the ability to work effectively as part of a team requires skills that must be practiced. In a national survey of 750 leading American companies, 71.4 percent of respondents mentioned "ability to work in teams" as an essential skill for MBA graduates—more important by far than knowledge of quantitative and statistical techniques.[6] If you want to get anything done—on the job or anywhere else—you must learn how to be a good team member.

Four important ideas about groups are introduced in this chapter to get you started learning about effective group membership. **First, groups exist to meet important human needs.** Schutz explained that groups meet needs for inclusion, affection, and control: a need to belong and be identified with others; a need for love and esteem from others; and a need to achieve and exert power over others and our environment.[7] Humans cannot meet these needs alone—participation with others is mandatory. In addition, these needs are so important that we willingly give of our own resources, especially time and energy, to participate in groups. For example, many people in Springfield, Missouri, worked to transform a decaying downtown space into Founders Park, a public green space in the city's center. Working in various groups, they selected the design, obtained necessary legal clearances, raised funds, publicized the project, and oversaw the construction. Numerous committee members worked hard, not only because the issue was so important to them, but also because they knew the project would succeed only if they worked collectively rather than individually. But participation in groups always requires trade-offs—you get something, but you give up something, too. In return for being included, getting to use your talents, and accomplishing something important to you, you give up some autonomy and the license to do whatever you want, whenever you want.

Second, the formation of groups is natural to humans; thus groups are everywhere. List all the small groups in which you participated during the past week, regardless of how briefly—and don't forget to list your family! Students in college classes average about 8 to 10, and sometimes list as many as 24 groups. For example, one student listed the following: family, Bible study, sorority, executive committee of sorority, study group in small group class, project group in marketing class, intramural volleyball team, car pool, and work group of clerks in clothing department. Our faculty colleagues often list even more groups than these. In fact, Goldhaber found that the average tenured faculty member served on six committees simultaneously and spent 11 hours per week in meetings![8]

Does this seem like a lot of groups? Consider this: Reliance on groups in our society is increasing and expected to increase further, perhaps dramatically. American managers are recognizing the value of participative decision making, with the small group as one important vehicle for encouraging employee participation and improving corporate decision making. The Ford Taurus and General Motors Saturn success stories are in large part the stories of successful group work. *Consumer Reports,* for example, praised Saturn for having a much better than average reliability record in its first year of production,[9] a far cry from the poor records of other General Motors cars throughout the 1980s. Years ago, Ouchi, developer of Theory Z management, warned American managers that their ability to counter Japanese competition depended on how well they learned to work in groups.[10] More recently, Waterman identified teamwork as a key element in companies that have kept their competitive edge.[11] Top management teams are recognized as the most influential groups in organizations today.[12] It seems that Americans are getting the message.

Why is group work successful? Groups are usually better problem solvers, in the long run, than solitary individuals because they have access to more information than individuals do, can spot flaws and biases in each others' thinking, and then can think of things an individual may have failed to consider. Moreover, if people participate in planning the work of solving the problem, they are more likely to work harder and better at carrying out the solution. Thus, participation in problem solving and decision making helps guarantee continued commitment to decisions and solutions.

Third, just because we often participate in groups, we cannot assume we participate effectively. Just doing it doesn't mean we do it well! And unless we know something about why a group is unproductive, we won't know what we can do about it and we can't help a group improve. We may laugh at the saying, "A camel is a horse designed by a committee," but when our own group's horse looks suspiciously like a camel, we're often helpless to know what to do about it.

Students often groan when we tell them a major portion of their grade will be based on a group project. Just recently, a student complained to one of us that her grade in a small group discussion course was unfair because it was based on her group's poor performance, not her outstanding individual performance. No doubt this student's opinions about group work are not positive. Sorensen calls this **grouphate.**[13] Grouphate captures the negative feelings many people have about group participation; some people may even loathe being a member of a group.[14] Interestingly, Sorensen found that grouphate is partly caused by lack of training in how to communicate effectively as a group member. It is in your best interest to overcome any grouphate you may have because students with negative feelings and attitudes about participating in groups have been less successful academically than those with more constructive and positive orientations toward group work.[15] We hope to reduce grouphate by providing you information about the process of group communication, effective group discussion, and productive teamwork.

Strong communication skills are central to effective discussion and productive teamwork. Donald Petersen, former CEO at Ford Motor Company, learned this during his rise at Ford. At first he envisioned his role as that of a solitary engineer designing cars, but later he discovered that a successful company requires interaction and teamwork: "Communication skills are crucial.

Grouphate

The feeling of antipathy and hostility many people have about working in a group, fostered by the many ineffective, time-wasting groups that exist.

And I mean that in both directions—not only the ability to articulate . . . in a good fashion, but to listen."[16]

Fourth, groups provide the vehicle by which the individual can make a contribution to the organization and the society as a whole. Larkin postulated that humans have a motivation to give. The basic ingredient cementing social cohesion is not the satisfaction of needs, but rather the availability for contribution. What best binds individuals to groups may not be so much the pressure to obtain necessities as the opportunities to give of one-self to something beyond merely self-interested acquisition.[17] The dignity of individuals, Lawson states, comes from people's contributions to something greater than themselves. People who give of their time, money, energy and other resources live healthier, happier, and more fulfilled lives; they report that their lives are more meaningful than those who do not.[18] For example, legendary baseball pitcher Nolan Ryan remembers the unity and team spirit of the 1969 pennant-winning New York Mets as a high point of his distinguished 27-year career.[19] We believe that the success of work-related committees stems largely from this need to contribute collaboratively with others.

Our focus is the communicative behavior of group members—what people say and do in groups. Although we will draw upon findings from other fields, we will concentrate on the process of communication among members, especially in Western cultures such as the United States, and on how you as a group member can influence this process. Moreover, we will use as examples groups from a variety of settings. Although groups in business and industry have captured a great deal of attention, group work is fundamental in all arenas of modern life. Thus, our examples come from the educational sphere, political life, sports and entertainment, health care situations, religious settings, social services, and community development organizations as well as the corporate and industrial realms.

Small group discussion, the interaction among group members, cannot be reduced to a set of prescriptions; it is far too complex for simplistic rules. Each element of group discussion influences every other element in the group system; we describe this interdependence in depth in Chapter 4. Because the only person you can directly control is yourself, this book is designed to promote your awareness of your own behavior in small groups and its implications for other members. We do give guidelines and suggestions for you to consider, yet we do so assuming that you will remember to take into account your group's entire and unique situation as you enact those guidelines.

In the remainder of this chapter, we present definitions of key terms we use throughout the book to reduce the possibility of misunderstanding. We also present information about the types of groups you will encounter in many different kinds of settings, provide a brief discussion of ethical behavior important to effective group functioning in Western cultures, and conclude with a description of the participant-observer perspective we hope you will adopt in your groups.

What Is Small Group Discussion?

Before we define how we view small group communication, we will begin with a big picture, then move to specifics. The first term requiring definition is **group.** What differentiates a collection of people from a *group* of people? Would you be able to identify what a group is and give your reasons for doing so? Don't worry if you have a hard time putting your own definition into words; no single definition of *group* exists among those who study groups for a living. Among the variety of definitions for group, we prefer Marvin Shaw's, who concluded that a group consists of "persons who are interacting with one another in such a manner that each person influences and is influenced by each other person."[20] Shaw argued that, of all the characteristics of groups, none were more important than *interaction* and *mutual influence.*

In our Grimm fairy tale, the Donkey, Dog, Cat, and Rooster simply collected in one place does not necessarily constitute a group unless there is reciprocal awareness and influence between them. If, for example, the Donkey forages in the woods for food and is approached separately by the Dog, Cat, and Rooster also foraging for food, Shaw would argue that no group exists yet because the Dog, Cat, or Rooster did not influence the Donkey. However, once the animals begin to interact with each other and talk about how to pool their efforts to acquire food, then we see a group emerging out of their interaction. Interaction assumes coordination of behaviors.[21] More fundamentally, interaction "requires mutual influence."[22]

The Donkey, Dog, Cat, and Rooster share a related key feature of a group: an **interdependent goal.** Interdependence exists when all group members succeed or fail together in the accomplishment of the group's purpose—in this case the food they want can be attained only if they coordinate their efforts. In addition, these animals coordinated their actions in the fable to frighten the robbers away. This logic extends to group members scattered geographically. If members interact and mutually influence each other by way of newsletters, telephone conversations, computer networks, closed-circuit TV, or radio, they still constitute a group.

The study of groups may include large groupings (e.g., whole societies) or small ones; our focus is on small groups. The notion that "each person influences and is influenced by each other" implies that members are aware of each other, and from this mutual awareness we ground our definition of *small* on perceptual awareness. A **small group,** therefore, is a group small enough that each member is aware of and able to recall each other group member, know who is and is not in the group, and recognize what role each is taking. We admit that this is fuzzy, but attempts to define *small* on the basis of number of members have never worked. At the low end, we can certainly perceive all members in a group of three. (We arbitrarily eliminate the dyad, or two-person unit, as a small group because dyads function differently from units of three or more.) At the high end, most of us can take in up to 11 members in a unit and, with training, may learn to handle 12 to 14.[23] But at the end of a semester, even a class as large as 25 may seem small to a teacher.

Interaction, mutual influence, and interdependence are all central features of a group. Coordinating behavior requires exchange of messages; thus, the most central feature of human groups is their communication (we use this term interchangeably with *interaction*). Verbal and nonverbal exchange among group members is where the work of the group gets accomplished. This exchange may be face-to-face or may use communication technology such as a computer or audioconferencing equipment. In this book, **small group discussion** refers to a small group of persons talking with each other (often face-to-face) in order to achieve some interdependent goal, such as increased understanding, coordination of activity, or a solution to a shared problem. We will now "unpack" this definition, which suggests several characteristics of small group discussion:

1. A small enough number of people for each to be aware of and have some reaction to each other (typically 3 to 7, rarely more than 15).

2. A mutually interdependent purpose, making the success of one member contingent on the success of all.

3. Each person having a sense of belonging, of being part of the group.

4. Interaction involving verbal and nonverbal channels, with words conveying the content of the discussion. This definition includes as "verbal" manual languages, such as American Sign Language and typed computer-mediated messages. The *emoticons* used in e-mail messages, such as :) to indicate smiling, count as nonverbal indicators. Members continuously respond to and adapt their actions to each other. The give and take of impromptu communication, rather than prepared speeches, is the essence.

5. A sense of cooperation among members. Although there may be disagreement and conflict, all members perceive themselves as searching for a group outcome that will be as satisfactory as possible to all, so that no one is frustrated at losing to another group member.

Some authors differentiate teams from small groups. Lumsden and Lumsden see teams as highly functioning groups in which members are committed to a goal, leadership is shared, and the team has forged a strong sense of identity.[24] Harris and Sherblom reserve *team* for those groups in which leadership is shared, such as in problem-solving or self-managed work groups.[25] We do not differentiate between teams and groups and sometimes use the terms interchangeably. In everyday life, a small group may be called a team (e.g., top management team), yet function no better than other groups of its type. Like Larson and LaFasto, we are interested in groups that function well, regardless of what they are called, and our intent is to provide you and your fellow group members with the tools you need to achieve top-notch performance.[26]

Discussion (Small Group Discussion)

A small group of people communicating with each other to achieve some interdependent goal, such as increased understanding, coordination of activity, or solution to a shared problem.

Human beings are social creatures and form groups naturally. Groups are so pervasive in our lives that we may overlook their importance. Even though negative experiences working in groups can turn many people away from group work, the fact of the matter is that effective small group interaction has profound practical consequences in our personal and professional lives.

1. People use groups to meet inclusion, control, and affection needs. Group participation allows people to make significant contributions to each other and society.

2. Being a group participant does not guarantee effective group behavior; group members have to work to coordinate their actions toward a shared goal.

3. Groups are not merely collections of individuals, but they involve interaction, interdependence, and mutual influence.

4. Small groups are not defined by the number of people in a group but by their limits of perceptual awareness.

5. Small group discussion highlights the key role communication plays in defining a collection of people as a small group with a sense of belonging, purpose, and collaboration.

Types of Small Groups

There are two major categories of small groups, *primary* and *secondary*. Each meets different human needs, but most of the groups to which you will belong contain elements of each category.

Primary Group

A group whose main purpose is to meet members' needs for inclusion and affection.

Primary groups exist chiefly to satisfy what are termed *primary* needs—needs for inclusion (affiliation, belonging) and affection (love, esteem). They are usually long term. Examples include a nuclear family, roommates, several friends who meet daily around a table in the student center, and co-workers who regularly share coffee breaks. Although such groups may tackle particular tasks, they exist mainly to provide personal attention and support for the members. The tasks they perform are less important than their primary purpose of providing affection. Members' talk, which seems disorganized and informal, is the end in itself. More than any other forces in our lives, primary groups socialize and mold us into the people we become; their importance is tremendous. For most of us, the family is our first group, where we learn communication patterns, functional and dysfunctional, that can last generations and affect all aspects of our lives.[27] Primary groups are not the main focus of this book; typically, primary groups are studied in interpersonal communication, sociology, and psychology courses. However, the interpersonal relationships at the heart of primary groups are very important to understanding small groups in general.

Secondary groups, like our group of animals in the opening fable, focus on task accomplishment and are formed for the purpose of doing work—completing a project, solving a problem, making a decision. Secondary groups, such as most work teams and problem-solving groups, meet primarily what are called secondary needs—needs for control and achievement. Such groups enable members to exert power over their environment and others. For example, the teams that worked to create Founders Park in downtown Springfield were secondary groups with a specific performance objective to be attained, and members had to coordinate their efforts in order to achieve that objective. All groups initiated to accomplish some task are more secondary than primary, although many task groups also help members achieve primary needs for socialization and affection.

As you may have discerned by this point, there are no *pure* primary or secondary groups. Although groups are classified as primary or secondary according to their major focus, primary groups also engage in work, and secondary groups also provide affection and belonging to their members. Thus, most groups blend primary and secondary characteristics and meet many human needs in addition to the ones for which they were initially formed. In fact, Anderson and Martin demonstrated that secondary group members are motivated by a number of factors that are more primary than secondary, including desires for pleasure and to escape. Such factors strongly influence secondary group members' communication behaviors, feelings of loneliness, and satisfaction with the group and are worth examining.[28]

In addition to the two major classifications just described, there are many other ways to categorize groups. The four categories described next exhibit both primary and secondary characteristics in varying degrees, with the fourth more purely secondary than the first three.

Activity Groups

Activity groups enable members to participate in an activity, both for the sake of doing the activity and for the affiliation provided by doing the activity with others. The following are examples: a book club whose members meet regularly to discuss a preselected book, bridge and poker clubs, road rally clubs, hunting and bird-watching groups, and numerous other interest groups. Members of such groups solve problems and make choices—when and where to meet, how to pay for their activities, how group membership is determined—but enjoyment of the activity and fellowship with others whose interests are similar are the main purposes.

Personal Growth Groups

Therapy and support groups are called collectively **personal growth groups.** They are composed of people who come together to develop personal insights, help themselves and others with personal problems, and grow as

---

Secondary Group

A group whose major purpose is to complete a task, such as making a decision, solving a problem, writing a report, or providing recommendations to a parent organization.

Activity Group

A group formed primarily for members to participate in an activity such as bridge, bowling, hunting, and so forth.

Personal Growth Group

A group of people who come together to develop personal insights, overcome personality problems, and grow personally through feedback and support of others.

individuals from the feedback and support of others. Goal interdependence is low because no purely group goal is sought; rather, members meet their individual needs for personal learning, awareness, and support in the context of the group. Examples include local chapters of 12-step programs such as Alcoholics Anonymous and Al-Anon, mutual support groups like gay or women's rights groups, outpatient groups for clients with personal adjustment problems, support groups for parents whose babies died of SIDS, cancer survivors' support groups, and therapy groups for spouse abusers.

Educational Groups

Small groups occur in educational contexts for a variety of purposes. The small groups we are interested in are those that involve individuals who come together, voluntarily or not, to understand or control events in their lives and the world around them better. Common **learning groups,** often called study groups, form so that members can understand a subject better by pooling their knowledge, perceptions, and beliefs. These tend to be voluntary and coordinated by interested students. Others, including cohorts, cooperative learning groups, and collaborative learning groups, are used by educators and often are not voluntary.[29] Cohorts, sometimes referred to as learning communities, are used by universities to group selected students around a program of study. Students often take a set of courses together. Cooperative learning groups are composed of students selected by teachers to work on a class assignment or topic. The group's output, often a report and presentation, is evaluated at the group level. Such assignments characterize a major component of many small group communication courses. Collaborative learning groups, similar to cooperative ones, are used to assess individual achievement. For example, students may be grouped to work on course papers where they tutor each other in an effort to improve their individual writing skills. In addition to learning about specific subject matter, members of such groups also learn skills of effective speaking, listening, critical thinking, and effective interpersonal communication.

Problem-Solving Groups

Problem-solving groups formed to address some condition or problem vary widely in their composition and functioning. Examples we have already mentioned include the Ford Taurus and General Motors Saturn development teams and the various Founders Park committees. Whatever their main function, problem-solving groups are so classified because they are created expressly to solve problems. There are many ways of describing subtypes of problem-solving groups. In this book, we deal with major subtypes prevalent in four modern organizational and social life: committees, quality control circles, self-managed work groups, and top management teams.

Committees **Committees** are groups that have been assigned a task by a parent organization or person with authority in an organization. Committees

Learning Group

A group discussing for the purpose of learning about and understanding a subject more completely.

Problem-Solving Group

A group whose purpose is finding ways to solve a problem or address a particular condition.

Committee

A small group of people given an assigned task or responsibility by a larger group (parent organization) or person with authority.

A committee discusses the content of a report.

may be formed to investigate and report findings, recommend a course of action for the parent group, formulate policies, or plan and carry out some action. All these tasks require discussion among members. Boards, councils, and staffs are special kinds of committees. For example, a *board of directors* is often called an *executive committee* and represents a larger organization. It may have extensive power to make and execute policy.

Committees can be classified as either *ad hoc* or *standing*. The **ad hoc** or **special committee,** established to perform a specific task, normally ceases to exist when that task has been completed. Ad hoc committees address all kinds of problems, such as evaluating credentials of job applicants, drafting bylaws, hearing grievances, planning social events, conducting investigations, devising plans to solve work-related problems, advising legislators on what to do about statewide problems, and evaluating programs and institutions. A *task force* is a type of ad hoc committee with members appointed from various departments of an organization or political body and usually charged with investigating a broad issue, such as how to ensure that rural areas receive needed health care. Once the task force or special committee has reported its action or recommendations, it disbands.

Standing committees are ongoing committees established through the constitution or bylaws of an organization to deal with recurring types of problems or to perform specific organizational functions. The most important standing committee of most organizations is called the executive committee, board, or steering committee. Usually this group is charged with overall management of the organization and can function for the entire organization when general membership meetings are not feasible. Other standing committees encountered commonly go under names such as membership committee, personnel committee, parking and traffic committee, program committee, bylaws committee,

Ad Hoc or Special Committee

A group that goes out of existence after its specific task has been completed.

Standing Committee

A group given an area of responsibility that includes many tasks and continues indefinitely.

and so forth. These groups continue indefinitely, even though the membership changes. Usually, some members of a standing committee are replaced annually so that the group includes both experienced members and those with a fresh perspective. Standing committees often meet regularly, such as the first Tuesday of every month, to resolve a number of problems at a single meeting.

Conference committees are composed of members who represent the interests of two or more other groups. The members serve as representatives of their constituent groups; their primary allegiance is often to the groups they represent rather than the conference committee. For example, a community's arts council may consist of representatives from the community theater, art museum, ballet, symphony, and jazz ensemble who meet to coordinate their scheduling, marketing, and publicity efforts so that individual events do not compete with each other. Delegates of the U.S. Senate and House of Representatives routinely meet in conference committees to resolve differences in legislation passed by each body. For example, a Senate-House conference committee recommended a $28.9 billion antiterrorism bill that reconciled differences between the original Senate and House versions. Often, conference committees do not have the authority to resolve matters themselves, but must submit their recommendations to their respective constituent groups for approval.

Conference Committee

A group composed of representatives from two or more groups; members' responsibilities are to represent the interests of their constituents.

Quality Control Circles   A **quality control circle** consists of workers (usually five to seven) in a company who either volunteer or are selected to meet regularly on company time to discuss work-related problems. Sometimes called *continuous improvement teams, cycle time reduction groups,* or just plain *quality circles,* their purpose is to improve some aspect of work life—efficiency, quality of finished products, worker safety, and so forth. Quality circles represent attempts to capitalize on the fact that groups usually make better and more readily accepted decisions about complex problems than individuals do, and that individuals actually performing the work are in the best position to recommend ways to improve it.

Quality Control Circle

A group of employees who meet on company time to investigate work-related problems and to make recommendations for solving these problems (also called a quality circle).

Self-Managed Work Groups   **Self-managed work groups,** also called *autonomous work groups* or *peer-led work teams,* are groups of workers given a defined area of freedom to manage their productive work within certain preset limits established by the organization. For example, an automobile assembly team may be responsible for assembling a car from start to finish. They may be given a deadline by which the car must be fully assembled, but within that limit the team members are free to elect their own leaders, plan their work procedures, and schedule individual assignments for the members. Members of self-managed work groups are often cross-trained, so each member can perform several jobs competently. This permits human and other resources to be allocated efficiently and effectively, gives workers the chance to develop a variety of skills, and reduces boredom. In the future, with more employees involved in self-managed work groups and quality control circles,

Self-Managed Work Group

A small group of peers who determine within prescribed limits their own work schedules and procedures.

sensitivity to group phenomena and skills in discussion leadership become increasingly important.

Top Management Teams (TMTs)   **Top management teams,** compared to self-managed work groups, encompass the upper echelon of management.[30] Their goal is not to deliver goods or services but to lead an organization. Many of today's organizations are so diversified that they cannot succeed using the typical chief executive officer (CEO)–chief operating officer (COO) model of managing. Instead, a team is formed because members' pooled talent exceeds that of the CEO and the COO. In other cases, a CEO may not want to select a COO, so he or she forms a team of managers to do the job of operating a company. TMTs have substantial power because they comprise some of the most influential members of the larger organization. They make highly complex strategic decisions with far-reaching consequences to the entire organization and themselves. For example, the Caterpillar TMT's decision to provide the U.S. government with heavy equipment during World War II resulted in the development of a worldwide distribution network that even today is central to Caterpillar's corporate success.[31]

In the same way that no group is purely primary or secondary, most small groups you encounter will combine elements of all four group types just described—activity, personal growth, learning, and problem solving. Several years ago, the Springfield City Council established an ad hoc task force to investigate and recommend solutions to the city's solid waste disposal problem. Members had to educate themselves about solid waste, various disposal options, and pros and cons of the options before they could make their recommendations to the city council. They also had to manage their own resources of time and information and be concerned with the comprehensive quality of life in the Springfield area. Thus, this group comprised elements of a learning group, problem-solving group, quality circle, and self-managed work group.

Top Management Team (TMT)

A team composed of top officers of an organization charged with making complex strategic decisions.

Recap: A Quick Review

Groups are pervasive in our everyday lives. They can be classified by purpose.

1. Primary groups, like family and friends, help us meet our needs for belonging and affection.

2. Secondary groups, those commonly referred to as task groups, help us meet our needs for control and achievement.

3. Subtypes of primary and secondary groups often mix the purposes of both. These include activity, personal growth, educational, and problem-solving groups such as committees, quality control circles, self-managed work groups, and top management teams.

Ethical Behavior of Group Members

For a group to perform effectively, its leader and members must behave ethically. **Ethics** refer to the "rules or standards for right conduct or practice."[32] Appropriate standards of behavior from the general culture apply also to behavior within groups; however, the unique nature of small groups requires attention, in our Western culture, to special ethical concerns regarding the treatment of speech, of people, and of information. When we interact with others in small groups, our actions have consequences to ourselves and others. This consequential nature of group communication requires that members ask not only what they *can* do in groups but also what they *should* do.[33] We offer the following five ethical principles to help you answer these sorts of questions.

1. **Members should be willing to speak and should not do anything to prevent others from speaking freely.** Groups work because several heads perform better than one, but that advantage will not be realized if group members are unwilling or afraid to speak freely in the group. All members should be willing to share their unique perspectives and help ensure that others feel free to share as well. The field of communication has evolved from what was originally the study of speech. Our field has a long and distinguished tradition, dating from Aristotle, that supports the value of free speech.[34] Each member of a group must feel free to share his or her knowledge, beliefs, and opinions within the group, according to the appropriate discussion rules established in the group.

2. **Group members should embrace diversity within the group.** Member diversity should not only be tolerated but encouraged and supported. Diversity stems from various factors that include, but are not limited to, race, ethnicity, age, religion, sexual orientation.[35] These factors contribute to differences in members' perspectives—the very differences that have the potential to enrich and enhance a group's performance. Groupings such as race, ethnicity, gender, and so forth, form what Orbe calls *co-cultures,* smaller groups that exist "simultaneously within, as well as apart from, other cultures"[36] in the United States. However, group members from such co-cultures run the risk of being marginalized, their perspectives and opinions ignored by members of the dominant culture. Orbe argues that co-culture members employ a number of strategies to have their perspectives heard. In short, they have to work harder to be included and have their opinions considered than do members of the dominant culture. The challenge to group members, particularly ones representing the dominant culture, is to make it possible for *all* members—regardless of co-culture—to contribute equally. Members who marginalize fellow group members both behave unethically and defeat the purpose of the group.

3. **Group members must conduct themselves with honesty and integrity.** Honesty and integrity take various forms. First, and most

obviously, group members should not intentionally deceive one another or manufacture information or evidence to persuade other members to their points of view.

Integrity implies that members should support group decisions, which may present challenges for the individual member. Sometimes you may be asked to do something for a group that violates your own personal values, beliefs, morals, or principles. For example, what if a group on which you serve decides to suppress information that is contrary to a decision the group wishes to make, and pressures you to go along? What will you do? Only you can answer that question. You may try your best to persuade the group to see things your way; you may decide to leave the group. But if you choose to stay with the group, make sure you can support, or at least live with, the group's actions and decisions.

Integrity also suggests that you are willing to place the good of the group ahead of your own individual goals. We believe that if groups are to function effectively, members should make public their private agendas so they are not operating from motives unknown to the other members. We have known individuals who are not able to become part of a team because they are unable or unwilling to merge their personal agendas with that of the group. These individuals make poor team members, and the group is better off without them.

4. **Group members should not disconfirm, belittle, or ridicule other members and should make sure they understand members before agreeing or disagreeing with them.** Deetz stresses that ethical interpersonal behavior should strengthen one's personal identity and should have mutual understanding as its goal.[37] Our first goal, as we interact, should be to strive to understand others to their satisfaction. If this happens, we will confirm and support each others' self-concept and identity, even when we disagree strongly.

5. **Group members should be thorough in gathering information and diligent in evaluating it.** Members should make a conscientious effort to find and present to the group all information and points of view relevant to the group's work. They should also set aside personal biases and prejudices when evaluating that information, and refrain from doing anything that short-circuits this process. Many consequential decisions are made in groups, from how best to get children to read to whether or not it is safe to launch a space shuttle in cold weather. These decisions will be only as good as the information on which they are based and the reasoning that members use to assess the information. It is absolutely crucial that group members consider all relevant information in an open-minded, unbiased way by employing the best critical thinking skills they can; to do otherwise can lead to tragedies such as the fatal decision to launch the space shuttle *Challenger*. It follows from this that members must credit or document the sources of

information they share with the group, and must not falsify data or information. We will return to the subject of ethical behavior at various points throughout the book.

The Participant-Observer Perspective

Participant-Observer

An active participant in a small group who at the same time observes and evaluates its processes and procedures.

A major purpose of this book is to help you develop a participant-observer perspective. A **participant-observer** is a regular member of the group who engages actively in its discussions, but at the same time observes, evaluates, and adapts to the group's processes and needs. Participant-observers direct part of their attention to participating in the group and part to assessing how the group is functioning; they try always to be aware of what the group needs at the moment. For example, if the group seems confused, a participant-observer will try to clarify; if group members seem tired of the task, a participant-observer may suggest a break. Because such members simultaneously pay dual attention to the group's processes and the content of the discussion, they can supply essential information, ideas, procedural suggestions, and interpersonal communication skills when needed.

Don't underestimate the value of knowing how to be a skillful participant-observer or its counterpart, the nonmember *consultant,* which we discuss in Chapter 7. Several former students of ours have landed wonderful jobs because they were able to demonstrate that they were effective team members and also that they were proficient in diagnosing and helping solve group problems. We hope this text gives you the tools you need to do both.

Some members supply valuable information but have little understanding of group processes. As long as the group is operating well, these members contribute needed facts and ideas, but they are of no help in resolving conflicts, reducing misunderstandings, offering procedural suggestions, or helping solve other process problems.

Social Loafer

A person who makes a minimal contribution to the group and assumes the other members will take up the slack.

Other people are members in name only; they are **social loafers** who watch and listen but contribute little, satisfied to let the rest of the members carry the workload. We all have experienced groups with social loafers—the committee member who makes no suggestions, the classmate in a discussion group who has not read the assignment to be discussed. This behavior may result from a lack of understanding of group processes or lack of confidence; it is inappropriate and unhelpful in any case.

In contrast to both these types of members, participant-observers who are competent communicators and have extensive knowledge about groups contribute to the quality of both the process and the product of the group. In a recent survey of real-life groups, Broome and Fulbright found, among other things, that members wanted stronger guidance about group methods, procedures, and techniques as well as fellow members skilled in the communication process.[38] To be an all-around valuable member of the group, you need both a participant-observer focus and information and expertise essential to completing the group's task. This is what *Effective Group Discussion* is designed to teach you.

Recap: A Quick Review

1. Successful groups depend on members acting ethically and understanding that how they choose to act and speak has consequences for themselves and others.

2. Ethical members treat speech, information, and others conscientiously, honestly, respectively, carefully, and open-mindedly.

3. Effective group members remember they not only behave in groups but also must observe the group processes and make any changes necessary to ensure the success of the group.

QUESTIONS FOR REVIEW

 Go to self-quizzes on the Online Learning Center at mbhe.com/galanes12 to test your knowledge of the chapter concepts

The Bremen Town Musicians, although a fable involving animals, reinforces a critical theme of this text: Small groups provide people with an invaluable way to solve complex problems. Reviewing the fable, we learn that individual skills, well coordinated, can produce amazing results.

1. What individual needs are being met by being a member of this group of would-be musicians?

2. What do these animals gain by devising a plan, together, as opposed to separately?

3. How are the unique features of a group evident in this fable? Which ones are not evident? How might you rewrite the fable to show these features?

4. Does this group meet the requirements do be defined a "small" group?

5. How does this initial primary group evolve into a secondary one?

6. Which ethical principles are most evident in this fable? Which ones are absent and how might they be displayed by the animals?

7. Select one of the animals. From its perspective how could it have behaved as a participant-observer in this group?

KEY TERMS

 Test your knowledge of these key terms by visiting the Online Learning Center website at mbhe.com/galanes12

Activity group
Committee
    Ad hoc or special committee
    Standing committee
    Conference committee
Discussion (small group discussion)
Ethics
Group

Grouphate
Interdependent goal
Learning group
Participant-observer
Personal growth group
Primary group
Problem-solving group
Quality control circle

Secondary group
Self-managed work group
Small group
Small group discussion (see discussion)
Social loafers
Top management teams

BIBLIOGRAPHY

Cathcart, Robert S., and Larry A. Samovar, eds. *Small Group Communication: A Reader*. 6th ed. Dubuque, IA: Wm. C. Brown Publishers, 1992, Sections 1 and 2.

Larson, Carl E., and Frank M. J. LaFasto. *TeamWork: What Must Go Right/What Can Go Wrong*. Newbury Park, CA: Sage, 1989.

NOTES

1. There are several versions of this tale. This one comes from www.bremen.de/info/skp/stadtmusikanten/townmusicians.htm. A children's animated version can be found at www.brementownmusicians.com.
2. Kurt W. Back, "The Small Group: Tightrope between Sociology and Personality," *Journal of Applied Behavioral Science* 15 (1979): 283–94.
3. Lawrence W. Frey, "Applied Communication Research on Group Facilitation in Natural Settings," in *Innovations in Group Facilitation: Applications in Natural Settings,* ed. Lawrence R. Frey (Cresskill, NJ: Hampton Press, 1995): 1–26.
4. Diane Cole, "Meetings That Make Sense," *Psychology Today* (May 1989): 14.
5. Bill Lawren, "Competitive Edge," *Psychology Today* (September 1989): 16.
6. Charles C. DuBois, "Portrait of the Ideal MBA," *The Penn Stater* (September/October 1992): 31.
7. William C. Schutz, *FIRO: A Three-Dimensional Theory of Interpersonal Behavior* (New York: Rinehart, 1958).
8. Gerald Goldhaber, "Communication and Student Unrest" (Unpublished report to the president of the University of New Mexico, undated).
9. "Road Test," *Consumer Reports* (April 1992): 266; (July 1992): 427.
10. William Ouchi, *Theory Z: How American Business Can Meet the Japanese Challenge* (Reading, MA: Addison-Wesley, 1981).
11. Robert H. Waterman, Jr., *The Renewal Factor: How the Best Get and Keep the Competitive Edge* (New York: Bantam Books, 1987).
12. Theodore E. Zorn and George H. Thompson, "Communication in Top Management Teams," in *New Directions in Group Communication*, ed. Lawrence R. Frey (Thousand Oaks, CA: Sage, 2002): 253–272.
13. Susan Sorensen, "Grouphate" (Paper presented at the International Communication Association, Minneapolis, May, 1981).
14. Joann Keyton and Lawrence R. Frey, "The State of Traits: Predispositions and Group Communication," in *New Directions in Group Communication,* ed. Lawrence R. Frey (Thousand Oaks, CA: Sage, 2002): 109.
15. K. A. Freeman, "Attitudes Toward Work in Project Groups as Predictors of Group Performance," *Small Group Research* 27 (1996): 265–282.
16. Quoted in Lisa Stroud, "No CEO Is an Island," *American Way* (November 15, 1988): 97.
17. T. J. Larkin, "Humanistic Principles for Organization Management," *Central States Speech Journal* 37 (1986): 37.
18. Douglas M. Lawson, *Give to Live: How Giving Can Change Your Life* (LaJolla, CA: ALTI Publishing, 1991).
19. Nolan Ryan, personal interview on the *Today Show* (May 25, 1993).
20. Marvin E. Shaw, *Group Dynamics: The Psychology of Small Group Behavior,* 3rd ed. (New York: McGraw-Hill, 1980): 8.
21. Donald G. Ellis and B. Aubrey Fisher, *Small Group Decision Making: Communication and the Group Process,* 4th ed. (New York: McGraw Hill, 1994): 5.
22. Shaw, *Group Dynamics,* p. 8.
23. Robert F. Bales, *Interaction Process Analysis* (Cambridge, MA: Addison-Wesley, 1950): viii, 35–39.
24. Gay Lumsden and Donald Lumsden, *Communicating in Groups and Teams: Sharing Leadership* (Belmont, CA: Wadsworth, 1993): 13–15.

25. Thomas E. Harris and John C. Sherblom, *Small Group and Team Communication* (Boston: Allyn and Bacon, 1999): 123–31.

26. Carl E. Larson and Frank M. J. LaFasto, *Team-Work: What Must Go Right/What Can Go Wrong* (Newbury Park, CA: Sage, 1989): 19.

27. Thomas J. Socha, "Communication in Family Units: Studying the 'First' Group," in *The Handbook of Group Communication Theory and Research,* ed. Lawrence R. Frey (Thousand Oaks, CA: Sage, 1999): 475–92.

28. Carolyn M. Anderson and Matthew M. Martin, "The Effects of Communication Motives, Interaction Involvement, and Loneliness on Satisfaction: A Model of Small Groups," *Small Group Research* 26 (February 1995): 118–37.

29. Terre H. Allen and Timothy G. Plax, "Exploring Consequences of Group Communication in the Classroom," in *New Directions in Group Communication,* ed. Lawrence R. Frey (Thousand Oaks, CA: Sage, 2002): 219–234.

30. Zorn and Thompson, "Communication in Top," 254–56.

31. J. Barney, "Looking Inside for Competitive Advantage," *Academy of Management Review* 9 (1995): 49–61.

32. *The Random House Dictionary of the English Language,* 2nd ed. unabridged (New York: Random House, 1987): 665.

33. See Rob Anderson and Veronica Ross, *Questions of Communication: A Practical Introduction to Theory,* 2nd ed. (Boston, MA: Bedford/St. Martin's, 1998), Chapter 10.

34. Ronald C. Arnett, "The Practical Philosophy of Communication Ethics and Free Speech as the Foundation for Speech Communication," *Communication Quarterly* 38 (Summer 1990): 208–17.

35. Brenda J. Allen, "'Diversity' and Organizational Communication," *Journal of Applied Communication Research* 23 (1995): 143–55.

36. Mark P. Orbe, "From the Standpoint(s) of Traditionally Muted Groups: Explicating a Co-cultural Communication Theoretical Model," *Communication Theory* 8 (February 1998): 2.

37. Stanley Deetz, "Reclaiming the Subject Matter as a Guide to Mutual Understanding: Effectiveness and Ethics in Interpersonal Interaction," *Communication Quarterly* 38 (Summer 1990): 226–43.

38. Benjamin J. Broome and Luann Fulbright, "A Multistage Influence Model of Barriers to Group Problem Solving: A Participant-Generated Agenda for Small Group Research," *Small Group Research* 26 (February 1995): 25–55.

Human Communication Processes in Small Groups

STUDY OBJECTIVES

As a result of studying Chapter 2 you should be able to:

1. Explain communication as a symbolic, personal, transactional process that is not always intentional.

2. Differentiate between the content and relationship dimensions of messages.

3. Explain the fallacy in each of five communication myths.

4. Give an example of a complete communication transaction and explain why such transactions are important.

5. Describe some of the differences between computer-mediated communication and face-to-face communication.

6. Identify and describe the four general listening preferences.

7. Identify and describe each of six pitfalls to effective listening.

8. Explain the process of active listening.

CENTRAL MESSAGE

Communication is a complex, symbolic process that group members must both observe and understand so they can coordinate their efforts to achieve the group goal.

Lam, Tamika, Ryan, Tyler, and Kelli were students in a small group communication course. Their major semester assignment was a service learning project in their community. These students shared an interest in the animal overpopulation of their city. For five weeks, they studied the animal overpopulation problem in their city and were looking forward to their first class presentation. They were eager to share the work they had accomplished so that they could actually begin to work for a local animal shelter as part of their solution to this problem. Their spirits were high because, for the most part, they had bonded and were working well together. Lately, though, Tyler had missed some meetings but seemed to have good excuses. The first sign of major trouble happened when they met to discuss their plan for the presentation. Tyler had not arrived and, after 20 minutes, Tamika, usually laid back, seemed on edge. She asked, "Man, what time is it already? Tyler is so late. We are 20 minutes into this meeting and need his stuff. I am tired of this." Kelli, in frustration, declared, "I'm tired of waiting on this jerk, too, okay?" Ryan defended Tyler by reminding everyone that he had sick parents and tried to come to meetings. Kelli shot back, "I have things I have to deal with too, and this is getting old. We are down to the wire and need his stuff. He did not even notify us this time!" Lam, sensing everyone was going to leave, switched directions with, "Let's just go ahead and get started and try to finish tonight. Ryan, did you bring the visual aids we will need?" The meeting proceeded without Tyler.

In Chapter 1 we made the case for recognizing small groups as our most important social formation, central to our lives and important to understand. Countless others in various disciplines seriously explore this important social unit. A psychological approach would direct your attention to the nature of individual members: their abilities, personality, and social characteristics. The effects on group dynamics of such variables as sex, open-mindedness, and intelligence would be explored. Sociologists focus on groups' social organization. They would explore the nature of such things as status and norms, their relationship to each other and their impact on group dynamics. A social psychologist would blend these interests. In communication, we focus on members' interaction and what happens as members discuss and work together; we also address what you can do to make your own communication as productive as possible.

Chapter 1 established the groundwork for your study of small groups and emphasized that interaction is central to the life of a group. As our student group shows, what and how we communicate with each other as group members creates the nature of the small groups we participate in. Communication is like the nerve network of a small group; it is the verbal and nonverbal process by which members forge themselves into a group, maintain the group, and coordinate their efforts. "Communication is the lifeblood that flows through the veins of the group. Communication is not just a tool that group members use; groups are best regarded as a phenomenon that emerges from communication."[1] No communication, no group.

Small group communication refers to the study of interaction among group members as well as to the large body of communication theory yielded by such study. We will examine in detail this body of theory and principles, and communicative behavior of group members will be the focus of this text. Early researchers studied group members and structure. Communication researchers, extending their interest in public speaking, began to explore the communication within groups and link members' communication to group outcomes such as the effectiveness of decisions and group climate. Now, as we have matured as a field, researchers have extended their interests into how ideas are developed, how communication creates and sustains group structure, how leadership is enacted by what people say and do, and how groups can best be studied. These trends are expected to continue and are being encouraged as appropriate directions for small group communication scholars.[2]

If you have previously studied communication, the next two chapters may be a review for you. Nevertheless, because communication scholars sometimes use key terms in different ways, we recommend that you at least survey these chapters to understand how we use key terms.

What Is Communication?

How do we define something so significant to group life? Many definitions of the term *communication* exist. We define **communication** as the process by which people create and send messages that are received, interpreted, and responded to by other people. The purpose of this process, for the small group, is to develop meaning that is shared sufficiently for the members to accomplish the group task. Meaning is never completely shared between two people, let alone among the four or five who typically constitute a small group. However, for group members to achieve their interdependent goal, at least *some* shared meaning must occur.

Communication
A process in which messages produced by people are received, interpreted, and responded to by other people.

Principles of Communication

In this section, we first present five principles of communication before we elaborate on the communication process in greater detail. In addition, we discuss several myths about communication. Different authors subscribe to different communication principles, but the following are the ones that are generally accepted by scholars and to us seem particularly important for understanding communication in small groups. We consider several of these principles in greater detail in Chapter 3.

1. **Human communication is symbolic.**
   This, perhaps, is the most important principle of communication. *Meaning* is not transferred directly from one person to another; rather, people send messages to each other that must be interpreted. In the

movie *Brainstorm,* the main character invented a headphone device that could transfer experiences directly from the brain of one person to another without first having to *encode* the experiences into words. Of course, we can't do this—yet! We must use verbal and nonverbal messages to send our thoughts to another person. In this encoding process, we convert our thoughts, feelings, beliefs, and experiences into the words, sounds, and gestures that we hope others will interpret as we mean them. The receiver then uses the reverse process of *decoding,* attending to what was sent and interpreting it, to try to determine what was meant.

Symbols are arbitrarily created by people to represent experiences, objects, or concepts. For example, there is no automatic or inherent reason why we call something we write with a *pen.* We could just as easily have agreed to call it a *dog, tree,* or *la plume.* Similarly, the *okay* gesture, the circle we make with thumb and forefinger, is an arbitrary symbol; it means something different in other cultures, such as in South America, where it means something obscene. This reliance on symbols is an important characteristic of human communication and is a major reason why meaning can never be shared exactly.

2. **Communication is personal.**

Meaning itself is not directly conveyed. The symbolic nature of communication is by definition arbitrary. Thus, the same word can have different meanings to different people. You may have heard the popular claim, "meanings are in people, not in words." This principle is even more important when we consider that many of the concepts we necessarily use in everyday conversation are abstract: fairness, excellence, effective. For instance, excellence to you may mean striving for an A grade on a project, with no typographical errors and all information thorough and complete; for a fellow group member, excellence may mean getting the project completed on time, even if there are mistakes and missing information. Both are using the same word or symbol, but aren't meaning the same thing at all! The more abstract the symbol, the more possible meanings there are for the symbol and thus the more ambiguous the symbol becomes. Your backgrounds, experiences, and the culture from which you came—all of these things affect the meanings you give to the words you and others use. We discuss in detail the effects of diversity and culture on the communication process in Chapter 5.

3. **Communication is a transactional process.**

This principle follows from the previous two. **Transactional** implies that participants in communication must cooperate and work together to achieve mutual meaning and understanding. From the previous example, if we know that the verbal symbol (i.e., word) *excellent* has different connotations to different people, and we want to make sure we

Symbol

An arbitrary, human creation used to represent something with which it has no inherent relationship; all words are symbols.

Transactional Process

All interactants mutually and simultaneously define both themselves and others during communication.

understand each other about our project, then we must work together, communicatively, to determine what we jointly mean by *excellent*. In addition, *transactional* implies that the sender-receiver roles occur simultaneously, not alternately. While I am describing what an excellent project means to me, I simultaneously see your frown and guess that you don't agree with my description. Thus, communication is *both* a sender *and* receiver phenomenon simultaneously for each person involved in the process. Finally, the concept of *process* implies that communication is an ongoing event with no clear beginning or end. If we argue about how excellent our project will be, then the next time we meet, we will carry the memory of that argument with us. Thus, communication is ever changing, not static, and constantly in flux.

In our opening story, Lam, Tamika, Ryan, Tyler, and Kelli believe that Tyler has a problem being "on time." Note Tamika's exclamation, "Tyler is so late." But what does it mean to be late? "Being on time" and "late" are interpretations of behavioral events (e.g., they agreed to meet at 2 PM; it is 2:20 and Tyler has not shown up). In this case, the group members are sharing with each other their own experiences of time and communicating, among other things, their understanding of responsibility.

4. **Communication is not always intentional.**
   This principle is sometimes stated as the communication axiom "You cannot NOT communicate," and not all communication scholars agree with this axiom.[3] For example, Infante et al. believe that for an event to "count" as communication, the sender must have intended to communicate with the receiver.[4] "You cannot NOT communicate" was never meant to imply that *all* behavior is communication, only that all communication in a social setting (e.g., a group) is behavior and behavior has no opposite (i.e., you cannot *not* behave). For instance, when two or more humans are in each other's perceptual awareness, they cannot stop sending nonverbal signals to each other, which they pick up, interpret, and respond to. Tyler's absence from his group communicates various things to his group. Thus, in a social setting, one probably cannot avoid communicating.[5] The way symbols are interpreted may not be the way they were intended; remember symbols vary in degree of arbitrariness, abstractness, and ambiguity. Tyler may not intend to communicate to his colleagues that he does not care enough for the business to be on time. Moreover, people do not always *know* what they intend, and may have multiple intentions for their words or actions.[6] Nevertheless, in a social setting like a group, you do not have the option of not communicating, because even silence will be interpreted by fellow group members.

5. **Communication involves content and relationship dimensions.**
   Any **message,** or any action, sound, or word used in interaction,[7] contains both dimensions simultaneously. The *content* or denotative dimension of

Message

Any action, sound, or word used in interaction.

the message is the subject, idea, or topic of the message—the *what* of the message. The *relationship* dimension of the message refers to what the message reveals about how the speaker views his or her relationship to the other participants—the *how* of the message.

At the content level, Tamika's first remark presents a fact—that Tyler has not arrived at the designated time—and an opinion—that the group could have finished its meeting if members had been able to start on time. Clearly, these colleagues feel angry and frustrated that Tyler has failed them again. Kelli's calling Tyler "a jerk" indicates that his behavior pattern is straining the good will of the others. Now notice Lam's final remark: "Let's just go ahead and get started . . . Ryan, did you . . . ?" This comment clearly illustrates the relationship level of communication, which concerns how the speaker views his or her relationship to the other members. Lam takes charge here by suggesting the group begin without Tyler, then asks Ryan for a report. At the content level, Lam seems to be making a procedural suggestion ("Let's get started") and asking Ryan for information. At the relationship level, however, Lam is saying, "I have enough authority in this group to suggest how to proceed, and I'm taking charge now." The rest of the members accept Lam's relational definition, and the meeting gets under way. Why? Lam is their leader, and he is behaving appropriately for his position. The actions of the others support this behavior and thus Lam's authority is sustained. In this instance Lam does not overstep his relational bounds.

The relationship dimension, which is often conveyed nonverbally through tone of voice and movement, can show that the speaker considers him- or herself to be dominant, subservient, or equal to the other members. Attitudes of arrogance, dominance, submissiveness, distrust, superiority, neutrality, or concern are not often stated; rather, listeners interpret them from nonverbal cues or how a message is expressed. Note that characteristics such as distrust, dominance, and neutrality convey even subtler distinctions of the relationship dimension of messages: responsiveness, liking, and power.[8] We convey *responsiveness* to others when we show them how much or how little we are interested in their communication through eye contact, posture, and facial expressions. Westerners generally express interest with sustained eye contact, whereas in other cultures sustained eye contact could be interpreted as disrespect for authority. In conversation, interactants who synchronize each other's facial expressions and posture may be expressing comfortableness with each other.[9] *Liking,* or for that matter dislike for others, can be expressed with smiles, friendly touching, and frowns. Considering the example above, expressions of anger, frustration, and labeling Tyler a "jerk" are indications of levels of liking or affection in the group. Finally, relationship-level meaning also contains expressions of *power* as we negotiate our status and influence with others. Perhaps both Tyler and Lam are in a power struggle over leadership. Tyler's absence can be seen as irresponsible or maybe Tyler is making the group wait for him. Making others wait can be used by people as an expression of status. Remember the last time you went for a doctor's visit or waited on a professor?! In this case, Lam responded to Tyler's absence by asserting his dominance, and his assertion was accepted by others in the group.

In our experience, these relationship-level meanings contribute to many of the misunderstandings we observe in small groups. To illustrate, what if Kelli had turned to Tamika and said, in a commanding tone of voice, "Tamika, you take notes for the meeting." Tamika would probably have wanted to say, "Who died and made you queen?" Group members often react strongly to a peer who seems to command and direct because the manner suggests superiority to the other members and perhaps dislike.

Myths about Communication

Misunderstandings about communication are perpetuated by a number of communication myths. Here are five of the most pervasive ones:

1. **I understand communication. I've been communicating all my life!**
   What if your 90-year-old Aunt Tilly said, "I know how to drive—I've been driving all my life!" Just because we do something often doesn't mean we do it well. Most people do not think reflectively about their communication behavior so they can improve it.

2. **All human problems are communication problems.**
   This statement trivializes the very real value differences that divide humans. Environmentalists who want to save the Bering Sea ecosystem, one of the world's richest and commercially valuable marine environments, may understand perfectly well the concern of fishermen who fear for their jobs and livelihoods—but they disagree over values and appropriate courses of action. Communicating more and better may do nothing to resolve their disagreements.

3. **If communicators use good communication techniques, they will automatically have good communication.**
   Becoming a good communicator does require practicing techniques of effective encoding and decoding. However, communication involves much more than that. The most important "skill" for improving communication involves having an attitude of wanting to be a good communicator. You can make mistakes with the techniques you use, but if people sense your basic good intentions they will often forgive your communicative lapses and you can be quite effective in coordinating meanings with them. Only if you *want* to be a good communicator can the skills and suggestions in most communication books help you. What promotes good communication? Almost always, group members' understanding of the communication process, their attitudes toward both the process and other people, and their abilities to listen enhance good communication.

4. **I didn't misunderstand him; he misunderstood me.**

   Both sender and receiver must cooperate to create clear, mutually understood messages; remember, communication is not linear but transactional. If a message is misunderstood, the effective communicator will accept a share of the responsibility (not blame!) and work to improve future transactions.

5. **Good communication achieves perfect understanding among participants.**

   Perfect understanding is impossible. Moreover, some messages are intended to mislead rather than enlighten. Have you ever answered vaguely to the question, "How do you like my new hairstyle?" In this case, the lack of clear, unambiguous communication purposefully avoids hurting someone's feelings. In addition, because communication is both symbolic and personal, the best we can do is come close enough to understanding that we can complete the work of the group.

A Description of a Communication Transaction

Now that we have looked at main principles and widespread myths about communication in general, let's go back to our definition of communication *(the process by which people create and send messages that are received, interpreted, and responded to by other people)* and use it to analyze a communication transaction. **Noise,** or interference with the participants' ability to achieve mutual understanding, can happen at any point in the communication process. Noise is always present to some extent; that doesn't mean that communication has broken down, but that the limitations of human communicating always make perfect understanding an impossibility.

To start the process, something occurs to a group member that he or she wants to share. That member then encodes the thought, feeling, or idea by putting it into words and gestures. This process, of course, happens without a lot of conscious thought. You typically don't stop to think how to arrange your face into a scowl when you are expressing your displeasure—you just *do* it. However, you probably have had the experience of intending to say something, but the words came out wrong, or the thought was not expressed as precisely as you would have liked. This glitch in encoding is a type of noise.

In small group communication, we usually assume the communicators are face-to-face. After the speaker has encoded the thought and sent it (i.e., spoken the words with accompanying nonverbal signals), another person must then receive the communication. This may sound simple, but the receiving process, which we call *listening,* is tricky, an additional source of noise. First, the receiver must *hear* what the speaker has said. Listeners often mishear or hear only part of what a speaker said. One of us attended a group meeting where a member said, "I don't have time to do that," but another member failed to hear the *don't,* and assumed the first member would handle a

---

Noise

Interference in the communication process; can occur at any step in the process, from the sender's original encoding of the message to the receiver's decoding of it.

particular task. Fortunately, a third member, who suspected the misunderstanding and clarified it, quickly straightened out the problem.

Once the receiver has physically heard the message sent, he or she must then *interpret* the message, another stage where noise interference often occurs. Major misunderstandings can occur during this step because of the symbolic and personal nature of communication. We may use the same words or gestures but mean very different things by them. For example, Raul comes to the first meeting of his group early. He greets everyone in a friendly way when they arrive, sits at the head of the rectangular table, and makes numerous suggestions. One member thinks, "Wow, I like his self-confidence. He'll really be an asset to the group." Another member thinks, "What an arrogant jerk. What makes him think he's in charge?" Note the different interpretations on the part of the receivers to the same actions. Later, as the members get to know each other better, they may modify their interpretations. The second member may conclude, "Well, he comes on a little strong to begin with, but actually he's really friendly and hard working."

A vital determinant of how we interpret messages comes from the culture in which we were raised. The culture or cultures we identify with give us the rules for what is appropriate communication behavior. Differing cultural rules can interfere with understanding in a small group. For example, consider our attitudes toward speaking in general. "Being quick on one's feet" in many speech communities of the United States means that people are expected to speak effectively and silence is often viewed negatively.[10] Silence is risky because it could mean a lack of connection with others, lack of information or knowledge, and even a dismissal of one's being (i.e., giving the silent treatment).[11] Other cultural groups, such as some Native American groups, appreciate silence and place a secondary value on speaking. Leon Rising Wolf, a member of the Blackfeet Nation, uses the phrase, "deeply communicative silence," to characterize his nation's communication style.[12] This form of communication is *listener active* and values a nonlinguistic copresence with another higher than the more *speaker active,* linguistic form of communication valued in other speech communities. Talking, for the Blackfeet, can be risky in that it may interfere with the connectedness participants experience or may presume a level of authority the communicator does not have. The effects of culture and diversity on small group communication are covered in more detail in Chapter 5.

The final step in the communication transaction is **feedback,** elaborated on in Chapter 4. Feedback in the context of a communication transaction is the listener's response to a message from the sender, and it provides a number of important functions in the communication process. First, it helps reduce the harmful consequences of noise that interfere with mutual understanding. For instance, a member who isn't sure she heard a speaker correctly could say, "I didn't catch that; could you run it by again?" Or a member who heard the speaker but isn't sure how to interpret the statement can say, "Does that mean that you can help me with that assignment, or not?" In addition, giving

Feedback

In the context of a communication transaction, this is the listener's response to a message from the sender.

feedback to other members implies, "I am listening to you and you are a valued member of this group." Chopra observed, for instance, that when group members did not give each other supportive feedback, retaliation, withdrawal, and defensive behaviors increased.[13]

In the groups to which you belong, notice whether there is a difference in how much members typically respond to each other. Are you, like most of us, more comfortable in groups in which members react openly and clearly (even to disagree), or in ones in which reaction is minimal? Do you agree with Jablin, who found that subordinates would rather have a boss disagree openly than ignore them, which is perceived as highly insulting?[14] We suggest you monitor your own feedback and change it if you routinely fail to respond to others.

Computer-Mediated Communication and Face-to-Face Communication in Small Groups

So far, we have discussed small groups that meet in real time and face-to-face. But since the advent of computers and more recently the explosion of Internet capabilities, groups no longer need to meet face-to-face in real time. **Computer-mediated communication,** or CMC, is the formal phrase used to refer to the use of computers to interact with others. CMC can take a variety of forms, including e-mail or electronic mail, chat rooms, electronic bulletin boards, Listservs, videoconferencing, and decision-making software. More and more group members use computer technology to communicate with each other between and during meetings. A question to ask is: "How different is computer-mediated communication from face-to-face communication?" To address this question, let's look at one kind of computer-mediated communication available to groups: the net conference.

Net conference is a general term used to refer to a conference electronically mediated by *networked* computers.[15] The *videoconference* is one of the more popular types of these kinds of conferences. Videoconferencing involves both audio and video net-mediated communication, whereas an audioconference can be as simple as a telephone conference call. Telephone conference calls are a popular way on college campuses of conducting job search interviews and oral defenses of dissertations when committee members attend different universities. In *computer conferences,* group members actually sit in front of their computers and send messages to each other that appear on their computer terminals. Types of net conferences vary in expense and usefulness. However, as the expense of travel for executives to attend face-to-face meetings continues to increase and as more and more organizations are created, even expensive net conferencing techniques will pay off in the long run. In addition, companies are becoming very sophisticated in their abilities to develop specialized computer software designed for their employees, linked to a network, to work simultaneously on any number of tasks.

Computer-Mediated Communication (CMC)

Group members' use of computers to communicate with one another.

Net Conference

A conference that takes place electronically over networked computers.

Although this kind of computer technology has its advantages, the question remains: "Do computer-mediated meetings have disadvantages in comparison to face-to-face group meetings?" Depending on the kind of net conference, participant nonverbal messages like facial expressions and body language are missing or exaggerated.[16] For example, during a videoconference participants can see each other; however, they are only as close to each other as the camera allows. This means that distance between participants is only simulated, *not* duplicated. And although you can see each other in a videoconference, you are not actually in each other's physical presence. Turn taking is easier face-to-face because in net conferencing there is often a delay of half a second. What happens then is that participants often overlap each other. In addition, participants are tied to their computer and this can restrict gestures. The sense of sharing, involvement, and team spirit can be low. Immediate verbal and nonverbal feedback usually does not occur or it is delayed. This could be harmful if the group is trying to build consensus about something, but it may not matter if participants are just trying to generate a list of ideas.[17]

Computer-mediated group communication versus face-to-face group communication brings up the issue of social presence. **Social presence** refers to how much group members perceive the communication medium is like face-to-face interaction socially and emotionally. This perception depends on the degree to which members perceive that other members are actually *there* during interaction.[18] *Asynchronous* communication, or communication where there is a delay between messages (e.g., e-mail), promotes less social presence than synchronous, more simultaneous communication. One factor that can influence social presence is the complexity of the group's task. The tougher the task, the less adequate some CMC can become because the medium's channels are not adequate. However, individuals using CMC can become very creative when it comes to creating the social presence of face-to-face communication. Several factors can improve the effectiveness of net conferences.[19] Each of these factors is somehow related to creating social presence. Sandwiching the conference between face-to-face meetings can enhance the sense of groupness between members. Using a trained moderator can improve the process. So will making sure that members are aware of the rules and guidelines for speaking, and they agree to abide by specified time limits. Tasks such as routine meetings and information sharing are more effective via a net conference. For much more complex tasks in which disagreement is likely to occur, face-to-face meetings are still preferable. However, computer conferences have been used effectively to help members in conflict achieve consensus. Table 2.1 compares the strengths of face-to-face and net conferences or what used to be called teleconference meetings.

Although CMC may appear to be a different kind of communication, the communicative processes involved are still symbolic, personal, transactional, and not always intentional, and they involve content as well as relationship dimensions. We will elaborate on CMC in later chapters.

Social Presence

The extent to which group members perceive that a particular communication medium is socially and emotionally similar to face-to-face interaction.

TABLE 2.1   Comparison of strengths

Teleconferences	Face-to-face meetings
• They can be useful for information sharing, routine meetings. • Quantity and quality of ideas are equal to face-to-face meetings. • In negotiations, evidence is more persuasive than personality. • Participants may pay more attention to what is said. • In conflict, more opinion change may occur than in face-to-face meetings. • Audioconferences/computer conferences are cost-effective.	• Face-to-face meetings are better when group cohesiveness and interpersonal relationships are important. • Group organization is easier to maintain. • Participants can exchange more messages more quickly. • Important nonverbal information (facial expressions, uses of space) is available. • People generally prefer face-to-face meetings. • Participants are more confident of their perceptions in face-to-face meetings.

Source: Adapted from Gene D. Fowler and Marilyn E. Wackerbarth, "Audio Teleconferencing versus Face-to-Face Conferencing: A Synthesis of the Literature," *Western Journal of Speech Communication* 44 (Summer 1980): 236–52.

Recap: A Quick Review

Communication is the lifeblood of group dynamics. It creates and sustains the character of any group.

1. Communication is a complex transactional process that involves the generation, transmission, receipt, and interpretation of verbal and nonverbal messages.

2. Effective groups share enough meaning to enable members to coordinate their behaviors in order to reach an interdependent goal.

3. Communication is an inexact process because it is a complex symbolic, transactional, and often unintentional process. Messages always include a content, or what, and relationship, or how, dimension. Relational dimensions send messages of responsiveness, liking, and power between members.

4. Misunderstandings between group members often are the result of communication myths that must be dispelled to improve group effectiveness.

5. Noise, or interference with members' understanding each other, can occur at any time. Thus, understanding is facilitated through feedback.

6. Computer-mediated communication poses special issues for group members if social presence is to be created and maintained in net conferencing and other forms of CMC.

Listening and Responding during Discussions

Earlier, we explained that communication involves encoding, sending, hearing, interpreting, and responding to messages. **Listening** involves hearing and interpreting. *Hearing* is a physiological process that involves the reception of sound waves by the ear. It is only the first element of listening, which also includes the *interpretation* of those sound waves (and other messages). A person with acute hearing may be a poor listener who does not interpret others' statements accurately or respond appropriately. In contrast, someone with considerable hearing loss may be a good listener who is motivated to understand others the way they want to be understood.

In 1996 someone estimated that every morning in the United States, 15 million meetings take place. Consider that in a six-person group, every time five minutes of information is repeated because of poor listening, a total of 30 minutes is wasted.[20] That is a lot of wasted time! Are you a good listener? Why? When you are not as effective a listener as you would like to be, what has happened? Read on to understand better how to improve your listening.

Good listeners remember four important things.[21] **First, good listeners pay attention to the context of what is said.** Have you ever been quoted "out of context"? If so, you know that context can change the entire meaning of what is said. Suppose Tiffany says she's not sure the president of her organization will read her group's entire report right away because the president is in the middle of performance reviews with all the committee heads. Saying "Tiffany said the president won't bother to read our report" seriously distorts what Tiffany said and ignores the context of the president's being too busy *at the moment* to give the report full attention.

Second, good listeners pay attention to the feelings of the speaker. Remember the affective component of a message? When Malcolm says, "Yes, that idea is fine," in a resigned, flat tone of voice, he's probably expressing a negative feeling about the idea, without actually saying so. A good listener will verify that interpretation: "Malcolm, you said you like it but you don't sound too enthused. Would you share your concerns with us?"

Third, good listeners help speakers make themselves clear by asking questions to clarify confusing behavior. For example, Shanda is a statistics whiz who completed all the computer analyses for your group's project. She knows her stats so well that she skips steps in explaining them to the rest of you, who are lost. You can help her communicate more clearly by asking her questions that encourage her to fill in the gaps.

Fourth, it is important to interpret silence carefully. Silence may mean that people don't understand what was said, that they don't agree, that they are apathetic, or that they are hoarding information as a power play. Or as we saw in our discussion of the Blackfeet, silence may mean a respect for the interconnectedness of the group members. Group leaders often mistake silence for agreement when it may be something else. Again, a well-timed question will help interpret silence correctly.

Listening

Receiving and interpreting oral and other signals from another person or source.

Poor listening is easier to detect in a dyad than in a small group where one person can "hide" for long periods of time.[22] Compare a nine-person group to a dyad. In a nine-person group, if all members are participating equally, then each member listens about 90 percent of the time! Thus, the social pressure on members to listen is not as intense in a group as it is in a dyad, and bad listening is easier to hide. Because people can fake listening, only when someone speaks do other participants have a basis for judging that person's listening behavior. Making irrelevant comments and asking questions about something that has already been explained are evidence of poor listening.

Most of us think we are good listeners, but evidence suggests otherwise. At times, group members are not even aware of the current topic of discussion. Berg found, for instance, that topics were switched about one time per minute in discussions he observed. Members were hardly listening or responding to what previous speakers had said.[23] This finding was confirmed by other investigators in a variety of cultures and situations.[24] Nichols and Stevens reported that students listening to lectures on which they knew they would be tested retained only about half the new information presented.[25] We have found that when members of small groups (whether college students or corporate personnel in training groups) are required to paraphrase what a previous discussant said to that person's satisfaction, they can do so only about half the time. This is true even when participants know that they will be assessed for accuracy in listening. How much, then, must group members misunderstand when they are *not* on guard?

The cost of poor listening is high. Jobs are completed incorrectly, shipments go awry, and people are hurt or killed because they or someone else didn't listen well. A good listener is, unfortunately, a rare commodity of great value to a group. Bechler and Johnson found that individuals who are perceived by their fellow group members as being skilled listeners (e.g., stayed focused on the discussion, maintained eye contact with the speaker, and so forth) are also perceived as being leaders.[26] In fact, we think good listening is one of the most important skills a leader can exhibit.

Listening Preferences

By now we hope you have gotten the idea that good listening in a group is an invaluable skill and poor listening can produce terrible group outcomes. We have mentioned why some of us are not very good listeners and suggested four things to remember if you want to improve your listening. In addition, you should understand that all of us bring to our group experiences different listening preferences, which if not recognized, can produce problems for the group. Have you ever thought that perhaps your strengths and weaknesses as a listener are tied to your learned listening preference?

Kittie Watson, a specialist in listening and small group communication, has identified four general listening preferences: people-, action-, content-, and time-oriented listeners.[27] No one preference is better than another because each has its advantages and disadvantages. The trick to managing different listening preferences is to be able to identify the listening preferences of all members, including yourself, in group interaction and shifting your preference to fit the needs of the group.

People-oriented listeners are concerned about how their listening behavior affects relationships. Appearing attentive and nonjudgmental, these listeners are the ones people go to when they want someone to listen to them. Behaviors indicative of this preference are the use of "we" more than "I," use of emotional appeals in discussion and debates, and willingness to show vulnerability. These members may be heard telling a personal story to calm down members who may be upset or angry. People-oriented listeners may also become distracted by others' problems, may avoid conflicts to maintain a sense of harmony, and may engage in too many side conversations during meetings.

Action-oriented listeners are focused on the job at hand. They help the group stay on task by remembering details and providing feedback about the goal. They enjoy listening to well-organized material. On the other hand, these members can appear overly critical, may interrupt too much if they believe the group is getting off track, and may lose interest if the discussion appears to be going nowhere.

Content-oriented listeners are the group members who really enjoy analyzing the things they hear and are drawn to highly credible sources. You may observe these members using graphs, quoting sources, bringing research to the group, and dissecting the information and arguments of others. These listeners can also be seen as overly critical and maybe even intimidating to other members. Their analytical skills, while valuable, may also slow the group down and can even serve to devalue information they do not see as important, such as anecdotes.

Time-oriented listeners can be identified by their attempts to schedule group meeting and activity times, their sensitivity to nonverbal cues that may indicate impatience, and their focus on moving the group along in a timely manner. The creative and spontaneous discussions so necessary to problem solving can pose difficulties for these listeners. They also discourage additional discussion as the group nears the end of its scheduled meeting time.

No one preference is the best. Preferences are learned, so you are not locked into one of them. A group member's preference is influenced by many factors, including the nature of the relationships between group members and time constraints. Practice participant-observation and observe the members in your group for behavioral patterns that identify their preferences. Be willing to shift your preference to suit the immediate needs of the group and be willing to encourage the productive use of all the preferences. Let's turn now to a discussion of some of the more common behaviors that stand in the way of our becoming better listeners and optimizing our listening preferences.

People-Oriented Listener

A listener who is sensitive to others, nonjudgmental, and concerned about how his/her behavior affects others; can become distracted from task by others' problems.

Action-Oriented Listener

A listener who focuses on the task, remembers details, and prefers an organized presentation.

Content-Oriented Listener

A listener who enjoys analyzing information and dissecting others' arguments; can be seen as overly critical.

Time-Oriented Listener

A listener sensitive to time; may be impatient or try to move group prematurely to closure.

Pitfalls to Listening Effectively

Our listening is impaired when we are tired, preoccupied, or overloaded with information and noise. But even when we are not bothered by such interference, we still may listen poorly as a result of bad habits. The following are behaviors that interfere with good listening:

1. **Pseudolistening.**

   Pseudolistening refers to faking the real thing. Pseudolisteners nod, smile, murmur polite responses, look the speaker in the eye, and may even give verbal support like "right" or "good idea." But behind the mask, the pseudolistener has "zoned off" on a daydream, a personal problem, sizing up the speaker, or mentally preparing a response. When such behavior is challenged, most pseudolisteners blame the speaker ("That stuff he was saying was boring") when they really hadn't given the speaker a chance.

2. **Sidetracking.**

   Related to pseudolistening is **sidetracking,** when you allow something another member said to send you off into your own private reverie. As a consequence, sometimes you may sidetrack the conversation in a completely inappropriate direction, thereby wasting the group's time.

3. **Focusing on irrelevancies and distractions.**

   Sometimes distractions such as background noises, room furnishings, and the air temperature make it difficult for us to concentrate on the speaker. At other times, undue attention to speaker characteristics such as dialect, appearance, or personal mannerisms causes us to miss important points. As one woman from Georgia said to her group: "Damn it, listen to what I have to say, not to how I speak. It makes me really mad when someone says, 'Oh, how you talk is so cute I just can't pay attention to what you are saying.'"

4. **Silent arguing.**

   Many people listen selectively for information that confirms views they already hold. When they hear information that contradicts their chosen positions, silent arguers carry on an internal argument that opposes what they think the speaker has said.

   You cannot mentally rehearse a reply at the same time you are striving to understand another. If you listen primarily to find flaws and argue them in your mind, you are unlikely to understand the speaker, the context of the remarks, and the meaning the speaker intends. We are not saying, "Don't argue." We are suggesting that you make sure you understand others first, well enough to be able to paraphrase their remarks *to their satisfaction,* before you disagree.

5. **Premature replying.**

   Similar to silent arguing, **premature replying** need not involve disagreement. Most commonly, a person prepares mentally to make a

---

Pseudolistening

Responding overtly as if listening attentively, but thinking about something other than what the speaker is saying.

Sidetracking

Spinning off on a private reverie unrelated to what another group member has said, or moving the conversation in a direction completely different from what was being discussed.

Premature Replying

Responding before you fully understand the comment or question.

remark before fully understanding the speaker's comment or question. Also, group members who know each other well think they know what others are going to say before they say it—but they aren't always right! Jumping to a conclusion before the other has finished speaking results in a disjointed discussion in which the subject keeps switching.

6. **Listening defensively.**
   When we feel psychologically threatened, we don't listen well. Feeling vulnerable, we generally quit listening in order to invent ways to defend ourselves and attack the perceived threat. This is called **defensive listening.** For example, later in the meeting of our student group, Kelli verbally attacks Tyler, who finally shows up. He defends himself by attacking Kelli back: "What's your problem? You've been riding my case all day!" Unfortunately, this won't help solve the group's problem. When we feel attacked is often the very time when we most need to understand the perceptions and values of the other person. Still later, after Tamika politely but directly confronts Tyler's behavior, his honest, nondefensive response to her indicates that he is not feeling attacked. You may have noticed that evaluation or judgment is part of most of these nonlistening behaviors. The sequence is entirely reversed from what it should be. Only *after* we understand each other's ideas are we able to judge appropriately. We need to be empathic listeners who try to understand what the other means *from his or her point of view,* with the motivation to receive information being greater than the motive to evaluate and criticize.[28]

   Now that you understand listening preferences and pitfalls and, we hope, want to improve your listening, we present some tested techniques to help you take responsibility for your listening habits.

Defensive Listening

Thinking of how to defend some aspect of one's self-image while appearing to listen to what another is saying.

Effective Listening in the Small Group

Listening is a key component of enhancing understanding between group members. Effective listening is an *active* process requiring as much effort as speaking. Engaged listeners show signs of physical activity, including an accelerated heartbeat and postural shifts. In contrast, heart rates of poor listeners frequently slow to the level of sleep! Listening involves a decision to listen. No matter how great the speaker is, it is the listener who chooses how to listen, to whom, and when. Thus, Watson reminds us, it is the listener who holds the power in small group interaction and, therefore, it is to our advantage to understand and use effective listening techniques.[29] One of the best techniques for increasing understanding is *active listening*.

Active Listening   A good test of how well you have been listening is a technique called **active listening.** This technique virtually forces the listener to understand a speaker before replying or adding to a discussion. The main rule is that you must state in your own words, or **paraphrase,** what you understand the previous speaker meant, then ask for a confirmation or correction

Active Listening

Listening with the intent of understanding a speaker the way the speaker wishes to be understood and paraphrasing your understanding so the speaker can confirm or correct the paraphrase.

Paraphrase

Restatement in one's own words of what one understood a speaker to mean.

of your paraphrase. Active listeners paraphrase; they do not repeat word for word. After all, a parrot can repeat, but that doesn't mean that the parrot has understood! A paraphrase in the listener's own words forces the listener to process the information cognitively, allowing the original speaker to determine whether the message was understood as intended or not. The original speaker can then reply to the paraphrase (i.e., give feedback) by accepting or revising it or asking the listener to try again. Only when the original speaker is fully satisfied that the listener has understood what was intended does an active listener proceed with agreement, disagreement, elaboration, change of topic, or whatever. The following dialogue illustrates the technique:

Ed: Requiring landowners to farm in such a way that topsoil is not lost is absolutely necessary if we really want to protect the Earth for our children. (opinion)

Gail: If I understand you, you think we should require that farming practices prevent possible erosion of the topsoil because erosion destroys the Earth for living things? (paraphrase of Ed's opinion)

Ed: Right, Gail. (confirmation and acceptance of the paraphrase)

Another example:

Consuelo: If every college graduate were required to demonstrate some competence in using a computer, that might help right at graduation. But computers are changing so rapidly that grads would be no better off in a few years, unless they kept up-to-date or had to use a computer all along. (opinion)

Taylor: Do I understand you right? Are you saying that a computer science course should *not* be required to get a degree? (attempted paraphrase of Consuelo's opinion)

Consuelo: No, just that it should be more than just how to use a computer. You ought to understand computers and what they do and don't do. (rejects the paraphrase and attempts to clarify)

Taylor: So you think there should be a requirement for a graduate to be able to explain what computers can and can't do, as well as be comfortable with a computer. (second attempt at paraphrasing Consuelo's opinion)

Consuelo: Yes, more than a course as such. (confirms Taylor's paraphrase)

Taylor: I agree with that idea and think we should also have a requirement for ability to investigate, organize, and write a term paper. (His paraphrase confirmed Taylor is now free to add his opinion, on a new topic, to the discussion.)

Every idea proposed in a discussion should be evaluated, but only when you are sure you understand it to the satisfaction of the speaker. Active listeners confirm their understanding *before* they express their positive or negative evaluation. Only at that point is critical listening in order, evaluation by the listener as to whether the statement is relevant, defensible, likely to be effective, was carefully thought through, and so forth.

Sometimes active listeners cannot hear adequately or are not confident of their understandings. If so, they will say so quickly, asking the speaker to repeat or clarify. Only then will they disagree, add more information, or express whatever is their honest reaction.

Active listening slows the pace of interaction. If you are not used to listening actively, you may at first find yourself with nothing to say for a moment after the other finishes speaking. Keep practicing; soon you will find yourself making spontaneous responses instead of preplanned or irrelevant remarks. Above all, don't pseudolisten, which often damages trust and cooperation.

Recap: A Quick Review

The most powerful group members are those who listen well. To listen is to make an active choice to attend and interpret.

1. People have four general listening preferences: action-oriented, content-oriented, people-oriented, and time-oriented.

2. Several pitfalls to good listening include focusing on irrelevancies, pseudolistening, sidetracking, silent arguing, premature replying, and defensive listening.

3. Active listening, when a listener paraphrases what a speaker has just said and asks for confirmation, facilitates mutual understanding.

QUESTIONS FOR REVIEW

 *Go to self-quizzes on the Online Learning Center at **mbhe.com/galanes12** to test your knowledge of the chapter concepts*

This chapter elaborates on the central feature of a group—its communication. Whether members function well or experience problems, like our student group, communication processes influence the character of a group.

1. Communication is, among other things, personal. What conclusions might be drawn about the personal attitudes of the students in our case toward each other and group processes?

2. Besides the obvious symbolic meanings of "late," what other meanings can be read into the remarks of the students?

3. What are the obvious content dimensions communicated in the students' remarks? What are they communicating to each other about their responsiveness, liking, and power?

4. What advice would you give this student group that reflects your understanding of the five communication myths?

5. Do these students give any hints to their listening preferences? If so, what are they?

6. How would you rewrite some of Lam's comments to show how he could have paraphrased what Kelli, Ryan, and Tamika said?

KEY TERMS

 Test your knowledge of these key terms by visiting the Online Learning Center website at **mbbe.com/galanes12**

Action-oriented listener
Active listening
Communication
Computer-mediated
    communication (CMC)
Content-oriented listener
Defensive listening

Feedback
Listening
Message
Net conference
Noise
Paraphrase
People-oriented listener

Premature replying
Pseudolistening
Sidetracking
Social presence
Symbols
Time-oriented listener
Transactional process

BIBLIOGRAPHY

Mader, Thomas F., and Diane C. Mader. *Understanding One Another: Communicating Interpersonally*. Dubuque, IA: Wm. C. Brown, 1990.

Roach, Carol A., and Nancy J. Wyatt. "Successful Listening." In *Small Group Communication: A Reader*. 6th ed. Robert S. Cathcart and Larry A. Samovar, eds. Dubuque, IA: Wm. C. Brown 1992, 301–25.

Stewart, John. *Bridges Not Walls*. 8th ed. New York: McGraw-Hill, 2002.

NOTES

1. Lawrence R. Frey, "The Call of the Field: Studying Small Groups in the Postmodern Era," in *Group Communication in Context: Studies in Natural Groups,* ed. Lawrence R. Frey (Hillsdale, NJ: Erlbaum, 1994): ix–xiv.

2. Richard Sykes, "Imagining What We Might Study If We Really Studied Small Groups from a Speech Perspective," *Communication Studies* 41 (1990): 200–211.

3. See especially Michael T. Motley, "On Whether One Can (Not) Not Communicate: An Examination via Traditional Communication Postulates," *Western Journal of Speech Communication* 54 (1990): 1–20.

4. Dominic A. Infante, Andrew S. Rancer, and Deanna F. Womack, *Building Communication Theory* (Prospect Heights, IL: Waveland Press, 1990): 8–10.

5. Janet B. Bavelas, "Behaving and Communicating: A Reply to Motley," *Western Journal of Speech Communication* 54 (1990): 593–602.

6. Glen H. Stamp and Mark L. Knapp, "The Construct of Intent in Interpersonal Communication," *Quarterly Journal of Speech* 76 (1990): 282–99.

7. Richard West and Lynn H. Turner, *Introducing Communication Theory: Analysis and Application,* 2nd ed. (New York: McGraw-Hill, 2004).

8. Alfred Mehrabian, *Silent Messages: Implicit Communication of Emotions and Attitudes,* 2nd ed. (Belmont, CA: Wadsworth, 1981).

9. Joseph Capella, "The Biological Origins of Automated Patterns of Human Interaction," *Communication Theory* 1 (1991): 4–35.

10. Judith N. Martin and Thomas K. Nakayama, *Experiencing Intercultural Communication:*

An Introduction (Boston, MA: McGraw-Hill, 2001): 102–103.

11. Donal Carbaugh, "'I Can't Do That!' but I 'Can Actually See Around Corners': American Indian Students and the Study of Public Communication," in *Readings in Intercultural Communication: Experiences and Contexts,* 2nd ed., eds. Judith N. Martin, Thomas K. Nakayama, and Lisa A. Flores (Boston, MA: McGraw-Hill, 2002): 138–148.

12. Ibid.

13. Amarjit Chopra, "Motivation in Task-Oriented Groups," *Journal of Nursing Administration* (1973): 55–60.

14. Fred Jablin, "Message-Response and 'Openness' in Superior-Subordinate Communication," *Communication Yearbook ii,* ed. Brent Ruben (New Brunswick, NJ: Transaction-International Communication Association, 1978): 293–309.

15. Tyrone Adams and Norman Clark, *The Internet: Effective Online Communication* (Fort Worth, TX: Harcourt, 2001): 112–19.

16. Ibid.

17. S. R. Hiltz and M. Turoff, "Virtual Meetings: Computer Conferencing and Distributed Group Support," in *Computer Augmented Teamwork: A Guided Tour,* eds. R. P. Bostrom, R. T. Watson, and S. T. Kinney (New York: Van Nostrand Reinhold, 1992): 67–85.

18. Everett M. Rogers, *Communication Technology: The New Media in Society* (New York: Free Press, 1986).

19. Compiled from Larry L. Barker, Kathy J. Wahlers, Kittie W. Watson, and Robert J. Kibler, *Groups in Process: An Introduction to Small Group Communication*, 3rd ed. (Englewood Cliffs, NJ:

Prentice Hall, 1987): 208 and Robert J. Johansen, J. Vallee, and K. Spangler, *Electronic Meetings: Technical Alternatives and Social Choices* (Reading, MA: Addison-Wesley, 1979): 113–15.

20. Kittie W. Watson, "Listener Preferences: The Paradox of Small-Group Interactions," in *Small Group Communication: Theory and Practice,* 7th ed., eds. Robert S. Cathcart, Larry A. Samovar, and Linda Henman (Madison, WI: Brown & Benchmark, 1996): 268–82.

21. Carol A. Roach and Nancy J. Wyatt, "Successful Listening," in *Small Group Communication: A Reader,* 6th ed., eds. Robert S. Cathcart and Larry A. Samovar (Dubuque, IA: Wm. C. Brown, 1992): 301–25.

22. Watson, "Listener Preferences," 270.

23. David M. Berg, "A Descriptive Analysis of the Distribution and Duration of Themes Discussed by Task-Oriented Small Groups," *Speech Monographs* 34 (1967): 172–75.

24. Ernest G. Bormann and Nancy C. Bormann, *Effective Small Group Communication,* 4th ed. (Minneapolis: Burgess, 1988): 120.

25. Ralph G. Nichols and Leonard Stevens, "Listening to People," *Harvard Business Review* 35 (1957): 85–92.

26. Curt Bechler and Scott D. Johnson, "Leadership and Listening: A Study of Member Perceptions," *Small Group Research* 26 (February 1995): 77–85.

27. Watson, "Listening Preferences," 271–75.

28. Charles M. Kelley, "Empathic Listening," in *Small Group Communication: A Reader,* 4th ed., eds. Robert S. Cathcart and Larry A. Samovar (Dubuque, IA: Wm. C. Brown, 1984): 296–303.

29. Watson, "Listening Preferences," 269.

Verbal and Nonverbal Messages in Small Group Communication

CENTRAL MESSAGE

Effective group members send and interpret verbal behaviors in conjunction with nonverbal behaviors and realize that all their actions are potential messages to other members.

STUDY OBJECTIVES

As a result of studying Chapter 3 you should be able to:

1. Describe the symbolic nature of language.

2. Explain the relationship between language and culture.

3. Discuss the complex interplay between language use and gender.

4. Describe the nature of bypassing, abstract language, and emotive words, including how they disrupt discussions and how to prevent or correct such disruptions.

5. Express your ideas during a discussion so that your statements are organized, clear, and relevant to the preceding remarks.

6. Explain three major principles of nonverbal communication.

7. Explain six major communicative functions performed by nonverbal behavior.

8. Name and give examples of eight types of nonverbal behavior, and explain how each contributes to communication among small group members.

For some months, a small neighborhood in Fresno, California, had been the site of vandalism resulting in damaged property. Neighbors were upset about what had happened to their quiet neighborhood. Taking the lead, a retired school teacher contacted her next-door neighbor, a small farmer from Laos. Together neighbors decided to ask three other families to join their efforts to stop these crimes. A meeting was called one evening in the hope that they could devise a plan of action. One neighbor entered the room carrying a stack of articles on how homeowners could best arm themselves. He took the chair at the head of the table and boldly asked when they were going to get this meeting going. Another neighbor shyly asked if everyone was present, only to be interrupted by the take-charge neighbor who proclaimed, "We have to stop those Hispanic gang bangers with the only thing they understand—force at the end of a gun barrel." The retired school teacher, thinking, "This guy is going to be trouble," asked him to please refrain from labeling all criminals as "Hispanic gang bangers" and noted that arming themselves was one option they would consider, but first they needed to hear from the rest of the group. At this point, the neighbor threw his papers on the floor, and pushing back his chair, isolated himself from the rest of the group. The small farmer then clarified that this meeting was not about reaching a decision but to hear the concerns of the neighbors and ask questions of a police officer who had been invited to the meeting.

Group communication begins before any member says a word. We begin to form opinions about each other on the basis of what we see and hear. One member quietly enters the room without looking at anyone and takes a seat in a corner: "Better not count on much from that one," you think. The next person, dressed in a dark business suit, strides confidently to the head of the table and deposits a briefcase: "Arrogant; will try to boss us around," you think. Members' clothing, looks, manners, where they sit, how much space they claim—all these and other nonverbal behaviors affect how relationships among members develop. Given the verbal and nonverbal behaviors of the boisterous neighbor in our story, what first impressions might you have drawn?

In Chapters 1 and 2 we argued that communication is the central feature of groups. Although discussion is the heart of group interaction, verbal and nonverbal messages operate together to create meaning; they are indivisible. Higginbotham and Yoder state, "It is impossible to study either verbal or non-verbal communication as isolated structures. Rather, these systems should be regarded as a unified communication construct."[1] We artificially separate verbal from nonverbal messages only to help you assess the contribution each makes to *meaning* during discussions. At different times and for various reasons we may attend more to the words or more to the nonverbal behaviors, but almost *no* group communicating is entirely verbal or nonverbal.

In this chapter, we first present an overview of the nature of language and its relationship to culture, some things that often go wrong when we speak to each other, and how informed word choices and arrangements can facilitate the group process. The latter part of the chapter summarizes research and theory about the characteristics of nonverbal communication.

Symbolically, he is a chien, hund, cane, perro, and dog; or Wolf to his best human pal.

The Nature of Language

Any language—Spanish, Vietnamese, English—consists of words and rules about how to use them. In addition, each community of users of a language (i.e., co-culture) develops its own unique language system. Cultures, co-cultures, corporations, families, clubs, and other groups often have their own languages that identify someone as belonging to that group or culture. For example, theater students call the *waiting room* the *green room.* Gloria's stepdaughter Molly and her friends call boys they don't like *corndogs.* "We were slashdotted" is the Internet colloquialism used when customers overwhelm and thus ruin a popular site such as a restaurant after a glowing review.

Language appropriateness depends on the situation and we all have learned to adapt our ways of speaking for a variety of situations. For instance, we use a different way of speaking when we meet someone in a church, synagogue, or mosque from the one we use during a tailgate party at a football stadium. Physicians explain a medical procedure to a patient differently from how they discuss the procedure among themselves. We must use the way of speaking shared by group members if we want to be understood and accepted.

Of all the characteristics of language, the most important to keep in mind is that all *language is symbolic.* You learned in Chapter 2 that words have no inherent meanings. As symbols, *words have no meaning or reality apart from the persons using them and responding to them.* Human communication is symbolic, and only if speakers and listeners have approximately the same **referent** for a word will they have perceptual similarity. *This cannot be taken for granted!* For instance, our neighborhood group at the beginning of the chapter had to decide collectively what *they* meant by "taking action" to restore their neighborhood, not just what *one member* may have meant.

Referent

Whatever is denoted by a symbol or statement.

FIGURE 3.1   One statement, different referents

Even if discussants speak the same language, they may use the same word to refer to different things. Consider the simple word *food*. As illustrated in Figure 3.1, when Joe says, "Let's go get some food," his referent is a cupcake and soft drink from the nearest vending machine. Mary envisions alfalfa sprouts on whole wheat bread, and Herbie pictures a five-course meal at a fine restaurant. Obviously, Joe's words have different meanings to these three people. If this were a group recommending a break for lunch, clarification would be necessary!

Clearly, we communicate effectively with symbols only when we have similar referents for them. Imagine that the leader of your group asks you to keep a "detailed" list of what the group discussed. The leader means "word-for-word account of the entire discussion," and you assume that "a broad description of major decisions" will suffice. Your group will have problems, even though neither of you was wrong. Each of you used the same symbol ("detailed") to refer to something different, which emphasizes the personal and transactional nature of communication—meanings are in people, not in words. To complicate matters, language is not static but dynamic; it changes constantly as our world changes. For instance, a bit of computer humor passed along the Internet poked fun at how language changes as our world changes. Remember when a *window* was something you hated to clean and a *ram* was the cousin of a goat? *Meg* was the name of your sister and *gig* was a job for the night. *Memory* was something you lost, a *CD* was a bank account, *log on* was adding fuel to a fire, and *backup* happened in your toilet. Now they all mean different things and that really *mega bytes*!

Language and Culture

Language and culture are intimately tied to each other in an ever-spiraling, reflexive relationship and together have a profound impact on shared understanding in group discussions. On one hand, language use helps to fashion the complex, multiple cultural realities you navigate daily; on the other hand, those cultural realities help give meaning to what you say and how you say it. We are all deeply immersed in language and as such there is not anything we perceive that is not somehow affected by our language.[2] A tenet of the commonly known Sapir-Whorf hypothesis is "The background linguistic system (in other words, the grammar) of each language is not merely a reproducing instrument for voicing ideas but rather is itself the shaper of ideas, the program and guide for the individual's mental activity, for his [or her] analysis of impressions."[3]

In other words, some scholars believe that language in fact *determines* how we experience our world; although such deterministic views have been softened, it is clear that our language systems help shape what we perceive in several fundamental ways.[4] How you behave verbally and nonverbally helps you identify as a member of any number of cultural groups, probably before you even say a word. In turn, your behavior is given meaning by placing it in any number of cultural contexts.

It is clear that our language helps shape what and how we experience our world. Several languages, for example, have more than one form of the pronoun *you*. A formal or polite version is used to address people who are strangers, while an informal version is used to address family and friends. A subtle variation in one pronoun affects relative formality, displays of respect, and perceptions of equity between people. Many Native American languages like the Hopi do not use past, present, or future verb tenses. These cultures privilege spontaneity and experience time as what happens in the present moment.

Language difficulties occur even between native speakers of the same language. One of our colleagues, a native-born Canadian, asked others to submit yearly activity reports in "point form." Faculty became confused until someone noted that to a Canadian "point form" means "outline form". Misunderstandings like these often become humorous or become jokes, like our Internet joke. Others are deadly. When an air traffic controller in Madagascar said, "Clipper 1736 report clear of runway," the American pilot of the Clipper thought he had been given clearance to take off. Instead, the controller meant, "Report that you have cleared the runway." Six hundred people died in the plane crash that followed.[5]

Culture is something that is learned or a set of expectations and behaviors we absorb. *Gender* behavior too can be viewed as largely culturally taught behaviors. With little conscious effort we learn to become *female* or *male* in the same way we learn to become a Hmong or Latina. Let's take a look at how language and culture are interrelated by looking at gender and language.

Language, Culture, and Gender

Gender

Learned and culturally transmitted sex-role behavior of an individual.

Sex

Biologically determined femaleness or maleness.

Learned characteristics and psychological attributes of masculinity and femininity are called **gender,** as opposed to our **sex** or biological characteristics. Researchers do not know precisely which differences have biological origins (i.e., sex differences) and which have cultural origins (i.e., gender differences); however, research suggests that many differences are learned, not inborn. Moreover, research findings are often inconsistent. Female and male gender roles have been changing so rapidly in the past 40 years, that differences observed many years ago do not necessarily hold true today. In addition, current research findings will almost certainly be out of date years from now because our roles as men and women continue to change.

We caution you that although there appear to be differences in the way men and women communicate, there are far more similarities between the genders than differences. Whether men and women represent two distinct communicative cultures is a highly contentious issue. Burleson argues that to study gender as a culture inaccurately characterizes men and women as more different than similar, promotes harmful stereotypes, and misrepresents differences that actually do exist in the communication between men and women.[6] Thus, to conceptualize communication between men and women as "intercultural communication" is not the same as identifying the cultural variables in male-female communication; in fact, it may obscure them.[7] We cannot resolve the issue here, but we want to introduce it to you so that you remember that we still have a lot to learn about sex and gender in small group communication.

An extensive review of findings about gender differences has been provided by Stewart et al.[8] In spoken communication gender differences have been observed in verbosity, interrupting, and initiating behaviors. Men talk more and interrupt more, but that may be changing, because research with college students did not find these differences. Women initiate more topics but, in part because men provide more minimal responses ("uh huh," or "yeah") without elaboration, more topics introduced by women are dropped in conversation than those introduced by men. Women often ask questions to *maintain* conversations; however, men usually ask questions to *acquire information.* Women speak more deferentially and tentatively. In the past, women were reported to ask more *tag* questions ("It's a good idea, *isn't it?*"), but recent research does not confirm those early findings.

Most researchers propose cultural rather than biological or psychological explanations for the differences that have been observed. For instance, Maltz and Borker concluded that men and women seem to have different rules about what constitutes friendly conversation, about how to conduct such conversation, and what certain behaviors mean.[9] For women, backchannel responses (mm-hmms) seem to mean, "I'm paying attention to you; keep talking," but for men they seem to mean, "I agree with you" or "I follow you so far." A male speaker receiving "mm-hmms" from a woman is likely to believe she agrees with him, but a woman speaker receiving only occasional "mm-hmms" from a man is likely to believe he is not listening. Men often complain that women *say* they agree with them, but it's impossible to tell what women *really* think; women often complain that men don't listen. Both complaints may stem from misunderstandings caused by two conflicting sets of cultural rules for conducting conversation.

The view that male-female differences in communication are primarily culture based is further supported by a review of gender comparison studies.[10] Mulac et al. characterize men's talk as direct, succinct, personal (heavy use of "I"), and instrumental (task-oriented). Women's talk is characterized as indirect, elaborate, contextual, and affective. Note that these differences are tendencies, not inviolable rules. The differences between men's and women's communication are attributed to cultural learning rather than biology. McCroskey et al. report that women display more facial and other signs of emotion than men.[11] In situations where males tend to sit or stand upright with their legs apart and hands on hips, women often clasp their hands together and fold their arms across their bodies. Women sit and stand closer to others, especially other females, than men do. Men sit closer to women than to other men, but require more personal space than females. Stewart et al. suggest that men's normal behavior signifies power and status, whereas women's conveys subordination.[12] Women display more signs of interpersonal liking (immediacy); men, more signs of power (potency). Both sexes display responsiveness, although the nature of the responsiveness differs.

In the small group field, gender differences have been investigated more than other intercultural phenomena. In an early summary of such research, Baird reported that women were more expressive (paying attention to the relationships among group members, expressing concern for others, displaying emotions) and men were more instrumental (oriented to the task, factual, analytical).[13] More recent research indicates that male-female behaviors have changed, but some differences still appear. For example, Smith-Lovin and Brody found that men interrupt women more often than other men, but women interrupt men and women equally.[14] Men give more supportive interruption attempts ("I agree. We should . . . ") in all-male groups, but the more women in the group, the less likely the men are to interrupt supportively. Men are less likely to yield to negative interruption attempts; women, much more likely to yield to them. They concluded that men seem to consider sex to be a status variable, whereas women do not, but the findings are more complex than previously thought. Women do not simply give in to higher-status individuals; instead, an interplay of sex, status, group composition, and gender salience affects the specific interaction.

There are questions about whether the differences exist. Verdi and Wheelan suggest that differences are exaggerated.[15] They found that all-male and all-female groups behaved the same, but mixed-sex groups behaved differently; group size seemed to be a more important factor than sex. Although early findings showed that men talked more than women, recent studies have produced mixed results. Mabry even found that women dominated group interaction and seemed to prefer interaction with other women more than with men, and that men showed subtle forms of resistance to a dominant presence of women.[16]

Some researchers have found that male leaders of small groups are more effective, but recent findings show that both men and women can behave in similar ways in groups, and neither sex is more effective than the other. Jurma and Wright observed that the leader's sex made no differences in members' perceptions of leaders who lost reward power during group discussions.[17] They concluded that men and women are equally capable of leading task-oriented groups. This conclusion is supported by Andrews, who noted that it is more important to consider the unique character of a group and the skills of the person serving as leader than sex.[18] She suggested that a complex interplay of factors (including how much power the leader has) influences effectiveness. Power was also a factor in Duerst-Lahti's study of successful, high-status businesswomen and men.[19] Contrary to the findings of others, women were not frozen out of conversations. The women talked more often but for shorter periods, gave more indications of verbal support, and freely challenged the men. They had power in the group, and their ideas and proposals were included in the final product. They seemed to have mastered the use of power just as effectively as the men.

Several studies suggest that, despite *actual* behavior, men and women are *perceived* differently. For instance, Carli found that men and women behaved similarly, but that women spoke more tentatively in mixed-sex dyads. However, they were more influential with men, but less so with other women, when they spoke tentatively.[20] Burrell et al. compared trained and untrained mediators of both sexes.[21] No male-female differences were observed in the behavior of trained mediators, but untrained female mediators were more controlling. However, the men, whether trained or not, were *perceived* as more controlling.

Shimanoff and Jenkins lament that an individual's gender alone can change how a person or message is heard and evaluated.[22] They stress that group members need to remember that they constitute a system; members' focus should not be on one person's fulfilling the role of leader but on leadership as the responsibility of all group members. Thus, group members should acknowledge and challenge sex role stereotypes which, if left unchecked, can deprive the group of valuable human resources. After all, group members have been found to be more satisfied and productive when the most qualified members lead, and research has shown repeatedly that such individuals are just as likely to be female as male.

Biological sex often serves as a status cue that may affect women's credibility in groups. Propp found that, in mixed-sex groups, information provided by women is evaluated more stringently.[23] Information introduced by males was twice as likely to be used by the group in its decision-making process. This was especially true when that information was new and not known generally by the rest of the members. Propp suggests that biological sex is used as a status cue, and this puts women's expertise at a disadvantage during decision making. In another study by Taps and Martin, how female behaviors were evaluated depended on whether the group was sex balanced or lopsided.[24] In all-female groups, women who gave *internal* accounts for their opinions (e.g., "Based on my previous experience, I think . . . ") were more influential and more well liked. However, the reverse was true for male groups with only one woman. In that case, women who gave *external* accounts (e.g., "Based on research done by Dr. Smith, I think . . . ") were more influential. In sex-balanced groups, the types of accounts didn't seem to matter. These findings have strong implications for how groups are constituted, especially in the workplace.

Other studies indicate that perceptions depend on factors other than gender. Canary and Spitzberg examined how men and women handled conflict episodes.[25] They concluded that the *approach* (i.e., using win-win strategies), not the sex, determined effectiveness, with each sex perceived as being equally effective.

About the only conclusions we can draw from this brief review are that gender expectations and behaviors are in a state of rapid flux, and that differences are largely a result of culture rather than sex. Remember, whatever is learned can be changed.

This discussion of language and culture has only scratched the surface, and is not intended to be exhaustive. It should encourage you to think about your own behavior with an eye toward sensitizing you to ethnocentric behavior that may cause problems in a group. We will explore further the impact of culture on group communication in Chapter 5 when we discuss ethnocentricity, race, class, and age. In the rest of this chapter, we will examine general characteristics of verbal and nonverbal behavior in small group communication.

Problems Resulting from Language Choices

The difficulties that face group members from different cultures can seem insurmountable. However, you have also seen how easy it is even for people who speak the same language to misunderstand each other. In addition, we have pointed out that an important ethical principle for group members is to make a sincere effort to comprehend one another. Fortunately, understanding that symbols (including all words) have no absolute or certain referents can help you prevent a variety of misunderstandings and problems common in discussions. Three of the most troublesome problems include bypassing, lack of clarity, and using emotive words.

Bypassing   **Bypassing** occurs when two discussants, like the air traffic controller and pilot, have different referents for the same word or phrase but think they have the same meanings, or when they think they disagree but really do

Bypassing

A misunderstanding that results from two people's not realizing they are referring to different things by the same words, or who have the same referent for different words.

not, because they use different words to indicate the same referent. For example, one of us observed a group arguing about whether *feminism* was good or bad. One young woman, believing feminism meant that men and women should have the same rights in the workplace, could not understand how another group member could be opposed to it. On the other hand, the man who disagreed with her believed *feminism* meant that women should be preferred over men and should receive higher salaries than men because of past discrimination and underpayment. This group wrangled for 15 minutes before someone, listening carefully, said, "I think you two actually agree," and asked each to explain what *feminism* meant. When they realized they had been using the word to refer to different phenomena, they were then free to discover that they actually *agreed* with each other that men and women performing the same work should receive the same pay.

Bypassing is particularly problematic when group members become self-righteous, with each believing the other is wrong or stupid. In the earlier example of the word *detailed*, if both you and the leader act as if the other's use of the word was wrong, then feelings will be hurt, as will the group's productivity. Our boisterous neighbor in our opening story insisted that "taking action" meant nothing less than using force to fight force. Instead, remember that it is normal for people to use words differently and that effective communication occurs only if discussants use the same code and definitions; they must be in agreement on the referents for their words at any given time. Whenever a symbol is used that could be misunderstood, ask for clarification: "What do you mean by *detailed?* How much detail do you want me to go into?" Taking a bit of extra time initially saves time in the long run.

Lack of Clarity   Two factors contribute to lack of clarity in discussions: abstractness and ambiguity. In discussions of ideas, many statements are necessarily **high-level abstractions,** lacking specific referents. Think of such terms as *justice, fairness, democratic, high quality, civil rights,* and so on. As members move away from terms referring to specific and unique items, the degree of abstractness increases, as does the potential for misunderstanding. Consider the following set of terms, each of which is more vague than the ones before:

> The 2006–2007 Curriculum Committee of the Department of Communication
>
> Departmental committee
>
> Committee
>
> Problem-solving group
>
> Small group
>
> Group
>
> Living system

High-Level Abstraction

A word, phrase, or statement commonly used to refer to a broad category of objects, relationships, or concepts; typically refers to intangibles such as love, democracy, and so forth.

When the first term is used among members of the Department of Communication, the picture in the listeners' minds is almost certain to be similar to the picture in the speaker's mind. However, when we talk of a *committee,* any one of many committees could come to mind. Only terms that name unique objects are likely to be completely clear. For example, one member of a group discussing classroom procedures and policies said, "Lecturing is a poor method of teaching." Another responded, "Oh, no it isn't." An argument ensued until a third member asked for **concrete** examples (lower-level abstractions). The speakers were then able to agree on specific instances of effective and ineffective lecturing, and particular contexts in which lecturing was either a good or a poor choice of teaching strategy. The vagueness thus reduced, the group agreed on a less abstract statement: "Lecturing, if well organized, filled with concrete examples, and done by a skilled speaker, can be an effective means of presenting factual information and theoretical concepts. It is usually less effective than discussion for changing attitudes or developing critical thinking skills."

Leathers found that highly abstract statements consistently disrupted subsequent discussion, with the degree of disruption increasing as the statements became more abstract. His groups contained "plant" discussants who were trained to make abstract statements like "Don't you think this is a matter of historical dialecticism?" After such a statement, most of the other discussants became confused and tense; some withdrew from further participation.[26]

Lack of clarity is also produced by **ambiguity,** or communication that could reasonably be interpreted in more than one way. Sometimes words can be interpreted in more than one way. For example, one of our colleagues once wrote in a letter of recommendation: "You will indeed be fortunate if you can get him to work for you." The writer meant that the person being "recommended" was a lazy employee and "you'll be lucky if you can get him to do any work." However, the recipient of the letter likely took it to mean that the future employer of this job candidate would be fortunate indeed to have such a promising employee.

A mixed message, one in which the words seem to imply one meaning but the actions indicate something different, can produce ambiguity, too. For example, the group leader might say, "Take as long as you like to consider this item," while at the same time looking at the clock and stuffing things into a briefcase. Such ambiguous messages are difficult to interpret and disrupt effective communication in the group.

Lack of clarity sometimes results when opinions are uttered in sentence fragments or in an evasive manner. Spontaneous participants quite commonly utter sentence fragments; they mention a subject, but never finish making a point about it, at least not in words. Sometimes, a nonverbal behavior—a shrug, a facial expression, a gesture—completes the sentence, but anyone not watching will miss the point, and those watching may misunderstand. A fragment like the following can confuse others:

> Maybe we should divide . . . there seem to be a lot of issues . . . a lot of confusing bits and pieces . . . will make a lousy solution.

Concrete

Low-level abstractions that refer to specific objects, experiences, and relationships; they thus help clarify abstract terms.

Ambiguity

Lack of clarity that occurs when a communication can be reasonably understood in more than one way.

This statement could have easily been said directly and clearly, leaving little doubt in listeners' minds about what was intended:

> Maybe we should divide our investigation of how student-athletes are treated academically by dividing the issue into component topics, such as recruitment, advising during orientation, advising after enrollment, and monitoring compliance with NCAA rules. Otherwise, we may get all these topics mixed up, overlook some problems, and produce an incomplete or shoddy report.

People use vague language for several reasons. Occasionally, a group member will try to enhance personal status by using technical jargon the others don't use. Sometimes, this is done to conceal ignorance of the issue. At other times, the speaker may be trying to cover up or evade answering the question directly, such as a politician saying: "Revenue enhancement is very important, and we will have to explore every available avenue for overcoming the economic paralysis caused by the deficit. No one likes new taxes, and I can promise you we'll investigate all options." (We think that means taxes are going up!) When you encounter this, don't be snowed by a show of technical expertise or jargon. Ask the speaker to explain in terms you know.

Members can and should try to prevent the confusion that results from abstractness and ambiguity by asking for clarification. Group members who are ethical strive for mutual understanding; this means they try to be clear and to help others make themselves clear. As a speaker, help produce clarity by using language appropriate to the particular group situation, by providing specific examples to illustrate the abstract terms you use, and by making your actions and words congruent. For example, the statement "I think we can produce an excellent report, one that addresses all three major aspects of the topic, uses references no older than two years, and is grammatically perfect" tells your listeners what you mean by "excellent." Encourage others to give you feedback, and welcome questions from other members as opportunities to improve mutual understanding.

As a listener, when you aren't sure what someone means, ask for clarification or for a specific illustration: "Jamal, you said we could take as long as we liked, but you seem rushed. Would you rather we table this discussion to a later meeting?" or "What do you mean by a 'detailed' report, Maria?" Paraphrase and ask the speaker to confirm or correct your understanding. Work transactionally *with* the speaker to create common meaning.

Lack of clarity because of abstractness and ambiguity can also plague groups that choose to use computers to communicate with each other formally and informally. The use, for example, of electronic mail or e-mail can help groups reduce the time they spend in face-to-face meetings.[27] This can be particularly beneficial for groups whose members may not live near each other or are simply very busy people. Although using e-mail may not be beneficial when the group is actually making decisions, it has been shown to help when they are initially tossing around ideas and when they are ready to map out the execution of their project.[28] Composing clear and accurate

- When you want to make a strong point, use asterisks (*point*).
- Book titles can be designated with underline marks.
- Avoid the use of special format codes such as color and boldface unless you know your group members can see them on their computers.
- Any acronyms like FtF (face-to-face) should only be used if they have been previously explained or defined—do not assume your group members understand them.
- Dates should be written out because 9/11/02 in one part of the world means September 11 and in other parts of the world November 9.
- Simplicity and conciseness are preferred on e-mail, not lengthy dissertations.
- Judiciously use your subject lines to cue people to the topic of your e-mail. This helps users decide which e-mails to read and which to avoid or save for later.

TABLE 3.1 E-mail rules for clarity

e-mail messages is just as important online as it is face-to-face. How might you do just that? Table 3.1 lays out some simple rules to follow when using e-mail.[29]

Emotive Words **Emotive words** evoke strong feelings in others; these words recall highly pleasant or unpleasant images and experiences. Some emotive words are the fighting, snarl, or trigger words that produce strong reactions—unthinking, instantaneous responses by a person reacting to the word as if it were the actual thing. For instance, the man mentioned earlier with the strong negative feelings about the word *feminist* had an image of feminists as man-hating, bra-burning, controlling females with no sense of humor. Powerful physiological reactions to words with highly negative connotations are normal, but they involve nonthinking responses. Group members are ethically obliged to strengthen, not weaken, one another's identity and self-concept; therefore, intentionally using emotive words to hurt someone or to see if you can get a rise out of someone is not only inappropriate; it is unethical.

When a person, or something he or she values, is called one of these negative terms, the response is usually defensive or hostile. Constructive, open-minded discussion ends. But this doesn't need to happen. You can state your opinion, even if it is controversial and others are likely to disagree, in a way that does not deliberately push somebody's "hot button." Most negative emotive words have neutral alternatives you can use instead. For example:

Negative Connotation	Neutral or Positive Connotation
Egghead	Intellectual
Broad	Woman
Manipulative	Persuasive
Jock	Athlete

Emotive Words

Words that evoke specific emotions, connote more than they denote, and serve as triggers for recalling pleasant or unpleasant experiences.

Why should we pay attention to such language? Groups can get side-tracked from their goals by hurt feelings and lost harmony. You want your ideas and opinions to get a fair shake in your group's discussions, but someone you have offended with an emotive word will be unable to consider fairly and objectively the merits of what you propose. So using such language hurts the group's ultimate outcome.

Group members must be sensitive to current usage and to the feelings of other group members; in other words, remember the *observer* part of being a good participant-observer. Sometimes the use of trigger words is not intentional. We might use a word and only afterward find out a group member was offended. These unintentional trigger words are referred to as **hidden antagonizers.** For example, a Caucasian group member with no prejudicial intention may say *colored,* and a black member may respond defensively. Our black students have told us they now prefer the term *African American* to *black,* which was the preferred term for many years. One member might say, "Nebraska has socialistic electric power distribution," meaning that such facilities are owned by the public and managed by a voter-elected board. Although *socialistic* is used appropriately to define a company owned by a social body (the citizens of Nebraska), some Nebraskans wouldn't take kindly to that adjective. *Publicly owned* would have been a better choice; it is equally descriptive, but doesn't carry the negative connotations of *socialistic*.

The use of sexist terms is a major problem for many groups. Terms that once were used interchangeably to refer to all people, as well as males specifically, are now rejected as biased against women. For instance, the word *man* has been used in the past when the person referred to could be either male or female (patrolman, chairman, businessman, postman). Language is dynamic; it changes to fit changing circumstances. What was once acceptable is now inappropriate. Any word that implies a sex criterion for filling a role or performing a task may disrupt many discussions. Ivy and Backlund, experts in gender and communication, propose, "If people would spend more time figuring out how a listener will best hear, accept, understand, and retain a message and less time figuring out how they want to say something to please themselves, then their communication with others would vastly improve."[30] We believe this is a worthwhile golden rule for managing all forms of potentially hurtful word choice.

The worst form of stigmatizing is name-calling. Adrenaline rises as we prepare to fight physiologically and psychologically when called by such names as *pig, chauvinist, feminazi, whitey,* or *nigger.* Name-calling is unethical. It deflects attention from the issues before a group, destroys trust, elicits defensive reactions, and does nothing to promote effective group discussion.

What can you do to prevent or reduce the negative effects of stigmatizing? First, recognize that people have feelings about everything and these feelings must be considered. When people or their beliefs are challenged, their concepts of self are also challenged and must be defended. Monitor your own behavior; be aware that your feelings and evaluations are just that—YOUR feelings and opinions, *not truths.* Take responsibility for your own opinions and express these

Hidden Antagonizers

Unintentional trigger words, not intended to offend, that do in fact provoke emotional reactions.

opinions provisionally: "It seems to me that . . . ," or "I don't like . . . ," for example, makes it clear you know you are expressing your opinion only.

Finally, when you hear someone else express a trigger term, you can reduce the potential harm by restating the emotive statement. For example, a statement like "Doctors are money-grubbing pigs at the American feed trough and we can't get health care reform because of their greed!" might be rephrased as follows: "Jamisha believes that health care reform will be difficult because physicians have strong concerns about losing their current incomes. What do the rest of you think?" Replacing the emotive terms with neutral ones and soliciting a variety of opinions and feelings allow the group to examine the idea objectively, in a mood of skeptical inquiry, so that the conclusion will be based on more complete information.

Stigmatizing and name-calling are unethical behaviors because they attempt to undermine other members' self-concepts. They sidetrack the group into arguments that deflect it from its goal and cause the group to reject what may be valuable information because it was poorly stated. Be sensitive to other group members in order not to stigmatize them, their values, or their beliefs. As a listener, rephrase stigmatizing statements so that they are neutral. That way, if members disagree, it will be on the merits of the idea, not because of the trigger words. If a member persists in stigmatizing others, make it clear—politely, but directly and firmly—that such behavior is not acceptable.

Improving Communication by Organizing Remarks

The ability to speak in a fluent and polished style is not essential to being a valuable group member but, as we have already discussed, clarity is. Organizing your remarks makes it easier for others to interpret them as you intend. The following are guidelines for organizing remarks:

1. **Relate your statements to preceding remarks.**
   Your statement should not appear to come out of the blue. You should connect it to the topic under discussion and, most of the time, to the immediately previous remark. For example, in a group investigating the loss of widely used library reference materials, Nguyen has just said, "A major problem for the library is replacing magazines with articles that have been cut out." You say, "Yes, that is a major reason why reference materials aren't available, and I *also* found out that every encyclopedia had articles removed. The librarian told me it costs $2,000 per year to replace them." Your remark will make sense to other group members because it relates directly to Nguyen's statement, it is relevant at this particular time in the discussion, and the point is clear.

2. **Speak concisely.**
   When other members' eyes glaze over, shut up; you've talked too long. State your ideas simply, briefly, and clearly—once! We all know participants who restate every point several times or use 200 words for what could be said in 20. This hogs "air time" and causes listeners to tune out.

3. **State one point at a time.**

   Usually, you should not contribute more than one idea in a single speech because a group can discuss effectively only one idea at a time. For instance, if you say, "Many people are injured when bumpers fail. Furthermore, I think cars should be required to have antilock brakes, and there's also a problem of the steering wheel that locks when the ignition shuts off," one person might reply about the bumpers, another about the brakes, and a third about the steering. A confused discussion will result. An exception to this guideline might be if you are submitting a multipoint report to the group, in which case it will help if you distribute a handout that lists or outlines the main points.

   In this section we have described the nature of spoken language and several of the pitfalls to avoid during small group discussion. We now turn to an equally important component of communication, nonverbal behavior.

Recap: A Quick Review

Verbal and nonverbal behaviors work together to create meaning and are the heart of group discussion.

1. Language, composed of words and the rules for their use, is fundamentally symbolic.
2. Language and culture are so intertwined as to be inseparable. Language helps shape cultural meanings in profound ways and thus is central to understanding how group members experience their worlds.
3. The characteristics and attributes of masculinity and femininity, or gender, are culturally influenced and enacted in language choices.
4. Gender stereotypes regarding expectations about how males and females should communicate can hinder a group if not understood and addressed.
5. How group members communicate to each other can produce three language challenges: bypassing, lack of clarity, and emotive words. Each of these can be managed effectively.

Nonverbal Behaviors in Small Group Communication

Nonverbal Behavior

Messages other than words to which listeners react.

Nonverbal behavior includes all behavior *except* the actual words themselves. They are vital to small group communication. For instance, Ray Birdwhistell, an early pioneer in the study of body-movement signals, believed that only about 35 percent of meaning is communicated verbally when people are face-to-face; the other 65 percent is evoked by nonverbal signals.[31]

Nonverbal behaviors supplement our words and tell listeners how to interpret our words. However, nonverbal codes are culture-bound. Most of what follows is about mainstream American culture and is *not necessarily valid* for people from other countries or from certain co-cultures of the United States. We address the effects of culture in Chapter 5; here, we first consider general principles about nonverbal communication, then the specific functions performed by nonverbal behaviors.

Principles of Nonverbal Communication

There are three major principles necessary for understanding nonverbal communication. These principles concern the flow of nonverbal behaviors, their lack of specificity, and what happens when nonverbal and verbal behaviors contradict one another.

1. **You cannot stop engaging in nonverbal behavior in a small group.**

   This is often stated as "you cannot *not* communicate" and means that, in the presence of another person, you cannot help performing behaviors that others can potentially receive and interpret (although the interpretation may be completely incorrect). One of us taught a small group seminar in which one member, afraid that others would get to know her too well, decided she would not communicate. She refused to look at the other members, made few verbal contributions, and even turned her chair slightly aside so that others could not see her face. Of course she communicated—that she did not care about other members and was "too good" for the rest of the group. Although this was not the message she intended, this was the meaning attributed to her by the others. You may not participate verbally, but you cannot be physically present without affecting the mood, climate, cohesiveness, and interpersonal relationships of the group. The question is not "Will I communicate?" but "*What* will I communicate?"

2. **Nonverbal behavior is highly ambiguous.**

   Consider what a smile can mean: feelings of friendship, agreement with a proposal, amusement, acknowledgment of another, gloating over someone's misfortune, feelings of superiority, or simple liking. To prevent misunderstandings, verbal clarification is needed.

3. **When nonverbal and verbal behaviors seem to contradict each other, people will usually trust the nonverbal behavior.**

   A fellow group member, fists clenched and brows drawn tight, shouts, "NO, I'M NOT MAD!" Do you believe him? Marriage counselors are taught to look for these discrepancies, such as the wife who says, "I love my husband," while she shakes her head to indicate "no." There is good reason why we tend to believe nonverbal elements when there is an inconsistency: Nonverbal behaviors are less subject to a

Nonverbal behaviors supplement the words.

person's conscious control. Few of us are able consciously to control sweating, blushing, blood pressure, tension levels of internal organs, and so forth. Most of the time in group meetings we are not fully aware of what our feet, hands, faces, and bodies are doing. Some of us have been taught to control our speech rate, vocal tone, or pitch; and most of us exercise considerable control over the words we utter. Thus, nonverbal communication is relatively spontaneous and easier to trust than the more easily manipulated stream of words. This is especially the case when the nonverbal and verbal behaviors conflict and less so when they are more congruent; then, we pay more attention to the verbal behaviors.

Just as nonverbal behaviors can be inconsistent with verbal ones, nonverbal behaviors are sometimes inconsistent with each other. For example, consider the group member who leans forward, nods at what you say, and seems to be paying rapt attention but stifles a yawn while sneaking a peek at the clock. What are you to make of that? The pattern of overall nonverbal behavior is more important than any individual behavior.

Sometimes, inconsistent nonverbal behaviors result from the sender's internal confusion or uncertainty. For example, a group member may both like and dislike different elements of someone's proposal; this genuine confusion may appear as mixed messages in the form of a positive head nod with a frowning face.

To avoid sending mixed messages, be honest and clear. If you as a speaker are confused, help other members interpret your remarks by honestly revealing your confusion. If you are confused or puzzled by the mixed messages of another, say so, and help the other person clarify his or her intent.

"Are you sure?"
Nonverbal behaviors
help us express
emotions.

Functions of Nonverbal Behavior

Awareness of the functions of nonverbal behavior will enable you to respond appropriately to others and make your own behaviors more clear to them. Nonverbal behaviors serve six major functions during group interaction:

1. **Supplementing the verbal.**
   Nonverbal behavior may repeat and reinforce the verbal message. For example, a person points to item three on a chart and simultaneously says, "Now look at the third item on our list of ideas." Sometimes, nonverbal behavior elaborates what is said. For instance, a discussant may say, "It will be about *this* high when it is finished," and holds his hand 3 feet from the ground.

2. **Substituting for words.**
   Many gestures are substitutes for spoken words. Thumb and forefinger forming an O with the other three fingers held out stands for *okay* in the United States, as does the thumbs-up signal. If a committee chair asks, "Are we ready to vote?" and members shake their heads from side to side, the group will not vote.

3. **Contradicting verbal behaviors.**
   As we discussed earlier, sometimes nonverbal behaviors contradict what a person says. For instance, a member might say, "Yes, I'll go along with that," but in such a way that you expect him or her to give no real support to the idea. In such a case, point out the contradiction and ask for clarification: "You said you'd go along with the proposal, but something about the way you said it sounded as if you really don't like it very much. What do you feel?"

4. **Expressing emotions.**

    As the previous example illustrates, our feelings are communicated more often by nonverbal behavior than by what we say. Say, "I agree with you," in a variety of ways, and notice how each seems to indicate a very different feeling. A smile or nod can signal, "I like your proposal." Negative feelings are communicated nonverbally as well. For instance, some vocal aspects of anxiety are immediately detectable.[32] Particular voice characteristics are associated with both passive and active feelings.[33] Vocal qualities, posture, and facial expressions can all communicate feelings.

    When group members engage in computer-mediated communication like e-mail or even some forms of net conferences, they are faced with the reality that they cannot see each other. We discussed in Chapter 2 how social presence is impacted by the use of computers. CMC lacks the emotional cues group members can normally get when they are face-to-face. **Emoticons** or typographical emotional symbols are used in CMC to convey emotions in plain text.[34] September 19, 2002, actually marks the 20th anniversary of one of the most popular emoticons—the smiley face :-). Scott Falhman of Carnegie Mellon University created this emoticon as a way to mark or indicate a joke in plain text. If you want to read about how his original post was tracked down, you can log onto http://research.microsoft.com/mbj/Smiley/Joke_Thread.html.

    Use emoticons in your e-mails to show the emotional tone of your remarks. For example, ;-) can mean flirtatious or sarcastic, :-D can mean laughing at you; :-* can mean a wry smile, and so on. Remember though that context can help you determine their judicious use. Their informal use among group members probably will not be a problem; however, if group members are e-mailing a business for information or to ask questions, emoticons should not be used. Emoticons are generally considered sophomoric and should be avoided in business communications.[35]

5. **Regulating interaction.**

    Certain nonverbal messages, called **regulators,** direct the flow of interaction among group members. For example, such things as leaning forward, taking an audible breath, or relaxing nonverbally communicate turn-taking. Turn-taking happens almost automatically, without much conscious thought, but discussion leaders also consciously employ head nods, eye contact, and hand movements to indicate who should speak next. Favorable nods indicate, "Keep talking," but lack of response or looking away may signal, "Shut up." Students raise their hands in classes to show they want to be recognized. Many of these regulatory cues are visual. A group that one of us observed had a blind member who could not see visual regulatory cues. He

Emoticons

Symbols and combinations of characters used in computer-mediated communication to help convey relational messages and social presence.

Regulators

Nonverbal behavior used to control who speaks during a discussion.

frequently talked out of turn or cut the other members' speaking turns short. The others were upset at what they perceived to be arrogant and self-centered behavior, but a discussion about regulatory cues helped the group discover the extent to which we depend on visual regulatory cues to regulate interaction. The discussion increased members' sensitivity to the communicative problems some blind people experience.

Turn-taking is problematic during computer-mediated communication.[36] When groups use net conferencing, they can be engaged in synchronous interaction. Although they can "talk to each other," so to speak, they will be out of sync with each other. There is about a half-second delay between speaking and hearing. When you begin to speak during a pause, the other person will probably start speaking before you are done. This delay of feedback throws off the ability of those using net conferences to respond to each other effectively. This timing problem affects the use of humor in net conferences (there is less compared to face-to-face) and amount of interaction (monologues are common in net conferences).[37]

6. **Indicating status relationships.**
Sitting at the end of the table indicates leadership or a desire for high influence in the group. A member who stakes out more than an average amount of territory at a table (briefcase, books, coffee cup, etc.) shows dominance or superiority, as does suddenly getting very close to another, a penetrating stare, loud voice, or a patronizing pat or other touch.[38] High-status members tend to have more relaxed postures than lower-status members. On the other hand, uncrossing arms and legs, unbuttoning a coat, and a general relaxation of the body often signal openness and a feeling of equality.[39] Emergence as a perceived leader has been related to shoulder, head, and arm gestures.[40] Body orientation, the angle at which a participant's shoulders and legs are turned in relation to the group as a whole or another person, indicate how much one feels a part of the group and often that one is more committed to a subgroup than to the group as a whole.[41]

Effective group members understand the principles and functions of nonverbal behavior we have just discussed and use their understanding to be sensitive to nonverbal behavior. For example, one of us observed a normally quiet group member fold his arms in a closed gesture in response to a statement made by the group's chair. The chair, recognizing that this gesture could be interpreted in a number of different ways, asked the member to share his opinions directly with the group. It turned out that the member strongly disagreed with the emerging group consensus for several excellent reasons the others had not considered. The chair's alertness and sensitivity helped make this member's information available to the entire group.

Types of Nonverbal Behaviors   Interpreting nonverbal behavior appropriately requires that we look at the *pattern* of behavior rather than at just a single cue. At the same time, we need to be aware of the various types of nonverbal behavior to avoid overlooking any. Those listed next are especially relevant to communication among group members. Proceed with caution in your study of nonverbal behavior. There is considerable cross-cultural variation in the types of nonverbal behavior exhibited by people from different cultures.

Physical Appearance   Members of a new group react to each other's appearances long before they begin to judge each other's expertise and competencies. The judgments may or may not be correct, but they are formed initially from nonverbal messages that cannot be concealed, such as race, sex, physique, and mode of dress. We attribute factors such as intelligence and likability to people on the basis of what we initially observe of them. Of course, we may change our judgments later, but they are formed initially from a variety of nonverbal messages.

Sex, body shape, and ethnicity particularly affect how group members interact with each other initially.[42] Interestingly, given how much American culture pays attention to physical attractiveness, no research to date has examined the impact of relative physical attractiveness of group members to group dynamics or outcomes.[43]

Cultural factors influence our responses to physical appearance as well. Americans apparently have a clear picture of what a leader should look like. We tend to be prejudiced against endomorphs (heavy bodies), whom we often perceive as lazy, sloppy, stupid, and undependable, but also as jolly and easy to get along with. Ectomorphs (tall and skinny) are perceived as frail, studious, and intelligent. Mesomorphs (muscular types) are more likely than others to be perceived as leaders. Height is particularly important. The taller a person is, the more likely she or he is to be looked up to, literally, as a leader; short people have to try harder to be seen as potential group leaders.[44] We often are not aware we have these prejudices, so it is especially important that we teach ourselves to react to what a person does rather than to physical appearance.

The appearance of group members matters not only to the group but also to outsiders. Groups do not operate in a social vacuum; how group members appear to others can affect their credibility and even their success during group presentations. The most famous rock band of all time, The Beatles, used black clothes early in their career to mimic the color of beetles.[45] When John Lennon was asked how much of their success was due to their sound rather than their appearance, he replied, "We could have managed, looking like we look and making worse records, or we could have managed, looking like the average pop singer and making our noise. But the combination makes a better impact. We have always looked different from the rest of the mob."[46]

Space and Seating   There have been many studies of how we use **proxemics,** or personal space and territory, to communicate. We signal our need to be included by how we orient our bodies to the group. The neighbor who wants to arm the neighborhood pushes his chair away from the group when another member of the group challenges him. A person who sits close to other members, directly in the circle in a flexible seating space, close to a circular table, or at a central point at a square or rectangular table signals a need to belong or a sense of belonging; a member who sits outside the circumference, pushed back from a table, or at a corner may be signaling a desire to withdraw. Sitting within range of touch indicates that we feel intimately or personally involved, whereas sitting from just outside touch distance to several feet away signals a more formal, businesslike relationship.[47] Patterson found that group members making collective (group) decisions sit closer together and in more of a circle than when making individual judgments.[48] Stacks and Burgoon discovered that closer distances (18 inches) make group members more persuasive and credible than distances of 36 or 54 inches.[49]

What is a comfortable distance varies from one individual or one culture to another. In South America, southern and eastern Europe, and Arab countries, people prefer to stand close, whereas in northern Europe, North America, and Japan, people prefer more space.[50] In fact, members of Arabic cultures feel reassured when they stand close enough to be able to smell their conversational partners. Westerners, however, are usually uncomfortable with such close contact and tend to back away, causing Arabs to mistrust their intentions.

In small groups, individuals usually try to place themselves at a comfortable conversational distance according to the norms of their own cultures. Naturally, this can cause problems if the participants are members of cultures with divergent norms about appropriate distance; they may interpret unexpected behavior of others as rudeness or aggressiveness. We know a New England native who becomes extremely uncomfortable in crowded spaces and perceives as pushy those who try to close the space. On the other hand, one of us had a friend from Alabama who kept moving closer to her co-workers in Ohio, who kept backing away. Finally, they began to joke about her "invasion of their personal space," and both she and her co-workers learned something about their own co-cultural rules.

Proxemics

The study of uses of space and territory between and among people.

Females tend to sit closer than males and tolerate crowding better. People of the same age and the same social status sit closer together than people of different ages and statuses. The better acquainted people are, the closer they tend to sit. Thus, members of a long-standing group characterized by high interpersonal trust would be comfortable sitting close together in a small room, but people just beginning to form into a group would need more space. Even so, humans are highly adaptable, so when a room or other constraint violates our preferred distances, we adjust, at least for a short time.

A member's status affects how others react to violations of space norms. Burgoon et al. found, for instance, that if low-status group members violated the group's norm regarding space, other members saw them as less persuasive, sociable, and attractive. In contrast, high-status members enhanced their status by moving closer than the group norm specified, and even more if they moved farther away.[51] Thus, it is generally advisable for you to follow group space norms rather than violate them, but if you are a high-status group member, you may have some leeway.

Leadership emergence in a group is related to space. Dominant people and designated leaders usually choose central positions in the group, such as at the head of a rectangular table or across from as many others as possible. Other members frequently avoid sitting next to a designated leader so the arrangement looks like a leader sitting facing a horseshoe.[52] This reinforces the leader's position, allows the leader a comprehensive view of the group, and facilitates the leader's coordination and control.

People sitting across from each other speak more often to each other than people sitting side by side.[53] However, when a group has a dominating leader, "sidebar" conversations tend to break out between people sitting next to each other. Thus, we can conclude that conversation normally flows across the circle, and leaders should sit where they can maintain eye contact with as many group members as possible.

Seating preferences have been found to vary across cultures. Summarizing research in this area, Ramsey explains that Americans show liking with close interpersonal seating, a forward lean, direct orientation toward the other, and eye contact. Leaders seem to gravitate to head positions, with high-status individuals sitting nearby. Similar behaviors occur in Japan, where the leader sits at one end of a rectangular table, and, the lower the rank, the farther away the seat. In some cultures, teachers and others need to be careful in assigning seats for fear of inadvertently violating cultural taboos about who may sit next to whom. In a few cultures, people sit opposite each other when they have differences to settle, but sit side by side in rows when eating or enjoying one another's company.[54] Most of what we know about seating patterns comes from research on Westerners; it may not hold true for people of other cultures.

Seating and spatial features of the group's environment, such as fixed-space permanent features like walls and doors and movable features like furniture, influence the group's interactions.[55] In a large room, group members may choose to sit closer together than normal. If a group is meeting in a space normally used for another activity, the normal use of that space may change the group's interaction; for example, meeting in a member's living room may encourage informality. Meeting around a formal conference table encourages somewhat formal interaction, whereas meeting in a lounge with comfortable sofas does not. Sometimes, simply rearranging a group's meeting place can turn a chaotic group into a productive one. One of us advised a student committee whose meetings were characterized by general disorganization, repetition, and sidebar conversations. The room used by the group was normally set up for large assemblies, with a head table on a raised platform at the front, which the members used for their discussions. The president sat at the center of the long table, with the rest of the members sitting on either side of her along one side of the table. Only the members directly next to the president could both see and hear her without great difficulty. The group was advised to stop using the table and instead to rearrange the chairs in a circle. After just one meeting, members reported substantial improvement.

Issues of proxemics take on a different meaning when group members are using different forms of net conferences like the ones we discussed in Chapter 2. *Paraproxemics* refers to the illusion of proximity individuals may have when they are using videoconferences for group business.[56] If the camera zooms in on a person, that may create intimacy; however, if that camera gets too close, members may become threatened. Remember too that being tied to your computer can limit the space you have to gesture or move. Keep in mind that while proximity can be simulated in net conferencing, it cannot be duplicated.

Eye Contact   Eye movements can signal disgust, dislike, superiority, or inferiority, as well as liking; the rules for eye contact are highly culturally dependent. For most middle-class white Americans, establishing eye contact is the first step to conversing. Americans use eye contact when they seek feedback, when they want to be spoken to, and when they want to participate more actively.[57] For many middle-class Americans, lack of eye contact is perceived as dishonesty, rudeness, apathy, or nervousness.[58] Burgoon reported that students given free choice of seating arrangements in small classes chose to sit in a circular or U-shaped pattern for their meetings so that they could maintain eye contact with as many other members as possible.[59] Although a stare may indicate competitiveness, in a cooperative group it shows friendship and cohesiveness.[60] Eye contact is important, but must be interpreted carefully in context with other verbal and nonverbal behaviors.

Americans prefer direct eye contact with their conversational partners, but in some cultures (e.g., most Native American cultures) this is perceived as rude, and in still others (e.g., Arabic cultures) intense staring is the norm.[61] Hispanic children are taught to lower their gaze to indicate respect, but this can backfire in cases where Hispanic children interact with members of the dominant American culture.[62] For example, white American teachers and police officers sometimes misinterpret a lowered gaze as sullenness. Many African Americans, too, tend to avoid eye contact, especially with someone of higher status.[63]

Facial Expressions   Facial expressions indicate feelings and moods. Without a word being spoken, you can perceive anger, support, disagreement, and other sentiments. Eckman et al. found that at least six types of emotion could be detected accurately from facial expressions.[64] People with poker faces, who change facial expression very little, tend to be trusted less than people whose expressive faces signal their feelings more openly. But even poker-faced people leak their feelings by physiological changes they can't readily control, such as sweating or blushing.[65] If group members show few facial expressions, watch for other revealing physiological signs.

The face is quick! Some expressions last a mere 200 milliseconds and your eye blinks are over in even less time. A net conference camera connected to a good Internet connection can transmit 24 frames every second. This can drop to 1 second or less during a bad connection. The consequence to group discussion is that many facial microexpressions are lost.[66]

Be careful assuming that facial expressions, such as smiling, mean the same in all cultures. For example, a smile in Japan may be a spontaneous expression of pleasure, but it may also represent the desire not to cause pain for someone else.[67] A smiling Japanese may say to you, "I just came from my mother's funeral." According to Japanese rules of etiquette, it is extremely bad form to inflict unpleasantness on someone else; thus, no matter how bad someone feels inside, a cheerful face must be presented to the world.

Movements   The study of how we communicate by movement is called **kinesics.** We reveal our feelings with bodily movements and gestures. We show tension by shifting around in a chair, drumming fingers, swinging a foot, or twitching an eye. Such behavior may signal frustration, impatience with the group's progress, or annoyance. Alert group members will attempt to track down the source of tension by pointing out the kinesic cues and asking what may be producing them.

According to Scheflen, body orientation indicates how open to and accepting of others a group member feels.[68] Members turn directly to those they like and away from those they do not like. Leaning toward others indicates a sense of belonging, whereas leaning away signals a sense of rejection. Members who sit at angles tangential to the rest of the group may not feel included or want to belong. In fact group members do change their body orientation significantly from one meeting to the next.[69] As they get to know, like, and trust each other, they tend to increase their eye contact and angle their bodies more directly toward each other.

When members are tuned in to each other, they tend to imitate each other's posture and movements, creating a *body synchrony*. Scheflen observed many instances of parallel arm positions, self-touching behavior, and leg positions

Kinesics

Study of communication through movements.

indicating congruity.[70] Several studies found that group members are more likely to imitate the movements and gestures of members with high status and power than those with low status.[71] We can infer who has power and status in a group by observing which members are mimicked by others.

In discussion groups, body movements often regulate the flow of discussion. For example, speakers often signal that they are finished speaking by relaxing and stopping hand gestures.[72] Scheflen reported that a speaker who is concluding a point makes a noticeable postural shift.[73] A listener can bid for the floor by leaning forward, waving a hand, and simultaneously opening the mouth.

Vocal Cues   Vocal cues, or **paralanguage,** are any characteristics of voice and utterance other than the words themselves. Included are variables such as pitch, rate, fluency, pronunciation variations, force, tonal quality, and pauses. Extensive research since the 1930s indicates that listeners attribute certain characteristics to speakers based on these vocal cues,[74] including such things as attitudes, interests, personality traits, adjustment, ethnic group, education, and anxiety level and other emotional states.[75] Tone of voice is an excellent indicator of a person's self-concept and mood. For instance, frightened people tend to speak in tense, metallic tones; anxious people have nonfluencies such as interjections, repetitions, hesitations, sentence correction, and even stuttering in their speech. Pierce relates the story of a woman from New York City who offended many guests by her bossiness at a party.[76] She appeared to be ordering everyone around, but Pierce observed that her words seemed perfectly polite and appropriate for the situation. It was her *intonation pattern* that was offensive. Her particular pattern, appropriate and customary for New York City dwellers, was perceived as domineering by persons from other areas.

How we react to statements such as "I agree" or "Okay" depends much more on the pitch patterns and tone of voice than on the words themselves. For example, sarcasm and irony are indicated primarily by a tone of voice that suggests the words should be taken *opposite* to what they seem to mean. Children generally do not understand sarcasm, and even one-third of high school seniors take sarcastic statements literally.[77] Sarcasm in a group is easily misunderstood.

In both movement and voice, animation tends to increase status within the group. People who speak quietly in a low key have little persuasive impact. They seem to lack much personal involvement with what they say. However, members whose vocal qualities change too extensively may be seen irrational, not to be trusted as leaders or credible sources. Taylor found, however, that excessive vocal stress was judged more credible than a monotonous vocal pattern.[78] You are advised to vary your vocal tone and use vocal cues to emphasize the verbal content of your remarks.

Cultural differences have been observed in the use of the **backchannel,** which refers to vocalizations such as *mm-hmmm, uh-huh,* and *yeah-yeah-yeah* that are uttered while another is speaking to indicate interest and active

Paralanguage

Nonverbal characteristics of voice and utterance, such as pitch, rate, tone of voice, fluency, pauses, and variations in dialect.

Backchannel

Nonverbal vocalizations such as mm-hmm and uh-huh that are uttered while another is speaking; partly determined by one's culture, can indicate interest and active listening.

listening. We showed this earlier in our discussion of language, culture, and gender. In addition, Caucasian Americans do not give such backchannel responses as frequently as African Americans, Hispanics, and people of southern European origins.[79] This can lead to friction if members who use the backchannel frequently think those who do not are not really attuned and listening well, whereas the less active backchannel responders perceive their fellow members as being rude for interrupting so often.

Dialect

A regional variation in the pronunciation, vocabulary, and/or grammar of a language.

Dialect may also cause misunderstandings. **Dialect** entails regional and social variations in pronunciation, vocabulary, and grammar of a language. Because dialect influences perceptions of a speaker's intelligence and competence, it can seriously affect employability and performance,[80] as well as credibility. Most countries, including the United States, Canada, Great Britain, and Japan, have regional and social class language deviations to the "standard" dialect. We tend to stereotype individuals with nonstandard dialects. People who use *dees* and *dose* instead of *these* and *those* are identified as lower-status speakers and accorded lower credibility ratings. Speakers of the general American dialect are rated higher than Appalachians and Bostonians on sociointellectual status, dynamism, and being pleasant to listen to. Those who speak a French-Canadian dialect are rated as poor and ignorant in comparison with those who speak an English-Canadian dialect. Teachers tend to rate students who use dialects other than general American as less confident and more ignorant.

It is important to be aware of judgment errors that result from such perceptions. However, as intercultural communication becomes more widespread, cultures become increasingly similar in some respects.[81] Surprisingly, William Labov, a renowned professor of sociolinguistics, has not found this to be the case with respect to dialect.[82] He predicted that, because of the homogenization of the American marketplace, he would find a standardization of dialect in the United States. In a three-year attempt to create a "phonological atlas" of the United States, he found that our dialects are stronger and more distinct than ever before. Even areas of the country, such as the West Coast, that have not had strong accents show regional dialects. For instance, "bed" in California is pronounced "bad"; in the Great Lakes region, it is pronounced "bud," and in the south, "bayed." Communities show their distinctiveness by how they speak; individuals show their uniqueness by consciously varying their accents.

Time Cues   Few of us think of time as a nonverbal dimension of communication. Perceptions of time are highly culturally dependent. Americans think of time as a commodity to be spent or saved. People in Western cultures tend to regulate their activities by the clock, but people in many other cultures act according to inner biological needs or natural events.

In the fast-paced culture of the American business world, being considerate of group members' time is important; Americans usually will allow only about a five-minute leeway before they expect an apology.[83] People who come late to meetings (except because of absolutely unavoidable circumstances) are judged to be inconsiderate, undisciplined, and selfish. Likewise, it is considered improper to leave a meeting before the announced ending time, unless some prior arrangement or explanation has been made. Forcing others to keep to your time schedule is the prerogative of high-status individuals.[84] It implies that your time is more important than that of the other members, and marks you as inconsiderate and arrogant.

Let's take a closer look at time and culture to understand better why individuals from different cultures may treat time differently. Hall describes the Spanish culture of New Mexico as *polychronic,* whereas the Anglo culture is *monochronic.*[85] The Spanish do several things at a time; the Anglos tend to do one thing at a time. The Spanish are casual about clocks and schedules; they are frequently late for appointments and meetings. Anglos are offended by such behavior. The cultures of Latin America, the Middle East, Japan, and France are polychronic, whereas the cultures of northern Europe, North America, and Germany are monochronic.[86] In these cultures, time is treated as a tangible *thing* that can be spent, killed, and wasted; time is perceived as more relational in communal cultures, which integrate task and social needs and hold more fluid attitudes about time.

Time also is a commodity in the group's interaction (i.e., "air time"). People can abuse this resource by talking too much or too little. Harper et al. found that persons who talked somewhat more than average were viewed favorably on leadership characteristics. Those who talked an average amount were the most liked. Extremely talkative members were regarded as rude and selfish, members the group could do without.[87] Derber refers to excessive talking as *conversational narcissism.*[88]

Touch   **Haptics** is the study of this important nonverbal dimension in interpersonal communication. It is vital to group maintenance in most primary groups and athletic teams, but may be nonexistent in many American work groups and committees. Studies of touch in group communication are sparse; most information about touch comes from work in interpersonal communication. The kind of touching people expect and enjoy depends on their acculturation and the type of relationship they share with others. For instance, touch between strangers, other than a handshake, tends to threaten most Americans.

Touch between individuals may occur to show play, positive feelings, or control, to get a job done, as part of a greeting or farewell; and of course we touch each other accidentally. Jones and Yarbrough found that *control touches* occur most often followed by positive affect touches.[89] *Control touches* are efforts to gain attention or request compliance and are most often accompanied by some sort of verbalization such as "Move over." Positive affect touches are most often signs of affection and associated with our primary groups but can occur in business settings. They found that some work teams may engage in spontaneous and brief touches to show support.

Touch among group members can strengthen unity and teamwork. Families join hands to say grace before a meal; football players pile on hands in a huddle; actors hug each other after a successful performance. The type of touch and its setting determines the reaction. Pats are usually perceived as signs of affection and inclusion. Strokes are generally perceived as sensual, inappropriate in

Haptics
The study of the perception of and use of touch.

a small group meeting. A firm grip on an arm or about the shoulders is usually a control gesture, interpreted as a "one-up" maneuver; among a group of equals, this may be resented. A gentle touch may be a means of getting someone to hold back and not overstate an issue. Many a group member has been restrained from saying something hostile by a gentle touch on the arm during a heated argument.

As with other nonverbal behaviors, people vary widely in the extent to which they accept and give touches. Andersen and Leibowitz found that people range from those who enjoy touch to those who react negatively to being touched.[90] For example, the handshake, a standard American greeting, is by no means universal. The willingness to touch hands suggests a belief in the equality of people.[91] This typically Western notion contrasts with the Hindu belief in a hierarchical society. Hindus greet each other by bringing their own palms together at the chest. Muslims, who according to the *Koran* are all brothers, hug each other shoulder to shoulder. The Japanese bow in greeting, but prefer to avoid physical contact. You can see how a culture's power distance (such as a belief in equality versus a belief in hierarchy) influences such things as the appropriate nonverbal form for a greeting, and also how easy it is for misunderstandings to occur in small groups with members of different cultures.

Often the unconscious nonverbal behaviors we have discussed determine how much we like or trust someone. We all have a tendency to like people we perceive as similar to us, but we are unaware that our feelings are often based on *nonverbal* similarity.[92] It is important for us to recognize this normal tendency and consciously suspend judgments of others in intercultural settings where the same nonverbal behaviors have different meanings.

Recap: A Quick Review

Nonverbal behavior not only functions in multiple ways but can also be categorized in numerous ways, each with its own cultural implication. Several categories are relevant to group communication.

1. Group member appearance is one of the first nonverbal behaviors judged by members.

2. Proxemics, or use of space and territory, can indicate things such as status, belonging, and comfort.

3. Eye contact is central to managing conversational dynamics.

4. Facial expressions indicate the feelings and moods of group members.

5. Kinesics involves body orientation and vocal characteristics.

6. The experience of time culturally can influence the rules of "being on time" and how members define the duration of speaking turns.

7. Touch, most important to interpersonal communication, also has serious implications to small group communication.

QUESTIONS FOR REVIEW

 Go to self-quizzes on the Online Learning Center at mhhe.com/galanes12 to test your knowledge of the chapter concepts

We began with a neighborhood group meeting for the first time. Despite the best of intentions misunderstandings and hard feelings emerged out of their verbal and nonverbal behaviors. Communication holds the secrets of effective group dynamics.

1. The most important characteristic of language is that all language is symbolic. How is this apparent in our neighborhood group?

2. How is the fact that language and culture are interconnected apparent in our story?

3. Are there any gendered characteristics of language operating in our story? Why should you be careful about drawing conclusions about gender and language?

4. Which language problems are the most obvious in our neighborhood group: bypassing, lack of clarity or the use of emotive words? How could some of their language problems have been avoided?

5. What are the three principles of nonverbal communication and their implications for this small group's communication?

6. What are the six functions of nonverbal behavior in small group communication? How does each function show itself in small group interaction?

7. Which of the eight major categories of nonverbal behaviors are most relevant to this neighborhood group?

8. How does space and seating impact group climate, status among members and leadership?

9. What are some different rules for eye contact group members might expect in a group with a mix of gender, age, and culture?

10. How do vocalics influence group interaction and in what ways may it have been relevant to the early dynamics of our neighborhood group?

11. How would computer technology change the perceptions and use of the categories of nonverbal behavior?

KEY TERMS

 Test your knowledge of these key terms by visiting the Online Learning Center website at mhhe.com/galanes12

Ambiguity
Backchannel
Bypass
Concrete
Dialect
Emoticons

Emotive words
Gender
Haptics
Hidden antagonizers
High-level abstractions
Kinesics

Nonverbal behavior
Paralanguage
Proxemics
Referent
Regulators
Sex

BIBLIOGRAPHY

Andersen, Peter A. "Nonverbal Communication in the Small Group." In *Small Group Communication: A Reader*. 6th ed. Robert S. Cathcart and Larry A. Samovar, eds. Dubuque, IA: Wm. C. Brown, 1992, 272–86.

Andersen, Peter A. *Beside Language: Nonverbal Communication in Interpersonal Interaction*. Palo Alto, CA: Mayfield, 1995.
Burgoon, Judee K. "Spatial Relationships in Small Groups." In *Small Group Communication: A*

Reader. 7th ed. Robert S. Cathcart, Larry A. Samovar, and Linda D. Henman, eds. Dubuque, IA: Brown & Benchmark, 1996, 241–53.

Burgoon, Judee K., David Buller, and W. Gill Woodall. *Nonverbal Communication: The Unspoken Dialogue*. New York: Harper & Row, 1989.

Condon, John C. *Semantics and Communication*. 3rd ed. New York: Macmillan, 1985.

Leathers, Dale G. *Successful Nonverbal Communication: Principles and Applications*. 2nd ed. New York: Macmillan, 1992.

NOTES

1. D. J. Higginbotham and D. E. Yoder, "Communication within Natural Conversational Interaction: Implications for Severe Communicatively Impaired Persons," *Topics in Language Disorders* 2 (1982): 4.

2. See John Stewart and Carol Logan, *Together: Communicating Interpersonally*, 5th ed. (New York: McGraw-Hill, 1998): 80–86.

3. John B. Carrol, ed., *Language; Thought and Reality: Selected Writings of Benjamin Lee Whorf* (New York: Wiley, 1956): 212–13.

4. Myron W. Lusting and Jolene Koester, *Intercultural Competence: Interpersonal Communication across Cultures* (New York: Harper-Collins, 1993).

5. "Englishes Are an International Language," *Michigan Today* (June 1995): 17.

6. Brant R. Burleson, "Proponents of 'Alien Cultures View' Need to Come Down to Earth," *Chicago Tribune* (November 23, 1997).

7. Aki Uchida, "Bring the 'Culture' Back In: A Culture-Building Approach to Gender and Communication," *Women & Language* XX (Fall 1997): 15–24.

8. Lea P. Stewart, Alan D. Stewart, Sheryl A. Friedley, and Pamela J. Cooper, *Communication between the Sexes: Sex Differences and Sex-Role Stereotypes*, 2nd ed. (Scottsdale, AZ: Gorsuch Scarisbrick, 1990): 43–114.

9. Daniel N. Maltz and Ruth A. Borker, "A Cultural Approach to Male-Female Miscommunication," in *Language and Social Identity*, ed. John J. Gumperz (Cambridge: Cambridge University Press, 1982): 195–216.

10. Anthony Mulac, Pamela Gibbons, and Stuart Fujiyama, "Male/Female Language Differences Viewed from an Inter-Cultural Perspective: Gender as Culture," paper presented at the Speech Communication Association Annual Convention (November 1990), Chicago.

11. James C. McCroskey, Virginia P. Richmond, and Robert A. Stewart, *One on One: The Foundations of Interpersonal Communication* (Englewood Cliffs, NJ: Prentice Hall, 1986): 244–47.

12. Stewart, Stewart, Friedley, and Cooper, *Communication between the Sexes*, 92–106.

13. John E. Baird, "Sex Differences in Group Communication: A Review of Relevant Research," *Quarterly Journal of Speech* 62 (1976): 179–92.

14. Lynn Smith-Lovin and Charles Brody, "Interruptions in Group Discussions: The Effects of Gender and Group Composition," *American Sociological Review* 54 (June 1989): 424–35.

15. Anthony F. Verdi and Susan A. Wheelan, "Developmental Patterns in Same-Sex and Mixed-Sex Groups," *Small Group Research* 23 (August 1992): 356–78.

16. Edward A. Mabry, "Some Theoretical Implications of Female and Male Interaction in Unstructured Small Groups," *Small Group Behavior* 20 (1989): 536–50.

17. William E. Jurma and Beverly C. Wright, "Follower Reactions to Male and Female Leaders Who Maintain or Lose Reward Power," *Small Group Research* 21 (1990): 97–12.

18. Patricia H. Andrews, "Sex and Gender Differences in Group Communication: Impact on the Facilitation Process," *Small Group Research* 23 (February 1992): 74–92.

19. Georgia Duerst-Lahti, "But Women Play the Game Too: Communication Control and Influence in Administrative Decision Making," *Administration and Society* 22 (August 1990): 182–205.

20. Linda L. Carli, "Gender, Language, and Influence," *Journal of Personality and Social Psychology* 59 (1990): 941–51.

21. Nancy A. Burrell, William A. Donahue, and Mike Allen, "Gender-Based Perceptual Biases in Mediating," *Communication Research* 15 (1988): 447–69.

22. Susan B. Shimanoff and Mercilee M. Jenkins, "Leadership and Gender: Challenging Assumptions and Recognizing Resources," in *Small Group Communication: Theory and Practice*, 7th ed., eds. Robert S. Cathcart, Larry A. Samovar, and Linda D. Henman (Madison, WI: Brown & Benchmark, 1996): 327–44.

23. Kathleen M. Propp, "An Experimental Examination of Biological Sex as a Status Cue in Decision-Making Groups and Its Influence on Information Use," *Small Group Research* 26 (November 1995): 451–74.

24. Judith Taps and Patricia Yancey Martin, "Gender Composition, Attributional Accounts, and Women's Influence and Likability in Task Groups," *Small Group Research* 21 (November 1990): 471–91.

25. Daniel J. Canary and Brian H. Spitzberg, "Appropriateness and Effectiveness Perceptions of Conflict Strategies," *Human Communication Research* 14 (1987): 93–118.

26. Dale G. Leathers, "Process Disruption and Measurement in Small Group Communication," *Quarterly Journal of Speech* 55 (1969): 288–98.

27. Tyrone Adams and Norman Clark, *The Internet: Effective Online Communication* (Fort Worth TX: Harcourt, 2001).

28. Jacob Palme, *Electronic Mail* (Norwood, MA: Artech House, 1995).

29. Adams and Clark, *The Internet*.

30. Diana K. Ivy and Phil Backlund, *Exploring Genderspeak: Personal Effectiveness in Gender Communication* (New York: McGraw-Hill, 1994): 17.

31. Ray L. Birdwhistell, lecture at Nebraska Psychiatric Institute, Omaha, NE, May 11, 1972.

32. J. Starkweather, "Vocal Communication of Personality and Human Feeling," *Journal of Communication* 11 (1961): 63–72.

33. Joel R. Davitz and Lois J. Davitz, "Nonverbal Vocal Communication of Feeling," *Journal of Communication* 11 (1961): 81–86.

34. Adams and Clark, *The Internet*.

35. Ibid.

36. Ibid.

37. J. Tang and E. Isaacs, "Studies of Multimedia-Supported Collaboration," in *Information Superhighways: Multimedia Users and Futures*, ed. S. Emmott (San Diego, CA: Academic Press, 1995): 123–60.

38. Erving Goffman, *Relations in Public* (New York: Harper & Row, 1971): 32–48.

39. Gerald E. Nierenberg and H. H. Calero, *How to Read a Person like a Book* (New York: Pocket Books, 1973): 46.

40. Edward A. Mabry, "Developmental Aspects of Nonverbal Behavior in Small Group Settings," *Small Group Behavior* 20 (1989): 192–203.

41. Stewart L. Tubbs, *A Systems Approach to Small Group Interaction* (Reading, MA: Addison-Wesley, 1978): 185.

42. Sandra Ketrow, "Nonverbal Aspects of Group Communication," in *The Handbook of Group Communication Theory & Research*, ed. Lawrence R. Frey (Thousand Oaks, CA: Sage, 1999): 251–87.

43. Ibid.

44. J. B. Cortes and F. M. Gatti, "Physique and Propensity," in *With Words Unspoken*, eds. L. B. Rosenfeld and J. M. Civikly (New York: Holt, Rinehart and Winston, 1976): 50–56.

45. Robert Freeman, *The Beatles: A Private View* (New York: Barnes & Noble, 1990): 46.

46. Ibid., p. 46.

47. Edward T. Hall, *The Silent Language* (Garden City, NY: Doubleday, 1959).

48. M. L. Patterson, "The Role of Space in Social Interaction," in *Nonverbal Behavior and Communication*, eds. A. W. Siegman and S. Feldstein (Hillsdale, NJ: Erlbaum, 1978): 277.

49. Don W. Stacks and Judee K. Burgoon, "The Persuasive Effects of Violating Spatial Distance Expectations in Small Groups." Paper presented at the Southern Speech Communication Association Convention, Biloxi, MS (April 1979).

50. William B. Gudykunst and Stella Ting-Toomey, *Culture and Interpersonal Communication* (Newbury Park, CA: Sage, 1975): 124–28.

51. J. K. Burgoon, D. W. Stacks, and S. A. Burch, "The Role of Interpersonal Rewards and Violations of Distancing Expectations in Achieving Influence

in Small Groups," *Communication* 11 (1982): 114–28.

52. R. F. Bales and A. P. Hare, "Seating Patterns and Small Group Interaction," *Sociometry* 26 (1963): 480–86; G. Hearn, "Leadership and the Spatial Factor in Small Groups," *Journal of Abnormal and Social Psychology* 54 (1957): 269–72.

53. B. Steinzor, "The Spatial Factor in Face to Face Discussion Groups," *Journal of Abnormal and Social Psychology* 45 (1950): 552–55.

54. Sheila J. Ramsey, "Nonverbal Behavior: An Intercultural Perspective," in *Handbook of Intercultural Communication,* eds. Molefi K. Asante, Eileen Newmark, and Cecil A. Blake (Beverly Hills, CA: Sage, 1979): 129–31.

55. Judee K. Burgoon, "Spatial Relationships in Small Groups," in *Small Group Communication: A Reader,* 6th ed., eds. Robert S. Cathcart and Larry A. Samovar (Dubuque, IA: Wm. C. Brown, 1992): 289–90.

56. Adams and Clark, *The Internet.*

57. James McCroskey, C. Larson, and Mark Knapp, *An Introduction to Interpersonal Communication* (Englewood Cliffs, NJ: Prentice Hall, 1971): 110–14.

58. Peter A. Andersen, "Nonverbal Communication in the Small Group," in *Small Group Communication: A Reader,* 6th ed., eds. Robert S. Cathcart and Larry A. Samovar (Dubuque, IA: Wm. C. Brown, 1992): 274.

59. Burgoon, "Spatial Relationships in Small Groups," 295.

60. R. V. Exline, "Exploration in the Process of Person Perception: Visual Interaction in Relation to Competition, Sex, and the Need for Affiliation," *Journal of Personality* 31 (1963): 1–20.

61. Donald Klopf, *Intercultural Encounters: The Fundamentals of Intercultural Communication* (Englewood, CO: Morton 1987): 177.

62. Stewart Tubbs and Sylvia Moss, *Human Communication,* 5th ed. (New York: Random House, 1997): 414.

63. Dorothy L. Pennington, "Black-White Communication: An Assessment of Research," in *Handbook of Intercultural Communication,* eds. Molefi K. Asante, Eileen Newmark, and Cecil A. Blake (Beverly Hills, CA: Sage, 1979): 387.

64. P. Eckman, P. Ellsworth, and W. V. Friesen, *Emotion in the Human Face: Guidelines for Research and an Integration of Findings* (New York: Pergamon Press, 1971).

65. R. W. Buck, R. E. Miller, and W. F. Caul, "Sex, Personality, and Physiological Variables in the Communication of Affect via Facial Expression," *Journal of Personality and Social Psychology* 30 (1974): 587–96.

66. Tyrone Adams and Norman Clark, *The Internet: Effective Online Communication* (Fort Worth TX: Harcourt, 2001): 119.

67. Branch Lotspiech, personal conversation, June, 1990.

68. Albert. E. Scheflen, "Quasi-Courtship Behavior in Psychotherapy," *Psychiatry* 28 (1965): 245–56.

69. Edward A. Mabry, "Development Aspects of Nonverbal Behavior in Small Group Settings," *Small Group Behavior* 20 (1989): 190–202.

70. Albert. E. Scheflen, *Body Language and the Social Order: Communication as Behavioral Control* (Englewood Cliffs, NJ: Prentice Hall, 1972): 54–73.

71. Judee K. Burgoon and T. Saine, *The Unknown Dialogue: An Introduction to Nonverbal Communication* (Boston: Houghton Mifflin, 1978).

72. S. Duncan, Jr., "Some Signals and Rules for Taking Speaking Turns in Conversations," *Journal of Personality and Social Psychology* 23 (1972): 283–92.

73. Scheflen, *Body Language and the Social Order.*

74. N. D. Addington, "The Relationship of Selected Vocal Characteristics to Personality and Perception," *Speech Monographs* 35 (1968): 492; Ernest Kramer, "Judgment of Personal Characteristics and Emotions from Nonverbal Properties of Speech," *Psychological Bulletin* 60 (1963): 408–20.

75. Davitz and Davitz, "Nonverbal Vocal Communication of Feeling."

76. Joe E. Pierce, "Life Histories of Individuals and Their Impact on International Communication," in *Intercultural and International Communication,* ed. Fred L. Casmir (Washington, DC: University Press of America, 1978): 525.

77. P. A. Andersen, J. F. Andersen, N. J. Wendt, and M. A. Murphy, "The Development of Nonverbal Communication Behavior in School Children Grades K–12" (Paper presented at the International Communication Association Annual Convention, Minneapolis, May, 1981).

78. K. D. Taylor, "Ratings of Source Credibility in Relation to Level of Vocal Variety, Sex of the Source

and Sex of the Receiver" (M.A. thesis, University of Nebraska at Omaha, 1984).

79. Peter A. Anderson, "Nonverbal Communication in the Small Group," in *Small Group Communication: A Reader,* 6th ed., eds. Robert S. Cathcart and Larry A. Samovar (Dubuque, IA: Wm. C. Brown, 1992): 278.

80. Klopf, *Intercultural Encounters,* 178.

81. Tubbs and Moss, *Human Communication,* 414.

82. William Labov, "Acute Inflection: Speech Patterns Buck National Homogeneity," *Civilization* (June/July 1999): 30.

83. Hall, *The Silent Language.*

84. Martin Remland, "Developing Leadership Skills in Nonverbal Communication: A Situational Perspective," *Journal of Business Communication* 3 (1981): 17–29.

85. Edward T. Hall, "The Hidden Dimensions of Time and Space in Today's World," in Cross-Cultural Perspectives in Nonverbal Communication, ed. Fernando Poyatos (Toronto: C. J. Hogrefe, 1988): 145–52.

86. Edward T. Hall, *The Dance of Life,* summarized in Gudykunst and Ting-Toomey, *Culture and Interpersonal Communication,* 128–30.

87. R. G. Harper, A. N. Weins, and J. D. Natarazzo, *Nonverbal Communication: The State of the Art* (New York: Wiley, 1978).

88. C. Derber, *The Pursuit of Attention* (New York: Oxford University Press, 1979).

89. Stanley E. Jones and A. Elaine Yarbrough, "A Naturalistic Study of the Meanings of Touch," *Communication Monographs* 52 (1985): 19–56.

90. P. A. Andersen and K. Leibowitz, "The Development and Nature of the Construct 'Touch Avoidance,'" *Environmental Psychology and Nonverbal Behavior* 3 (1978): 89–106.

91. Klopf, *Intercultural Encounters,* 178.

92. Walburga von Raffler-Engle, "The Impact of Covert Factors in Cross-Cultural Communication," in *Cross-Cultural Perspectives in Nonverbal Communication,* ed. Fernando Poyatos (Toronto: C. J. Hogrefe, 1988): 96.

The Small Group as a System

STUDY OBJECTIVES

As a result of studying Chapter 4 you should be able to:

1. List and explain the major input, throughput, and output variables in a small group system and provide examples of their interdependence.
2. Define the main terms and types of variables pertaining to systems.
3. Describe the main concepts of the bona fide group perspective.
4. Describe the characteristics of an effective discussion group.

CENTRAL MESSAGE

All components of a small group operate interdependently with one another, and the group itself is interdependent with its environment. To understand a group fully, we must examine the components in relationship to one another, not in isolation.

During one traumatic week, the church board—one minister and three lay people—of a new Unity church faced nearly insurmountable challenges. On Monday the board chair suffered a stroke; on Wednesday the minister died. The remaining members, in shock, recruited three other members to help carry on the work. The board had been working to establish a second Unity church in Springfield, Missouri, following an unpleasant church split two years earlier. The new church had just gotten off the ground when these tragedies occurred, but members, committed to the project, decided to keep the church going. The board elected Bill, a lawyer, as chair. Sally, a widowed secretary whose husband had been a minister, agreed to serve as secretary. The other members included Marina, a college professor; Sunni, director of a university speech and hearing clinic; and Norm, a massage therapist who was also an accomplished musician. No paid employees worked for the church—all the work was accomplished by volunteers, including board members.

Among the challenges board members faced were how to handle Sunday services without a minister, how to pay for the lease they had recently signed on an older building, and how to overcome opposition to the new congregation, from the denomination's headquarters and the original church's minister. The board quickly decided they needed additional expertise so they soon added two more members: Don, a retired business owner, and Gary, a maintenance worker. The members had diverse experiences and expertise, but they all shared a similar vision for the church and common values to guide them in their work. The board met every week for two years. At the end of that time, members could point to several important accomplishments: Sunday services were held every week and attendance had increased from about 40 members to about 90 members per Sunday; bylaws had been approved by the congregation; the board, originally an informal, self-selected board, was voted in by the congregation; enough money had been set aside to cover a minister's salary for six months; and, most important of all, the formerly renegade congregation had received official approval from the denomination's headquarters and was now "legal."

We have already discussed how pervasive small groups are in our daily lives and why we should study them. In this chapter we will use the church board we just introduced to illustrate the basic principles of general systems theory, a framework for understanding small groups. We periodically present dialogue from the church board to illustrate how various principles of systems theory may appear communicatively. Once you have a communication-based model for understanding systems principles, you can recognize the principles operating in any group.

The Systems Perspective

When a new person joins a group, the group changes in some ways. For example, when a new baby is brought into a family, all family relationships will change, including between the parents, between the other children, and between the parents and the children. In addition, new relationships must be accommodated—between everyone else and the new baby. This illustrates the idea of a **system**—a set of relationships among interdependent, interacting components and forces. General systems theory is built upon an analysis of living entities—including groups and organizations—as they attempt to remain in dynamic balance with the environment by making constant adjustments.

The systems framework helps you keep track of all the individual components of a small group as they interact in a complex whole. The "group as system" metaphor has long been dominant among small group communication scholars because, in part, a key premise of the systems approach is that *communication* links the relevant parts of a system together.[1] We like the approach because it places the role of communication to the forefront of what we study and helps students manage the complexity of small group communication. Even when we focus on a small part of the puzzle (e.g., leadership or problem solving), the systems framework reminds us that each piece of the puzzle interacts with every other piece.

However, the systems perspective has been criticized by some scholars. For instance, some have questioned how useful the perspective is because it appears to be a philosophical framework rather than a useful explanatory framework.[2] Others have said that the systems approach focuses too much on a group's dynamic balance, or *homeostasis*. In other words, systems theorists assume that a system's goal is to maintain stability; thus, the systems framework calls more attention to how groups stay the same rather than how they change. Our point here is not to elaborate on or refute these specific concerns, but to let you know that this is one of several theories used to understand small group communication. In previous chapters we have explained the fundamentals of communication. We now begin the process of examining how communication helps shape the small group system.

Principles of a System

One of the most important system principles is that of **interdependence,** which states that the parts of a system do not operate in isolation but continuously affect each other, as well as the system as a whole. The new baby affects every other family member. Similarly, if the usually cheerful chair of a committee comes to a group meeting in a grouchy mood, the other members may feel uneasy and the group's normally effective decision-making processes may be impaired. In the church board we described, every decision was accomplished through open discussion that emphasized member interdependence. For example, for Sunday services to proceed without a hitch, the worship coordinator had to book the speaker and print the programs; the decorator had to make sure that the flowers were in place and the hymnals distributed; and the hospitality coordinator had to unlock the building and

System

An entity made up of components in interdependent relationship to each other, requiring constant adaptation among its parts to maintain organic wholeness and balance.

Interdependence

The property of a system such that all parts are interrelated and affect each other as well as the whole system.

make the coffee. If anyone failed to do his or her job, the service as a whole would be hurt.

A column by George Will in *Newsweek* dramatically illustrates the principle of interdependence and also reminds us that, because we are all interdependent, actions we take sometimes have unanticipated consequences.[3] When the Lincoln Memorial was illuminated at night, the lights attracted insects, which attracted the spiders that fed on them, which then attracted the birds that fed on the spiders. To keep the monument beautiful for visitors, workers scrubbed the bird droppings and the spider webs that accumulated, but the act of scrubbing the marble made it susceptible to the exhaust fumes from the traffic in Washington, D.C. Lighting the monument, intended to have a positive effect, also set in motion a chain of events that is contributing to the monument's deterioration. We cannot know in advance all the effects our actions will cause.

Nonsummativity

The property of a system that the whole is not the sum of its parts, but may be greater or lesser than the sum.

Another key principle is the system property of **nonsummativity** (nonadditivity), which states that the whole system is not just the sum of its parts. It may be either greater or less than the sum of its parts, with either positive synergy or negative synergy operating. Sports fans know they will lose money on a basketball or football game if they add up the statistics for each player, arrive at team totals, and bet on the team with the higher total. On any given day, a so-called poor team can play beyond its apparent potential (positive synergy), or a terrific team can have an off day (negative synergy). Why? Because each team or group is a living system in which everything is interdependent, and no one can predict precisely how the new system will function during any particular time or how the parts will affect one another.

A team takes on a life of its own and becomes a real, living entity that is *based* on members' abilities, but is not just a totaling up of their skills. For example, the Southwest Missouri State University Lady Bears basketball team, whose players are shorter, slower, and less experienced than many top-tier women's teams, won the National Invitational Tournament in 2005 and has occasionally played in the semifinal rounds of the National College Athletic Association tournament. On the other hand, the knowledgeable, intelligent, and dedicated scientists and managers at NASA collectively made a flawed decision in 1986 to launch the space shuttle *Challenger,* which exploded just after liftoff.

No one can predict whether a group will experience positive or negative synergy. In our classes, we have often had groups composed of bright students whose final products disappointed us. However, Salazar has posited that the amount of ambiguity a group faces and how it handles the ambiguity play major roles.[4] Ambiguity determines the types of obstacles a group will encounter. Whether the obstacles are dealt with in a helpful or disruptive way determines whether a process loss (negative synergy) or gain (positive synergy) will occur. In any case, the communication behavior of the members is the principal determining factor for process gains or losses.

The principle of **equifinality** (literally, *equal ends*) suggests that different systems can reach the same outcome even if they have different starting places; the related principle of **multifinality** states that systems starting out at the same place may reach different end points. Both principles refer to the same idea: It is impossible to predict where a system will end up by knowing only where it starts out. For example, we occasionally give our students an early group assignment of giving a class presentation based on a chapter of this text as a way to jumpstart the group formation process. As you might imagine, we have observed a variety of approaches to carrying out this assignment, even though the groups have been given the same charge and the same material. Some groups have chosen to lecture from the text; others have created role plays and interactive exercises based on chapter material; still others have incorporated clips from current films to illustrate concepts. Some groups of outstanding students have done fabulous presentations; others have not. We find it impossible to predict what our students will do or even how well they will do!

Odds were against the church board's success. A splinter group from the same original congregation had tried to start a new church years before; it had failed. But our church board, composed of ordinary yet dedicated individuals, succeeded. We have observed similar outcomes in many contexts: government, community and voluntary organizations, business, education. For example, one group of students turned in, at the last minute, a mediocre final paper because members had not been able to find a way to handle interpersonal conflict between two of them. By the end of the semester, none of them ever wanted to see the others again. Early in the semester, though, we predicted that this group of A students would turn in an A paper. In the same class, another group of average students had "jelled"—members liked each other, wanted to do a good job, and were willing to put in extra effort toward the task. They turned in a draft of the paper a week early, so we could pre-grade it with comments. They then took those comments and put the final finishing touches on what was an outstanding paper. They had a party to celebrate their success. As you can imagine, the communication among members is the key to where a group ends up.

The systems perspective helps keep us from oversimplifying our understanding of how a group functions and perhaps missing something important. For example, systems theory emphasizes **multiple causation,** the fact that whatever happens in a system is not the result of a single, simple cause, but is produced by complex interrelationships among multiple forces. For example, several factors contributed to the church board's successful efforts, including the board's shared leadership, Bill's democratic coordination, the commitment and expertise of the members, the fact that creation of a new congregation filled a need in the community, and probably some fortuitous factors, such as the availability of an affordable location.

Equifinality

The system's principle that different systems can reach the same end point.

Multifinality

The system's principle that systems starting out at the same place can reach different end points.

Multiple Causation

The principle that each change in a system is caused by numerous factors.

Groups are living systems that operate under the following principles:

1. A system is a set of relationships among interdependent components, such as members of a group.

2. Two advantages of the systems perspective for examining small groups: It helps organize the complexity of small group communication and places communication at the center of what links all the components together.

3. Groups, as systems, exhibit interdependence—each component affects each other component.

4. Groups and other systems are nonsummative—as with sports teams, sometimes systems perform better than expected (positive synergy) and sometimes worse (negative synergy).

5. Groups exhibit equifinality and multifinality—you cannot predict where a system ends from where it starts.

6. What happens in a group or other system has multiple causes—you cannot point to one factor as being the one and only reason why something happens.

Variables of a System

A small group system works when members use communication to transform information and other resources into outcomes that are tangible (e.g., a written report; a group presentation) or intangible (e.g., a decision; increased cohesiveness among members). The following section examines in detail how this process occurs by examining the **variables** of a system, which are its characteristics or dimensions.

System variables have been classified into three broad categories: *input, throughput,* and *output.* In a small group, **input variables** are components from which a small group is formed and that it uses to do its work, including the members; the reasons for the group's formation; resources such as information, expertise, money, and computer technology; and environmental conditions and forces that influence the group. In the church committee, members with their diverse areas of expertise were inputs. For instance, both Sunni and Sally had examples of bylaws from other churches, and Bill knew what to do to incorporate and receive tax-exempt status. All this information, possessed by individuals and shared with the group, served as resource input variables that ultimately affected both the group's deliberations and its success. Consider this exchange, after the minister died:

Sunni: I'm in shock from the past week, but I don't want to give up.

Norm: Me, neither. We're just on the verge of creating something that people have been wanting for two years, and I want to see us keep going.

Variables

Observable characteristics or qualities that can vary.

Input Variables

The energy, information, and raw material used by an open system, which is transformed into output by throughput processes.

Marina: Me, too. It's really important for me to have a church where I feel comfortable, so I'm willing to give whatever time is necessary to pull this off!

Members communicated the high level of commitment they brought to this daunting task and their willingness to see it through—important input variables.

    Throughput variables of a group involve how the group actually transforms inputs into final products—how the system functions, what it actually does. Examples include roles, rules, and norms; procedures the group follows; the group's leadership; communication among members; and all the other things that are part of the process as the group works toward completing its task. In our church board, observe how certain rules and procedures evolved. First, the members complimented each other and affirmed their commitment to the group's task. This led to a pattern of expressing cohesiveness and mutual respect, which later made it easier for members to contribute freely and frankly. Bill operated as a democratic chair who supported the group's norms of equality and shared leadership. This helped other members feel comfortable to jump in with suggestions or comments. Look at the following exchange:

Bill: Well, here's draft one of the bylaws! They aren't carved in stone. I suggest that everybody take them home, read them carefully, and come prepared with changes next week. Then we can make the changes and have them copied and distributed for the congregation to look at. Sound OK?

Norm: Hang on a second, Bill. We said we were going to give these to Reverend Lacy [minister of another congregation who agreed to give the denomination's perspective] for feedback. That will take longer than one week.

Bill: You're right; I forgot. Let's schedule our discussion of the bylaws after Norm gets Reverend Lacy's perspective.

In this exchange, chair Bill's original suggestion is challenged, politely, by Norm. Bill acknowledges that he made a mistake and backtracks. This illustrates a throughput process that is democratic, in which members can contribute without fear of repercussion and the leader has no more power to control events than the others do.

    Output variables of a group are the results or products of the group's throughput processes, including the tangible work accomplished (such as written reports, items built, and policies developed), changes in the members (such as increases in commitment and increased self-confidence), the group's effect on its environment, and changes in the group's procedures. The church board's most obvious output *to its environment* was the formation of a church now serving many people in southwest Missouri. *Within*

Throughput Variables

The actual functioning of a system, or how the system transforms inputs into outputs.

Output Variables

Anything that is produced by a system, such as a tangible product or a change in the system; in a small group, includes such things as reports, resolutions, changes in cohesiveness, and attitude changes in members.

the group, though, strong bonds of affection, cohesiveness, and pride at a job well done are examples of intangible outputs that developed. In one meeting, after the group had been together for over a year, members articulated their feelings:

Don: As much as we complain about how much work we have to do, look at our finances! We have nearly half a year's salary in the minister's fund.

Bill: I know. At times when I'm swamped and feel like giving up, I think about what we've created and I'm energized again.

Marina: When I get discouraged about all that we *haven't* done and all the things that have fallen through the cracks, I think about how enthusiastic the congregation is, and how wonderful you all are, and I'm overcome with gratitude!

Gary: Speaking of gratitude, I haven't told you all how hesitant I was to be part of this group at first. You all have a lot more education than I do, and I didn't feel like I could express myself as well. But this has been one of the best experiences of my life, and I'm grateful for your encouragement and support.

Clearly, this is a cohesive, supportive group. Could Gary admit something like this if he didn't trust the others?

A System and Its Environment

A system may be either *open* or *closed,* depending on the degree to which it interacts with its **environment,** or the setting in which the group exists. A group that is an **open system** interacts freely with its environment, with resources, information, and so forth, flowing freely between the environment and the group. For example, a classroom group that solicits relevant information from the instructor, other classmates, friends outside class, and media or news sources is an open system. The church board had a high degree of interchange between itself and the congregation that constituted the main part of its environment, which made it an extremely open system. The board meetings were open and anyone from the congregation could attend them. In addition, the board held "town meetings" once every couple of months, at which congregation members were invited to share their opinions about the running of the church. In contrast, a **closed system** has relatively little interchange between the group and its environment. Its boundaries are more solid and it is limited in its ability to adapt to the environment. A cloistered monastery, where monks interact with each other but have little contact with outsiders, illustrates a closed system. However, there is no completely closed human system.

One specific type of interchange between a group and its environment is **feedback,** which is the environment's response to output it has received from

---

Environment

The context or setting in which a small group system exists; the larger systems of which a small group is a component.

Open System

A system with relatively permeable boundaries, producing a high degree of interchange between the system and its environment.

Closed System

A system, such as a small group, with relatively impermeable boundaries, resulting in little interchange between the system and its environment.

Feedback

A response to a system's output; it may come in the form of information or tangible resources and helps the system determine whether or not it needs to make adjustments in moving toward its goal.

the group. It can come in the form of information or tangible resources and helps the system determine whether or not it needs to make adjustments to reach its goals. For instance, a car company that sells many cars (outputs) receives money for those cars (response to the outputs). This positive consumer response to the cars also provides the company with the information that it will likely reach its profit goals. One goal of the church board was having its bylaws approved by its denomination's Ministerial Association. To achieve this goal, the board actively sought feedback:

Sally: I used to know people at the association, but everyone I knew has moved on. The association's approval is critical—if they don't like our bylaws, we won't get official approval as a church.

Sunni: Is there any way we can get a preliminary reaction, before we send our final draft?

Norm: Yes—remember Reverend Lacy, from Columbia? She said she'd help us however she could, and she's on a couple of committees at the association. She could look at the bylaws and tell us how the association is likely to react.

Reverend Lacy did have several suggestions for modifying the bylaws. Her reaction (feedback) to the draft of the bylaws (the output) produced several changes in the bylaws that strengthened them and enhanced their chances of being approved. This is similar to the student group mentioned earlier, in which members asked one of us to pregrade the paper so that they could improve it. This feedback from the professor helped them achieve their goal of receiving an A.

As you can see, input, throughput, and output variables are not separable; everything influences and is influenced by everything else. For example, attitudes affect interaction, which in turn affects the outcome, which then returns to affect attitudes.

Just as input, throughput, and output variables are interdependent, so is a group highly interdependent with its **environment,** the setting in which the group exists. Many small group researchers have criticized small group research for ignoring the effect of the group's environment on the group.[5] Some group researchers have implied that the quality of a group's output is entirely or largely within a group's control. They have suggested that as long as the group has skilled and knowledgeable members (inputs) and effective leadership with helpful norms such as a conscientious attitude and good listening behaviors (throughputs), then the group will produce high-quality outputs. This oversimplifies the case because most groups are *not* self-contained entities but in fact are highly dependent on their environments. For instance, Broome and Fulbright asked real-life group members what factors hurt their efforts.[6] They found that organizational factors beyond a group's control often had strong negative effects on a group's performance.

Hirokawa and Keyton asked members of actual organizational groups what factors helped and hindered their groups' progress.[7] Several factors fell into an organizational category—whether the group got assistance from the parent organization, including continuing informational support as needed. These two studies strongly support the view that the group's environment—not just input and throughput factors—substantially influences a group's success; however, environmental factors are often beyond the group's control. We explore this concept in more detail in the following section.

Bona Fide Group Perspective

The perspective that focuses naturally-occurring groups with stable but permeable boundaries and are independent with their environment.

The Bona Fide Group Perspective   You have probably participated in a classroom group assigned to complete a project. To what extent do you think your classroom group is similar to or different from a "real" group in an organization? Do you think those differences are important? Communication scholars Linda Putnam and Cynthia Stohl developed *bona fide group theory* in large part to correct what they perceived as naïve assumptions about groups; in particular, they wanted to call attention to the importance of a group's context, or environment, which they believed most group scholars failed to acknowledge.[8] The **bona fide group perspective** states that bona fide (i.e., genuine, naturally occurring) groups have stable but permeable boundaries and borders and are interdependent with their environments. Earlier group studies seemed to imply that what happened inside a group—the internal process—was the appropriate focus for small group communication inquiry; but Putnam and Stohl demonstrated that, if we really want to understand a group, we must understand that group's relationship with its environment.

First, bona fide groups have stable but permeable boundaries. The boundaries must be recognizable; otherwise there would not be a group, but they are not rigid—they shift due to four factors. First, group members have multiple group memberships—they belong to several groups at once, and sometimes their roles conflict. For example, you may want to agree with your group on a proposal to distribute organizational resources differently, but if the proposal will cause your department to lose resources, the department members will expect you to argue against it, no matter how you may feel personally. You aren't entirely a free agent as a group member. Second, group members represent other groups, whether they want to or not. We know several female faculty who constantly are asked to serve on committees to ensure that women's concerns are adequately represented. Third, group membership often fluctuates, with old members leaving and new members joining the group. In many cases, these fluctuations are required by the organization's bylaws. For instance, once the church's steering committee became an official board, voted by the members, it was required to hold yearly elections and term limits were imposed. Bill, the original chair, was organized and efficient. Dirk, a newer member who became chair, loved to tell jokes and often got the group off task. Consequently, the board meetings became longer but were more fun (for some people). Finally, group identity formation refers to the varying levels of commitment and belonging members feel to different groups they belong to. New members of the church board, who had not experienced the death of the minister, the anxiety of conforming to the denomination's requirements, and the weekly steering committee meetings, did not bring with them the same intense dedication. However, they did bring in fresh perspectives and creative ideas that ultimately changed the way things were done.

Second, bona fide groups are interdependent with their relevant contexts, which means that a group both influences and is influenced by its environment. Four factors contribute to this interdependence. First, members experience intergroup communication, which means that they interact constantly with members of other groups, exchanging information and ideas. In our church board, Bill, the lawyer, talked to his office partners about the board and vice versa. These interactions simultaneously influenced both groups. Second, groups must coordinate their actions with other groups. Church committees such as the finance committee, building committee, and worship committee had to work with the board for things to go smoothly. Third, members must negotiate their autonomy and jurisdiction. For example, the church's worship committee wanted to make substantial changes in the order of service and the elements included in the service. But it had to negotiate with the board to determine to what extent the committee had the authority to make changes and how to manage those changes in the least disruptive way. Fourth, groups must make sense of their relationships with other groups. Members have perceptions of other people and groups within an organization, and these perceptions may shift over time. For example, one campus department, generally perceived as uncooperative and self-serving, offered to give up a faculty position to another department that was short-staffed. The second department, caught by surprise, had to rethink its perceptions of the first; in subsequent interactions, these two departments began to form alliances and coalitions that would once have been unthinkable.

The bona fide group perspective is consistent with systems theory in its focus on the relationship between a group and its environment. This is an important advantage because most groups are part of a larger organizational structure and must interact with individuals and other groups within that structure. Interestingly, for groups dealing with complex tasks in a very uncertain environment, how often members communicate *within* the group is not as important to their performance as is how often they interact with others *outside the group*.[9] This demonstrates how important it is for groups to match their internal abilities to process information with the external informational demands of the environment they are embedded in. Even nonorganizational groups are also part of an environment. For instance, the environment of a family may be the neighborhood or the general society in which it lives.

The *bona fide group perspective*'s most recognized contribution is its focus on the embeddedness of smaller groups in larger systems and recognizing that those boundaries are not only permeable but fluid.[10] Identifying a *group* then is not as straightforward as traditional definitions of *group* would lead us to believe. Complicating matters is the reality that many of these smaller groups use computer technology to do their business and interact with their environment. The use of these technologies has prompted even bona fide group theorists to take a second look at this ever complicated relationship between a group and its environment.[11]

Bona Fide Virtual Groups

Most of the research in small group communication has focused on groups whose members meet face-to-face. We began to speculate in Chapter 1 about how group processes may change in groups whose members do not meet face-to-face. The reality of our global world is that many companies that might not otherwise ever collaborate on tasks now do so with the help of computer technology that allows the members of multiple groups to interact with each other without being on the same site. For instance, the Boeing 767 airplane is the result of collaboration between Boeing engineers, who designed the fuel and cockpit; Aeritalia SAI engineers, who developed the fins and

FIGURE 4.1   Model of a small group as a system

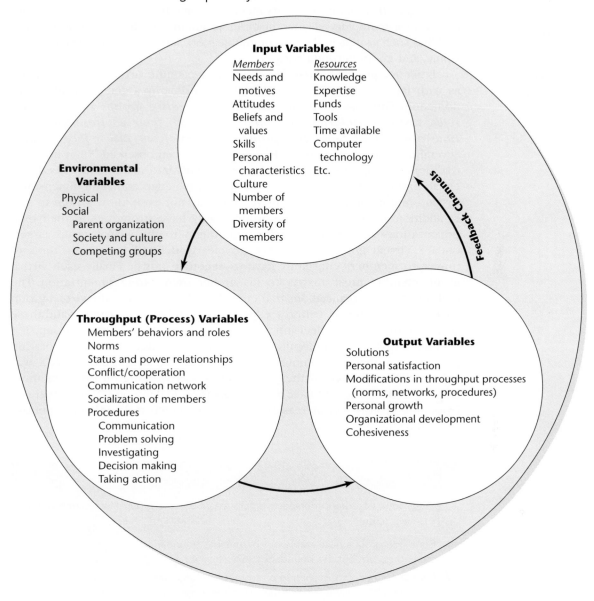

Input Variables

Members   *Resources*
Needs and   Knowledge
  motives   Expertise
Attitudes   Funds
Beliefs and   Tools
  values   Time available
Skills   Computer
Personal   technology
  characteristics   Etc.
Culture
Number of
  members
Diversity of
  members

Environmental Variables

Physical
Social
    Parent organization
    Society and culture
    Competing groups

Feedback Channels

Throughput (Process) Variables

Members' behaviors and roles
Norms
Status and power relationships
Conflict/cooperation
Communication network
Socialization of members
Procedures
    Communication
    Problem solving
    Investigating
    Decision making
    Taking action

Output Variables

Solutions
Personal satisfaction
Modifications in throughput processes
  (norms, networks, procedures)
Personal growth
Organizational development
Cohesiveness

rudder; and multiple Japanese firms, whose responsibility was the main body of the plane.[12]

Modern-day organizations are rapidly changing. Their employees do not necessarily work in the same place or at the same time. Entire organizations are virtual—that is, they are not an "office" but a network of members connected by computer who may never see each other face-to-face, but contact

Collaborating Group

Collaborating Group
A group whose members come from different organizations to form a temporary alliance for a specific purpose.

each other via electronic mail (e-mail) or videoconferencing. The **collaborating group** is one in which its members come from different organizations and form a temporary alliance in order to attain a particular purpose.[13] You will find such groups in the telecommunication, aerospace, motor vehicle, electronic, and computer industries.

Bona fide group theorists have begun to examine virtual groups because, as with face-to-face groups, collaboration is primarily a communicative phenomenon. They ask, *How do virtual collaborative groups manage their roles, tasks, boundaries, and interaction with their environments?* and *How are virtual bona fide groups different from face-to-face groups?* Several differences, particularly in degree, have been observed.[14] For instance, traditional groups usually know where to find information they need, but collaborating virtual groups may be so cutting-edge and multidimensional that no one member has the answer and may not even know whom to ask. In addition, members of virtual groups likely have strong ties to their own organizations and consider their commitment to the virtual group as secondary. Virtual groups often have no clearly defined formal positions of power, so members constantly have to negotiate power. Finally, each virtual group member must answer to his or her own parent organization. The multiple parent organizations that contributed members to the virtual group have their own norms, cultures, expectations, and even demands—and these all affect the internal decision-making processes of the virtual group. For example, UNIX is a computer system that resulted from collaboration between a number of computer companies. At the same time as UNIX was being developed, each of these companies was working on products unrelated to UNIX but could have affected decision making on UNIX. Virtual collaborating groups will increase in the future, which makes them important to understand.

Recap: A Quick Review

The bona fide group perspective calls attention to a group's interaction with its environment:

1. Bona fide groups have stable but permeable boundaries; there is a clearly defined group, but the boundaries shift constantly.

2. Four factors affect this shifting of a group's boundaries: multiple group memberships members have; the fact that members serve as representatives of other groups to the group in question; the fluctuation in group membership, with old members leaving and new members joining; and the varying strength of identity with the group (i.e., commitment, loyalty) that members feel.

3. Bona fide groups are interdependent with their environments, simultaneously influencing and being influenced by the environment.

(continued)

(continued)

4. Four factors contribute to this interdependence: intergroup communication, as members interact with people in other groups; the need for the group to coordinate its work with other groups; the group's negotiation to determine its autonomy and the scope of its jurisdiction; and the way a group makes sense of its relationship with other groups.

5. Bona fide group scholars have begun to examine virtual collaborating groups whose members do not meet face-to-face, but interact using technology such as computers. Members of these groups belong to different parent organizations, but come together virtually to complete their tasks.

6. Virtual collaborating groups face distinct challenges: the cutting edge information they need may be hard to find; members may have primary commitments to their parent organizations; power must be continually negotiated; and decisions made within the parent organizations can affect the decision process within the group.

Communicating across Boundaries

In our previous discussion, we emphasized that contemporary groups constantly interact with their environments. Ancona and Caldwell suggest that groups need members who serve as **boundary spanners** by constantly monitoring the group's environment to bring in and take out information relevant to the group's success.[15] Boundary spanners serve three main functions. The first is initiating transactions to import or export needed resources, such as information or support. For instance, in our example of an effective group, Norm contacted Reverend Lacy for advice about organizing the new congregation and help in gaining approval from the association. Second boundary-spanning function consists of responding to initiatives of outsiders. Someone may ask a group member what the group discussed at a particular meeting; that member must then decide whether and what information to relate. The final function involves changes in the membership of the group—new people may be brought into the group either temporarily or permanently. For example, in an unorthodox move, members decided to invite Gary's wife, Christy, to attend church board meetings in his place as a nonvoting member during a two-month stretch when he was unable to attend meetings. This enabled Gary to keep up with the board information and maintain, through Christy, relationships that he had formed. The management of the group's relationship with the environment is crucial and can spell success or failure for the group. If the church board had decided to be secretive and not share openly with the congregation what was discussed and decided at board meetings, the congregation would have been unlikely to support the church with time, energy, and resources.

Boundary Spanner

A group member who monitors the group's environment to import and export information relevant to the group's success.

FIGURE 4.2
Boundary spanner
functions and
strategies

Boundary Spanner Functions

1. Initiate transactions between the group and its environment to import and export resources.
2. Respond to the initiatives from outsiders.
3. Initiate temporary or permanent group membership.

Boundary Spanner Strategies

1. Ambassador.
2. Task coordinator.
3. Scout.
4. Guard.

Ancona and Caldwell, in a five-year study of product-development teams, further explored the behaviors of boundary spanners.[16] Their research uncovered key strategies these team members use to carry out their functions as boundary spanners. (See Figure 4.2.) When Norm solicited feedback from Reverend Lacy, he was acting in an *ambassadorial capacity* for the church group. Ambassadors check out the environment to see who supports the group; bring in information from the environment in summary form; and may also attempt to persuade outsiders to the desires, goals, and importance of the group. Strategies involving *task coordination* occur when members coordinate technical issues and thus tend to talk laterally across all relevant groups. Members may address design problems, coordination of schedules and deadlines, and securing resources needed by the group. *Scouting* activities involve general scanning of the outside for relevant information and ideas that can be used by the group, including figuring out what the competition is doing. Ambassadorial, task-coordination, and scouting strategies all involve the group engaging its environment proactively. The last strategy, *guarding,* is characterized by actions by the group to close itself off from the environment. These efforts can be seen as a way the group has of controlling information that may damage its profile.

Ancona and Caldwell argue fervently that a pattern of isolation is not beneficial to productive groups.[17] Successful product teams engaged in consistent communication with their environment. High levels of ambassador activity as well as task coordination are necessary if product teams are to perform well. Groups that remain cut off from their environments are low performers even if they believe they have the necessary information to complete the task or that their output will be judged independent of their process. Although this research involved production teams, any task group should heed Ancona and Caldwell's call for consistent and extensive communication across group boundaries.

Characteristics of Effective Problem-Solving Groups

A secondary group's effectiveness can be determined only by comparing its accomplishments (outputs) with its stated goals and assessing its impact on its environment. The standards summarized in Figure 4.3, represent the ideal input, throughput, output, and environmental variables toward which discussion groups should strive, even though most will fall short.

Input Variables

1. **Members share basic beliefs and values about the purpose of the group.**
   For instance, if one member of a project group believes deeply that the project is worthwhile and intends to commit substantial time to it but another member thinks the assignment is busywork and decides to "blow it off," the group will not reach consensus or interact smoothly. Ideally, members *want* to be part of the group and are dedicated to the group's purpose. In our story about the effective church board, members made their commitment to the group and its purpose clear: "It's really important to me to have a church where I feel comfortable" and "I'm willing to give whatever time necessary to pull this off!" Furthermore, a group performs more effectively when members bring different perspectives, information, and approaches to a problem, but share basic values and goals for the group.

2. **Members understand and accept the group's purpose.**
   One of us had a student group with one member who, no matter how the others tried to help him, never seemed to "get" what the group's assignment was. The group spun its wheels trying to get everyone on the same page about what the group was supposed to do. In the church board, if half the group thought that their purpose was to become a viable church by finding another congregation with which to merge, but the other half thought their purpose was to create a self-sustaining congregation, both halves would have been pulling the church in different directions. Goal clarity is important; the group's area of freedom and limitations are understood by the members and by the parent organization.

3. **The number of members should be as small as possible, so long as the necessary variety of perspectives is represented.**
   That means that diversity of backgrounds and perspectives is needed (otherwise, why form a group?), but when a group is too large, not everyone can participate. A main reason to form a group is to bring multiple points of view to an issue or problem, but if a group is too large, it becomes unwieldy and frustrates those who cannot participate. Sometimes, for political reasons (so all the "right" areas will be represented), a group ends up being larger than ideal, but try to keep the group as small as you need to.

FIGURE 4.3

The following represent *ideal* input, throughput, output, and environmental characteristics. Your groups may not reach these ideals, but these are goals to shoot for.

Ideal Input Variables

1. Members share basic beliefs and values about the purpose of the group.
2. Members understand and accept the group's purpose.
3. The number of members should be as small as possible, so long as the necessary variety of perspectives is represented.
4. Group members know what the group's relationship is to other groups and organizations, and what resources they can count on from these groups and organizations.
5. The group has enough time to do its work.
6. The group's meeting is comfortable and allows members to discuss without distractions.

Ideal Throughput Variables

1. Members are dependable and reliable.
2. Members express themselves well interpersonally and are considerate of other members.
3. Members' roles are relatively stable, understood, and accepted by all.
4. Members have relatively equal status.
5. Norms and rules are understood and followed or discussed openly and changed when they don't work.
6. Communication flows in an all-channel network.
7. Procedures are efficient and members contribute to developing them.

Ideal Output Variables

1. Members perceive that the group's purpose has been achieved.
2. Members are personally satisfied with their respective roles in the group, the discussion and group work process, and their relationships with other members.
3. Cohesiveness is high.
4. The leadership structure of the group is stable.
5. The group's culture reflects its unique qualities and values.
6. The parent organization (if one exists) is strengthened as a result of the small group's work.

Ideal Environmental Factors

1. The environment (usually an organization) should publicly recognize the accomplishments of the group and reward the group *as a group*.
2. The environment should supply whatever informational resources the group needs.
3. The environment should supply whatever resources and expertise the group needs.
4. The environment should provide a supportive atmosphere for the group.

4. **Group members know what the group's relationship is to other groups and organizations, and what resources they can count on from these groups and organizations.**
   Group members know how they relate to the organization that created the group, where they fit in the big picture, and how they relate to other groups and the environment. The church board, for example,

knew that the original church from which it split would *not* supply resources, information, or help, but that compatible denominations would provide speakers and consultation help to the new board.

5. **The group has enough time to do its work.**

   If research is needed to understand the problem, group members should have enough time to do it thoroughly. Groups need time to work through all the phases of the problem-solving process or to digest and process information and ideas. In short, members must have and commit enough time to do their work as a group thoroughly and well. For example, they should not try to find a solution to a city's congested traffic in a 40-minute meeting. Our church board met every week for two years before it considered its main goals met.

6. **The group's meeting place is comfortable and allows discussions without distractions.**

   A committee that has no adequate room in which to meet regularly will expend much energy just finding and changing meeting places and trying to get members to those places. A quality circle cannot discuss problems well in a noisy assembly room, nor can a personnel committee evaluate job candidates in a room where strangers compromise privacy by wandering in and out.

Throughput Variables

1. **Members are dependable and reliable.**

   A member who undertakes an assignment can be counted on to carry it out, whether that involves gathering information, typing and distributing a report, or scheduling a Sunday speaker for the service. Members can be counted on to attend scheduled meetings, notify the group if this is not possible, and perhaps send a knowledgeable substitute in their place if appropriate.

2. **Members express themselves well interpersonally and are considerate of other members.**

   In the church board, although Gary felt insecure about his ability to express ideas, he was willing to share his opinions, he did so clearly, and he was encouraged by the other members. Group members should express their ideas with sensitivity so that they don't evoke defensiveness in others. Bill, although he was the group's chair, often followed his own suggestions by saying, "Sound OK?" or "Is that all right with all of you?" This affirmed his respect for the others' opinions.

3. **Members' roles are relatively stable, understood, and accepted by all.**

   There is both sufficient role definition to permit members to predict each other's behavior (e.g., on the church board Marina was consistently task oriented and organized and Bill was consistently democratic). Roles are sufficiently flexible so that anyone can make needed contributions to either the task or interpersonal relationships (for instance, other members besides Marina were task oriented and organized, and Marina also contributed to the positive feelings: "I'm overcome with gratitude!"). There is an equitable division of labor. The leadership position has been settled satisfactorily, but all members share leadership functions.

4. **Members have relatively equal status.**
On the church board, Bill's external status as a lawyer was relatively high, but that didn't stop Norm, the massage therapist, from saying, "Hang on a second, Bill. . . . That will take longer than one week," when he reminded Bill of the need for Reverend Lacy's perspective. That was possible because inside the group, the status of members was relatively equal. Equal status promotes teamwork. Members spend their energies achieving the goals of the group, not competing against each other for power and position. When all members feel equal, they freely contribute ideas, opinions, and suggestions; they don't hold back. This gives the group more information to work with.

5. **Norms and rules are understood and followed or are discussed openly and changed when they don't work.**
For example, our church board had a habit of searching for diverse opinions, which is why Marina supported Bill when he suggested putting one or two people on the bylaws committee who were most vocal about limiting the power of the minister. The church board operated with a norm of open discussion and consensus.

6. **Communication flows in an all-channel network.**
A high proportion of remarks is directed to the group as a whole, not to individual members. There are no sidebar conversations during the group meeting, yet members are free to approach any and all other members when a meeting is not in progress. Members build on each other's ideas.

7. **Procedures are efficient and members contribute to developing them.**
In a problem-solving group, all members understand and follow the group's procedures. Sometimes, a member will share a specific discussion technique or procedure appropriate to the group's purpose. For example, in the church board, Marina had often used focus groups, and she offered to organize focus groups during a congregational town meeting so that the board could learn how the congregation thought things were going. Furthermore, when procedures need to be changed, the group participates in deciding what those changes should be. For example, after the board had reduced its meetings to every other week, Norm questioned this procedure by noting the problems it created ("Things really pile up in two weeks . . . "). But he invited others'

opinions ("Does anyone else feel bothered by this, or is it just me?"), and the group discussed this thoroughly before deciding to return to weekly meetings.

Output Variables

1. **Members perceive that the group's purpose has been achieved.**
   Members support the best decisions and solutions to problems. The church board members talked about several accomplishments they had achieved, including receiving bylaws approval from their congregation and their association, and saving enough money for half a year's salary for a minister. Solutions decided upon by a group should be accepted by most or all of the people affected.

2. **Members are personally satisfied with their respective roles in the group, the discussion and group work process, and their relationships with the other members.**
   For example, Bill says, "I think about what we've created and I'm energized again," and Gary says, "I'm grateful for your encouragement and support." The fact that at one point the board decided to meet more frequently, not less, indicates a high degree of satisfaction with the activity.

3. **Cohesiveness is high.**
   Members have a strong sense of identification with the group and give it high priority among competing demands for their time and attention. Cohesiveness among board members was evident ("This has been one of the best experiences of my life . . ."). A high degree of trust exists among members, as when Gary revealed his original insecurity about being a member of the board.

4. **The group's leadership is stable and reliable.**
   If asked independently, each member would identify the same person(s) as leader of the group and as choice for leader in the future. For example, Bill emerged as the group's designated leader because he organized well, was democratic, and put in considerable work. He was drafted to coordinate the steering committee and was later elected board chair. Members shared in leading the group when their areas of expertise were relevant to the group's task.

5. **The group creates a culture that reflects its unique qualities and values.**
   Each group creates a culture or personality that is different from every other group. In effective groups, that culture is a positive one that supports the values of the members and reflects to the members what is most important in that group. For example, church board members sometimes stopped a discussion for a brief prayer, particularly if a disagreement was under way. The prayer reminded members that disagreeing with ideas was acceptable but being disagreeable to other people was

not. These brief prayer breaks were an important part of the group's culture. Clearly, in a different kind of group, prayer breaks would not have been appropriate or welcomed.

6. **The parent organization (if one exists) is strengthened as a result of the small group's work.**
   The organization is better off as a result of the group's work. In the church board's case, this requirement clearly was met. The board helped create a viable church that grew, received its denomination's approval, and eventually hired its first minister.

Environmental Factors

1. **The environment (usually an organization) should publicly recognize the accomplishments of the group and reward the group *as a group.***
   Praise and recognition for one's efforts are highly motivating. In contrast, ignoring someone's efforts is demoralizing. Group members will be motivated to work efficiently and productively when they know there will be praise and other rewards for their efforts. The church board was publicly recognized and thanked by the congregation at several points during the process of creating the new congregation.

2. **The environment should supply whatever informational resources the group needs.**
   Nothing is more frustrating to group members than to be given a task but not the information or data needed to complete the task. In addition, as members begin their work, they often find that they need information they had not anticipated. It is especially important that the parent organization continue to give the group access to whatever information members find they need to complete their task in a timely manner.

3. **The environment should supply whatever resources and expertise the group needs.**
   Sometimes organizations provide initial training and orientation for group members, especially for brand new groups, but often forget that groups may need continuing training and access to specialized procedures and expertise. For instance, a problem-solving group may benefit from bringing in a consultant to help them develop their creativity as a group. Ideally, the group's environment is supportive of such group needs and continues to supply resources, training, expertise, coaching, or whatever else a group needs to be productive.

4. **The environment should provide a supportive atmosphere for the group.**
   Groups are sometimes demoralized when their efforts are consistently second-guessed or interfered with by the parent organization. In addition,

organizations sometimes tend to load a group, particularly one that has been successful in the past, with too many priorities to handle well. Instead, the ideal environment for a group is a nurturing and supportive one that gives the group room to negotiate without stifling or overburdening it. Few groups you experience may measure up to these standards as well as the church board did. However, you now have a model of an effective small group as a basis for comparison and should be able to spot at least some of the sources of difficulty in any group that is not producing satisfactory outputs.

QUESTIONS FOR REVIEW

 Go to self-quizzes on the Online Learning Center at mhhe.com/galanes12 to test your knowledge of the chapter concepts

This chapter used the case study of the church board to illustrate many of the concepts discussed in the chapter. Reread the case study and refer to the recap boxes, if necessary, to discuss the following questions:

1. In what ways did the church board demonstrate the system principles of interdependence, nonsummativity, equifinality, multifunality, and multiple causation?

2. The board demonstrated considerable interaction with its environment, particularly with the congregation it represented. How do you see the two main principles of the bona fide group perspective (permeable boundaries and interchange with the environment) operating in the church board? What effects did these exchanges seem to have?

3. In what ways did board members serve as boundary spanners? What boundary-spanning functions and strategies did members employ, and what were the effects on the board and the congregation?

4. In many ways, this board demonstrated the input, throughput, output, and environmental factors that are considered to be ideal. What examples of the board's inputs, throughputs, outputs, and environmental factors were particularly striking to you? Were any of these factors less than ideal? If so, what effects did this have on the board?

KEY TERMS

 Test your knowledge of these key terms by visiting the Online Learning Center website at mhhe.com/galanes12

Bona fide group perspective	Feedback	Open system
Boundary spanners	Input variables	Output variables
Closed system	Interdependence	System
Collaborating group	Multifinality	Throughput variables
Environment	Multiple causation	Variables
Equifinality	Nonsummativity	

BIBLIOGRAPHY

Katz, Daniel, and Robert L. Kahn. *The Social Psychology of Organizations*. 2nd ed. New York: Wiley, 1978. See Chapter 2.

Mabry, Edward A. "The Systems Metaphor in Group Communication." In *The Handbook of Group Communication Theory and Research.* Lawrence R. Frey, ed. Thousand Oaks, CA: Sage, 1999, 71–91.

Putnam, Linda L., and Cynthia Stohl. "Bona Fide Groups: An Alternative Perspective for Communication and Small Group Decision Making," in *Communication and Group Decision Making,* 2nd ed. Randy Y. Hirokawa and M. Scott Poole, eds. Thousand Oaks, CA: Sage, 1996, 147–78.

Von Bertalanffy, Ludwig. *General System Theory*. New York: George Braziller, 1969.

Wood, Julia T., Gerald M. Phillips, and Douglas J. Pedersen. "Understanding the Group as a System." In *Small Group Communication: A Reader.* 6th ed. Robert S. Cathcart and Larry A. Samovar, eds. Dubuque, IA: Wm. C. Brown, 1992, 5–17.

NOTES

1. Edward A. Mabry, "The Systems Metaphor in Group Communication," in *The Handbook of Group Communication Theory and Research,* ed. Lawrence Frey (Thousand Oaks, CA: Sage, 1999): 71-91.

2. Stephen W. Littlejohn, *Theories of Human Communication,* 7th ed. (Belmont CA: Wadsworth/Thomson Learning, 2002).

3. George F. Will, "A New Level of Worrying," *Newsweek* (July 22, 1996): 72.

4. Abran J. Salazar, "Understanding the Synergistic Effects of Communication in Small Groups: Making the Most Out of Group Member Abilities," *Small Group Research* 26 (May 1995): 169-99.

5. Benjamin J. Broome and Luann Fulbright, "A Multistage Influence Model of Barriers to Group Problem Solving: A Participant-Generated Agenda for Small Group Research," *Small Group Research* 26 (February 1995): 25-55; Cynthia Stohl and Michael E. Holmes, "A Functional Perspective for Bona Fide Groups," *Communication Yearbook* 16 (1993): 601-14; Jeremy Rose, "Communication Challenges and Role Functions of Performing Groups," *Small Group Research* 25 (August 1994): 411-32.

6. Broome and Fulbright, "A Multistage Influence Model."

7. Randy Y. Hirokawa and Joann Keyton, "Perceived Facilitators and Inhibitors of Effectiveness in Organizational Work Teams," *Management Communication Quarterly* 8 (May 1995): 424-46.

8. The information about bona fide group theory is synthesized from the following sources: Linda L. Putnam and Cynthia Stohl, "Bona Fide Groups: A Reconceptualization of Groups in Context," *Communication Studies* 41 (1990): 248-65; Linda L. Putnam and Cynthia Stohl, "Bona Fide Groups: An Alternative Perspective for Communication and Small Group Decision Making," in *Communication and Group Decision Making,* 2nd ed., eds. Randy Y. Hirokawa and M. Scott Poole (Thousand Oaks, CA: Sage, 1996): 147-78; Lawrence R. Frey, "Group Communication in Context: Studying Bona Fide Groups," in *Group Communication in Context: Studies of Bona Fide Groups,* 2nd ed., ed. Lawrence R. Frey (Mahway, NJ: Erlbaum, 2003): 1-20; and Cynthia Stohl and Linda L. Putnam, "Communication in Bona Fide Groups: A Retrospective and Prospective Account," in *Group Communication in Context: Studies of Bona Fide Groups,* 2nd ed. Lawrence R. Frey, ed. (Mahway, NJ: Erlbaum, 2003): 399-414.

9. Deborah G. Ancona and David F. Caldwell, "Bridging the Boundary: External Activity and Performance in Organizational Teams," *Administrative Science Quarterly* 37 (December 1992): 634-65.

10. Jennifer H. Waldeck, Carolyn A. Shepard, Jeremy Teitelbaum, W. Jeffrey Farrar, and David Seibold, "New Directions for Functional, Symbolic Convergence, Structuration, and Bona Fide Group

Perspectives of Group Communication," in *New Directions in Group Communication,* ed. Lawrence R. Frey (Thousand Oaks, CA: Sage, 2002): 3–24.

11. Cynthia Stohl and Kasey Walker, "A Bona Fide Perspective for the Future of Groups," in *New Directions in Group Communication,* ed. Lawrence R. Frey (Thousand Oaks, CA: Sage, 2002): 237–52.

12. Ibid.

13. Ibid.

14. Ibid.

15. Deborah G. Ancona and David F. Caldwell, "Beyond Task and Maintenance: Defining External Functions in Groups," *Group & Organization Studies* 13 (December 1988): 468–94.

16. Deborah G. Ancona and David F. Caldwell, "Bridging the Boundary: External Activity and Performance in Organizational Teams."

17. Ibid.

Developing the Group

The information in Part I provided the foundation for understanding small groups and concluded with a discussion of systems theory, our primary conceptual framework. In Part II, we begin our discussion of how small groups begin to form by focusing on two key factors influencing this process. The first factor is the group's diversity, shaped partly by cultures represented by the members. The second factor involves the members themselves, including how their individual characteristics and interactions help shape their roles in the group. Inputs, including the group's diversity and its members, strongly influence the group's throughput processes.

Diversity and the Effects of Culture

CENTRAL MESSAGE

The United States is a pluralistic culture composed of many different co-cultures that strongly influence members' communicative behaviors. Diversity in groups is a fact of life *now* and will only increase in the future, which makes it imperative for small group members to recognize, understand, adjust to, and embrace their differences.

STUDY OBJECTIVES

As a result of studying Chapter 5 you should be able to:

1. Define culture and explain why knowledge of cultural differences in communication is important for effective group discussion.

2. Explain the advantages that can come from diversity in groups and organizations.

3. Describe six major dimensions on which cultures differ.

4. Explain why race, socioeconomic class, and generational differences may be viewed as cultural differences, and describe the differences that have been observed.

5. Describe the public dialogue technique and explain how it can help increase understanding among members of different cultures.

6. Describe the ethical principles group members should use to address and embrace cultural differences.

Martha, who grew up and attended college in New York City, had always wanted to work in California. During spring semester of her senior year, with her degree in computer science almost in hand, Martha landed a job interview with a software development firm in Silicon Valley. The firm's software development team, a self-managed work group, was responsible for its own interviewing and hiring. Members wanted to have a strong sense of any person they were considering for a position—Would that person be a good "fit" with the rest of the team?—and they had a good track record. Martha would spend an entire day with the team, attending their meetings, shadowing various members, eating lunch with them, and so forth. The team wanted to see how she handled herself in the kinds of work situations that were everyday occurrences for them.

Martha prepared carefully for her interview. She read up on the company, knew the kinds of software it was known for, updated her portfolio of college projects, and selected her clothes for the interview very carefully—new navy blue suit, matching pumps, white shell, discreet jewelry. She was ready!

Martha's first inkling that something might go wrong occurred when team representative Jorge met her at her hotel. Jorge was wearing jeans, a San Francisco 49ers' cap, and a T-shirt with a fish tie handpainted on the front. When they got to the company's building, she noticed that all the workers were similarly dressed—casually, with a certain irreverent style. Team members asked her to talk a bit about her background before they started their meeting, and she relaxed a bit. After all, she had prepared for how to sell herself. About five minutes into her presentation, Jorge interrupted to suggest that he take her on a tour of the building before the next meeting. They left, and the other team members began to talk. "Thinks a lot of herself, doesn't she" said Akimi. "She talks so fast I couldn't follow half of what she said," complained Scott. "She's wired pretty tight," agreed Montana. The group concluded that Martha would probably not be a good fit with the culture of this particular team, in part because she didn't seem like a team player. Within a half hour of first meeting her, they decided not to extend her a job offer.

This story underscores four important points we make in this chapter. First, diversity among group members presents a tremendous challenge to small groups because it forces members to pay more careful attention to their communicative behavior and to give up preconceived stereotypes if the group is to succeed. Second, diversity stems from several sources, including someone's culture, which is the focus of this chapter. Third, cultural differences can exist even among individuals from the same country who speak the same language and have similar educations, as Martha's failed job interview demonstrated. Finally, although diversity is challenging, it represents a potentially valuable group resource and should be embraced, not eliminated.

In this chapter, we consider a member's culture to be an input factor that is a major determinant of that member's behavior. In the following chapter, we consider several personal characteristics that also affect individual behavior.

Information about culture fills textbooks! Our goal is to present you with a framework for understanding cultural differences, but we do not pretend to cover culture in depth. Instead, we hope this framework helps you appreciate the difficulty cultural and co-cultural differences create in small groups. We also believe this offers you a tool for diagnosing what has gone wrong and how it can be repaired.

In this century, Americans of Asian, Hispanic, African, Middle-Eastern, and eastern European ancestry will outnumber Caucasians of western European ancestry. Called the "browning of America" by *Time* magazine,[1] this phenomenon will have a profound effect on *all* forms of communication. In addition, age differences will affect communication behavior in the United States. Allen notes that, for the first time, four different generations must work together.[2] Transactions between people of different ethnic, racial, and age groups require patience and attention to the communication process. You don't have to leave the United States for this phenomenon to affect you. The change, already well under way, will come to you; you will soon participate in groups with people whose backgrounds are markedly different from your own, if you haven't already.

We use the term *diversity* to encompass a wide variety of differences, including ethnicity, race, age, social class, education, and sexual preference, among others.[3] Contemporary approaches to diversity go beyond tolerance of differences; they celebrate and capitalize on differences without necessarily trying to force assimilation into the dominant culture of the United States.[4] These approaches demand sensitive and effective communication. Haslett and Ruebush, in their review of how individual and cultural differences can affect a group, conclude that, unless group members are sensitive, groups can experience highly differential rates of participation, poor management of conflict, and factionalism between in-groups and out-groups.[5] Good communication can reduce this so that the potential benefits can be realized. Table 5.1 summarizes the potential competitive advantages that effective diversity management offers an organization.

Recent studies suggest that cultural diversity can be a real plus. Diversity can enhance a group's performance, assuming that the group's communication process allows members to integrate their diverse perspectives.[6] McLeod and her associates explicitly studied the effects of ethnic diversity on a brainstorming task.[7] They compared ethnically homogeneous (all-Anglo American) groups with ethnically diverse (Anglo, Asian, African, and Hispanic American) groups and found that the diverse groups came up with more creative solutions. However, they also found that the diverse groups had more negative feelings about their groups than the homogeneous groups. To us, these findings highlight the importance of studying the effects of culture; diversity can be an important source of energy and creativity in all areas of American work, but only if we can appreciate and work *with* our differences, not against them.

The culture(s) in which a person is raised profoundly affects every aspect of that person's communication behavior, starting with the interpretation

TABLE 5.1
Competitive advantages of effective diversity management

Resource acquisition	Companies known for effective diversity management develop reputations as desirable places to work, and thus can recruit a highly skilled labor pool.
Marketing advantage	As markets become diverse, a diverse workforce provides increased awareness and competitive advantage.
System flexibility	Appreciation of varying viewpoints produces greater openness to ideas and helps a company handle challenges and changes.
Creativity	Diverse viewpoints enhance creativity, decision making, and performance.
Problem solving	Diverse viewpoints lead to better decisions because a wider range of perspectives is considered and issues are analyzed more thoroughly and critically.
Cost reduction	Failure to integrate all workers leads to higher turnover, absenteeism, and so forth; effective diversity management saves money.

Source: Information taken from T. H. Cox and S. Blake, "Managing Cultural Diversity: Implications for Organizational Competitiveness," *Academy of Management Executive* 5 (1991): 45–56; cited in Susan Kirby and Orlando C. Richard, "Impact of Marketing Work-Place Diversity on Employee Job Involvement and Organizational Commitment," *Journal of Social Psychology* 140 (June 2000).

Ethnocentric

The belief that one's own culture is inherently superior to all others; tendency to view other cultures through the viewpoint of one's own culture.

process we discussed in Chapter 2. Communication among people of diverse backgrounds (hence with diverse communication patterns) is challenging. Unfortunately, most people are **ethnocentric:** they believe their personal native culture is superior and judge everyone else's behavior by the norms of their own culture. But successful communication among culturally diverse individuals requires them to give up their ethnocentricity.[8] The software development team members who interviewed Martha couldn't get past her New York style, with its fast-paced talk and aggressive verbal pattern. In relaxed California, that style says "She thinks she's all that," but in New York, people are taught to promote their accomplishments and talents when given an opportunity. The team concluded, ethnocentrically, that Martha was not a team player because she promoted her accomplishments and spoke fast without pausing for others to jump in. They interpreted her actions through their own cultural filter.

This software development team isn't unusual. Many of us stereotype the behavior of cultural groups different from our own, then negatively evaluate that behavior. Speicher's analysis of a conflict between an African American male and a white female concluded that the participants' failures to recognize cultural differences contributed to the conflict and to each person's negative evaluation of the other person.[9] Leonard and Locke examined stereotypes held by African Americans about Caucasian Americans, and vice versa.[10] Each group evaluated the other negatively on the basis of the group's stereotypical

Effective groups, more and more, require sensitivity to cultural differences.

communication behavior. African Americans had worse impressions of the Caucasian Americans than the other way around, but neither group's evaluations suggested a supportive climate for communication. Perhaps enhanced cultural understanding can begin to undo such negative assessments.

In this chapter we try to sensitize you to how other cultures and co-cultures differ from the "dominant culture" of the United States, thereby improving your communication in groups. Instead of presenting a laundry list of cultures and the characteristics associated with each (a lengthy catalog!), we focus primarily on several broad dimensions on which cultures differ. We offer three important caveats. First, from the vast and growing field of intercultural communication, we present only information we believe to be most relevant to small group communication. Second, in many instances we are overgeneralizing. For example, when we say that "white, middle-class Americans prefer direct eye contact," we know there is a lot of variation in the preferences of white, middle-class Americans. We urge you to remember that often *there will be as much within-group as between-group variation,* especially for pluralistic cultures such as the United States. Third, there has been relatively little research on intercultural communication *within small groups.* Although much is known about how Mexicans and Arabs behave *within* their own cultures, almost nothing is known about how Mexicans and Arabs behave when they work *together* in the same small group. In many instances, we are making logical, best guesses about what happens when individuals of different cultures must interact within the same setting. We rely heavily on findings from studies of interpersonal intercultural communication, applying them to small group settings.

We have already used several terms in common usage, but now we define them according to our usage in this book. These terms are *culture, cultural identity, co-culture, intracultural,* and *intercultural communication.*

What Is Culture?

Culture

The patterns of values, beliefs, symbols, norms, procedures, and behaviors that have been historically transmitted to and are shared by a given group of persons.

Cultural Identity

The identification with and acceptance of a particular group's shared symbols, meanings, norms, and rules for conduct.

Culture refers to the pattern of values, beliefs, symbols (including language), norms, and behaviors shared by an identifiable group of individuals. During enculturation, or becoming part of a culture, you are taught how to perceive the world, to think, to communicate, and to behave. The teaching is done both formally and informally as you learn the lifestyle of the family and community. Small primary groups, starting with the family, are vital to this process and are the chief way individuals become enculturated. This process happens so gradually and automatically that, unless something happens to make us question our behavior, we rarely are aware of how culture affects us; our own culture's effect on us is invisible, unless we make a point of looking for it. **Cultural identity** refers to the degree to which a person learns, accepts, and identifies with the symbols, meanings, and standards of behavior common to a particular group.[11] Individuals are *taught* such things as language, how and when to speak, how to perceive the world, what is and is not appropriate behavior, and so forth. As with most of us, members of Martha's interview team were oblivious to how their cultural identities affected both their own communication behavior and their interpretation of Martha's behavior. Consider, for example, the culture shock that faces New Orleans natives forced to relocate after Hurricane Katrina's devastation, including the painful identity change that will occur for many of them.

Our definition of *culture* is intentionally broad. *Culture,* as we define it, refers to *any* group of people with a shared identity. For example, a *cultural grouping* can refer to ethnicity (black, white, Hispanic, Greek), a professional grouping (college students, communication professors, nurses, accountants), an interest grouping (hunters, duplicate bridge players), an age group (baby boomers), or even socioeconomic class (working class, middle class). In short, any symbol system that is "bounded and salient" to individuals may be termed a culture.[12]

Co-culture

A grouping that sees itself as distinct but is also part of a larger grouping.

Sometimes a grouping that sees itself as distinct, but is part of a larger culture, is termed a **co-culture.** We use the term *co-culture* rather than the more common *subculture* because we agree with Orbe's argument that *subculture,* which simply refers to size—a smaller grouping within a larger culture—can also imply inferiority.[13] Co-culture, on the other hand, reminds us that "no one culture is inherently superior over co-existing cultures,"[14] although one culture may dominate. Co-cultural groupings can form on the basis of any shared identity. For example, your coauthors consider themselves to be part of the co-culture *professional educators.* We share certain values and beliefs with other professional educators that are very important to us: a belief in the value of education, similar ideas about what does and does not constitute a good education, a desire to place education high on a list of funding priorities, and so forth. When we interact with professional educators (at our universities, at professional conferences, during chance encounters on airplanes, etc.), we take these beliefs for granted—we accept them as "givens." Other examples of co-cultural groupings include rural and urban; white collar and blue collar; eastern, southern, western, and midwestern United States; Roman Catholic and Jewish; and many more.

Each of us belongs to several different co-cultures simultaneously. For example, Gloria is white, middle-class, Greek American; Kathy is white, middle-class, a military brat. Whether a particular co-cultural identification is important in a given circumstance depends on the specific features of that circumstance. Gloria's identification as a Greek American is more salient when she attends the Greek festivals in Little Rock and Cincinnati than when she attends professional conferences. Kathy thinks of herself as a military brat when she talks about how much she has moved or when she attends high school reunions with those who went to Wagner High School on Clark Air Force Base in the Philippines.

It is important to understand your culture because it affects *everything* you do, particularly your communication behavior.[15] The behaviors and attitudes we adopt from our culture are learned and lasting. Cultures do change, but slowly. During **intracultural communication** (among individuals from the same culture or co-culture), much of the communication behavior can be taken for granted. But during **intercultural communication** (among individuals from different cultures or co-cultures), participants must be alert to the added potential for misunderstanding.

Our opening story of Martha was chosen to emphasize that intercultural communication is not limited to encounters between people from different countries. An Anglo American manager talking to an Arabic counterpart certainly represents an instance of intercultural communication, but so does a native of Cupertino, California, talking to someone from New York City. In fact, a conversation between people from different countries can be more *intra*- than *inter*cultural (e.g., as between an Anglo American and an Anglo Canadian).

In a sense, *every* act of communication has intercultural elements because each individual is a *unique* blend of learned behaviors.[16] Intercultural communication is a continuum with *intercultural* communication at one end and *intracultural* communication at the other.[17] All encounters are more or less intercultural, but none is purely one or the other. Thus, communication among members of an Inuit family living in a remote area of Alaska will be almost purely *intra*cultural, whereas a conference of Japanese and American legislators who do not speak each other's languages would be extremely *inter*cultural. The more intercultural communication becomes, the greater the potential for communication malfunctions.

Now that we have introduced you to these important terms, we turn to a discussion of six broad characteristics that differ from culture to culture and significantly influence group members' communication behaviors. As mentioned earlier, this information is not a list of characteristics and the cultures associated with them, although we provide cultural examples to illustrate. It is a framework to help you understand where communication differences originate, diagnose misunderstandings, and decide how you will act.

Intracultural Communication

Interaction between and among individuals from the same culture or co-culture.

Intercultural Communication

Interaction between and among individuals from different cultures or co-cultures.

A group member's culture or co-culture has a major influence on that member's communication behavior:

1. The pluralism of U.S. society and the fact that societal diversity is increasing guarantees that groups of the future will be increasingly culturally diverse.

2. The more similar group members' cultures are, making the communication more intracultural, the easier it will be for them to take communication for granted; however, the increase in diversity, making communication more intercultural, demands that members try to understand and embrace their differences.

3. Diversity confers a number of competitive advantages, including creativity and problem solving.

4. Ethnocentricity—judging someone's behavior through the lens of your own culture—creates unnecessary problems in groups.

5. We all simultaneously belong to several co-cultures, smaller cultures within the larger one, whose values and communication patterns may be very important to us.

Cultural Characteristics That Affect Communication

A number of researchers have investigated particular characteristics that differ across cultures.[18] We focus on six that are especially relevant for communication in small groups. These are *worldview; individualism versus collectivism; power distance; uncertainty avoidance; masculinity versus femininity;* and *high- versus low-context communication.* As with intra- and intercultural communication, each dimension will be thought of as a continuum. We describe each end of the continuum, but recognize that cultures do not fall exclusively at one end or the other. Cultures are complex; they exhibit the following characteristics in varying degrees. These characteristics are summarized in Table 5.2.

Worldview

Worldview

One's beliefs about the nature of life, the purpose of life, and one's relation to the cosmos.

Worldview encompasses how we perceive the nature of the world around us, our relationship to it, and the purpose of life. Every culture has a worldview that serves to explain why things are the way they are and where humans fit into the grand scheme of life; this cultural characteristic is highly resistant to change. For example, people with cultures from a *being* orientation believe that fate controls all human events and are more likely to "go with the flow" because they believe their destinies are predetermined. In contrast, people from cultures with a *doing* orientation believe people can control, or at least strongly influence, events and adopt a "make it happen" worldview.[19] The United States has a *doing* orientation. For instance, Americans usually ask, "What do you do for a living?" when they first meet someone.

TABLE 5.2   Dimensions of culture and associated characteristics

Worldview	"Being" Orientation	"Doing" Orientation
	Go with the flow. Fate controls human events. Patience is valued.	Make things happen. People control events and are in charge of their own fates. Prefer getting to the point quickly.
Collectivism/Individualism	Collectivism	Individualism
	Group is standard of reference; group is valued over individual. Value harmony and conformity. Value slow consensus building.	Individual is standard of reference; individual is valued over group. Value dissent and diversity. Value debate and disagreement.
Power Distance	High Power Distance	Low Power Distance
	Status differences maximized. Status hierarchy based on birth/position in society is normal; people are not created equal. Prefer authoritarian, directive leadership.	Status differences minimized. Status hierarchy based on birth/position in society unfair; people are created equal. Prefer democratic, participative leadership.
Uncertainty Avoidance	High Uncertainty Avoidance	Low Uncertainty Avoidance
	Uncomfortable with ambiguity. Prefer clear rules and norms, high structure. Prefer structured leadership.	High tolerance for ambiguity. Comfortable with loose, flexible rules. Prefer democratic leadership.
Masculinity/Femininity	Masculinity	Femininity
	Value assertive behaviors. Value achievement. Emphasize objectivity, control. Prefer autocratic leadership.	Value caring, nurturing behaviors. Value relationships with others. Emphasize subjectivity. Prefer participative leadership.
High/Low Context	High Context	Low Context
	Message carried by the context, nonverbal content. Culturally homogeneous; much meaning can be safely assumed. Prefer indirect communication.	Meaning carried by the words, verbal content. Culturally diverse; meaning cannot be taken for granted. Prefer clear, direct communication.

Other cultures want to know who you *are* rather than what you do: Who are your parents? Your family? Are you a person of good character? Such cultures, which include some Asian and many Native American cultures, conceive of life as a river that flows; it is more appropriate for people to flow with the river than try to navigate against it. But *doing* cultures, such as that of North America and some western European cultures, believe the opposite. Sayings such as "If at first you don't succeed, try, try again" indicate a worldview that hard work, with or against the river, is expected.

In terms of communication behavior in groups, members with *being* orientations value patience, allowing events to proceed at their own pace without forcing them to a conclusion. Americans, from our strong *doing* orientation, want to get to the point in a hurry so we can get things done. When members representing both orientations meet in a group, consensus may be impossible.

Individualism versus Collectivism

Individualistic Culture

Culture in which the needs and wishes of the individual predominate over the needs of the group.

Collectivist Culture

A culture in which the needs and wishes of the group predominate over the needs of any one individual.

Some cultures place higher value on individual goals, but others value group goals more. Gudykunst and Ting-Toomey note that in **individualistic cultures** the development of the individual is foremost, even when this is at the expense of the group, whereas in **collectivist cultures** the needs of the group are more important, with individuals expected to conform to the group.[20] As is suggested by the terms, conformity is valued in collectivist cultures, but diversity and dissent are more esteemed in individualistic cultures. People in the United States admire the person who "marches to a different drummer." The identity of *I* takes precedence over *we,* so we give high priority to *self*-development, *self*-actualization, and individual initiative and achievement. We go so far as to encourage group members to leave a group if they feel their individual values, beliefs, and preferences are being compromised. This contrasts with most Asian and Native American cultures. For example, a Chinese proverb states, "The nail that sticks up is pounded down." This means that if a member is standing out from the group, the group has the right—even the obligation—to force the individual to conform. In collectivist cultures, the goals, wishes, and opinions of the in-group (the dominant group) always prevail; such cultures value cooperation within the group and slow consensus building rather than direct confrontation in which individual opinions are debated.

Members of collectivist cultures tend to place strong emphasis on extended family, with communication centering on the family. A Nigerian student told us how unfriendly he thought Americans were when he first came to the United States. His friends on campus said "hello" to him, but kept walking to class. In Nigeria, with its collectivist culture, his friends would have inquired about his mother, father, brothers and sisters, aunts, uncles, and so forth. He would have had a long conversation about their respective families. Imagine his shock when he experienced the individualistic "get down to business" focus of the American students!

This distinction between collectivist and individualistic cultures is important in mixed-culture small groups, primarily because of the effect on communication behaviors. For example, members of individualistic cultures, who see themselves as relatively more independent than interdependent, value verbal clarity more than members of collectivist cultures.[21] Recent research has found, in bargaining situations, the collectivist buyers and sellers earned higher joint profits.[22] The seller's collectivism was the key factor.

Power Distance

Cultures differ with respect to their preferred **power distance,** which is the degree to which power or status differences are minimized or maximized.[23] In low power-distance cultures, such as Austria, Israel, and New Zealand, people believe that power should be distributed equally. The United States is a relatively low power-distance culture. We prize equality under the law; our Declaration of Independence asserts that "all men are created equal." We regard it as unfair for some to receive privileges accorded to them only by accident of birth instead of being earned by hard work or merit. In contrast, high power-distance cultures, such as the Philippines, Mexico, Iraq, and India, generally have a rigid, hierarchical status system and prefer large power distances. In high power-distance cultures, people believe that each person has his or her rightful place, that leaders or others with power should have special privileges, and that the authority of those with power should not be questioned.

Hofstede noted that larger cultures usually develop higher power distances. Larger groups need more formalized leadership and communication structures to maintain themselves than smaller groups do. Power tends to be concentrated in the hands of a few people, with others accepting the fairly rigid hierarchy as normal and desirable.[24] And who counts most in the hierarchy varies considerably. For example, consider the following scenario. A man is in a small boat with his mother, wife, and child when it capsizes. Only he can swim and he can save only one of the other three. Whom should he save? Rubenstein found that *all* of the Arabs he asked would save the mother because a man has only one mother, but can always get another wife and child. In contrast, of 100 American college freshman, 60 said they would save the wife and 40, the child. They laughed at the idea of saving the mother.[25] This represents a fundamental difference in how Arabs and Americans view the world.

Lustig and Cassotta have summarized research that examines how power distance might affect small group communication.[26] They found that power distance is related to leadership styles and preferences, conformity, and discussion procedures. High power-distance cultures value authoritarian, directive leadership, whereas low power-distance cultures value participative, democratic leadership. We Americans tend to assume, ethnocentrically, that everyone wants a chance to participate in decisions that affect them. That reflects our deeply held cultural values stemming from our relatively low power-distance culture. However, an American group leader trying to use a participative leadership style in a group of Mexicans or Filipinos is likely to be seen as inept or incompetent. Power distance is also related to the discussion procedures members prefer. Participation in group discussions and decisions is preferred by persons who believe their individual opinions should be valued regardless of status (i.e., low power-distance cultures), but decision making by the leader, with minimal participation from the group, is the norm in high power-distance cultures. People from high power-distance cultures believe it is appropriate for low-status group members to conform to the desires of high-status members; however, in low power-distance cultures, members will be less likely to conform.

Power Distance
The degree to which a culture emphasizes status and power differences among members of the culture; status differences are minimized in low power-distance cultures and emphasized in high power-distance cultures.

Uncertainty Avoidance

Uncertainty Avoidance

The degree to which members of a culture avoid or embrace uncertainty and ambiguity; cultures high in uncertainty avoidance prefer clear rules for interaction, whereas cultures low in uncertainty avoidance are comfortable without guidelines.

Uncertainty avoidance refers to how well people in a particular culture tolerate ambiguity and uncertainty.[27] Does unpredictability make us anxious or eager? Low uncertainty avoidance cultures have a high tolerance for ambiguity, are more willing to take risks, have less rigid rules, and accept a certain amount of deviance and dissent. Great Britain, Sweden, and Hong Kong are such countries. The software group in our opening case seemed pretty laid back and free of many rules (except the one about being laid back!). At the other end of the continuum are countries such as Greece, Japan, and Belgium, where people prefer to avoid ambiguous situations. These cultures establish rules and clear-cut norms of behavior that help individuals feel secure. All members of the culture are expected to behave in accordance with the standards of behavior, and dissent is not appreciated. People from such cultures often have a strong internalized work ethic. The United States is a fairly low uncertainty avoidance culture.

When low and high uncertainty avoidance individuals come together, they may threaten or frighten each other.[28] Low uncertainty avoidance people, such as most Americans, are perceived as too unconventional by their high uncertainty avoidance counterparts. On the other hand, high uncertainty avoidance people are seen as too structured or uncompromising by the low uncertainty avoiders.

Uncertainty avoidance affects preferences for leadership styles, conformity, and discussion processes.[29] Cultures high in uncertainty avoidance rely on clear rules, consistently enforced, with the leader expected to structure the work of the group and behave autocratically. They prefer structure and clear procedures. In contrast, low uncertainty avoidance cultures prefer democratic leadership approaches. High uncertainty avoidance cultures value predictability and security; nonconformist behavior threatens this predictability. Conformity to the leader and group opinion is the norm for high avoidance cultures, whereas dissent and disagreement are tolerated, even encouraged, in low avoidance cultures. Lustig and Cassotta postulate that high uncertainty avoidance members should produce groups with greater task orientation, whereas low uncertainty avoidance members should display a more relationship-oriented focus. In part, this may have been a major problem between Martha and the software design group; they wanted someone who would fit with the other members, suggesting that the relationship focus was key, but Martha seemed to be more task (and "me") focused, which violated their expectations.

Masculinity versus Femininity

Masculinity (as applied to culture)

The quality of cultures that value assertiveness and dominance.

Femininity (as applied to culture)

The quality of cultures that value nurturing and caring for others.

Masculinity refers to cultures that value stereotypical masculine behaviors such as assertiveness and dominance.[30] This is contrasted with **femininity,** referring to cultures that value behaviors such as nurturing and caring for others. Masculine cultures, which include Japan, Austria, Mexico, and Venezuela, prize achievement, accumulation of wealth, aggressiveness, and what we would call "macho" behavior. Feminine cultures, which include the Scandinavian countries, The Netherlands, and Thailand, value interpersonal relationships, nurturing, service to and caring for others, particularly the poor and unfortunate. The United States is a moderately masculine culture.

Lustig and Cassotta observe that masculinity and femininity affect a number of preferences related to small groups.[31] Masculine cultures are more comfortable with a controlling, directive leadership. Such cultures value objectivity and control, qualities exhibited by authoritarian leaders. Feminine cultures, which value relationships and subjectivity, prefer a more participative, democratic leadership style. Stereotypical masculinity, with its emphasis on assertiveness and ambition, does not value conformity highly. In contrast, femininity, which stereotypically values cooperation and group-based decision making, expects and values conformity. Finally, social roles between men and women are more clearly differentiated in high masculine cultures. Males are more likely to undertake task-related roles and females, socioemotional ones. This affects the roles performed in small groups, including who will compete for the leadership role and whether women will be accepted in leadership and other high-status positions.

Low- versus High-Context Communication

The final cultural characteristic we will consider is low- versus high-context communication.[32] In **low-context communication,** the primary meaning of a message is carried by the verbal, or explicit, part of the message, whereas in **high-context communication,** the primary meaning is conveyed by certain features of the situation. In other words, in a high-context culture, what is *not* said may be more important in determining meaning than what *is* said. In high-context cultures, there is such a high degree of consensus that words aren't needed; members of the culture share the same understandings and can take much for granted. For example, one of our students who is Roman Catholic said she was completely comfortable during a recent trip to Europe when she attended Roman Catholic religious services in Italy and France. Despite the fact that she spoke no Italian or French, she knew from the context exactly what to do and when. In low-context cultures, such as those of Germany, Switzerland, the Scandinavian countries, and the United States, direct, clear, and unambiguous statements are valued. The suggestions we provided in Chapter 3 for conducting organized and effective group discussions are appropriate for low-context cultures such as ours. We expect people to state precisely what they mean so that there can be little room for doubt, no matter what the situation (i.e., context) happens to be. The same verbal message given in different contexts means about the same thing. For example, "No, I don't agree with that idea" means much the same thing whether you are in a meeting of co-workers, at the family dinner table, or meeting with your church board. In contrast, high-context cultures such as China, Japan, and South Korea

Low-Context Communication

Communication wherein the primary meaning of a message is carried by the verbal or explicit part of the message.

High-Context Communication

Communication wherein the primary meaning of a message is conveyed by features of the situation or context instead of the verbal, explicit part of the message.

prefer ambiguity, with several shades of meaning possible, because this helps preserve harmony and allows people to save face. In China, instead of "No, I don't agree with that idea," you are more likely to hear, "Perhaps we could explore that option." You would have to be well versed in Chinese communication patterns to know whether that statement means "No, we don't like it" or "We like it very much, but we must build consensus slowly" or "We don't know whether we like it or not until we explore it more fully." Moreover, you would also have to be astute at reading clues in the situation—for instance, is this in reaction to the boss's suggestion, or to a younger co-worker's? Complicated, isn't it? To us, with our low-context bias, it seems as though the Chinese are beating around the bush.[33]

Low-context cultures also tend to be individualistic, and high-context cultures tend to be collectivist.[34] Collectivist cultures operate by consensus of the group; individuals try not to risk offending another member of the group because this might upset a delicate balance of agreement and harmony. Apparently, ambiguity allows individuals to express opinions tentatively rather than directly without the risk of affronting others and upsetting the balance. Because low-context cultures such as the United States display cultural diversity in which little can be taken for granted, verbal skills are probably more necessary, and thus more valued.[35] In a high-context culture such as Japan, the high degree of cultural homogeneity means that more can be taken for granted (and thus remain unspoken) during the communication process. In fact, most Japanese value silence more than we do and are suspicious of displays of verbal skills.[36]

Imagine how difficult group communication can be when members from a high-context culture try to interact with members from a low-context culture. One of us observed a student group that included Qing-yu, who was from Taiwan. The American students were used to lively debate and accustomed to speaking out in favor of or in opposition to one another's ideas, but in Qing-yu's culture, disagreement is indicated very subtly. Qing-yu's quiet, subdued behavior in the group irritated the American students, who kept trying to get her to behave more like them. The harder the Americans tried to force her to take a stand, get to the point, and be direct, the more she retreated into her familiar orientation of ambiguity and indirectness. The misunderstanding was severe.

The six characteristics we have just discussed determine what is considered appropriate verbal and nonverbal communicative behavior in a particular culture. (See also Table 5.2, p. 117.) In the previous chapter, we discussed several effects of cultural differences on nonverbal communication. Here, we focus on language issues related to cultural or co-cultural differences. Nonverbal signals are inherently ambiguous and readily subject to misinterpretation, whether cultural differences exist or not. But language *seems* more precise. We may be tempted to assume that verbal language is less susceptible to cultural misunderstanding—but we would be wrong! The following section describes communication issues related to cultural and co-cultural differences.

Cultures differ along several dimensions, which provide a framework for understanding and comparing different cultures and co-cultures, although there is considerable variability *within* every culture:

1. The worldview of *doing* implies that people can make things happen, but the *being* worldview implies the opposite—people should go with the flow because fate is in charge.

2. Collectivist cultures value the group over the individual and expect conformity and consensus building; individualistic cultures elevate the individual over the group and value dissent.

3. High power-distance cultures emphasize status differences, whereas low power-distance cultures minimize them. Authoritarian, directive leadership is expected in high power-distance cultures, but participative leadership is valued in low power-distance ones.

4. Cultures high in uncertainty avoidance dislike ambiguity and prefer clear rules and procedures; low uncertainty avoidance cultures are comfortable with loose, flexible rules and procedures.

5. High masculine cultures emphasize achievement and assertive behavior; high feminine cultures value relationships and nurturing behavior.

6. In high-context cultures, the meaning of the message is conveyed less by the words than by the situation, or context; ambiguous communication that preserves harmony is expected. In low-context cultures, words convey the intent of a message, with clear, direct communication valued.

Communication Challenges Posed by Co-Cultures

Earlier we described cultural and co-cultural communication rules and patterns as things that are learned, expectations and behaviors that we absorb. The United States contains many co-cultures, some of them more visible than others. We now examine differences in the characteristics and communication patterns based on race, age, and socioeconomic class.

Co-Cultural Differences Based on Race: African American Communication Patterns

In this section we focus on communication differences observed between African Americans and Caucasian Americans. We do not intend to imply that relationships between Hispanics and European Americans, or Asians and African Americans, are not equally important. In fact, in the near future, Hispanics will be the largest minority group in the United States as they are now in California, with profound implications for communication. However, we elected to discuss black-white communication because misunderstandings here appear to be among the most serious and volatile at this time. African Americans and Caucasian Americans perceive each other as threatening and have generally negative evaluations of each other;[37] it seems especially important to help each group understand the other. We remind you again that even though we discuss African American communication patterns as though African Americans were a uniform group, this is not the case. So to some extent we are stereotyping the communication patterns of both groups. We take this risk with you because we think it is important that you know and be sensitive to the fact that some communication differences have cultural origins. We agree with Orbe, who notes that the considerable diversity *within* the African American community has been largely ignored by researchers.[38]

Foeman and Pressley have summarized research that describes "typical" (although we caution you again that there is no such thing as "typical") black communication, particularly in organizational settings.[39] Black culture in the United States is an oral culture, so verbal inventiveness and virtuosity of expression are highly valued. What many whites perceive as boastfulness Foeman and Pressley call *assertiveness,* which takes both verbal and nonverbal forms (for instance, trying to top someone else's boast, strutting across the street). Black managers are perceived as forthright or overly reactive. In a conflict, for instance, a black is more likely to confront an individual directly, whereas a white manager is more likely to approach the problem indirectly. Consequently, some blacks perceive whites as underreactive, but some whites see blacks as overreactive. Degree of responsiveness (expressiveness) differs; blacks are more likely to respond both verbally and physically (e.g., gesturing often with their hands), whereas whites tend to focus on verbal responses. Blacks make less direct eye contact, but they compensate by standing closer to their conversational partner than most whites. These differences in cultural communication patterns can create serious misunderstandings. For instance, a white expecting more eye contact may be likely to repeat or rephrase statements in order to get the expected signs of understanding (such as eye contact), whereas the black person feels the white person is being condescending.

The black culture is more collective than the more dominant white culture of the United States. For example, Penington examined the interactions of middle-class African American and European American mother-daughter dyads.[40] While both sets of dyads used similar communication strategies to negotiate their relationships, the African American dyads expressed more intensity and greater desire for closeness. The European American dyads expected greater autonomy and preferred more individualism.

African Americans and European Americans express themselves verbally in different ways. Blacks are more playful than most whites in their use of language and relish playing verbal games. Foeman and Pressley explain that blacks *signify* (or hint) at questions rather than asking them directly because they perceive disclosure of personal information to be voluntary; thus, questions are implied so that the person being asked will not feel vulnerable or obliged to answer.[41] In addition, blacks use the backchannel (or *call-response*) to indicate interest and involvement in the discussion. For example, in black churches the services resemble a dialogue, with congregation members freely calling *Amen, Go ahead, Preach* to the minister; such responses would be less frequent in most white churches. Differences in black-white uses of the backchannel, as we discussed earlier, can create misunderstandings and cause hurt feelings.

One of us noticed an illustration of these verbal differences. The week after John Kennedy, Jr., was killed in an airplane crash, Rev. Jesse Jackson was being interviewed by Cokie Roberts in a television tribute to Kennedy. In response to a question about Kennedy's work with the disadvantaged, Rev. Jackson began to speak movingly and at length about the young man. He was using the cadences and extended style of many black preachers, and it was clear that he was just getting started when Cokie interrupted him to say, "So in other words, there was substance to [Kennedy]." In one short sentence, Cokie, who seemed a little frustrated at how long it was taking Rev. Jackson to answer her question, summarized concisely what he had been saying and went on to her next question. The "typical" white, to-the-point style bumped up against the "typical" flowery, elaborated style of black preachers in an interesting way.

In the United States, it is often difficult for someone from one co-culture to participate fully in a group dominated by members of a different co-culture. Many African Americans, including some of the most successful, say they must behave cautiously and carefully in groups of Caucasian Americans; they can never fully relax.[42] In many ways they have developed bicultural competencies—one set of behaviors for African American groups; another for primarily Caucasian groups. This balancing act can be exhausting, but many African Americans believe that if they do not conform to the communication rules of the dominant European American culture, they will pay a high price.

Co-Cultural Differences Based on Age

Over our many years of teaching, we have noticed more "nontraditional" (i.e., older) students in our classes than was true 25 or 30 years ago. We have also noticed that events that helped shape us as teachers, such as the assassination of President John F. Kennedy, Vietnam, and Watergate, are things our students know only from their history books. Age and generational differences have produced interesting challenges for us and for our students, who increasingly must participate in multigenerational groups.

Orbe notes that co-cultural patterns come from the lived experiences of members of the co-culture.[43] The significant events people live through together contribute to formation of the worldview and communication preferences co-cultural group members exhibit. Hicks and Hicks have examined such events with respect to the four generations that currently predominate in the United

States, and have identified a number of key differences that challenge members of different age groups to communicate effectively.[44] The following generational descriptions are, of course, overgeneralizations; however, significant happenings—political assassinations, the explosion of the Internet—have significantly influenced each generation's values and approach to life.

The **builder generation,** born from 1901 to 1945, lived through the Great Depression and World War II. They experienced the four-term presidency of Franklin Roosevelt, the polio epidemic, the Japanese attack on Pearl Harbor, the U.S. drop of atomic bombs on Hiroshima and Nagasaki, and the Red Scare fear of communism. Most were adults during the 1950s economic boom, when ordinary people could buy houses, appliances, and cars for the first time. This generation tends to be cautious about money, defers gratification, and believes in discipline, self-sacrifice, and working toward the common good. Members tend to value conformity and traditional role relationships between the sexes; they can lack spontaneity.

The **boomer generation,** about which much has been written, grew up when television became widely available. Born from 1946 to 1964, boomers experienced the divisiveness of the Vietnam War, political assassinations in the United States, the civil rights movement, the advent of the birth control pill, and the massive mistrust of government precipitated by Watergate. This is a confident generation, willing to challenge authority and tackle big causes. Their sheer size—for a long time this was the largest generation—means that they have been catered to by marketers and producers. Thus, boomers believe they are right all the time, are self-absorbed, and feel free to break rules when they think that's best for them. They also are willing to work hard and expect to be fulfilled in their work.

The **X generation,** born from 1965 to 1976, are sandwiched between two very large generations. They were the first to experience divorce on a massive scale and many became latchkey children. They feel abandoned or emotionally neglected, and have a higher suicide rate than the other generations. They believe they are entitled to the good life, and they don't want to wait for it. They want to prove themselves, but feel the boomers aren't giving them a chance to do so. They are flexible, are comfortable with pluralistic points of view, and are used to change. X-ers display commitment to diversity, which they value more than conformity.

The final generation, the **net generation,** was born between 1977 and 1997. This is the largest generation in terms of numbers, but they are too young yet to have made their influence fully felt. Net-geners are the first fully wired generation—they grew up with computers, e-mail, answering machines, cell phones, voice mail, CDs, and DVDs. They have never known a world without AIDS. Major influences include the Internet and the death of Princess Diana. Members of this generation are in touch with their friends constantly through electronics, even though their friends may be widely scattered. Net-geners have been doing collaborative work ever since their elementary school days; they are comfortable in group settings, are open minded and tolerant, and are

Builder Generation

Individuals born before 1945; key experiences include the Great Depression and World War II.

Boomer Generation

Individuals born from 1946 to 1964; key experiences include the Vietnam war, the civil rights movement, and Watergate.

X Generation

Individuals born from 1965 to 1976; key experience includes divorce on a massive scale.

Net Generation

Individuals born from 1977 to 1997; the first truly "wired" generation, comfortable with technology in all forms.

nonlinear thinkers. But they also don't like to conform to bureaucracy and organizational rules.

Generational differences can severely tax the resources of a group if members aren't sensitive to them. When e-mail was just becoming widely used at her university, Gloria chaired a university committee that included builders, boomers, and a Net-gen student representative. The boomers had become used to using computers and e-mail; the student had grown up with computers. One builder refused to use e-mail for communication; he preferred written memos. Because he was a valuable group member in every other way, Gloria chose to accommodate him by printing out hard copies of all e-mail messages and sending them to him via campus mail. Today, years later, everyone uses e-mail, although some builders and boomers have not learned to navigate the net with the ease of the X-ers and Net-geners.

One of us observed a classroom group with difficulties caused in part by generational value differences. The boomer member, who was the age of the Net-geners' mothers, attempted to organize the work of the group, to establish regular meeting times, and to coordinate the library research of the group. In her journal, one of the Net-gen students lamented that she felt "ordered around" by her mother and was having a hard time accepting this boomer student as a peer. She wanted to disagree and to suggest alternative ways of finding information—such as using the Internet for research—but felt uncomfortable about contradicting somebody who reminded her of her mother. Eventually, partly because of the sensitivity of the boomer member, this group was able to talk and joke about their generational differences and to learn from one another. One particularly interesting difference in this group was that the Net-gen students thought of the Internet *first* as a way to research a topic, whereas the boomer thought first of print sources.

Age or generational differences in small groups have not been investigated much. Two recent studies of media use found generational differences. Kuo found that X-ers in Taiwan used electronic media significantly more than others.[45] Shah et al. found different patterns of media usage for informational purposes, with builders using newspapers, boomers using television, and X-ers using the Internet.[46] Timmerman, in his study of age and racial diversity of baseball and basketball teams, found both age and racial diversity related to impaired performance on basketball teams.[47] This negative relationship between diversity and performance seems to be a relatively recent phenomenon of the last 20 years. Timmerman speculates that diversity is likely to be more challenging for teams in which task interdependence is high, as in basketball. These results support further study into the effects of generation-related co-cultural differences.

Co-Cultural Differences Based on Socioeconomic Class

As with generational differences, the effects of socioeconomic class differences in small groups likewise have not been widely investigated. However, numerous studies attest to differences in communication patterns based on socioeconomic class. We like to think we belong to a classless society, but we don't. For example, during the news coverage of Hurricane Katrina's aftermath, it became clear that the disaster plan had been constructed by middle- and upper-class Americans and was based on middle-class assumptions (such as everyone has access to a personal car with which to evacuate). This failure to understand behaviors and life patterns of individuals from lower socioeconomic classes was devastating for the New Orleans poor, who had no way to leave the city before the storm. Socioeconomic class is not based solely on income. Jackman found that class distinctions are also determined by education, job authority, and skill.[48] In addition, people are readily able to classify others by socioeconomic class. Jackman's research participants showed a high degree of consensus when they were asked about the social class into which particular occupations fit. Furthermore, class differences produce differences in values and communication patterns. Ellis and Armstrong examined television depictions of middle-class and non-middle-class (lower-class and poor) families and found implicit messages about how people of different classes communicate.[49] For instance, middle-class males used longer sentences and generally more complex speaking patterns than non-middle-class males. Middle-class people of both sexes used more adverbs. The word *ain't,* never used by middle-class speakers, served to mark someone as non-middle class.

Communication within the family exhibits class-based communication patterns. Ritchie discovered that families of parents whose jobs entailed a high degree of openness and autonomy in the workplace—in other words, parents of higher socioeconomic class—demonstrated greater conversational orientation within the family, and less conformity.[50] The families that Jordan observed showed relationships among social class, perceptions of time, and media usage.[51] Parents in middle- and upper-class families socialized their children to observe deadlines and structure their time. They used a linear, sequential structure for activities in the home by encouraging their children to do one thing at a time and to complete one task before going on to another. They planned their schedules in advance and adhered to them. The working-class families used looser organizational patterns and tended to do several things at once, such as watch television, eat dinner, and talk to each other at the same time. Schedules were not planned in advance or were changed spontaneously. Jordan speculates that a family's use of time may be related to the perception of time as a resource, which itself may be class based. For instance, middle- and upper-class families perceived time as a scarce commodity that should be managed well and not wasted, and taught their children to perceive time in the same way. In such families, media usage, particularly watching television, was not seen as a particularly good use of time. Working-class parents did not perceive media use as either a good or bad use of time. Interestingly, working-class parents were more concerned about the *content* of media usage than upper- or middle-class parents. These preferences can produce subtle differences in what individuals from different socioeconomic classes accept as normal or appropriate in a group.

We could find no studies that looked at the effect of class differences within small groups. However, in our own teaching, we have observed the effects (usually bad ones) of communication differences that are class based. A recent book by Payne describes several of the key communication patterns, related to the co-cultures of class, that can cause problems.[52] Payne, a teacher and principal, has been successful in working with both children and adults from backgrounds of what she calls *generational poverty,* in which a family has experienced socioeconomic poverty for at least two generations. Payne notes that the communicative and daily living rules differ greatly for people from poor, middle, and wealthy classes. Each class experiences its own ethnocentricity, assuming that its rules are both known and appropriate. Middle-class individuals, who include many of the teachers, managers, and professionals in the United States, assume that "everyone knows the rules" for how to do things. But the poor and the wealthy have different values and communicative rules! What are some of those differences?

Middle-classes value achievement and believe they can affect the future with the choices they make in the present. Individuals in generational poverty focus on the present. They believe the future is controlled by fate and they cannot do much to change it. Wealthy classes respect the past; they make decisions based on tradition and history. They prize social connections.

Payne notes that different classes use discourse in different ways. Individuals from backgrounds of generational poverty use discourse as a form of entertainment. For all discourse, they use the casual register—an informal meandering conversational style the middle class uses only between friends. It is characterized by vague word choice, incomplete sentences, reliance on nonverbal signals to complete thoughts, and a limited vocabulary of 400 to 800 words. The narrative pattern is circular, wherein the speaker talks around an issue before getting to the point. This contrasts significantly with the formal register style middle-class and wealthy speakers use for most conversations. Formal register uses complete sentences, standard sentence construction and syntax, a more extensive vocabulary, and specific words; and the speaker gets right to the point. In Table 5.3, the story of Cinderella, told in both casual and formal discourse, illustrates some of these differences.

The formal register version is told in chronological order, from beginning to end, and demonstrates cause, effect, and conclusion. It follows the typical problem-solving pattern of sequential logic—first one thing happens, then the next, then the next. The casual register version is more entertaining and relies on audience participation. The narrator expects others to jump in and help tell the story. For middle-class readers, the story will appear disorganized. However, and this is an important point to remember, the story has its own logic, an emotionally based one, in which the most important emotional elements are highlighted first.

These differences are interesting, but their point here is to highlight the potential challenges of diverse groups. Imagine how frustrating it can be if you think it is important for a speaker to get right to the point, and you encounter someone in your group with a wandering narrative style. Similarly,

TABLE 5.3
Cinderella, in formal
and casual register

Formal Register Version (abbreviated because of familiarity)

Once upon a time, there was a girl named Cinderella. She was very happy, and she lived with her father. Her father remarried a woman who had three daughters. When Cinderella's father died, her stepmother treated Cinderella very badly and, in fact, made her the maid for herself and her three daughters. At the same time in this land, the King decided that it was time for the Prince to get married. So, he sent a summons to all the people in the kingdom to come to a ball. Cinderella was not allowed to go, but she was forced to help her stepsisters and stepmother get ready for the ball. After they left for the ball, and as Cinderella was crying on the hearth, her fairy godmother came and, with her magic wand, gave Cinderella a beautiful dress, glass slippers, and a stagecoach made from pumpkins and mice. She then sent Cinderella to the ball in style. There was one stipulation. She had to be home by midnight.

At the ball, the Prince was completely taken with Cinderella and danced with her all evening. As the clock began striking midnight, Cinderella remembered what the fairy godmother had said and fled from the dance. All she left was one of her glass slippers.

The Prince held a big search, using the glass slipper as a way to identify the missing woman. He finally found Cinderella; she could wear the glass slipper. He married her, and they lived happily ever after.

Casual Register Version (bold type indicates the narrator; plain type indicates audience participation)

Well, you know Cinderella married the Prince, in spite of that nasty old stepmother. Pointy eyes, that one. Old hag! **Good thing she had a fairy godmother or she never would've made it to the ball.** Lucky thing! God bless her ragged tail! Wish I had me a fairy godmother. **And to think she nearly messed up big time by staying 'til the clock was striking 12. After all the fairy godmother had done for her.** Um, um. She shoulda known better. Eyes too full of the Prince, they were. They didn't call him the Prince for no reason. **When she got to the ball, her stepsisters and stepmother didn't even recognize her she was so beautiful without those rags.** Served 'em right, no-good jealous hags. **The Prince just couldn't quit dancing with her, just couldn't take his eyes off her. He had finally found his woman.** Lucky her! Lucky him! Sure wish life was a fairy tale. Kind like the way I met Charlie. Ha ha. **The way she arrived was something else—a coach and horseman—really fancy. Too bad that when she ran out of there as the clock struck 12 all that was left was a pumpkin rolling away and four mice!** What a surprise for the mice! **Well, he has to find her because his heart is broken. So he takes the glass slipper and hunts for her—and her old wicked stepmother, of course, is hiding her.** What a prize! Aren't they all? **But he finds her and marries her. Somebody as good as Cinderella deserved that.** Sure hope she never invited that stepmother to her castle. Should make her the maid!!

Source: Ruby K. Payne, *A Framework for Understanding Poverty* (Highlands, TX: aha! Process, Inc., 2001, 47-48 (Reprinted by permission).

can you envision how rude and boring it must seem to someone with a colorful, spiraling narrative style to be paired with a sequential, get to-the-point partner? That is why we think it is important for group members to understand each other's rules and assumptions.

Challenges for Co-Cultural Group Members

This discussion of race, age, and social class has only scratched the surface and is not intended to be exhaustive. It is intended to encourage you to think about your own behavior with an eye toward sensitizing you to ethnocentric behavior that may cause problems in a group. Orbe suggests that members of co-cultures that are not part of the dominant culture can become marginalized in groups and organizations.[53] If they want their views represented, they must expend energy thinking about how their communication affects and is received by members of the dominant culture. There are a number of strategies they use, but they may or may not be successful in being heard.

Two recent studies by Kirchmeyer indicate that minority members of groups are often the lowest contributors.[54] Two plausible explanations for this are that minorities may lack a sense of belonging to the group and that, although they may be skilled in communication within their own culture, they may lack the skills to communicate effectively in groups composed primarily of whites. Because minority status affected contribution levels, Kirchmeyer cautions that multicultural groups may not be using the multiple perspectives of all their members in the final products. This view is supported by Teboul's study of minority hires in organizations.[55] He notes that minority new hires encounter more setbacks in becoming truly part of their organizations, experience more relational isolation, and learn that certain relational doors are closed to them. This represents a significant loss to all of us. Whether we are black or white, young or old, middle class or poor, Protestant or Jewish, urban or rural, we must begin to recognize that differences are just that—differences!

In the film *The Color of Fear,* eight men of different races discuss their pesonal experiences with racism. Communication scholar Tadasu Imahori, who is Japanese American, discusses his reaction to watching the European American in the film deny that racism is a problem in this country.[56] He observes that he can easily relate with the other men who had experienced racism but were unable to convince the white man of the validity of their experiences. This illustrates a main point we want to convey in this chapter: It is imperative in small groups to invite and acknowledge the experiences, perceptions, and viewpoints of all members. Someone's perspective may be different, but this does not make it invalid, wrong, uneducated, or stupid. We must learn to manage diversity effectively. Failure to do so has hurt members' feelings, demonized individuals who represent the dominant culture of the United States, fostered reverse discrimination, pinpointed certain groups or individuals as being responsible for all diversity-based problems, reinforced stereotypes, and demoralized everyone.[57] When we don't embrace and

FIGURE 5.1   Steps in the Public Dialogue process

1. Facilitators and notetakers trained in the microskills of facilitation are selected.
2. Questions are planned in advance and open ended enough to elicit a variety of opinions. (For example, "If our community were the best it could be, what would it look like?")
3. Groups of six to eight are formed, each with a trained facilitator and notetaker.
4. Ground rules are reviewed. (For example, "Participants should listen respectfully and are encouraged to invite the speaker to elaborate," and "Participants should not interrupt.")
5. The facilitator starts the discussion and keeps it flowing while the notetaker writes down the main ideas; the notetaker is encouraged to co-facilitate where appropriate.
6. At the end of the discussion (typically 60 to 90 minutes), the notetaker reviews the notes with the participants.
7. Notes are later compiled (if there are several groups operating at the same time) and distributed to all participants.
8. Often, an action plan is developed from the information (for example, deciding how to reach the "ideal community" on participants' experiences).

encourage group diversity, we deprive groups of the ideas, creativity, and problem-solving efforts of *all* members.

Public Dialogue: A Process to Encourage Appreciation for Differences We have talked at length about the importance of sensitivity to cultural differences, but sometimes appreciating differences is easier said than done. The Public Dialogue process is specifically designed to promote such appreciation by encouraging respectful, interested listening.[58] Based on the communication theory Coordinated Management of Meaning, it is ideally suited to situations where individuals must be able to coordinate their actions (such as in a small group) but hold different perspectives, perhaps as a result of their different cultures. In Public Dialogue, groups of six to eight individuals discuss issues that may be sensitive or controversial. The groups are led by facilitators and notetakers trained in the microskills of facilitation: leading with genuine curiosity, listening, enriching the conversation by asking questions, and recording what participants say. The discussion questions, carefully preplanned, are open ended to elicit a variety of opinions. Participants, with the encouragement of the facilitator, are trained to listen appreciatively so that they genuinely understand someone else's point of view, even if they do not agree with it.

The Public Dialogue process is credited by Cupertino's city manager with helping that city prevent the explosion of a powder keg based on race. Cupertino's Asian population grew from 17 to 42 percent in a decade, leading to tensions and misunderstandings. The carefully constructed dialogues invited community members to talk about what they wanted in their community. One outcome was the creation of Citizens of Cupertino Cross Cultural Consortium, a volunteer group that encouraged continuation of the dialogues. The procedure's steps are summarized in Figure 5.1.

Behaving Ethically in Intercultural Interactions

By now, you know that what is considered rhetorically sensitive and appropriate communication depends on the culture. If communication rules differ in each individual culture, are there any universal or overarching principles that preserve the integrity of individual cultures, yet let members of those cultures work together? Kale suggests two broad principles that should govern intercultural interactions: We should protect the worth and dignity of all human beings, and we should act in such a way as to promote peace among all people.[59] The following ethical guidelines follow from these broad principles:

1. **Communicate in a way that extends empathy and respect to all members of the group.**

    Similar to the ethical principle described in Chapter 1, this principle requires that you work to understand others as they want to be understood. This is more challenging between group members of different cultures because there are fewer "givens," but there are things you can do. First, remember that all discussions are to some extent intercultural; be aware of and sensitive to cultural differences and view them as potential strengths for a group, not liabilities. Resist making judgments about the intelligence or motives of others. Encourage all members to get to know each other beyond the task demands of the group. Finally, initiate discussion of the differences. You will help group members move toward greater understanding and empathy if you explicitly acknowledge differences and willingly discuss them, not in a judgmental way but as an opportunity to learn more about your fellow group members and yourself.

2. **Work to incorporate the key cultural values of all members into the group's procedures and outputs.**

    Of course this is easier said than done, but failure to do this denigrates the cultural values of those members who are ignored. This also means that all members must adjust their normal ways of interacting to accommodate differences. Bantz's work with an intercultural research team provides several specific suggestions for managing cultural diversity.[60] In that team, explicitly establishing common goals and deadlines addressed the needs of members high in uncertainty avoidance, and differences in power distance norms were handled by segregating tasks and varying the leadership styles accordingly. Differing needs for cohesion were addressed by alternating task and social aspects of the work. Notice that these ways of handling the diversity recognized the legitimacy of the differing cultural norms, showed the members' ability to adapt, and demonstrated respect for all concerned—all ethical goals.

    Specific suggestions to help you put these ethical principles into effect in your small groups are summarized in Figure 5.2.

FIGURE 5.2
Guidelines for
ethical intercultural
interaction

In intercultural small group communication,

Remember that every discussion is intercultural to some extent. Because we each have unique backgrounds, we do not use verbal and nonverbal signals to mean exactly the same things.

Recognize and accept differences; view them as strengths of the group, not liabilities. Instead of judging others as wrong for behaving in ways different from yours, recognize that each of us is the product of our culture. Resolve to learn from each other, not try to change each other.

Resist making attributions of stupidity or ill intent; ask yourself whether the other member's behavior could have cultural origin. When another member's behavior seems rude, inconsiderate, or unusual, ask yourself whether you could be observing a cultural difference in what is considered appropriate behavior before you decide the other member is worthless to the group.

Be willing to discuss intercultural differences openly and initiate discussion of differences you observe. Instead of being uncomfortable or pretending that differences do not exist, be willing to ask for and share information about cultural norms and rules. When you observe differences, you can enrich everyone's understanding by pointing them out and initiating a discussion about how cultures vary.

Be willing to adapt to differences. Instead of insisting that others follow the prescriptions of your culture, be willing to adapt your behavior to different cultural practices when appropriate. Try to incorporate the key values and needs of each culture into the group's procedures and outputs.

Recap: A Quick Review

We simultaneously belong to several co-cultures that present communicative challenges when we interact in groups with individuals from other co-cultures:

1. African Americans and Caucasian Americans, in general, misunderstand and evaluate each other negatively. In general, the African American co-culture is more collective, expressive, and verbally playful than that of the dominant Caucasian American culture. Blacks seem overreactive to whites, but whites seem underreactive to blacks.

2. For the first time, four different generations (builders, boomers, X-ers, and Net-geners) must work together in many organizations and groups. Each of these groups was influenced by different experiences and world events, which shaped their view of the world and can make communication between generations challenging.

(continued)

(continued)

3. Differences in socioeconomic class have not been widely researched, but there are different communication "rules" for the co-cultures of wealth, middle class, and poverty. In the co-cultures of wealth and the middle class, communication in organizational groups uses formal register, with complete sentences, standard sentence construction, and a linear organizational pattern. Individuals from generational poverty use casual register almost exclusively and tell stories in a circular, meandering style that is negatively evaluated by middle-class listeners.

4. Public Dialogue, a small group technique that encourages respectful and appreciative listening, can help members from different cultures and co-cultures understand and appreciate each other.

5. Two principles govern ethical intercultural communication: communicating with empathy and respect and, as much as possible, incorporating the cultural values of all members into the group's procedures and outcomes.

QUESTIONS FOR REVIEW

 Go to self-quizzes on the Online Learning Center at mbhe.com/galanes12 to test your knowledge of the chapter concepts

This chapter focused on the types of cultural differences that created challenges for groups composed of members from different cultural and co-cultural groups. One example of those challenges was presented in our opening case of Martha, who lost the job with the software design team.

1. How do the intercultural dimensions discussed in the chapter serve as a framework for assessing the differences in communication pattern between the software design team and Martha? Where were the biggest sources of friction between the two?

2. Martha and the design team were all fairly recent college graduates; all were either from generation X or the net generation. What are the main differences between these two groups and, if Martha had gotten the job, where would you expect to see the most serious communication challenges?

3. The software team included one Hispanic member (Jorge) and one African American member (Scott). How might these co-cultural differences have created challenges with Martha, if she had gotten the job?

4. If the software team and Martha had been more culturally tuned in, how might they have bridged their initial ethnocentric reactions? If you had been either Martha or one of the members of the team, and you had seen the entire interview disintegrating, is there anything you could have said or done to save it?

KEY TERMS

 Test your knowledge of these key terms by visiting the Online Learning Center website at mbhe.com/galanes12

Boomer generation
Builder generation
Co-culture
Collectivist cultures
Cultural identity
Culture
Ethnocentric
Femininity (as applied to culture)
High-context communication

Individualistic cultures
Intercultural communication
Intracultural communication
Low-context communication

Masculinity (as applied to culture)
Net generation
Power distance

Uncertainty avoidance
Worldview
X generation

BIBLIOGRAPHY

Allen, Brenda J. *Difference Matters: Communicating Social Identity.* Long Grove, IL: Waveland Press, 2004.

Hicks, Rick, and Kathy Hicks. *Boomers, X-ers, and Other Strangers: Understanding the Generational Differences that Divide Us.* Wheaton, IL: Tyndale, 1999.

Lustig, Myron W., and Laura L. Cassotta, "Comparing Group Communication across Cultures: Leadership, Conformity, and Discussion Processes." In *Small Group Communication: A Reader.* 6th ed. Robert S. Cathcart and Larry A. Samovar, eds. Dubuque, IA: Wm. C. Brown, 1992, 393–404.

Lustig, Myron W., and Jolene Koester, eds. *Among Us: Essays on Identity, Belonging, and Intercultural Competence.* New York: Longman, 2000.

Payne, Ruby K. *A Framework for Understanding Poverty,* new revised edition. Highlands, TX: aha! Process, Inc., 2001, especially Chapters 1 through 4.

Porter, Richard E., and Larry A. Samovar. "Communication in the Multicultural Group." In *Small Group Communication: A Reader.* 6th ed. Robert S. Cathcart and Larry A. Samovar, eds. Dubuque, IA: Wm. C. Brown, 1992, 382–92.

NOTES

1. William A. Henry, "Beyond the Melting Pot," *Time* (April 9, 1990): 29–35.

2. Brenda J. Allen, *Difference Matters: Communicating Social Identity* (Long Grove, IL: Waveland Press, 2004): 5.

3. C. W. Von Bergen, Barlow Soper, and Teresa Foster, "Unintended Negative Effects of Diversity Management," *Public Personnel Management* 31 (Summer 2002). Accessed on Internet, July 20, 2002.

4. John M. Ivancevich and Jacqueline A. Gilbert, "Diversity Management," *Public Personnel Management* 29 (Spring, 2000). Accessed on Internet July 20, 2002.

5. Beth Bonniwell Haslett and Jenn Ruebush, "What Differences Do Individual Differences in Groups Make?" in *The Handbook of Group Communication Theory and Research,* ed. Lawrence R. Frey (Thousand Oaks, CA: Sage, 1999): 115–138.

6. Martha L. Maznevski, "Understanding Our Differences: Performance in Decision-Making Groups with Diverse Members," *Human Relations* 47 (May 1994): 531–52; Haslett aand Ruebush, "What Differences Do Individual Differences in Groups Make?"

7. Poppy Lauretta McLeod, Sharon Alisa Lobel, and Taylor H. Cox, Jr., "Ethnic Diversity and Creativity in Small Groups," *Small Groups Research* 27 (May 1996): 248–64.

8. Young Yun Kim and Brent D. Ruben, "Intercultural Transformation: A Systems Theory," in *Theories in Intercultural Communication: International and Intercultural Communication Annual,* Vol. 12, eds. Young Yun Kim and William B. Gudykunst (Newbury Park, CA: Sage, 1988): 299–321.

9. Barbara L. Speicher, "Interethnic Conflict: Attribution and Cultural Ignorance," *Howard Journal of Communication* 5 (Spring 1995): 195–213.

10. Rebecca Leonard and Don C. Locke, "Communication Stereotypes: Is Interracial Communication Possible?" *Journal of Black Studies* 23 (March 1993): 332–43.

11. Mary Jane Collier and Milt Thomas, "Cultural Identity: An Interpretive Perspective," in *Theories in Intercultural Communication: International and Intercultural Communication Annual,* Vol. 12, eds. Young Yun Kim and William B. Gudykunst (Newbury Park, CA: Sage, 1988): 113.

12. Ibid., 103.
13. Mark P. Orbe, "From the Standpoint(s) of Traditionally Muted Groups: Explicating a Co-cultural Communication Theoretical Model," *Communication Theory* 8 (February, 1998): 1–26.
14. Ibid., 2.
15. Donald W. Klopf, *Intercultural Encounters: The Fundamentals of Intercultural Communication* (Englewood, CO: Morton, 1987): 27–30.
16. Larry E. Sarbaugh, "A Taxonomic Approach to Intercultural Communication," in *Theories in Intercultural Communication: International and Intercultural Communication Annual*, Vol. 12, eds. Young Yun Kim and William B. Gudykunst (Newbury Park, CA: Sage, 1988): 22–38.
17. Young Yun Kim, "On Theorizing Intercultural Communication," in *Theories in Intercultural Communication: International and Intercultural Communication Annual*, Vol. 12, eds. Young Yun Kim and William B. Gudykunst (Newbury Park, CA: Sage, 1988): 12–13.
18. E. Glenn (with C. G. Glenn), *Man and Mankind: Conflict and Communication Between Cultures* (Norwood, NJ: Ablex, 1981); Edward T. Hall, *Beyond Culture* (New York: Anchor Press, 1977); Geert Hofstede, *Culture's Consequences: International Differences in Work-Related Values* (Beverly Hills, CA: Sage, 1980); F. Kluckhohn and F. Strodtbeck, *Variations in Value Orientations* (New York: Row, Peterson, 1961); Charles H. Kraft, "Worldview in Intercultural Communication," in *Intercultural and International Communication*, ed. Fred L. Casmir (Washington, DC: University Press of America, 1978): 407–28; Larry E. Sarbaugh, "A Taxonomic Approach to Intercultural Communication."
19. Kluckhohn and Strodtbeck, *Variations in Value Orientations*.
20. William B. Gudykunst and Stella Ting-Toomey, *Culture and Interpersonal Communication* (Newbury Park, CA: Sage, 1988): 40–43.
21. Min-Sun Kim and William F. Sharkey, "Independent and Interdependent Construals of Self: Explaining Cultural Patterns of Interpersonal Communication in Multi-Cultural Organizational Settings," *Communication Quarterly* 43 (Winter 1995): 20–38.
22. Deborah A. Cai, Steven R. Wilson, and Laura E. Drake, "Culture in the Context of Intercultural Negotiation: Individualism-Collectivism and Paths to Integrative Agreements," *Human Communication Research* 26 (October 2000): 591–617.
23. Hofstede, *Culture's Consequences*.
24. Ibid.
25. Moshe F. Rubenstein, *Patterns of Problem Solving* (Englewood Cliffs, NJ: Prentice Hall, 1975): 1–2.
26. Myron W. Lustig and Laura L. Cassotta, "Comparing Group Communication across Cultures: Leadership, Conformity, and Discussion Procedures," in *Small Group Communication: A Reader*, 6th ed., eds. Robert S. Cathcart and Larry A. Samovar (Dubuque, IA: Wm. C. Brown, 1992): 393–404.
27. Hofstede, *Culture's Consequences*.
28. Myron W. Lustig and Jolene Koester, *Intercultural Competence: Interpersonal Communication across Cultures* (New York: HarperCollins, 1993).
29. Lustig and Cassotta, "Comparing Group Communication across Cultures."
30. Hofstede, *Culture's Consequences*.
31. Lustig and Cassotta, "Comparing Group Communication across Cultures."
32. Hall, *Beyond Culture*.
33. Linda Wai Ling Young, "Inscrutability Revisited," in *Language and Social Identity,* ed. John J. Gumperz (Cambridge: Cambridge University Press, 1982): 79.
34. Gudykunst and Ting-Toomey, *Culture and Interpersonal Communication,* 45.
35. Roichi Okabe, "Cultural Assumptions of East and West," in *Intercultural Communication Theory: International & Intercultural Communication Annual,* Vol. 7, ed. William B. Gudykunst (Beverly Hills, CA: Sage, 1983): 21–44.
36. Donald W. Klopf, "Japanese Communication Practices: Recent Comparative Research," *Communication Quarterly* 39 (Spring 1991): 130–43.
37. Leonard and Locke, "Communication Stereotypes."
38. Mark P. Orbe, "Remember, It's Always Whites' Ball: Descriptions of African American Male Communication," *Communication Quarterly* 42 (Summer 1994): 287–300.
39. Anita K. Foeman and Gary Pressley, "Ethnic Culture and Corporate Culture: Using Black Styles in Organizations," *Communication Quarterly* 35 (Fall 1987): 293–307.
40. Penington, Barbara A. "Communicative Management of Connection and Autonomy in African American and European American Mother-Daughter Relationships," *Journal of Family Communication* 4 (2004): 3–34.

41. Foeman and Pressley, "Ethnic Culture and Corporate Culture," 295-307.

42. Mark P. Orbe, "Remember, It's Always Whites' Ball."

43. Mark P. Orbe, "From the Standpoint(s) of Traditionally Muted Groups."

44. Rick Hicks and Kathy Hicks, *Boomers, X-ers, and Other Strangers: Understanding the Generational Differences that Divide Us* (Wheaton, IL: Tyndale, 1999).

45. Cheng Kuo, "Consumer Styles and Media Uses of Generation X-ers in Taiwan," *Asian Journal of Communication* 9, no. 1, (1999): 21-49.

46. Dhavan V. Shah, Nojin Kwak, and R. Lance Holbert, " 'Connecting' and 'Disconnecting' with Civic Life: Patterns of Internet Use and the Production of Social Capital," *Political Communication* 18 (April 2001): 141-162.

47. Thomas A. Timmerman, "Racial Diversity, Age Diversity, Interdependence, and Team Performance," *Small Group Research* 31 (October 2000): 592-606.

48. Mary R. Jackman, "The Subjective Meaning of Social Class Identification in the United States," *Public Opinion Quarterly* 43 (Winter 1979): 443-62.

49. Donald G. Ellis and Blake Armstrong, "Class, Gender, and Code on Prime-Time Television," *Communication Quarterly* 37 (Summer 1989): 157-169.

50. David L. Ritchie, "Parents' Workplace Experiences and Family Communication Patterns," *Communication Research* 24 (April 1997): 175-87.

51. Amy B. Jordan, "Social Class, Temporal Orientation, and Mass Media Use within the Family System," *Critical Studies in Mass Communication* 9 (December 1992): 374-86.

52. Ruby K. Payne, *A Framework for Understanding Poverty*. Highlands, TX: aha! Process, Inc., 2001.

53. Mark P. Orbe, "From the Standpoint(s) of Traditionally Muted Groups."

54. C. Kirchmeyer and A. Cohen, "Multicultural Groups: Their Performance and Reactions with Constructive Conflict," *Group & Organization Management* 17 (1992): 153-70; C. Kirchmeyer, "Multicultural Task Groups: An Account of the Low Contribution Level of Minorities,"

Small Group Research 24 (February 1993): 127-48.

55. J. C. Bruno Teboul, "Racial/Ethnic 'Encounter' in the Workplace: Uncertainty, Information-Seeking, and Learning Patterns among Racial/Ethnic Majority and Minority New Hires," *The Howard Journal of Communication* 10 (April–June 1999): 97-121.

56. Tadasu Todd Imahori, "On Becoming 'American,'" in *Among Us: Essays on Identity, Belonging, and Intercultural Competence*, eds. Myron W. Lustig and Jolene Koester (New York: Longman, 2000): 68-77.

57. Stella Ting-Toomey, "Rhetorical Sensitivity Style in Three Cultures: France, Japan, and the United States," *Central States Speech Journal* 39 (Spring 1991): 28-36; Mary Jane Collier, "A Comparison of Conversations among and between Domestic Culture Groups: How Intra- and Intercultural Competencies Vary," *Communication Quarterly* 36 (Spring 1988): 122-44.

58. The information about Public Dialogue is synthesized from the following sources: Kimberly A. Pearce and W. Barnett Pearce, "The Public Dialogue Consortium's School-Wide Dialogue Process: A Communication Approach to Develop Citizenship Skills and Enhance School Climate," *Communication Theory* 11 (2001): 105-123; Kimberly A. Pearce, *Facilitating Dialogic Communication: Basic Facilitation Training Manual.* (Public Dialogue Consortium, 2001); W. Barnett Pearce and Kimberly A. Pearce, "Extending the Theory of the Coordinated Management of Meaning (CMM) Through a Community Dialogue Process," *Communication Theory* 10 (2000): 405-423; and Donna Krey, "Cupertino Asks, 'Can We Talk About Diversity?'" *Western City.* Magazine online. Archived. Accessed December 12, 2002 from http://www.westerncity.com/CupertinoDec99.htm.

59. David W. Kale, "Ethics in Intercultural Communication," in *Intercultural Communication: A Reader,* 6th ed., eds. Larry A. Samovar and Richard E. Porter (Belmont, CA: Wadsworth, 1991).

60. Charles R. Bantz, "Cultural Diversity and Group Cross-Cultural Team Research," *Journal of Applied Communication Research* 21 (February 1993): 1-20.

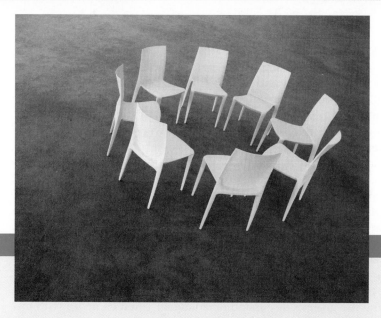

The Members and Their Roles

CENTRAL MESSAGE

The number of members, their personal characteristics, and their attitudes are input variables that help shape the group's throughput processes, including the interaction and the development of member roles.

STUDY OBJECTIVES

As a result of studying Chapter 6 you should be able to:

1. Know how many members should compose a specific small group.

2. Describe characteristics such as communication apprehension, cognitive complexity, self-monitoring, preference for procedural order, and egalitarianism/authoritarianism and explain how each can affect problem-solving discussions.

3. Describe attitudes that influence how effective a group can be, including grouphate, a sense of responsibility for the group's success, willingness to communicate, and open-mindedness.

4. Differentiate between formal and informal roles and describe how informal roles emerge from within the group.

5. Describe task-oriented, maintenance (relationship-oriented), and self-centered behaviors that constitute members' roles.

6. Explain how group members can manage the conflicts that arise when membership in one group competes with membership in another.

Advertising agencies typically accomplish much of their work in teams. A client—a restaurant, a line of cosmetics, a nonprofit organization—is assigned a team of individuals. One particular agency we know about had an exceptionally productive and successful team of five people. Ben, the team's leader, was the head of retail advertising and handled the meetings. Candi, the account executive, served as liaison between the agency and the client. The others described her as "buttoned down." Marija was the media buyer, Vinnie was the art director, and Toni was the copywriter. The team members took it as a matter of personal pride that they were often given the most demanding clients and toughest assignments. The team also represented a variety of perspectives and work styles. Such a combination often derails a team if members don't know how to work with others whose styles, perspectives, and approaches are different. But members of this team worked well together. Ben and especially Candi were highly task focused and able to keep everyone on track. Both took seriously their responsibilities for keeping the project within budget. But they both truly appreciated Vinnie and Toni who, although sometimes taking the group's discussion on a tangent, often came up with just the right theme, just the right visual image, or just the right slogan for a particular ad campaign. Marija, the number cruncher, had an excellent command of figures about how much exposure per dollar various media would provide. Toni, though usually fulfilling a creative role, consistently helped the team focus on the project by asking lots of questions about the client, the target market, the product, and the main images the client wanted to project. In other circumstances, it would be easy to imagine this group self-destructing over differences in work styles, but these open-minded, committed, and competent members had learned both to appreciate and to work with their differences, and they were highly successful.

Both the individual characteristics of members and their mix affect how a small group functions and how productive it is. LaFasto and Larson, in their study of outstanding teams of all sorts, discovered that excellent team members possessed two overall competencies, a working knowledge of the problem and the ability to work in a team.[1] They found six specific factors that mattered the most: experience, problem-solving ability, communication that was both open and supportive, a desire to act rather than be passive, and a personal style that was positive and optimistic. Members of the advertising team mentioned in our story demonstrated all of these characteristics. Productive group members are, or become, skilled and knowledgeable regarding the group's task, really want the group to succeed, and are communicatively competent collaborators. The right people can make group work rewarding, even joyous. Whether we like it or not, group members evaluate each other on such things as their perceived interaction skills and, more often than not, dislike is often based on *lack* of interaction skills. In Chapter 5 we discussed cultural influences that affect member behaviors. Here, we describe how the number of members and their individual characteristics can help produce a winning team.

Group Size

Theoretically, each member brings some different knowledge, perspectives, and skills relevant to the group's purpose. For complex, nonroutine problems, groups of individuals with diverse skills, information, and perspectives are more effective than homogeneous groups.[2] But that does *not* mean the more, the better. At some point, increasing members costs more in coordination time and energy than it adds. Hare concludes that adding members helps when diverse skills and points of view are needed for a particular task, but that apparent advantage becomes a disadvantage if the increase in group size makes consensus difficult or action impossible.[3] What should be our guiding principle for group size? Thelen's principle of **least-sized groups** says we should strive for a group as small as possible, but that has all the expertise and diverse points of view necessary to complete the task well.[4]

Least-Sized Group
The principle that the ideal group contains as few members as possible so long as all necessary perspectives and skills are represented.

As group size increases, the complexity of interpersonal relationships increases geometrically. In a three-person group, only three two-person relationships can exist, but in a group of 10 members there can be 45! As numbers increase, so does the discrepancy in the amount of talking done by different members, with a tendency for one person to do relatively more talking.[5] Leadership becomes more centralized and formal, with increasing demands on designated leaders to regulate and keep order. Increased size creates several specific problems: lower member satisfaction and cohesiveness, higher competitiveness, increased aggressiveness, increased withdrawal, and fragmentation of work,[6] although some of the negative effects of group size can be offset by a teambuilding program,[7] which we discuss in Chapter 8. On the other hand, groups of fewer than four members can produce tension and may feel constrained.[8] Somehow, we must strike a balance between diversity and size.

As groups get larger, they are harder to coordinate, have less equal participation rates, and are less satisfying than smaller groups.

Other factors being equal, a group of five to seven members is an optimal size for participant satisfaction and cohesiveness. This size is small enough for informal interaction, gives everyone a chance to speak up, keeps down social loafing (nonparticipation), and facilitates consensus decisions, yet provides the diverse information and points of view needed for quality decisions. In practice, many groups are larger for reasons that have little to do with efficiency or effectiveness (such as for political reasons). Our advertising group was the perfect size for effective group work.

Traits and Personality Characteristics

A small group's most important resource is its members. A group cannot be productive if members are lazy, uncooperative, or incompetent. Your personal traits, personality characteristics, and attitudes are major factors that help determine whether a group succeeds or fails. Hirokawa and his colleagues analyzed stories group members told to explain why groups succeed or fail.[9] Members who were knowledgeable and skillful, had high motivation for the group task, were willing to listen and to share information, and expressed pleasure, excitement—as well as fear—about the task were perceived to help a group succeed. On the other hand, group failure was attributed to members who were selfish and resentful, were either overconfident and cocky or demonstrated no enthusiasm for the task, failed to share information, and were poor listeners. Your traits, personality characteristics, and attitudes are the fundamental building blocks that contribute to your competence as a group member. You can use this chapter as a tool to evaluate yourself and determine where you might need to change.

Trait

A relatively enduring, consistent pattern of behavior or other observable characteristic.

Attitude

A network of beliefs and values, not directly measurable, that a person holds toward an object, person, or concept; produces a tendency to react in specific ways toward that object, person, or concept.

A **trait** is a consistent pattern of behavior or other observable characteristic. Traits are influenced by both genetics and environment. Some people talk about traits (e.g., your eye color) as being unchangeable. However, human behavior stems from complex causes; we believe that many of the traits and trait-like characteristics group members exhibit can be modified. When we refer to traits and personality characteristics in this section, we acknowledge that you may have a predisposition to behave in a certain way, but we also think you have some ability to change your behavior. Our behavior is also determined by our attitudes. An **attitude** is a cluster of values and beliefs held by someone about another person or types of people, an object, or a concept. We cannot measure attitudes directly, but we infer them from what people say and do. Why should we study individual traits, characteristics, and attitudes in a small group course? Research has confirmed that some traits and attitudes are better for groups than others.[10] For instance, an extremely individualistic attitude makes it hard for someone to operate well as a member of a team.

A number of personal traits have been shown to influence behavior in groups, including psychological sex type[11] and verbal argumentativeness.[12] We will now discuss five general traits and characteristics that have a significant bearing on the type of group member someone can be. These traits are communication apprehension, cognitive complexity, self-monitoring, preference for procedural order, and egalitarianism-authoritarianism.

Communication Apprehension

Communication apprehension is the anxiety or fear that people experience when they try to speak in a variety of social situations, including in small groups. Sometimes called *shyness* or *reticence*, communication apprehension (CA) is one of the most well-researched characteristics in the field of communication. It can manifest as severe anxiety about speaking in public to one other person, or in groups, which is our main focus here. James McCroskey and his associates, particularly Virginia Richmond, have studied CA extensively and note that high CA has far greater negative repercussions in group settings than other settings.[13] For example, McCroskey and Richmond say that high CA group members speak much less than members low in CA, choose seats where leaders can overlook them, make more irrelevant comments, are less likely to become a group's leader, and are likely to express strong agreement, even when inwardly they disagree. High CAs are perceived as making little contribution to the group, with others seeing them as less desirable members than low CAs. High CAs even have a lower opinion of *themselves* than other members have of them.[14]

> **Communication Apprehension (CA)**
>
> Anxiety or fear of speaking in a variety of social situations, including in group settings; reticence; shyness.

Reticence about speaking may have a cultural origin. Porter and Samovar explain that in certain cultures, particularly high-context ones, people do not speak as much as people in low-context cultures such as that of the United States.[15] They do not rely on verbal communication to the same extent and are sometimes suspicious of people who talk a lot. A member of this type of culture may have a very difficult time adapting to the noisy, verbal, direct communication style of most Americans. It is particularly important for others in the group to recognize this possible source of reticence to communicate and to demonstrate patience.

If you are relatively high in CA as a group member, what can you do? Your college or university may have a center where you can learn such helpful techniques as *systematic desensitization* or *cognitive restructuring*. Although fearful of group settings, if high CAs are willing to engage in small group activities, this exposure itself may lessen their anxieties.[16] McCroskey and Richmond add that an in-depth understanding of the communication process and of specific skills can help, too. We hope you will have that understanding by the time you finish this course.

Cognitive Complexity

How members act in discussions of complex problems, especially when there are wide differences among members' perspectives and preexisting beliefs, is seriously affected by a trait psychologists call *cognitive complexity*. Related to

Cognitive Complexity

How well developed a group member's construct system for interpreting signals is; cognitively complex individuals are able to synthesize more information and think in more abstract and organized terms than are cognitively simple individuals.

but different from general intelligence, **cognitive complexity** refers to an individual's ability to interpret multiple signals simultaneously: how differentiated, abstract, and organized someone's ability to process information is. In common terms, this is a measure of complex-to-simplistic thinking—do you think in only either/or terms, or can you perceive shades of gray? During discussion, people high in cognitive complexity use more complex arguments in speaking, can integrate their goals with those of others in these arguments, and do a better job of building on others' feelings and beliefs than people lower in cognitive complexity.[17] Cognitively complex members ask more questions and provide more objective information during discussions of class policies than do their less developed classmates; they do not presume to know the other's viewpoint. Less cognitively complex members use their own frames of reference as if these are also the viewpoints of others. During group decision making, high complexity persons can arrive at consensus much better than less complex persons, who speak as if they already know what their fellow group members believe and have experienced.[18] If you think you are low in cognitive complexity, you can begin to assume less, ask more questions, and check out what you think others want, feel, and think. For example, Candi, our advertising group's account executive, was highly cognitively complex. She constantly asked questions to understand the client's point of view, she absorbed the massive amounts of information Marija gave her about which media outlets were likely to reach the client's target audience, and she was a master at weaving the client's ideas and suggestions together with the recommendations offered by the advertising professionals.

Self-Monitoring

Self-Monitoring

The extent to which someone pays attention to and controls his or her self-presentation in social situations; high self-monitors are able to assess how others perceive them and adapt their behavior to elicit a desired response.

A third cognitive variable important to how we interact with others in problem solving is called *self-monitoring*. **Self-monitoring** refers to the degree to which a person monitors and controls self-presentation in social situations: High self-monitors pay careful attention to the social cues other group members send and, from these cues, they infer how their own behavior is being received and interpreted; then, if necessary, they can adapt their behavior so that it is more appropriate to the situation.[19] In short, there are two elements to self-monitoring: the ability to perceive how others are responding to you and the ability to adjust your behavior so that others will respond more favorably. In contrast, low self-monitors rely only on their own internal cues and attitudes; thus, they say and do what they want without much consideration about how others are responding to them. High self-monitors, then, are keenly aware of whether others' responses to their behavior suggest approval or disapproval of that behavior. They can adjust their behavior to achieve desired responses better than low self-monitors by displaying behaviors and role functions appropriate to the group. Modifying behavior instead of following initial inclinations "... is the primary mechanism by which high self-monitors emerge as leaders."[20] In other words, sensitivity to cues from others is not sufficient; flexibility and skill in *adjusting one's behavior* as a small group member is also necessary. We discuss how self-monitoring is related to leadership emergence in Chapter 9.

Overlapping the trait of self-monitoring is the characteristic called **rhetorical sensitivity.** Rhetorically sensitive persons monitor what they say, adapting their statements to how they think other members of the group may react.[21] You might have doubts about the ethical standards of self-monitors who are rhetorically sensitive, but we do not. The rhetorically sensitive person is not a *reflector* who says what she thinks others want her to say, or a *noble self* who says whatever comes to mind. Rather, before speaking out, rhetorically sensitive people search consciously for the most effective way to express their point in order to help ensure that other members give their points the fairest possible hearing. They are careful not to insult or inflame other members.

Ben, the retail advertising division head who was our advertising team's leader, was good at phrasing suggestions so that clients could give them a fair hearing. For example, a client who owned a chain of shoe stores thought it would be funny to have a cartoon kangaroo (kangaroos have huge feet) wearing women's high heels (an image Ben thought would keep women away in droves). Instead of saying, "Oh, that's a great idea!" (as a reflector would) or "That's one of the dumbest things I've ever heard!" (as a noble self would), he responded in a sensitive way: "I think the kangaroo image is really funny, particularly if you think about kangaroos wearing high heels. I'm not sure it will do what you want, though. Our research shows that women are sensitive about their feet sizes—on average, they would rather be wearing a size or two smaller. Calling attention to large feet will send women to other stores." Ben was true to his belief, but didn't insult the client by how he stated that belief.

Preference for Procedural Order

A fourth cognitive trait desirable in members of problem-solving groups is the ability to think critically and systematically. Gouran reported a tendency for most discussion participants to accept inferences without challenging them, even when patently flawed reasoning was involved.[22] For thorough evaluation of proposed solutions, groups need individuals skilled in all aspects of critical thinking along with group procedures that encourage thorough critical evaluation of all solutions. Critical thinking and systematic thinking may be linked in a personality trait referred to as **preference for procedural order** (PPO), the need or desire to follow a clear, linear structure during problem solving. Putnam described the rationale for such a personality measure, development of a questionnaire for measuring it, and why it is important to group problem solving.[23] Later research by Hirokawa and associates suggests that high PPO persons do much better in choosing among alternatives when a highly structured problem-solving procedure (such as is presented in Chapter 10) is followed by the group. High PPO persons did not seem to think as clearly as possible during loosely structured

Rhetorical Sensitivity

Speaking and phrasing statements in such a way that the feelings and beliefs of the listener are considered; phrasing statements in order not to offend others or trigger emotional overreactions.

Preference for Procedural Order

A trait characterized by need or desire to follow a clear, linear structure during problem solving and decision making.

discussions. However, groups of low PPO persons who are comfortable with less structured discussion did equally well whether following a procedure of high or low structure. No mixed-PPO groups were considered, but this research suggests that systematic procedures would improve (or at least not reduce) the output quality of most decision-making groups.[24]

In the ad team, copywriter Toni and art director Vinnie are low in PPO, but Candi is particularly high, with Marija just behind her. Early in its formation, these differences caused irritation and frustration. Ben, the leader, hoping to prevent a small problem from becoming a major one, facilitated a discussion about work style preferences; the group talked through how structured their meetings would be. While Toni and Vinnie like completely unstructured meetings, which drive Candi and Marija nuts, they can adapt to structure. Once they realized how anxiety-producing the lack of structure was to Candi and Marija, they willingly adapted. Ben now sends an agenda out in advance, and the members have learned to tease each other (with respect!) about their differences ("Candi's stress level just spiked; we'd better get back to the agenda.")

As with the ad team, most groups usually include members with varying preferences for order and structure. Half the students Pavitt surveyed preferred a linear structure during decision making, while the other half preferred a looser "reach testing" process.[25] Groups whose members' preferences are similar will have an easier time working together, but with patience and good will, members can adjust to each others' preferences, like the ad team, and learn to appreciate their differences. If you want to test your own PPO level, use the scale in Chapter 7.

Egalitarianism/Authoritarianism

Egalitarianism and *authoritarianism* are contrasting ways of seeing human relationships. **Egalitarianism** is the belief that all people are equally important; this is a tenet of the U.S. Declaration of Independence. Egalitarian people encourage full participation by all group members; they tend to be free of bigotry and stereotypes. They abhor bossiness and dictatorial behavior in themselves and others. In contrast, members high in **authoritarianism** prefer a controlling leader and will dominate a group when they are placed in leadership positions. However, it may surprise you to know that high authoritarians accept uncritically the information and ideas expressed by or attributed to authorities, experts, and leaders. As group members, they tend to follow the leader without questioning. They ask opinions of others less often, act less friendly, and make more directive comments ("Do this now!") than egalitarians.[26]

Egalitarianism and authoritarianism are, in part, culturally based. Lustig and Cassotta note that members of high power-distance cultures, which include the Philippines, Mexico, India and Venezuela, have been socialized to accept clear distinctions between leaders and followers, and thus should be more comfortable with authoritarian group leadership.[27] Similarly, cultures high on masculinity, which value control, objectivity, and assertiveness, are also likely

Egalitarianism

Belief in the equality of all people; results in the preference for including all group members in problem solving, not just a few high-status members.

Authoritarianism

Tendency to accept uncritically the information, ideas, and proposals of authority figures such as a high-status group member or leader; results in preference for strong leaders and follower subservience.

to prefer authoritarian leadership. In contrast, cultures high in femininity or low in power distance, such as the Scandinavian countries, should favor democratic leadership. Individualism may be related to egalitarianism as well. In individualistic cultures, where self-initiative is rewarded, democratic leadership is likely to be preferred.

In the dominant culture of the United States, we value egalitarian behavior and expect our group leaders to involve us in decision making. Can you imagine the ad team in our opening case succeeding if Ben tried to control everything? Within the group, everyone is not only free to but expected to speak up, challenge ideas, and make suggestions. As we have noted, though, other cultures do not assume that everyone has an equal right to participate; they expect the leader to assume strict, authoritarian control. However, for most of the groups you will experience in the United States, you are safest to adopt an egalitarian position.

In our experience, personality differences and differences in how members approach work create the most frustration in groups. The differences themselves are not the problem; the problem occurs because members do not know how to work with (much less appreciate) people who are very different from themselves. We encourage you to put those differences on the table where you can discuss them and figure out how to capitalize on them. Toni and Vinnie have come to appreciate Candi's ability to keep track of all details of a project without letting anything fall through the cracks; Candi and Marija rely on Toni's and Vinnie's creative sparks to generate excitement and make their meetings fun.

Recap: A Quick Review

A number of input factors, including size and member characteristics, affect how effective a group will be.

1. Groups need diversity, but too many members make coordination difficult. Groups should be *least-sized:* as small as possible, so long as the necessary diversity of perspective and opinion is represented. Usually, five to seven members are an ideal number.

2. Members with communication apprehension about speaking in groups can impair a group's functioning. They don't contribute to the discussion, make irrelevant comments, express agreement when they don't agree; and they are seen by others as less desirable members. Sometimes, reticence about speaking can have a cultural origin; some cultures do not rely on verbal communication as much as the dominant culture of the United States.

3. Ideally, group members are high in cognitive complexity, which helps them handle complex information, weave a variety of perspectives together, and help a group arrive at consensus. Cognitively complex members assume less and ask more questions.

(continued)

(continued)

4. Members high in self-monitoring are tuned in to social cues about how others are responding to them and are able to adjust their behavior so that others will respond more favorably. They think carefully before speaking and are rhetorically sensitive.

5. Members high in preference for procedural order prefer a linear, structured process for problem solving and actually perform better when they can use such a process. Members low in preference for procedural order like a looser structure, but can perform well either way.

6. Egalitarian members believe all members are equally important, but authoritarian members have extreme respect for authority, are bossy as group leaders, but may blindly follow someone else's leadership. In the United States, we expect egalitarian behavior that encourages everyone to participate and contribute.

Communicative Attitudes and Behaviors

Your attitudes and behaviors in a group cannot be untangled from your traits and personality characteristics, and they are fully as important to a group. Other members *most* appreciate someone who will work hard on behalf of the group; they *least* appreciate someone who is there in name only or whose attitude is negative or cynical.[28] We turn now to several of the key attitudes that influence group work: grouphate, a sense of responsibility for the group's success, willingness to communicate, and open-mindedness.

Grouphate

Grouphate, first described by Sorensen, was discussed in Chapter 1.[29] It is the utter hatred that many people feel about working in groups—they dread the thought and will go to great lengths to avoid group work. One of our students hated groups so much that he tried to get his classroom group to fire him before the final project so that he could work alone. He deliberately missed meetings, failed to turn in assignments, and behaved obnoxiously—but his group members were too nice to remove him from the group, so everyone suffered! Hating group work can be debilitating in today's society. In one study, Freeman placed master of business administration students in groups to complete a number of projects throughout the semester.[30] The students' attitudes about working in groups predicted the students' grades better than their grade point averages, previous work experiences, and scores on standardized tests. The high-performing groups had members with positive attitudes about group work, but the low-performing groups did not. As we have noted throughout this text, group work is increasing in *every* facet of modern life, so if you don't want your academic and work careers derailed, you need to overcome the grouphate you may feel.

Keyton and Frey, in their review of group member traits, discuss a grouphate scale developed with colleagues.[31] (You can assess your own grouphate by taking this survey in Chapter 7). These researchers correlated the grouphate scale with one that measured what things members liked about group interaction and what they didn't like. They found that some individuals were apathetic about groups and didn't care much about them one way or the other. Others, highly involved, both liked and disliked several aspects of groups. Another set of individuals routinely hated most things about groups; this set contrasted with those individuals who routinely liked most things about groups. These researchers also found that all-male groups exhibited the highest levels of grouphate and all-female groups the lowest, with mixed groups in the middle. Interestingly, the amount of these individuals' past experiences with groups did not affect their grouphate, but it *did* lower their communication apprehension in groups. Sorensen, however, found that training in how to communicate effectively as a group member *did* reduce grouphate. If you have grouphate, we are hoping it will lessen with the understanding you gain from reading this text.

A Sense of Responsibility for the Group's Success

Perhaps the most important attitude of ideal small group members is summarized by the phrase *a sense of responsibility for the success of the group*. Constructive members feel a personal responsibility to do whatever they can to help the group achieve its goals. They are *dependable*. Responsible members put accomplishment of group goals ahead of selfish wants. They are guided by a number of ethical standards, such as:

1. No member has a right to act in a way that would be disastrous if all members acted that way.

2. No member has a right to expect more effort from other members than he or she makes for the group.

3. Every member should faithfully carry out assignments for the group, and, if he or she cannot do so, should immediately notify the group and explain what went wrong.

4. A member should share any relevant information and ideas for the group to use in solving problems.

The extent to which group members naturally feel a collective responsibility for the group may in part be culturally based. In extremely collectivist cultures, there is no "self" separate from the group. Members of collectivist cultures, by definition, naturally put the good of the group ahead of their own individual good and do not perceive this as the sacrifice that someone from an individualistic culture would perceive it. Perhaps the ultimate in feeling responsibility for and to a group was exemplified in the 1980s film *Black Rain,* in which the Japanese detective said he would willingly commit ritual suicide if he failed to meet his obligation to the group.

You can observe behaviors that suggest members are committed to a group. For instance, members will use pronouns such as *we, us,* and *our* rather than

FIGURE 6.1
Assertiveness lies between aggressiveness and nonassertiveness

you or *your*. Members volunteer to do more than their fair share of the group's work and can be counted on to get it done. In the ad team, when Candi's mother died, Marija voluntarily picked up some of Candi's commitments and met with a number of clients in her absence. In our student project groups, social loafers cause the greatest friction among members. In sum, the valuable group member is fully responsible and trustworthy. If you refuse to act that way, other members are better off without you; maybe they can replace you with a useful member.

Willingness to Communicate

To be a productive member, your *willingness to communicate* must be greater than your communication apprehension or your need to protect yourself from disagreement or embarrassment. People who have relevant information or see flaws in proposals but do not speak up actually harm the group. They are excess baggage, sucking the energy out of a group and taking up space that a contributing member might have occupied. Can you imagine how successful the ad team would be if Marija decided not to share with the group information about which television show or magazine best matched the target market for a particular ad campaign? It is important, though, that you communicate in an effective, *assertive* way.

Assertiveness refers to communicative behavior that reflects respect both for oneself and for other group members. Assertive people communicate openly to other members as equals. Assertiveness lies on a continuum, illustrated in Figure 6.2, between **passiveness** (nonassertiveness) and **aggressiveness** in communicating. Aggressive people are highly dominant and often authoritarian; they try to force ideas and practices on others. They call names, demand, insult, threaten, command, shout, pound the table, and frequently drown out others who are speaking. Rather than challenging information or reasoning, they attack other people. Emotional bullies, their motto is, "My way or the highway!" Aggressive behavior may stem from psychopathology, from cultural practices, inability to handle frustration, or just a lack of verbal skills for dealing constructively with conflict.[32] No matter what the cause, this behavior destroys productive discussion, cohesiveness, and teamwork. We think that both aggressive and passive behavior violate the ethical principles described in Chapter 1 and earlier in this chapter. If you want to know how assertive your communication or that of your fellow group members is, you may want to complete the assertiveness rating scale shown in Figure 7.3 in Chapter 7.

Passive discussants, like high CAs, go along with a majority rather than argue, even when they disagree. In going along despite doubts, they are unethical,

Assertiveness

Behavior that shows respect both for your own and others' rights, in contrast to passive and aggressive behavior.

Passiveness

Nonassertive behavior that allows one's own rights and beliefs to be ignored or dominated, often to avoid conflict; impairs good decision making.

Aggressiveness

Behavior designed to win or dominate that fails to respect the rights or beliefs of others.

FIGURE 6.2
Passive "yessers"
do not express
genuine agreement

untrue to themselves, and therefore untrue to the group. Passive members tend to make little eye contact, speak so softly they are hard to hear, and won't resist aggressors. The stereotyped "yessers" shown in Figure 6.3 epitomize passive behavior. Their motto might be, "We'll do it your way; nothing is worth fighting about." The most harmful type of passive member engages in **passive-aggressive behavior,** which is highly destructive to teamwork. Passive-aggressives attempt to get their way subtly; they sabotage rather than confront in the way an assertive person does. Instead of saying, "I don't like that policy" or "I disagree," they may be late with an assigned report, "forget" to carry out an assignment, fail to attend a meeting, or neglect to do their share of the group work.

In contrast to both aggressors and passives, assertive members disagree openly and explain why. They explain what they think as clearly as possible and state what they want. Even more important, they try hard to understand the information, ideas, perspectives, and wants of other members, and to co-orient so that a mutually satisfactory decision may be found. Consider this exchange from the ad team:

Ben: I think we should recommend that the Ozarks Glass Studio buy a full-page, color ad in *417 Magazine* to promote its glassblowing classes.

Marija: Ordinarily I might agree with you, but Ozarks Glass Studio has a natural demographic—people who like the arts, people who hang out downtown, and people who have plenty of time and disposable income. That matches the demographic of the public radio station, which I think is a better buy.

Passive-Aggressive Behavior

Behavior that appears on the surface to be cooperative but subtly sabotages group work, such as when members "forget" to carry out an assignment.

417 Magazine hits business people, but public radio here hits business people and arts-oriented folks. *(Marija went on to provide specific facts and figures.)*

Notice, in this exchange, that Marija neither caved in to Ben nor tried to shout him down. She assertively stated her position and attempted to persuade with facts. That's what she *should* do as a good group member—speak up!

Open-Mindedness

Another attitude helpful to group work is *open-mindedness.* Open-minded members welcome new information and ideas, are curious, and are low in prejudice. Hirokawa et al.'s research credited member openness, effective listening, and information as factors in a group's success,[33] and LaFasto and Larson observed that effective members are open to the ideas and opinions of the other members.[34] Open-minded members are low in the trait called **dogmatism.** The more dogmatic people are, the less willing they are to try to understand new ideas, to listen to or accept evidence that contradicts their present beliefs, and to base conclusions on the total pool of information available to the group.[35] Arguments based on evidence and sound reasoning can change the positions of open-minded members, but will not influence dogmatic ones whose decisions are based more on prior beliefs, internal needs, and emotions than a desire to know the truth and be logically consistent. In the previous example from the ad team, Ben was persuaded by Marija's argument about why public radio was a better vehicle for Ozarks Glass Studio than *417 Magazine,* even though he loved the magazine and often recommended it to clients.

Similar to cognitively simple people, dogmatic people see things in either-or, black-or-white terms. One of us, while discussing the merits of collective bargaining with several highly educated individuals, was dismayed to hear such dogmatic utterances as, "I'm just against unions in principle. They're wrong. I wouldn't even consider joining one." Others said, "Unionism is good. Management just doesn't care about us who do the real work." Neither statement demonstrates open-minded use of evidence or reasoning, and neither makes allowance for exceptions. People who talk like this, without qualification, question, or evidence, can block group consensus.

Ideally, group members would all be open-minded. Dogmatic members create roadblocks to group co-orientation and unity. A little self-monitoring can help a lot. *Ask* for points of view that differ from yours, and be sure you listen actively to them. If you observe dogmatism to be a problem in a continuing group, tackle the problem head-on by describing it. Keep reminding the group that mutual respect is essential for group cooperation and for effective performance.

We have been discussing the individual characteristics and attitudes members bring with them to a small group. These are examples of input variables that exist as a group is formed and that are important as the group engages in its work. Members' characteristics and attitudes influence their communicative behavior in groups, and this behavior—the key element in a group's

Dogmatism

A tendency to hold rigidly to personal beliefs; closed-mindedness to evidence and reasoning contrary to one's beliefs.

throughput process—affects the roles that develop. We discuss roles and their development in the next section.

Development of Group Roles

When they hear the term *role,* most people think of parts in a play or movie. Play scripts contain interlocking roles, each of which is a different character in the cast. A member's **role** represents the cluster of behaviors performed by that member and the overall functions those behaviors perform for the group, just as an actor's role consists of all the lines and actions of the character in the play. Like Brad Pitt, whose various film roles have included a spy in *Spy Games,* a tragic alter ego in *Fight Club,* and a paid assassin in *Mr. and Mrs. Smith,* individuals enact many diverse roles in the numerous groups to which they belong. In one group the role might be *daughter* or *son;* in another, art director; and in yet another, *church treasurer.* A given individual might be a leader in one group and play a supporting role in another. The role a person enacts in any particular group is a function of that person's personality, abilities, and communication skills, the talents of the other members, and the needs of the group as a whole.

Role

A pattern of behavior displayed by and expected of a member of a small group; a composite of a group member's frequently performed behavioral functions.

Formal versus Informal Roles

There is a difference between a member's *formal role,* sometimes called a *positional role,* and that member's *informal,* or *behavioral role.* A **formal role** refers to a specific position with a set of expectations for fulfilling that position. For example, a group's *chair* is expected to call meetings, distribute agendas, and coordinate the other members' work. A group's *secretary* is responsible for taking notes, distributing minutes, and handling correspondence. Members who hold these roles are usually elected or appointed to them. Often, the duties associated with formal roles are written into a group's bylaws or operating procedures.

An **informal role** refers to a unique role created as a result of a member's behaviors. Informal roles reflect the traits, personality characteristics, habits, and preferences of the members in a particular group. They are not specified in advance, but evolve through the interaction among members and are based on members' behaviors. To understand how informal roles form, we need to distinguish between a *behavior* and a *behavioral function.* A **behavior** is any verbal or nonverbal act by a group member; a **behavioral function** is the effect that behavior has on the whole group. For example, the joke Yukiko tells in her group is the *behavior.* But Yukiko's joke can serve a variety of *functions,* depending on what else has been going on in the group. If her joke relieves tension during an argument, it has a positive function; but if Yukiko's jokes are constantly getting the group off track and members are tired of it, the function is negative. Some behavioral functions are common to all groups and widely shared by members, such as providing information or offering opinions. Others may become the exclusive domain of one member, such as mediating conflicts between members or telling jokes.

Even though formal roles are specified and informal ones are not, members bring their own personalities, preferences, attitudes, and so forth to the formal roles they fill. Think about a group or organization you belong to with a formal designated leader (such as a chair or president). If you have experienced several individuals filling that role, you know that each one brings in his or her special "flavor" to the position. For example, the Curriculum Committee in one of our departments has rotated the chair position for several years. One chair was serious and highly task oriented; his meetings were particularly efficient. Another with a great sense of humor liked to joke around; his meetings took longer but were more fun. A third, who was well connected with other groups in the university, constantly brought in information about the curricular changes occurring in other departments; her focus was, "How do our changes fit in the university's bigger picture?" You can see that, even if a role is formal, each person in that role will enact it somewhat differently.

Role Emergence

The informal role a particular member holds in a small group is worked out in concert with the other members, primarily through trial and error. In a review of how roles develop, Anderson, Riddle, and Martin concluded that members negotiate their roles by observing others and particularly observing how others respond to their behaviors.[36] For example, Ty-isha may have a clear idea of how the group can accomplish its tasks; she will make attempts to structure the group's work: "I suggest we first make a list of all the things we need to do to finish our project." If no one else competes to supply that structuring

---

Behavior

Any observable action by a group member.

Behavioral Function

The effect or function a member's behavior has on the group as a whole.

function, and if the other members see that structuring behavior as helpful to the group, they will reinforce and reward Ty-isha's statements and actions: "Okay, Ty-isha that sounds like a good idea." This reinforcement, in turn, is likely to elicit more of those structuring behaviors from Ty-isha. On the other hand, if several members are also competent to structure the group's work, the group members collectively will reinforce the actions of the member they perceive to be the most skilled in this performance area. If Ty-isha is not reinforced as the group's "structurer," she will search for some other way to be valuable to, and valued by, the group. For instance, she may help clarify the proposals of the other members ("In other words, are you saying that . . . ") or become the group's critical evaluator ("I think there are two major flaws with that proposal."). *Every member needs a role that makes a meaningful contribution to the group.*

Because an individual's role depends on the particular mix of people in the group, that person's role will vary from group to group. A major principle of small group theory is this: *The role of each group member is worked out in the interaction between the member and the rest of the group* and continues to evolve as the group evolves. Thus, a well-organized person may end up leading one group and playing a supporting role in another, depending on the characteristics and competencies of all members relative to one another.

In addition, members' roles are fluid and dynamic as members respond to others and to shifting conditions in a group. Most people demonstrate flexibility as they enact their roles in a group[37]; a member who supplied information will also support another member's suggestion, for example. Sometimes, consistent with the bona fide group perspective discussed in Chapter 4, external forces in the environment create internal changes in group roles. Apker, Propp, and Zavaba-Ford found that changing societal and professional expectations about the role of nurses led to changes in how nurses actually operated among themselves and with physicians in health care settings, particularly with respect to their degree of authority and autonomy.[38]

Classifying Group Roles

Group researchers have developed a variety of systems for classifying group roles. Hare, in a 1994 historical review of research about group roles, recommends that group researchers describe roles in terms the group members themselves would understand.[39] One such system is the functional role classification system described by Benne and Sheats.[40] These researchers classified members' roles on the basis of the functions those roles performed for the group. They defined three main categories of behavior: task, maintenance (socioemotional), and individual. Task behaviors directly affect the group's task. Maintenance or socioemotional behaviors affect the relationships among members, thus indirectly affecting the task. Individual behaviors are self-centered behaviors that help neither the task nor the relationships, but function to satisfy the individual at the expense of the group.

FIGURE 6.3 Task and social/relational impact of member behaviors

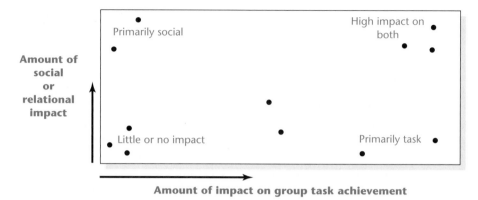

Although Benne and Sheats's system was first described many years ago, recent research verifies its usefulness as a classification system. Mudrack and Farrell, noting that there has been little direct empirical investigation into this system, investigated how well this three-category system describes typical member behaviors from the perspective of the members themselves.[41] They found that the task, maintenance, and individual distinctions Benne and Sheats described hold up. Although their study suggested a five-category model as being most precise, the addition of the two factors (one was a task subcategory; the other, a maintenance subcategory) actually did not measurably improve the usefulness of the model. Mudrack and Farrell concluded that the three-category system—task, maintenance, and individual—is fairly accurate.

To some extent, all classification systems oversimplify the situation by suggesting that a remark or nonverbal behavior performs only one function in a group; in fact, remarks are fluid and affect both dimensions. For example, assume Teresa says to Mona and Melvin, "I think you guys are bypassing each other, and you should listen more carefully." That statement, even though it focuses on the ways members are relating to each other (a socioemotional concern), also has a bearing on the task accomplishment of the group, especially if Melvin and Mona start paying better attention to each other. Moreover, Teresa's statement implies that she has the right to intervene to improve the group's process, which says something about her relationship to the group. Thus, although many researchers consider actions to be *either* task- *or* relationship-oriented, it is more accurate to say that an act may have considerable impact on *both* dimensions.[42] In fact, Mudrack and Farrell found that the gatekeeper role, a maintenance role we describe later, and the information-seeker role, a task role, straddled both categories.[43] Figure 6.5 depicts these two major dimensions and illustrates how individual acts can affect each dimension to a greater or lesser degree.

Most researchers agree that both task and socioemotional needs must be met for a group to be effective. For example, the ad team's members attended to the task and socioemotional needs of the group. Candi and Marija made sure that the group had all the information it needed to perform well and kept the group on track, but they also participated in the teasing and joking that made meetings fun. Ben provided agendas for the group's meetings, but he also sometimes brought in snacks or treated the group to happy-hour celebrations when something great happened. Toni and Vinnie had a great sense of fun and play, but they made sure their visual and textual images for ad campaigns were done on time and on target. We turn now to a look at the specific kinds of behaviors that contribute to a group's success (or not!). What follows is a list of behavioral functions, based on Benne and Sheats's classification, that groups need to achieve their goals. Figure 6.6 illustrates the roles three group members might enact using various combinations of the following behaviors.

Task Functions   **Task functions** affect primarily the task output of the group. Some of the most helpful, with statements that exemplify those functions, are:

Task Functions

Task-oriented member behaviors that contribute primarily to accomplishing the goals of a group.

- *Initiating and orienting:* proposing goals, plans of action, or activities; prodding the group to greater activity; defining position of group in relation to external structure or goal. ("Let's assign ourselves tasks to finish before the next meeting.")
- *Information giving:* offering facts and information, evidence, or personal experience relevant to the group's task. ("Last year, the ad campaign spent $200,000 for TV spots.")
- *Information seeking:* asking others for facts and information, evidence, or relevant personal experience. ("Juan, how many campus burglaries were reported last year?")
- *Opinion giving:* stating beliefs, values, interpretations, judgments; drawing conclusions from evidence. ("I don't think theft of materials is the worst problem facing the library.")
- *Clarifying:* making ambiguous statements clearer; interpreting issues. ("So does 'excellent' to you mean that the report should be perfect grammatically?")
- *Elaborating:* developing an idea previously expressed by giving examples, illustrations, and explanations. ("Another thing that Toby's proposal would let us do is . . .")
- *Evaluating:* expressing judgments about the relative worth of information or ideas; proposing or applying criteria. ("Here are three problems I see with that idea.")
- *Summarizing:* reviewing what has been said previously; reminding the group of a number of items previously mentioned or discussed. ("So,

by next week, Marija will have the media research finished and Toni will have the preliminary drawing of the logo for us to see.")

Coordinating: organizing the group's work; promoting teamwork and cooperation. ("If Meagan interviews the mayor by Monday, then Joyce and I can prepare a response by Tuesday's meeting.")

Consensus testing: asking if the group has reached a decision acceptable to all; suggesting that agreement may have been reached. ("We seem to be agreed that we'll accept the counteroffer.")

Recording: keeping group records, preparing reports and minutes; serving as group secretary and memory. ("I think we decided that two weeks ago. Let me look it up in the minutes to be sure.")

Suggesting procedure: suggesting an agenda of issues, or special technique; proposing some procedure or sequence to follow. ("Why don't we try brainstorming to help us come up with something new and different!")

Maintenance Functions

Relationship-oriented member behaviors that reduce tensions, increase solidarity, and facilitate teamwork.

Maintenance (Relationship-Oriented) Functions **Maintenance functions** influence primarily the interpersonal relationships of members. We think the following seven functions, with sample statements, are especially vital to task groups:

Establishing norms: suggesting rules of behavior for members; challenging unproductive ways of behaving as a member; giving negative response when another violates a rule or norm. ("I think it's unproductive to call each other names. Let's stick to the issues.")

Gatekeeping: helping some member get the floor; suggesting or controlling speaking order; asking if someone has a different opinion. ("Ruben, you look like you want to make a comment. Do you want to say something about the proposal?")

Supporting: agreeing or otherwise expressing support for another's belief or proposal; following the lead of another member. ("I think Joi's right; we should examine this more closely.")

Harmonizing: reducing secondary tension by reconciling disagreement; suggesting a compromise or new alternative acceptable to all; conciliating or placating an angry member. ("Jared and Sally, I think there are areas in which you are in agreement, and I would like to suggest a compromise that might work for you both.")

Tension relieving: making strangers feel at ease; reducing status differences; encouraging informality; joking and otherwise relieving tension; stressing common interests and experiences. ("We're getting tired and cranky. Let's take a 10-minute break.")

Dramatizing: evoking fantasies about people and places other than the present group and time, including storytelling and fantasizing in a vivid way; testing a tentative value or norm through fantasy or story. ("That reminds me of a story about last year's committee . . .")

Showing solidarity: indicating positive feeling toward other group members; reinforcing a sense of group unity and cohesiveness. ("Wow, we've done a great job on this!" or "We're all in this together!")

Whereas the preceding functions are necessary to effective small group functioning, there is another category of functions detrimental to the group. They represent an individual member's hidden agenda.

Self-Centered Functions   **Self-centered functions** refer to those member behaviors that serve the performers' unmet needs at the expense of the group. We think the following three are especially harmful:

Withdrawing: avoiding important differences; refusing to cope with conflicts; refusing to take a stand; covering up feelings; giving no response to the comments of others. ("Do whatever you want, I don't care," or not speaking at all.)

Blocking: preventing progress toward group goals by constantly raising objections, repeatedly bringing up the same topic or issue after the group has considered and rejected it. ("I know we already voted, but I want to discuss it again!") It is *not* blocking to keep raising an issue the group has not really listened to or considered.

Status and recognition seeking: stage hogging, boasting, and calling attention to one's expertise or experience when this is not necessary to establishing credibility or relevant to the group's task; game playing to elicit sympathy; switching subject to area of personal expertise. ("I think we should do it the way I did it when I won the 'Committee Member of the Year' award.")

This list is by no means exhaustive; it could be expanded considerably with such categories as *special interest pleading, advocating, confessing,* and similar harmful functions. Self-centered functions manipulate and use other members for selfish goals that compete with what the group needs.

Although researchers believe that both task and maintenance roles are essential to effective group functioning, task roles seem particularly important to group members themselves, according to Mudrack and Farrell.[44] Members clearly recognized the contributions task roles make to the group effort, but did not seem to value the contributions of the maintenance roles, nor did they *de*value the individualistic roles. Mudrack and Farrell recommend that researchers continue to study how members evaluate these categories of roles.

We cannot emphasize enough how important it is for you to understand the types of roles a small group needs and how you, as a group member,

Self-Centered Functions

Actions of a small group member, motivated by personal needs, that serve the individual at the expense of the group.

FIGURE 6.4 Roles
of three members of
the advertising
group

Candi
IDEA LEADER

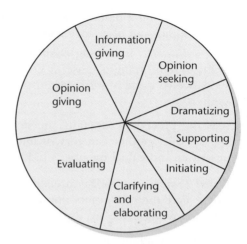

Marija
DEVIL'S ADVOCATE

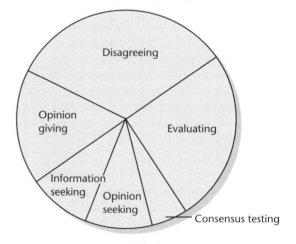

Vinnie
SOCIOEMOTIONAL LEADER

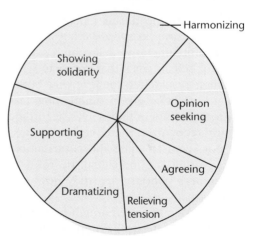

can perform appropriate roles for the group. Plas, writing about the importance of participatory management approaches in American industry, says:

> One of the keys to working well within teams is learning how to differenti-
> ate roles—process roles as well as task roles. Successful teams—no matter
> where you find them—are made up of individuals who know how to define
> roles for themselves and how to work with the roles that other team mem-
> bers have adopted.[45]

Role Management across Groups

Just as important to understanding the role structure of your group is the recognition that members bring role expectations into the group from other groups. The bona fide group perspective discussed in Chapter 4 has been instrumental in reminding us that group members are often simultaneously members of other groups. One implication of this fact is that our roles in one group may or may not be in conflict with the time and commitment expec- tations of our roles in other groups. One implication of this fact is that our roles in one group may conflict with the time and commitment expectations of our roles in other groups. For instance, the fact that ad team leader Ben was president of the local Public Relations Society of America chapter affected how much time he could devote as a member of his local Rotary Club. How do we manage the roles in our church or community groups with our roles in work and family groups? Michael Kramer studied a community theater group in order to answer such a question.[46]

Most of us desire and seek membership in what Kramer calls "life enrich- ment groups" such as church and community volunteer groups. We can also experience difficulty in managing our time and commitment in those groups as they clash with the time and commitment demands of our family and work groups. The trick is not only creating but also maintaining, then negotiating, the roles in these life enrichment groups so we can maintain a balance among all our groups.

Kramer discovered that members of the theater group expressed to others the importance of home and work commitments *and* showed how important the theater group was to them. Part of the negotiation of conflicting intergroup roles was to talk about the importance of both sets of roles while also showing the sacrifice made to the theater group. People who could not balance their home or work role commitments with the theater group simply did not try out for the production. Those who did join the group would talk to co-workers and family members about their participation in the theater group as part of negoti- ating the role commitments in both.

When people experience conflicts between multiple group member- ship commitments, they can either segment or integrate them.[47] These the- ater members segmented their theater roles by time of day and by limiting the amount of time they committed to the theater roles. During the day their work or family roles took precedence, whereas at night their theater roles were more important. They also made it clear early in production that they would commit to this group for six weeks. Limiting their amount of time is possible because the theater group had a finite life span compared to their work and family groups. However, Kramer warns that as more and more of us work at home, this kind of segmentation may not be possible, which may make negotiation of multiple intergroup roles more difficult for people.

Recap: A Quick Review

Members bring their various personal characteristics and attitudes into a group as inputs and then begin to interact with one another; in so doing, they shape the group's roles.

1. A role represents the clusters of behaviors a member performs in the group. Formal (positional) roles result from specific positions that members fill and typically are described in a group's bylaws or operating procedures. Informal (behavioral) roles result from members' behaviors and evolve from the group's interactions.

2. A behavior is any action a member performs; a behavioral function is the effect of that behavior on the group. Telling a joke (the behavior) may be positive (e.g., if it relieves tension) or negative (e.g., if it makes fun of another member).

3. Informal roles emerge from the members' interactions with one another. As a member acts, others reinforce (or not) that person's actions. When the actions are reinforced, that member will continue to perform those functions. When the actions are not reinforced, the member will search for behaviors that will be more valued by the others.

4. Members' behaviors can be classified into three categories: task functions, which primarily affect the group's task; maintenance (or relationship-oriented) functions, which serve to strengthen relationships among members; and self-centered functions, which serve the individual member's needs ahead of the group's. Behaviors can have simultaneous effects in more than one category.

5. Members of actual groups readily acknowledge the contributions of task roles to the group's work, but do not always recognize the value of maintenance roles and do not always perceive the negative effects of self-centered roles.

6. Members generally belong to more than one group simultaneously, which can create conflicts in expectations. In managing roles that compete for a member's time and energy, talking about the importance of both sets of roles and demonstrating willingness to make sacrifices help a member balance competing role demands.

QUESTIONS FOR REVIEW

 *Go to self-quizzes on the Online Learning Center at **mbhe.com/galanes12** to test your knowledge of the chapter concepts*

This chapter used the advertising team to illustrate key concepts and to give you a mental picture of the concepts discussed. Consider the advertising team as you reflect on the following questions:

1. From what you know about the members of the ad team, to what extent do you think each member demonstrated communication apprehension, cognitive complexity, self-monitoring, preference for procedural order, and egalitarianism/authoritarianism? Give specific examples as evidence for your opinion.

2. In many ways, this team's members had ideal attitudes about communicating in groups. How did they demonstrate their lack of grouphate, their sense of responsibility for the group, willingness to communicate, and open-mindedness? What do you think would have happened to the group if any one of the members had not had the "right" attitudes for group success?

3. From what you know about the members, what behavioral functions did each one perform, and how did these behavioral functions merge to shape each member's role? Did there seem to be any roles missing that you think the team should have had? Did there seem to be any competition among members for a particular role?

KEY TERMS

 *Test your knowledge of these key terms by visiting the Online Learning Center at **mbhe.com/galanes12***

Aggressiveness	Dogmatism	Passiveness
Assertiveness	Egalitarianism	Preference for procedural order
Attitude	Formal (positional) role	Rhetorical sensitivity
Authoritarianism	Grouphate	Role
Behavior	Informal (behavioral) role	Self-centered function
Behavioral function	Least-sized groups	Self-monitoring
Cognitive complexity	Maintenance function	Task function
Communication apprehension	Passive-aggressive behavior	Trait

BIBLIOGRAPHY

A. Paul Hare. "Roles, Relationships, and Groups in Organizations: Some Conclusions and Recommendations." *Small Group Research* 34 (April 2003): 123–154.

Keyton, Joann, and Lawrence R. Frey. "The State of Traits: Predispositions and Group Communication." In *New Directions in Group Communication,* Lawrence R. Frey, ed. Thousand Oaks, CA: Sage, 2002, 99–120.

LaFasto, Frank, and Carl Larson. *When Teams Work Best: 6,000 Team Members and Leaders Tell*

What It Takes to Succeed. Thousand Oaks, CA: Sage, 2001, 1–32.

McCroskey, James C., and Virginia P. Richmond. "Communication Apprehension and Small Group Communication." In *Small Group Communication: A Reader.* 6th ed. Robert S. Cathcart and Larry A. Samovar, eds. Dubuque, IA: Wm. C. Brown, 1992, 361–374.

NOTES

1. Frank LaFasto and Carl E. Larson, *When Teams Work Best: 6,000 Team Members and Leaders Tell What It Takes to Succeed* (Thousand Oaks, CA: Sage, 2001): 1–32.

2. Susan E. Jackson, "Team Composition in Organizational Settings: Issues in Managing a Diverse Work Force," in *Group Process and Productivity,* eds. Stephen Worchel, Wendy Wood, and Jeffry A. Simpson (Newbury Park, CA: Sage, 1992): 138–73.

3. A. Paul Hare, "Roles, Relationships, and Groups in Organizations: Some Conclusions and Recommendations," *Small Group Research* 34 (April 2003): 123–154.

4. Herbert A. Thelen, *Dynamics of Groups at Work* (Chicago: University of Chicago Press, 1954): 187.

5. Robert F. Bales et al., "Channels of Communication in Small Groups," *American Sociological Review* 16 (1952): 461–68.

6. J. A. Schellenberg, "Group Size as a Factor in Success of Academic Discussion Groups," *Journal of Educational Psychology* 33 (1959): 73–79; E. B. Smith, "Some Psychological Aspects of Committee Work," *Journal of Abnormal and Social Psychology* 11 (1927): 73–79; Richard B. Powers and William Boyle, "Common Dilemma Choices in Small vs. Large Groups" (Paper presented at American Psychological Association, Anaheim, CA, August 1983).

7. Albert V. Carron and Kevin S. Spink, "The Group Size–Cohesion Relationship in Minimal Groups," *Small Group Research* 26 (February 1995): 86–105.

8. Phillip E. Slater, "Contrasting Correlates of Group Size," *Sociometry* 21 (1958): 129–39.

9. Randy Y. Hirokawa, Daniel DeGooyer, and Kathleen Valde, "Using Narratives to Study Task Group Effectiveness," *Small Group Research* 31 (October 2000): 573–91.

10. Brian H. Spitzberg, "Interpersonal Competence in Groups," in *Small Group Communication: A Reader,* 6th ed., eds. Robert S. Cathcart and Larry A. Samovar (Dubuque, IA: Wm. C. Brown, 1992): 431.

11. James Joseph A. Diliberto, "A Communication Study of Possible Relationships between Psychological Sex Type and Decision-Making Effectiveness," *Small Group Research* 23 (August 1992): 379–407.

12. Dean Kazoleas and Bonnie Kay, "Are Argumentatives Really More Argumentative? The Behavior of Argumentatives in Group Deliberations over Controversial Issues" (Paper presented at the Speech Communication Association Conference, New Orleans, LA, November 1994).

13. James C. McCroskey and Virginia P. Richmond, "Communication Apprehension and Small Group Communication," in *Small Group Communication: A Reader,* 5th ed., eds. Robert S. Cathcart and Larry A. Samovar (Dubuque, IA: Wm. C. Brown, 1988): 405–19.

14. K. W. Hawkins and R. A. Stewart, "Effects of Communication Apprehension on Perceptions of Leadership and Intragroup Attraction in Small Task-Oriented Groups," *Southern Communication Journal* 57 (1991): 1–10.

15. Richard E. Porter and Larry A. Samovar, "Communication in the Multicultural Group," in *Small Group Communication: Theory and Practice,* 7th ed., eds. Robert S. Cathcart, Larry A. Samovar, and Linda D. Henman (Boston, MA: McGraw-Hill, 1996): 306–15.

16. Rebecca B. Rubin and F. F. Jordan, "Effects of Instruction on Communication Apprehension and Communication Competence," *Communication Education* 46 (1997): 104–14.

17. Susan L. Kline, Cathy L. Hennen-Floyd, and Kathleen M. Farrell, "Cognitive Complexity and Verbal Response Mode Use in Discussion," *Communication Quarterly* 38 (1990): 350.

18. Ibid., 357–58.

19. Robert J. Ellis and Steven F. Cronshaw, "Self-Monitoring and Leader Emergence: A Test of Moderator Effects," *Small Group Research* 23 (1992): 114–15; see also Robert J. Ellis, Raymond S. Adamson, Gene Deszca, and Thomas F. Cawsey, "Self-Monitoring and Leadership Emergence," *Small Group Behavior* 19 (1988): 312–24.

20. Ellis and Cronshaw, "Self-Monitoring and Leader Emergence," 123.

21. Roderick P. Hart, Robert E. Carlson, and William F. Eadie, "Attitudes toward Communication and the Assessment of Rhetorical Sensitivity," *Communication Monographs* 47 (1980): 2–22.

22. Dennis S. Gouran, "Inferential Errors, Interaction, and Group Decision-Making," in *Communication and Group Decision Making,* eds. Randy Y. Hirokawa and Marshall Scott Poole (Beverly Hills, CA: Sage, 1986): 93–111.

23. Linda L. Putnam, "Preference for Procedural Order in Task-Oriented Small Groups," *Communication Monographs* 46 (1979): 193–218.

24. Randy Y. Hirokawa, Richard Ice, and Jeanmarie Cook, "Preference for Procedural Order, Discussion Structure, and Group Decision Performance," *Communication Quarterly* 36 (1988): 217–26.

25. Charles Pavitt, "Describing Know-How about Group Discussion Procedure: Must the Representation be Recursive?" *Communication Studies* 43 (Fall 1992): 150–70.

26. William A. Haythorn, Arthur Couch, D. Haefner, P. Langham, and L. F. Carter, "The Behavior of Authoritarian and Equalitative Personalities in Groups," *Human Relations* 3 (1956): 54–74; Stanley Milgram, "Some Conditions of Obedience and Disobedience to Authority," *Human Relations* 9 (1965): 57–76.

27. Myron W. Lustig and Laura L. Cassotta, "Comparing Group Communication Across Cultures: Leadership, Conformity, and Discussion Processes," in *Small Group Communication: Theory and Practice,* 7th ed., eds. Robert S. Cathcart, Larry A. Samovar, and Linda D. Henman (Boston, MA: McGraw-Hill, 1996): 316–26.

28. Gloria J. Galanes (Unpublished research based on interviews with individuals identified by peers as excellent group leaders, 2002).

29. Susan Sorensen, "Grouphate" (Paper presented at the International Communication Association, Minneapolis, May 1981).

30. Kimberly A. Freeman, "Attitudes toward Work in Project Groups as Predictors of Academic Performance," *Small Group Research* 27 (May, 1996): 265–282.

31. Joann Keyton and Lawrence R. Frey, "The State of Traits: Predispositions and Group Communication," in *New Directions in Group Communication,* ed. Lawrence R. Frey (Thousand Oaks, CA: Sage, 2002): 99–120. The scale was developed by Keyton, Harmon, and Frey in "Grouphate: Its Impact on Teaching Group Communication" (Paper presented at the National Communication Association Conference, San Diego, November, 1996).

32. Dominic A. Infante and Charles J. Wigley III, "Verbal Aggressiveness: An Interpersonal Model and Measure," *Communication Monographs* 53 (1986): 61–67.

33. Randy Y. Hirokawa, Daniel DeGooyer, and Kathleen Valde, "Using Narratives to Study Task Group Effectiveness."

34. LaFasto and Larson, *When Teams Work Best*.

35. Milton Rokeach, *The Open and Closed Mind* (New York: Basic Books, 1960).

36. Carolyn M. Anderson, Bruce L. Riddle, and Matthew M. Martin, "Socialization Processes in Groups," in *The Handbook of Group Communication Theory and Research,* ed. Lawrence R. Frey (Thousand Oaks, CA: Sage, 1999): 139–163.

37. Hare, "Roles, Relationships, and Groups in Organizations," 128–141.

38. Julie Apker, Kathleen M. Propp, and Wendy S. Zavaba Ford, "Negotiating Status and Identity Tensions in Healthcare Team Interactions: An Exploration of Nurse Role Dialectics," *Journal of Applied Communication Research* 33 (May 2005): 93–115.

39. A. Paul Hare, "Types of Roles in Small Groups: A Bit of History and a Current Perspective," *Small Group Research* 25 (August 1994): 433–48.

40. Kenneth D. Benne and Paul Sheats, "Functional Roles of Group Members," *Journal of Social Issues* 4 (1948): 41–49.

41. Peter E. Mudrack and Genevieve M. Farrell, "An Examination of Functional Role Behavior and Its Consequences for Individuals in Group Settings," *Small Group Research* 26 (November 1995): 542–71.

42. A. J. Salazar, "An Analysis of the Development and Evolution of Roles in the Small Group," *Small Group Research* 27 (1996): 475–503.

43. Mudrack and Farrell, "An Examination of Functional Role Behavior."

44. Ibid.

45. Jeanne M. Plas, *Person-Centered Leadership: An American Approach to Participatory Management* (Thousand Oaks, CA: Sage, 1996): 88.

46. Michael W. Kramer, "Communication in a Community Theater Group: Managing Multiple Group Roles," *Communication Studies* 53 (2002): 151–70.

47. Ibid., 162–65.

Group Observation and Evaluation Tools

Groups can often benefit from learning about themselves. Sometimes members can initiate and lead a group in evaluating itself. At other times, it is more helpful to bring in an outside consultant to provide an objective perspective. Chapter 7 presents a variety of assessment and evaluation tools you can use to learn about yourself or your group or to conduct a systematic evaluation of another group. We present this information here to encourage you to practice using these tools as you study the various group communication concepts discussed in the rest of this text.

PART III

Tools for Assessing and Evaluating Groups

CENTRAL MESSAGE

It is healthy for members periodically to evaluate themselves, their fellow members, and the group because information from such assessments can suggest specific areas for improvement. Sometimes a group can benefit from the observations of outside consultants, including students who understand group communication processes.

STUDY OBJECTIVES

As a result of studying Chapter 7 you should be able to:

1. Explain the benefits of assessing your own behavior as a group member and reflecting on it.

2. Explain the benefits of conducting regular group evaluations.

3. Explain the benefits of having a consultant observe and work with a group.

4. Prepare a consultant's observation guide appropriate for observing a small group.

5. Report observations in ways that are helpful to group members.

6. Devise and use instruments for assessing yourself, your fellow members, and your group as a whole and that you can use when you consult for another group.

Sam, the CEO of a small plant that manufactured specialized circuit boards, decided to hire a consultant to help his executive committee overcome several problems. The committee met weekly and consisted of the department managers: Roger, manufacturing; Elgin, quality assurance; Angela, sales and marketing; and Frank, the comptroller. The team had made several costly mistakes in the past several months, which Sam thought were caused by misunderstandings between members, on top of the pressures caused by an expanding business. In one instance, Angela had promised an early delivery to a customer on the basis of what she thought Roger had said, but the circuit boards weren't ready and the company lost the customer. Things didn't seem to be improving, and Sam didn't know whether the problems were due to his leadership style, the competence of the members, ineffective communication at the weekly meetings, or something else.

Sam had already done what he knew to do. He found a rating scale on the Internet so that members could assess their own preference for procedural order. Group members had fun with this—they enjoyed learning that they were pretty low in preference for procedural order—but group meetings did not seem to improve. He also distributed brief questionnaires after one meeting to learn whether members thought the meetings were productive and worthwhile. He discovered that members didn't particularly think the meetings were worth their time, but they didn't give specific suggestions for improvement. Sam decided he needed the objective and informed opinion only an outsider could provide.

Enter Susanna, organizational trainer and consultant who specialized in team performance and teambuilding. First, she gathered all the information she could about the team by interviewing Sam and reading the group's memos and minutes. This didn't take her long because committee minutes were kept sporadically. She observed three meetings, which highlighted to her what some of the problems might be, and took extensive notes so that she could provide specific examples to the members. As a last step, she interviewed each of the group members to gain their perspectives on the meetings and their own performance.

Susanna prepared her feedback for the group. She had a long list of things she could mention, but she didn't want to overwhelm or demoralize the team. She selected the few she thought were most problematic, beginning with "housekeeping." The team did not operate with an agenda, nor was anyone regularly assigned to take notes. She noted that the team met in an employee break room that had snacks handy, but because other employees wandered in and out, the room was noisy and distracting. She observed that at each meeting, nearly every member was called away at least once by a secretary or subordinate to answer a question or take a phone call.

In her report, Susanna recommended that Sam provide members with an agenda at least a day or two before the meeting, and that if members didn't want to rotate the job of taking minutes, Sam's secretary could attend the meetings specifically for that function. She suggested that members find another place to meet—even if that had to be away from the plant, at a private meeting room in a restaurant over breakfast, for example. She also recommended that members not allow their secretaries or subordinates to interrupt the meeting, except for a dire emergency.

The next recommendations concerned the process of discussion itself. Susanna praised the group for their obvious dedication to the company and their creativity in solving problems. She noted, however, that because there had been several costly misunderstandings, members exhibited signs of distress and distrust, which she thought they could overcome. Susanna gave the group several examples of how their discussion was disorganized, with members jumping from one topic to another without concluding a topic. At any given moment, there could be three different topics under discussion, and it was easy to mishear or misunderstand information. She affirmed that their problems were solvable and gave them several suggestions for how the group could monitor its own discussion process. She spoke privately with Sam about his somewhat lax leadership style and recommended that he keep firmer control of the meetings.

Finally, Susanna designed a training program for the group to take place during a weekend retreat. The program succeeded in improving the members' basic communication skills and featured several teambuilding activities to help the group begin to recover some of the trust eroded by recent mistakes.

This case study illustrates several points we want to make in this chapter. First, it is completely appropriate for members to conduct assessments of their own behavior. Most people like learning about themselves, and there are numerous surveys and scales designed to assess particular characteristics. Sometimes, such information is used only by each individual member. Often, that's enough to encourage members to reflect about how their own behavior contributes to the group. Sometimes, group members all take the same scale and want to discuss their findings within the group, as Sam's group did regarding their preference for procedural order.

Second, it's a good idea for group members regularly to assess the group as a whole, including the behavior and participation of their fellow members. Experienced group leaders routinely conduct periodic "how are we doing" sessions in which the topic of the group discussion is the group itself and how well it functions. This information is usually shared with the group as a whole, but sometimes a leader wants members to have the safety of anonymity, so members may complete a group assessment survey that only the leader will see.

Finally, most groups can benefit from outside assessment. It is hard as a group member to split your attention between participating in the group at the same time you are observing the group process. You can't do both in the same instant; instead, your attention shifts back and forth between one and the other, which makes it likely that you'll miss something. Sometimes, you will know *exactly* what a group needs, but other times you won't have a clue—you just know it needs help! That was Sam's position, and that is why he sought the services of an outside consultant who could be free just to observe without having to participate.

This chapter discusses all three of these processes: self-assessment, member and group assessment, and outside consultation. We also provide tools and instruments you can use for these kinds of assessments. As you read through the rest of this text, you are encouraged to use these assessments, to modify them, or to create your own so that you can make the most of your group experience.

Internal Assessment: Members Evaluate the Group

Knowledgeable group members can do a lot to make their groups effective. By the time you finish this text, you should have an idea of what needs to improve and how you can contribute. You have many resources available to you for assessing yourself, one another, and your group.

Self-Assessment

Do you enjoy learning about yourself? Most people do, and members of groups often enjoy taking personality and other assessments for that purpose. There are many such assessments available in textbooks and on the World Wide Web.

FIGURE 7.1   Grouphate

The following scale provides information about the extent to which you like or dislike working in groups. Indicate how much you agree or disagree with each statement by circling the appropriate response. Add the numbers you have circled. The higher the number, the more you experience grouphate.

Statement	Strongly Agree	Agree	Neither	Disagree	Strongly Disagree
1. I like working in groups.	1	2	3	4	5
2. I would rather work alone.	5	4	3	2	1
3. Group work is fun.	1	2	3	4	5
4. Groups are terrible.	5	4	3	2	1
5. I would prefer to work in an organization in which teams are used.	1	2	3	4	5
6. My ideal job is one in which I can be interdependent with others.	1	2	3	4	5
Total					

Adapted from Joann Keyton and Lawrence R. Frey, "The State of Traits: Predispositions and Group Communication," in Lawrence R. Frey, ed., *New Directions in Group Communication* (Thousand Oaks, CA: Sage, 2002): 109.

You can take such self-assessments for the sole purpose of learning about yourself, but you can also use the information to prompt group discussion about the effect a particular member characteristic has on the group as a whole. For example, members of a group we know answered questionnaires to learn their preferred conflict management styles. Their group leader then facilitated a discussion of their styles; the members used this opportunity to reflect and talk about how others perceived their behavior and how their actions influenced the group. Often, self-rating scales are easily changed to ones that can be used to rate the other participants.

Grouphate and Preference for Procedural Order were discussed in Chapter 6; Figure 7.1 presents a short questionnaire to help you assess your level of grouphate, and Figure 7.2 assesses how much you like group discussion

FIGURE 7.2 Preference for procedural order

The following scale assesses your preference for procedural order. Indicate how much you agree or disagree with each statement by circling the appropriate response. Add the numbers you have circled. The higher the number, the more you prefer orderly, systematic group discussions.

Statement During Group Work, I	Strongly Agree			Neither			Strongly Disagree
1. Request or suggest deadlines for the group to follow.	7	6	5	4	3	2	1
2. Request or suggest agendas, task lists, or ranking of alternatives.	7	6	5	4	3	2	1
3. Request or make statements about group goals.	7	6	5	4	3	2	1
4. Suggest signposts to signal the start of group meetings.	7	6	5	4	3	2	1
5. Summarize/integrate contributions of members during a meeting.	7	6	5	4	3	2	1
6. Suggest or request division of labor among group members.	7	6	5	4	3	2	1
7. Suggest ways to implement a task or course of action.	7	6	5	4	3	2	1
8. Request direction about procedures for the group to follow.	7	6	5	4	3	2	1
9. Ask questions and make comments to clarify specific procedures.	7	6	5	4	3	2	1
10. Keep discussions task-related by following agenda topics.	7	6	5	4	3	2	1
Total							

Adapted from Linda L. Putnam, "Preference for Procedural Order in Task-Oriented Small Groups," *Communication Monographs* 16 (August 1979): 212.

FIGURE 7.3
Assertiveness rating scale

Name _____   Date _____

The check mark on each scale indicates my best judgment of my own degree of assertiveness as a participant in the discussion.

	Nonassertive	Assertive	Aggressive
Behavior			
Getting the floor			
	yielded easily	usually refused to let others take over or dominate	interrupted and cut others off
Expressing opinions			
	never expressed personal opinion	stated opinions, but open to others' opinions	insisted others should agree
Expressing personal desires (for meeting times, procedures, etc.)			
	never, or did so in a pleading way	stated openly, but willing to compromise	insisted on having my own way
Sharing information			
	none, or only if asked to do so	whenever information was relevant, concisely	whether relevant or not; long-winded, rambling
Manner			
Voice			
	weak, unduly soft	strong and clear	loud, strident
Posture and movements	withdrawn, restricted	animated, often leaning forward	unduly forceful "table pounding"
Eye contact			
	rare, even when speaking	direct but not staring or glaring	stared others down
Overall manner			
	nonassertive	assertive	aggressive

to be orderly and organized. A self-rating of assertiveness is provided in Figure 7.3; to change this scale from a self-rating scale to an other-rating scale, change the wording slightly: Instead of asking about your "best judgment of my own" degree of assertiveness, ask about your "best judgment of Sally's degree of assertiveness." Figure 7.4, the Ross-DeWine Conflict Management

FIGURE 7.4   Ross-DeWine Conflict Management Message Style instrument

Directions: Below you will find messages that have been delivered by persons in conflict situations. Consider each message separately and decide how closely this message resembles the ones that you have used in conflict settings. The language may not be exactly the same as yours, but consider the messages in terms of similarity to your messages in conflict. There are no right or wrong answers, nor are these messages designed to trick you. Answer in terms of responses you make, not what you think you should say. Give each message a 1–5 rating on the answer sheet provided according to the following scale. Mark one answer only.

In conflict situations, I

1	2	3	4	5
never say things like this	rarely say things like this	sometimes say things like this	often say things like this	usually say things like this

_____ 1.   "Can't you see how foolish you're being with that thinking?"
_____ 2.   "How can I make you feel happy again?"
_____ 3.   "I'm really bothered by some things that are happening here; can we talk about these?"
_____ 4.   "I really don't have any more to say on this . . . " (silence)
_____ 5.   "What possible solution can we come up with?
_____ 6.   "I'm really sorry that your feelings are hurt—maybe you're right."
_____ 7.   "Let's talk this thing out and see how we can deal with this hassle."
_____ 8.   "Shut up! You are wrong! I don't want to hear any more of what you have to say."
_____ 9.   "It is your fault if I fail at this, and don't you ever expect any help from me when you're on the spot."
_____ 10.   "You can't do (say) that to me—it's either my way or forget it."
_____ 11.   "Let's try finding an answer that will give us both some of what we want."
_____ 12.   "This is something we have to work out; we're always arguing about it."
_____ 13.   "Whatever makes you feel happiest is OK by me."
_____ 14.   "Let's just leave well enough alone."
_____ 15.   "That's OK . . . it wasn't important anyway . . . You feeling OK now?"
_____ 16.   "If you're not going to cooperate, I'll just go to someone who will."
_____ 17.   "I think we need to try to understand the problem."
_____ 18.   "You might as well accept my decision; you can't do anything about it anyway."

Scoring:
  Self-oriented: Add items 1, 4, 8, 9, 10, 16, 18
  Other-oriented: Add items 2, 6, 13, 14, 15
  Issue-oriented: Add items 3, 5, 7, 11, 12, 17
  Roseanna G. Ross and Sue DeWine, "Assessing the Ross-DeWine Conflict Management Message Style (CMMS)," *Management Communication Quarterly*1 (February 1988): 389–413.

Message Style Instrument, is the conflict styles assessment completed by the group mentioned above. When you score this instrument as indicated, you learn to what extent your conflict style is self-oriented (motivated to win, to get what you want), other-oriented (motivated to maintain the relationship with the other person), or issue-oriented (motivated to work with the other person to solve the problem or issue). Finally, Figure 7.5 provides a self-rating scale that a discussion leader can use to evaluate his or her own performance. Had Sam completed this, he might have had an "ah ha!" reaction to realize where his leadership behaviors could have been modified to help the group.

Member and Group Assessment

One of the most effective group leaders we know conducts regular assessments of her group. Sometimes, she takes a few moments at the end of the meeting to ask members whether they thought the goals of the meeting were accomplished and what could have been done better. At other times, she distributes a more formal questionnaire asking for specific evaluation of some aspect of the group—problem solving, goal setting, or even her own performance as leader. Stopping to ask, "How are we doing?" can help a group completely change its direction or fine-tune an already effective process.

Almost any characteristic of individual behavior can be evaluated with an appropriate scale. Many different types of scales, surveys, and forms are available for this purpose; most of these instruments are easily modified. If a group cannot find a preexisting scale that suits its purpose, members or the leader should feel free to create a scale tailored specifically for what the group needs to know. Examples of two participant rating scales are provided in Figures 7.6 and 7.7. Figure 7.6 is a simple rating form, originally designed by students, that can be given to each participant and quickly tallied. Participants can complete these scales anonymously about each other, then distribute them to the person being rated. We use something similar in our classes to help students in project groups understand how their behavior is perceived by others. In some cases, what students *think* they are doing and how they are *actually* coming across can be very different. One young woman perceived herself as being good at spotting potential problems with the group's plans; her group members dreaded working with her because she disagreed with *everything*—she didn't know when to turn it off. The participant reaction forms gave her an alternative "reading" of her behavior, which she was able to modify. The participant rating form in Figure 7.7 has a similar purpose but is more comprehensive. The rating form in Figure 7.8 is designed to evaluate the leader. Originally devised for rating Air Force personnel as discussion leaders, it has been modified substantially over the years and is quite thorough.

The rating forms discussed thus far look at the individual behaviors of members and leaders, but sometimes group members want to assess the performance of the group as a whole. Members can assess any aspect of a group and its discussion: group climate, norms, interpersonal relationships, speaking,

Instructions: Rate yourself on each item by putting a check mark in the "Yes" or "No" column. Your score is five times the number of items marked "Yes." Rating: *excellent*, 90 or higher; *good*, 80–85; *fair*, 70–75; *inadequate*, 65 or lower.

	Yes	No
1. I prepared all needed facilities.	____	____
2. I started the meeting promptly and ended on time.	____	____
3. I established an atmosphere of supportiveness and informality by being open and responsive to all ideas.	____	____
4. I clearly oriented the group to its goal and area of freedom.	____	____
5. I encouraged all members to participate and maintained equal opportunity for all to speak.	____	____
6. I listened actively, and (if needed) encouraged all members to do so.	____	____
7. My questions were clear and brief.	____	____
8. I saw to it that unclear statements were paraphrased or otherwise clarified.	____	____
9. I used a plan for leading the group in an organized consideration of all major phases of problem solving and all components of vigilant interaction.	____	____
10. I saw to it that the problem was discussed thoroughly before solutions were considered.	____	____
11. I actively encouraged creative thinking.	____	____
12. I encouraged thorough evaluation of all proposed solutions, both for effectiveness and negative consequences.	____	____
13. I integrated related ideas or suggestions and urged the group to arrive at consensus on a solution.	____	____
14. I prompted open discussion of substantive conflicts.	____	____
15. I maintained order and organization, promptly pointing out tangents, making transitions, and keeping track of the passage of time.	____	____
16. I saw to it that the meeting produced definite assignments or plans for action and that any subsequent meeting was arranged.	____	____
17. All important information, ideas, and decisions were promptly and accurately recorded.	____	____
18. I was able to remain neutral during constructive arguments, and otherwise encourage teamwork.	____	____
19. I suggested or urged establishment of needed ethical standards and procedural norms.	____	____
20. I encouraged members to discuss how they felt about group process and procedures.	____	____

FIGURE 7.5
Discussion leader self-rating scale

FIGURE 7.6
Participant rating scale

Date _____

_____   Observer _____

(Name of participant)

1. Contributions to the *content of the discussion* (relevant information, issue-centered arguments, adequate reasoning, etc.).

5	4	3	2	1
outstanding in quality and quantity		fair share		few or none

2. Contributions to *efficient group procedures* (agenda planning, responding to prior comments, summaries).

5	4	3	2	1
always relevant, aided organization		relevant, no aid in order		sidetracked, confused group

3. Degree of *group orientation and cooperation* (listening to understand, responsible, agreeable, group centered, open-minded).

5	4	3	2	1
very responsible and constructive				self-centered

4. *Speaking competency* (clear, to group, one point at a time, concise).

5	4	3	2	1
brief, clear, to group				vague, indirect, wordy

5. *Overall value* to the group.

5	4	3	2	1
most valuable				least valuable

Suggestions:

Participant's name _____

Instructions: Circle the number that best reflects your evaluation of the discussant's participation on each scale.

Superior				Poor	
1	2	3	4	5	1. Was prepared and informed.
1	2	3	4	5	2. Contributions were brief and clear.
1	2	3	4	5	3. Comments relevant and well timed.
1	2	3	4	5	4. Spoke distinctly and audibly to all.
1	2	3	4	5	5. Willingness to communicate.
1	2	3	4	5	6. Frequency of participation [if poor, too low( ) or high( )].
1	2	3	4	5	7. Nonverbal responses were clear and constant.
1	2	3	4	5	8. Listened to understand and follow discussion.
1	2	3	4	5	9. Open-mindedness.
1	2	3	4	5	10. Cooperative, team orientation.
1	2	3	4	5	11. Helped keep discussion organized, followed outline.
1	2	3	4	5	12. Contributed to evaluation of information and ideas.
1	2	3	4	5	13. Respectful and tactful with others.
1	2	3	4	5	14. Encouraged others to participate.
1	2	3	4	5	15. Overall rating as participant.

Comments: Evaluator _____

FIGURE 7.7
Discussion participant evaluation scale

FIGURE 7.8
Comprehensive
leader rating scale

Date _____ Leader _____

Time _____ Observer _____

Instructions: Draw a line through any item not applicable to the discussion you have just observed. Use the following scale to evaluate the designated leader's performance as discussion leader.

5—superior   4—above average   3—average   2—below average   1—poor

Personal Style and Communicative Competencies

To what degree did the leader:

_____ Show poise and confidence in speaking?

_____ Show enthusiasm and interest in the problem?

_____ Listen well to understand *all* participants?

_____ Manifest personal warmth and a sense of humor?

_____ Show an open mind toward all new information and ideas?

_____ Create an atmosphere of teamwork?

_____ Share functional leadership with other members?

_____ Behave democratically?

_____ Maintain perspective on problem and group process?

Preparation

To what degree:

_____ Were all needed physical arrangements cared for?

_____ Were members notified and given guidance in preparing to meet?

_____ Was the leader prepared on the problem or subject?

_____ Was a procedural sequence of questions prepared to guide discussion?

Leadership Techniques

To what degree did the leader:

_____ Put members at ease with each other?

_____ Equalize opportunity to speak?

_____ Introduce and explain the charge or problem so that it was clear to all?

_____ Control aggressive or dominant members with tact?

_____ Present an agenda and/or procedural outline for group problem solving?

_____ Encourage members to modify the procedural outline?

_____ State questions clearly to the group?

_____ Guide the group through a thorough analysis of the problem before discussing solutions?

_____ Stimulate imaginative and creative thinking about solutions?

_____ Encourage the group to evaluate all ideas and proposals thoroughly before accepting or rejecting them?

_____ See that plans were made to implement and follow up on all decisions?

_____ Keep discussion on one point at a time?

_____ Rebound questions asking for a personal opinion or solution to the group?

_____ Provide summaries needed to clarify, remind, and move group forward to next issue or agenda item?

_____ Test for consensus before moving to a new phase of problem solving?

_____ Keep complete and accurate notes, including visual chart of proposals, evaluations, and decisions?

_____ If needed, suggest compromise or integrative solutions to resolve conflict?

_____ (Other—please specify_____)

Instructions: On the basis of behaviors and interaction you observed, rate the degree to which the group measured up to each criterion.

Poor		Fair		Average		Good		Excellent
1		2		3		4		5

1 2 3 4 5   1. Concerns of all members were established regarding the problem.

1 2 3 4 5   2. Components of the undesirable situation and obstacles to change were clearly described.

1 2 3 4 5   3. The goal was clearly defined and agreed upon by all members.

1 2 3 4 5   4. Possible solutions were listed and clarified before extensive evaluation of them.

1 2 3 4 5   5. Criteria for evaluation were previously understood and accepted, or discussed and agreed upon by all members.

1 2 3 4 5   6. Based on facts and reasoning, predictions were made regarding the probable effectiveness and possible negative consequences of each proposed solution.

1 2 3 4 5   7. Consensus was achieved on the most desirable/acceptable solution.

1 2 3 4 5   8. A realistic plan was developed for implementing the solution and, if appropriate, for evaluating its effectiveness.

1 2 3 4 5   9. Overall, the problem-solving process was thorough, vigilant, and systematic.

FIGURE 7.9
Problem-solving procedure scale

listening, problem-solving effectiveness, and so forth. For example, the composite scale in Figure 7.9, based on a similar one developed by Patton and Giffin, can identify deficiencies in problem-solving procedures.[1] The set of scales in Figure 7.10 was developed by Larkey to allow members of a diverse work group to evaluate how well the group manages its diversity.[2]

One common type of assessment is the **postmeeting reaction form (PMR),** which is a questionnaire given to participants at the end of a meeting to get objective feedback for improving future discussions. Usually anonymous, PMRs encourage candid and honest assessments. PMR forms are often handed out by a group's leader, but they can be planned by other group members. They can also be used by instructors, consultants, or planners of large conferences to evaluate a class, program, or conference. PMR results should be tallied and fed back to the group as soon as possible after members complete them; if a group has access to the right computer software, ratings can be entered and tallied

Postmeeting Reaction Form (PMR)

A form, completed after a discussion, on which group members evaluate the discussion, the group, and/or the leader.

Instructions: Answer each question on the basis of what you have observed and experienced in your workgroup.

Inclusion	Agree				Disagree
1. If someone who is not included in the mainstream tries to get information or makes a request, others stall or avoid helping them out in subtle ways.	5	4	3	2	1
2. It seems that the real reason people are denied promotions or raises is that they are seen as not fitting in.	5	4	3	2	1
3. I have to prove myself more and work a lot harder to get into that next position because of my gender or ethnic background.	5	4	3	2	1
4. It's hard to get ahead here unless you are part of the old boys' network.	5	4	3	2	1

Ideation

5. When people from different backgrounds work together in groups, some people feel slighted because their ideas are not acknowledged.	5	4	3	2	1
6. People are reluctant to get involved in a project that requires them to balance ideas from different gender and racial points of view.	5	4	3	2	1
7. Individuals with different backgrounds have a difficult time getting their ideas across.	5	4	3	2	1
8. Individuals in our group have a difficult time really listening with an open mind to the ideas presented by those of another culture or gender.	5	4	3	2	1

Understanding

9. When people who are culturally different or of different genders work together in our group, there is always some amount of miscommunication.	5	4	3	2	1
10. Women and people of color are interpreted differently than white males, even when they say the same thing.	5	4	3	2	1
11. Whenever I've confronted someone for giving me a hard time because of my race or gender, they have denied the problem.	5	4	3	2	1

Treatment

12. Some people in our group are "talked down to" because they are different.	5	4	3	2	1
13. People's different ways of talking or acting cause them to be treated as less competent or smart.	5	4	3	2	1
14. Performance evaluations seem to be biased against those who are different, because supervisors focus on very traditional ways of getting work done.	5	4	3	2	1
15. You can just feel a difference in the way some people are treated or talked to because they are different.	5	4	3	2	1

Instructions: Check the point on each scale that best represents your honest judgment. Add any comments you wish to make that are not covered by the questionnaire. Do not sign your name.

1. How clear were the *goals* of the discussion to you?

   very clear   somewhat vague   muddled

2. The *atmosphere* was

   cooperative and cohesive   apathetic   competitive

3. How well *organized and vigilant* was the discussion?

   disorderly   just right   to rigid

4. How effective was the *leadership* supplied by the chairperson?

   too autocratic   democratic   weak

5. *Preparation for this meeting* was

   thorough   adequate   poor

6. Did you find yourself *wanting to speak* when you didn't get a chance?

   almost never   occasionally   often

7. How satisfied are you with the *results* of the discussion?

   very satisfied   moderately satisfied   very satisfied

8. How do you feel about *working again* with this same group?

   eager   I will   reluctant
   Comments:

FIGURE 7.11
Postmeeting
reaction (PMR) form

1. How do you feel about today's discussion?

   excellent _____ good _____ all right _____ so-so _____ bad _____

2. What were the strong points of the discussion?

3. What were the weaknesses?

4. What changes would you suggest for future meetings?

(You need not sign your name.)

FIGURE 7.12
Postmeeting
reaction (PMR) form

simultaneously. The feedback provided by PMRs helps members and the leader adjust so they can be more effective in reaching their goals. Two examples of PMR forms are shown in Figures 7.11 and 7.12. Although both are designed to be completed anonymously, groups can also set aside the last five or so minutes of a meeting for an open postmeeting discussion about how members felt about the meeting. Figure 7.12, in particular, can guide such a discussion.

Recap: A Quick Review

Groups can benefit when members take the time to assess themselves, each other, and the group as a whole.

1. Numerous instruments, such as personality inventories and rating scales, can help members learn about themselves; several examples were presented, but others can be found in textbooks and through the Internet.

2. Sometimes the information is given only to the member, but often members discuss within the group what they learned about themselves and how their behaviors affect the group.

3. Members can assess each other's behavior, thus providing valuable feedback to each other; any of the instruments and scales used for self-assessment can be modified to be used for assessing other members or the leader.

4. Groups should regularly evaluate their meetings and their processes so that they can make needed adjustments.

5. Any element of a group—its norms, decision making, leadership, and so forth—can be evaluated; questionnaires and rating scales can be specifically tailored to focus on the specific areas you most want to evaluate.

6. Postmeeting reaction forms are questionnaires used to evaluate specific meetings; they can be designed to evaluate specific areas of a meeting (such as the group's decision-making effectiveness) or can be more general (such as evaluating whether members thought a meeting was effective).

Calling for Outside Help: The Consultant

Consultant

A nonparticipant observer who works with a group to determine what it needs, then helps by providing information, special techniques, and procedures.

Sometimes, even the most knowledgeable group members or leaders may become so immersed in discussion of a particular issue that they lose sight of the process, or they just can't distance themselves enough to take an objective look. That's when a **consultant,** an observer who does *not* participate in the group's discussion, can be a real asset in spotting what might be wrong and helping a group fix its problems. Evaluating a group's process has been shown to be beneficial to both small groups and the organizations that created them.[3]

The consultant does not need to be a paid professional—our students can and have served as consultants to groups and organizations both on and off campus. By the time you finish this chapter, you will know how to plan and conduct an observation of a group. You may also be able to use that experience as a student consultant to help land a job. For example, one of our students included a copy of the small group consulting project she completed as a class assignment in her job portfolio. A prospective employer, whose organization wanted to move to more group- and team-based work, recognized her potential value to the company and hired her on the strength of that class consulting project.

In this section, we describe the functions consultants perform, suggest strategies for planning your consultation, and give you more examples of instruments that are particularly useful for observing and consulting. We also remind you that the scales and questionnaires already presented can be used by consultants in addition to the members themselves, so don't forget about them when you put on your consultant hat.

Practice First

The best thing you can do to become an effective consultant is to practice. You need to train your eyes and ears in what to observe and how best to gather the information you need. There are many groups you can observe in their natural settings, such as most meetings of boards, councils, and government committees for whom a "sunshine law" exists. Many groups will open their meetings to you if they know you are a student and you promise to maintain the confidentiality of the group's private business.

Observing as part of a team will increase your learning. A team can take in more than an individual, and team members learn a lot from sharing and discussing their individual insights. An observation team may be able to arrange a fishbowl setup, with observers sitting in a circle outside the discussion group. Sometimes, all observers will focus on the same aspects of group discussion, such as leadership sharing; at other times, each member watches for and reports on a different phenomenon (e.g., Martha observes leadership sharing, Xiuchen concentrates on how the group uses information).

Consultants generally provide three functions for the groups they consult for: they *remind* a group of techniques or principles of discussion it has overlooked, they *teach* a group new procedures and techniques to improve the group's performance, and they *critique* a group's performance. Sometimes, consultants do all three of these at once.

Reminding Often group members need only to be reminded of principles and techniques they already know but have temporarily overlooked in the excitement of a lively argument. A reminder is like a coach during pauses in a football game. When the consultant notices some difficulty with the group's communication process, he or she may remind the group of the principles or techniques that have temporarily been overlooked. Having a reminder can improve a group's decision quality. Schultz et al. trained certain group members to serve as reminders, intervening whenever they observed symptoms of defective group decision making.[4] The reminders were instructed not to be aggressive but to remind the group by providing timely questions and suggestions: "Maybe we shouldn't make our final choice until we've looked at all the alternatives."

Reminders, particularly those who were regular group members and not the emergent leaders of their groups, significantly affected decision quality.

Teaching   Sometimes a consultant can be a helpful teacher by providing basic information about small group processes. Many of the people who participate in groups of all kinds have never studied small group communication and don't know what is normal and what isn't. Just by taking a small group communication course, you are ahead of many group leaders and managers who may have been thrown into a group with no training.

A teaching consultant can provide specialized information or ideas for procedures and techniques designed to solve specific group difficulties. Examples of such procedures are provided throughout this text.

Critiquing   Many consultants, teachers, and trainers provide a group with **critique,** a descriptive analysis and evaluation of the group's strengths and weaknesses. Communication specialists on corporate training and development staffs are often called on to provide evaluations of both groups and individual members to managers, but even students can provide thoughtful critique. Greenbaum and associates claim that failure to evaluate adequately the procedures and output of the quality circles is often a major factor in the demise of quality circle programs.[5]

In general, a consultant's critique should cover at least four aspects of a group's discussion processes and culture: (1) inputs to and content of the problem-solving discussion; (2) the group process, including patterns of verbal interaction, member roles (including any ego-centered behavior and ethical lapses), communication process, decision making, and problem solving as a whole; (3) the group product, including how well it has been evaluated by the group, how appropriate it is to the goals or problem described by the group, and how committed members seem to be to making it work; and (4) leadership, especially the role of the designated leader and the sharing of leadership functions.[6]

Giving Feedback   No matter what consulting function you provide, there are guidelines you should follow when you deliver feedback. Following these guidelines will increase the chance that members will be willing to hear what you say instead of getting defensive.

1. Give the group a chance to correct itself first. Don't jump in right away when you observe a problem; see if the group will figure something out on its own.

2. Focus on the most important issues or problems. Don't overwhelm a group by noting every single thing you think could be improved because that will bog members down and could demoralize them.

3. Stress the positive first; look for things to point out that the members and leader are doing well before you point out where improvements are needed.

4. Focus on communication processes and procedures, not the *content* of discussion.

Critique

Analysis and assessment of something, such as identification of strengths and weaknesses in a small group's process and interaction.

5. Don't give orders, try to force the group to change, or argue. Ultimately, it is up to the members whether or not they want to take your advice. Present your observations, back them up with specific examples, but leave members free to decide whether or how your feedback will be used.

6. Speak (or write) clearly, precisely, and briefly. If the group asks for an explanation, elaboration, or demonstration of a technique, prepare it carefully and don't ramble.

7. Phrase most of your remarks as descriptions of what you have observed, questions, and suggestions. Susanna did this for the executive team: "Did you notice that in the space of only four minutes, the team has discussed _____, _____, and _____?"

8. If you need to correct a member's or leader's behavior, do so privately so that you don't embarrass that person in front of the group. To the group, focus on trends and tendencies rather than singling someone out (unless it is to praise them).

9. Don't bluff. If a group asks for information or procedures you aren't familiar with, admit it and explain that you will research these for the group and bring the information back at a subsequent meeting.

Ethical Principles for Consultants

After observing a discussion, a consultant usually makes a detailed feedback statement to the group that describes selected aspects of the discussion and assesses the group's strong and weak points. When you do so, respect both the individual members and the group as an entity. Behave so that the group will welcome other observers and consultants in the future. The ethical standards that apply to observers are analogous to those that universities use when faculty and students conduct research involving human subjects. Group members, like research participants, deserve the same type of protections. As consultant, adhere to the following standards of personal conduct:

1. Do not harm group members either physically or psychologically by your observation and feedback. Don't knowingly cause embarrassment, emotional upset, physical danger, and so forth. For example, it *would* be unethical for a consultant to make fun of a group member in front of the rest of the group, but it *would not* be unethical to speak with that member privately to describe the effect of the offending behavior on the group.

2. Tell the truth. It is unethical to tell a group that a critique will not be given to a superior when in fact it *will*. It is also unethical to tell a group that you think its decision-making procedures are careful when in fact you think they are sloppy.

3. Make your criticism constructive. When you point out a problem, you should also suggest what to do to correct it, as Susanna did when she recommended that the group find a different meeting room, that Sam

4. provide an agenda, and that his secretary take minutes. You are there to help, not to judge.

4. Respect the privacy and confidentiality of group members at all times. It is not ethical to share with outsiders what you have observed in a specific group unless: (1) you told the group you were going to do so before observing and the group granted you permission to do so; or (2) you so thoroughly disguise the identity of the group and its members (as in a statistical summary) that no one can possibly identify the group and members in your report. In addition, it is not ethical to receive confidential information from one member and share it with another without permission. Finally, unless a group meeting has been legally declared open to the public, you should not report details or the substance of group business to outsiders.

When you report findings of your observations (for instance, reporting to your teacher or class), you will need to get permission to do so from the group members *before* you do your observing. The members observed may be more willing to let you report if you offer to use pseudonyms instead of real names. In general, treat observed persons just as you would want to be treated if your roles were reversed.

Planning the Consultation

When you first consult for a group, you may feel overwhelmed by all that goes on. Planning your observation and consultation in advance will help you focus on variables most important to your purposes and functions as a consultant. You may first want to talk with the group's leader or the person responsible for the group's output for background material about the group, such as what its purpose is, the history of the group, how effective it is perceived to be, and so forth. One way to cope with information overload is to record the group's discussion on audio- or videotape (but only after obtaining permission from the group) for more detailed analysis at a later time. That way, you will worry less about missing something important and can make notes about parts of the discussion to review later.

The questions in Table 7.1 can guide you in selecting a more limited list of questions for a specific observation. If you have been asked to consult, this

TABLE 7.1   Questions to help guide your observation

Group Purpose/Goals
What is the group's purpose?
Do members clearly understand and accept the group's purpose?
Has the committee achieved a clear understanding of its charge?
Do members seem to know and accept limits on their area of freedom?
Can members describe what sort of output is needed?

(continued)

Setting

How adequate are meeting facilities, such as seating arrangement, privacy, and comfort?
How adequate are facilities for recording and displaying group progress (information, ideas, evaluations, decisions, and so on)?

Communication Skills and Network

How competently do members encode verbally and nonverbally?
How carefully are members listening to understand each other?
How equally is participation spread among the members?
Is the network of verbal interaction all-channel or unduly restricted?

Group Culture, Norms, and Communication Climate

To what degree is the group climate characterized by openness, trust, and teamwork?
What attitudes toward each other and the content of information and ideas are members manifesting?
Are cultural, work style, or personality differences interfering with the group's effectiveness?
Are any self-centered hidden agenda items interfering with progress toward the goal?
Are any norms interfering with cohesiveness and progress?
Are arguments being expressed sensitively and being managed to test ideas and achieve consensus, or to win?

Role Structure

Is there a designated leader?
If so, how well is this person performing the role? With what style? Are others encouraged to share in leader functions?
If not, how is leadership distributed? Are any needed services missing?
Are all necessary functional roles being provided?
Are there any ego-centered behavioral roles?

Problem-Solving and Decision-Making Procedures

How vigilant are the group's problem-solving procedures?
Do members seem to be adequately informed or are they planning how to get needed information before reaching decisions?
Are information and ideas being evaluated thoroughly for effectiveness and possible negative consequences, or accepted without question?
Are criteria shared by all group members, or explicitly discussed and agreed upon?
Are there any tendencies toward groupthink?
Has some procedure or agenda for the discussion been accepted by the group? If so, how adequate is it and how well is it being used?
Are information, interpretations, proposals, and decisions being recorded?
Are these provided in some record visible to the entire group?
How creative is the group in finding alternatives?
How frequently are summaries being made and used to focus and move discussion toward the goal?
How are decisions being made?
If needed, is the group making adequate plans to implement its decisions? To evaluate the adequacy of its actual solution(s), and possibly make changes later?
Might procedural changes or special techniques such as brainstorming, committee procedural rules, Nominal Group Technique, or computer charting be beneficial to the group?

list can help you decide which processes are going well so that you can focus on characteristics that group members may want to change.

Obviously, you cannot consider all these questions at the same time. Concentrate on the one or two factors that seem most important or most problematic for the group. With increased experience you will discover that you can pay attention to more factors, or rapidly scan what is happening and then decide where to focus your attention.

More Instruments for Observing and Consulting

The final section of Chapter 7 is devoted to presenting more instruments and techniques for observing and evaluating groups. Just as the instruments presented early in the chapter can be used by observers and consultants, the instruments presented here can be used by group members themselves as part of a group's self-asssessment, especially if a member is designated to observe a particular meeting. Feel free to use the instruments as presented or adapt them to suit specific situations and needs.

Verbal Interaction Analysis

Verbal Interaction Analysis

An analysis of who talks to whom and how often during a discussion.

A diagram of a **verbal interaction analysis** reveals who talks to whom, how often each member participates orally, and whether the group has members who dominate or who do not speak up. The information at the top of Figure 7.13 identifies the group, time, and members involved, in this case the six members of the G.E. Tigers. Each circle represents a group member, and the arrows represent lines of communication connecting each member to every other member. The longer arrows pointing to the center of the circle represent communication to the group as a whole. The circles and arrows should be drawn in advance. Each time a member speaks, a short cross mark is made on the shaft of the appropriate arrow.

Verbal interaction diagrams are easier to interpret when the cross marks are represented as numbers and percentages in a chart, like the ones in Figures 7.14 and 7.15. Judging from the numbers shown in this example, who do you think was discussion leader of the G.E. Tigers? Are there any other reasoned inferences you can make about this group from the data? You could modify this procedure and instrument to capture the frequency of some nonverbal behaviors such as eye contact and body angles.

Content Analysis

Content Analysis

An analysis of the content (topics, behaviors, specific words or ideas, fantasy themes, etc.) of a group's discussion.

Content analysis procedures examine the actual content of remarks (e.g., topics discussed, types of remarks) made during a discussion. One type of content analysis focuses on who performs what behaviors and how often. From such a descriptive analysis, members' roles can be described. The examples in Figures 7.16 and 7.17 classify members' behaviors during the observed discussion. Specific behaviors are listed along the left side of the chart, and the

Group ___G.E. "Tigers"___

Time _____

Begin ___1:03___

End ___1:54___

Place ___Conf. Rm. 14___

Observer ___Snow___

FIGURE 7.13
Verbal interaction
diagram

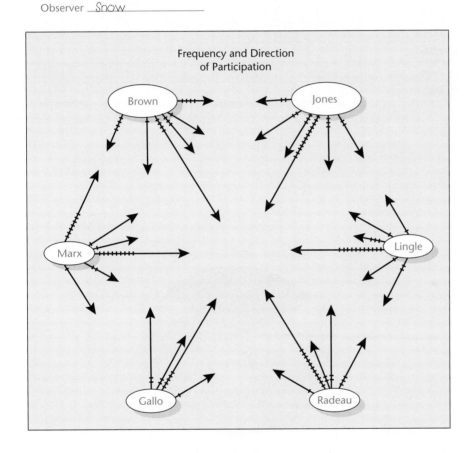

Frequency and Direction
of Participation

participants' names in the cells at the head of each column. Each time a member speaks, the observer judges what the behavior was and places a tally mark in the appropriate cell of the chart. After the discussion the tally marks are converted to numbers and percentages, as shown in Figure 7.17. They can also be converted to pie charts such as the one shown for Jodi in Figure 7.18. From this analysis, can you tell who is probably task leader of this group? Who is the social or maintenance leader? Do any individuals seem to be interfering with the group's progress toward its goal?

FIGURE 7.14
Displaying data
from a verbal
interaction diagram

Group	G.E. "Tigers" Q.C.					Place	Conf. Rm. 14		
Observer	Snow					Date	11-5-02		
Beginning time	1:03					Ending time	1:54 pm		

TO:

FROM:	Brown	Jones	Lingle	Radeau	Gallo	Marx	Group	Total Percent
Brown	–	5	2	4	2	5	5	23 / 16.1
Jones	3	–	3	4	4	3	13	30 / 21
Lingle	2	2	–	3	2	4	12	25 / 17.5
Radeau	3	3	4	–	0	2	12	24 / 16.8
Gallo	3	3	2	0	–	0	6	14 / 9.8
Marx	8	2	2	3	2	–	10	27 / 18.9
Total number / percent	19 / 13.3	15 / 10.5	13 / 9.1	14 / 9.8	10 / 7	14 / 9.8	58 / 40.6	143 / 100

FIGURE 7.15
Another way to
display data from a
verbal interaction
diagram

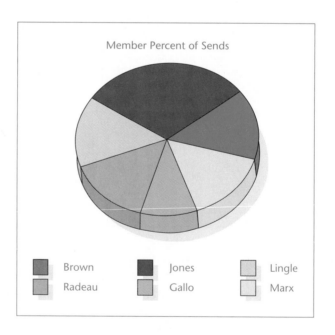

Member Percent of Sends

■ Brown   ■ Jones   ■ Lingle
■ Radeau   ■ Gallo   ■ Marx

Group_____ Place _____ Observer_____

Date _____ Beginning time _____ Ending time _____

Participants' Names

Behavioral Functions						
1. Initiating and orienting						
2. Information giving						
3. Information seeking						
4. Opinion giving						
5. Opinion seeking						
6. Clarifying and elaborating						
7. Evaluating						
8. Summarizing						
9. Coordinating						
10. Consensus testing						
11. Recording						
12. Suggesting procedure						
13. Gatekeeping						
14. Supporting						
15. Harmonizing						
16. Tension relieving						
17. Dramatizing						
18. Norming						
19. Withdrawing						
20. Blocking						
21. Status and recognition seeking						

FIGURE 7.16
Content analysis of behavioral functions of members

FIGURE 7.17
Displaying data from analysis of behavioral functions of members

Group __EXECUTIVE COMMITTEE__   Place __CU LOBBY__
Observer __ANDY__   Date __11 – 14 – 02__
Beginning time __4:30 P.M.__   Ending time __6:30 P.M.__

Participants' Names

Behavioral Functions	Mary	John	Edna	Dave	Jodi	Total (number / percent)
1. Initiating and orienting	5	3				8 / 5.7
2. Information giving	6	5		2	3	16 / 11.4
3. Information seeking			3			3 / 2.1
4. Opinion giving	8	8	4	2	1	23 / 16.4
5. Opinion seeking			2			2 / 1.4
6. Clarifying and elaborating			3			3 / 2.1
7. Evaluating	2	4			1	7 / 5
8. Summarizing	2					2 / 1.4
9. Coordinating	8					8 / 5.7
10. Consensus testing				3		3 / 2.1
11. Recording			5			5 / 3.6
12. Suggesting procedure	3		6			9 / 6.4
13. Gatekeeping			1	5		6 / 4.3
14. Supporting	2		2	6		10 / 7.1
15. Harmonizing				3	2	5 / 3.6
16. Tension relieving					6	6 / 4.3
17. Dramatizing		5			3	8 / 5.7
18. Norming				4		4 / 2.9
19. Withdrawing		1				1 / .7
20. Blocking	2	5				7 / 5
21. Status and recognition seeking		4				4 / 2.9
Total (number / percent)	38 / 27.1	35 / 25	26 / 18.6	25 / 17.9	16 / 11.4	140 / 100

A content analysis can be developed for virtually any set of categories that can be used to classify member behavior, including types of statements (e.g., questions, answers, opinions), styles of conflict management (e.g., self-oriented, other-oriented, issue-oriented), and so forth. It is important for the observers to classify the remarks consistently so that the same behavior is classified in the same way by two observers, or by one observer at two different times.

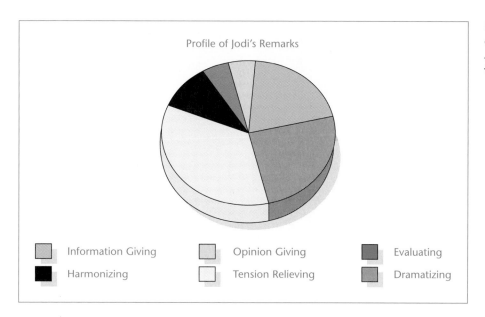

Profile of Jodi's Remarks

■ Information Giving   ■ Opinion Giving   ■ Evaluating

■ Harmonizing   □ Tension Relieving   ■ Dramatizing

FIGURE 7.18 Pie chart displaying Jodi's behavioral functions

SYMLOG: Drawing a Snapshot of a Group

SYMLOG, which is an acronym for the System for the Multiple Level Observation of Groups, is both a theory and a methodology that permits a three-dimensional diagram to be constructed of a group.[7] Such diagrams can be constructed by outside observers and consultants or by the group members themselves. Examples of such diagrams are provided in Figures 7.19 and 7.20. (Instructions for producing a simplified SYMLOG-like diagram are included in the *Instructor's Manual*.) You can see, even without detailed information about SYMLOG theory, that the first group (Figure 7.19) is fragmented and polarized, but the second (Figure 7.20) is unified and cohesive.

SYMLOG theory rests on the assumption that behavior of each group member in a group can be classified along each of three independent dimensions: dominant versus submissive; friendly versus unfriendly; and task-oriented versus emotionally expressive.[8] SYMLOG may be used in one of two ways. With the scoring method, external observers score the verbal and nonverbal behaviors of members as they interact in real time. The rating method is easier, requiring no special training; external observers or group members themselves complete a 26-question rating scale evaluating each member's behavior. The results are tallied in a particular way so each member can be placed on the SYMLOG diagram.

Each of the three dimensions is represented by a pair of letters that anchor the pole positions. For example, *P* (positive) stands for *friendly* and *N* (negative) stands for *unfriendly* behavior. On the diagram, the more friendly a member is toward the other members of the group, the farther the circle is placed to the right. The more unfriendly members are located farther to the left. (In Figure 7.19, Ed is the most friendly and Ann the most unfriendly.) Task

SYMLOG

SYstem for the Multiple Level Observation of Groups, both a theory about member characteristics and effects on group interaction, and a methodology that produces a three-dimensional "snapshot" of a group at a given point in time.

FIGURE 7.19   SYMLOG diagram of a noncohesive group

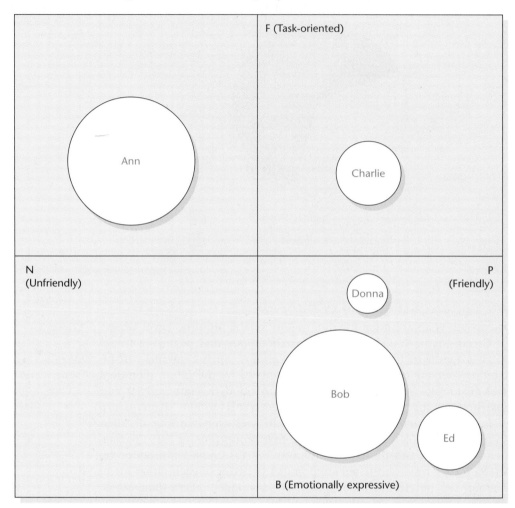

orientation is represented by *F* (forward); the more task-oriented a member is, the closer he or she is to the top of the diagram. Emotional expressiveness is represented by *B* (backward); these members are closer to the bottom of the diagram. (In Figure 7.19, Ann is the most task-oriented, and Ed the most emotionally expressive.) The third dimension is depicted by the size of a member's circle; dominant members have larger circles than submissive ones. (In Figure 7.19, Ann and Bob are the most dominant, Donna the most submissive.)

You can readily see that the group shown in Figure 7.19 is not cohesive. Ann is dominant, task-oriented, and negative toward her fellow members. She tries to dictate what happens in the group. Bob is dominant, but friendly and emotionally expressive, which gets the group off track frequently; almost certainly, Bob's behavior clashes with Ann's desire to stick to the task. Charlie, who

FIGURE 7.20   SYMLOG diagram of a unified, productive group

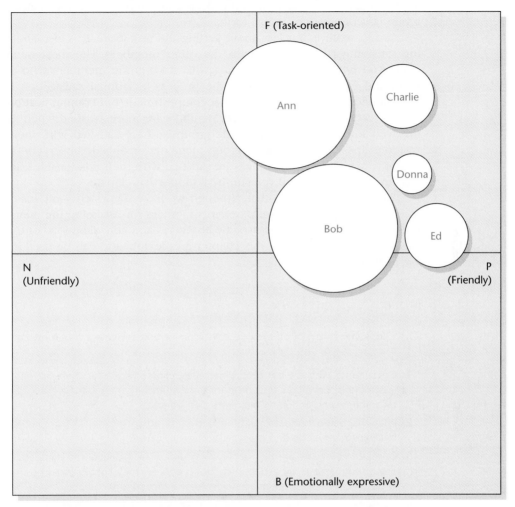

is moderately dominant, task-oriented, and friendly, is in the ideal position for a democratic, group-centered leader, but he's all by himself. Just by looking at the diagram you can tell that these people do not work well as a team. Members are dissimilar, they clash, there appears to be little cohesiveness, and there are wide variations in the degree of participation members exhibit.

The diagram in Figure 7.20 tells a different story. This group seems unified, with all members in the upper-right-hand quadrant (which Bales calls the *decision-making quadrant*). Members are sufficiently task-oriented to complete the group's assignment, but friendly enough toward each other that their interaction is probably harmonious. This is a picture of a productive and efficient group. As you can see, a SYMLOG analysis provides a "snapshot" of a group as a whole system whose component parts (the members) operate interdependently.

SYMLOG is a particularly helpful tool because it so clearly displays such aspects as the degree of cohesiveness, the degree and type of member participation, group task orientation, and so forth.

Group work is not just about getting the task done. It is also about forming satisfying relationships with the other members. The most memorable teams you will experience are those that have group members who do good work and enjoy one another in the process. Relational satisfaction has not been studied as extensively as task accomplishment, but communication scholars are recognizing its importance. Members are more satisfied when they feel involved, know they belong to the group, and are satisfied with their group relationships.[9] SYMLOG helps group members or outside observers "see" the extent to which group members are satisfied with their relationships, are cohesive and productive, and operate in a supportive climate.

We remind you again that, although we have suggested some instruments as particularly useful for self-assessment, others for assessing the members or the group, and others to be used by observers and consultants, all of the methods we have presented in this chapter are flexible and can be used in a variety of ways.

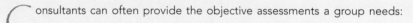

Recap: A Quick Review

Consultants can often provide the objective assessments a group needs:

1. Consultants, who are not group members, can serve the functions of reminding members of principles they have forgotten, teaching members procedures and techniques, and critiquing a group's performance.

2. Knowledgeable students can be effective consultants; their skills are enhanced through observation and practice.

3. Consultants must plan their observations in advance because it is impossible to pay attention to every aspect of a group equally; they should focus on the most important or most problematic aspects of a group's interaction.

4. Consultants must give feedback sensitively and cannot force a group to change; ultimately, the group decides whether and how to accept the consultant's feedback.

5. Consultants must treat members ethically, the way they would want to be treated; they can be guided by the procedures that universities have established for how to treat research participants.

6. Verbal interaction diagrams describe who talks to whom and how often.

7. Content analysis can be constructed to evaluate any type of content, including topic of discussion, types of questions, and style of managing conflict.

8. SYMLOG, which is both a theory and a methodology, can help members or consultants gain insight into how a group functions; it is especially useful for assessing the group's cohesiveness or lack of it.

QUESTIONS FOR REVIEW

 Go to self-quizzes on the Online Learning Center at mbhe.com/galanes12 to test your knowledge of the chapter concepts

The case study that opened this chapter concerned Sam, who had tried several ways to assess and improve his executive committee's performance, but who elected to bring in Susanna as an outside consultant.

1. Do you think Sam's choice to ask members to assess their own preference for procedural order was a good choice? Why do you think he selected that scale? Were there better choices for him?

2. Sam also asked his group to assess how meetings were going. Given what you know about this group, what would you have done if you were Sam?

3. What were the specific issues that Susanna identified as problems for this group?

4. What do you think a verbal interaction diagram, content analysis, and SYMLOG diagram might have shown regarding the executive committee?

5. What would you have advised the group to do to improve performance?

KEY TERMS

 Test your knowledge of these key terms by visiting the Online Learning Center Web site at mbhe.com/galanes12

Consultant
Content analysis
Critique

Postmeeting reaction forms
(PMRs)

SYMLOG
Verbal interaction analysis

BIBLIOGRAPHY

Bales, Robert F. *SYMLOG Case Study Kit.* New York: Free Press, 1980.

Schwarz, Roger M. *The Skilled Facilitator: Practical Wisdom for Developing Effective Groups.* San Francisco: Jossey-Bass, 1994.

Wheelan, Susan A. *Creating Effective Teams: A Guide for Members and Leaders.* Thousand Oaks, CA: Sage, 1999.

NOTES

1. Linda K. Larkey, "The Development and Validation of the Workforce Diversity Questionnaire: An Instrument to Assess Interactions in Diverse Work Groups," *Management Communication Quarterly* 9 (February 1996): 296–337.

2. Bobby R. Patton and Kim Giffin, *Problem-Solving Group Interaction* (New York: Harper & Row, 1973): 213–14.

3. Patricia M. Fandt, "The Relationship of Accountability and Interdependent Behavior to Enhancing Team Consequences," *Group & Organization Studies* 16 (1991): 300–12; Harold H. Greenbaum, Ira T. Kaplan, and William Metlay, "Evaluation of Problem-Solving Groups," *Group & Organization Studies* 13 (1988): 133–47.

4. Beatrice Schultz, Sandra M. Ketrow, and Daphne M. Urban, "Improving Decision Quality in the Small Group: The Role of the Reminder," *Small Group Research* 26 (November 1995): 521–41.

5. Greenbaum et al., "Evaluation of Problem-Solving Groups."

6. Ibid., 137–39, 145.

7. Robert F. Bales and Stephen P. Cohen, *SUMLOG:A System for the Multiple Level Observation of Groups* (New York: Free Press, 1979). Space constraints prevent including a complete description of SYMLOG theory and methodology here; we refer readers who are interested in learning to construct a complete SYMLOG diagram for their groups to the following workbook: R. F. Bales, *SYMLOG Case Study Kit* (New York: Free Press, 1980). The *Instructor's Manual* for this text includes instructions and necessary forms for completing a simplified SYMLOG-like diagram so that students can have a better idea of what SYMLOG does.

8. Lynne Kelly and Robert L. Duran note that, in some recent writings, Bales refers to the third dimension as acceptance versus nonacceptance of authority, a designation that seems more appropriate when assessing group member values as opposed to behaviors; in "SYMLOG: Theory and Measurement of Small Group Interaction," *Small Group Communication: A Reader,* 6th ed., eds. Robert S. Cathcart and Larry A. Samovar (Dubuque, IA: Wm. C. Brown, 1992): 220–33.

9. Carolyn M. Anderson, Matthew M. Martin, and Bruce L. Riddle, "Small Group Relational Satisfaction Scale: Development, Reliability, and Validity," *Communication Studies* 52 (Fall 2001): 220–33.

Small Group Throughput Processes

When individuals with diverse backgrounds, personalities, and perspectives begin to interact as members of a small group, they create the group's throughput processes. The two chapters in this section focus on several key throughput processes. Chapter 8 examines the roles of tension among members, group fantasy, member socialization, norms, and group climate in the creation of a group's culture. Chapter 9 focuses on group leadership, one of the most important small group throughput processes.

Communication and Group Culture: Tensions, Fantasy, Socialization, Norms, and Climate

CHAPTER 8

CENTRAL MESSAGE

When individuals collaborating on an interdependent goal begin to interact, their communication shapes them into a group with its own unique culture. This group culture is a function of how group members manage their social and task challenges, the group's fantasy life, status hierarchy, socialization patterns, emergent norms, and climate.

STUDY OBJECTIVES

As a result of studying Chapter 8 you should be able to:

1. Describe the structuration process whereby member communication creates and maintains the group.

2. Describe primary and secondary tension and explain how members' management of their task and social concerns gives rise to the major phases through which most groups pass.

3. Describe how a status hierarchy develops in a group and explain the implications that such a hierarchy has on group dynamics.

4. Describe how fantasy chains contribute symbolically to the formation of a small group's culture.

5. Define group socialization and describe the phases of socialization.

6. Explain how group rules and norms develop; be able to recognize, state, and describe their effect on the group.

7. Explain cohesiveness and describe nine techniques for enhancing it in a small group.

8. Differentiate supportive from defensive communication behaviors and explain how they contribute to a group's climate.

9. Describe teambuilding and illustrate how it can be used to increase group cohesiveness, including cohesiveness in virtual teams.

Six medical school faculty members, three psychiatrists with M.D.s, a psychologist, and two social workers, were selected by their deans to develop an instructional program to teach new methods for identifying psychological disorders.[1] All six members were outstanding teachers and competent in their respective areas. They were given the freedom to develop any program they wished as long as it could be funded by outside grants.

During their first meeting, the members decided to base all group decisions on sound reasoning. Julian was selected leader, perhaps because of his "take charge" nature. The members insisted that he was expected to encourage input by all members and equalize member influence. Julian made strong efforts to meet their expectations because he strongly believed that their best decisions would be those based on input from all members. He even went so far as to consult books on small group communication for ideas about how best to equalize participation and influence.

However, the group ran into problems over time. First, group members, strongly entrenched in the medical culture, afforded the M.D.s greater clout. As a result, those without medical degrees found that their comments lacked influence. They talked less and less, did not push for their ideas, and after meetings would complain to each other. Second, the group was under pressure to continue to seek funding or their project would end. This pressure led to Julian's increased influence because his contacts enabled him to secure funds for two years.

Soon the group formed into a small clique with Julian as its aggressive leader. He talked more than any other member. When he rephrased others' remarks, he did so in a way that mirrored his own ideas. The non-M.D.s came to rely on his interpretations and lost influence in the group. Conflicts were not dealt with in a constructive manner and meetings were tense. Despite all their best intentions, Julian found himself the leader of an autocratic clique. How did this group's initial democratic spirit get away from the members? We will look for answers in this chapter and the one that follows.

Our central theme has been identifying small group verbal and nonverbal communication as the most important throughput variable of small group dynamics. In this chapter, we describe how communication is the factor that enables a group to emerge from a collection of individuals. The system perspective continues to serve as our framework. Small group social systems are created in *and* through the communicative behavior of group members to produce output variables such as status hierarchies, norms, and climates. Likewise, small groups can change themselves by revising their interaction and, as we saw with our medical group, can go astray from their original intentions. Note that these group characteristics can be discussed as *both* throughput and output variables because the development of group processes (throughput) is also one of the accomplishments (outputs) of small group interaction. The "pecking order" of the medical group emerged out of their interaction (as output) and simultaneously served to guide and give sense to their discussion (as throughput). Rather than focus on individual characteristics, as we did in Chapter 7, we turn to the effect of member behavior on the group as a whole.

The Interplay between Communication and Group Culture

We discussed *culture* in Chapter 5 as a group of individuals that can be identified by its shared patterns of values, beliefs, symbols, language, rules, and so forth. We discussed different ethnicities, international groupings, and race, gender, class, and age as culture. In this chapter we see that small groups themselves develop unique cultures, just as societies and other larger groupings do. When we talk about culture and small groups, we mean three things: Members bring their own cultural experiences into the group as input variables, each group develops its own unique small group culture (output), and the members' communicative processes create and maintain the group's culture (throughput and output).

Group culture is the pattern of values, beliefs, norms, and behaviors that are shared by group members and that shape a group's individual "personality". Many factors weave together to create a group's culture, including the content and pattern of interactions, the roles members enact and their interrelationships, and the norms and rules guiding the group's interactions. Each group has a unique mix of members, purposes, rules, and behaviors that cannot be duplicated exactly in other groups. For instance, some groups behave informally, with lots of joking and low power distance. Other groups display hostility, aggressive verbal behavior, and divisive conflict. Still others adhere to strict, formal interaction rules with polite, controlled communication. How do these differences come about? We examine some of the processes most important to the development of a group's culture in this chapter.

> **Group Culture**
> The pattern of values, beliefs, and norms shared by group members, developed through interaction and incorporating members' shared experiences in the group, patterns of interaction, and status relationships.

Structuration Theory and Group Culture

A group's culture is always dynamic, never static. As a system, a group continually evolves by adapting to its changing circumstances and environment. Communication among members is the means by which members create and sustain their group culture. Anthony Giddens's structuration theory and its application to small group dynamics by Marshal Poole and his associates helps us understand the central role communication plays in the emergence of group culture. Where does a group's culture come from and how is it sustained? **Structuration** is the idea that any social system's rules, operating procedures, and resources emerge out of the verbal and nonverbal communication between members. Their subsequent use of those rules and resources sustains the system and give the appearance of stability. However, members may change the rules and resources or use them differently, thereby changing the nature of the social system.

> **Structuration**
> The concept that a group creates and continuously recreates itself through members' communicative behaviors; the group's communication both establishes and limits how the group develops.

Structuration theory was applied to the dynamics of the small group in 1980.[2] Individuals form a small group by exchanging verbal and nonverbal messages that ultimately establish the norms and rules shaping members' behaviors; the group's structure is composed of rules and resources. *Rules* are guidelines for how actions are to be done. In our opening case, we see the rule that all decisions will be based on sound reasoning. *Resources* are those aspects (e.g., materials and possessions) of a group that are used by members to control the behavior of other members. In our opening case, one resource is the higher status afforded the M.D.s. Rules and resources are used by group members to interact with each other, and they help them interpret member actions.

The theory of structuration embraces three important assumptions.[3] First, the behavior of group members is constrained by such things as the general rules of the society in which they live, the structures of the particular group in which they find themselves, and the behavior of the other members. For example, the rules of corporate America frown on executives' settling their differences with a fistfight. Members of a group that has developed a formal, polite atmosphere would be embarrassed by a member who slaps another on the back and says, "Hey, babe, how's your sex life?" The other members would disapprove of the offending member's behavior and, if the behavior continued, might try to remove that person from the group. The medical group in our opening story was constrained by the presence of the M.D.s and the need to secure external funding.

The second important assumption is that people can choose whether or not to follow the rules of the group. Although there may be unpleasant consequences for a member who doesn't follow a group's rules, there is no *law,* like the law of gravity, that forces conformity. In our medical group, despite all attempts by Julian and members' original wishes, a majority of them did not follow the "spirit" of democracy.

The third important assumption of structuration is that group creation is a process; the group creates itself initially and also continuously *re-creates* itself, changing in incremental ways, always in a state of *becoming,* with communication as the instrument for this creation and constant re-creation. This incrementalism is often the reason groups like our medical group can find themselves "off track" long after the initial changes start happening; the patterns sneak up on you and become entrenched.

Structuration theory places our focus on how group members' behaviors are always in the process of structuring their groups. If the group dynamics remain the same, it is because members are continuously using the same rules and resources, and if the dynamics change it means the members have acted in a way to change the structure.

The theory of structuration is quite complex. However, the main point remains: The *communication among members* is what creates group rules in the first place; and once rules and structures are in place, communication is what keeps them there, or changes them, as the case may be. Suppose a company appoints a group of several managers to develop long-range strategy. Two members, Mauricio and Cary, have worked together before and naturally call each other by first names. Mauricio introduces Cary to Carol, an acquaintance of hers, by his first name, and pretty soon the rest of the group members are calling each other by first name instead of Mr., Ms., or Dr. As they wait for the meeting to begin, members talk about mutual interests such as sports and jazz music, and several find common outside interests with other members. Norms of informality and friendliness have begun to develop among these members, and these norms will begin to affect other aspects of the communication among members, such as how they deal with disagreement. For instance, assume that, at a later group meeting, Cary says, in a formal and accusing tone of voice, "I respectfully disagree with the proposal offered by my esteemed colleague Ms. Hernandez," and continues to make a formal speech relating his objections. The rest of the members will probably say something like: "When did we get so formal, Cary? What's the big deal here? Why are you sounding like a prosecutor?" What they are saying, in another way, is: "We've developed norms of informality and friendliness, which you are violating. Your behavior seems inappropriate to us." Of course, Cary can choose to continue in his formal, prosecutorial way; but if he does, that may either change the informality and friendliness norms to ones more formal and adversarial, or it may cause the other members to ignore Cary and ostracize him from the group.

A variety of internal and external factors influences the types of structures groups create, including member characteristics and preferences, the nature of the group's task, and such structural dynamics as the interplay between important (but perhaps conflicting) values. The members of the medical group valued democratic principles, but the pressure to get the job done and the deference given to a medical degree led members to encourage controlling leadership.[4] This contradiction produced tension within the group and an eventual split. Sunwolf and Seibold found several conflicting values in their study of jury decision making resulting from numerous contradictions between internal and external factors.[5] For instance, although the jury was told to use judicial resources should any confusion occur, the jury developed the norm that no jury member could send a note outside the group asking for help before first securing permission from the group. In addition, several members of the jury struggled with reporting inappropriate behavior to the court. The expectations that the law should be followed clashed with the social rule of not telling on your friends. Sunwolf and Seibold concluded: "One of the inherent contradictions of group life in jury deliberations occurs in situations in which the attempt to obey the directive to maintain their group's existence simultaneously requires them to collaborate in a reluctant cover-up of member misconduct."[6] These examples also illustrate the point we made in Chapter 4 regarding the fluid nature of boundaries between groups and their multiple environments. Often these boundaries are constructed in group interaction while simultaneously serving to connect the group to *and* separate it from its environment.

Adaptive
Structuration Theory

A version of structuration theory that focuses on how the rules and resources of computer technology are used in the structuration process.

Structuration processes can also be found in a group's use of computer technology, which further confirms the central role of communication in creating and maintaining group culture.[7] **Adaptive structuration theory** is a particular version of structuration theory introduced by Poole and DeSanctis to show how the structures (i.e., the rules and resources) of computer technology get used during small group decision making.[8] GDSSs are computer-based hardware and software systems designed to improve the quality and speed of group problem solving, especially idea generation, information organization, evaluation of options, and decision making. For example, several GDSSs help groups brainstorm.

Poole and DeSanctis look at which rules and features of GDSSs are actually used by the group, how they are used, and how such use influences group outcomes.[9] They conclude that the technology itself becomes an integral part of producing and reproducing the group system. A GDSS has two important characteristics: its spirit, or intention, and the features built into the technology. The spirit refers to the goals the technology is designed to achieve. The features are the rules of how the GDSS is supposed to be used. Both elements work together. A particular GDSS's rules may promote or detract from its spirit, or intent, depending on how the group members actually adapt the GDSS. For instance, a particular GDSS may intend to generate discussion by all group members. Its rules are designed to support this goal because the facilitator is supposed to paraphrase each remark before a new one is entered on the computer screen. However, a particular group may decide to skip this step, thus violating the rule for how the GDSS is supposed to be used. This may undermine the GDSS's spirit. Poole and DeSanctis hypothesized that if groups use the GDSS faithfully, following both the rules and the spirit, if members are comfortable with the GDSS, and if they agree about how the GDSS should be used, then the group will produce more predictable outcomes than groups that act contrary to the spirit of the GDSS, are not comfortable with it, and do not agree about how it is to be used. Research has found that the more restrictive the design of a particular GDSS, the less the group tries to control the GDSS and the more the group tries to work *with* it. In addition, using the GDSS the way it was designed to be used produces greater group consensus than adapting it contrary to its intent. We will further discuss GDSS use in group decision making in Chapter 11.

We agree with Poole that structuration captures the complexity of human behavior by recognizing that, although human beings are free agents, certain limitations and constraints keep their behaviors in small group systems within certain boundaries while recognizing that change is possible.[10] Yet at the same time it offers a "way out" for members with little power who, by enacting changes in behavior over time, can change the group's structure. It also explains why unintended consequences can occur in group interaction. The communicative focus of structuration theory reminds us to look at the *communicative behavior* of members to learn about a group.

Recap: A Quick Review

Communication and emergent group culture are inseparable processes, each influencing the other. The secrets of group life are found in the group's communication among its members.

1. Groups actively create and maintain their own group culture through a process called structuration. Group members use rules and tangible resources to create their own cultures and in so doing create a unique group identity (structure) that is sustained and changed through their communication.

2. Group culture is dynamic and always unfinished, acting simultaneously as a throughput and output variable of the group system. Although difficult, group members can choose to change their dynamics by changing their patterns of interaction to produce a new set of constraints.

3. Adaptive structuration theory, applied to how secondary small groups use computer technology, cautions group members to follow the rules faithfully if they want the technology to be implemented effectively without damaging their problem-solving dynamics.

Negotiating Task and Social Dimensions of Group Culture

Somehow, what starts as a collection of individuals with various, often conflicting, goals must become a group that functions as a whole with an interdependent purpose. A group's culture emerges from the communicative dynamics of the members. Group members must manage tensions and negotiate status among themselves. As the members handle their multiple challenges of getting the job done and managing relationships with one another, their communication begins to assume identifiable patterns.

A number of researchers have studied how groups develop and change over time; they have found that the emergence of group culture progresses through identifiable phases. This is an evolutionary process that happens gradually, without clear demarcations to separate phases.[11] However, predictable phases of group development can be identified by the types of interactions that occur. Bales was one of the first to investigate a group's progression through these predictable phases.[12] He identified two concerns that group members face and must manage effectively if they are to fulfill their mission successfully: *socioemotional* and *task* concerns. First, members must develop the kinds of interpersonal relationships that provide stability and harmony, allowing the group to function cooperatively. Second, they must attend to the group's job. Bales noted that groups tend to cycle between these concerns, initially focusing on socioemotional issues and then moving to task concerns; however, they eventually move back and forth between socioemotional and task concerns as they work to finish their charge.

Primary Tension

Tension and discomfort in members that stems from interpersonal (i.e., primary) sources, including the social unease that occurs when members of a new group first meet or during competition for power among members.

Secondary Tension

Work-related tension found in the differences of opinion among members as they seek to accomplish their task.

Primary and Secondary Tension   Early in the group's *formation phase,* the socioemotional dimension predominates as members attempt to negotiate the kinds of relationships they will have with each other. **Primary tension** results from the interpersonal relationships among members and is described by Bormann as being "the social unease and stiffness that accompanies getting acquainted."[13] Primary tension is displayed in behaviors such as extreme politeness, apparent boredom, yawning and sighing, frequent long pauses, and tentative statements uttered in soft tones. Members are asking themselves, "Will they like me? Will this be a group I enjoy working with?" The politeness and apparent boredom are only a façade intended to cover the tensions we all feel when we are with people we don't know well. If these tensions are not managed effectively, groups will structure themselves into patterns of over-politeness, formality, and hesitancy to disagree, which can impair their ability to think critically when they attend to their task.

What kinds of actions can group members take to manage their primary tension effectively? Several choices can help them reduce their primary tension. Members can take time to get acquainted with each other. They can talk about themselves, their backgrounds, interests, hobbies, and experiences relevant to the group's purpose, feelings about being groups, and so on. Actively sharing information about each other is a characteristic of cohesive groups.[14] It may benefit the group to have a social hour or party, with no formal agenda. Joking, laughing together, and finding common interests can help diminish primary tensions. Even if time together seems at a premium, groups can spend a few minutes introducing themselves. Even groups whose members have worked together over the course of many meetings typically spend a few minutes early in a meeting chitchatting and confirming their relationships before getting down to work.

In the *production phase* of a group's life cycle, when the group has reached socioemotional maturity, task- or job-related behaviors emerge to present a different set of challenges: the management of secondary tensions. **Secondary tension** is work-related tension found in the differences of opinion among members as they seek to accomplish their task. It is inevitable, because members perceive problems differently and disagree about goals, the means for achieving them, and the criteria they use to evaluate ideas. These tensions are the direct result of the need to make decisions *as a group.*

Secondary tension looks and sounds different from primary tension. Voices become loud and strained. There may be long pauses followed by two or more members' talking at once. Members twist and fidget in their seats, bang fists on the table, wave their arms, interrupt each other, move away from each other, and may even leave the room. They may try to shout each other down, call each other names, or aggressively question each other's intelligence or motives. Some may be very vocal while others may sit stiffly and awkwardly, not knowing what to do.

One of the biggest challenges for a small group is to create and reinforce a culture that manages secondary tension effectively. Too often, group members ignore secondary tension because dealing with it can be uncomfortable, even painful. The medical group at the beginning of the chapter began with a desire to use sound reasoning in its discussions, but members did not act to create a culture of sound reasoning. Instead, they allowed certain members more status than others and, over time, reinforced patterns of antagonism that divided them. Had they made a different set of choices, they could have redirected the quality of their group culture.

Managing secondary tension effectively can lead to several advantages for the group. First, attempts to duck the tension-producing issue don't work. Bormann points out, "The problem . . . if ignored or dodged will continue to . . . impede progress. Facing up to secondary tensions realistically is the best way to release them."[15] Second, groups that find integrative versus divisive ways to manage their secondary tension experience greater cohesiveness. Members teach each other, through their interactions, that they can disagree with each other yet still experience a sense of trust and commitment. In contrast, the medical group members taught each other that it was OK to be told what to do and that talking behind one another's back was acceptable; this fostered distrust between members. Finally, group members can learn to welcome the tensions because they force members to look more carefully at task-related issues, which can ultimately help them develop a better final outcome.

Secondary tensions are inevitable; the key to whether they help or hurt a group depends on how they are managed by the group. Bales discovered three categories of behaviors typically reduced secondary tension among members: agreeing, showing solidarity, and tension release.[16] Showing agreement is socially rewarding to the person agreed with, as if to say, "I value you and your opinion." Solidarity is shown by indicating commitment to the group. Using *we* to refer to the group, speaking well of members, offering to help, expressing confidence in the group, and talking about the importance of the group and its task are all ways to show solidarity and move members away from an "us versus them" attitude. Humor can help to release tension, so long as the humor does not ridicule another member or is used to ignore the disagreement. In *Pattern for Industrial Peace,* Whyte described how a union staff representative did this by using fishing photos whenever the discussion between the representatives of the steel company and union got overheated with secondary tension.[17]

These socioemotional and task concerns reflected in primary and secondary tension are interrelated. That is, the choices that members make as they negotiate these issues affect both dimensions at the same time. At the very first meeting, a group must begin the process of forming into a functioning group culture by establishing the interpersonal relationships, leadership and role structures, norms, status hierarchy, and climate that enable it to work effectively. The group must concurrently deal with its task: what its charge is, how the task should be approached, who is to do what, and so forth. Although interpersonal concerns may dominate the group's early focus, task concerns are still present and are affected by how the group sets its interpersonal tone. As a group matures socioemotionally, more and more time can be devoted to its task; how members work together can affect their interpersonal relationships. At no time is either issue—task or relationship—absent from the group or unaffected by choices made in the other dimension. This interplay between socioemotional and task concerns can be observed in the way status hierarchies help structure how members relate to each other and also how the work gets done.

Status Hierarchy   The six members of our medical group were recognized experts in their fields of study—their individual competence was unquestioned. Over time, the way they chose to interact *with* each created a culture in which certain members were treated with more value than others. The status hierarchy that emerged did not, in the long run, serve them well.

Status refers to the relative importance, prestige, and power of a member in a small group. You saw in Chapter 6 that, as roles emerge, each person is placed in a sort of pecking order, like the one you saw emerge in the medical group. Several advantages accrue to members of high status. High status is socially rewarding, so such members feel important and worthwhile. Other group members defer to them, grant them a disproportionate share of the group's attention, agree with their proposals, and seek their advice and opinions. People occupying formal, high-status roles (e.g., manager or CEO) may be given such tangible signs of status as large offices, private secretaries, and powers not granted to other members.

Effects of status are numerous. High-status members talk more than low-status members and address each other more often than do low-status members, who address their remarks more often to high-status members than to each other.[18] Low-status members also send more positive messages to high-status members than to other low-status members.[19] Low-status members are interrupted more, and their comments are ignored more often than the comments of those with higher status. High-status members tend to talk more to the group as a whole, whereas low-status members express most of their comments to individuals.

In addition to being granted a number of psychological or material rewards, high-status members are expected to meet certain responsibilities within the group. They are expected to work especially hard to accomplish the group's goals, and to uphold the group's norms. They may lose status by failing to fulfill the group's expectations, although they may be given additional leeway to bend the rules, called **idiosyncracy credit,** that other members do not receive.[20] This means that, for members who have made an exceptionally valuable contribution to the group, certain rules can be bent. Recent research confirms this view. Estrada et al. found a high correlation between idiosyncracy credit and leadership—the group members to whom others were willing to award idiosyncracy credit also were perceived as leaders.[21] When this was the case, the group's performance was enhanced. However, they also found some low-performing groups in which idiosyncracy

---

Status

The position of a member in the hierarchy of power, influence, and prestige within a small group.

Idiosyncracy Credit

Additional leeway in adhering to group norms, given to a member for valuable contributions to the group.

credit was not related to group leadership. Estrada et al. speculate that in such groups the members' attention is diverted from the task.

Status within a small group may be *ascribed* or it may be *earned*. At first, before members know each other well and are sure what their respective contributions will be to the group, status is **ascribed** on the basis of each member's position outside the small group. It is based on such things as wealth, education, occupation, personal fame, or position in the group's parent organization. For example, a committee composed of a company CEO, the vice president of manufacturing, a senior accountant, two employees from the marketing division, and a college student intern in marketing will initially have that order of ascribed status. However, status can also be **earned** or achieved on the basis of a member's individual contributions to the group. The intern who conducts considerable research on behalf of the group and is a key contributor will have higher earned status than the senior accountant who completes no assignments. In some instances, the importance of variables that contribute to ascribed status, such as sex, appears to be shifting, as we noted in Chapter 5.

One of the supposed benefits of computer-mediated communication (CMC) in a group is that status differences are minimized because in many CMC groups, members remain anonymous; thus status cues aren't visible. However, Scott's recent review of communication technology and its effects questions this assumption.[22] For one thing, anonymity is largely irrelevant in organizational groups—members are identified and know with whom they work. Influence from the face-to-face context carries over to the CMC context. True anonymity, however, can minimize ascribed status social cues. Flanagin et al. found that men in CMC situations tried to make the CMC interaction more like a face-to-face (FTF) interaction, but women in CMC situations tried to preserve reduced social cues of CMC interaction. These authors speculate that reducing the status-lowering social cues gives women greater influence in the group, whereas maintaining the status cues of FTF interaction enhances the influence of men.[23]

Ideally, a group's relationships and relative status differences are somewhat flexible so that different members can become more influential as their particular knowledge and skills are pertinent to the issues or problems facing the group at any point in time. Wood found that paying undue attention to ascribed status differences negatively affected a group's ability to accomplish its task.[24] It is important to note that lower status does not mean *of little value*. Lower-status members are not necessarily unhappy in the group; cohesive groups value the contributions of each member, and each member knows it. Only when members say things such as "We could have done just as well without Morgan and Jolene on this committee," can we infer that lower status definitely means "inferior." More typically, everyone in the group might follow the lead of a normally quiet, low-status person who seems to have just the information or ability the group most needs at a given moment. That person might later slip back into a more usual low-profile position, but the contribution will have been noted and appreciated.

Ascribed Status

Status due to characteristics external to the group, such as wealth, level of education, position, physical attractiveness, and so forth.

Earned Status

Status earned by a member's valued contributions to the group, such as working hard for the group, providing needed expertise, being especially communicatively competent, and so forth.

Recent research by Bonito suggests that members take into account both external status characteristics and member behaviors in the group when they make judgments about the value of their own and others' participation in a group.[25] External status characteristics—age, gender, appearance—contribute to expectations about how and how much someone will participate in a group. Although status differences have been found to be related to differential rates of participation, they are not reliable predictors. Members' behavior in the group and contribution to the task also influence others' perceptions of their participation. People differ with regard to which factors they pay more attention to. In any case, rigid status hierarchies based on external status characteristics can diminish the participation of all members.

Fantasy Themes

A continuing theme of ours is that group cultures are produced by the interaction among group members. We have discussed primary and secondary tension challenges, emergent status hierarchies, and their impact on group culture. We turn now to one of the most powerful ways in which group culture is created: through *fantasy*. Technically, **fantasy** refers to "the creative and imaginative shared interpretation of events that fulfill members' psychological or rhetorical need to make sense of their experience and to anticipate their future."[26] Fantasy, in this sense, does not mean fictitious or unreal. It means that during certain periods of the group's interaction, rather than discussing events happening in the here and now of the group, the members are telling stories, relating past events, and sharing anecdotes that have a bearing *at the unconscious level* on the group's process. In other words, group members rarely set out consciously to establish the group's culture. Instead, they just talk. Some of that talk appears to be tangential to the group's real task, but in fact it meets psychological and rhetorical needs of the members.

When a group member says something not directly related to the present task of the group, that member has introduced a fantasy. This happens often during a discussion, with many fantasies going no further. However, sometimes group members pick up on the fantasy introduced by one group member and elaborate on it. Several members join the fantasy by adding their pieces to the story, in a kind of group storytelling. A fantasy that members elaborate on is called a **fantasy chain,** first described by Bales.[27] During a fantasy chain the speed of the interaction typically picks up, voices become louder, and a sense of excitement can be detected. The mood is electric. A fantasy chain may last from as little as half a minute to as much as half an hour. Eventually the chain peters out, often when one member pulls the group back on task. Fantasy chaining is a way members create shared images of the group and its environment. In Chapter 2 we noted that communication is transactional; during fantasy chaining, group members transact, without preplanned intent, to create meaning for the group. This storytelling activity plays a crucial role in structuration of a group's culture.[28]

Fantasy

A statement not pertaining to the here-and-now of the group that offers a creative and meaningful interpretation of events and meets a group's psychological or rhetorical need.

Fantasy Chain

A series of statements by several or all group members in which a story is dramatized to help create a group's view of reality.

Fantasy chains develop in a fairly predictable way.[29] First, some form of ambiguity or uncertainty exists in the group. One member begins the fantasy by introducing a core image that somehow relates to the uncertainty. Other members spread that core image by adding their own elements to the fantasy, creating a group metaphor, rather than just an individual one. Finally, when the fantasy chain has ended, the group members have converged on a particular picture of the group's reality.

Fantasies are *about* something; the content of the fantasy is called the **fantasy theme.** There is an obvious or *manifest* theme to the fantasy chain, and a *latent,* or below-the-surface theme that, when examined, reveals the culture, values, and norms of the group. Often, fantasies have heroes and villains, plot lines, and a well-developed ethical structure that gives moral or psychological guidance to a group. To interpret the latent meaning of a fantasy, Bales suggests looking for a sudden insight rather than trying to analyze the fantasy systematically.

Fantasy is rooted in the theory of **symbolic convergence,** which was articulated and developed by Bormann. Symbolic convergence theory acknowledges that humans are storytelling creatures who create and share meaning through talk.[30] *Convergence* refers to the fact that during interaction the private symbolic worlds of individuals often overlap, or converge. When that occurs, as it must to some extent in a group or there would be no group, meaning is shared; the symbolic, personal communication of two or more individuals constructs a shared reality that bonds the individuals, helps them discover how they feel about certain events, reveals shared values, and guides them to action. In other words, symbolic convergence theory "accounts for the creation and maintenance of a group consciousness through shared motives, common emotional activity, and consensual meanings for events."[31] We will now turn from this fairly abstract discussion to several specific examples of how fantasy helps shape a group's reality.

In the short and simple fantasy chain below, members of a student group are planning publicity for their annual Career Day seminar.[32] Chris asks Kevin what the previous year's group did for publicity:

Fantasy Theme

What the actual content of a fantasy or fantasy chain is about.

Symbolic Convergence

The theory that humans create and share meaning through talk and storytelling, producing an overlapping (convergence) of private symbolic worlds of individuals during interaction.

Discussion

Chris: Kevin, do you know what they did last time?

Kevin: Yeah, somewhere I've got a list here. All they really did was put an ad in the school paper and then sent around this tacky memo to the faculty about a week ahead of time asking them to announce it in classes. It was embarrassing!

Commentary

Chris asks a direct, task-relevant question.

Kevin answers Chris, but introduces the fantasy about the "embarrassing" performance of last year's group.

Deirdre: I can't believe that's all they did!	Deirdre, animated, picks up on Kevin's criticism of the previous group.
Lori: It was John's fault—he didn't want to do *anything,* and the group didn't do anything!	Lori adds her part.
Tony: What a bunch of lazy wimps!	Tony contributes.
Chris: We've already done more than they ever did, and we've just gotten started.	Chris contributes, and adds the idea that *this* group has already done better than the last one.
Kevin: I know! We're going to look a lot better than they did!	Kevin adds to Chris's idea.
Lori: Okay, I like trashing those guys as much as you do, but we're really getting off track.	Lori stops the fantasy by getting the group back on track.

In this segment, the group starts out addressing its task directly, but quickly gets off task as members enjoy trashing the previous year's group. Kevin introduces the fantasy, with all group members participating in the fantasy chain until Lori, the group's designated leader, stops the chain and returns the group to its task.

What function has this fantasy served? The manifest theme of the fantasy is "Last year's group did a rotten job of publicity." Remember, though, that fantasies help create shared meanings for the *present* group. In this sequence, trashing the previous group builds up the performance of the present group by comparison, as hinted at in Chris's comment, "We've already done more than they ever did." By saying what a lousy group the previous year's group was, this group is not so subtly saying, "We're so much better." The group is setting standards of excellence, establishing norms of professionalism missing in the previous group that motivate the members to do better.

Fantasies perform several functions for small groups. **First, they help the members create the group's unique identity.**[33] The student group helped define itself as an excellent, hard-working, professional team by comparing itself favorably with the previous group.

Second, fantasies help a group deal with threatening or difficult information that members might feel reluctant to address directly. To illustrate, Morocco related the story of the first meeting of a research group whose student members believed their leaders were not providing them with enough direction.[34] One student recalled seeing a film about an experiment in which baby monkeys were deprived of maternal nurturing. The other members, who had seen the movie in school, began to contribute by adding details and developing a plot and dramatic images associated with the movie. The social and sexual development of the monkeys in the movie had been impaired by the lack of parental care, and this image served to symbolize the reality that these group members were *currently* experiencing. In essence, the group said, "The lack of attention and help on the part of the leaders will ultimately harm us."

Third, fantasies help direct a group's actions by subtly endorsing or condemning particular courses of action. For example, Putnam and her associates describe a contract bargaining situation between two committees, one of teachers and the other of administrators.[35] The administrators constructed a fantasy chain about one of the teachers, whose constant head nodding reminded them of a woodpecker or a toy bird bobbing up and down on a cup. Their fantasy theme created a shared image of the teachers as well meaning but inexperienced. Later during the bargaining situation, the teachers appeared to renege on a proposal they had earlier accepted. The administrators could have made a big deal of this by escalating the conflict, but the image of the teachers as inexperienced rather than unscrupulous led them to perceive the teachers' actions as an innocent mistake. This benevolent interpretation by the administrators gave the teachers latitude to err without derailing the bargaining process. The effect was to maintain good feelings all around. The fantasy, in part, inspired this outcome by molding the administrators' perceptions of the teachers' shortcomings.

Finally, fantasies can be entertaining and fun for the group. In the previous example, the administrators' committee kept itself happily entertained by imagining the teacher who nodded constantly as a woodpecker and a whirligig bird. Fantasies help groups exercise their imaginations and creativity. They are powerful shapers of a group's culture and show concretely the interplay between communication and group culture.

Recap: A Quick Review

Secondary group dynamics are not just about a group's task. Small groups are composed of human beings; thus, the negotiation of interpersonal relationships is just as important to group dynamics as managing the task.

1. Primary and secondary tensions between group members are to be expected when groups come together for the first time and begin to work on the task. The choices that group members make when facing these tensions affect their success in the long run.

2. Group member interactions around task and social challenges eventually produce a pattern of power relationships that guide, reinforce, and modify the status of each member relative to each other. Uncritical acceptance of the ascribed status of members can harm the group's culture.

3. When groups face the challenges of negotiating task and socioemotional concern, they often engage in creative, often playful fantasizing in the face of uncertainty. These "digressions" are woven together by all group members; this results in a collective new version of their group identity, which in turn redirects how members act toward each other and their task.

The significant role that communication between group members plays in the emergence of a group's culture cannot be overstated. We have used structuration theory to explain this dynamic between communication and culture; we have also discussed how structuration processes operating in task and socioemotional challenges as members manage tensions, jockeying for status, and group fantasies. In these discussions, we implied that the group maintained a consistent membership. But what happens to these dynamics when new members enter the group? How do individuals and groups socialize new members and become changed themselves in the process?

Group Socialization of Members

When we hear the word *socialization,* we generally think about someone who is learning to become part of a group or even society at large. Just as children are socialized into families and society, people are socialized into newly formed and established groups. Typically, socialization processes have been studied in organizational research focusing on how the organization molds the newcomer to its culture.[36] Recent research in communication has begun to take seriously not only the socialization process in small groups but it also recognizes the active role the new member plays in affecting the existing small group culture.

Group Socialization

The social influence and change process during which both newcomers and established members adjust to one another.

Carolyn Anderson, Bruce Riddle, and Matthew Martin define **group socialization** as a reciprocal process of social influence and change in which both newcomers and/or established members and the group adjust to one another. It is the process using verbal and nonverbal communication to create and re-create a group's unique culture and group structures, engage in relevant processes and activities, and pursue individual and group goals.[37] This definition supports our belief in the central role of communication in all group processes, including the socialization of members.[38] This definition is lengthy, so let's take it apart and apply it to an example. Consider what happened to the following theater group. Actors had been practicing for weeks, but one week before opening night, leading man Richard was told he needed emergency surgery—immediately! The cast was devastated. Of course, cast members were worried about Richard, but they also were concerned about losing six weeks of rehearsals, during which the troupe had developed into a cohesive group. The director thought about canceling the show, but she asked an experienced actor friend of hers to assume Richard's role. Opening night was delayed a week to give Ted time to learn the lines and the troupe time to integrate a new member.

First, the adapting and adjusting that happen when a new group forms or when a new member enters a group occur through group member communication. Periods of adjustment are often filled with uncertainty, and group members typically communicate with each other in an effort to reduce the anxiety brought on by the uncertainty. You can see this when group members talk to each other about how to make decisions, how to handle conflict and how to behave and discuss what their roles will be when a new member joins a group.[39] If the community theater members do not talk to each other about the new cast member, welcome him into the troupe, and see his presence as a way to move in new directions, then his willingness to replace Richard will be wasted.

Second, members' definition highlights the fact that effective socialization requires a balance between individual member and group goals and satisfaction.[40] The new cast member, the director, and the rest of the troupe must have similar goals and levels of comfort if his replacing Richard is to be a positive experience.

Third, their definition emphasizes that socialization is an ongoing process involving not only the new member, but also the rest of the group. As a member of the troupe what might you do to help Ted? If you were the director, what might you do to help Ted and the cast negotiate a new formation phase so that they can focus on the play? If you were Ted, what could you do to help others feel comfortable with you? Understanding the phases of group socialization can help you further consider what this troupe can do to negotiate Ted's entrance into the cast effectively.

Phases of Group Socialization

Anderson and colleagues describe five phases of group socialization: antecedent, anticipatory, encounter, assimilation, and exit.[41] Each phase has unique communication needs. As you study the phases, remember the following things: This model assumes that group members are typically also members of other groups and that socialization involves both newly forming groups and established groups dealing with new members. It also assumes that groups may move through these phases at different speeds and may revisit one or more of these phases as they accept or reject new members, and finally that behaviors in one phase have a ripple effect through the other phases.

In the **antecedent phase,** group inputs, including individual characteristics, listening styles, and cultural differences, affect a group's throughput and output variables. All members, including Ted in our previous example, bring to a group their own attitudes, motives, and communication traits, which profoundly influence how ready and able they are to be socialized into a group and to engage in group work and relationship building. For instance, consider *grouphate,* described in Chapter 6.[42] Many of the ideas and attitudes people bring to new or existing groups are based on previous experiences in groups. In our classes, we repeatedly hear students verbalize their dislike for anything resembling group work because of horrific experiences in the past. If you feel this way, you may be pessimistic about joining a group and accepting a new member.

Another antecedent factor that affects group socialization is motives for communicating in groups. Recall our discussion of listening styles. Some of us listen in order to sustain the relationships in the group and others to make

Antecedent Phase

Prior to group socialization, the phase in which group members' individual characteristics affect their readiness and willingness to socialize members effectively.

sure the work gets done. Others focus their listening on meeting a time schedule and others on only information from trusted sources. These listening preferences, linked to our motives for communicating, influence the effective socialization of members. For instance, those members who communicate in order to build relationships rather than control others or distance themselves from others report more satisfaction with the group. Those who communicate in order to accomplish the work talk more in the group. Members highly motivated for both reasons are likely to be more willing to engage the socialization process.[43]

Communication apprehension and verbal aggressiveness are two other antecedent factors influencing group socialization. Group members who are not comfortable talking in groups (communication apprehension) would make it hard to participate actively in socialization. Remember that if socialization in groups is to be effective, members have to communicate with each other to reduce the uncertainty inherent in the socialization experience. On the other hand, verbally aggressive group members may be quite comfortable talking but attack others when they express disagreement. This communication alienates others and does not promote positive socialization experiences.[44]

Anticipatory Phase

During group socialization, the phase in which members' expectations of each other and the group set the stage for what will occur during socialization.

The **anticipatory phase** of group socialization involves all the initial expectations members have of each other and the group. These expectations are the grounds for what the individual anticipates will happen over the course of the group's life. Suppose the director had enthusiastically talked about Ted's talents, thereby leading the cast to anticipate a master actor and great opening night. In turn, Ted had been told about the great cast he was joining. Both parties would anticipate a successful experience. However, if their expectations were not accurate, socialization could be a disaster. In both examples, the more the expectations differ from the actual experience, the more the members will experience anxiety and perhaps even anger.

Socialization involves *both* individual expectations (Ted) and group expectations (cast). Individuals enter new or existing groups with all sorts of expectations, including estimating how well they will be received and how much they will be respected as an individual. Ted may predict that he will be well received and although he is stepping in for Richard, the cast will understand that he brings his own interpretation to the role. If he is wrong, this can produce a negative experience and stressful entry into the group—even perhaps an unsuccessful adjustment. For the cast their anticipatory phase begins when Ted decides to take over for Richard. If cast members are open to the adjustment ahead of them, they are more likely to socialize Ted into the group successfully.

Group socialization is enhanced when groups systematically have in place ways to welcome new members.[45] In the case of our community theater cast, this could include a meeting with Ted in which members introduce each other and talk about their expectations; an informal dinner with Ted; and a tour of the theater, stage, and dressing rooms. These kinds of activities or *audition practices* help both the new member and the group draw more realistic expectations and experience less primary tension during socialization.[46]

The third phase of group socialization is the **encounter phase:** The learning that takes place in all forms of socialization begins in earnest in this phase when the expectations of the anticipatory phase meet the realities of the group and lasts for an indefinite period.[47] During this time the individual and the group create or adjust the group's norms, culture, climate, status hierarchy, and leadership structure.

Earlier in our discussion of group socialization we alluded to how important it is to negotiate a balance between individual and group goals. During this phase, members also negotiate their roles in the group. The addition of a new member can disrupt the roles already established in a newly forming or existing group. Communication about individual role expectations and careful assessment of what the group needs are necessary if socialization is to be a positive experience. For instance, newcomers who proactively seek information about role expectations are socialized more effectively than those who do not seek this kind of information.[48]

The **assimilation phase** is characterized by a member's full integration into the group and its structures.[49] New members are comfortable with the group culture and show an active interest in both the group's task and relationships. In turn the existing members accept the new member. Members blend productively and supportively, enacting the kind of communication necessary to sustain the group's culture. If this integration does not occur smoothly, as is often the case, secondary tension can throw the group back into the anticipatory and encounter phases. Do not let these regressions surprise you because, over a group's life span, members will often have to negotiate the good fit between themselves and the group.

The fifth phase of group socialization is the **exit phase:** Earlier we remarked that group socialization is a process that continues over the course of a group's life. This process is experienced at both the individual and the group level and actually ends when the new member leaves or when the group ceases to exist. Exiting a group can be a difficult transition to make and is one group members often minimize.[50] If a member leaves, such as Richard in our community theater example, the group must deal with why he left, how he left, how his departure changes their communication, and what comes next. When an entire group disbands, members deal with variations of the same issues.

Group turnover is common. How many times have you watched as a member left, and then found yourself dealing with the loss and the adjustment to a new member? This process can be filled with uncertainty and resentment or it can be managed quite well. One way a group can effectively manage turnover is to develop a positive group attitude toward turnover—see it as a way to redefine who you are. When an entire group ends, do not treat it lightly—how you disband can and does impact the kind of experiences you take into the next group. Keyton recommends that groups give themselves an opportunity to say good-bye and process their experience.[51]

Encounter Phase

During group socialization, the phase in which member expectations meet the realities and members begin to adjust to each other in actuality.

Assimilation Phase

During group socialization, the phase in which members are fully integrated into the group and its structures.

Exit Phase

During socialization, the phase that encompasses the process members experience when a member leaves the group or the group disbands.

Group socialization is a complex process spanning the entire cultural life of a group. Recognizing its characteristics deepens our understanding of group development and reminds us that groups usually must adapt to losing and gaining members. Socialization involves important input, throughput, and output variables. Looking at socialization through the lens of structuration theory reminds us that how members socialize newcomers into the group can reinforce existing rules or be a powerful change agent to promote better processes of socialization.

Our discussions of socialization and structuration of group culture have consistently mentioned the importance of the group's rules. In the following section we take a closer look at rules of group culture.

Recap: A Quick Review

Just as larger social cultures socialize new members, small groups initially socialize each other and do so again when a new member comes into the group.

1. The addition of new members into groups challenges the existing group's way of doing things and how members relate to each other. In socializing a new member, group members teach the new member *how* he or she is expected to behave, thereby reinforcing current group expectations.

2. Group socialization is the responsibility of both the new member and the group; it represents a delicate balance of individual and group goals and satisfaction.

3. The group socialization process is dynamic and can be captured in five interrelated stages: antecedent, anticipatory, encounter, assimilation, and exit stages.

4. How a group ends is just as important as how it begins.

Development of Group Norms

When individuals begin to interact as members of a group, the full range of human behaviors is potentially available to them. Perhaps they will listen politely to each other, or maybe they will interrupt and insult one another. Somehow, the members must develop a set of rules and operating procedures to coordinate their individual behaviors into a system. Some **rules** are formalized guidelines for behavior that may be written down and taken into the group as an input variable. For example, *Robert's Rules of Order*, Newly Revised, is used by many organizations as a guide for governing face-to-face interaction.[52] Robert includes an entire section of rules that apply to any committee of an organization using his parliamentary manual.

However, most of the normal operating procedures for a group are developed gradually, with unspoken consent of the group members. For instance, if Kara comes late to a meeting and other members make a point of chastising her, Kara will likely arrive on time for subsequent meetings and the group

Rules
Statements prescribing how members of a small group may, should, or must behave, which may be stated formally in writing, or informally as in the case of norms.

has "decided" on a rule that members should arrive on time. Such an informal rule, or **norm,** is seldom written down; instead, it is "an idea in the minds of the members of a group, an idea that can be put in the form of a statement specifying what the members . . . should do, ought to do, are expected to do, under given circumstances."[53] This section focuses on these norms: prescriptions from group behavior that emerge out of group communication and are an important process variable of group interaction.

Norms reflect cultural beliefs about what is appropriate or inappropriate behavior, as we discussed in Chapter 5. Although the norms of an individual group may be specific to that group, chances are they will mirror general cultural norms. For instance, if physical violence is prohibited by the general culture, with disagreements handled through discussion, then a group established in the context of this larger culture will likely use discussion instead of physical violence to settle disputes. As Shimanoff stated,

> When group members come together for the first time, they bring with them past experiences and expectations regarding cultural and social rules and rules for specific groups they assume may be similar to this new group. It is out of these experiences and expectations as well as its unique interaction . . . that a particular group formulates its rules.[54]

Norms are not imposed by an authority outside the group but are imposed by members on themselves and each other through their communication. Various types of peer pressure, ranging from slight frowns to ostracism, enforce them. It is important for group members, particularly new members, to be aware of these norms because to violate them may mean punishment, loss of influence, and perhaps exclusion from the group.

Norms guide and regulate the behavior of group members. They govern how and to whom members speak, how they dress, what they talk about and when, what language may be used, and so on. The whole process of communication among group members is rule-governed.[55] Rarely do norms specify absolutes; rather, they indicate ranges of acceptable and unacceptable behavior. A particular group may endorse a prompt starting time for its meetings. However, being 4 minutes late may be tolerated without comment, but coming 15 minutes late would not.

The development of group norms may be obvious in groups where members meet face-to-face. However, our earlier discussion of adaptive structuration theory showed that group members can and do appropriate into their group interaction the particular rules of computer technology, making those rules their own. Students using e-mail as part of a course have been shown to develop their own way of using this kind of computer-mediated communication.[56] Some groups used it to chat, others to coordinate schedules, and others to talk to those who were not present. Further, conformity to the emergent norms increased over time.

During the formation stage of a new small group, norms are developed rapidly via the structuration process described earlier, often without members'

Norm

An unstated informal rule, enforced by peer pressure, that governs the behavior of members of a small group.

realizing what is occurring. The group's first meeting is particularly critical in establishing that group's norms. At that time, behaviors typical of primary tension in the formation phase—speaking quietly, suppressing disagreement, making tentative and ambiguous statements—can become norms if not challenged. Norms usually evolve over time and exist below the level of conscious awareness of most members. Often, a norm is brought to a group's awareness only after a member violates it, a new member questions it, or an observer points it out.

Conformity, or following group norms over time, helps reinforce those norms.[57] Conformity to group norms helps the group function as a whole and work in an environment with less ambiguity. In addition, group members can show each other acceptance and loyalty to the group through their conformity. Conformity to group norms, although contrary to the individualism valued by some cultures, remains an important way group members have of measuring the reasonableness of their own behaviors, ideas, and opinions.

How quickly do group members conform to norms? Five conditions seem to influence conformity to group norms.[58] First are individual characteristics. For example, older people are less likely to conform. Second, members follow well-articulated and well-enforced norms more. Third, the more members who conform to the norm, the more likely it is that others will follow. Fourth, highly cohesive groups tend to generate more conformity to their norms. Finally, members who support the goals of their group are more likely to follow that group's norms.

General norms direct the behavior of the group as a whole, whereas *role-specific norms* concern individual members with particular roles, such as the designated leader. The medical group discussed in our chapter opening developed a general norm related to rational decision making. Role-specific norms for Julian included his rephrasing and redefining of the others' ideas. He also developed the norm of talking more than the others. Examples of each type of norm follow:

General Norms (Applicable to Every Member)	**Role-Specific Norms (Applicable to Specific Members)**
Members should sit in the same position at each meeting.	The leader should prepare and distribute an agenda in advance of each meeting.
Members should address each other by first names.	The leader should summarize from time to time, but other members may do so if a summary is needed.
Other members should not disagree with the chair's ideas.	The secretary should distribute minutes of the previous meeting at least three days before the next meeting.

No one may smoke during meetings.

Members may leave the meeting to get something to drink, but should return to their seats promptly.

Members should arrive on time for meetings.

Gulshan may play critical tester of all ideas by asking for evidence.

Terrell should tell a joke when the climate gets tense during an argument.

Julian should restate other members' remarks in his own words.

If norms generally exist below the level of conscious awareness, how can group members discover what their norms are? Norms can be inferred and confirmed by observation. New members, especially, should be sensitive to the group's norms so that they do not inadvertently violate important ones. There are two types of behavior to watch for especially:

1. **Behaviors that occur repeatedly and with regularity, by one or all members:**

   Repetitions of a behavior are evidence that a norm exists regulating it. Thus group members should look for answers to questions such as: "Who talks to whom?" "How do members speak?" "What kind of language do they use?" "What do they talk about and for how long?" "Where do they sit?" "When do they move about and for what reasons?" and "How is the group brought to order?"

2. **Punishment of a member for infraction of a rule:**

   The strongest evidence of a norm is a negative reaction or punishment directed at a member who does not conform to the norm. Deviance from a group norm may take several forms: nonconformity to a general norm (e.g., avoiding sound reasoning); specific role deviance (e.g., secretary not distributing the minutes); deviance from gender, class, age, ethnic social role expectations (e.g., nurse questioning the M.D.'s opinion); and breaking from past patterns (Julian begins to defer to the faculty members on the committee).[59]

   Observers looking for norms should pay attention to behaviors that elicit negative reactions, ranging from a bit of head shaking, to surreptitious and disapproving glances passing between members, to forceful negative comments or even threats. Notice behaviors to which members react with gestures of rejection, such as frowns, head shaking, and tongue clucking. What acts do members studiously ignore, as if out of embarrassment? Listen for negative comments: "It's about time you got here," "Let's stick to issues and not go blaming each other," and "Maybe you'll have your report ready for our next meeting." Note, particularly, those actions that elicit negative responses from more than one person, a sure bet that a norm important to the group has been infringed. Weaker support for the existence of a norm is provided when violators correct themselves and the other members visibly approve the correction.

Changing a Norm

Norms have a tremendous effect on the processes and outcomes of the group. Group members should not only be aware of them, but also act to change them if they appear to be detrimental. Just because members conform to a norm does not mean the norm is good for the group overall. For instance, a norm implying that low-status members may not disagree with high-status members interferes with the critical evaluation of ideas, as we saw in our medical group. Or groups that permit members to criticize ideas as soon as they have been proposed may find that members are reluctant to make innovative suggestions, so creativity is stifled. In such cases, individuals should not "sit back and take it" but work to change the rules. Small persistent changes can be effective because they are not as noticeable to those who may resist the change.[60] A social worker in our medical group was successful in temporarily moving the group into a more democratic climate. She decided to refuse Julian's attempts to rephrase her comments, which in turn helped him be more aware of his pattern of changing other's ideas to reflect his own. The group managed this new pattern for a while, but when a crisis arose, members, including Julian, fell back into old ways. Had the social worker persisted in her attempts, she might have been successful in changing the autocratic norm.

Using a full frontal assault, particularly one that may be perceived as a personal attack, will not be successful either and will make the person demanding the change seem like a deviant. Instead, following a few simple guidelines can help you change norms without unnecessary trauma. First, the member desiring the change must establish an identity as a loyal member of the group and speak not as an outsider but as a member committed to the group's well-being. Second, the member should carefully observe the offending behavior and keep a record of how often it occurs and what the consequences are to the group. Armed with specific information and obvious concern for the good of the group, the member is ready for the next step, constructive confrontation.

The member should pick an appropriate time, indicate his or her concern with something that appears to be causing trouble for the group, state the specifics calmly and clearly, then ask whether other members share the concern. For instance, rather than saying, "We never get started on time and I'm sick and tired of it," the member should say instead: "For the past four meetings, we have started our work anywhere from 15 minutes to half an hour late. We seem to have a rule that we don't have to observe our announced starting time, which makes our meetings run late. Two of us have another committee meeting directly following this one, and for each of these late meetings we have missed the conclusion of our business. This means that we need to spend additional time at the next meeting bringing everyone up-to-date. Does anyone else share my concern?" The norm now has been brought to the attention of the group and becomes part of the surface agenda of the group where it can be discussed openly. If the member is wrong about the norm, the group can correct the perception without disparaging the concern. However, if the individual is right, the group will appreciate the concern and likely decide to change the norm. Even if the other members agree to a new norm, they may still need gentle reminders until the new behavior becomes habituated, part of "our way of doing things."

Although norms are usually developed generally without conscious intent, they are not fixed in stone and can be changed, with persistence, as the group's situation warrants. But always keep in mind a valuable lesson from structuration theory—any change in group interaction may have unforeseen consequences.

Recap: A Quick Review

Central to group structuration is understanding how group members use pre-existing general norms of behavior and also create their own norms, often implicitly, which in turn guide group communication until changes occur and new norm(s) alter group interaction.

1. Norms are informal rules that often emerge out of group members' tendencies to conform; they then guide future group task and social expectations.

2. Conformity to group norms is a function of five interrelated conditions: individual tendency toward conformity, number of group members following the norm, how well the norm is articulated and supported, level of group cohesiveness, and degree to which group members support the group goal.

3. Evidence of a group norm can be found in repetitious behavior and the degree to which nonconformity is punished.

4. Changing a group norm should involve thoughtful planning around when to bring up the norm with the group, careful description of the norm and its perceived consequence to the group, and presentation to the group in a manner that shows loyalty to the group identity as a whole.

Development of a Group's Climate

We began this chapter by recognizing that small groups develop their own cultural identities as they meet task and socioemotional challenges, socialize members, and create implicit norm structures. We also showed how fantasy themes can powerfully craft their symbolic realities. It is only fitting that we end this chapter with a discussion of group climates. Climates reflect the emotional tenor of a group's culture and show once again how important it is to recognize the key role that socioemotional dynamics play in shaping the group culture.[61] **Group climate** refers to a group's emotional and relational atmosphere. How well do members work together? Do they seem to like each other? Are members' identity and relational needs being met? Is the atmosphere tense or relaxed? In this section, we discuss two elements that contribute to group climate: cohesiveness and supportiveness.

Group Climate

A group's emotional and relational atmosphere.

Cohesiveness

When the U.S. women's soccer team won the 1999 World Championship, star Mia Hamm said, "Everything I am I owe to this team."[62] By all objective measures, this team presented a stellar example of unity, trust, and teamwork. The cohesiveness and commitment of the members drove them to achieve outstanding individual effort. For example, Michelle Akers battled chronic fatigue syndrome and bad knees for a long time, yet she was one of the mainstays of the team. This was a cohesive and productive team, the likes of which may never be seen again in soccer. What creates the kind of climate that would lead Mia Hamm to credit her team rather than herself for her performance?

Cohesiveness refers to the common bonds and sentiments that hold a group together. When a group is high in cohesiveness, the relationships among members are, on the whole, attractive to them; they have a high degree of "stick togetherness" and unity. Highly cohesive groups behave differently from less cohesive groups. They display more characteristics of primary groups than less cohesive groups.[63] They have higher rates of interaction. Members express more positive feelings for each other and report more satisfaction with the group, such as was demonstrated by the women soccer players choosing to go out to dinner together. Members are willing to cooperate and collaborate with each other.[64] In addition, cohesive groups exert greater control over member behaviors.[65] High cohesiveness is associated with increased ability to cope effectively with unusual problems and to work as a team in meeting emergencies. Although results of individual studies have been mixed, two recent meta-analyses of cohesiveness research have found that, in general, highly cohesive groups are more productive.[66] The nature of the task influences the cohesiveness-productivity relationship.[67] If the task is one that requires a high degree of coordination and interdependence among members, with communication an essential factor in the group's task completion, then cohesiveness enhances productivity, such as was demonstrated by the women's soccer team.

There are several dimensions to cohesiveness. Two studies support the idea that cohesiveness can involve *both* personal relationships and commitment to the group's goal.[68] Cohesiveness that is due to interpersonal attraction and liking produces different results than cohesiveness that is based on commitment to the task or goal. Chin et al. also found two factors that contribute to cohesion: belonging and morale.[69] Belonging refers to whether a member feels a part of the group—without this, that member won't want to associate with the other members. Without high morale, group members won't be motivated to work on the task.

There is an optimum level of cohesiveness beyond which performance decreases.[70] Cohesive groups are productive only when the members have both high acceptance of organizational goals implicit in the group's task *and* a strong drive (motivation and enthusiasm) to complete the task.[71] Groups that are highly cohesive but socially oriented rather than task-oriented may end up accomplishing nothing.[72]

Cohesiveness

The degree of attraction members feel for the group; unity.

We noted in our discussion of primary tension that highly successful and cohesive groups tend first to get acquainted and interested in each other as people. This type of self-disclosure increases cohesiveness, commitment to the task, and productivity.[73] Members can be heard saying, "I'm proud of our group; we really thrash out ideas until we arrive at the best; then we team up." However, recall that high cohesiveness can also pressure members to conform to the majority or to high-status members' desires, which can result in a less-than-thorough critical evaluation of ideas, leading to what is called *groupthink,* which we discuss in Chapter 11.

Although high cohesiveness can be associated with pitfalls such as groupthink, cohesiveness can produce great results. A group that accomplishes its objectives, provides members with satisfaction in their participation, offers prestige in belonging, and is successful in competing with other groups is very attractive to its members.

Cohesiveness is fostered to the extent that members know and like each other as individuals, by their frequency of interaction, and by the amount of influence each exerts on the group. In addition, some evidence suggests that cohesive groups cooperate in creating a dominant sensory metaphor as a group, and that cohesiveness can be monitored through metaphor.[74] For example, when a group is first established, various members indicate their understanding by saying, "I see," "I hear you," or "I grasp that." Each of these metaphors for "I understand" concentrates on a different sense—sight, sound, or touch. In cohesive groups, members tend to symbolically converge on a particular sensory metaphor. If the visual metaphor is "chosen," for example, members will all start saying, "I see," "I've got the picture," and "I've spotted a flaw." This happens below the level of conscious awareness like fantasy chaining and indicates that the members have influenced each other in subtle but significant ways.

Interestingly, open disagreement is more frequent in highly cohesive groups, probably because a climate of trust gives each member the security needed to openly disagree on issues, facts, and ideas.[75] On the other hand, if high-status members indicate that they perceive disagreement to be a personal affront and demand compliance, then cohesiveness may become groupthink and be maintained at the expense of high-quality decision making.

Cohesiveness, then, is generally desirable. Here are our suggestions to enhance cohesiveness:[76]

1. **Allow time for members to get to know each other.**
   Members do not have to become best friends, but it helps if they feel comfortable with one another. The performance of even short-term teams benefits if members spend time getting to know one another.[77]

2. **Set clear, attainable group goals.**
   One of the most important characteristics that differentiates high-performing, cohesive teams from mediocre ones is having a compelling goal that is clear.[78]

3. **Treat members like people, not machines.**
   The efficient, highly oiled machine is *not* the best metaphor for the kinds of groups we have been discussing. Group work is not just about meeting control needs and task accomplishment, but meeting needs for inclusion and affection as well.[79]

4. **Develop a group identity, with group traditions and rituals.**
   Develop nicknames for the group, insignia indicating membership, or mascots for the group. Encourage traditions and rituals that give added meaning to the group's culture. Encourage the group to develop a rich fantasy life.

5. **Stress teamwork.**
   Members, especially selected leaders or high-performance members, should avoid talking about "my accomplishments." A friend of ours, who has since become an effective group leader, told us she failed in her first leadership assignment because she kept taking credit for work the group had completed. She demoralized the team.

6. **Get the group to recognize good work.**
   Encourage members to compliment and praise one another. Coach DiCicco talked about how one of his players, Michelle Akers, inspired him.[80] Low-status members, especially, need attention and recognition. Look for ways to support other members with their group work assignments, but also with non-group-related activities.

7. **Reward and celebrate group accomplishments.**
   Although many organizations reward individual performance, groups should be rewarded *as groups.* These can be tangible or intangible rewards, including recognition dinners, public praise, letters of commendation, and so forth. Outstanding leaders look for things to celebrate and do so in a variety of ways.[81]

8. **Support both disagreement and agreement.**
   Highly cohesive groups show more disagreement, with conflict encouraged not repressed. Often, when conflicts are resolved, group members feel closer than ever and are more cohesive.

9. **Have fun!**
   Teamwork isn't only about completing work—it's about enjoying and appreciating your fellow group members. Having fun, laughing together, enjoying a non-task-related activity, can help unify a group.

Building Cohesiveness and Productivity in Virtual Teams   A **virtual team** is one in which the members' interactions take place primarily through some combination of electronic systems, such as telephone, computer, fax, and videoconferencing, instead of face-to-face.[82] Virtual teams must do what face-to-face teams do—accomplish work and promote good team relationships—but because members typically do not work in the same location or meet in

Virtual Team

A group that meets primarily or exclusively through some combination of electronic means (computers, telephones, videoconferences, and so forth).

person regularly, they face additional challenges. Jarvenpas has identified nine behaviors that help build trust in virtual teams, including social communication, communication that conveys enthusiasm, methods to deal with technological and task uncertainty, individual initiative, predictable communication, substantive and timely feedback, positive leadership, transitions from procedure to task focus, and calm reactions to crisis.[83] Virtual teams are relatively new, but they are becoming more common throughout corporate America. The following suggestions will help you form a cohesive, productive virtual team.[84] Specific directions for group leaders follow in Chapter 13.

1. **Establish an identity for the team.** Make sure that all members know who is on the team, where they are located, and how they can be reached via e-mail, telephone, and so forth. Some team leaders ask members to post a picture with brief biographical information on a team Web site, so that all members can see and know a bit more about their fellow team members.

2. **Manage the team's uncertainty: Clarify the team's purpose, specific outcomes to be achieved, and time line.** Face-to-face teams have the luxury of allowing the team's goals and chronology to evolve, at least to some extent, but virtual team members need this spelled out specifically when the team is formed.

3. **Manage technology issues: Make sure members agree on the technology to be used, have been trained in it, and are reasonably comfortable with it.** Satisfaction with technology comes in large measure from comfort with it. A team member who can't use the technology appropriately will shy away from virtual teamwork—no one wants to look dumb in front of his or her peers. In addition, members should standardize what they will use. If the team will be preparing a document to which everyone contributes, agree in advance which word processing program will be used and so forth.

4. **If possible, have the members meet face-to-face, particularly at the beginning of their work as a virtual team.** Although this isn't always practical or possible, it helps build a team feeling. This may be the single most important thing a manager can do to promote trust and teamwork.

5. **Make sure members know the communication rules to be used for the team's business.** Sometimes, virtual communication can seem abrupt or even rude because many of the nonverbal cues that provide context or can soften a negative message are missing. Members, particularly if they are new to the technology, must be encouraged to be more precise with their language because the primary messages, at least on computers, are conveyed through text. In addition, it may be helpful for the group's leader, with the input of the group, to establish expectations, such as for how often members will be expected to check into

the virtual meeting site, and so forth. Members should, of course, observe common courtesies with each other.

6. **Have a virtual location—chat room, bulletin board, folder— where the team's documents and records are kept.** Face-to-face teams have minutes and memos to help them keep track of the task. Virtual teams can also have access to such organizing information, which helps them keep on task and captures the group's collective memory.

7. **Encourage regular communication, including informal social communication among members.** Regular, predictable, and frequent interaction, using whatever electronic forms the team has agreed to, helps keep members connected to each other and aware of each other. In addition, as with face-to-face teams, encouraging informal, nontask communication helps build trust and a satisfying team experience.

Supportiveness

LaFasto and Larson's work with numerous kinds of teams over many years has revealed that there are significant differences in climate between high-performing teams and ones that are merely OK (or worse):

> With rare exceptions, members of effective teams describe the atmosphere of the team in positive terms. The team is relaxed, comfortable, informal, fun, warm. Teams that are good at problem solving have a way of making their members feel accepted, valued, and competent. Members of poor teams, on the other hand, tend to describe the climate as tense, overly critical, political, cynical, inhibiting, cold, or too stiff and formal.[85]

The members of excellent teams are consistently described as supportive, interested, and willing to help the rest of the members succeed.[86] For instance, they bolster other members' confidence, pitch in to help each other, and listen well to each other. Nonsupportive members, in contrast, are "me" oriented, disinterested in the others, and do only the jobs they are assigned. They may be social loafers. LaFasto and Larson make a point that supportive members care deeply about the work of the group, and freely challenge ideas and opinions.

Supportive Climate

A group climate in which each member is valued and appreciated.

Defensive Climate

A group climate in which members attack and belittle each other, and where members feel they have to defend themselves from possible attack.

What LaFasto and Larson observed is consistent with what Gibb observed many years ago.[87] Gibb observed members of many teams and asked them what behaviors were helpful and not helpful within the team. The two opposite communication climates he defined, a supportive climate and a defensive one, are created by the communication among members. It is what members do and say, how they treat each other, that creates the group's climate.

A **supportive climate** is one that values each member. Members know they are wanted and appreciated, that their ideas and opinions are important to the group. Members behave toward one another in the most ethical of ways, confirming and supporting each other. Members build each other up. However, in a **defensive climate,** members tear each other down and violate the ethical principle, mentioned in Chapter 1, that states that members should not belittle or ridicule one another. Defensive climates carry an element of

FIGURE 8.1   Supportive and defensive communication

Supportive Communication	Defensive Communication
Description: Tries to understand other points of view; takes responsibility for one's own opinions and beliefs.	**Evaluation:** Judges and criticizes; blames other people.
"I've noticed that, for the last few meetings, we've started 15 minutes after the announced starting time."	"What's the MATTER with you people? Is there some REASON why we can't get started on time?"
Problem orientation: Tries to solve the problem; enlists others' help; invites others' ideas.	**Control:** Tries to be in charge; dominates; insists on having one's own way.
"What do you all think we should do?"	"Here's what I've decided we're going to do."
Spontaneity: Open, honest, genuine communication.	**Strategy:** Manipulative communication that tries to steer the group in a particular direction.
"That's a great idea! One problem I see with it is . . ."	"Don't you think it would be better if . . .?"
Empathy: Demonstrates caring and understanding; shows members they are valued.	**Neutrality:** Demonstrates lack of understanding and lack of concern; indifference.
"Congratulations! That's a great job, but we're really going to miss you."	"You're leaving? Can I have your office?"
Equality: Minimizes status differences and power distance; encourages members to contribute equally.	**Superiority:** Makes status differences clear; maximizes power distance; pulls rank.
"Nice to meet you, Suzie. Go ahead and call me Gloria, not Dr. Galanes."	"Nice to meet you, Suzie. I'm Dr. Galanes."
Provisionalism: Expresses opinions tentatively; open to others' ideas and opinions.	**Certainty:** Expresses opinions dogmatically and with no room for others' opinions; know-it-all attitude.
"Right now I'm leaning toward Option A, but I'd like to know what you all think."	"Option A is the ONLY thing that will work!"

judgment, which makes members feel as if they are being evaluated and found wanting. If you have ever worked in a defensive climate, you know that only a portion of your energy is being directed to the group's task. Much of it is going to protect yourself from psychological attack. Members feel as if they have to walk on eggshells around their fellow group members. You can't do your best work that way, so ultimately the group's work suffers.

Gibb described six dimensions of group climate, which we discuss here and summarize in Figure 8.1. It is very important to note that defensiveness and supportiveness are conveyed as much—or more—through nonverbal messages as through verbal ones. In particular, defensiveness is often conveyed through paralanguage. When you read the defensive statements we provide as examples, imagine they are being said in a snotty or sarcastic tone of voice.

In much the same way that face-to-face groups create supportive and defensive climates, virtual groups that meet only online create such climates as well. In describing her participation in an e-mail discussion list devoted to the television series *Dr. Quinn, Medicine Woman,* Bird notes that the communication among members contributed to creating a nurturing community.[88] Bird observes that the list is generally free of flaming and insults, largely because the list owner is "overwhelmingly" supported by members in taking disciplinary action when members step out of line. Members receive a code of conduct from the list owner when they first subscribe, which participants themselves actively enforce. People are removed from the list for using profanity, racist comments, and personal invective, although members will give those who inadvertently violate the rules, particularly new members, a second chance. Participants, who are almost all women, freely disagree with each other—sometimes vehemently—but they generally disagree respectfully. Members express that they feel listened to and believe that they belonged to a virtual family or community. Bird describes a high level of trust and openness in this community, and although she does not use the word "supportive," what she describes is just that—a supportive, virtual group.

Teambuilding

Teambuilding

A set of planned activities designed to increase teamwork, cohesiveness,or other aspects of group performance.

Sometimes a group needs something out of the ordinary to help it develop or improve its cohesiveness. *Teambuilding* is the current term for special programs designed to accomplish such goals. **Teambuilding** refers to any planned program of activities designed to enhance teamwork or improve a group's performance. In addition to enhancing group climate, teambuilding activities can be used to improve group decision making, help members learn more effective ways of handling conflict, increase creativity, and improve communication skills and many other group throughput processes. Often, teambuilding activities occur during retreats that take groups out of their normal settings and encourage them to focus on the teambuilding topic.

The best teambuilding programs are tailored to meet the unique needs of each specific group. Tony DiCicco, coach of the women's soccer team, understood this principle well. He helped create a unified, high-performance team out of diverse individuals ranging from the quiet, intense Briana Scurry to the gregarious, funny Julie Foudy. He learned that women respond well to challenges but poorly to chastisement. So, for example, he showed them videos "catching them being good" rather than replays of mistakes. The team participated in trust walks guided by a motivational psychologist. Other common strategies are used in teambuilding sessions (see Figure 8.2).

Teambuilding activities can be effective and lasting. For instance, Carron and Spink found that a teambuilding program helped a very large group increase its cohesiveness.[90] Glaser described a three-day teambuilding retreat designed for department leaders of a fire management unit.[91] The teambuilding topics included communication skills, consensus building, and problem solving; and three years later, members continued to report substantially improved teamwork.

FIGURE 8.2   Guidelines for teambuilding sessions

A teambuilding session may be planned by a group's leader (see Chapter 13), one of the members, a subgroup within the group, or an outside consultant or facilitator. The following are suggestions for teambuilding planners.[89]

1. **Define the purpose of the teambuilding activity.** The observation and evaluation tools in Chapter 7 can help you pinpoint key areas to address that meet the needs of the group.

2. **Take the group out of its usual setting for the teambuilding activities.** This will enhance concentration on the teambuilding activities and decrease distractions.

3. **Teambuilding sessions must be planned with clear objectives** to give the process focus, yet flexible enough to allow adaptation to the teambuilding process as it unfolds.

4. **Help the group members appreciate the strength in their own diversity.** Often, group members who work with each other day in and day out can lose sight of the fact that their differences can be beneficial to the group rather than frustrating.

5. **Stay tuned to the importance of blending work and meaningful ritual.** The richness of a group's culture is reflected in its rituals, celebrations, and other symbolic activities that serve to coordinate a strong identity.

Recap: A Quick Review

A group's climate is felt and seen in its emotional and relational atmosphere. Cohesive climates emerge out of patterns supportive group interaction.

1. Group cohesiveness is observed in high member satisfaction, constructive and supportive behaviors, effective coping behaviors in the face of difficulties, and more control over group member behavior.

2. Cohesiveness, while obviously a characteristic of the socioemotional quality of the group culture, is also closely tied to the group's commitment to its goal (or task).

3. Highly cohesive groups, contrary to common assumptions about cohesiveness, show higher rates of open disagreement than do less cohesive groups.

4. Cohesiveness can be facilitated by teamwork, clear goals, allowing time for members to get to know each other, rewarding accomplishments, creating group identity and the rituals to reinforce it, allowing the group time to play, and supporting open disagreement in climates of trust.

5. Virtual groups face the same challenges that face-to-face groups do in creating cohesive climates; in addition, they must consider how their computer technology can both facilitate and impede their cohesiveness.

6. Patterns of supportiveness versus defensive behaviors should be reinforced if a group is to build cohesive climates.

7. Teambuilding is a special set of procedures that group members can use to build cohesiveness; the procedures are out of the ordinary but may be necessary.

QUESTIONS FOR REVIEW

 Go to self-quizzes on the Online Learning Center at mhhe.com/galanes12 to test your knowledge of the chapter concepts

Why do some groups manage to build the kind of group cultures that facilitate success and others fall apart? We argue that the secrets are found in the group's communication among its members and its environment. The medical team of unassailable member competence just could not "get it together." Consider their group and the others mentioned in this chapter when you review these questions.

1. How would you describe the structuration process of the medical group as they try to develop an instructional program? How do they end up creating a group that moves them away from a democratic spirit?

2. How would you describe secondary tension to this group and what would you recommend to them as ways to better negotiate this tension?

3. What are the communicative dynamics of both ascribed and earned status in Julian's behaviors as well as the other members of the medical group? How might Julian's idiosyncracy credit help and harm the group culture?

4. What might a fantasy chain look like in the medical group? How could it have helped them move back to their desire for a more democratic spirit?

5. Ted graciously agrees to take Richard's place in the acting troupe shaken by Richard's departure. What are critical actions that Ted and the troupe must try to make if they are to move through the stages of socialization effectively?

6. Consider your responses to question 5. What kinds of norms do your responses suggest would help this group effectively negotiate a new member and change into a more productive group culture?

7. What would a defensive climate sound and look like in the acting troupe? What are the major norms implied in your description, and how would you propose that the troupe could change any one or more of those norms?

8. Consider the special context and challenges to cohesiveness of virtual groups. How would you lead a teambuilding activity for this kind of group?

KEY TERMS

 Test your knowledge of these key terms by visiting the Online Learning Center Web site at mhhe.com/galanes12

Adaptive structuration theory
Cohesiveness
Conformity
Fantasy
Fantasy chain
Fantasy theme
Formation phase
Group climate
    Defensive climate
    Supportive climate

Group culture
Group socialization
    Antecedent phase
    Anticipatory phase
    Assimilation phase
    Encounter phase
    Exit phase
Idiosyncratic credit
Norm
Primary tension

Production phase
Rules
Secondary tension
Status
    Ascribed status
    Earned status
Structuration
Symbolic convergence
Teambuilding
Virtual team

BIBLIOGRAPHY

Bormann, Ernest G. *Small Group Communication: Theory and Practice,* 3rd ed. New York: Harper & Rowe, 1990, Chapters 5, 7 and 8.

Clark, Neil. *Teambuilding: A Practical Guide for Trainers.* New York: McGraw-Hill, 1994.

Ellis, Donald G., and B. Aubrey Fisher. *Small Group Decision Making: Communication and the Group Process.* 4th ed. New York: McGraw-Hill, 1990, Chapter 5.

Feldman, Daniel. "Development and Enforcement of Group Norms." *Academy of Management Review* 9 (1984): 47–53.

Larson, Carl E., and Frank M. J. LaFasto. *Teamwork: What Must Go Right/What Can Go Wrong.* Newbury Park, CA: Sage, 1989.

Lipnack, Jessica, and Jeffrey Stamps. *Virtual Teams: Reaching Across Space, Time and Organizations with Technology.* New York, Wiley, 1997.

Poole, Marshall S. "Group Communication and the Structuring Process." In *Small Group Communication: A Reader.* 7th ed. Robert S. Cathcart, Larry A. Samovar, and Linda D. Henman, eds. Dubuque, IA: Brown & Benchmark, 1996, 85–95.

NOTES

1. This story is a modified version of a case found in Marshall S. Poole, "Group Communication and the Structuring Process," in *Small Group Communication: A Reader,* 7th ed., eds. Robert S. Cathcart, Larry A. Samovar, and Linda D. Henman (Dubuque, IA: Brown & Benchmark, 1996): 89–91.

2. Bryan Seyfarth, "Structuration Theory in Small Group Communication: A Review and Agenda for Future Research," in *Communication Yearbook* 23, ed. Michael Roloff (Thousand Oaks, CA: Sage, 2000): 341–79.

3. Marshall S. Poole, David R. Siebold, and Robert D. McPhee, "Group Decision Making and the Structurational Process," *Quarterly Journal of Speech* 71 (1985): 74–102; Marshall S. Poole, David R. Seibold, and Robert D. McPhee, "A Structurational Approach to Theory-Building in Decision-Making Research," in *Communication and Group Decision Making,* eds. Randy Y. Hirokawa and Marshall S. Poole (Beverly Hills, CA: Sage, 1986): 237–64; and Poole, "Group Communication and the Structuring Process," 85–95.

4. Poole, "Group Communication and the Structuring Process."

5. Sunwolf and David R. Seibold, "Jurors' Intuitive Rules for Deliberation: A Structurational Approach to Communication in Jury Decision Making," *Communication Monographs* 65 (1998): 282–307.

6. Ibid., 303.

7. Seyfarth, "Structuration Theory in Small Group Communication."

8. Craig Scott, "Communication Technology and Group Communication," in *The Handbook of Group Communication Theory and Research,* ed. Lawrence Frey (Thousand Oaks, CA: Sage, 1999): 432–72.

9. Seyfarth, "Structuration Theory in Small Group Communication."

10. Poole, "Group Communication and the Structuring Process."

11. B. Aubrey Fisher and Randall K. Stutman, "An Assessment of Group Trajectories: Analyzing Developmental Breakpoints," *Communication Quarterly* 35 (Spring 1987): 105–24.

12. Bales, *Interaction Process Analysis.*

13. Ernest G. Bormann, *Discussion and Group Methods: Theory and Practice,* 3d ed. (New York: Harper & Row, 1990): 132–39.

14. David B. Barker, "The Behavioral Analysis of Interpersonal Intimacy in Group Development," *Small Group Research* 22 (February 1991): 76–91.

15. Bormann, *Discussion and Group Methods,* 139.

16. Robert F. Bales, *Interaction Process Analysis* (Reading, MA: Addison-Wesley, 1950).

17. William F. Whyte, *Pattern for Industrial Peace* (New York: Harper, 1951).

18. J. I. Hurwitz, A. F. Zander, and B. Hymovitch, "Some Effects of Power on the Relations among

Group Members," in *Group Dynamics: Research and Theory,* 3rd ed., eds. D. Cartwright and A. Zander (New York: Harper & Row, 1968): 291–97.

19. Dean C. Barnlund and C. Harland, "Propinquity and Prestige as Determinants of Communication Networks," *Sociometry* 26 (1963): 467–79.

20. E. Hollander, "Conformity, Status, and Idiosyncracy Credit," *Psychological Review* 65 (1958): 117–27.

21. Michelle Estrada, Justin Brown, and Fiona Lee, "Who Gets the Credit? Perceptions of Idiosyncracy Credit in Work Groups," *Small Group Research* 26 (February 1995): 56–76.

22. Craig R. Scott, "Communication Technology and Group Communication," in *Handbook of Group Communication Theory and Research,* ed. Lawrence R. Frey (Thousand Oaks, CA: Sage, 1999): 432–72.

23. Andrew J. Flanagin, Vanessa Tiyaamornwong, Joan O'Connor, and David R. Siebold, "Computer-Mediated Group Work: The Interaction of Member Sex and Anonymity," *Communication Research* 29 (February 2002): 66–93.

24. Carolyn J. Wood, "Challenging the Assumptions Underlying the Use of Participatory Decision Making Strategies: A Longitudinal Case Study," *Small Group Behavior* 20 (1989): 428–48.

25. Joseph A. Bonito, "The Effect of Contributing Substantively on Perceptions of Participation," *Small Group Research* 31 (October 2000): 528–53.

26. Ernest G. Bormann, "Symbolic Convergence Theory and Communication in Group Decision Making," in *Communication and Group Decision Making,* eds. Randy Y. Hirokawa and Marshall S. Poole (Newbury Park, CA: Sage, 1986): 221. For a thorough review of the development and use of symbolic convergence theory, see Ernest G. Bormann, John F. Cragan, and Donald C. Shields, "Three Decades of Developing, Grounding, and Using Symbolic Convergence Theory," in *Communication Yearbook* 25, ed. Willam B. Gudykunst (Thousand Oaks, CA: Sage, 2001): 271–313.

27. Robert F. Bales, *Personality and Interpersonal Behavior* (New York: Holt Rinehart and Winston, 1970): 105–8, 136–55.

28. Eric E. Peterson, "The Stories of Pregnancy: On Interpretation of Small-Group Cultures," *Communication Quarterly* 35 (1987): 39–47.

29. Catherine C. Morocco, "Development and Function of Group Metaphor," *Journal for the Theory of Social Behavior* 9 (1979): 15–27.

30. Bormann, "Symbolic Convergence Theory."

31. Linda L. Putnam, Shirley A. Van Hoeven, and Connie A. Bullis, "The Role of Rituals and Fantasy Themes in Teachers' Bargaining," *Western Journal of Speech Communication* (Winter 1991): 87.

32. This fantasy chain is a slightly expanded version of the one that occurs near the beginning of the leadership segment, part 1, of the videotape ancillary to this text, *Communicating Effectively in Small Groups.*

33. Morocco, "Development and Function of Group Metaphor," 15–27.

34. Ibid.

35. Putnam, Van Hoeven, and Bullis, "The Role of Rituals and Fantasy Themes in Teachers' Bargaining."

36. Bruce Riddle, Carolyn Anderson, and Matthew Martin, "Small Group Socialization Scale: Development and Validity," *Small Group Research* 31 (October 2000): 554–72.

37. Carolyn Anderson, Bruce Riddle, and Matthew Martin, "Socialization Processes in Groups," in *Handbook of Group Communication Theory and Research,* ed. Lawrence Frey (Thousand Oaks, CA: Sage, 1999): 139–63.

38. Ibid.

39. Riddle et al., "Small Group Socialization Scale."

40. Ibid.

41. Anderson et al., "Socialization Processes in Groups."

42. Joann Keyton, *Group Communication* (Mountain View, CA: Mayfield, 1999): 115.

43. Anderson et al., "Socialization Processes in Groups," 147.

44. Ibid., 148.

45. Ibid., 149.

46. Stewart Sigman, "The Applicability of the Concept of Recruitment to the Communication Study of a Nursing Home: An Ethnographic Case Study," *International Journal of Aging and Human Development* 22 (1985–86):

215–33. See also Melanie Booth-Butterfield, Stephen Booth-Butterfield, and Jolene Koester, "The Function of Uncertainty Reduction in Alleviating Primary Tension in Small Groups," *Communication Research Reports* 5 (1988): 146–53.

47. Anderson et al., "Socialization Processes in Groups," 151.

48. K. E. W. Morrison, "Information Usefulness and Acquisition During Organizational Encounter," *Management Communication Quarterly* 9 (1995): 131–55.

49. Anderson et al., "Socialization Processes in Groups," 152.

50. Ibid., 164.

51. Joann Keyton, "Group Termination: Completing the Study of Group Development," *Small Group Research* 24 (1993): 84–100.

52. Henry M. Robert, *Robert's Rules of Order,* Newly Revised (Glenview, IL: Scott, Foresman, 1990): 471–521.

53. George C. Homans, *The Human Group* (New York: Harcourt Brace Jovanovich, 1950): 123.

54. Susan B. Shimanoff, "Coordinating Group Interaction via Communication Rules," in *Small Group Communication: A Reader,* 6th ed., eds. Robert S. Cathcart and Larry A. Samovar (Dubuque, IA: Wm. C. Brown, 1992): 255.

55. Shimanoff, "Coordinating Group Interaction."

56. Tom Postmes, Russell Spears, and Lea Martin, "The Formation of Group Norms in Computer-Mediated Communication," *Human Communication Research* 26 (July 3): 341–71.

57. J. Dan Rothwell, *In Mixed Company*, 4th ed. (Fort Worth, TX: Harcourt, 2001): 63.

58. Steven Beebe and John Masterson, *Communicating in Small Groups,* 6th ed. (New York: Addison-Wesley, 1999): 82–83.

59. Gay Lumsden and Donald Lumsden, *Communicating in Groups and Teams,* 3d ed. (Belmont, CA: Wadsworth/Thomson Learning, 2000): 281.

60. Poole, "Group Communication and the Structuring Process."

61. Joann Keyton, "Relational Communication in Groups," in *Handbook of Group Communication Theory and Research,* ed. Lawrence R. Frey (Thousand Oaks, CA: Sage, 1999): 192–222.

62. Information for this story was compiled from several sources. Most information came from

Mark Starr and Martha Brant, "It Went Down to the Wire . . . and Thrilled Us All," *Newsweek,* (July 19, 1999): 45–54; with additional information from Bill Saporito, "The New Dream Team," *Time* (July 19, 1999): 60–67; and David Leon Moore, "Goalkeepers: Don't Expect Any Handouts," *USA Today* (Friday, July 9 1999): 1C–2C.

63. David B. Barker, "The Behavioral Analysis of Interpersonal Intimacy in Group Development," *Small Group Research* 22 (February 1991): 76–91.

64. Carolyn M. Anderson, Bruce L. Riddle, and Dominic A. Infante, "Decision-Making Collaboration Scale: Tests of Validity," *Communication Research Reports* 15 (1999): 245–55.

65. Harold L. Nixon II, *The Small Group* (Englewood Cliffs, NJ: Prentice Hall, 1979): 74–76.

66. Charles R. Evans and Kenneth L. Dion, "Group Cohesion and Performance," *Small Group Behavior* 22 (1991): 175–86; Stanley M. Gully, Dennis J. Devine, and David J. Whitney, "A Meta-Analysis of Cohesion and Performance: Effects of Level of Analysis and Task Interdependence," *Small Group Research* 26 (November 1995): 497–520.

67. Gully et al., "A Meta-Analysis of Cohesion and Performance."

68. M. E. Johnson and J. G. Fortman, "Internal Structure of the Gross Cohesiveness Scale," *Small Group Behavior* 19 (February 1988): 187–96.

69. Wynne W. Chin, Wm. David Salisbury, Allison W. Pearson, and Matthew J. Stollak, "Perceived Cohesion in Small Groups: Adapting and Testing the Perceived Cohesion Scale in a Small-Group Setting," *Small Group Research* 30 (December 1999): 751–66.

70. Lynne Kelly and Robert L. Duran, "Interaction and Performance in Small Groups: A Descriptive Report," *International Journal of Small Group Research* 1 (1985): 182–92.

71. Charles N. Greene, "Cohesion and Productivity in Work Groups," *Small Group Behavior* 20 (1989): 70–86.

72. Wood, "Challenging the Assumptions."

73. Frederick G. Elias, Mark E. Johnson, and Jay B. Fortman, "Task-Focused Self-Disclosure: Effects on Group Cohesiveness, Commitment to the Task, and Productivity," *Small Group Behavior* 20 (1989): 87–96.

74. William F. Owen, "Metaphor Analysis of Cohesiveness in Small Discussion Groups," *Small Group Behavior* 16 (1985): 415–26.

75. Barker, "The Behavioral Analysis of Interpersonal Intimacy."

76. Synthesized from Ernest G. Bormann & Nancy C. Bormann, *Effective Small Group Communication,* 2nd ed. (Minneapolis: Burgess, 1976): 70–76; and Gloria J. Galanes (unpublished research based on interviews with peer-nominated excellent leaders, 2002).

77. Vanessa Urch Druskat and D. Christopher Kayes, "Learning versus Performance in Short-Term Project Teams," *Small Group Research* 31 (June 2000): 328–53.

78. Larson and LaFasto, *TeamWork;* Frank LaFasto and Carl Larson, *When Teams Work Best: 6,000 Team Members and Leaders Tell What It Takes to Succeed* (Thousand Oaks, CA: Sage, 2001): 65–83.

79. Ernest G. Bormann and Nancy C. Bormann, *Effective Small Group Communication,* 4th ed. (Edina, MN: Burgess, 1988): 74–76.

80. Bill Saporito, "The New Dream Team," *Time* (July 19, 1999): 60.

81. Gloria J. Galanes (unpublished research).

82. Anthony M. Townsend and Samuel M. DeMarie, "Are You Ready for Virtual Teams?" *HR Magazine* 41 (September 1996): np; accessed via EBSCOhost on World Wide Web, August 2, 2002.

83. Sirkka Jarvenpas, quoted in Carla Joinson, "Managing Virtual Teams," *HR Magazine* 47 (June 2002): np; accessed via EBSCOhost on World Wide Web, August 2, 2002.

84. Synthesized from the following sources: Joinson, "Managing Virtual Teams;" Jessica Lipnack and Jeffrey Stamps, *Virtual Teams: Reaching Across Space, Time, and Organizations with Technology* (New York: Wiley 1997); Townsend and DeMarie, "Are You Ready for Virtual Teams?"

85. LaFasto and Larson, *When Teams Work Best;* 68.

86. LaFasto and Larson, *When Teams Work Best,* 14–15.

87. Jack R. Gibb, "Defensive Communication," *Journal of Communication* 11 (1961): 141–48.

88. S. Elizabeth Bird, "Chatting on Cynthia's Porch: Creating Community in an E-mail Fan Group," *Southern Communication Journal* 65 (Fall 1999): 49–65.

89. Suggestions synthesized from Neil Clark, *Teambuilding: A Practical Guide for Trainers* (New York: McGraw-Hill, 1994); Glenn M. Parker, *Team Players and Teamwork* (San Francisco: Jossey-Bass, 1991); Glenn H. Varney, *Building Productive Teams: An Action Guide and Resource Book* (San Francisco: Jossey-Bass, 1989); and our own experiences.

90. Albert V. Carron and Kevin S. Spink, "The Group Size–Cohesion Relationship in Minimal Groups," *Small Group Research* 26 (February 1995): 86–105.

91. Susan R. Glaser, "Teamwork and Communication: A Three-Year Case Study of Change," *Management Communication Quarterly* 7 (February 1994): 282–96.

Perspectives on Leadership in Small Groups

CENTRAL MESSAGE

Small group leadership is an interactive phenomenon; it results from communicative behaviors appropriate to group task and relational goals, other members' behaviors, the context, and other contingencies.

STUDY OBJECTIVES

As a result of studying Chapter 9 you should be able to:

1. Define the concepts of *leadership, leader, leadership emergence,* and *designated leader.*

2. Explain the five sources of interpersonal influence (power) in a group and how they are involved in small group leadership.

3. Describe the process of leadership emergence.

4. Explain traits, styles, and function approaches to small group leadership and the strengths and weaknesses of each approach.

5. Describe the unique focus of each of the contingency approaches to small group leadership.

6. Name and describe nine communicative competencies important for small group leaders.

7. Explain how leaders and members are interdependent, describe the LMX model and transformational leadership.

8. Explain *distributed leadership* and why it is an appropriate model for small, task-oriented groups.

Jennifer, Robyn, Jiang, and Andreas comprise the broadcast advertising team in the corporate offices of a California-based retail company. Jennifer is the team's designated leader and their broadcast media buyer. Jiang, their promotions coordinator, is responsible for planning and directing promotional events, such as the back-to-school campaign, which coincide with the television and radio advertisements. He also makes sure that all of Jennifer's business records are kept up-to-date. Andreas, their production coordinator, assists Jennifer in writing, producing, and directing all television and radio commercials. Robyn, their broadcast advertising coordinator and Jennifer's administrative assistant, is primarily responsible for creating and maintaining working relationships with television and radio sales representatives. The company's quarterly profits are directly tied to successful media campaigns, which themselves are directly tied to how well this team works together.

Jennifer has been associated with the company for well over 20 years and is highly regarded in the advertising community. But everything does not always run smoothly for this broadcast advertising team. Although highly respected by her peers, Jennifer feels she must be in control of all tasks and the team's socioemotional environment. She tends not to let other members of the team make mistakes or create their own successes.

Her leadership style poses problems for team members in a couple of ways. High turnover is common in this division. New employees are regularly being trained, often inadequately. New employees are never fully informed about their job responsibilities because Jennifer tightly controls the flow of information to them, but she is often too busy to work with them. Too often, they learn how and what they are supposed to do when they have been reprimanded by Jennifer for making a mistake. This creates resentment among the team and costs the company money for wasted time. Further resentment is created by her desire to control their socioemotional environment. For instance, if Andreas writes a poor advertising script, she expects one of his coworkers to tell him rather than convey the bad news herself. Yet this retail company is successful in part because the broadcast advertising group produces effective advertising. At what point is ineffective leadership considered a problem? Who is responsible for change? Is the character of a group solely determined by one person's behaviors? If you were an outside consultant, what would you say to this division? These and other issues will be touched on in this chapter.

According to Larson and LaFasto, the final ingredient for effective group performance is team leadership, with the right person serving in the leadership role.[1] Because small groups are everywhere, you will certainly have your turn serving as a small group leader. This can be a source of self-esteem, recognition, and appreciation; it can also be a nightmare.

Much of the conventional wisdom about what makes a good leader is simply wrong. Many people hold oversimplified beliefs about effective leadership that interfere with their learning to function well as small group leaders.

We hope this chapter and Chapter 13 will dispel those beliefs, as well as help you discover the communication competencies you must develop to perform well as a leader.

In Chapter 9 we examine the concepts of *leader* and *leadership,* describe the process of leadership emergence, review historical and contemporary perspectives about leadership, examine the relationship between leaders and members, and develop an argument in favor of *distributed leadership* for most small task-oriented groups. In Chapter 13 we focus on the duties commonly expected of small group leaders in our culture and provide specific suggestions on how to perform them.

Leadership and Leaders

In previous chapters we have discussed the importance of several input, throughput, and output variables to the success of a small group system. Leadership is a central factor in whether the group can get the job done and, at the same time, maintain respect among members. Whether your group has a person called a leader or not does not matter. What *does* matter, if the group is to function effectively, is that it has *leadership.* Why? Because leadership is a process, whereas *leader* refers to a person. Let's look more closely at the distinction and its relevance to small group communication.

Leadership

Leadership as a process is captured in Hackman and Johnson's definition: "Leadership is human (symbolic) communication which modifies the attitudes and behaviors of others in order to meet group goals and needs."[2] We use their definition because it extends the essential role of *communication* in group dynamics into leadership processes. Leadership is accomplished through communication—what a leader actually says and does in interaction. Leadership involves persuasion and discussion, not psychological coercion or physical violence. Through human symbolic behaviors, leaders *modify* the positions of group members, which implies that good leadership involves flexibility regarding the group's conditions and the characteristics of its members. In addition, leadership consists of those behaviors that help the group achieve its goals, not those that run counter to those goals. Leadership, then, does not exist in a vacuum but is a shared property of the group and is created through group communication.

Too many people forget these central features of leadership and equate leadership with power. Leadership does involve power; however, all members of a group can influence group interaction with their power resources.[3] What power resources might the members of the broadcast-advertising team have to pull off successful advertising campaigns while working for a superior with strong control issues?

> **Leadership**
> Influence exerted through communication that helps a group achieve goals; performance of a leadership function by any member.

Power

The potential to influence behavior of others, derived from such bases as the ability to reward and punish, expertise, legitimate title or position, and personal attraction.

Sources of Influence (Power)   The ability to influence others stems from **power** that is derived from a particular source, or base. Leaders and followers transact to create a relationship based on perceived power. Leaders can influence the conduct of others to the extent that their power is perceived and acknowledged by followers. The sources of power identified by French and Raven include reward, punishment, legitimate, referent, and expert.[4]

Leaders can *reward* followers by giving them both tangible and intangible items such as special attention, acknowledgment, compliments, personal favors, special titles, money, and material goods. For instance, Lucas found that telling members they were high performers within their work teams (whether they were or not) and giving them a high-status job title actually increased their satisfaction, performance, commitment to the organization, and decreased turnover.[5] Jiang, the broadcast advertising team's program coordinator, is in a position to reward Jennifer with up-to-date business records. Jennifer may come down hard on her broadcast-advertising team, but she lets them leave early and gives the team free tickets to social events like concerts and baseball games. Leaders can also *punish* by withholding these same items. For example, Jennifer withholds information from new employees by tightly controlling it and disrupts the group's socialization of new members by refusing to spend time with them. *Coercion* is a special form of punishment power that uses threats or force to "influence" others. Although good leaders may effectively use punishment (especially the fear of losing something important, such as belonging to the group or the respect of the others), they do not use hardball tactics to coerce or force compliance. Coercion breeds resentment, sabotage, and rebellion, which are not desirable small group outcomes. We do not consider coercion to be genuine leadership as we define it.

Legitimate power stems from a special position or role acknowledged by the followers. For instance, in a police task force, lieutenants are accepted as having the right to give orders to sergeants, who themselves may give orders to patrol officers. Jennifer was designated the leader of the broadcast advertising team, which made her leadership legitimate. However, legitimate power includes only influence that is accepted as appropriate by followers. Thus, a committee chair does not have the right to tell members how to dress or wear their hair, although a supervisor might be given such power.

Referent power is based on attraction or identification with another person. Robyn's relationships with television and radio sales representatives are built around her referent power and thus affect how successfully the broadcasting advertising team produces its media campaigns. Some referent leaders have charisma and others want to associate with them and imitate their behavior. For example, one of us skipped a class in high school because the referent leader of our small group of friends suggested it. Ideally, however, leaders model positive behaviors for the other members to admire and emulate, such as listening, considering all sides of an issue, and keeping remarks orderly. The more leaders are admired and respected, the more members copy their behavior, and thus the greater their power to influence the group.

Expert power comes from what others believe a member knows or can do. The person with expert power is influential because he or she is perceived as having knowledge or skills vital to the group. Jennifer's 20 years of service to the company and the high regard with which she is held by the advertising community help establish her expert power base within the team. If your group is responsible for producing a panel discussion for the rest of your class and you happen to be the only member who has ever participated in a panel discussion, you have expertise the others value, which gives you power in that particular group.

Usually a leader's power stems from more than one source. The more sources on which a person's power rests, the more that person has the potential to dominate a group. Conversely, the more these bases of power are distributed among members, the more likely verbal participation is to be shared, decision making to be collaborative, and satisfaction to be high. In other words, leadership can be provided by all members' exercising their influence in service to the group goal. We expand on this idea later.

Leaders

The term *leader* refers to a person, or sometimes to a special position occupied by a person.[6] A **leader** in a small group is a person who influences the behavior of others through communication. We use the term *leader* to refer to three related types of individuals: a person who exerts influence toward achievement of a group's goal, a person who is perceived by the others as being a leader, and a person who has been appointed or elected to a leadership position (e.g., chair, team leader, coordinator, or facilitator). A person elected or appointed to a leadership position is called a **designated leader.**

Having a designated leader can help provide stability to a group. Numerous studies have shown that small groups with stable leadership are more effective in goal achievement than small groups without it. A group whose energy is siphoned off in a leadership struggle produces poor outcomes, dissatisfied members, and low cohesion.[7] In contrast, groups with designated leaders *accepted by the members* have fewer interpersonal problems and often produce better outcomes than groups without designated leaders.[8] The implication is clear: Even in a group in which influence (and thus leadership) is widely shared, someone must coordinate the flow of communication and the work of the members.

Having the title *designated leader* gives someone legitimate power, like Jennifer, but that person must still earn the respect and support of other members. A designated leader's behavior will be evaluated and may frequently be challenged by the members. If the designated leader's power rests solely on the legitimacy of the title, someone else with more broadly based power will likely emerge as a more influential informal leader.

Even though all members of a small group bear responsibility for the success or failure of the group, the designated leader shoulders special

Leader

A person who uses communication to influence others to meet group goals and needs; any person identified by members of a group as leader; a person designated as leader by election or appointment.

Designated Leader

A person appointed or elected to a position as leader of a small group.

Designated leaders greatly affect small groups.

responsibility for the group's work. As Stech and Ratliffe put it, both "group members and outsiders tend to hold the leader accountable for group beliefs, proposals, actions, and products."[9] This confers tremendous obligation on the designated leader to attend to how the group is functioning as a system and to ensure that needed leadership services are provided. Not all leaders in a group are designated. The person perceived by other group members as the leader or the person who is influencing the group toward its goal may, over time, have emerged as leader from interaction among the group members.

Leadership Emergence

The process by which someone emerges as the leader of an initially leaderless group in which all members start out as equals.

Leadership Emergence   The process of **leadership emergence,** whereby one individual who starts out on an equal footing with other members and emerges to be perceived as the group's leader, has been charted by Aubrey Fisher, known for his focus on the dynamics of small group decision making.[10] He developed his model (refer to Figure 9.1) from his own conclusions after listening to numerous hours of audiotaped small group interaction. The model is a description of member contention for leadership after one or more members make a move toward leadership.

The three-stage model presumes that all members are potential candidates for leadership. Stage 1 is characterized by one or more members' (see, for example, member E) falling from consideration almost immediately. Such members may perceive themselves as unable to lead or uninterested in leading for a number of reasons (e.g., too busy). Also, if some members exhibit behaviors others see as nonleaderlike (e.g., quiet, uninformed, or dogmatic) they will be eliminated.[11]

FIGURE 9.1 A model of emergent leadership

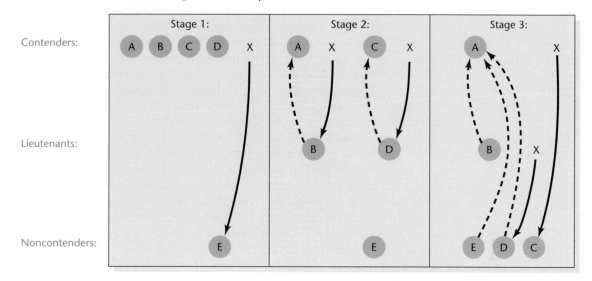

Stage 2 is characterized by the remaining members' bids for leadership being supported by other members. A and C are still in contention and enlist the help of B and D, who back out of contention but serve as ***lieutenants*** to A and C, respectively. Notice that two cliques or coalitions form around both A and C. Fisher noted that stage 2 can be lengthy, with verbal sparring typical. Eventually, one contender fails at her or his bid and drops out. The candidate that falls out of contention usually is too directive and communicatively offensive to others (e.g., talks too much, is manipulative).[12]

In stage 3, C falls out completely and A is left as leader. Member E's support may or may not be important. If E's activity stays low, his or her support is not significant. However, if E becomes active, both A and C might vie for E's support because alliance with E could be extremely important to either one. Member D could also shift support to A during C's failed attempt to emerge as leader.

Fisher's model (Figure 9.1) is basic and can involve several variations. For instance, leadership emergence may involve only two stages. It can occur painlessly and quickly when only one member secures a lieutenant and the rest of the group follows along. Sometimes an early leader emerges who is later deposed, which causes the leadership emergence process to recycle back to stage 2. Finally, the leadership emergence process may not involve a stage 3 if the two contenders cooperate as coleaders.

You will note that while Fisher's model describes general processes based on the quantity and quality of communication, there is a sense that some personal characteristics (e.g., skills in verbalizing) are associated with who emerges as leader. In fact, it has been popular to explain leadership emergence by searching for the personal characteristics of the emergent leader.

Personal Characteristics of Emergent Leaders   Several studies of leadership have found a number of characteristics associated with emergent leaders. One of these is **self-monitoring,** discussed briefly in Chapter 6, which refers to individuals' abilities to monitor, in a given situation, both social cues and their own actions.[13] High self-monitors are sensitive to contextual cues, socially perceptive, and able to respond flexibly according to what seems needed at any given time. Zaccaro et al. found that more than half the variance of leadership emergence was explained by self-monitoring.[14] This was confirmed by Ellis and Cronshaw, who found that males who were high self-monitors emerged as leaders because they were better able to adapt their behaviors to fit the needs of the group.[15] However, this was not true for women, probably because female high self-monitors, who are sensitive to subtle clues, sometimes sense that their leadership behavior is perceived as inappropriate. They may then modify their actions to tone down that leadership behavior. These authors discovered that high self-monitors do in fact monitor social cues and are able to modify their responses; they are more likely to emerge as leaders across situations. However, low self-monitors, whose actions are motivated more by internal than external cues, can also emerge as leaders in situations in which they have favorable attitudes toward expressing leadership; they will not emerge as leaders if they hold unfavorable attitudes about leadership.[16]

Verbal style, together with the content of communication, also is associated with leadership emergence.[17] Consistent with earlier studies, Baker found that members whose communication style was quiet, tentative, or vague were perceived as uncommitted to the group and not knowledgeable about the group's task. These members were quickly eliminated as potential leaders because others did not believe they contributed ideas or helped organize the group. Those who did emerge as leaders made more attempts to suggest procedures for the group and thus helped get the group organized. The emergent leader's participation profiles were high in procedure giving, moderate in idea giving, and low in stating opinions. Leaders' and members' styles were consistent in what Baker describes as mundane style: informal, unimaginative, ordinary. High-status members who were not leaders had a dramatic style that, though unusual, was tolerated because of their perceived helpfulness to the group.

Pescosolido found that informal, or emergent, leaders of groups strongly influence the other group members' perceptions about their ability to get the job done, particularly early in the group's life.[18] Such leaders seemed to be able to help members make sense of information and events in a positive way. Early on, they are able to shape the group's perceptions about what its capabilities are, and to set expectations for group success.

Years ago, biological sex was associated with group leadership in that males were more likely to emerge than females. However, biological sex has not been a useful predictor of who will emerge as a leader in a group. Psychological gender, on the other hand, may be more useful. Regardless of sex,

---

Self-Monitoring

An individual's ability to monitor other people's reactions to his/her behavior and adjust in response.

those individuals enacting a masculine communication style (i.e., independent, self-reliant, willing to take a stand) emerged more often as leader than those enacting feminine and nonandrogynous communication styles.[19] Generally, groups appear to choose leaders on the basis of performance, most especially task performance. Hawkins observed mixed-sex groups and analyzed transcripts of their communication.[20] She found that task-relevant communication, not gender, was the factor that explained who emerged as leader. Furthermore, she found no significant differences in the amount of task-relevant remarks contributed by men and women. Sex, gender, and leader emergences are difficult processes to unravel. Shimanoff and Jenkins remind us that research, time and again, provides evidence that men and women lead equally well and group members are equally satisfied with both male and female leaders.[21]

This finding about the importance of task-focused communication is consistent with the findings of De Souza and Klein.[22] They hypothesized that the nature of the task would affect leadership emergence. They found that although the type of task did not influence emergence, members' individual abilities to contribute to the task and their commitment to the group goal were associated with their emergence as leaders. They also discovered that groups with emerged leaders outperformed those without them. This latter finding is supported by Kurth, who found that group members themselves considered groups with emerged leaders more successful.[23]

Sometimes a group member will emerge as a leader even though the group already has a designated leader. Wheelan and Johnston followed four individuals identified by their peers as *informal leaders* in groups with formal leaders.[24] They found that the behavior of such leaders did not completely follow the behavior either of traditional emergent or designated leaders. Such individuals did talk more than most of their fellow members, but their talk was not more task-oriented, as is true with emergent leaders. Member leaders contributed more to the socioemotional aspect of the group, but not always in a positive way. They were more likely to challenge the designated leaders. They built coalitions with other members and generally displayed anti-authority positions. Wheelan and Johnston note that the presence of such members can have a substantial effect on the group's interaction but that too little is known about such members; they call for more research into informal member-leaders.

What can we learn from this discussion of leadership emergence? First, even if a group has a designated leader, one or more group members can also emerge as leaders. Emergent leaders appear to lead primarily through referent, expert, and reward power. Without a title or a legitimate base of power, they rely on communication skills to lead and, by definition, have the support of other group members. Designated leaders would do well to act like the kind of person who would also emerge as a leader. Remember that each group's situation is different. The type of task as well as the personalities and preferences of the members influences the kind of leadership accepted by a group.

Second, if your group does not have a designated leader, one will emerge. Rather than list the rules for leader emergence, we turn the tables to list what any group member can do to *avoid* emerging as a leader:[25]

- Miss as many meetings as possible.
- Say very little in group meetings.
- Volunteer readily to be the group's recorder.
- Do what you are told by other members.
- When you do contribute to the group, be dogmatic, verbally aggressive, and act like you know it all—especially early in the group's history.
- When you can, play the role of joker.
- Show disdain for leadership.

The secrets of effective leadership have been sought for years, as you will learn in the next section. As with other social scientific phenomena, the study of leadership has moved from simplicity to complexity.

Recap: A Quick Review

Leadership is a process central to small group dynamics. Although a group may not have a leader, it must have leadership to move effectively toward its goal.

1. Leadership is often defined as a process involving communication efforts to influence others toward group goals. The nature of the interpersonal influence may stem from reward, legitimate, referent, coercion, or expert power.

2. *Leader* is a term used to identify a person or position. Groups can have designated or emergent leaders, and sometimes both.

3. Leadership emergence can be described in a general three-stage model depicting how one person can, over time, become perceived as the group's leader. Several kinds of behaviors, such self-monitoring and verbal style, are related to leadership emergence.

4. Informal leaders who emerge in groups that already have designated leaders usually rely on referent, reward, and expert power.

Theoretical Approaches to Leadership

In this next section, we present several of the most important approaches to the study of leadership. The most useful contemporary theories are based on models of communication. We urge you not to become rigidly attached to any one theory because all of them contain useful insights; moreover, new discoveries may simplify the complexity that currently exists.

Traits Approaches

Our discussion of leadership emergence has focused on communication characteristics, broadly, and specific personal characteristics often referred to as traits. A *trait* is a characteristic of a person. Some traits, such as eye color or height, are unchangeable; others, such as self-monitoring, are subject to some control. The **traits approach** to leadership examines how traits are related to leadership and assumes that leaders are more likely to have certain traits than other group members are. You just read how several traitlike characteristics have been associated with leadership emergence.

The earliest studies of leadership (from before the Christian epoch through the 1950s) assumed that people were collections of relatively fixed traits, with one leadership situation being much like another. Trait approach researchers looked for the trait or traits that distinguished leaders from followers. They believed that leaders were a special class of people who were born, not made. Social scientists used a number of personality measures in an effort to discover the traits of leaders. Some studies found that leaders tended to have higher IQs and were taller, more attractive, and larger than nonleaders.[26]

You may have heard this approach to leadership taken to the extreme; for example, during election years, some people try to predict who will be elected president of the United States by physical characteristics alone. Male leaders typically brush their hair to the left (Al Gore brushed his from the right). Only 5 of 42 presidents have been left-handed (all front runners in the 2000 U.S. election were right-handed). Taller presidential candidates enjoy a 3 to 1 advantage over other contenders. And, finally, some say "royal" blood is the best predictor in a presidential election; George W. Bush is the most "royal" of any president.[27] As you might guess, no one has been able to find the trait or set of traits that can be used to explain leadership. There simply is no trait or combination of traits that leaders have that other members do not also have.

Modern trait approaches examine a variety of complex personality characteristics such as enthusiasm, verbal facility, creativity, critical-thinking ability, and self-confidence. Although they are labeled traits, they seem to represent behaviors that leaders perform rather than invariable, unchangeable characteristics. In short, this approach, although intuitively appealing, has been less than helpful to us in our attempts to understand complex leadership processes. Personality characteristics are not easily measured and, most important, this approach does not help distinguish between good and bad leaders nor does it explain why leadership changes in a group.[28] Stogdill noted that "leadership is a relation that exists between persons in a social situation, and that persons who are leaders in one situation may not necessarily be leaders in other situations."[29]

We believe that his conclusion that leadership is not a universal set of traits is valid; however, it seems equally clear that people with the ability to adapt their behaviors and who possess communication skills that help clarify the group's task and motivate other members will be influential in

Traits Approach

The approach to leadership that assumes that leaders have certain traits that distinguish them from followers or members of a group.

FIGURE 9.2   Comparison of autocratic, democratic, and laissez-faire leadership styles

	Autocratic	Democratic	Laissez-faire
Characteristics	Theory X assumptions. Directive; controlling. Speaks with certainty. Gives orders; makes assignments. Makes decisions for group.	Theory Y assumptions. Participative; invites input. Speaks provisionally. Makes suggestions; helps structure group time. Involves group in decisions.	Asks group to take charge. Doesn't necessarily voice opinion. Expects group to decide everything.
Typical statements	"I've decided that this is what you're going to do . . ."	"What ideas would you suggest for getting this done?"	"Whatever you decide is okay with me."
Useful when	Group members are unmotivated, uninterested, or unfamiliar with task. Emergency situations occur.	Group members are knowledgeable, interested. Group has time to discuss and deliberate.	Group members are experts, have worked together before, can assume group leadership.

groups.[30] Foreshadowing our discussion of other approaches, we may say that appropriate leader behaviors in a group are shaped by the needs of the group.

Styles Approaches

Styles approaches focus on the pattern of behaviors a leader exhibits in a group. Early style theorists attempted to discover whether there was one ideal style for small group leaders. More recent style theorists have looked at styles in relationship to member and task characteristics.

Considerable research has examined the behaviors of designated leaders classified as *democratic, autocratic,* and *laissez-faire*, which are summarized in Figure 9.2. **Democratic leaders** encourage members to participate in group decisions, including policy-making decisions ("What ideas do you have for organizing our task?"). **Laissez-faire leaders** take almost no initiative for structuring a group, but they may respond to inquiries from members ("I don't care; whatever you want to do is fine with me."). **Autocratic leaders** tightly control their groups, making assignments, directing all verbal interaction, and giving orders ("Here's how I've structured your task. First, you will . . . "). They ask fewer questions but answer more than democratic leaders and make more attempts to coerce but fewer attempts to get others to participate.[31]

Styles Approach

The leadership approach that studies the interrelationship between leader style and member behaviors.

Democratic Leaders

Egalitarian leaders who coordinate and facilitate discussion in small groups, encouraging participation of all members.

Laissez-Faire Leaders

Do-nothing designated leaders who provide minimal services to the group.

The autocratic and democratic styles of leadership described here correspond closely with the Theory X and Theory Y assumptions described by management theorist Douglas McGregor.[32] Theory X assumes that people don't like to work and must therefore be compelled by a strong, controlling leader ("boss") who supervises their work closely. In contrast, Theory Y assumes that people work as naturally as they play and are creative problem solvers who like to take charge of their own work. Leaders who accept the assumptions of Theory Y behave democratically by providing only as much structure as a group needs, allowing members to participate fully in decision making and other aspects of the group's work.

Research findings have been consistent about the effects of leadership style on group output.[33] Democratically led groups are generally more satisfied than autocratically led groups; most people in American culture prefer democratic groups. Autocratic groups often work harder in the presence of the leader, but they also experience more incidents of aggressiveness and apathy. Democratic groups whose leaders provide some structure and coordination are better problem solvers and their members are more satisfied than those in laissez-faire groups without structure. Research continues into the complex relationship among leadership style, satisfaction, and productivity. A recent meta-analysis found a correlation between style and productivity only when the type of task was taken into account.[34] Democratic leadership is more productive in natural settings and, in laboratory settings, seems to produce higher productivity on moderately or highly complex tasks.

The link between democratic leadership and satisfaction is not guaranteed. A recent analysis of this relationship by Foels et al. found that members' satisfaction depends on a number of moderating factors.[35] The relationship is stronger in artificial laboratory groups than in bona fide groups and in larger groups. Perhaps larger groups are less cohesive than smaller groups, and instituting a democratic style may affect member satisfaction because it softens the reduced, size-based cohesiveness. Finally, the democratic leadership-satisfaction relationship was stronger the more males there are in the group, but only in artificial groups. In both real and artificial groups, women are less satisfied with autocratic leadership and more satisfied with democratic leadership. Men in real groups prefer autocratic leadership; their satisfaction fell with democratic leadership. In contrast, in artificial groups, the more male the group, the greater the satisfaction with democratic leadership. Foels et al. think this may occur in part because artificial groups are composed of college students, with more liberal views of what is appropriate leadership, whereas in the work world, men are generally accustomed to a more task-oriented, directive style.

Satisfaction with leadership style is highly culture-dependent as we alluded to earlier. Lustig and Cassotta note that an autocratic style will be preferred in cultures with high power distance, such as Mexico, the Philippines, and India.[36] Similarly, cultures that demonstrate a stereotypically masculine orientation, including Japan, Austria, and Venezuela, would likewise prefer autocratic leadership.

Autocratic Leaders

Leaders who try to dominate and control a group.

The problem with styles approaches to leadership is that they oversimplify the complexities of groups as open systems. Although a leadership style that provides some degree of structure appears to be the most desirable for both productivity and satisfaction in the United States, several contingent factors (including cultural values) affect how much structure and control a particular group seems to need; that is, you cannot separate any one style from the situation that leaders and followers find themselves in.[37] Even Jennifer, designated leader of the advertising team in our opening story, who typically engages in a controlling leadership style, finds herself adjusting to the situation and to the peculiarities she discovers in each new employee. Group needs do not remain constant over time. Early on, members may appreciate a leader like Jennifer but, over time, grow to resent her style. Clinging to the notion that one style fits all groups and situations is dangerous. A number of factors, such as group member experience, how well members know each other, their history of success, the nature of the task, time deadlines, and so forth, all contribute to any style's success.

Functions Approach

Functions Approach

The study of functions performed by leaders; the theory that leadership is defined by the functions a group needs and can be supplied by any member.

The **functions approach** brings to mind the discussions of member roles in Chapter 6 and the key task and socioemotional dimensions of group culture in Chapter 8. This approach is grounded in two assumptions: (1) For any group to reach its goal, both task and social functions have to be performed, and (2) the performance of these task and social functions is generally the responsibility of *all* group members.

Task and social dimensions must be performed by someone in the group. The functions approach posits that one or more members must first diagnose what functions are needed and then take the actions necessary to perform those functions. Designated leaders are expected to do this effectively. If there is no designated leader, then *who* performs these functions is a good predictor of who is likely to emerge as a leader. This approach sets the stage for viewing group leadership behavior as a property of the group and a function of the interaction between leader(s) and the other group members.

Several researchers have attempted to identify specific task and maintenance functions needed for effective leadership. One of the earliest category systems for studying behavioral functions was the Interaction Process Analysis developed by Bales.[38] Benne and Sheats identified a variety of task and maintenance functions they claim are productive for the group, along with a set of functions that are counterproductive.[39] Several of the Benne and Sheats functions are included in the lists in Chapter 6. Fisher identified four functions performed by leaders, whom he saw as providing a mediating function between group events and activities and the final outcome:

1. Leaders provide sufficient information, as well as the ability to process and handle considerable information.

2. Leaders enact a variety of functions needed within the group.

3. Leaders help group members make sense of decisions made and actions performed within the group by doing such things as supplying good reasons for those actions.

4. Leaders focus on the here and now, stopping the group from jumping to unwarranted conclusions or adopting stock answers too quickly.[40]

Another major function of leadership is captured in Weick's metaphor of *leader as medium*.[41] Task groups usually confront a variety of interpersonal and task obstacles that must be overcome. One of the most difficult is the need to reduce a vast amount of complex and often equivocal information to an understandable level. Goal achievement requires group members to devise a set of rules and procedures for narrowing the number of plausible interpretations so that they can devise an appropriate course of action. Weick says that the basic function of leadership is to assist the group in creating an organizing scheme of rules and procedures for problem solving. The leader is the medium, or mechanism, through which this is accomplished. As you saw from our story of the broadcast advertising team, their leader Jennifer does not do a very good job of helping her employees narrow down plausible interpretations for any number of work tasks, especially their job responsibilities. She is a poor *medium*.

Contingency Approaches

All **contingency approaches** assume that group situations vary, with different situations requiring different leadership styles. These approaches explicitly acknowledge that factors such as members' skills and experience, cultural values, the type of task, and the time available affect the type of leadership likely to be effective. Contingency approaches acknowledge the complexity of small group systems, with all factors such as task, members, and environment affecting each other interdependently.

Not only do most current researchers accept contingency assumptions, but so do group members. Wood asked members of continuing small groups with task, social, and dual task-social objectives what they expected of designated leaders. Members expected different behaviors of the leaders depending on the group's focus, although a moderate degree of team spirit was expected by leaders of all types of groups.[42] Griffin found that the amount of structuring and directive behavior expected from supervisors depended on the level of growth needs of subordinates. People with high growth needs (i.e., who enjoy challenging jobs) most preferred participative, considerate supervisors, whereas employees with lower growth needs preferred more autocratic leadership.[43] For instance, perhaps the members of the broadcast advertising team in the opening case have high growth, since they do not take well to Jennifer's autocratic behaviors. A complex relationship was found among member needs, leadership style, and member satisfaction,

Contingency Approaches

The study of leadership that assumes that the appropriate leadership style in a given situation depends on factors such as members' skills and knowledge, time available, the type of task, and so forth.

giving credence to the general contingency hypothesis of leadership in small discussion groups.

Downs and Pickett also examined contingencies of leader style and member needs.[44] Groups of participants with high social needs were most productive with task-oriented procedural leaders and least productive with no designated leader. Groups of people low on interpersonal needs did equally well with designated leaders who provided task structuring only, with leaders who provided both task structuring and socioemotional leadership, and with no designated leader. Groups with some members high and some low in interpersonal needs performed somewhat better without a designated leader.

The contingency approach is also supported by Skaret and Bruning, who noted that satisfaction involves a complex interaction between leader behavior and work group attitudes.[45] The following traits of followers influence the type of leadership they preferred: degree of authoritarianism and dogmatism, need for achievement, and locus of control (whether one feels in control of one's own life or governed by fate).[46] From the research and theory surveyed, we can safely conclude that a discussion leader needs to be flexible, adapting to situational contingencies, but that in almost all situations in the United States, a democratic structuring approach will be productive, or will at least not be counterproductive.

Fiedler's Contingency Model   Some contingency approaches assume that there are limits to leaders' abilities to adapt; in other words, people are relatively inflexible. Some leaders have styles they prefer and use more effectively than other styles. Fiedler's contingency model of leadership reflects this view. He concluded that there are three factors upon which appropriate leader behaviors are contingent: leader-member relations, task structure, and strength of leader position (or legitimate) power.[47] The central thesis of Fiedler's work is that individuals' personal needs and characteristics make them suited for leadership only in certain types of contingencies, so it is more productive to match prospective leaders to situations than to try to change the individual's style. This also implies that a group's leadership situation will remain relatively stable. Extensive application has been made of this theory in placing supervisory personnel. According to Fiedler, problem-solving groups are generally best served by democratic structuring leaders with concerns for people, rather than by autocratic or nonstructuring leaders. However, in other types of situations (for instance, during emergencies or in leading primary groups), either a more autocratic or a more relationship-oriented style would be more productive.

Hersey and Blanchard's Situational Model   Other contingency approaches assume that people are flexible enough to adapt their behavior to meet the needs of many groups. Representative of this approach is the model of leadership adaptability and style developed by Hersey and Blanchard.[48] Leadership behaviors can be located along two dimensions, relationship orientation

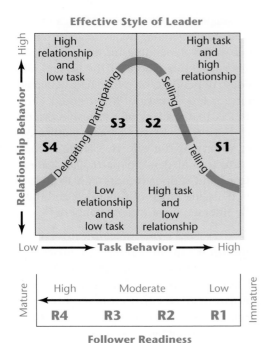

Effective Style of Leader

High Relationship Behavior → Low

High relationship and low task	High task and high relationship
S3	S2
S4	S1
Low relationship and low task	High task and low relationship

Low ——→ **Task Behavior** ——→ High

Mature | High | Moderate | Low | Immature
R4 | **R3** | **R2** | **R1**

Follower Readiness

FIGURE 9.3   Task and relationship needs of maturing groups

Source: Adapted from P. Hersey and K. Blanchard, *Management of Organizational Behavior; Utilizing Human Resources,* 7th ed. Englewood Cliffs, NJ: Prentice Hall, 1996. (Reprinted by permission.)

(giving socioemotional support) and task orientation (coordination efforts, instructions, advice, and so forth). A leader can be high on one, both, or neither dimension. (Figure 9.3 illustrates these dimensions.) However, whether a leader is effective depends on his or her ability to adapt to the needs of the members at all points during the life of the group. For instance, a new group of inexperienced members who may be unwilling or unable or who may simply not have the information to complete the task on their own are in low readiness. In this case, *telling* (low relationship and high task) may be an effective leadership style. Through close supervision and direction, group members can improve their readiness so that they require less task direction later on. As members need less direction about the task, the leader can focus on the relationships among members. *Participating* (high relationship and low task) styles recognize a level of maturity in members, with the leader able to facilitate shared responsibility for the group. Any group member may be supported in performing leadership behaviors. The fully mature group is one in which members are both able and willing to perform and need little direction and encouragement. In such groups, leaders can shift to a *delegating* (low relationship and low task) style in which responsibility is turned over to the group as a whole.

Hersey and Blanchard's model places great faith in the leader's ability to adapt to the needs of the group as the group's situation changes over time. There is support for believing that many leaders are flexible, as the self-monitoring studies reported earlier suggested. Wood found, for example, that the discussion leaders she observed demonstrated behavioral flexibility. The comments of the designated leader varied depending on the stated purpose of the discussion and the previous success or failure of the committee. Leaders tended to compensate as needed, depending on what had occurred at previous meetings, by providing more or less structure. Wood noted, "The most important and obvious conclusion is that leaders of purposive discussions do engage in adaptive behavior."[49] Her results have been confirmed. Sorenson and Savage observed greater variety in the effective leaders' communicative styles than in those of ineffective leaders. In particular, leaders should attend to the degrees of dominance and supportiveness they exhibit.[50] Drecksell, too, found that leaders covered a wide range of functions, and their interaction was more complex than the interaction of other members.[51]

Communicative Competencies Approach   In an attempt to provide a model that acknowledges contingencies without overwhelming us with complexity, Barge and Hirokawa recently proposed a Communication Competency Model of Group Leadership.[52] The **communicative competencies model** is based on the assumptions that leadership involves behaviors that help a group overcome obstacles to goal achievement, that leadership occurs through the process of communication, and that communication skills (competencies) are the means used by individuals to lead small groups. This model maintains the task and relationship distinctions noted by many researchers, but provides an organizing scheme for the overwhelming array of facts and conjectures relating to group leadership. We consider it a contingency approach because it assumes that the actual context facing the leader and group is constantly shifting, so the task and relational communicative competencies needed vary from moment to moment. Group leaders must be highly flexible to draw from a personal repertoire of such competencies. Knowing the behaviors and competencies that distinguish effective task group leaders can help you select a group's leader wisely and learn to be a better leader yourself. The following are specific communicative competencies exhibited by effective discussion leaders. Both task and relational competencies are needed.

> **Communicative Competencies Model**
>
> The model that assumes that the communication-related skills and abilities of members are what help groups overcome obstacles and achieve their goals.

1. **Effective small group leaders communicate actively, clearly, and concisely.**

    Numerous studies have found emergent leaders to be high in verbal participation, although not necessarily the highest in a group.[53] Reynolds found that leaders maintained their influence by staying involved in group discussion and decision making.[54] But amount of talk alone is only a small part of verbal competency; Russell found that group leaders had higher levels of communicative skills than other members.[55]

    What are these skills? Lashbrook found that leaders were perceived as speaking more clearly and fluently than other members.[56] Facility in verbalizing problems, goals, values, ideals, and solutions characterizes effective discussion leaders. Barge and Hirokawa theorized that the more complex the group's task, the more ambiguous the member roles; and the more negative the climate, the more important are the leader's communication skills.[57]

2. **Effective group leaders communicate a good grasp of the group's task.**

   Above all else, their communication behaviors reveal extensive knowledge about the task, skills for organizing and interpreting that knowledge, and an understanding of procedures that facilitate task accomplishment. They have technical know-how, are credible to the members, and know when to ask others for help.[58]

3. **Effective group leaders inspire team members' confidence in themselves.**

   Effective leaders set clear expectations and let their members know they have confidence in members' abilities. The leaders that Jung and Sosik studied empowered their members, which affected both the members' collective confidence and their performance.[59] LaFasto and Larson found that effective leaders bolster members' self-assurance by providing clarity about performance goals, by assigning members responsibilities that demonstrate the leader's trust in them, and by accentuating the positive.[60] These authors note that we like to be around positive people who make us feel competent. Showing confidence in team members increases their desire to achieve while it decreases their fear of failure. This can produce extraordinary successes.

4. **Effective group leaders skillfully mediate information and ideas supplied by all members.**

   Such leaders are especially competent in analysis of statements and in the kinds of critical thinking that lead to thorough evaluation and integration of information. They are good at providing structure to unorganized information, at asking probing questions to bring out pertinent information, and at evaluating inferences and conclusions drawn from information. They help all members focus on activities relevant to the group's goal.[61]

5. **Effective group leaders express their opinions provisionally.**

   Most Americans prefer their leaders not to express ideas dogmatically. Maier and Solem demonstrated that groups whose leaders suspended judgment and encouraged full consideration of minority viewpoints produced better solutions than did other groups.[62] Moreover, groups whose leaders withheld their opinions about solutions until later in a discussion produced more and better alternatives to a solution than groups whose leaders expressed their opinions early.[63] Groups prefer open-minded leaders.[64]

6. **Effective group leaders express group-centered concern.**
   From interviews with 90 successful leaders in various professions, Bennis and Nanus reported "there was no trace of self-worship or cockiness in our leaders."[65] Larson and LaFasto found that outstanding team leaders "articulate the team's goal in such a way as to inspire a desire for and eventual commitment to the accomplishment of the goal" and exhibit personal commitment to that goal in both words and deeds.[66] Furthermore, such leaders readily confront members who are more self- than group-centered.[67]

7. **Effective group leaders model a collaborative climate by respecting and supporting others.**
   LaFasto and Larson's excellent leaders worked to establish a collaborative climate and to make it safe for group members to communicate.[68] Building on his studies of democratic leaders, Rosenfeld claimed that when "people are equals with whom they work, the rewards and punishments are to be shared."[69] Such leaders are sensitive to nonverbal signals and the feelings these signify. Kenny and Zaccaro reported that leadership depends heavily on competencies in perceiving the needs and goals of members, then adjusting behaviors to these needs.[70] Effective discussion leaders are courteous.

   This may be particularly important in a virtual environment, where members don't normally (or ever) interact face-to-face. Oakley suggests that defensive communication may find a "natural home" in the impersonal atmosphere of a virtual team because members are typically chosen on the basis of their expertise, and thus may be tempted to present opinions and information as "certain and unchallengeable."[71] She recommends that team leaders make a special effort to promote the social aspects of team work and to help align members' priorities with organizational priorities in a way that will interest and excite them.

8. **Effective group leaders promote celebration of diversity and sensitive diversity management.**
   Effective group leaders make sure to include *all* members in the team's work and play. Team members perceive them as impartial, not showing favoritism to particular members.[72] Leaders also make time for group members to get to know one another and learn to appreciate one another as individuals. Watson et al. found that the performance of ethnically diverse teams especially benefited from leadership that focused on relational aspects of the team.[73] In contrast, focus on the task was more effective for teams that were not diverse.

9. **Effective group leaders share rewards and credit with the group.**
   As Fiedler and Chemers pointed out, "Leadership is an amazing ego-involving activity."[74] Leaders are often tempted to take credit for the accomplishments of the group and to consolidate their personal power. But effective leaders share as equals both within the group and when

dealing with outsiders. They give credit to the group for accomplishments and work to develop the leadership competencies of all members.[75] In short, effective leaders are skilled in communicating appreciation for efforts of members.

The Relationship between Leaders and Followers

All contingency approaches assume an interdependent relationship between the communication behavior of the leader and the behavior, skills, preferences, and expectations of the members. In fact, although we discuss leaders and members separately, we do so only for convenience; leader-member behaviors form a unit, an interdependent system. Whether a leader's behaviors are effective depends in large part on both the perceptions and behaviors of the other members.

Most people in our culture want their leaders to perform structuring behaviors and to be considerate as well. Pavitt and Sackaroff found that experienced group members expected leaders to be enthusiastic and organized, and to encourage participation from all members as well as suggest procedures for the group.[76] This was confirmed by Ketrow, who found that a person who served as a procedural specialist was identified most often as a group's leader, and the task specialist was perceived as being most influential.[77] Infante and Gordon discovered that subordinates preferred a communication style they described as *affirming* (relaxed, friendly, and attentive) and low in verbal aggressiveness (attacks on others' self-concepts).[78]

One characteristic that may affect what members perceive and prefer is sex. Several studies suggest that women enact leadership differently than men, perhaps because members perceive different behavior as appropriate for men and women. Andrews found that although men and women had equal potential as leaders, women were uncomfortable calling themselves *leader* and preferred the designations *organizer* or *coordinator,* apparently because they perceived a stigma attached to the leader label.[79] This finding is supported by Owen, who noted that women distance themselves from the label of *leader*.[80] He also observed that women became leaders by outworking men in a group and that they used more themes of cohesion. Women's leadership behavior is likely constrained by expectations of members. Watson found, for instance, that women who enacted a dominant approach were less influential than women who enacted a considerate approach to leadership, especially with males.[81] However, women gave dominant female leaders higher ratings of effectiveness, but, regardless of style, women liked female bosses less than men did. Watson suggests a problem-solving approach for female leaders that takes into account the difficulties women sometimes have in dealing with perceptions of others.

Leader-Member Exchange (LMX) Model

One model that has looked systematically at the nature of the interdependent relationship of leader-member behaviors and perceptions is the **Leader-Member Exchange (LMX) model,** which suggests that supervisory leaders develop different kinds of leadership relationships with different members, depending on leader and member characteristics. Members differ in the amount of *negotiating latitude* they are allowed by leaders; a member with a high negotiating latitude is given a great deal of leeway to design and perform his or her job, whereas a member with low negotiating latitude is not accorded such freedom by the leader. Generally, members with higher negotiating latitude are more satisfied and more committed to the organization or group. The member's degree of negotiating latitude is transacted through a reciprocal interaction process with the leader, whose impression of the member's capabilities helps determine in large part what degree of negotiating latitude will be permitted.[82]

McClane found support for an interaction between leader and member characteristics, with the best leader-member fit determined by congruence on the need for power.[83] Leaders with high power needs gave greater negotiating latitude to members with high power needs; likewise, leaders with low power needs gave greater negotiating latitude to members with low power needs. Characteristics such as sex, locus of control, and need for achievement were not related. Clearly, leaders with high power needs take a different approach to forming groups than leaders with low power needs; both types of leaders appear to be more comfortable with members who share their assumptions about the appropriate use of power. By extension, members are more likely to be satisfied with leaders who share their assumptions by rewarding them with higher negotiating latitude.

Leader-Member Exchange (LMX) Model

The leadership model based on the finding that supervisors develop different kinds of leadership relationships with their subordinates, depending on characteristics of both the leader and members.

In a different study, McClane compared groups with wide variations in the amount of negotiating latitude and groups with little variation.[84] His results suggest that high differentiation (having some members with high negotiating latitude and some with little latitude in the same group) may have an undesirable effect on a group, particularly if the members accorded high negotiating latitude are seen as an elite core group with the rest feeling like hired hands. These results have been confirmed by Lee, who found that members with little negotiating latitude perceived less fairness than members with high latitude.[85] Those members who thought things were fair also perceived the work group's communication to be more cooperative. Although it is normal for leaders to interact differently with different members, clearly, they must tread carefully in doing so.

The foregoing discussion is designed to remind us that neither the leader nor the members operate in a vacuum; instead, their interactions are shaped by each other. Models such as the LMX remind us that, even though we isolate leadership and treat it as an individual variable for study purposes, in fact it is a *system-level* variable that is a property of the group as a whole, not of the individual called the group's leader.

The foregoing discussion is designed to remind us that neither the leader nor the members operate in a vacuum; instead, their interactions are shaped by each other. LMX and even the contingency models remind us that, even though we isolate leadership and talk about it separately for discussion and research, in fact it is a process and property of the group as a whole, not of the individual perceived or called the *leader*. Contemporary transformational leadership models try to capture this interdependence between leaders and followers in a different way.

Transformational Leadership

The concept of **transformational leadership** emerges out of contemporary organizational structures and subsequent discussions of management philosophy.[86] Traditional models of leadership assume that leaders trade rewards for group or team member performance.[87] Leaders use their bases of power to influence group members to do things for the group. However, communication itself is also a powerful way through which an inspirational leader can transform group members so that they perform beyond original expectations.[88]

Transformational leaders do not use rewards or even punishment to sustain their influence; instead, they use creative and dramatic messages to craft a powerful inspirational vision that motivates members to exceed expectations. Bass describes four characteristics of transformational leadership.[89] First, these leaders give the kind of *individual attention* to group members that we discussed in the LMX models. They coach, advise, and treat members as unique individuals who *matter* to the group. Second, these leaders are charismatic, portraying a spirit of confidence that is attractive. Members

Transformational Leadership

Transformational leadership empowers group members to exceed expectations by rhetorically creating a vision that inspires and motivates members.

find them *inspirational* in their communication, which in turn motivates them, through symbols and rhetorical visions, to aim higher. Third, transformational leaders blend their socioemotional skills with an *intellectual stimulation* that is contagious, encouraging members to be sharp critical thinkers and problem solvers. Finally, here is the bottom line: These leaders are able to inspire members of a group or team and thus *empower* them. When people are empowered, they have been given the freedom to discover their own self-efficacy—self-determination and confidence in their ability to perform.[90]

When subordinates in an organization are given the freedom to control their jobs and are supported by superiors who value their worth, they are generally more satisfied.[91] They believe that their supervisors are fair, they report fewer problems, and they rate their performance higher than those under more controlling supervisors. What do you think the members of the broadcast advertising team think about themselves and their work under Jennifer's less-than-transformational style of leadership?

The Case for Distributed Leadership

Distributed Leadership

The concept that group leadership is the responsibility of the group as a whole, not just of the designated leader; assumes that all members can and should provide needed leadership services to the group.

We have said several times that small group leadership is the property of the group, not the individual who happens to hold the title of leader. We believe strongly that although a group's designated leader or emergent one bear a lot of responsibility for coordinating and structuring the group's activities, all members can and should be equally responsible for the leadership of the group. The idea of **distributed leadership** explicitly acknowledges that the leadership of a group is spread among members, with each member expected to perform the communication behaviors needed to move the group toward its goal. A group that distributes leaderships is, in Hersey and Blanchard's terms, mature; the designated leader can largely withdraw from both task and relationship activity because the group members themselves are able to supply these for the group. Remember, a group may be able to function without a leader, but it cannot function without leadership. For example, Counselman described a group that had been active for 17 years without a designated leader.[92] Various leadership functions had been picked up by members of the group. The most important of these were providing structure, gatekeeping, setting group norms, and adhering to the group's task. We know this is unusual; most groups can and should use the services of a designated leader. However, this case verifies the important point that we made earlier about locus of leadership in a group: It belongs to the group.

Barge provided support for the distributed leadership concept when he compared two models of group leadership—one in which the leader was an active, directive influence in the group; and a leaderless model, in which all members engaged in the leadership process.[93] He discovered that the better predictor of group productivity was overall leadership activity, as opposed to the activity of the designated leader alone. In contrast to what we might expect, the more productive groups were not more controlling or directing. Instead of demonstrating a sender mode, the productive groups enacted a listener mode, reflecting a more contemplative approach with increased sensitivity to the environment and the other members. Barge concluded that although an individual leader's behavior may not necessarily help a group achieve its goals, the overall group leadership behavior does.

Gastil's studies of small group democracy also provide support for distributed leadership. Gastil says that democratic leadership distributes responsibility among members, empowers them by improving their general abilities and leadership skills, and helps the group in its decision-making process.[94] In examining factors that interfere with small group democracy, he notes that all the obstacles he identified were negatively related to comprehension and showing consideration for other members.[95] Listening, in other words, is potentially an important communication skill for members of groups with distributed, democratic leadership.

These findings affirm for us the concept that we have of an ideal group. We are not suggesting doing away with designated leaders. Instead, we invite you to consider what an ideal, responsible, mature group looks like, one in which all members of the group accept responsibility for its leadership. Members understand enough about the group process to know what functions are needed at what times, and they can supply those functions skillfully. Each member has, and acts on, a personal commitment to the group. Each member can step into the leadership position and function effectively, with the support and contribution of the other members. Leadership is distributed throughout.

Recap: A Quick Review

Leadership involves an interdependent relationship between leader and followers; it is a process that involves all group members.

1. The LMX model of leadership highlights the benefits of the leader's nurturing unique relationships with each group member.

2. Transformational leadership is a contemporary philosophy of leadership stressing the ways a dynamic and creative leader can use rhetoric and powerful symbols to empower group members. A vision is crafted that motivates group members to exceed expectations.

3. Distributed leadership is an extension of functional leadership in that it promotes the idea that all members of a group can enact behaviors that effectively move the group toward its goal. Once members develop into a mature group, the leader can step back and let the task and social dimensions be managed by the members themselves.

QUESTIONS FOR REVIEW

Go to self-quizzes on the Online Learning Center at mhhe.com/galanes12 to test your knowledge of the chapter concepts

This chapter scrutinized the complexity of group leadership. Consider the broadcast advertising team led by Jennifer. Members have problems, in part due to Jennifer's leadership style, but they also produce successful advertisements.

1. Pinpointing the leader of this group is easy. Why? In your own words, how would you describe the leadership of this group?

2. What types of interpersonal influence can you observe in this team? How might the way members use their power explain why they can produce effective advertising, even though they also have leadership problems?

3. Jennifer is this group's designated leader. Could any other member emerge as an informal leader? How?

4. Why are traits and styles approaches inadequate to explaining the leadership of this team, once you examine the team's dynamics?

5. How can functions and contingency approaches help explain why this team is successful, even with its leadership challenges?

6. What communication competencies are found in this group? Which competencies does Jennifer seem to lack?

7. What advice would you give this team to help members move to a more transformational or a distributed model of leadership?

KEY TERMS

Test your knowledge of these key terms by visiting the Online Learning Center Web site at mhhe.com/galanes12

Autocratic leaders
Communicative competencies model
Contingency approaches
Democratic leaders
Designated leader
Distributed leadership

Functions approach
Laissez-faire leaders
Leader
Leader-Member Exchange (LMX) model
Leadership
Leadership emergence

Power
Self-monitoring
Styles approaches
Traits approach
Transformational leadership

BIBLIOGRAPHY

Barge, J. Kevin, and Randy Y. Hirokawa. "Toward a Communication Competence Model of Group Leadership." *Small Group Behavior* 20 (1989): 167–89.

Bennis, Warren, and B. Nanus. *Leaders: The Strategies for Taking Charge*. New York: Harper & Row, 1985.

Cathcart, Robert S., Larry A. Samovar, and Linda D. Henman. *Small Group Communication: Theory and Practice*. 7th ed. Madison, WI: Brown & Benchmark, 1996, Section 7.

Hackman, Michael Z., and Craig E. Johnson. *Leadership: A Communication Perspective*. Prospect Heights, IL: Waveland Press, 1991.

Larson, Carl E., and Frank M. J. LaFasto. *TeamWork: What Must Go Right/What Can Go Wrong*. Newbury Park, CA: Sage, 1989.

NOTES

1. Carl E. Larson and Frank M. J. LaFasto, *Team-Work: What Must Go Right/What Can Go Wrong* (Newbury Park, CA: Sage, 1989): 118.

2. Michael Z. Hackman and Craig E. Johnson, *Leadership: A Communication Perspective* (Prospect Heights, IL: Waveland Press, 1991): 11.

3. E. Hollander, "Leadership and Power," in *The Handbook of Social Psychology 3,* vol. II, eds. G. Lindzey and Elliot Aronson (New York: Random House, 1985): 485–537.

4. John R. P. French and Bertram Raven, "The Bases of Social Power," in *Group Dynamics: Research and Theory,* 3rd ed., eds. Dorwin Cartwright and Alvin Zander (New York: McGraw-Hill, 1981): 317.

5. Jeffrey W. Lucas, "Behavioral and Emotional Outcomes of Leadership in Task Groups," *Social Forces* 78 (December 1999): 747–78.

6. Marvin E. Shaw, *Group Dynamics: Research and Theory,* 3rd ed. (New York: McGraw-Hill, 1981): 317.

7. Ernest G. Bormann, *Discussion and Group Methods,* 2nd ed. (New York: Harper & Row, 1975): 253–69; Nancy L. Harper and Lawrence R. Askling, "Group Communication and Quality of Task Solution in a Media Production Organization," *Communication Monographs* 47 (1980): 77–100.

8. E. P. Hollander, *Leadership Dynamics* (New York: Free Press, 1978): 13–16.

9. Ernest Stech and Sharon A. Ratliffe, *Working in Groups* (Skokie, IL: National Textbook Company, 1976): 201.

10. Donald Ellis and B. Aubrey Fisher, *Small Group Decision Making: Communication and the Group Process* (New York: McGraw-Hill, 1994): 203–6.

11. Ernest G. Bormann, *Small Group Communication: Theory and Practice,* 3rd ed. (New York: Harper & Row, 1990): 205–14, 291–92; John C. Geier, "A Trait Approach to the Study of Leadership in Small Groups," *Journal of Communication* 17 (1967): 316–23.

12. John C. Geier, "A Trait Approach to the Study of Leadership in Small Groups," 316–23.

13. M. Snyder, "Self-Monitoring Processes," in *Advances in Experimental Social Psychology,* vol. 12, ed. L. Berkowitz (New York: Academic Press, 1979).

14. Stephen J. Zaccaro, Roseanne J. Foti, and David A. Kenny, "Self-Monitoring and Trait-Based Variance in Leadership: An Investigation of Leader Flexibility across Multiple Group Situations," *Journal of Applied Psychology* 76 (1991): 308–15.

15. Robert J. Ellis and Steven F. Cronshaw, "Self-Monitoring and Leader Emergence: A Test of Moderator Effects," *Small Group Research* 23 (February 1992): 113–29.

16. Steven F. Cronshaw and Robert J. Ellis, "A Process Investigation of Self-Monitoring and Leader Emergence," *Small Group Research* 22 (November 1991): 403–20.

17. Deborah C. Baker, "A Qualitative and Quantitative Analysis of Verbal Style and the Elimination of Potential Leaders in Small Groups," *Communication Quarterly* 38 (Winter 1990): 13–26.

18. Anthony T. Pescosolido, "Informal Leaders and the Development of Group Efficacy," *Small Group Research* 32 (February 2001): 74–94.

19. Judith A. Kolb, "Are We Still Stereotyping Leadership? A Look at Gender and Other Predictors of Leader Emergence," *Small Group Research* 28 (1997): 370–93.

20. Katherine W. Hawkins, "Effects of Gender and Communication Content on Leadership Emergence in Small Task-Oriented Groups," *Small Group Research* 26 (May 1995): 234–49.

21. Susan Shimanoff and Mercilee M. Jenkins, "Leadership and Gender: Challenging Assumptions and Recognizing Resources," in *Small Group Communication: Theory and Practice,* 7th ed., eds. Robert S. Cathcart, Larry A. Samovar, and Linda Henman (Madison: WI: Brown & Benchmark, 1996): 327–44.

22. Gita De Souza and Howard J. Klein, "Emergent Leadership in the Group Goal-Setting Process," *Small Group Research* 26 (November 1995): 475–96.

23. Lita Kurth, "Democracy and Leadership in Basic Writing Small Groups" (Paper presented at the Annual Meeting of the Conference on College Composition and Communication, March 1995).

24. Susan A. Wheelan and Frances Johnston, "The Role of Informal Member Leaders in a System Containing Formal Leaders," *Small Group Research* 27 (February 1996): 33–55.

25. Ellis and Fisher, *Small Group Decision Making*, 210–12.

26. Ralph M. Stogdill, *Handbook of Leadership: A Survey of Theory and Research* (New York: Free Press, 1974): 63–82; Marvin E. Shaw, *Group Dynamics*, 2nd ed. (New York: McGraw-Hill, 1976): 274–75 and Chapter 6.

27. "Predictions: If the Crown Fits . . . ," *Newsweek*, August 23, 1999, p. 8.

28. Ellis and Fisher, *Small Group Decision Making*, 182.

29. Ralph M. Stogdill, "Personal Factors Associated with Leadership: A Survey of Literature," *Journal of Psychology* 25 (1948): 64.

30. Charles Pavitt and Pamela Sakaroff, "Implicit Theories of Leadership and Judgments of Leadership among Group Members," *Small Group Research* 21 (1990): 374–92.

31. Lawrence B. Rosenfeld and Timothy B. Plax, "Personality Determinants of Autocratic and Democratic Leadership," *Speech Monographs* 42 (1975): 203–8.

32. Douglas McGregor, *The Human Side of Enterprise* (New York: McGraw-Hill, 1960).

33. Ralph K. White and Ronald Lippett, "Leader Behavior and Member Reaction in Three 'Social Climates,'" in *Group Dynamics: Research and Theory,* 2nd ed., eds. Dorwin Cartwright and Alvin Zander (Evanston, IL: Row, Peterson, 1960): 527–53; William E. Jurma, "Effects of Leader Structuring Style and Task-Orientation Characteristics of Group Members," *Communication Monographs* 46 (1979): 282; Malcom G. Preston and Roy K. Heintz, "Effectiveness of Participatory versus Supervisory Leadership in Group Judgment," *Journal of Abnormal and Social Psychology* 44 (1949): 344–45; George Graen, Fred Dansereau, and Takau Minami, "Dysfunctional Leadership Styles," *Organizational Behavior and Human Performance* 7 (1972): 216–36; Norman R. F. Maier and Ronald A. Maier, "An Experimental Test of the Effects of 'Developmental' vs. 'Free' Discussions on the Quality of Group Decisions," *Journal of Applied Psychology* 41 (1957): 320–23; William E. Jurma, "Leadership Structuring Style, Task Ambiguity and Group Members' Satisfaction," *Small Group Behavior* 9 (1978): 124–34.

34. John Gastil, "A Meta-Analytic Review of the Productivity and Satisfaction of Democratic and Autocratic Leadership," *Small Group Research* 25 (August 1995): 384–410.

35. Rob Foels, James E. Driskell, Brian Mullen, and Eduardo Salas, "The Effects of Leadership on Group Member Satisfaction," *Small Group Research* 31 (December 2000): 676–701.

36. Myron W. Lustig and Laura L. Cassotta, "Comparing Group Communication across Cultures: Leadership, Conformity, and Discussion Processes," in *Small Group Communication: Theory and Practice,* 7th ed., eds. Robert S. Cathcart, Larry A. Samovar, and Linda D. Henman (Boston: McGraw-Hill, 1997): 316–26.

37. Ellis and Fisher, *Small Group Decision Making*, 184.

38. R. F. Bales, *Interaction Process Analysis* (Cambridge, MA: Addison-Wesley, 1950).

39. Kenneth D. Benne and Paul Sheats, "Functional Roles of Group Members," *Journal of Social Issues* 4 (1948): 41–49.

40. B. Aubrey Fisher, "Leadership as Medium: Treating Complexity in Group Communication Research," *Small Group Behavior* 16 (1985): 167–96.

41. Karl Weick, "The Spines of Leaders," in *Leadership: Where Else Can We Go?* eds. M. McCall and M. Lombardo (Durham, NC: Duke University Press, 1978): 37–61.

42. Julia T. Wood, "Alternative Portraits of Leaders: A Contingency Approach to Perceptions of Leadership," *Western Journal of Speech Communication* 43 (1979): 260–70.

43. R. N. Griffin, "Relationships among Individual, Task Design, and Leader Behavior Variables," *Academy of Management Journal* 23 (1980): 665–83.

44. Cal W. Downs and Terry Pickett, "An Analysis of the Effects of Nine Leadership–Group Compatibility Contingencies upon Productivity and Member Satisfaction," *Communication Monographs* 44 (1977): 220–30.

45. David J. Skaret and Nealia S. Bruning, "Attitudes about the Work Group: An Added Moderator of the Relationship between Leader Behavior and Job Satisfaction," *Group & Organization Studies* 11 (1986): 254–79.

46. M. L. Chemers, "Leadership Theory and Research: A Systems-Process Integration," in *Basic Group Processes,* ed. P. B. Paulus (New York: Springer-Verlag, 1983): 9–39.

47. Fred E. Fiedler, *A Theory of Leadership Effectiveness* (New York: McGraw-Hill, 1967).

48. Paul Hersey and Kenneth Blanchard, *Management of Organizational Behavior: Utilizing Human Resources*, 7th ed. (New York: Prentice-Hall, 1996).

49. Julia T. Wood, "Leading in Purposive Discussions: A Study of Adaptive Behaviors," *Communication Monographs* 44 (1977): 152–65.

50. Ritch L. Sorenson and Grant T. Savage, "Signaling Participation through Relational Communication: A Test of the Leader Interpersonal Influence Model," *Group & Organization Studies* 14 (September 1989): 325–54.

51. Gay L. Drecksell, "Interaction Characteristics of Emergent Leadership" (Unpublished doctoral dissertation, University of Utah, 1984).

52. J. Kevin Barge and Randy Y. Hirokawa, "Toward a Communication Competency Model of Group Leadership," *Small Group Behavior* 20 (1989): 167–89.

53. Charles G. Morris and J. R. Hackman, "Behavioral Correlates of Perceived Leadership," *Journal of Personality and Social Psychology* 13 (1969): 350–61.

54. Paul D. Reynolds, "Leaders Never Quit: Talking, Silence, and Influence in Interpersonal Groups," *Small Group Behavior* 15 (1984): 411.

55. Hugh C. Russell, "Dimensions of Communicative Behavior of Discussion Leaders" (Paper presented to Central States Speech Convention, Chicago, April 1970).

56. Velma J. Lashbrook, "Gibb's Interaction Theory: The Use of Perceptions in the Discrimination of Leaders from Nonleaders" (Paper presented at the Speech Communication Association, Houston, December 1975).

57. Barge and Hirokawa, "Toward a Communication Competency Model."

58. Frank LaFasto and Carl Larson, *When Teams Work Best: 6,000 Team Members and Leaders Tell What It Takes to Succeed* (Thousand Oaks, CA: Sage, 2001): 130–35.

59. Dong L. Jung and John J. Sosik, "Transformational Leadership in Work Groups: The Role of Empowerment, Cohesiveness, and Collective-Efficacy on Perceived Group Performance," *Small Group Research* 33 (June 2002): 313–36.

60. LaFasto and Larson, *When Teams Work Best*, 121–30.

61. Fisher, "Leadership as Medium," 205–7.

62. Norman R. G. Maier and A. R. Solem, "The Contributions of a Discussion Leader to the Quality of Group Thinking: The Effective Use of Minority Opinions," *Human Relations* 5 (1952): 277–88.

63. Lance E. Anderson and William K. Balzer, "The Effects of Timing of Leaders' Opinions on Problem-Solving Groups: A Field Experiment," *Group & Organization Studies* 16 (March 1991): 86–101.

64. Franklyn S. Haiman (From a paper given at the Speech Communication Association Annual Conference, Chicago, December 1984).

65. Warren Bennis and Burt Nanus, *Leaders: The Strategies for Taking Charge* (New York: Harper & Row, 1985): 57.

66. Larson and LaFasto, *TeamWork*, 121–23.

67. Ibid., 135.

68. LaFasto and Larson, *When Teams Work Best*, 108–20.

69. Lawrence B. Rosenfeld, *Now That We're All Here . . . . Relations in Small Groups* (Columbus, OH: Charles E. Merrill, 1976): 76.

70. D. A. Kenny and S. J. Zaccaro, "An Estimate of Variance Due to Traits in Leadership," *Journal of Applied Psychology* 68 (1983): 678–85.

71. Judith G. Oakley, "Leadership Processes in Virtual Teams and Organizations," *Journal of Leadership Studies* 5 (Summer 1998): 3–17.

72. LaFasto and Larson, *When Teams Work Best*, 121–28.

73. Warren E. Watson, Lynn Johnson, and George D. Zgourides, "The Influence of Ethnic Diversity on Leadership, Group Process, and Performance," *International Journal of Intercultural Relations* 26 (February 2002): 1–16.

74. Fred E. Fiedler and Martin M. Chemers, *Leadership and Effective Management* (Glenview, IL: Scott, Foresman, 1974): 5.

75. Larson and LaFasto, *TeamWork,* 126–27.

76. Pavitt and Sackaroff, "Implicit Theories of Leadership and Judgments of Leadership among Group Members," 374–92.

77. Sandra M. Ketrow, "Communication Role Specializations and Perceptions of Leadership," *Small Group Research* 22 (November 1991): 492–514.

78. Dominic A. Infante and William I. Gordon, "How Employees See the Boss: Test of Argumentative and Affirming Model of Supervisors' Communicative Behavior," *Western Journal of Speech Communication* 55 (Summer 1991): 294–304.

79. Patricia Hayes Andrews, "Sex and Gender Differences in Group Communication: Impact on the Facilitation Process," *Small Group Research* 23 (February 1992): 74–94.

80. William Foster Owen, "Rhetorical Themes of Emergent Female Leaders," *Small Group Behavior* 17 (November 1986): 475–86.

81. Carol Watson, "When a Woman Is the Boss: Dilemmas in Taking Charge," *Group & Organization Studies* 13 (June 1988): 163–81.

82. G. B. Graen and T. A. Scandura, "Toward a Psychology of Dyadic Organizing," in *Research in Organizational Behavior* 9, eds. L. L. Cummings and B. Shaw (Greenwich, CT: JAI, 1987): 175–208.

83. William E. McClane, "The Interaction of Leader and Member Characteristics in the Leader-Member Exchange (LMX) Model of Leadership," *Small Group Research* 22 (August 1991): 283–300.

84. William E. McClane, "Implications of Member Role Differentiation: An Analysis of a Key Concept in the LMX Model of Leadership," *Group & Organization Studies* 16 (March 1991): 102–13.

85. Jaesub Lee, "Leader-Member Exchange, Perceived Organizational Justice, and Cooperative Communication," *Management Communication Quarterly* 14 (May 2001): 574–589.

86. Gay Lumsden and Donald Lumsden, *Communicating in Groups and Teams: Sharing Leadership*, 4th ed. (United States, 2004).

87. Bernard M. Bass, "From Transactional to Transformational Leadership: Learning to Share Vision," *Organizational Dynamics* (Winter 1990): 19–31.

88. Lumsden and Lumsden, *Communicating in Groups and Teams: Sharing Leadership*.

89. Bass, "Leadership and Empowerment: A Social Exchange Perspective."

90. Lumsden and Lumsden, *Communicating in Groups and Teams: Sharing Leadership*, 268.

91. Tiffany Keller and Fred Dansereau, "Leadership and Empowerment: A Social Exchange Perspective," *Human Relations* (1995): 127–46.

92. Eleanor F. Counselman, "Leadership in a Long Term Leaderless Group," *Small Group Research* 22 (May 1991): 240–57.

93. J. Kevin Barge, "Leadership as Medium: A Leaderless Group Discussion Model," *Communication Quarterly* 37 (Fall 1989): 237–47.

94. John Gastil, "A Definition and Illustration of Democratic Leadership," *Human Relations* 47 (August 1994): 953–75.

95. John Gastil, "Identifying Obstacles to Small Group Democracy," *Small Group Research* 24 (February 1993): 5–27.

Preparing for Problem-Solving Discussions: Informational Resources for the Group

We now prepare to explore in depth how you can make a group's problem-solving and decision-making procedures as effective as possible. A group's output can be only as good as its input and throughput allow. As with cooking or building a house, it's important to use the best possible materials, in this case, information. Groups that gather as much relevant information as possible *before* they begin their problem-solving or decision-making procedures will produce better outputs—decisions, solutions, reports, recommendations—than groups whose inputs are inadequate.

This Internal Appendix is designed to help you improve your input resources by assessing the information you have, deciding what additional information you need, and then obtaining it, evaluating it, and organizing it for easy referencing by the group. The four steps, in order, are (1) review and organize your present stock of information and ideas, (2) gather additional information you need, (3) evaluate all the information and ideas you have collected, and (4) organize the information and ideas into a tentative outline. This comprehensive information-gathering procedure is especially useful for important problems and decisions when making a mistake would be costly or worse. In such cases, the search for information should be exhaustive and the evaluation thorough. For problems with little danger of causing a costly mistake, the group can adapt the procedure or focus on just those steps that are most relevant.

Review and Organize Your Present Stock of Information and Ideas

You probably already have some information about the subject. Taking a systematic inventory of the information you currently have saves time and makes it easier for you to recall what you have when you need it.

1. **Place the problem or subject in perspective.**
   To what is it related? What will it affect, and what affects it? For example, when the church board mentioned in Chapter 4 decided on a new location for the church, it had to consider the financial condition

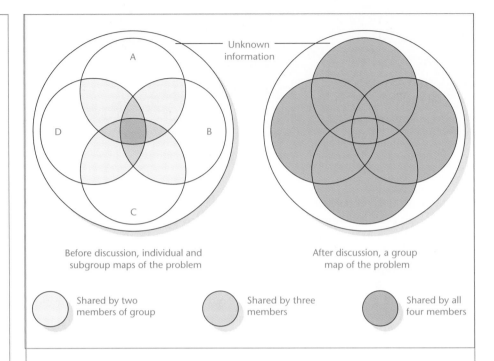

Unknown information

A

D

B

C

Before discussion, individual and subgroup maps of the problem

After discussion, a group map of the problem

Shared by two members of group

Shared by three members

Shared by all four members

of the church, long-range plans, the availability of public transportation and parking facilities, types of activities planned for the church, and so forth.

2. **Make an inventory of information you have about the subject.** As much as possible, each member needs to be on the same page as a group begins its problem-solving process. However, an advantage of group work is that members bring different perspectives, information, opinions, and so forth to the discussion. Members *should* represent different points of view; they should pool their collective knowledge and resources by sharing what they know, which they can do by mapping the problem thoroughly.

In mapping, participants share all they know about a problem: facts, conditions, complaints, circumstances, factors, happenings, relationships, effects, and so forth. Someone—the group recorder or a volunteer— keeps track of the information that members share. Before the mapping process begins, as illustrated in Figure IA.1, two or three members may have shared some information, but very little information was shared by all four. Some information was unknown by any of them. After the mapping process, all four members share what they all know, ideally. Furthermore, members are in a better position to assess what they *don't* know and to plan a strategy for finding that information.

3. **Organize the information into a rough draft of a problem-solving outline.**

   Look over the information for main issues, topics, or questions about the problem. You may want to use the guidelines suggested in Chapters 10 and 11.

4. **Look for deficiencies.**

   The rough draft will reveal where the group has gaps in its information and will suggest specific information you need and opinions or ideas that need to be supported.

Gather Information You Need

You are now ready to plan how to correct the gaps in your knowledge and thinking. *Planning* is important; otherwise, haphazard information gathering produces "garbage in" that results in "garbage out" conclusions.

For complex problems, you cannot expect to deal with all this information in a single meeting. Even if members are familiar with the topic in advance, you need time to think about the information and spot gaps. This usually takes two meetings, often more. The following two-step procedure helps ensure that the group overlooks nothing important:

1. **The group should identify and list all the major issues or topics, along with subtopics, that it needs to explore further.**

   These issues were suggested by the rough outline produced during step 1 above. Add additional topics or deficiencies as they occur to you. Produce a list of all additional information needed.

2. **The group should assign research responsibilities to individual members.**

   Distribute items from the list produced in step 1 equitably to the members and establish deadlines to complete the research. This increases individual responsibility and involvement. Ideally, members can choose voluntarily the topics of most interest to them. A group secretary or chair should keep track of who has agreed to undertake what research.

Ideally, members should work together for this common background study, with two or more of you examining each major source on the topic. This helps offset individual perceptual biases and helps prevent the group from relying on one "specialist" for each topic. However, time constraints often force members to work alone during the information-gathering stage. That makes it especially important for each member to be conscientious and thorough.

Ways of gathering information are suggested below. Because this information is likely to have been covered in previous communication and composition classes, we review it only briefly.

Self-Monitoring   Why related to leadership emergence

Robert J. Ellis and Steven F. Cronshaw, " Self-Monitoring and Leader Emergence: A Test of Moderator Effects," in *Small Group Research,* 23(February 1992): 113–29.

"It is possible that low and high self-monitors are equally effective at identifying the needs of a group, but only high self-monitors are proficient at modifying their behavior to respond to such needs." p. 124

Note Taking

Information and ideas slip from memory or become distorted unless we make accurate and complete notes. Saying that a key piece of information appeared "in a book by some DNA researcher" is useless because fellow members cannot evaluate the credibility of the information or the source. The best system of note taking is to record each bit of information or data on a separate index card or directly into a database via a laptop computer, along with the topic heading and the full bibliographic reference, as shown in Figure IA.2

Note cards and databases provide both accuracy and flexibility. They can be arranged in groups to help synthesize and interpret the evidence collected. They can be sorted in a variety of ways and consulted with ease during a discussion without the researcher's having to leaf through a disorganized notebook.

Three important sources for gathering information useful to problem-solving discussions are direct observation, reading, and individual or group interviews.

Reading: Print and Electronic Sources

Often, a print or electronic encyclopedia, such as Encarta, can provide a helpful overview of a topic, although usually this overview will not provide much depth.

For many topics and problems, the major source of information will be books, journals, newspapers, government documents, and other printed materials, whether in hard copy or online through the Internet. First, it is important to narrow down the print sources likely to yield relevant information. To do that, you need to compile a **bibliography,** which is a list of published sources on a particular topic or issue. Although ideally you would like to locate and evaluate all recent printed information on your topic before making any final decision, that is not always possible. Internet sources are especially helpful here. Be sure, however, that you do not limit yourself to only one or two sources or to sources that support only one point of view. This will produce a bias in your information with no way to cross-check validity.

Bibliography

A list of sources of information about a topic; usually includes books, journal or magazine articles, newspaper stories, interviews, and so forth.

To compile your bibliography as efficiently as possible, first prepare a list of key terms—descriptors—on the topic. For instance, a group investigating, "What type of lottery should our state conduct?" might use the following descriptors: *lottery, sweepstakes, gambling, crime, revenue,* and *betting.* Once you start your search, you may encounter additional terms, such as *victimless* or *wagering.* A reference librarian's help is indispensable in using printed sources of all kinds, including *Sociological Abstracts, Psychological Abstracts, ERIC, Facts on File,* and others. The abstract sources are significant time savers because they provide brief summaries of articles or books so that you can determine whether you should read the entire publication for details.

Most of these sources are now accessible by computer. Computerized databases such as *ComAbstracts, Communication and Mass Media Complete, InfoTrac, PsychInfo, EBSCObost,* and *Lexis-Nexis* can be invaluable in locating information about a topic. Although some of these databases may entail a fee, they make it extremely easy for you to locate relevant items quickly, so they are usually worth the money. The list of descriptors your group generates provides a starting point for a computer file search.

Most of the electronic databases work the same way. Once you enter the database, often from your university or public library, you can search the database by key word, title, or author. For instance, in gathering information about capital punishment, key words such as *capital punishment, death penalty, death row, lethal injection,* or *electric chair* might be entered. If you know that John Smith has written a number of articles about capital punishment, you could search by author name, *John Smith.* Generally, this search will produce a list of articles pertinent to your topic. If your list is too long, you can refine it by adding additional key words: *capital punishment* and *Missouri,* for example. Sometimes, in addition to the article's title, you can see an abstract, or summary, of the article. More and more often, articles are available full text online. Utilizing electronic search help can save you a lot of time.

Even if you do not have access to electronic databases, the World Wide Web itself serves as a giant electronic database. By using a **search engine** such as Yahoo.com, Google.com, AltaVista.com, or Infoseek.com, you can search the Web for items related to key words you enter. Many search engines attempt to rank-order the items they send you, so that the ones that seem most relevant appear first; but this process is not foolproof, so you may end up with information overload. Even so, you will want to try this to see what you do get.

In addition, seeking out the home page of organizations relevant to your topic can be both efficient and helpful. For instance, if your group is investigating the effects of drinking and driving, you may want to type into your search engine *Students Against Drunk Driving* to see what hits you get. If you do that, you will find that the first website listed is called *Students Against Destructive Decisions,* which is the name for SADD. On that site are several buttons linking you to specific information helpful to your research.

Remember that when you cite research you obtained from the Web, you must provide the reader with enough information to locate the website you

Search Engine
Software that allows you to search the Web for items related to key words you enter.

used. That means you need, at minimum, the Universal Resource Locator (URL) for the site, any links you clicked to get deeper into the site, the specific paragraph from which you obtained your specific information or your quoted material, and the date on which you accessed the material.

A good library manual, available at virtually every college or university library, helps in building a bibliography and locating print materials. Also helpful are bibliographies of bibliographies, such as *A World Bibliography of Bibliographies and Bibliographic Sources* and *Bibliographic Sources*. Bibliographies are also found at the end of most books, doctoral dissertations, and research articles. Do not overlook indexes to periodicals, such as *The Readers Guide to Periodical Literature, The New York Times Index,* and *Education Index*. Federal and state government publications, in special sections of many libraries, also contain vast amounts of information. The *Monthly Catalog of U.S. Government Publications* and the *Monthly Checklist of State Publications* will help you locate relevant information in these publications. Other useful sources include the *Congressional Quarterly Weekly Report* and the *Congressional Digest*. Many of these, such as *CQ Weekly,* are now online.

Even while you start to compile a bibliography, you can begin reading. A good strategy is for all members of the group to read some of the same things to provide a common background, then divide up the rest of the bibliography. When you evaluate a book for usefulness, read the index and table of contents for clues. Skim rapidly until you find something pertinent to your group; then read carefully. Take notes of the most important ideas and facts, and make copies of particularly valuable information for the rest of the group.

For controversial problems or topics, read as many contrasting interpretations and viewpoints as possible. For example, before developing a campus policy regarding use of laboratory animals for research, study the writings of those who favor and oppose using animals. Although it is easier to remember opinions that support your own, making an effort to understand other points of view is essential for effective group discussion and problem solving. Doing that will also help you increase your level of cognitive complexity.

Direct Observation

Many times, needed information can come only from firsthand observation by group members, and often only direct observation can breathe life into a table of statistics or survey results. For example, a group of students trying to improve conditions in a self-service coffee shop of a student union spent time observing and recording how many customers did and did not bus their waste materials, the kinds of litter on the floor and tables, and the placement and condition of waste containers. In their final report, they were able to provide brief examples from their observations, which made their report more vivid and compelling.

Surveys

Sometimes a group may decide that it wants more comprehensive or representative information than members can gather through observation alone. In that case, members may construct a survey to be given to individuals whose opinions are important to the group. Entire courses are devoted to construction of valid and reliable surveys, and we don't intend to provide details here. However, many student groups have designed simple, clear surveys to uncover additional information that they cannot get any other way. The student group investigating the coffee shop constructed an easy-to-take, short survey to learn who used the coffee shop, what time of day patrons were most likely to use it, what they liked best about it, and what they liked least. Patrons could pick up the one-page survey as they entered the shop, complete it in less than a minute or two, and drop it off in a specially designated box at the door. The students compiled the survey information and included it in their report.

Individual and Group Interviews

Sometimes you need firsthand information or explanations by a knowledgeable individual; interviews can help you obtain information you cannot get in other ways. Members of the group described earlier that observed the operation of the campus coffee shop also interviewed a number of customers to determine how they felt about its condition and to ask their reasons for not busing their wastepaper and leftovers. They also interviewed the manager to determine why materials that contributed to litter were being used. Most people are flattered to be asked for their information and opinions, but remember that your interviewees are busy and would prefer that you read first, then interview them for clarification.

Interview questions may be open-ended ("Why do you eat in the snack shop?") or closed-ended ("If trash containers were more conveniently located, would you use them? Yes ——— No ———"). In-depth interviews using open-ended questions often yield unexpected information and provide richer data. However, answers to open-ended questions are more difficult and time-consuming to tally. In contrast, closed-ended questions can be asked of many people quickly and are easily tabulated if formulated properly. You may want to use both.

It is invalid to generalize findings from a casual or haphazard sample to a larger population. For example, interviews about location of a new sanitary landfill with 50 people who happen to enter a particular door of city hall will not provide an accurate picture of the beliefs of residents of that city, or even of people who go to city hall. A scientifically designed sample (a *representative* sample) must be taken if results of interviews are to be generalized to members of a larger population.

Focus Group Interviews   Individual interviews can be time-consuming; *Focus groups* allow several people to be interviewed at the same time. In a

focus group, participants are encouraged to talk in an unstructured way about a topic presented to them by a trained facilitator, who often simply announces the topic and lets participants respond freely. This free-association discussion is usually tape-recorded for later content analysis. Focus groups have long been used in advertising and marketing research to discover potential markets and possible directions for innovation. Today, politicians use them to gauge voter reaction to issues; organizations, to identify problems, interests, and concerns of employees; and many different kinds of groups, to research particular issues. As an information-gathering technique, focus groups provide two advantages. They use researchers' time efficiently, and, because participants discuss issues in a group, they help spark ideas the focus group participants might not think of during an individual interview.

Focus groups are extremely versatile; the format can range from completely unstructured to somewhat structured. For example, one of us served on a focus group for a lawyer preparing to take a major product liability case to court. In front of two focus groups, he briefly presented both sides of the case by sharing the major evidence and arguments from both sides. After he finished, the focus groups went into separate rooms to discuss the evidence while video cameras recorded the discussion. The groups did not have to reach agreement; instead, participants were encouraged to talk freely about which evidence was or was not convincing. Later, the lawyer and his staff analyzed the videotaped discussions to determine where their case was strong, where it needed bolstering, and what the major issues would be from a jury's perspective. This let them sharpen and focus their arguments during the actual trial, which the lawyer won.

Other Information Sources

Useful information may crop up anywhere, anytime. You may hear something relevant to your topic or problem while listening to the radio or watching television. Some televised material, such as the program content of C-SPAN, is cataloged and available for purchase or rent. Lectures or public speeches are another source of information. An idea may occur to you when you are not consciously thinking about the group's problem—for example, while riding to school, jogging, or talking with friends. Most of us find it helpful to keep a small notepad or a few note cards with us so that we can jot down ideas when they occur, lest we forget or distort them. The important thing is to be alert to unexpected information and record it promptly.

Evaluate the Information and Ideas You Have Collected

The information and ideas you have gathered must be evaluated for accuracy and credibility. Many of your ideas may collapse in the presence of contradictory information, or some of your information may be spurious, from suspect sources, in direct contradiction to other evidence, or irrelevant. Now is the time for the group to cull the misleading, unsubstantiated, or wrong information so that your decision or solution will not be faulty.

In Chapter 10, we will discuss ways you can evaluate information and reasoning, including information you get from the World Wide Web. For now, focus on the following questions:

1. **Are the sources believable?**
   Is the person a recognized expert? Is there anything—vested interest, known bias—that could have biased his or her opinion? For instance, ideas about medical care in the United States from representative physicians, insurance agents, and pharmaceutical salespeople are likely to be biased in different ways.

2. **Is a clear distinction made between facts and inferences?**
   Are opinions stated as though they are facts? Can the facts be verified by independent credible sources?

3. **Are statistical data validly gathered, analyzed, and explained?**
   Was the sample representative? Were appropriate statistical procedures used to analyze the data? Are the results appropriately generalized, or overgeneralized?

4. **Are conclusions (inferences) supported by good reasoning?**
   Are there any reasoning errors that call the conclusions into question? Can you draw different but equally valid conclusions from the same set of evidence?

Organize Your Information and Ideas

The most efficient way to organize the group's information is to write a tentative outline. Ask yourself, "What are the questions that must be answered by our group to understand the problem or subject fully?" Your answers can serve as tentative main points in your outline. In addition, your outline helps make the problem-solving process, discussed in Chapters 10 and 11, more systematic and less likely to omit something important.

Once you have decided on some tentative major issues or topic areas, you can arrange your notes into piles, one per issue or outline item. Some of the piles can be further divided into subheadings. For example, information concerning the nature of the problem might be arranged under such subheadings as "who is affected," "seriousness of the problem," "contributing causes," "previous attempts to solve the problem," and so forth. Organizing your information like this makes it easier for you to locate pertinent information when a topic arises during group discussion, helps you prepare questions the group needs to consider, and generally helps you and the group conduct an orderly and comprehensive discussion of a complex topic.

When you prepare for a problem-solving discussion, your outline is likely to contain some possible solutions you have found or thought of. You may have evidence or reasoning that shows how similar solutions were tried on a similar problem or even some suggestions about how to implement a plan. However, such thinking and planning should be *tentative*. It is easy to become dogmatic about an issue after you have spent hours preparing to discuss it, but it is absolutely essential that your mind be open. Group members should resist coming to a discussion prepared to defend their solutions against all comers. Remember that experts at the cutting edge of their fields are usually less dogmatic and sure of themselves than people who know much less.

We emphasize again that the information-gathering strategies we have suggested here can be modified to suit the particular needs of the group. For consequential decisions that will affect many people, something like this full procedure should be used. However, for relatively minor problems with few risks of making a mistake, the group can focus on the parts of this procedure most relevant to the group's problem.

Now that your group has high-quality, relevant information—good input material—to use, we turn to the crucial topic of the group's throughput processes. Two of the most critical are the group's problem-solving and decision-making procedures—how can the group make the best use of the information that members have gathered?

Improving Group Outputs

Problem solving and decision making are the reasons most secondary groups exist. Because problems solved by groups affect us all, we need to understand how to make the problem-solving and decision-making processes in groups the best they can be. Part V describes the nature of both processes, provides vital information to improve them, and explains how conflict can enhance group problem solving and decision making. After you read Part V, you should have a solid understanding of strategies you can use when your group is faced with solving problems, whether those are simple or complex ones.

PART

V

Problem Solving and Decision Making in Groups I: Defining a Problem, Finding and Evaluating Options

CENTRAL MESSAGE

Groups need to have a plan when they begin to tackle problems; several procedures can help groups organize their problem-solving process, including the general Procedural Model of Problem Solving, an adaptable procedure that is introduced in this chapter and concluded in the next.

STUDY OBJECTIVES

As a result of studying Chapter 10 you should be able to:

1. Describe the relative advantages and disadvantages of group and individual problem solving and decision making.

2. Understand and be able to explain why a group should systematically structure its problem-solving process.

3. Explain the steps in the Procedural Model of Problem Solving (P-MOPS), the Single Question Format, and the Ideal Solution Format.

4. Explain why the first three steps in the P-MOPS procedure are important.

5. Describe and be able to use a problem census.

6. Describe the four types of questions groups address during problem solving: questions of fact, conjecture, policy, and value.

7. Describe the brainstorming, brainwriting, and electronic brainstorming procedures for finding many solutions to a problem.

8. Define critical thinking and describe how to evaluate information and reasoning, including from the World Wide Web.

9. Describe five common fallacies that inhibit critical thinking.

T he city of O'Fallon, Missouri, just west of St. Louis, has experienced phe-nomenal growth during the last two decades. In the early 1990s, city officials knew they would have to find a long-range solution to the city's water treatment problems.[1] O'Fallon was on a deep well system, and the drop-ping water table signaled that the city couldn't stay on that system forever. Officials sought a long-term solution that would be both cost-effective and effi-cient. In a series of meetings, they determined their criteria for an effective solution: Whatever they decided to do had to provide high-quality water to the citizens of O'Fallon and also give the city long-term control over costs. Next, city officials had to investigate what their options were; they discovered three realistic possibilities. They could interconnect with other water districts to buy water from them, they could build a traditional-style water treatment plant, or they could build a membrane treatment plant. Finally, in another series of small group meetings, they evaluated these options.

Buying water from the surrounding districts would be easy, but this option left the city at the mercy of other districts in terms of both quality and cost. The traditional water treatment plant would be cheaper to build initially, but required more chemicals to treat the water and was likely to need future upgrades as the Environmental Protection Agency continues to tighten water quality standards. The membrane treatment system, which would be more expensive initially, needed fewer chemicals to provide high-quality water and provided the best long-term control over costs. Officials concluded that the membrane treatment system best met their two main criteria. It was the first membrane treatment system built in Missouri.

In addressing this issue, city officials in O'Fallon demonstrated the prob-lem solving and decision making throughput activities central to small groups. In the next two chapters, we consider those two critical small group processes: problem solving and decision making. We also look at the quality of the outputs produced through these processes.

Problem Solving and Decision Making

A **problem** is a discrepancy between the current state—what actually *is* happening—and a desired goal—what *should* be happening. **Problem solving** is the comprehensive, multistep procedure a group uses to move from its cur-rent state—which is unsatisfactory in some way—to the desired goal. It involves creating and discovering solutions, evaluating them, choosing among them, and putting them into effect. In O'Fallon, the problem was clear: The city's need for water would soon outstrip the plant's ability to provide it; doing nothing was not an option. The desired goal was clear: to secure enough good water for all citizens, affordably, into the foreseeable future. In order to solve the problem, city officials had to figure out what the issues were, determine what they hoped to accomplish, discover what their options were and evalu-ate them, then select what they thought was the best option. Finally, they had

---

Problem

The discrepancy between what should be happening and what actually is happening.

Problem Solving

A comprehensive, multi-stage procedure for moving from a current unsatisfactory state to a desired goal, and developing the plan for reaching the goal.

to implement their solution by building the membrane plant. This problem-solving process took many months.

In the course of solving the water problem, O'Fallon officials had to make many different decisions. **Decision making** refers to the act of choosing among alternatives. The most obvious choice the O'Fallon group made was selecting the membrane treatment plant, but, in fact, the group made many less obvious decisions on the way to the solution. For example, they had to decide who should be involved in the process, what the main issues were, what their main criteria would be, what sort of process they would use to make the decision, where they would meet, what their time frame would be, how they would go about getting the information they needed, and so forth. Thus, although problem solving and decision making refer to different processes, in fact they are so inextricably linked that we have chosen to discuss them together.

Decision Making
Choosing from among a set of alternatives.

Group versus Individual Problem Solving and Decision Making

Groups can be much better problem solvers and decision makers than individuals. At their best, groups achieve an **assembly effect** in which the decision is qualitatively and quantitatively better than the best individual judgment of any one member or the averaged judgments of all the members. In this kind of synergy, the whole becomes greater than the sum of its parts. For example, a recent study of managers in a drug rehabilitation center showed that the group members' interactions created a type of collective intelligence superior to just the addition of their individual contributions.[2] Other studies, too, have found evidence of the assembly effect.[3] However, only when group members interact and work *interdependently* on the task is synergy possible; groups whose members work *independently* do not achieve this result.[4] If group members complete individual assignments on their own and then later compile their individual products into the final group product without discussing each members' individual work *as a group,* then that group will probably not achieve an assembly effect. It is the communication among members that allows synergy to occur.[5]

Assembly Effect
The decision of group members collectively is better, qualitatively and quantitatively, than adding or averaging the individual judgments of the members.

However, there are trade-offs and the advantages must be balanced against the disadvantages. On the positive side, members can compensate for each others' weaknesses, with each member's information complementing the others'.[6] By sharing what they know, members give the group a larger pool of information and ideas to draw from. In addition, group members can spot each other's errors, recognize truth, and process more information than individuals can.[7] They also provide different perspectives to a problem. For example, an O'Fallon taxpayer may feel differently about the cost of building an expensive membrane treatment facility than the city manager does, but both perspectives need to be taken into account. Groups can also get much more done than an individual can. Can you imagine the time it would take for *one person* to do just the preliminary research that

O'Fallon needed about types of treatment facilities, costs, and so forth? Instead, group members and their staffs spent a lot of time finding the needed information. Another advantage is that group involvement in decision making increases acceptance of a decision.[8] For instance, when workers have a voice in changing a work procedure, they are more productive than when the change is imposed on them.[9] Block and Hoffman wrote, "The effectiveness of gaining members' commitment to change through use of group decision is unquestioned."[10] Finally, as we noted in Chapter 1, groups meet our human needs for belonging and affection. On the flip side, though, groups usually take more time to make decisions than individuals take. One of us participated on a committee revising the *Faculty Handbook;* out of curiosity, a member calculated how many person-hours went into the project, and it was staggering. Sometimes group members can experience pressures to conform and may cave in to that pressure, even if they don't agree. Finally, when the group process goes badly, relationships among members can become strained, sometimes permanently, and the parent organization can be harmed.

Factors Affecting Quality of Group Outputs

Several factors affect whether the quality of a group's output will be better than what an individual can produce, including the type of task, the abilities of the members, and the type of communication they engage in. First, groups are better at **conjunctive tasks,** in which each member possesses information relevant to solving a problem, but no one member has all the needed information. However, groups are not better at **disjunctive tasks,** which require little or no coordination and which the most expert member working alone can answer correctly.[11] Often, groups cycle between conjunctive and disjunctive tasks and must know when to switch from individual to group decision making. Pacanowsky, for instance, notes that teams can be more efficient when members work individually, then pool their insights to create a team-designed solution.[12] The key is to recognize which type of task you are working on and which type of strategy is most suitable.

The abilities of members are another input factor that affects output quality. Salazar et al. found that group potential, as defined by individual members' abilities, strongly influences group performance.[13] Gruenfeld and Hollingshead determined that members with high *integrative complexity*—the ability to engage in highly complex reasoning processes—produced group interaction that was more complex and better able to incorporate diverse points of view into the ultimate decision, especially on conjunctive tasks.[14] Similarly, Scudder et al. discovered that when members are predisposed to process information cognitively—that is, they have a high *need for cognition*—decision quality is improved.[15] Laughlin et al. ascertained that overall decision-making performance was hurt by weaker members, whose impaired abilities to reason and hypothesize correctly affected the entire group.[16] All these authors

Conjunctive Task

A task where each member has relevant information, but no one member has all the information needed; thus, a high level of coordination among members is necessary.

Disjunctive Task

A task in which members work on parts of the group problem independently, with little or no coordination and group discussion needed.

recommend further investigation into the relationship between member abilities and group performance.

Communication among members, *the* essential group throughput process, affects the quality of a group's output. Verbal interaction itself, not just a summing of individual members' perceptions of opinions, contributes to the increased quality that groups usually exhibit.[17] Salazar et al. suggest that task-relevant communication is perhaps even more important than originally thought.[18] Communication that was goal directed, with issues handled systematically and assertions documented, was associated with increased decision quality. Effective groups do a better job of sharing and providing information[19]; focus more of their talk on understanding and establishing criteria for evaluating decisions[20]; and spend more time analyzing the problem, establishing group procedures, and evaluating alternatives.[21] Their findings are consistent with Scudder et al., who discovered that groups whose members carefully assessed their options produced better decisions.[22]

Bona fide group members themselves were asked which behaviors they have experienced either help or hurt small group decision making.[23] Three factors emerged as being important. By far the most influential factor is the full participation of all group members, and includes such behaviors as encouraging members to contribute, to disagree, and to elaborate on their suggestions. The second two factors pertained to how group members establish the group's climate. Negative socioemotional behaviors—being sarcastic, expressing dislike, personal attacks—hurt decision making, but positive socioemotional behaviors—respecting and supporting others' ideas—improved it. Clearly, *both* input *and* throughput factors affect a group's output.

The Need for Structure in Group Problem Solving

When you have a problem to solve as an individual, what do you do? In the early 1900s, philosopher John Dewey asked people this question; most people told him they reflected carefully about the problem, thought of options for solving it, evaluated those options, selected one, then implemented their choice. Based on what he learned about individual problem solving, Dewey developed the Reflective Thinking Model of decision making, which serves as the basis for several different *group* problem-solving models. Each of these models, which we describe in more detail later, provides a logical structure for group members to follow as they begin to solve a problem. But why do groups need structure? Why can't they just jump in and start talking about the problem? They can—but without guidelines, group problem solving can be pretty haphazard.[24] Typically, someone mentions a problem, someone else suggests a way to solve it, the group briefly discusses the idea, then it is adopted or something else is proposed, and the group is off on another topic. Groups often flit from idea to idea and this random process is unlikely to produce a good solution. Organizing problem-solving discussions helps groups balance participation, improve reflectiveness, coordinate group members' thinking, and establish important ground rules for proceeding.[25]

Sometimes, when we advise our students to structure their group problem solving systematically, they think we intend to dismiss the value of intuition, that flash of insight that helps you find a solution. Nothing could be further from the truth! We value intuition and have often gotten inspiration from an intuitive "ah ha" moment. Use your intuition—but don't rely on it alone, particularly when your decision will affect others. That's when you really need to evaluate the problem and your potential solutions thoroughly.

There is ample evidence that discussions in groups using a problem-solving structure are rated higher in quality and produce better decisions. In one early study by Brilhart, participants following a highly structured problem-solving procedure made a greater proportion of statements relevant to the issue than when the leader did not use a problem-solving structure to guide the group.[26] Scheidel and Crowell found that groups not instructed in how to use problem-solving guidelines tended to spiral from discussing problem issues to discussing solutions, a sequence called "reach testing."[27] Observers rate the quality of such discussions lower than discussions organized with a structure such as reflective thinking.[28] Even participants low in task orientation rate structured discussions higher than those in which the leader fails to help organize the problem-solving procedure.[29] Poole concluded that following a structured procedure often provides logical priorities and reminds group members of something they forgot to do in an earlier stage (such as analyze the problem thoroughly before proposing solutions).[30] As long as the logical priorities are incorporated into a sequence (e.g., problem analysis before proposing solutions), no single structure seems to be better than another. In a study by Brilhart and Jochem, the quality of final decisions reached by following three different problem-solving structural outlines was not significantly different (although the participants preferred one of the structures to the others).[31] Both Bayless and Larson reported results confirming that no one structure produced the best final decisions, but Larson also found that using *no* structural pattern for problem solving produced distinctly worse solutions.[32]

Some people believe that following a systematic linear procedure is not normal for small groups, but trainers in business and industry invariably recommend teaching corporate personnel systematic procedures before they institute participative management groups such as quality circles or self-managed work teams. For example, researchers associated with a scientific research and development corporation argued forcefully for a highly systematic, structured problem-solving format to prevent scientists from making the kinds of mistakes often attributed to random error.[33] They note that systematic problem solving is not a rigid set of techniques but "a matter of effective *communication* and data *handling*."[34] Group participants themselves seem to want methods and procedures to help them function more effectively. Broome and Fulbright found that experienced group participants identified that "methodological deficiencies" (e.g., gaps in knowing what to do at the right time and how to do it) were significant barriers to effective group problem solving.[35] They asked for tested procedures to help them deal more productively with complex problems.

The Functional Perspective of Group Problem Solving and Decision Making

We have noted that procedures improve group problem solving and decision making, but that no particular procedure seems to be superior to another. That is because a procedure itself is not the key factor in determining performance; what procedures *do* is oblige group members to pay attention to the *functions* necessary for a group to do a good job of problem solving or decision making.[36] That is the heart of the **Functional Perspective,** which states that the communicative actions of group members determine decision-making and problem-solving performance.[37] This is similar to the functions approach to leadership discussed in Chapter 9.

The Functional Perspective assumes that group members are motivated to make the best choice possible, that the choice isn't obvious, that they have access to the information and other resources they need, and that they have the cognitive ability and communication skills necessary for the task.[38] For many years, Gouran, Hirokawa, and their associates have investigated what communicative functions need to be performed for a group to succeed, and they have determined that groups must meet five fundamental task requirements:

1. Group members must understand the issue to be resolved.

2. Members must determine what minimal characteristics any acceptable alternative must have.

3. They must determine what those relevant and realistic alternatives are.

4. They must carefully examine those alternatives against the previously determined characteristics necessary for an acceptable choice.

5. They must select the alternative that seems most likely to have the characteristics needed.

Critical thinking is at the heart of this perspective, which encourages group vigilance—careful and thorough analysis of a group's problem and the possible options it can choose from—in the problem-solving and decision-making processes. Groups that are successful know how to overcome factors that impair problem solving and are willing to review their work—and even to start over—if members believe they have overlooked something or made a mistake.[39]

Productive groups usually address the five essential tasks in a more or less organized sequence, although the sequences may vary from discussion to discussion.[40] The biggest single error by groups that reach faulty solutions is omission of one or more of these steps, or failure to be thorough in discussing

Functional Perspective

The approach to group problem solving that focuses on the necessary communicative functions group members must perform for the group to do an effective job of problem solving and decision making.

them. Both laboratory studies of group problem solving using college students and a field study of committees in a large utility company support the premises of the Functional Perspective.[41] In a Midwestern manufacturing firm, Propp and Nelson discovered continued support for the importance of addressing these issues.[42] They found that the most consistent predictor of group performance was vigilant attention to the nature of the problem or task facing the group. In addition, they found that this particular group addressed another issue: *What procedures should we use to address how we want to solve our problem?* Handling this concern effectively appears to be most important when a group faces several difficult decisions. Finally, groups with the highest-quality decisions not only use a vigilant decision-making procedure but also are willing to second-guess their work by retrospectively questioning their previous choices.[43] Because the Functional Perspective focuses on how competent *communication* is related to the quality of solutions and decisions, it continues to be a fruitful area for future research.[44]

In short, the Functional Perspective focuses our attention on the communicative functions that a group must perform to produce high-quality outputs. We turn now to *how* group members can help ensure that their groups attend to the functions necessary for success. In the next section, we describe three problem-solving guidelines that groups can use to keep their thinking systematic and on track.

Problem-Solving Guidelines

As we have noted, failing to use a structured procedure does not doom a group to fail. However, using a structured procedure helps ensure that a group addresses all the functions necessary for effective problem solving. You are less likely to omit something critical if you use a structured procedure. In fact, even groups that aren't given a procedure tend to develop one anyway because they seem to sense, intuitively, that one is needed. There are many different types of structured processes that groups can use, often based on Dewey's Reflective Thinking Model mentioned earlier. Some versions are called *standard agendas,* and all are designed to help groups organize their problem-solving procedures. We briefly present three different procedures to give you an idea of the types of tools available to groups (these are summarized in Figure 10.1). Each of them addresses the issues of the Functional Perspective, although in slightly different ways. We then explore one of those procedures—the Procedural Model of Problem Solving (P-MOPS)—in detail and use it as an extended example of how groups can use structured guidelines.

The Procedural Model of Problem Solving (P-MOPS)

The **Procedural Model of Problem Solving (P-MOPS)** is a general procedure, modeled according to the sequence originally described by Dewey, that can be adapted to fit any group problem-solving situation. The acronym

Procedural Model of Problem Solving (P-MOPS)

An adaptable, five-step general procedure for structuring a group's problem-solving process.

FIGURE 10.1   Comparison of the questions addressed by three problem-solving guidelines

The Procedural Model of Problem Solving (P-MOPS)	The Single Question Format	The Ideal Solution Format

1. What is the nature of the problem facing the group?
2. What might be done to solve the problem we've described?
3. What are the probable benefits and possible negative consequences of each proposed solution?
4. What seems to be the best possible solution that we can all support?
5. How will we put our decision into effect?
	1. What is the single question that, when answered, means that the group knows how to accomplish its purpose?
	2. Collaboration
	  A. What principles should we agree on in order to maintain a reasonable and collaborative approach throughout the process?
	  B. What assumptions and biases are associated with the single question identified in step 1, and how might they influence the discussion?
	3. What issues or subquestions must we answer to fully understand the complexities of the overall problem?
	4. What are the two or three most reasonable answers to the subquestions?
	5. Among the possible solutions, which one is most desirable?
		1. Does everyone agree on the nature of the problem?
		2. What would be the ideal solution from the point of view of all interested people or groups involved?
		3. Which conditions within the situation could be changed to achieve the ideal solution?
		4. Of all the solutions available, which one best approximates the ideal solution?

P-MOPS has a double purpose: It helps us remember the full name of the model and, as a pun, it reminds us that the purpose of this (or any) model is to "mop up" all the details or logical necessities for high-quality problem solving. We call this a *general* model because it can be adjusted to fit all the contingencies facing a group.

The following are the major steps:

Step 1: Problem description and analysis: *What is the nature of the problem facing the group?*

Step 2: Generating and elaborating on possible solutions: *What might be done to solve the problem we've described?*

Step 3: Evaluating possible solutions: *What are the probable benefits and possible negative consequences of each proposed solution?*

Step 4: Consensus decision making: *What seems to be the best possible solution we can all support?*

Step 5: Implementing the solution chosen: *How will we put our decision into effect?*

The model assumes that the leader has formulated a written outline containing specific questions about all the issues the group must consider. For complex problems, the group should be invited to participate in identifying all the subquestions so that no important contingency is overlooked. You can see that this is a linear procedure whose focus is equally distributed, in sequence, on the critical functions identified in the Functional Perspective. Later in this chapter and the next, we explore each P-MOPS step in detail. For now, we want to give you an overview of the procedure.

The Single Question Format

The **Single Question Format** is less highly structured than P-MOPS, but also addresses the functional issues critical to effective decision making. This technique has been developed and tested over the last 30 years by Larson and LaFasto.[45] One thing that differentiates it from other formats is its focus on problem or issue analysis, thereby helping prevent a group from becoming prematurely solution-minded. Individuals who are low in preference for procedural order may prefer this less-structured format, which still addresses the key functions but focuses group members on the goal they want to reach. The steps are as follows:

Step 1: Identify the problem: *What is the single question that, when answered, means that the group knows how to accomplish its purpose?*

Step 2: Create a collaborative setting

    2A: Agree on principles for discussion: *What principles should we agree on in order to maintain a reasonable and collaborative approach throughout the process?*

    2B: Surface any assumptions and biases: *Which assumptions and biases are associated with the single question identified in step 1, and how might they influence the discussion?*

Step 3: Identify and analyze the issues (subquestions): *Before individuals respond to the single question in step 1, what issues or subquestions must be answered in order to fully understand the complexities of the overall problem?*

Step 4: Identify possible solutions: *Based on an analysis of the issues, what are the two or three most reasonable solutions to the problem?*

Step 5: Resolve the single question: *Among the possible solutions, which one is most desirable?*

A group using the Single Question format may spend considerable time in step 1, but once that has been done, the group's attention is focused and the goal is clear. Different from P-MOPS and the Ideal Solution format that we next discuss, the Single Question format explicitly addresses issues of group climate and how members will interact with one another and requires members to discuss, in advance, what they will do to establish a collaborative climate.

The Ideal Solution Format

The **Ideal Solution Format,** also developed by Larson, focuses the group's attention on what the ideal solution would look like, and it recognizes that different groups likely have different ideal solutions.[46]

> **Step 1: Identify the nature of the problem:** *Does everyone agree on the nature of the problem?*
>
> **Step 2: Identify the ideal solution:** *What would be the ideal solution from the point of view of all interested people or groups involved?*
>
> **Step 3: Identify the conditions that must change:** *Which conditions within the situation could be changed to achieve the ideal solution?*
>
> **Step 4: Select the most ideal solution:** *Of all the solutions available, which one best approximates the ideal solution?*

Ideal Solution Format
A problem-solving format that takes individual perspectives into account by asking a group to focus on what the ideal solution would do.

The Ideal Solution format acknowledges the different perspectives that individual members and groups may have and encourages open discussion of what would look ideal from each of these perspectives. A simple procedure to follow, it is particularly useful when members and the groups they represent must accept the solution.[47] It also can capture group members' imaginations, as they envision the possibilities of what an ideal solution could do.

All three of the guidelines presented are easy to follow and address the functions important to effective problem solving and decision making. Each requires problem analysis. The Single Question Format focuses on the goal and the climate that members create, the Ideal Solution Format focuses on what the solution can do for the group, and P-MOPS distributes members' attention fairly evenly to the key functions. All of these techniques are adaptable to suit a group's particular situation.

Recap: A Quick Review

Group problem solving and decision making are key throughput processes that largely determine the quality of a group's output.

1. Problem solving (a multistep procedure that includes analyzing a problem, creating or finding solutions, evaluating the solutions, choosing the best, and implementing it) and decision making (the act of choosing) are intertwined.

(continued)

(continued)

2. Groups can achieve an assembly effect when members work interdependently, share what they know, and compensate for one another's mistakes, so usually group decisions are superior to individual decisions.

3. Groups do better than individuals on conjunctive tasks, when members have good cognitive abilities and communication skills, when they all participate, and when they create a positive group climate.

4. Without structure, group problem solving is haphazard and its ultimate products are of lower quality.

5. The Functional Perspective focuses on five key functions that a group must perform to succeed. Structured guidelines help ensure that these functions are fulfilled, but no structured guideline is superior, although using *any* guideline works better than using none.

6. Three common guidelines are the Procedural Model of Problem Solving (P-MOPS), the Single Question Format, and the Ideal Solution Format. These guidelines are similar, but each has its own particular focus.

Using P-MOPS to Address Complex Problems

We turn now to an in-depth discussion of P-MOPS, which we believe is one of the most flexible procedures available to groups and which can be adjusted for any type of problem, simple or complex. In this chapter, we address the first three steps of P-MOPS. We conclude with the final two steps in the next chapter and, at the end of the P-MOPS discussion, we show two adaptations of P-MOPS so that you can see how others have applied it. Depending on the problem, your group may not have to take every question equally into account.

Step 1 of P-MOPS: Problem Description and Analysis

In many ways, this is a deceptively simple step, but if a group faces a complex problem, this step alone can take a long time to determine. The question to be addressed in step 1 is *What is the nature of the problem facing the group?* Subquestions to think about are listed here.

1A: Understand the Charge and Area of Freedom

The **charge** is the assignment given to the group, usually by a parent organization or individual. Sometimes a group develops its own charge; neighbors who band together to try to reduce speeding in their neighborhood are not given the charge by an outside body, but develop it out of mutual interests. The charge specifies what a group is to do; it usually includes the group's **area of freedom,** or amount of authority it has, along with any limitations it faces. Are there budget restrictions? Is the recommendation to be kept private or

Charge

A group's assignment or task, often given by a parent organization or individual.

Area of Freedom

The amount of authority and limitations a group has.

shared? Are there things the group should not do? For example, a Student Services Committee was charged by the vice president for Student Affairs with recommending improvements to services for evening students in a written report to be given to him. Ignoring their charge and area of freedom, committee members produced a report recommending that two individuals be fired and that the budget be reallocated, with more money for student services. They copied and distributed their report to the entire administrative staff of the college, including the two whose positions they wanted to eliminate. Needless to say, they ignored their charge and exceeded their area of freedom.

Make sure that all members of your group understand the charge: What is the group supposed to do? By what time frame? What resources does the group have (e.g., money, computer time, secretarial help)? What should the group *not* do? What will the final product be (e.g., a written report, an oral recommendation)? Who receives the final product?

1B: Understand the Type of Question to Be Addressed

There are four common types of questions that groups address: *questions of fact, questions of conjecture, questions of value,* and *questions of policy.*[48] Gouran and Hirokawa note that it is important to know which type of question you face because each question requires a different discussion emphasis. A **question of fact** asks whether something is true or not, whether something actually happened or not. For example, O'Fallon's city officials needed to determine whether the water table in the area was actually falling. They relied on objective, credible experts to help make that determination. A **question of conjecture** asks a group to speculate, or make an educated guess, about what might or could happen in the future. O'Fallon officials asked, *Based on what we know is true right now about the water table and the population growth, how long do we think the current water treatment facility will be able to handle the demand?* As you can see, making a *good* educated guess depends on having accurate information and facts. A **question of value** refers to what is right, good, preferable, or acceptable. In O'Fallon, the group had to decide how much members valued local control of their water supply. One of the cheapest alternatives, in the short run, was to buy water from neighboring districts—but that would put O'Fallon at the mercy of others! *How important is it,* officials asked, *to keep control of our water supply and pricing?* A **question of policy** asks what course of action a group will take: *What are we going to do, recommend, decide about something?* The bottom line for O'Fallon was a decision about which option to choose: buying water from another district, building another treatment plant, or building a state-of-the-art membrane plant.

As you can see, it is usually easier to decide questions of fact (although that is not always the case, as with some jury deliberations) than questions of conjecture or value. Sometimes, members' perspectives and values are so different that they will answer questions of conjecture or value differently. And,

Question of Fact

A question that asks whether something is true or not, or actually happened or not.

Question of Conjecture

A question that asks a group to speculate or make an educated guess about something.

Question of Value

A question that asks whether something is right, good, preferable or acceptable.

Question of Policy

A question that asks what course of action a group will take.

What does this problem question mean to us?
What are our charge and area of freedom?
What is unsatisfactory at present?
Who (or what) is affected?
When, where, and how?
How serious do we judge the problem to be?
How long has the problem existed?
Do we need to gather any additional information to assess the nature and extent of the problem adequately?
What conditions have contributed to the problem?
What appear to be causative conditions?
What precipitated the crisis leading to our discussion?
What exactly do we hope to accomplish (the goal, desired situation)?
What obstacles to achieving the desired goal exist?
What information do we need before we can find a satisfactory solution?
What additional subquestions must we answer?
How might we find answers to these subquestions?
What are the answers to these subquestions?
How can we summarize our understanding of the problem to include the present and desired situation and causal conditions?

of course, if those are answered differently, members will choose to decide things differently. You can also see that, with complex problems, groups have to deal with all four types of questions, as the examples from O'Fallon show. But groups should understand what questions they must address so that members know where to put their efforts. For instance, if the group must come to consensus about a question of value, then members must share what they believe and be willing to look for common values that they all agree on, so that they can recommend a solution that does not violate those mutual values. That isn't always possible.

1C: Focus on the Problem

Focus on the problem before jumping in to try to solve it. What would you think if you drove your car to a mechanic, who said, "You need new valves," before even looking under the hood? Focusing on the problem is the equivalent of looking under the hood. Getting solution-minded too quickly is a common problem; writers concerned with business groups have noted this tendency and the harm it can cause.[49] Questions to guide your analysis of a problem are presented in Table 10.1.

ID: State the Problem Appropriately

One thing that will help prevent you from getting solution-minded too quickly is stating the group's problem in the form of a single, unambiguous

Solution Questions	Problem Questions
How can I transfer a man who is popular in his work group but slows down the work of other employees in the group?	How can I increase the work output of the group?
How can we increase the publicity for our club's activities so that attendance will be increased?	What can we do to increase attendance at our club's activities?

FIGURE 10.2
Solution versus problem questions

problem question, which focuses on the issue or the goal. In contrast, a **solution question** implies or suggests the solution within the question itself. What if O'Fallon officials had asked themselves, "How can we negotiate the best costs for water with other districts before we run out?" instead of "What should we do to ensure that our city has high-quality and affordable water?" The second, a problem question, leaves the door open for many different options, but the first channels group members' thinking into only one option, negotiating with other districts for water. Examples of solution versus problem questions are shown in Figure 10.2.

Problem Question

A question that focuses the group's attention on the issue or problem; does not suggest any particular type of solution in the question itself.

Solution Question

A question in which the solution to a problem is implied in the question itself.

IE: Map the Problem

We discussed mapping a problem in the Internal Appendix; the same principles apply here. Group members should take the time to share what each person knows about the issue or problem so that if one person knows something, the others do as well. Mapping the issue tends to minimize the potential problem of a *hidden profile,* in which information held in private by individuals favors a less effective solution, but all the information together favors the best solution.[50] In other words, if members chose to share all the relevant information they hold privately, the group would find the best solution. Unfortunately, members freely discuss information they *already* know in common, but tend to hold on to their own unique information without sharing it. Henningsen and Henningsen found that as groups moved away from hidden profiles and were willing to share what each member knew separately, they made better decisions.[51] The mapping process described earlier encourages this pooling of information. During this first step of P-MOPS, group members should be encouraged to ask any and every question they think needs an answer before proceeding.

Using the Problem Census to Discover Problems

How do groups find problems to address? Up to this point, we have assumed that a group already has a problem to solve—either because someone has given the group the task of solving it or because the group became aware of the

TABLE 10.2   Steps in the problem census

1. Group members sit in a semicircle facing a board or flip chart.
2. The leader (or person designated to conduct the census) explains the purpose and procedures.
3. Members present problems one by one, in round-robin fashion, until all problems have been presented.
4. The leader posts each item as the member presents it. The leader or members can ask for clarification and elaboration, but cannot argue. The problem statement may be condensed so that it is concise enough to fit on the chart. Chart pages are removed and fastened to the wall so that all items are visible.
5. Some questions may be easily answered then and there; if so, they are removed from the list.
6. Members establish a priority order for the remaining items. Sometimes, members have a sheet of 5 or 10 stickers to place on the items they think are most important. All items remain on the list, but voting or attaching stickers prioritizes the list.
7. Each remaining item is dealt with in turn over the course of the group's deliberations. Often, a member will volunteer to do the legwork of preparing the discussion guideline for a particular problem.

Problem Census

A technique in which group members are polled for topics and problems that are then posted, ranked by voting, and used to create agendas for future meetings.

problem and decided on its own to tackle it. Sometimes, particularly in organizations or continuing groups, forward-thinking leaders try to anticipate what problems loom on the horizon rather than waiting for them to become obvious. The **problem census** is a "posting" technique used to identify important issues or problems that will need to be addressed. Thus, it is often used to build an agenda for future problem-solving meetings or discovering problems encountered by organization members. The group makes a list of all concerns, problems, questions, or difficulties that any member would like to discuss. The group establishes a priority order for which issues to take on first; some of the issues or problems may be minor and can be answered or handled then and there. The remaining problems are developed into an agenda for the group to work on over time, with individual members usually taking the lead in discussing particular issues. A university department where one of us worked conducted, at the beginning of the school year, a problem census that developed into the department's agenda for the year. Faculty members first listed all the problems they thought should be addressed and assigned themselves to research and present an outline of each problem for eventual problem solving by the entire group. Table 10.2 presents the steps of the problem census, with brief instructions for each step.

Step 2 of P-MOPS: Generating and Elaborating on Possible Solutions

The question to ask here is, *What* might *be done to solve the problem?* Notice that we phrased this as "might" not "should." That phrasing is intentional; at this stage, you don't want to squash members' creative ideas by getting too

1. Members are presented with the problem, which can range from specific *(What should we name our new pudding?)* to abstract *(How can we improve living conditions in the residence halls?)*
2. Members are encouraged to generate as many solutions as possible, under the following rules:
A. No evaluation is permitted. No one is allowed to criticize, laugh at, or negatively react to any idea.
B. Quantity is sought. Members should try to generate as many solutions as they can. The facilitator should prod them to think of more if there is a lull.
C. Innovation is encouraged. Wild and crazy ideas are encouraged—you never know which one will spark just the right solution for the group.
D. Hitchhiking is encouraged. Members can piggyback on each other's ideas to build on them and extend them.
3. All ideas are written down so that the entire group can see.
4. All ideas are evaluated, but at another session or after a substantial break.

TABLE 10.3   Steps in brainstorming

focused on trying to decide something. You want good ideas to choose from. Here are principles that can help a group capture a wealth of good ideas:

2A: Identify as Many Good Ideas as You Can

Ultimately, you will need to evaluate all the ideas that you have identified to assess how likely they are to succeed, but for now, try to capture as many ideas as possible so you have plenty to choose from. The Functional Perspective lists having an array of relevant and realistic alternatives as one of the essential functions for effective problem solving.[52] This process may be lengthy, but members should guard against adopting the first solution that seems to solve the problem—that solution may not be the best one!

Using Brainstorming to Discover Alternatives

One technique to help you find or create good ideas is **brainstorming,** which was developed in the advertising industry, whose business it is to create innovative advertising campaigns.[52] In order for a group's creativity to be released, members must feel safe in a nonthreatening environment free of judgment.[53] Because critical evaluation kills creativity, the main principle behind brainstorming is "no evaluation" during the brainstorming process. Evaluation of ideas—a necessary component of critical thinking—takes place *after* group members have listed all the ideas they can think of. The steps for conducting a brainstorming session are briefly described in Table 10.3.

   True brainstorming is harder than it looks. Staying nonjudgmental isn't easy! Members have a natural tendency to comment about suggestions: "That sounds great!" or "That's a goofy idea!" To stifle this tendency, some organizations have creative ways to remind members not to evaluate. For instance, in

Brainstorming

A technique for stimulating creative thinking by temporarily suspending evaluation of alternatives.

one company, members bring squirt guns to meetings to squirt anyone who criticizes an idea during a brainstorming session. In another company, offending members get nerf balls thrown at them.[54]

Brainstorming is widely used wherever a group needs many solutions or creative ideas to choose from. Such industries as banking, engineering and design, marketing, medicine, education, government, decorating, and food science, to name just a few, use the technique, often in conjunction with other techniques, as we have shown here.

Brainwriting

Individual brainstorming in writing before group discussion of items.

Brainstorming has several variations, including **brainwriting,** which capitalizes on the fact that group members are sometimes more productive when they work alone, but in the presence of others. During brainwriting, members are given a specified time limit—10 or 15 minutes—to write down as many ideas as they can generate about the problem. They are encouraged to write as fast as they can without stopping and, as with brainstorming, to piggyback on their own ideas. When the time is up, members share their ideas, round-robin, and proceed as with regular brainstorming. Brainwriting can overcome some of the obstacles of traditional brainstorming, including the inhibition of some participants, having one or two dominant speakers monopolize the session, or the group's fixating on just a few ideas.[55]

Electronic Brainstorming (EBS)

Brainstorming on computers linked to a large screen that displays all responses, but no one knows who contributed which items.

Electronic brainstorming (EBS) is another variation; it capitalizes on the fact that anonymity can remove inhibitions. Members sit at computer terminals and type in their ideas, which are sent via computer to a large screen visible to all. No one knows who contributed which idea. EBS groups often generate more ideas, and more high-quality ideas, than oral brainstorming groups or members working alone.[56] Members were less fearful of being evaluated and were more satisfied with EBS than with oral brainstorming. Anonymous EBS is an excellent method to use in a large group in particular.[57]

Sosik and Avolio compared anonymous and identified EBS groups to determine how much a facilitator influences how group members use the technology.[58] When facilitators tried to stimulate creativity with comments such as "Remember to be innovative when offering our views" and "Let's understand each other's views" the creativity was actually *negatively* affected. Apparently, the comments, even in anonymous EBS groups, introduced an element of judgment too early in the process, which hurt the generation of ideas. When comments were offered in an effort to spur creativity, they were instead perceived as judgmental and violated members' expectations of EBS. These authors stress that leaders and facilitators must be carefully trained in how to use the technology so that they don't misuse it.

2B: Defer Judgment during Discussion to Identify Options

Even if you aren't using brainstorming or a similar technique, the "no judgment" rule of brainstorming is a good one to apply when an idea is just beginning to form during a group's discussion. Evaluation stifles innovation and creativity. When you are developing ideas, don't also try to evaluate them—yet.

Absolute (*Must* Be Met)	Relative (*Should* Be Met)
Entertainment must not cost over $400.	Location should be convenient, that is, within 30 minutes' driving time for all members.
Must be enjoyable to members and their families. (*Enjoyable* means: provide a variety of activities designed to appeal to people ranging in age from 3 to 80.)	Facilities should be comfortable; for example, shelter in case of rain, electrical outlets, hot and cold running water, restroom facilities, and so on.

FIGURE 10.3
Absolute versus relative criteria to guide plans for a club's annual picnic

2C: Discuss Criteria for Evaluating Solutions

The group must establish **criteria,** or standards against which to evaluate the various options, and group members must agree on criteria before they can begin to evaluate their options. Criteria establish the group's standards and express the values shared by members. Two people with different values will use different criteria to evaluate options, thereby arriving at quite different solutions. For example, Rubenstein asked Arab students and American students whom they would save if their boat capsized and they could save only one other person beside themselves: wife, child, or mother. *All* the Arabs chose the mother (your mother holds a unique and irreplaceable position in your life), but *none* of the Americans did—they split about evenly between the child and the wife.[59] In this case, Arab values and American values supported widely divergent criteria for deciding whom to save. Unless a group can agree about criteria, consensus may be impossible.

Criteria

Standards against which alternatives are evaluated.

    Some criteria *must* be met and are *absolute,* but with others, *relative* criteria, the group has some leeway. (Examples of absolute and relative criteria are shown in Figure 10.3.) For example, O'Fallon city officials held water quality as an absolute standard—whatever solution they developed, the water had to be of "high quality." But criteria should be measurable, if possible; criteria such as "high quality" are abstract, so a group should quantify its criteria. For example, "high-quality water" may mean water that has certain specified maximum levels of heavy metals, particulates, and bacteria. Water quality engineers and the Environmental Protection Agency helped the O'Fallon officials specify what "high quality" meant to them.

    Theorists have argued about whether and when a problem-solving discussion should include a step for establishing explicit criteria. Many people place it during the problem analysis step, before talking about solutions. Still others suggest that criteria are better discussed after the group has accumulated all possible solutions first. Evidence provides no simple, single answer to this. Brilhart and Jochem found that decision quality was not affected by *when* criteria were discussed, or whether discussion of criteria was a separate step in the problem-solving outline or not. However, significantly more participants wanted criteria discussed explicitly and preferred to discuss them *after* brainstorming, not before.[60]

If criteria are well known, they may not need to be discussed at all. Hirokawa et al. explored the importance of *evaluation clarity* in applying criteria.[61] Evaluation clarity is high when criteria are clearly presented to the group as part of the charge or the presentation of the problem and are understood by all members. Evaluation clarity is low when standards are not presented to the group, are fuzzy, or are understood differently by different members. These authors concluded that when evaluation clarity is high, decision quality is not much affected by whether members discuss or use evaluation criteria; but when evaluation clarity is low, decision performance is strongly related to whether members establish and use explicit criteria.

Although advice from the research is mixed, and if the criteria are part of the group's charge or otherwise clearly understood, you do not have to discuss them; however, we think it's never wrong to discuss criteria. For one thing, group members may have misjudged their degree of understanding of and agreement about criteria! Discussing criteria explicitly, even briefly, may save you from unnecessary misunderstanding or disagreement when you begin to evaluate options. *When* you discuss criteria is up to you, although members seem to like brainstorming options before discussing criteria, which is why we place this step at the end of the Generating Solutions step of P-MOPS.

Recap: A Quick Review

Understanding how to use guidelines such as the P-MOPS procedure can be useful to groups, whether the problem is simple or complex:

1. During step 1, problem description and analysis, members must understand their charge and area of freedom, or limitations, and must know whether they are facing questions of fact, conjecture, value, or policy.

2. Groups should focus on the problem before beginning to identify solutions; they can help ensure this by starting with a good problem question as opposed to a solution question, which suggests the type of solution within the question and which can narrow members' thinking.

3. Group members should share what they each know individually about a problem by mapping it so that as much information as possible is held in common.

4. Many groups and organizations deliberately seek out problems to work on; the problem census technique helps group members identify issues that can be built into the group's working agenda.

5. During step 2, generating and elaborating possible solutions, the group's goal is to identify as many relevant and realistic options as it can.

(continued)

(continued)

6. Brainstorming and its variant brainwriting can help groups identify a wealth of creative options; evaluation is not permitted during a brainstorming session so that creativity isn't stifled.

7. Group members should discuss criteria, or standards, for evaluating the options; absolute criteria must be met, but a group has leeway about whether to meet its relative criteria.

8. Whether group criteria have to be discussed explicitly depends on evaluation clarity; when clarity is high, meaning that criteria are clear and members agree on them, it isn't essential to discuss criteria explicitly.

Step 3 of P-MOPS: Evaluating Possible Solutions

Once the problem has been thoroughly analyzed, with alternatives accumulated and criteria clearly understood by all members, the group is ready to evaluate alternatives. For the best alternative to surface, the pros and cons of each solution must be explored, as members ask, *What are the probable benefits and possible negative consequences of each proposed solution?* Group members must employ their sharpest critical thinking skills to ensure thorough evaluation of all options.

3A: Establish a Collaborative Climate for Evaluation

Your critical thinking task will be facilitated if you engage in some preparation work first. Members are more willing to think critically when the group's climate is collaborative and supportive, and when that climate explicitly supports critical thinking. Use the best communication skills you can—listen to understand, help other group members make their points, and encourage everyone to participate. We discussed the factors that contribute to a supportive climate in Chapter 8; here is the place to be particularly mindful of the way you interact with others. Ethical behavior is paramount; trickery, manipulation, deception, coercion—all ethical breaches are unacceptable.

Some groups discuss explicitly the type of atmosphere they want to create and how they will do that. An acquaintance of ours who works in marketing for a Fortune 500 company asks group members to think of the best group or team they've ever been part of, then to think of how the present group could become as good as their "best" group. This prompts members to establish their own norms of mutual respect, careful listening, and commitment to the task.

3B: Establish Norms That Promote Critical Thinking

Critical thinking is the systematic examination of information and ideas on the basis of evidence and logical or probable reasoning, rather than intuition or hunch. Unfortunately, many groups do not encourage critical thinking skills.

Critical Thinking

The systematic examination of information and ideas on the basis of evidence and logic rather than intuition, hunch, or prejudgment.

For instance, Meyers et al. found that group arguments in undergraduate groups consisted of simple assertions almost half the time and that members seldom cited rules of logic or used criteria as standards.[62] But to evaluate options thoroughly, you must make critical thinking a team effort. Groups evaluate both information and reasoning.

Evaluating Information   *Information*—facts, ideas, opinions, data—is the raw material from which a group's decision is made. A group's final decision can be only as good as the information inputs used by the group. Members must evaluate information for accuracy, credibility, and relevance to the group's decisions.

Distinguishing between Facts and Inferences   It is especially important to distinguish between facts and inferences, opinions, and preferences. Often, group members state opinions as though they were facts, thus leading other group members to accept what may be erroneous conclusions.

Fact

A verifiable observed event; a descriptive statement that is true.

A **fact** can be verified as *true* or *false*. Facts either exist or do not exist; they are not open to argument. A *statement of fact* is a declarative statement that describes an observation of some event. "It is raining outside" is a statement of fact if it really is raining and someone could verify that fact (e.g., by looking out the window). Present events are relatively easy to verify. If the statement of fact refers to a past event, that past event must have actually been observed by somebody. If several independent sources report the same information as fact, you can be more confident than if it comes from only one source.

Inference

A statement that goes beyond fact, involves some degree of uncertainty or probability, and cannot be checked for accuracy by direct observation.

An **inference** is an opinion that goes beyond what was actually observed; it makes a leap from a fact to a conclusion based on that fact. A *statement of inference* contains an opinion, preference, or conclusion. For example, "The Springfield metropolitan area is growing rapidly" is a statement of inference that goes beyond the *fact* that the area's population was 228,118 in the 1980 census and 325,721 in the 2000 census. *Rapidly* is a relative term; whether this inference is valid depends on what we compare the growth rate to: average growth rate for metropolitan areas in the United States, average growth rate for Missouri metropolitan areas, recent growth rate for areas of similar size, and so on. Thus, inference *is arguable*. Figure 10.4 provides examples and further descriptions of facts and inferences.

Evaluating Survey and Statistical Data   Factual-type statements, including statistics or the results of surveys, need to be evaluated carefully for dependability. Surveying is a sophisticated operation. The questions and who asks them can make a big difference in the results. Ask the following questions when evaluating statistics: Who commissioned the study? How were the data gathered and analyzed? How were questions phrased? You may need the help of an expert to evaluate and interpret statistical data properly, especially if you are basing an important conclusion on those data.

Statements of Fact	Examples
• Are limited to description.	• The population of the Springfield metropolitan area recorded in the 2000 census was 325,721.
• Can be made only *after* observation.	• On August 9, 2005, Gloria Galanes lived with two cats.
• Are as close to certain as humans can get.	• The university library's catalog contained 2,437,532 volumes on July 8, 1996.
• Only a limited number of facts exist.	• After instituting lotteries, three states reduced their tax rates.

Statements of Inference and Opinion	Examples
• Go beyond what was observed directly.	• Springfield is growing rapidly.
• Can be made at any time without regard to observation.	• Gloria Galanes likes cats.
• Can be made by anyone, observer or not.	• The heart of a good university is its library.
• Entail some degree of probability, inferential risk, or uncertainty.	
• An unlimited number can be made about anything.	• We should legalize casino gambling to reduce the state income tax.

FIGURE 10.4
Comparing statements of fact and statements of opinion and inference

Evaluating the Sources and Implications of Opinions   When first introduced to the differences between facts and opinions, some students act as if statements of opinion are less valuable in a discussion. Hardly so! Facts provide the basis for discussion and debate. As we discussed regarding types of questions, groups must deal not only with what has already been verified but also determine priorities of values, ethics, goals, and procedures acceptable to all. Members make inferences about what will probably happen *if* they adopt each possible alternative. For example, facts regarding AIDS and how it is spread are fairly well known, but what a particular board of education will *do* about it depends on the values, opinions, and judgments about policies that will be acceptable to the community.

All people have an equal right to express their opinions, but opinions themselves are not all equal. Opinions *can* be evaluated for their validity and appropriate use of fact. First, consider the source of the opinion.

1.   Is this person (or other source) a recognized expert on the subject? How do other experts in the field regard this person? If their opinions are different, how might this be explained?

2. Does the source have a vested interest that might have influenced the opinion? For example, a flood victim, insurance agent, politician, and taxpayer will have different opinions about whether government should reimburse victims of natural disasters for all their losses.

3. How well does the source support the opinion with documented evidence? Is the evidence well organized, with supporting statistics and tables and clear reasoning?

4. How consistent is this opinion with others expressed by the source? If not consistent, is there an acceptable explanation for the person's inconsistency?

Second, consider the implications of the opinion. Where does the conclusion lead, and is that acceptable to the group? For example, a writer may argue that outlawing private ownership of handguns would protect us from accidents and murderers. What are the implications of this statement? That dangerous devices should not be allowed in the hands of citizens at large? That only nonessential dangerous tools that could potentially be used as murder weapons should be restricted? That eventually all potential murder weapons should be restricted? When a group decision depends on opinions, it is important to test these opinions for what they assume and imply.

Evaluating the information available to the group is only the first element of critical thinking. It is equally important to evaluate how both information sources and group members reason from this information.

Evaluating Reasoning   Valid reasoning connects information with conclusions in an appropriate and defensible way. Once you have evaluated the information (raw data), you must also look at how speakers and writers reason from that information. Are their conclusions logical and plausible? Here is where *group* decision making can be clearly superior to individual decision making, because one member is usually able to spot a flaw or a reasoning error, called a **fallacy,** that another member missed. Several common fallacies observed in group discussions include overgeneralizing, making *ad hominem* attacks, suggesting inappropriate causal relationships, posing a false dilemma, and making faulty analogies.[63]

Fallacy

A reasoning error.

Overgeneralizing   An **overgeneralization** is a conclusion that is not supported by enough data. Because something is true about one or a few instances, someone claims it is true of all or most instances of the same type. For example, when a person concludes that because *some* college students have defaulted on their government-guaranteed loans, *most or all* college students are irresponsible, that person has overgeneralized. Generalizations are not automatically wrong. After all, that is what statistics do—help us generalize appropriately from a relatively small sample to a large population. The problem occurs when we *over*generalize. To test generalizations, ask whether evidence other than personal testimony is being offered to support the generalization and how many cases the generalization is based on.

Overgeneralizing

Assuming that because something is true about one or a few items, it is true of all or most items of the same type.

Ad Hominem *Attacks*   An *ad hominem* **attack** is a statement that attacks a person instead of pointing out a flaw in the person's argument. The attack diverts the group's attention so that members debate the merits of the person rather than his or her position on the issue. *Ad hominem* attacks may be explicit ("You can't trust women or minorities to evaluate affirmative action laws fairly!") or veiled ("Why do you think someone *like that* could help our group?"). In any case, they are a subtle form of name-calling. Determining the credibility of the person supplying information is important, but *ad hominem* attacks condemn individuals on the basis of characteristics irrelevant to the validity of opinions or accuracy of information they provide. And they do *not* help evaluate the arguments advanced by the person for or against some proposal.

Ad Hominem Attack

An attack on a person rather than his or her argument.

Suggesting Inappropriate Causal Relationships   Sometimes people assume that because two events are related or occurred close to each other in time, one must have caused the other. Common sense suggests that events usually have multiple and complex causes. To suggest that one single event causes another almost always oversimplifies a relationship among numerous variables. For example, we overheard a newscaster say that because female graduates of women-only colleges were more likely to serve on the boards of Fortune 500 companies than graduates of coeducational schools, attendance at women's colleges probably caused greater career achievement. This is a preposterous statement! Numerous factors influence career achievement. For instance, many women's colleges are both highly selective and expensive; their students are often bright, grew up in families who own or are connected to Fortune 500 companies, and can afford to attend expensive schools. Attendance at women-only colleges may indeed provide women with greater opportunities for engaging in leadership activities. More likely, native ability, economic resources, and family connections "cause" both attendance at women-only colleges and career achievement. Whenever you see causal connections being posited, look for other reasons why the events might be linked. Only when alternative explanations have been eliminated can a causal connection be accepted as probably true, and then only tentatively.

False Dilemmas   A **false dilemma** poses an either–or choice that implies, wrongly, that only two courses of action are possible. For example, either the university builds a new parking lot *or* students have to walk miles to get to class. Either sex education is taught by the parents *or* by the schools. Each of these statements ignores the fact that other options exist to accomplish both goals—in other words, the dilemma is false. The university could provide a shuttle bus service to transport students from faraway parking lots, schedule classes early or late to alleviate parking crunches at certain times, or set up a car-pooling service to improve the parking situation. Children can be taught sex education by their parents; their teachers; their ministers, priests, or rabbis; committees composed of teachers and parents working together; teams of clergy and parents; and so forth. Just because a writer or speaker does not

False Dilemma

Either–or thinking that assumes, incorrectly, that only two choices or courses of action are possible.

offer you alternatives should not blind you to their existence. Whenever you are offered an either–or choice, look for additional options.

Faulty Analogy

An incomplete comparison that stretches a similarity too far; assuming that because two things are similar in some respects, they are alike in others.

Faulty Analogies   A **faulty analogy** is a comparison that stretches a similarity too far. Comparisons help us understand issues more vividly, but all comparisons have limitations. Author Gloria's orange tabby cat may look and act like a tiger, but he does not eat 10 pounds of meat per day and cannot hurt you if he jumps on your lap. We have heard many students complain (we have even complained ourselves!), "You can't really learn how to be a public relations professional in college. It would be like trying to learn to swim from a book, but never getting in the water." At first glance, this remark hits home because there *are* limitations to what you can learn in school. Examining the analogy more closely, however, reveals that many classroom activities and assignments prepare students for professional practice. Public relations majors practice writing for a variety of audiences, learn principles of graphic design and use them to design materials for a variety of clients, put together dynamic oral presentations, write job specifications and budgets for proposed projects, and so on. All of these are activities that public relations professionals carry out in professional practice. Whenever you hear an analogy being offered as an argument, ask yourself three things: (1) What two things are being compared? (2) How are they similar? and, more important, (3) How are they different or where does the comparison break down? Always ask, "Is the conclusion warranted by *this* analogy?"

The fallacies we have just presented are among the most common, but by no means are they the only ones you will encounter. The important thing is for you and your fellow group members to be alert to mistakes in reasoning so that you will not be led by faulty reasoning to make poor decisions.

Evaluating Information and Reasoning from the World Wide Web

The foregoing information pertains to all sources of information, regardless of the method you used to acquire the information. But because anyone can post virtually anything on the World Wide Web, evaluating Web-based sources poses unique problems. Adams and Clark suggest using six evaluation criteria that look at accuracy, authority, audience, purpose, recency, and coverage.[64]

Accuracy.   How do you know information from the Web is accurate? You can't know beyond any doubt, but three factors can help you. First, be suspicious of information that has not passed through any editorial checks. Some Web-based sources, such as those maintained by credible news organizations such as CNN, carry information that has been screened. Accept with caution information that seems to bypass editorial checks. Second, determine whether multiple sources verify the same information. Finally, use your common sense. If something seems too good or too incredible to be true, don't accept it automatically. We found a Web site that advertised manbeef—human meat for food consumption. It was a spoof, but some people accepted it as true.

Authority.   Ask what the source of the information is, and determine whether you would trust that source. Collective or corporate authority, such as CNN or the American Medical Association, adhere to stricter standards for information than most individuals do. Find the information's home page to determine who is providing it and whether there may be bias.

Audience.   For whom is the information being offered? Web designers have particular audiences in mind. Information is tailored to reach particular audiences. It may be too technical, too jargon-filled, or too simplistic for your purposes. It may also be slanted to appeal to a particular audience.

Purpose.   Why is this information being offered? It may be intended to inform, persuade, or entertain you, or advocate for something. You can gain some clue to this by paying attention to what comes after the dot. A .gov ending is sponsored by the government, for instance, and is probably intended to inform. A .com signifies a commercial enterprise and is probably trying to sell you something. Organizational sites are probably advocating a cause or course of action.

Recency.   How current is the site? The Internet allows information to be placed instantly, but some sites are not monitored or updated frequently. A site's date may be the date it was created or the date it was last modified—it isn't always clear. Many sites have an e-mail address that allows you to ask questions or give feedback to the site owners. Use this to find out more.

Coverage.   Is your topic covered in enough depth? The Internet's speed can work against depth of coverage, but, often, you can link to additional sites that touch on your topic. Use a variety of sources to get sufficient information.

These suggestions aren't foolproof, but they will help you gauge the value and usefulness of Web-based information. Don't just accept something because it's on the Web. Remember, on the Internet, no one knows if you're a dog! Up to this point, we have discussed the first three steps of the P-MOPS procedure in detail. Essentially, we have established the foundation for the act of *deciding*, which we discuss in the next chapter.

Recap: A Quick Review

How well a group evaluates the pros and cons of its alternatives affects how good its solution or decision will be:

1. Step 3 requires a group to evaluate all the options it has identified; ideally, members have a collaborative, cooperative climate for this as well as norms that promote critical thinking—the systematic examination of ideas based on evidence and reasoning.

(continued)

(continued)

2. In evaluating information, members must distinguish between facts, which are not arguable, and inferences (or opinions), which are.

3. Evaluating survey and statistical data may require the help of an expert, since how the questions are asked and the data gathered can influence the results.

4. When members evaluate sources and opinions, they try to determine whether the source is credible unbiased, supports his or her opinion with evidence, and whether that opinion is consistent with those of other experts.

5. When members evaluate reasoning, they look for fallacies, which are reasoning errors.

6. Five common fallacies are *overgeneralizing* (drawing a conclusion based on one or just a few cases); *ad hominem* attacks (attacking the person instead of the argument); suggesting *inappropriate causal relationships* (assuming that because two events are related, one caused the other); a *false dilemma* (acting as if only two choices exist, when likely there are several); and making a *faulty analogy* (stretching a comparison too far).

7. Because anyone can post something on the World Wide Web, members need to evaluate information from the Web carefully.

8. Ask if Web information is accurate (has the information passed some kind of screening or review before being posted?); whether the source is a credible authority; who the audience is for the information; what its purpose is (paying attention to the ending helps—you can guess that .com represents a site that wants to sell something); how recent or current the site is; and coverage of the topic (is the topic covered in depth?).

QUESTIONS FOR REVIEW

 Go to self-quizzes on the Online Learning Center at mbhe.com/galanes12 to test your knowledge of the chapter concepts

The opening case in this chapter concerned a group of officials in O'Fallon, Missouri, who were faced with finding a long-term solution to the city's water treatment problems. Reread the case, if necessary, to answer the following review questions:

1. How systematic in its problem-solving approach did the O'Fallon group seem to be? Do you think they achieved the assembly effect?

2. How well did they seem to meet the functions identified by the Functional Perspective as being necessary for good problem solving?

3. What types of questions did the group have to deal with in the course of solving its problem? Do some types of questions seem harder to resolve than others? If so, which ones?

4. What were the criteria against which the group compared its three realistic options? Why do you think the solution chosen—the membrane treatment facility—met the criteria better than the others? Where were the others weaker?

5. How critical was the O'Fallon group's thinking? What examples in the story lead you to that conclusion?

KEY TERMS

Test your knowledge of these key terms by visiting the Online Learning Center Web site at mhhe.com/galanes12

Ad hominem attack	Electronic brainstorming (EBS)	Problem questions
Area of freedom	Fact	Problem solving
Assembly effect	Fallacy	Procedural Model of Problem
Brainstorming	False dilemma	Solving (P-MOPS)
Brainwriting	Faulty analogy	Question of conjecture
Charge	Functional Perspective	Question of fact
Conjunctive tasks	Ideal Solution Format	Question of policy
Criteria	Inference	Question of value
Critical thinking	Overgeneralization	Single Question Format
Decision making	Problem	Solution questions
Disjunctive tasks	Problem census	

BIBLIOGRAPHY

Gouran, Dennis S., and Randy Y. Hirokawa, "Effective Decision Making and Problem Solving in Groups: A Functional Perspective." Randy Y. Hirokawa, Robert S. Cathcart, Larry A. Samovar, and Linda D. Henman, eds. *Small Group Communication, Theory and Practice: An Anthology.* Los Angeles, CA: Roxbury, 2003, 27–38.

Hirokawa, Randy Y., and Marshall S. Poole, eds. *Communication and Group Decision Making.* Beverly Hills, CA: Sage, 1986, 81–111.

Larson, Carl E., and Frank M. J. LaFasto. *TeamWork: What Must Go Right/What Can Go Wrong.* Newbury Park, CA: Sage, 1989.

Shaw, Marvin E. *Group Dynamics.* 3rd ed. New York: McGraw-Hill, 1981, Chapter 10.

Worchel, Stephen, Wendy Wood, and Jeffry A. Simpson, eds. *Group Process and Productivity.* Newbury Park, CA: Sage, 1992.

NOTES

1. Patrick Banger, personal interview, March 18, 2002.

2. Francois Cooren, "The Communicative Achievement of Collective Minding: Analysis of Board Meeting Excerpts," *Management Communication Quarterly* 17 (May 2004): 517–551.

3. Brant R. Burleson, Barbara J. Levine, and Wendy Samter, "Decision-Making Procedure and Decision Quality," *Human Communication Research* 10 (1984): 557–74; Herm W. Smith, "Group versus Individual Problem Solving and Type of Problem Solved," *Small Group Behavior* 20 (1989): 357–66.

4. Patricia Fandt, "The Relationship of Accountability and Interdependent Behavior to Enhancing Team Consequences, *Group & Organization Studies* 16 (1991): 200–12.

5. Charles Pavitt and Kelly Kline Johnson, "An Examination of the Coherence of Group Discussions," *Communication Research* 26 (June 1999): 303–21.

6. Mark F. Stasson and Scott D. Bradshaw, "Explanations of Individual-Group Performance Differences: What Sort of 'Bonus' Can Be Gained through Group Interaction?" *Small Group Research* 26 (May 1995): 296–308.

7. Patrick Laughlin, Scot W. VanderSteep, and Andrea B. Hollingshead, "Collective versus Individual Induction: Recognition of Truth, Rejection of Error, and Collective Information Processing," *Journal of Personality and Social Psychology* 61 (1994): 50–67.

8. M. L. Chemers, "Leadership Theory and Research: A Systems-Process Integration," in *Basic Group Processes*, ed. P. B. Paulus (New York: Springer-Verlag, 1983): 19–20; Randy Y. Hirokawa, "Consensus Group Decision Making, Quality of Decision and Group Satisfaction: An Attempt to Sort Fact from Fiction," *Central States Speech Journal* 33 (1982): 407–15.

9. Lester Coch and John R. P. French, Jr., "Overcoming Resistance to Change," *Human Relations* 1 (1948): 512–32.

10. Myron W. Block and L. R. Hoffman, "The Effects of Valence of Solutions and Group Cohesiveness on Members' Commitment to Group Decision," in *The Group Problem Solving Process*, ed. L. Richard Hoffman (New York: Prager, 1979): 121.

11. Herm W. Smith, "Group versus Individual Problem Solving and Type of Problem Solved," *Small Group Behavior* 20 (1989): 357–66.

12. Michael Pacanowsky, "Team Tools for Wicked Problems," *Organizational Dynamics* 23 (Winter 1995): 36–51.

13. Abran J. Salazar, Randy Y. Hirokawa, Kathleen M. Propp, Kelly M. Julian, and Geoff B. Leatham, "In Search of True Causes: Examination of the Effect of Group Potential and Group Interaction on Group Performance," *Human Communication Research* 20 (June 1994): 529–59.

14. Deborah H. Gruenfeld and Andrea B. Hollingshead, "Sociocognition in Work Groups: The Evolution of Group Integrative Complexity and Its Relation to Task Performance," *Small Group Research* 24 (August 1993): 383–405.

15. Joseph N. Scudder, Richard T. Herschel, and Martin D. Crossland, "Test of a Model Linking Cognitive Motivation, Assessment of Alternatives, Decision Quality, and Group Process Satisfaction," *Small Group Research* 25 (February 1994): 57–82.

16. Laughlin et al., "Collective versus Individual Induction."

17. Burleson et al., "Decision Making Procedure and Decision Quality."

18. Salazar et al., "In Search of True Causes."

19. Michael E. Mayer, Kevin T. Sonoda, and William B. Gudykunst, "The Effect of Time Pressure and Type of Information on Decision Quality," *Southern Communication Journal* 62 (Summer 1997): 280–92.

20. Elizabeth E. Graham, Michael J. Papa, and Mary B. McPherson, "An Applied Test of the Functional Communication Perspective of Small Group Decision-Making," *Southern Communication Journal* 62 (Summer 1997): 269–79.

21. Kathleen M. Propp and Daniel Nelson, "Problem-Solving Performance in Naturalistic Groups: A Test of the Ecological Validity of the Functional Perspective," *Communication Studies* 47 (Spring/Summer 1996): 35–45.

22. Scudder et al., "Test of a Model."

23. Michael E. Mayer, "Behaviors Leading to More Effective Decisions in Small Groups Embedded in Organizations," *Communication Reports* 11 (Summer 1998): 123–32.

24. Irving L. Janis and Leon Mann, *Decision Making: A Psychological Analysis of Conflict, Choice, and Commitment* (New York: Free Press, 1977); Irving L. Janis, *Groupthink: Psychological Studies of Foreign-Policy Decisions and Fiascoes,* 2nd ed. (Boston: Houghton-Mifflin, 1983).

25. Susan Jarboe, "Procedures for Enhancing Group Decision Making," in *Communication and Group Decision Making,* 2nd ed., eds. Randy Y. Hirokawa and Marshall Scott Poole (Thousand Oaks, CA: Sage, 1996): 345–83.

26. John K. Brilhart, "An Experimental Comparison of Three Techniques for Communicating a Problem-Solving Pattern to Members of a Discussion Group," *Speech Monographs* 33 (1966): 168–77.

27. Thomas M. Scheidel and Laura Crowell, "Developmental Sequences in Small Groups," *Quarterly Journal of Speech* 50 (1964): 140–45.

28. Dennis S. Gouran, Candace Brown, and David R. Henry, "Behavioral Correlates of Perceptions of Quality in Decision-Making Discussions," *Communication Monographs* 45 (1978): 62; William E. Jurma, "Effects of Leader Structuring Style and Task Orientation Characteristics of Group Members," *Communication Monographs* 46 (1979): 282–95.

29. Jurma, "Effects of Leader Structuring Style."

30. Marshall S. Poole, "Decision Development in Small Groups II: A Study of Multiple Sequences in Decision Making," *Communication Monographs* 50 (1983): 224-25; Decision Development in Small Groups III: A Multiple Sequence Model of Group Decision Development," *Communication Monographs* 50 (1983): 321-41.

31. John K. Brilhart and Lurene M. Jochem, "Effects of Different Patterns on Outcomes of Problem-Solving Discussions," *Journal of Applied Psychology* 48 (1964): 175-79.

32. Ovid L. Bayless, "An Alternative Model for Problem-Solving Discussion," *Journal of Communication* 17 (1967): 188-97; Carl E. Larson, "Forms of Analysis and Small Group Problem Solving," *Speech Monographs* 36 (1969): 452-55.

33. Charles M. Kelly, Michael Jaffe, and Gregory V. Nelson, "Solving Problems," *Research Management* 30 (1987): 20-23.

34. Ibid.

35. Benjamin J. Broome and Luann Fulbright, "A Multi-Stage Influence Model of Barriers to Group Problem Solving: A Participant-Generated Agenda for Small Group Research, *Small Group Research* 26 (February 1995): 25-55.

36. Randy Y. Hirokawa, "Why Informed Groups Make Faulty Decisions," *Small Group Research* 18 (1987): 3-29.

37. The principles of the Functional Perspective are summarized succinctly in Dennis S. Gouran and Randy Y. Hirokawa, "Effective Decision Making and Problem Solving in Groups: A Functional Perspective," in *Small Group Communication, Theory and Practice: An Anthology,* eds. Randy Y. Hirokawa, Robert S. Cathcart, Larry A. Samovar, and Linda D. Henman (Los Angeles, CA: Roxbury, 2003): 27-38. Other relevant sources include Dennis S. Gouran and Randy Y. Hirokawa, "Functional Theory and Communication in Decision-Making and Problem-Solving Groups: An Expanded View," in *Communication and Group Decision Making,* 2nd ed., eds. R. Y. Hirokawa and M. S. Poole (Thousand Oaks, CA: Sage, 1996): 55-80; Randy Y. Hirokawa, "Communication and Group Decision Making Efficacy," in *Small Group Communication: A Reader,* 6th ed., eds. Robert S. Cathcart and Larry A. Samovar (Dubuque, IA: Wm. C. Brown, 1992): 165-77; Randy Y. Hirokawa and Kathryn Rost, "Effective Group Decision

Making in Organizations: A Field Test of the Vigilant Interaction Theory," *Management Communication Quarterly* 5 (February 1992): 267-88; Randy Y. Hirokawa, "Group Communication and Decision-Making Performance: A Continued Test of the Functional Perspective," *Human Communication Research* 14 (1988): 487-515; Dennis S. Gouran, "Inferential Errors, Interaction, and Group Decision Making," in *Communication and Group Decision Making,* eds. R. Y. Hirokawa and M. S. Poole (Beverly Hills, CA: Sage, 1986): 93-111; Randy Y. Hirokawa, "Discussion Procedures and Decision-Making Performance: A Test of the Functional Perspective," *Human Communication Research* 12 (1985): 59-74. Randy Y. Hirokawa, "Group Communication and Problem-Solving Effectiveness II: An Exploratory Investigation of Procedural Functions," *Western Journal of Speech Communication* 47 (1983), 59-74.

38. Gouran and Hirokawa, "Effective Decision Making and Problem Solving in Groups."

39. Ibid., 28-30.

40. Randy Y. Hirokawa, "Group Communication and Problem-Solving Effectiveness II;" Marshall S. Poole and Joel A. Doelger, "Developmental Processes in Group Decision-Making," in *Communication and Group Decision Making,* eds. R. Y. Hirokawa and M. S. Poole (Newbury Park, CA: Sage, 1986): 35-61.

41. Hirokawa and Rost, "Effective Group Decision Making," 20-22.

42. Kathleen M. Propp and Daniel Nelson, "Problem-Solving Performance in Naturalistic Groups: A Test of the Ecological Validity of the Functional Perspective," *Communication Studies* 47 (1996): 35-45.

43. Randy Y. Hirokawa, "Why Informed Groups Make Faulty Decisions, " *Small Group Behavior* 18 (1987): 3-29.

44. John F. Cragan and David W. Wright, "The Functional Theory of Small Group Decision Making: A Replication," *Journal of Social Behavior and Personality* 8 (1993): 165-74.

45. Carl E. Larson, "Forms of Analysis and Small Group Problem-Solving," *Speech Monographs* 36 (1969): 452-55; Frank LaFasto and Carl Larson, *When Teams Work Best: 6,000 Team Members and Team Leaders Tell What It Takes to Succeed,* (Thousand Oaks: Sage, 2001): 84-90.

46. Carl E. Larson, "Forms of Analysis and Small Group Problem-Solving"; Alvin A. Goldberg and Carl E. Larson, *Group Communication: Discussion Processes and Applications* (Englewood Cliffs, NJ: Prentice Hall, 1975).

47. Alvin A. Goldberg and Carl E. Larson, *Group Communication: Discussion Processes and Applications*.

48. Types of questions and their relationship to effective problem solving and decision making are discussed in detail in Dennis S. Gouran and Randy Y. Hirokawa, "Effective Decision Making and Problem Solving in Groups."

49. For example, see Kelly, Jaffe, and Nelson, "Solving Problems"; Norman R. F. Maier and R. A. Maier, "An Experimental Test of the Effects of 'Developmental' vs. 'Free' Discussions on the Quality of Group Decisions," *Journal of Applied Psychology* 41 (1957): 320–23; and Randy Y. Hirokawa, "Group Communication and Problem-Solving Effectiveness: An Investigation of Group Phases," *Human Communication Research* 9 (1983): 291–305.

50. David Dryden Henningsen and Mary Lynn Miller Henningsen, "Examining Social Influence in Information-Sharing Contexts," *Small Group Research* 34 (August 2003): 391–412.

51. Ibid., 407–409.

52. Alex Osborn, *Applied Imagination,* rev. ed. (New York: Scribner, 1975).

53. Paul Kirvan, "Brainstorming: It is More than You Think," *Communication News* 28 (1991): 39–40.

54. Michael Schrage, "Meetings Don't Have to Be Dull," *The Wall Street Journal* (April 29, 1996): A22.

55. Graham Hitchings and Sara Cox, "Generating Ideas using Randomized Search Methods: A Method of Managed Convergence," *Management Decision* 30 (1992): 58.

56. R. Brent Gallupe, Alan R. Dennis, William H. Cooper, Joseph S. Valacich, Lane M. Bastianutti, and Jay F. Nunamaker, Jr., "Electronic Brainstorming and Group Size," *Academy of Management Journal* 35 (June 1992): 350–70.

57. See also Joseph S. Valacich, Alan R. Dennis, and T. Connolly, "Idea Generation in Computer-Based Groups: A New Ending to an Old Story," *Organizational Behavior and Human Decision Processes* 57 (1994): 448–68.

58. John Sosik and Bruce Avolio, "Inspiring Group Activity: Comparing Anonymous and Identified Electronic Brainstorming," *Small Group Research* 29 (1998): 3–31.

59. Moshe F. Rubenstein, *Patterns of Problem Solving* (Englewood Cliffs, NJ: Prentice Hall, 1975): 1–2.

60. Brilhart and Jochem, "The Effects of Different Patterns."

61. Randy Y. Hirokawa, John G. Oetzel, Carlos G. Aleman, and Scott E. Elston, "The Effects of Evaluation Clarity and Bias on the Relationship between Vigilant Interaction and Group Decision-Making Efficacy" (paper presented at the Speech Communication Association Convention, November, 1991).

62. Renee A. Meyers, David R. Siebold, and Dale Brashers, "Argument in Initial Group Decision-Making Discussions: Refinement of a Coding Scheme and a Descriptive Quantitative Analysis," *Western Journal of Speech Communication* 55 (Winter 1991): 47–68.

63. Much of the following information is distilled from M. Neil Browne and Stuart M. Keeley, *Asking the Right Questions: A Guide to Critical Thinking,* 7th ed. (Englewood Cliffs, NJ: Prentice Hall, 2004).

64. The following information is taken from Tyrone Adams and Norman Clark, *The Internet: Effective Online Communication* (Fort Worth, TX: Harcourt, 2001): 166–75.

Problem Solving and Decision Making in Groups II: Deciding and Implementing

STUDY OBJECTIVES

As a result of studying Chapter 11 you should be able to:

1. Describe and explain the importance of the final two steps in the problem-solving process, making the decision and implementing it.

2. Understand the differences between decisions made by the leader, by the leader's consulting with members, by majority vote, and by consensus, including the advantages and disadvantages of each method.

3. Explain five guidelines for making group decisions by consensus and the reasons for these guidelines.

4. Describe the phases many groups experience during decision making and explain several factors that may influence these phases.

5. Describe the group polarization effect and explain how it can impair effective decision making.

6. Describe groupthink and its symptoms; explain how it can impair effective decision making and how members can counteract it.

7. Describe and be able to use the RISK technique to second-guess a group's tentative choice and the PERT technique to keep track of implementing a complex solution.

8. List and describe seven characteristics of problems that can help a group decide how to tailor its problem-solving procedures.

9. Describe various technologies available to help groups and explain how teleconferences and group support systems, in particular, can both help and hinder group problem solving.

CENTRAL MESSAGE

The work that a group has accomplished during the problem analysis, solution generation, and solution evaluation steps sets up how good a decision the group makes and how effectively that decision is implemented. Several things can go wrong during the process, but vigilant group members can prevent these and also can take advantage of technological aids available to help groups.

At a university where one of us worked, registration staff members calculated that they were spending thousands of dollars processing all the courses that students dropped and added during a single quarter. In the days before computerized registration and fee payment, each of these drop-adds had to be processed by hand—a time-consuming and expensive process. The registration staff discussed ways to cut the number of drop-adds. Staff members concluded that students were scheduling classes without careful planning and forethought, so they decided to penalize "frivolous" drop-adds by imposing a fee on each one. But because they realized that some drop-adds were "legitimate," they included a procedure whereby the student's academic adviser could waive the drop or add if the student's reason was a legitimate one (such as failing a prerequisite course!). Remember, this was before computerized scheduling; the new procedure meant that a paper form had to be completed for *each course* dropped or added, and if the fee was to be waived, another form was needed for *each course* whose fee was waived. It turned out that most students had legitimate reasons for dropping and adding courses, often because their work schedules changed from one quarter to another. The bottom line was that the Registration Office processed nearly twice as many paper forms as before, at greater cost than the old, free drop-add system. After a couple of years, this new system was abandoned in favor of the old one.

To us, this example suggests at least three flaws in the registration staff's problem-solving and decision-making processes. First, the staff made assumptions about *why* students dropped and added classes, and the assumptions (students are irresponsible and don't plan ahead) were flat out wrong! This indicates that the staff didn't do its homework to learn why students dropped and added classes. The real reasons had to do partly with the fact that students were required to schedule for the upcoming quarter three months before the quarter began! A lot can change in three months, including work schedules. Second, it seems as if the staff didn't do a thorough job of developing its options to reduce the numbers of drop-adds. Staff members seemed to latch onto the first "solution" that fit their preconceived ideas about why the students were drop-adding. Finally, staff members didn't pretest their solution first, either by asking the advisers for their opinions or by trying the process on a limited scale or as a pilot project before they involved the entire university.

Using P-MOPS to Address Complex Problems, Continued

In this chapter, we continue our discussion of problem solving and decision making by focusing on the final steps of the problem-solving process, deciding on a solution and implementing it. We discuss what can go wrong and how technology can be used to help a group; we also present two procedures, RISK and PERT, that can improve the deciding and implementing steps.

Step 4 of P-MOPS: Consensus Decision Making

The group's entire work comes down to this point, making the actual decision. The question the group must address is: *What seems to be the best possible solution that we can all support?*

4A: Decide What Decision-Making Method to Use

Groups may use a number of different methods to make decisions. Among the most common are the four described here; their advantages and disadvantages are outlined in Figure 11.1.

Decision Making by the Leader   Sometimes a designated or emergent leader thinks the problem through alone and announces a decision. Group members are then given instructions for executing the decision. The resulting

FIGURE 11.1   Comparing advantages and disadvantages of four common decision-making methods

Decision-Making Method	Advantages	Disadvantages
By the Leader	• Can be high-quality decision if leader is an expert. • Is fast. • Group avoids anxiety/responsibility of decision making.	• Lacks others' input, so may not be high quality. • Members may not support decision. • May cause resentment, reduced cohesiveness, lack of motivation for future.
By the Leader, with Consultation	• Can be high-quality decision. • Can be faster than having group decide. • Especially useful if group cannot come to consensus. • Members appreciate opportunity to participate.	• Members may resent decision if their input isn't used. • "Losing" side may not support decision. • May encourage members to duck hard work of developing consensus.
By Majority Vote	• Familiar procedure for Americans. • Each vote counts equally. • Decision can be reached quickly.	• Minority side may stay silent out of fear. • Minority may resent outcome and not support it. • Majority is not always right; decision may be flawed.
By Consensus	• All members support decision. • Members more satisfied and committed to decision. • Decision can be high quality, because all viewpoints are taken into account.	• Usually takes more time. • Members may feel pressured to conform. • May be hard or impossible to achieve.

solution may or may not be a high-quality one, but other outcomes of such control by the leader may be resentment, lowered cohesiveness, half-hearted support for the decision, and unwillingness to contribute to subsequent decisions. Members may even sabotage the decision. We once observed a group of faculty members who became furious that their designated leader had made an important decision without consulting them. They called a special meeting to overturn his decision. After discussing their options, they proceeded to make *exactly the same* decision that he had made. Clearly their distress was not about the *content* of the decision—it was about the *process* and their belief that the leader had disenfranchised them.

Decision Making by the Leader in Consultation with Members   Often, a group leader reserves the right to make a decision, but wants input from the group. The leader consults with members, individually or as a group, then makes the decision based on that consultation. This is an appropriate method to use when the leader alone is responsible for the decision, such as a department head who must determine annual budgets, but who wants to broaden his or her base of knowledge. It is also an effective method when a group cannot come to consensus. One of us was responsible for deciding which teaching area a new faculty position should represent. The broadcast journalism, print journalism, and media production faculty each argued that the new position should fill teaching needs in those individual areas; the group could not achieve consensus. The various arguments and proposals helped your coauthor make the decision, and even though some faculty were disappointed, they all believed they had the opportunity to be heard.

Majority Decision

Decision made by vote, with the winning alternative receiving more than half the members' votes.

Decision Making by Majority Vote   Making a **majority decision** through voting by a show of hands, saying *aye,* or with written ballot is probably the procedure used most often to settle a difference of opinion in democratic groups. On the plus side, everyone has an equal opportunity to influence the decision by speaking, each vote counts equally, and the decision is reached more quickly than if the group's norms require a consensus decision. The numerical power of the majority wins—no problem if the vote is unanimous. But usually the vote is split, with minority members (losers) sometimes doubting that their ideas have been understood fully and treated fairly. People in a minority may even remain silent for fear of being ridiculed for opinions that deviate from the majority opinion. Not only does the quality of the decision sometimes suffer, but the group's cohesiveness and commitment to the decision may be lowered. When a group's bylaws *require* that a vote be taken, the group may want to discuss an issue until consensus has been reached, then vote to confirm it "legally."

Consensus Decision

A choice that all group members agree is the best one that they all can accept.

Decision Making by Consensus   A **consensus decision** is one that all members agree is the best that everyone can support. It may be, but is not necessarily, the alternative most preferred by all members. When a true consensus has been reached, the output is usually better and members are more satisfied and likely to accept the outcome. However, reaching consensus may take much more time than other procedures. Furthermore, unanimity— the state of perfect consensus in which every group member believes that the decision achieved is the best that could be made—is not at all common. Sometimes a true consensus cannot be achieved, no matter how much time is spent in discussion.

More than just the merit of the decision is involved when a group strives for consensus. Certain personality traits, values, and other characteristics of the members affect a group's ability to achieve consensus, as we mentioned in Chapter 6. For example, Beatty found that groups with members similar in decision-rule orientation were more likely to achieve consensus.[1] Three common decision-rule orientations are attempts to minimize losses (a conservative, pessimistic approach), attempts to maximize gains (a risk-taking, optimistic approach), and the maximum expected utility approach (an attempt to derive the highest average payoffs no matter whether a pessimistic or optimistic future is envisioned). Beatty noted that the degree of comfort that members felt with the decision was more important in achieving consensus than the quality of the decision itself. Groups with members whose decision-rule orientations were similar had an easier time achieving consensus. Thus, more than just the merit of the decision is involved when a group strives for consensus.

Consensus may be superficial when some members accommodate to other higher-status members, including "experts" who express their opinions with exceptional force, a designated leader, or a large majority. One of us once completed "Lost on the Moon," a group decision-making exercise in which the group is asked to rank the usefulness of several items to astronauts lost on the moon. Her group included several electrical and mechanical engineers with considerable scientific and technical expertise. She readily conceded to these experts. Interestingly, her individual ranking of the items was better than the group's ranking, but she was swayed by the engineers' confidence in their knowledge. Even though it may be uncomfortable to be the group's opinion deviate, do not suppress your opinions. Conflict is likely. Expect it and welcome it, particularly the type of constructive argument that enhances critical thinking. In the next chapter we present specific suggestions to help you manage conflict.

Suggestions for Achieving Consensus   The process of reaching consensus gives all members an opportunity to express how they feel and think about the alternatives, and an equitable chance to influence the outcome. For important decisions, it is worth the time. Here are some discussion guidelines outlined by Hall for making consensus decisions:

1. **Don't argue stubbornly for your own position.** Present it clearly and logically. Listen actively to others and consider all reactions carefully.

2. **Avoid looking at a stalemate as a win–lose situation.** Rather, see whether you can find a next best alternative acceptable to all.

3. **When agreement is reached too easily and too quickly, be on guard against groupthink.** Through discussion, be sure that everyone accepts the decision for similar or complementary reasons and really agrees that it is the best that can be reached. Don't change your position just to avoid conflict.

4. **Avoid conflict-suppressing techniques, such as majority vote, averaging, coin tossing, and so forth, except as a last resort.** Although they prevent destructive interpersonal conflicts, they also suppress constructive substantive arguments.

5. **Seek out differences of opinion, which are helpful in testing alternatives and evaluating reasoning.** Get every member involved in the decision-making process. The group has a better chance of selecting the best alternative if it has a wider range of information and ideas.[2]

4B: Understand Phasic Progression during Decision Making

Groups often cycle through predictable phases as they attempt to solve problems and make decisions. Bales and Strodtbeck were among the first to identify this **phasic progression.**[3] During the *orientation* phase, members orient themselves to the task and to one another, if they do not already know each other. In the *evaluation* phase, they decide what they collectively think about the problem or decision. Finally, during the *control* phase, the group has reached enough socioemotional maturity for members to concentrate on completing their task. For each new problem they confront, groups will tend to cycle through all three of these stages, returning to an orientation stage for a new problem once a decision has been reached about a previous problem.

Phasic Progression

The movement of a group through fairly predictable phases or stages, each of which is characterized by specific kinds of statements.

Fisher's Model of Group Phases   Later, Fisher observed that experienced decision-making groups pass through four phases as they work toward deciding among a group of alternatives.[4] These phases are orientation, conflict, decision emergence, and reinforcement. They can be identified by the kinds of interactions that occur in each.

Orientation   During the orientation phase, members develop a shared understanding of their task, the facts about available options, and how to interpret them. Signs of disagreement are minimal; ambiguous and favorable remarks are common. This makes sense because, when group members are uncertain about the facts or concerned about how others will perceive them, they refrain from making strong statements of disagreement that might offend another member. In this early stage, a member is more likely to say, "Well, that idea sounds like it might work, but maybe we should take time to think about it some more," than to say, "That's not going to work at all—we're going to have to try a lot harder if we are to come up with a decent solution." The first remark is ambiguous and tentative; the second is clear and definite.

Conflict   During the conflict phase, members offer initiatives, take stands, disagree, offer compromises, argue for and against proposals, and generally discuss ideas in a more open manner than during orientation. Ambiguous remarks fall to a low level in this phase, but disagreeing and agreeing remarks are common. For instance, Selena says, "I think we should get more information about the impact this might have before we proceed much further." Andrew replies, "Naw, we have all the information we need right now to decide." Then Tina supports Selena: "I agree with Selena. We need to know a lot more or we might really mess things up." Members argue for and against proposals, with most people taking sides. Wishy-washy behavior disappears as opinions are expressed clearly and forcefully.

Decision Emergence   For a group to achieve its goal, it must move, somehow, from a position where each member argues a particular point of view to a position where members are willing to be influenced by one another. This movement is signaled by the reappearance of ambiguity in the group. Whereas the earlier ambiguity served as a way of managing primary tension, now it helps resolve secondary tension by allowing the members to back off from staunchly held positions and save face at the same time. It would be hard on a member's self-image to switch suddenly from "I think we should accept the first proposal" to "OK, let's reject the first proposal." A transition is needed; the ambiguity provides this transition, which allows the member to move from "I think we should accept the first proposal" to *"Maybe* you are right. There might be some problems with the first proposal that I hadn't considered. Let's look at it more closely before we decide." Members move gradually toward a common group position. Near the end of this phase a consensus decision emerges, sometimes suddenly. The members usually know when this point is reached, and they all indicate support for the decision. (If this does not occur, then the group may need to resolve its disagreement by majority vote.)

Reinforcement   After a group has accomplished its primary objective, it doesn't just immediately move on to a different problem or disband. Members reinforce each other and themselves for a job well done. They say such things as, "Wow, it took a long time, but we got some really important things done," or "I really like the proposal. It's going to work beautifully," or "I'm proud of us for coming up with this. You guys are super and this has been a rewarding experience." Members pat each other on the back and reinforce the positive feelings they have toward the decision and toward each other. This good feeling carries over to the next meeting.

　　Fisher believed that unless some outside factor (like severe time pressure) interferes with the group's natural decision-making process, these phases will follow each other in a predictable way, although the proportion of time spent in each phase may vary from decision to decision. It is important to recall, however, that he studied interaction in previously developed groups that had already passed through their formation stage.

Poole's more recent investigations have called into question the idea that most groups experience exactly the same phases, in the same order.[5] Group decision making is more complex than unitary sequences suggest. A number of factors influence not only what phases groups experience, but also in what order the phases occur.[6] For example, some groups experience long, drawn-out conflict phases with little socioemotional integration after the conflict. Others experience lengthy periods of idea development with no overt conflict.

Poole's contingency model of group decision making describes three types of factors that affect phasic progression: objective task characteristics, group task characteristics, and group structural characteristics.[7] *Objective task characteristics* include such factors as goal clarity and potential impact of the decision. For example, if the group's goal is clear at the beginning of the process, members may be able to shorten the orientation phase. *Group task characteristics* include such factors as time and population familiarity. Members are more likely to spend extra time orienting themselves to the task and arguing the merits of various options for a novel task that is unfamiliar to them than for a familiar one. Finally, *group structural characteristics* refer to how members of the group work together and include such factors as cohesiveness, conflict, and history. Members who have experienced divisive conflict may either run away from potential arguments in the group or may approach group meetings with their defenses up and boxing gloves on. As you can see, group decision making is complicated, with numerous factors potentially influencing phasic progression.

Fisher's work provides the link between a group's development stages of formation and production with its decision-making stages. For each new major decision a group faces, members must reorient themselves to each other and to the group's new task, argue for and against the various options available, *decide* something, and achieve some sort of closure through reinforcement of the decision. Thus, from our review of work on phasic progression and from our own experience, we envision a group cycling repeatedly through phases like those Fisher described while moving gradually forward from early formation to full and efficient production. This movement is captured in the spirals of Figure 11.2.

This back-and-forth spiral movement is typical of many continuing groups. Scheidel and Crowell observed the spiral-like progression of a group's problem-solving process and noted that a group does not move in a clear, straight line toward a decision.[8] This spiral-like effect has been observed by others. Sabourin and Geist described the collaborative nature of group decision making as a process in which group members build on each other's proposals.[9] Fisher and Stutman also observed the messy, but ultimately progressive, nature

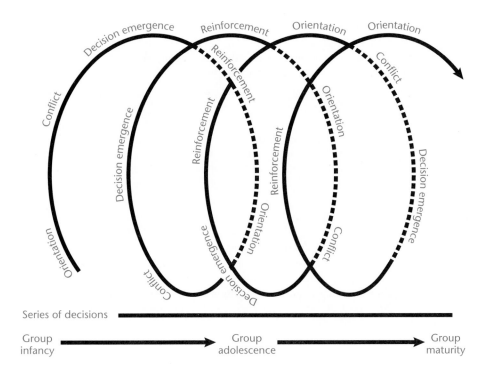

FIGURE 11.2
Decision making within the development of a small group

of the spiral model.[10] However, a recent investigation by Pavitt and Johnson suggests that this spiraling movement is not universal.[11] They found great variation in the spiraling exhibited by the groups that these authors analyzed, ranging from little or no spiraling to much more than the spiral model indicates. Even so, it may be especially helpful for members high in preference for procedural order to know that such messy cycling between problem analysis to a decision and solution discussion is normal; they can better endure the frustration they feel when a group's progress seems to be "two steps forward, one step back."

Recap: A Quick Review

After groups have identified and evaluated their options, they must make a choice and implement that choice.

1. When groups prepare to make their choice, they must first decide what decision-making method to use.

2. The leader can make the choice, but members may resent it; they are less likely to resent it if the leader consults with members first (unless the leader ignores the input).

(continued)

(continued)

3. Members can use the well-accepted method of majority voting; however, those in the minority may feel misunderstood or not heard.

4. In consensus decision making, members accept the option they believe is the best that they can all agree to; members are satisfied with the decision, but the process can be lengthy and consensus may be impossible.

5. When a group uses consensus decision making, members should not stubbornly argue for their own positions and should be willing to listen to other points of view, seek out differences of opinion, avoid conflict-suppressing techniques (such as majority voting) and, instead of assuming a win-lose position, look for areas about which they can agree.

6. Many groups experience phases during the course of decision making; Bales first identified the phases of orientation, evaluation, and control that he saw repeated regularly during decision making.

7. Fisher described four phases: orientation, in which group members orient to themselves and the task; conflict, in which members take positions and argue for and against them; decision emergence, in which members begin to coalesce around a particular alternative; and reinforcement, in which members bolster their choice and celebrate their success.

4C: Understand What Can Go Wrong during Decision Making

Groups *can* make better decisions than individuals (see Chapter 10), but they don't always reach their potential, even when they achieve consensus. For example, Burleson studied 10 groups that achieved consensus and found that, although eight of them had better decisions than their individual members acting alone, two of them produced worse decisions.[12]

Several factors interfere with effective decision making. One factor is that group members may not actually exchange the information they have as individuals (similar to the *hidden profile* discussed in Chapter 10)[13] or use well the information they do share,[14] with their decisions suffering as a result. Decision making seems to improve when groups are smaller and members have little common information. Apparently, this forces members to share what they do have.

Wood observed several factors that impede decision making, including members who don't have the needed skills or information and members whose social needs prevent them from attending to the task.[15] Poor operating procedures, including the failure to provide structure for the decision-making process and failure to test for consensus, hurt decision quality. Finally, adhering to ascribed (external) status characteristics impaired open and honest communication, which prevented critical thinking. Very cohesive groups with high-performance expectations perform well,[16] and groups that approach decision making systematically make better decisions than groups that do not.[17] Group interaction itself can promote collective inferential error if members accept unusual cases as representative (i.e., overgeneralizing), passively accept specialized knowledge without questioning it, or create hypothetical scenarios with no basis in fact.[18]

Two phenomena pose particular problems for effective decision making: group polarization and groupthink.

Group Polarization   Group members can and should influence each other, but such influence can produce the **group polarization** tendency, which refers to the finding that group members often make decisions that are more extreme (either more risky or more cautious) than the individual members' initial preferences.[19] In other words, group members push themselves *further* in a particular direction than where they initially started. Two explanations have been proposed for this.[20]

Social Comparison Theory (SCT) focuses on psychological factors; it suggests that as members get to know each other's values, they want to appear "correct" and may exaggerate opinions in the direction that they believe the group values positively. For example, if you are mildly liberal politically and you are in a group that seems to value liberal thought, then you might be tempted to exaggerate how liberal you are. Thus, if the group or cultural norm favors risk (as with many business decisions in our culture), the group will shift toward risk; if caution is the cultural norm (as with a decision affecting a child's life), the group shifts toward caution.

The second explanation for group polarization focuses on cognitive factors. *Persuasive Arguments Theory* (PAT) says that the number, salience, and novelty of arguments in a particular direction persuade members to move in that direction. Thus, if members favor risk (or caution), there will be more and stronger arguments presented in favor of risk (or caution); the persuasive power of these arguments shifts the group in that direction.

Studies have found support for both SCT and PAT. Whether SCT or PAT better explains choice shift in a specific group may depend on conditions within the group. For example, Hale and Boster found that as the task became more ambiguous, SCT seemed to explain shifts better, but as task ambiguity decreased, PAT made more sense.[21] Kaplan and Miller discovered that the type of task mattered; SCT explanations prevailed for tasks requiring judgment, but PAT explained the choice shifts better for intellective tasks that had correct answers.[22]

An intriguing study of burglar behavior by Cromwell et al. supports the concept of group polarization and confirms that both cognitive and emotional factors come into play during group decision making.[23] Burglars themselves believe they take more risks when working with others, but the evidence suggests otherwise. Burglars normally rate potential targets on the basis of the risks associated with those targets. When burglars work in groups, one burglar may point out risks the others miss, so they collectively take into account risk cues they may not have noticed working alone. For example, in one group of three burglars, two rated a particular house a 6 (with 10 the lowest risk), but the third burglar, a woman, pointed out that the time was nearly 3 PM, school

---

Group Polarization

The tendency for group members to make decisions that are more extreme (more risky or cautious) than they would make individually.

would soon be out, and many children were likely to be playing nearby. The burglars collectively reassessed the risk as 2.

At the same time, burglars working together apparently increase each other's excitement and egg each other on. In the same study, Cromwell et al. found that burglars in groups were more likely to go on multiple burglary sprees, hitting multiple targets, something that individual burglars did not and would not do. These findings about burglar risk and caution, which seem incompatible, can be reconciled as follows. Burglars deciding to commit a crime experience high rates of arousal, which is increased by the presence of others. This social facilitation effect can lead to increased risk taking. However, assessing a particular site for degree of risk is actually a low-arousal state that requires cognitive information-processing skill, which seems to be helped by the presence of others. Thus, both cognitive and psychological factors appear to be involved in decision making, and both are affected by the participation of others. It is interesting to note that one of the major advantages for group decision making—that several heads are better than one—is distinctly helpful during the information-processing phase of decision making, even for burglars.

Thus, decision making can be impaired or improved by the particular norms and arguments that prevail in a group. Being aware of these normal group tendencies can help group members guard against bias in decision making.

Groupthink

The tendency of some cohesive groups *not* to subject information, reasoning, and proposals to thorough critical analysis.

Groupthink   Another factor that can significantly impair critical thinking in a small group is groupthink. Coined by Irving Janis, **groupthink** occurs when a highly cohesive group wants to maintain consensus so much that it suppresses confrontation and disagreement, so that the group's decisions are not carefully thought through.[24] The group's balance tilts toward maintaining cohesiveness and harmony rather than toward thinking critically. Janis compared two decisions by President John F. Kennedy's National Security Council. The first, a disastrous one, occurred when the United States decided to invade Cuba at the Bay of Pigs shortly after Fidel Castro had established a communist government there. The second is considered a model of effective group decision making; it was the 1963 decision to blockade Cuba when missile sites were discovered there and ships with nuclear warheads to arm them were photographed on their way from the Soviet Union. Janis was intrigued by the fact that essentially the same group of people made decisions of such divergent quality. He found the reason *not* in the individual decision makers' personalities or intentions, but in the *throughput processes* they used. Groups making effective decisions and proposing high-quality alternatives are willing to engage in open conflict, challenge one another's reasoning, and test all information and ideas for soundness. Janis found that Kennedy's advisers did not thoroughly test information before making the Bay of Pigs decision, which explains how such well-educated, intelligent individuals, in the face of evidence to the contrary, *as a group* allowed such a stupid decision to be made.

Please note that just because a group decision turns out badly does not automatically mean groupthink is the culprit. Sometimes decisions go awry because of factors over which the group has no control or can't have known about. What makes a decision faulty because of groupthink is the group's failure to consider all the information available *at the time of the decision* in a thorough and unbiased way. Highly cohesive groups are particularly vulnerable to the groupthink trap because that very cohesion creates a general desire to keep the members together on a decision. This then leads to pressure for consensus and touches off a fear of anything that seems to threaten the cohesion, particularly conflict. The pressure to achieve consensus is particularly acute in groups experiencing time pressures and with leaders who have a preferred alternative that they attempt to promote.[25]

Groupthink is revealed in the type of communication that members exhibit. Cline compared the conversations of groupthink and non-groupthink groups and found several surprising differences.[26] Although levels of disagreement were similar in both sets of groups, the groupthink groups exhibited significantly higher levels of *agreement,* and these agreements were simple, unsubstantiated ones. Group members ended up making statements and agreeing with themselves. In contrast, the agreements exhibited in the non-groupthink groups were substantive in nature, with different speakers providing different evidence and lines of reasoning to support their assertions. Cline concluded that in groupthink, concern for positive relationships and cohesiveness overrides critical thinking.

Groupthink is a common phenomenon in government, business, and educational groups. It has been implicated in a number of disastrous policy decisions, including NASA's 1986 decision to launch the space shuttle *Challenger,* which exploded just after takeoff.[27] It has also been linked to a number of clearly unethical decisions made in American business, including Beech-Nut's decision to market phony apple juice, E. F. Hutton's decision to kite checks, and Salomon Brothers' illegal bidding in Treasury auctions.[28] In all these decisions, group members had information that should have forewarned them of impending failure, but biases affected how they processed the information; desire for harmony and cohesiveness sabotaged the decision-making process. It seems that when informational and normative pressures (pressures stemming from group norms) compete, the influence of norms supporting agreement outweighs the pressure to share and evaluate information.[29]

Groupthink is not inevitable in a cohesive group. Aldag and Fuller remind us that such antecedents of groupthink as high cohesiveness and directive leadership do not inherently produce dysfunctions in a group.[30] Bernthal and Insko discovered that high socioemotional cohesiveness was most likely to produce groupthink symptoms, especially when it was paired with low task-oriented cohesiveness.[31] This was confirmed by the meta-analysis of cohesiveness by Mullen et al., who found that cohesiveness based on interpersonal attraction among members can produce the kinds of problems associated with group-think, but cohesiveness based on commitment to the task has the opposite effect.[32] The effects of cohesiveness are magnified when a group must decide unanimously instead of by majority rule.[33]

A revised model of groupthink that takes these and other factors into account has been proposed by Neck and Moorhead, who add time pressure and importance of the decision as factors contributing to groupthink.[34] These authors believe that two moderating factors, the role of the leader and how methodical the group's decision-making processes are, determine whether the antecedent conditions of cohesiveness, time, and importance will actually produce groupthink. The leader's behavior is particularly important. A leader with a closed communication style discourages member participation in decisions, discourages diverse opinions, states his or her opinions at the outset of a discussion, and does not emphasize the importance of making a wise decision. When groupthink conditions are present, this style is more likely to produce groupthink than an open style that encourages participation.

Symptoms of Groupthink   How can you recognize groupthink? The symptoms of groupthink identified by Janis and others fall into three main categories:

1. **The group overestimates its power and morality.**

    A group may be so optimistic that it overestimates the chances for its programs to succeed. For example, the group of men behind the burglary of the Democratic National Headquarters, which eventually led to the Watergate hearings and President Nixon's resignation in disgrace, believed that they had a morally determined duty to protect the American public by gathering intelligence, no matter how, to help the president.

2. **The group becomes closed-minded.**

    Either a high-status leader or the group has a preferred solution, and the group closes itself off to any information contrary to this preference. This sounds like the group proposing its "solution" for drop-adds. A group may also stereotype outside figures who disagree so that it doesn't have to pay attention to what they might have to say. NASA officials were so biased in favor of launching that they ignored or devalued information provided by engineers who opposed the *Challenger* launch.

3. **Group members experience pressures to conform.**

    Pressure to conform manifests itself in a variety of ways. First, members censor their own remarks, exemplified in Figure 11.3. If you think everyone else in the group favors a proposal, you will tend to suppress your own doubts and fears. Second, the group members have a shared illusion of unanimity, manifested by the amount of simple agreement

FIGURE 11.3   Groupthink in action

Reprinted with permission of King Features Syndicate.

discovered by Cline.[35] Because individuals do not express doubts openly, the members think they all agree. Consensus is assumed rather than obtained.[36] Third, a member who does venture a contradictory opinion will experience direct pressure from the rest of the group to conform: "Why are you being so negative, Jim? The rest of us think it's a good idea." The group may also have a number of self-appointed *mindguards* who "protect" the group by deliberately preventing dissonant information from reaching the group—by stopping outsiders from addressing the group, failing to mention contrasting points of view contained in research materials, and so forth. Finally, in groups with rigid status hierarchies, lower-status members are less likely to contradict higher-status members and will avoid issues they think may produce conflict.[37] These conformity pressures are especially dangerous when a group *must* achieve consensus. The need for consensus can lead to an "agreement norm," which curtails disagreement, ultimately causing the decision to suffer.[38]

Preventing Groupthink   Critical thinking is the responsibility of all group members; when each member takes that role seriously, tendencies toward groupthink will be minimized. Here are specific suggestions for preventing groupthink:

1. **Each member should assume the role of critical evaluator.**
   Every member should use his or her best critical thinking skills on

behalf of the group. Occasionally, the group may assign a specific individual to serve as a *devil's advocate* or *reminder*, who is charged with constructively criticizing the ideas brought to the group. Ideally, this role rotates among members so that the criticism doesn't become associated with a particular individual.

2. **Independent subgroups can be formed to work on or evaluate the same issue.**

   The competition of rival subgroups, even friendly ones, can make the subgroups more careful and thorough in their work. In addition, the clash between subgroups can spark novel or creative solutions.

3. **The group should prevent its own insulation from outside information.**

   This, too, was a key problem for the Bay of Pigs group and, currently, with NASA; some members served as *mindguards*, keeping what they perceived as contradictory information away from the other members of the group. But this information was exactly what could have benefited the group and prevented that disastrous decision! This is likely what happened to the registration staff deciding to charge fees for dropping and adding classes—they didn't seek feedback from anyone but themselves in making the decision.

   Leaders, in particular, can take steps to offset insularity. They can encourage members to get feedback on tentative proposals from trusted associates outside the group, then report back to the group. Leaders can also arrange for outside experts to discuss their views with the group, thereby helping to ensure a broadly based foundation for making the decision.

4. **Leaders should refrain from stating their preferences at the beginning of a problem-solving or decision-making session.**

   Janis found President Kennedy's stated preferences to be one of the main forces leading to the terrible Bay of Pigs decision. Group members may want to defer to or please the leader, but this can impair decision making.

5. **Group members can suggest and use appropriate technology to encourage thorough problem solving.**

   There are many relatively inexpensive computer programs, which we will discuss later in the chapter, designed to keep a group focused on the task. Some systems allow members to react anonymously so that the effects of conformity pressure and strong leadership can be minimized. Miranda found that even when a group is predisposed to groupthink, group support systems helped prevent groupthink and promoted effective decision making.[39]

4D: Second-Guess the Tentative Choice before Fully Committing to It

As consensus begins to emerge in a group, or after a group has chosen an alternative in another way, members should, if possible, consider that choice a tentative one and second-guess it, perhaps in a meeting held especially for that purpose. Hirokawa's research shows that one of the most crucial functions a group should perform is assessing the potential negative consequences of a decision.[40] This can be especially difficult near what group members believe is the end of their problem-solving process. When groups sense closure, they begin reinforcing their hard work, as we discussed earlier in this Chapter. Hirokawa found that when members of effective groups begin to screen the alternatives, they first spot the serious defects.[41] Once they find an alternative they like, they switch strategies and begin to detail the positive aspects of the alternative. It can be really hard at this point to revisit their choice, but that is exactly what members should do to ensure they haven't overlooked a fatal flaw. The RISK technique can help them do that.

Using the RISK Technique to Second-Guess the Choice   The **RISK technique** is designed specifically to allow a group or organization to assess how a proposed policy or change might negatively affect the individuals and groups involved.[42] The six basic steps in the RISK technique are summarized in Table 11.1:

1. The leader describes the proposed solution or change in policy in detail and asks members to think of any risks, fears, or problems they may have about the proposal.

2. Members brainstorm, as a group or individually with the brainwriting process described in the last chapter, to discover all potential problems with the solution or change in policy.

RISK Technique

A small group procedure for identifying and dealing with all risks, fears, doubts and worries that members have about a new policy or plan before it is implemented.

---

1. The leader describes the proposed solution or change in policy in detail.
2. Members brainstorm, alone or as a group, to discover all potential problems with the solution or change in policy.
3. Problems are posted, round-robin fashion, on a chart for all to see. Members can add to the list as they think of new problems.
4. A master list of all problems is compiled and distributed to all participants, who can add additional problems to the list.
5. Risks are discussed one at a time. Minor risks or ones easily handled are removed from the list.
6. Serious risks are compiled into an agenda for future problem-solving discussions.
7. If the risks cannot be resolved, the proposed plan should be reconsidered.

TABLE 11.1 Steps in the RISK technique

3. Problems are posted, in round-robin fashion, on a chart for all to see. As with brainstorming, members are encouraged to add to the list whenever they think of a new problem. The individual posting the problems may ask for clarification or elaboration, but it is *absolutely imperative* for that person to remain nonjudgmental. The moment members feel threatened or intimidated, they will clam up and the most serious risks won't be surfaced. Don't rush this process! Often, the risks that people privately think are most serious will be offered after a lull in the process.

4. After the RISK meeting, a master list of all problems is compiled and distributed to all participants, who can add additional problems to the list. The participants or the group leader may choose to circulate this list to others who will be affected by the decision for their input as well.

5. At a second RISK meeting, the risks are discussed one at a time, after giving everyone another chance to add risks to the master list. If members perceive that a risk is minor or easily handled, they can decide to remove it from the list. Members are encouraged to share their feelings—doubts, fears, concerns—at this meeting.

6. The remaining risks, the ones thought to be serious enough for further discussion, are compiled into an agenda and handled the same way as items in a problem census. Members investigate the risks and lead the group in a discussion of them.

7. If the risks cannot be resolved, the proposed plan should be reconsidered. The discussion of risks in step 6 may reveal a way to make the proposal acceptable by modifying it, but if that is not the case, the group should consider discarding it.

Using the RISK procedure can benefit the entire organization as well as the group. If the Registration Committee had been willing to use this procedure, especially if they had invited others to the meeting who would be affected by the change in drop-add procedures, they would have discovered the fatal flaw in their plan. As it was, their proposal turned out to be expensive in terms of money, time, and loss of goodwill from the students.

Once the group has developed its solution and made its choice, it is ready for the final phase of this problem-solving discussion: implementation.

Step 5: Implementing the Solution Chosen

The group is now ready to implement its solution. Members must now decide *What will we do to put our solution into effect?* Sometimes a group will hand this task off to a different group or individual, but here we are assuming that the same members who made the choice are responsible for carrying it out. Sometimes the implementation process is almost as complex as the entire

TABLE 11.2   Steps in the PERT procedure

1. Describe the final step (how the solution should appear when fully operational).
2. Enumerate any events that must occur before the final goal is realized.
3. Order these steps chronologically.
4. If necessary, develop a flow diagram of the process and all the steps in it.
5. Generate a list of all the activities, resources, and materials needed to accomplish each step.
6. Estimate the time needed to accomplish each step; then add all the estimates to get a total time for implementing the plan.
7. Compare the total time estimate with deadlines or expectations and correct as necessary (by assigning more people or less time to a given step).
8. Determine which members will be responsible for each step.

problem-solving process; someone needs to see that the group has worked out all necessary details. The group must answer the following questions: *Who will do what, when, and by what date? Do we need any follow-up evaluation of how well our solution is working? If so, how will we do that?*

Use PERT to Keep Track of Implementation Details

For complex problems involving the entire group, the **Program Evaluation and Review Technique (PERT)** can help members keep track of implementation details. Sometimes a solution is very complicated, involving a variety of materials; people whose work must be coordinated; and steps that must be completed in a specific sequence. Think of what is involved in remodeling a large building on campus or constructing something like the space shuttle. PERT was developed to expedite such detailed operations so that they can be done efficiently and so that people can keep track of each step of the process. The procedure can be simplified to help even a student project group keep track of who is responsible for what. The main points of PERT[43] are summarized in Table 11.2 and an example of a simple PERT chart for a student project group is provided in Figure 11.4.

We have just described all the P-MOPS steps. There is one more thing we would like to mention. P-MOPS is a sequential process, but sometimes groups realize in a later step that they forgot to consider something in an earlier step. In that case, it is perfectly appropriate (in fact, recommended) that the group recycle back to the earlier step. Sometimes it's hard to go back to a step you thought you had finished, but group members should be willing to do that instead of following the procedure just for the sake of following the procedure! After all, that is the strength of the procedure and that is why groups that use procedures fulfill more completely the functions necessary for effective problem-solving: The procedure reminds members of something they may have forgotten.

Program Evaluation and Review Technique (PERT)

A procedure for planning the details to implement a complex solution that involves many people and resources.

FIGURE 11.4 Sample PERT chart for a student group project

Date	Aretha	Barney	Candy	Denzil	Entire Group
Tues Sep. 5	Report on prelim observ.		Report on prelim observ.		Decide group to observe; decide variables
Thu Sep. 7		Prelim report, conflict	Prelim report, ldship	Prelim report, roles	Discuss prelim reports; decide methods of analysis
Tues Sep. 12		Complete lib research, Conflict	Complete lib research, Leadership	Complete lib research, Roles	
Thu Sep. 14		Observe group, 8 PM	Observe group, 8 PM	Have observ materials ready; survey, SYMLOG	
Tues Sep. 19		Complete SYMLOG of group	Complete SYMLOG of group		Meet after class, discuss preliminary findings
Thu Sep. 21			Observe group, 8 PM	Observe group, 8 PM Have tape recorder ready	
Tues Sep. 26					Discuss overall observations; listen to tape
Thu Sep. 28		Complete first draft, Conflict	Complete first draft, Leadership	Complete first draft, Roles	
Mon Oct. 2	Begin overall editing and typing	Final draft, Conflict; Intro done	Final draft, Leadership; Conclusion done	Final draft, Roles	Look at each other's sections to improve style
Tues Oct. 3					
Wed Oct. 4					
Thu Oct.. 5					
Fri Oct. 6	Editing and typing done	Tables and charts to Aretha (conflict)	Table/Charts to Aretha (leadership)	Tables/Charts to Aretha (roles)	
Sat Oct. 7	Proof; make copies			Proof; make copies	
Sun Oct. 8	Distribute copies to all by 8 PM	Assemble full report by 5 PM	Assemble full report by 5 PM	Make large charts for class presentation	
Mon Oct. 9		Read full paper	Read full paper	Read full paper	Rehearsal at Aretha's 7 PM
Tues Oct. 10					Final presentation to class

Recap: A Quick Review

M any things can affect the process of decision making, which requires vigilance on the part of group members.

1. Among the factors that can impair decision making are the fact that members often do not share the information they have as individuals with each other, they do not use a systematic process for decision making, they fail to test for consensus, or they pay too much attention to ascribed (external) status characteristics.

2. Group polarization, the tendency of groups to make decisions that are more extreme than the individuals in the group would make on their own, can hurt decision making by shifting members too far toward either risk or caution.

3. Social Comparison Theory, the psychological explanation posited for polarization, assumes that members want to look good to each other on the values important to the group, so they exaggerate their opinions in the direction the group seems to value.

4. Persuasive Arguments Theory, the cognitive explanation for polarization, assumes that the number, novelty, and salience of the arguments that members hear from each other pushes them in a particular direction.

5. Support has been found for both explanations, depending on the type of task and degree of ambiguity of the group's situation.

6. Groupthink, the failure of group members to think critically and use all their information effectively, has been blamed for several disastrous decisions, including the failed U.S. invasion of Cuba at the Bay of Pigs and the launch of the shuttle *Columbia*.

7. During groupthink, the group overestimates its power and the rightness of its cause and becomes closed-minded, and members are pressured to conform.

8. Members can prevent groupthink by assuming the role of critical evaluators, by forming subgroups to evaluate the same issue, preventing insulation from outside information by soliciting credible opinions and information, and using appropriate technology to help the problem-solving process. Leaders should refrain from biasing the group by stating their preferences too early.

9. The RISK procedure allows a group to second-guess its tentative choice by asking members (and perhaps others) to identify any problems they see with the choice.

10. PERT charts help group members and the leader keep track of the many details involved in implementing a solution.

Now that you understand the entire P-MOPS procedure and how it is used for complex problems, we discuss how you can modify the procedure to fit specific problems.

Tailoring P-MOPS to Fit a Specific Problem

You shouldn't think of P-MOPS as a rigid procedure that you have to follow no matter what. Instead, think of it as a flexible procedure that is easily adaptable for a variety of problems. For example, if your group is charged with solving a problem that is complex, touches a lot of people, may be costly, and affects quality of life (such as figuring out how to handle O'Fallon's city's water supply problems described in the previous chapter), you need to make sure that you make the most carefully thought-out decision possible. Very likely, you will want to use all the steps of P-MOPS. But if your group is charged with planning a party for your service club, you don't run a big risk of making a mistake. You can skip or shorten some of the steps. How do you know the best way to adjust? You can consider the characteristics of your particular problem.

Problem Characteristics

In his classic synthesis of group dynamics, Shaw described five characteristics of problems that small groups tackle: *task difficulty, solution multiplicity, intrinsic interest, cooperative requirements,* and *population familiarity.*[44] To these we add *acceptance requirements* and *technical requirements.* Only the most general steps in the problem-solving procedures will be the same for all problems.

Task difficulty refers to the problem's complexity—hence, the effort, knowledge, and skill needed to achieve the goal. Groups generally are asked to tackle complex problems, those for which a number of different perspectives must be considered. For instance, consider recent government task forces assigned to recommend improvements in the American health care system, reduction of the budget deficit, or improvement of learning levels of high school graduates—problems beyond the capacity of any single person. Thorough problem analysis and mapping will be needed.

Solution multiplicity refers to the number of conceivable or feasible alternatives for solving the problem. There are usually only a few useful ways to get from your residence to your classroom, but there are innumerable ways to decorate your living room. Structured procedures like *brainstorming* have long been available to help us think of more possible alternatives when solution multiplicity is even moderately high.[45]

Ideally, groups would discuss only intrinsically interesting problems. In actuality, people are assigned to committees that deal with a variety of problems, some of little interest to them. **Intrinsic interest** was defined by Shaw as "the degree to which the task in and of itself is interesting, motivating, and attractive to the group members,"[46] reminding us of Larson and LaFasto's finding that outstanding teams had clear, elevating goals. When group members

Task Difficulty
Degree of problem complexity and effort required to solve a problem.

Solution Multiplicity
Extent to which there are many different possible alternatives for solving a particular problem.

Intrinsic Interest
Extent to which the task itself is attractive and interesting to the participants.

are highly interested in their task, they want to share control of the group's procedures, but when interest is low, they are happy to let the discussion leader assume control.[47] Our experience verifies this finding: If interest is high, members at first want to express opinions and feelings and will resist strict procedural control. After they have vented their feelings, they are more likely to accept procedural control of the problem-solving procedure.

The phrase **cooperative requirements** means the degree to which coordinated efforts are essential to satisfactory completion of a task. In other words, the task is conjunctive. Increased complexity requires members to talk to each other, share information, and cooperate, in short, to be competent communicators.

The **population familiarity** dimension is the level of members' knowledge about and previous experience with the task. It is no surprise that groups with experienced members tend to perform better than groups with inexperienced ones.[48] When population familiarity is low to start, the problem-solving procedure should concentrate on analysis of the problem. But sometimes very knowledgeable people become smug and unwilling to think of new approaches. Then procedures to increase innovation may be essential.

The **acceptance requirements** dimension refers to the extent to which a proposed solution must be acceptable to people whom it will affect. Legislation enacted to solve public problems has often backfired when acceptance requirements were overlooked. A task force recently created a planning and zoning ordinance for a county near where one of us lives; but citizen groups, although acknowledging a need for some such law, refused to accept it. The United States has experienced epic struggles over laws controlling alcohol, marijuana, and driving. Sometimes a group must give heavy consideration to the acceptability of a solution; at other times, little or none.

The **technical requirements** characteristic of a problem refers to whether it must match some standard of technical excellence or be technically feasible. For instance, U.S. automakers have had to rethink their quality control procedures, and some have done so with great success. O'Fallon city officials required the water from whatever water treatment solution they selected to meet certain standards for safety and taste.

Use common sense when you modify P-MOPS. One of us spent two hours in a staff meeting trying to decide what would be the most appropriate gift for the college's board of trustees whose terms had expired. What a waste of time! Heavy problem analysis, which the group leader insisted on, was unnecessary—there was no possibility of making a mistake because all the options were appropriate. In fact, the staff would have been happy to have the leader select the gifts, with or without consultation. Examples of P-MOPS modifications suggested by a problem's characteristics are shown in Figure 11.5.

Examples of discussion outlines are provided to give you a mental model of how a leader might structure the group's problem-solving process. Examples of two leaders' outlines adapting P-MOPS are presented in Figures 11.6 and 11.7. In Figure 11.6, the outline deals with all the complexities of parking on an urban campus. From the outline, you can see how major criteria were

---

Cooperative Requirements

The degree to which members must coordinate their efforts for a group to complete its task successfully.

Population Familiarity

The degree to which members of a group are familiar with the nature of a problem and experienced in solving similar problems.

Acceptance Requirements

The degree to which the solution for a given problem must be accepted by the people it will affect.

Technical Requirements

The degree to which the solution for a given problem is technically feasible or must meet standards of technical excellence.

FIGURE 11.5
How problem
characteristics
suggest ways to
adapt P-MOPS

Problem Characteristic	Adaptation of Problem-Solving Procedure
1. Intrinsic interest is high.	A period of ventilation before systematic problem solving.
2. Task difficulty is high.	Detailed problem mapping; many subquestions.
3. Solution multiplicity is high.	Brainstorming.
4. Cooperative requirements are high.	A criterion step, creating and ranking explicit criteria.
5. High level of acceptance is required.	Focus on concern of people affected when evaluating options.
6. High level of technical quality is required.	Focus on evaluating ideas, critical thinking; perhaps invite outside experts to address group.
7. Population familiarity is high.	Focus on criteria and creation of multiple options.
8. Need only one or a few stages of the problem-solving process.	Shorten procedure to only steps required.

arrived at and used to evaluate proposals. Figure 11.7 is a leader's simple out-line for structuring discussion of a problem with few solutions and for which discussion time was limited. Figure 11.8 uses the Single Question format for a discussion about the Springfield area's solid waste disposal problem, and Figure 11.9 shows how O'Fallon city officials might have used the Ideal Solution format to discuss their water treatment problem.

Using Technology to Help a Group's Problem Solving and Decision Making

In the last decade, technological hardware and software that we previously only dreamed about are now affordable and show great promise for helping groups, as we discussed in Chapter 2. Ranging from simple to highly complex, a variety of systems are available. For example, conference calls use existing telephones and phone lines. Electronic mail (e-mail) lets group members communicate via their personal computers asynchronously, whenever it is convenient for the individual member.[49] Group writing systems permit multi-authored document writing, in which members create, analyze, edit, and revise a single document simultaneously.[50]

There are a number of computer-mediated communication (CMC) systems to choose from. Instant messaging (IM) allows for rapid-fire messages compared to e-mail and voice mail messages that often build up. An IM user clicks on the name of another user's IM handle to begin an immediate chat session. People

PROBLEM QUESTION: What should be done to improve student parking at Southwest Missouri State University?

I. What is the nature of the problem that students encounter with parking at SMSU?
    A. What is the scope of our concern with student parking?
        1. Do any terms in the question need to be clarified?
        2. What authority do we have?
        3. Do we need to determine the authority and duties of departments involved with campus parking?
    B. What is now unsatisfactory about student parking?
        1. What have we found to be unsatisfactory?
            a. Have any studies been done?
            b. What complaints have students been making?
        2. Does any other information exist about student parking that we need to consider?
    C. What goals does the committee hope to achieve by changes in parking that we need to consider?
    D. What obstacles may stand in the way of improving parking for students?
        1. What do we know about what is causing the problem(s) we've described?
        2. How much interest do involved persons have in this problem?
        3. What limits are there on resources that might be needed?
            a. Funds?
            b. Space?
            c. Personnel?
            d. Other?
        4. Are there any other obstacles to changing student parking?
    E. How shall we summarize the problem(s) with student parking at SMSU?
        1. Do we all perceive the problem the same?
        2. Should we subdivide the problem?
Used with permission of Greg Gravenmeier, student in John Brilhart's class.

FIGURE 11.6
Using P-MOPS to structure a complex question about student parking

I. What sort of written final exam should we have for our class?
    A. How much authority (area of freedom) do we have?
    B. What facts and feelings should we take into account as we seek an answer to this question?
II. What are our objectives (criteria) in deciding on the type of exam?
    A. Learning objectives?
    B. Grades?
    C. Type of preparation and study?
    D. Fairness to all?
III. What types of written final exams might we have?
IV. What are the advantages and disadvantages of each?
V. What will we recommend as the form of our written exam?

FIGURE 11.7
Using P-MOPS to structure a simple question with limited discussion time about a final exam in a college class

FIGURE 11.8
Using the Single
Question format to
structure discussion
about solid waste
disposal methods

1. *What is the single question . . . ?*
   What is the most environmentally benign, politically acceptable, and economically feasible way to dispose of solid waste from Springfield and the surrounding counties?
2. *Collaboration*
   A. *What principles should we agree upon in order to maintain a reasonable and collaborative approach throughout the process?*
      - We will solicit all viewpoints and treat them with respect.
      - We will listen carefully to each other and not interrupt.
      - We will treat each other with respect.
      - We will do what we think is best for the citizens of O'Fallon and not for ourselves personally.
   B. *What assumptions and biases are associated with the single question identified in step 1, and how might they influence the discussion?*
      - We assume that there are better methods than our current method.
      - We believe that sometimes new technology isn't necessarily tested well.
      - We tend to be biased in favor of low-cost alternatives so that rates won't rise.
      - We don't like being vulnerable to surrounding communities for water or for reasonable rates.
3. *What issues or subquestions must we answer to fully understand the complexities of the overall problem?*
      - How could the solid waste of Springfield be disposed of?
         ○ How much will each feasible method cost?
         ○ What will facilities and start-up cost?
         ○ What will continuing operation cost?
         ○ Will the method generate enough revenue to pay its costs?
      - What might be the harmful effects of each method?
         ○ How will each method affect water, air, land, and the environment?
         ○ What health hazards might each method create?
      - What problems might we have getting voters to accept each method?
         ○ What group or groups opposed each method?
         ○ How well has this method been accepted elsewhere?
      - How well has this method worked in other places?
         ○ How dependable has it been?
         ○ What personnel training is required?
         ○ How long will this method serve Springfield?

   (The task force engaged in extensive research efforts, including paying consultants, hiring an engineering consulting firm, and making several trips to observe facilities used by other cities.)
4. *What are the two or three most reasonable answers to the subquestions?*
      - The Materials Recovery Facility (MRF) emerges as the best choice.

   (The task force recommended the MRF with composting and limited landfill usage to voters. After an extensive information campaign, voters approved the MRF.)

FIGURE 11.9
Using the Ideal
Solution format for
O'Fallon's problem
about water
treatment

1. *Does everyone agree on the nature of the problem?*
   ○ Geologists have evidence that the water table is dropping.
   ○ Construction of new deep wells is not feasible due to the dropping table.
   ○ The problem will become a crisis in about 10 years.
2. *What would be the ideal solution from the point of view of all interested people or groups involved?*
   ○ What do the geologists prefer? (protection of the water table)
   ○ What do voters prefer? (low cost with high quality)
   ○ What do elected officials prefer? (not raising taxes; long-term solution)
   ○ What does the health department prefer? (safety)
   ○ What do surrounding cities and counties prefer? (ability to sell water for profit)
   ○ What do environmentalists prefer? (no degradation of the environment)
   (Analysis of the preferences of interested parties revealed three main criteria that emerged: The solution must provide high-quality water; it must be cost-effective and efficient; it must give the city long-term control over costs.)
3. *Which conditions within the situation could be changed to achieve the ideal solution?*
   ○ The current system cannot be expanded safely or reliably.
   ○ Voters could be educated about the long-term benefit of building a membrane treatment plant and would likely support it when they see the eventual cost savings.
4. *Of all the solutions available, which one best approximates the ideal?*
   ○ The membrane treatment facility best meets all criteria.

who use IM like how quickly they can access others, but the jury is out on the impact of IM on worker productivity.[51] Some systems permit members to coordinate their calendars electronically to find convenient times to meet.

Instructors increasingly use asynchronous electronic bulletin board services (BBS) and synchronous chat environments, like the Internet Relay Chat (IRC), to facilitate classroom learning.[52] Such computer-mediated systems let teachers and classmates talk to each other when it is convenient and can equalize participation, increase learner self-responsibility, allow learners to see different perspectives, give them time to think about how best to construct a message, and prepare them for computer-mediated communication in their future professions.[53]

Pena-Shaff and associates compared both BBS and IRC in the classroom; their findings have important implications for small groups. BBS services allow group members to post asynchronous messages and are particularly useful when the group wishes to promote critical thinking and reflection.[54] BBS discussions are generally structured, reflective, and focused on the task and topic. The downside to BBS is that it does not promote collaboration and social interaction. Group members need to be motivated to use it. In contrast, the synchronous character of text-base "talk," such as IRC, does promote collaboration and works well for brainstorming.[55] IRC is more informal. Members feel more pressured to reach consensus, yet find it difficult to do so. The freewheeling nature of chat rooms, which helps members initially explore issues, also allows members to get offtrack easily. Once offtrack, it is hard to get the discussion back on track. Thus, although chat rooms allow for interaction in real time and provide immediate feedback, similar to face-to-face interaction, the talk can be confusing, with content and flow reflecting "messy" thinking.

Practically speaking, your group first needs to decide whether you want to use an electronic bulletin board service or a chat room. Your answer depends on whether you want free-wheeling discussion, as is appropriate during problem analysis, idea generation, brainstorming, and so forth, or critical evaluation, as is appropriate when a group is evaluating options and trying to decide something. Either way, consider the following guidelines:[56]

1. Make sure all members know where the chat room or bulletin board is located and how to access it.

2. Guarantee that the chat room or bulletin board is private so that outsiders do not interrupt your group's discussions.

3. Select a group member as moderator to facilitate discussion and help ensure more equal participation. Allowing members to review an agenda prior to discussion can help. Group members may rotate the moderator role.

4. Moderators and group members should motivate each other to contribute and collaborate. This is harder in real time, but can be fostered.

5. Use emoticons with reservation. Emoticons can be misread or misunderstood, especially if group members don't know each other.

6. Remember that instant message chatting, in particular, can easily become derailed, so be conscious of staying on task.

As you can see, CMC to help problem solving can take several forms, each with its own advantages and disadvantages. Weigh the pros and cons against the type of group you are in, the task you face, the nature of your leadership, and member characteristics. We next discuss two key ways that technology can help groups problem-solve: teleconferences and group support systems.

Teleconferences

Teleconference

A meeting of participants who communicate via mediated channels such as television, telephone or computer rather than face to face.

We introduced you to net conferences in Chapter 2 in our discussion of how computer-mediated communication compares to face-to-face communication. Here, we will elaborate on how net conferences can be used in group problem solving and decision making. **Teleconferences** or net conferences are electronically mediated meetings that allow members of a group to meet even though they may be spread out geographically. For example, author Gloria lives in Missouri, Kathy lives in California, and our editors Jennie and Suzanne live in New York; we confer by teleconference when we begin to prepare revisions of this text. Teleconferences save the travel time and expense of face-to-face meetings when members have to travel long distances to attend. Teleconferences can be *videoconferences,* which let members see and hear each other; *audio-conferences,* which let members hear but not see each other; and *computer conferences,* which allow members to send messages to one another that are displayed on computer monitors—like the IRC used in classrooms.

Videoconferences are still expensive for most companies, but audioconferences, including telephone conference calls, are routine. Computer conferences are becoming increasingly sophisticated and accessible, with a number of companies developing their own specialized software for employees linked to a network that lets them work simultaneously on a variety of tasks. Recent studies have shown that decisions made by computerized conference groups were just as good as ones made by face-to-face groups, but computer groups were less likely to come to agreement.[57] The *type* of computerized technique seems to make a difference. Murrell found that using the window method, which permits each participant to see the responses of all other participants at once (which is more like face-to-face communicating), produced higher decision quality than a message system that required participants to complete a message before they could interact.[58] Some studies, in fact, have found that computer conferences can provide advantages over face-to-face meetings. Dubrovsky et al. discovered that electronic mail conferences minimized inequalities due to status and expertise.[59] Hiltz et al. suggest that computer programs permitting anonymity may help create greater and more equal participation.[60] On the other hand, computer-mediated group decision making leads to more delays, more outspoken advocacy, and more extreme decisions (i.e., group polarization) than face-to-face meetings.[61]

From more than 100 studies of teleconferencing, we can develop practical guidelines for making them more productive.[62] For audioconferencing, speakerphone equipment is readily available, relatively inexpensive, and requires no special studios. It can be set up in any office. However, audioconferences lack "social presence."[63] The sense of sharing, belonging, and recognition of each other as individuals can be low because many key nonverbal cues are absent and electronic equipment can fail at the most inopportune times. On the other hand, there is higher potential for *greater* equality participation, depending on the skill of conference leaders and type of technology.

For teleconferencing to work best, Johansen et al. recommend that the participants hold an extended face-to-face conference beforehand to form a sense of "groupness."[64] For instance, your authors and editors of this book supplement their teleconferences with an annual face-to-face meeting during the national communication conference. A postconference meeting can be useful as well. It seems that for complex tasks, particularly when there is likelihood of disagreement, face-to-face meetings are still preferable, with teleconferences well suited to routine meetings and information sharing. Several factors can improve routine teleconferences, including using a trained moderator, ensuring that participants are aware of the rules and guidelines for speaking, and ensuring that all speakers abide by specified time limits.[65]

Several computer-related innovations promise to improve the effectiveness of mediated meetings, even those involving complex tasks. Several texts offer specific instructions about how to set up a teleconference effectively and how to optimize the conversation and collaboration among members.[66]

Group Support Systems (or Group Decision Support Systems)

Group Support Systems (GSS) or Group Decision Support Systems (GDSS) are computer-based hardware and software systems designed to improve the quality and speed of group problem solving. They are sometimes called *groupware computer-supported cooperative work (CSCW),* or *electronic meeting systems (EMS).*[67] Specifically, GSS help groups perform the functions associated with effective problem solving, including generating ideas, organizing information, evaluating options, and making decisions.[68] Different GSS address different problem-solving processes.[69] For example, some focus on the idea generation step of brainstorming. Others attempt to improve the entire decision-making process by providing the structure that groups often need but don't otherwise receive. Two of the most commonly known systems are GroupSystems and Software Assisted Meeting Management (SAMM); both include modules to help groups in every area of problem solving, such as group management, brainstorming, analysis, policy formation, evaluation and voting, exchanging comments on topics, and so forth. GSS are usually used in conjunction with face-to-face meetings and may require specialized training of the meeting leader and the members. They are especially helpful when members want to evaluate solutions because they offer ways to structure group interaction so that members can honestly react to each other's suggestions and ideas.

GSS are fairly new, so you may not have seen one in operation. The following example should help you picture what some sophisticated systems can do. One of us attended a meeting of a local school board that was having trouble achieving closure on agenda items at its regular meetings. Members found themselves wandering offtrack, going in a completely different direction from that provided in the agenda. They accepted the offer made by university faculty members to help them by using GSS technology. The school board members met in a room specially designed to accommodate GSS meetings. The room had 12 individual computers linked to each other. The computers were configured in a U shape, with a large overhead projection system, visible to all, at the open end of the U. One faculty member served as group facilitator by organizing the discussion of the two agenda items that the school board president most wanted to complete: deciding what issues to emphasize and what promotional strategies to use in the upcoming school bond levy. The facilitator stood under the projection screen at the open end of the U. The other faculty member served as the chauffeur, running the computer system for the meeting. He, too, was visible behind the operation desk at the top right of the U. Both the facilitator and chauffeur had specialized training in how to use the system.

At their individual computer stations, group members brainstormed about their first item, the issues to be addressed in the campaign. Each member worked alone; then, when all were ready, they sent their suggestions to the central computer with a keystroke. The master list then appeared on the overhead screen. No one knew who had made which suggestions. The facilitator and chauffeur clarified vague items and combined like items. Group members were then given the chance to make comments, again anonymously, and send them to the screen. With the help of the facilitator, face-to-face discussion occurred concerning several items. Finally, members ranked all the items and sent them to the system, which automatically tallied the rankings and provided an overall ranking and rating of each item. The rankings and ratings were displayed in numerical and bar graph form, which provided visual reinforcement for the members' opinions. Face-to-face discussion followed, with members easily coming to consensus (or realizing that they already had achieved consensus). They addressed the second issue in the same way.

School board members reacted enthusiastically. The visual display of ratings and rankings emphasized to some of the long-winded members that consensus had already been achieved, so further discussion was unnecessary. Both the facilitator and the chauffeur reminded the school board that the system was designed to *support,* not replace, effective group discussion. GSS help groups do what they *should* do, but often *don't* do without computer support: analyze carefully, evaluate thoroughly, and give everyone a chance to participate. They also make record keeping easy because the computer provides an automatic history of all the items that were listed, the comments about each, and the rankings and ratings of each.

GSS are rapidly increasing in number, ease of use, and effectiveness. People can use GSS for most of their work or for just one problem-solving task, as the school board did. GSS can allow members to remain anonymous, as with the school board, so that *who* submitted a particular comment, idea, criticism and so forth is not identified. When members are anonymous, they are less inhibited, status differences are reduced, quality of participation is improved, and dominance by some members is reduced.[70]

Although anonymity provides important benefits to a problem-solving group, it can also pose problems. Members who don't see each other may not identify with each other or with the group. This lack of identification can lead to hollow or empty decisions. Scott warns that groups should not favor anonymity at the expense of face-to-face meetings—groups should work to combine both modes of communication.[71]

Three specific disadvantages have been observed with GSS.[72] First, all group members are not equally comfortable using computers and may not want to use computer technology as part of their problem-solving activities. At Kathy's university, the administration requires all course grades to be submitted online. Some faculty resist the mandate either because they do not feel competent using computers or they dislike technological advances being forced on them. Second, GSS procedures may actually structure group inter-action too tightly. Groups adapting GSS must find an effective balance between how the GSS are intended to be used and the group's own unique way of using the system, which could be detrimental to the group. For example, some GSS are designed to allow members to remain anonymous, but sometimes members try hard to figure out who contributed what, circumventing the pre-sumption of anonymity. Third, sometimes managers or group leaders do not want employees or other group members to have full access to information easily obtained via computers; they may try to thwart use of GSS.

Effectiveness of GSS   In our discussion of adaptive structuration theory in Chapter 8, we explained that groups use the rules and resources of tech-nology in such a way that their use helps produce and reproduce the group system. Therefore, it is vital for group members to understand exactly how the group as a whole is affected by the way they use computer software. On balance, GSS seem to be effective. Olaniran reported that computer-mediated groups produced more ideas than face-to-face groups.[73] However, they took a longer time to come to consensus. Decision quality was best when groups used a combination of computer-mediated and face-to-face discussion, as did the school board we just described. Poole and his associates, who have studied GSS extensively, noted several benefits.[74] GSS seem to focus mem-bers' attention on problem-solving procedures and improves organization of the decision-making process. GSS also spark insight into the decision process, although it takes time for members to learn a system and orient themselves to it. Jessup and Valacich, in their extensive review of GSS research, concluded that computer-supported decision making is as good as or better than traditional decision making.[75] GSS in larger groups seem to help members sustain their task focus better, and they end up spending less time in meetings.

Whether GSS improve problem solving or not depends on a variety of fac-tors. One of the most important is the level of GSS support, which refers to how sophisticated a system is and how much intervention it provides into the group's natural problem-solving process. Benbasat and Lim found that more sophisticated level 2 support produced better decisions and higher satisfac-tion than level 1 support.[76] This is consistent with Sambamurthy et al., who concluded that simpler is not always better.[77] The particular system used must be well matched to the task, according to Farmer and Hyatt.[78] For exam-ple, some complex tasks require that information to be processed via many channels, including audio, video, and screen sharing. However, for other tasks, having an audio channel alone might be sufficient, as is the case with our audioconferences with our editors for this text.

Familiarity with the system is another factor influencing GSS effective-ness. Hollingshead et al. observed that computer group members' poor initial performance seemed to be related to their unfamiliarity with using computer support, but those differences disappear over time.[79] They also noted that face-to-face groups are likely to outperform computer-mediated groups on intellective tasks, in which there is a correct answer, and negotiation tasks, in which members must reconcile their competing interests. These researchers warn managers planning to institute computer-mediated work groups that there may be initial declines in performance and dissatisfaction until members become comfortable with the technology.

The presence of a facilitator also affects GSS performance. Poole et al. were surprised by their findings that, although groups using GSS exhibited more organized decision processes, they did not demonstrate improved critical thinking or more thorough evaluation of options.[80] These authors noted that the groups they studied had no facilitator support; they postulate that this, along with the level of GSS support as discussed earlier, may have been a key factor hampering GSS effectiveness. Ideally, a facilitator should have a strong conceptual understanding of the technology and its capabilities, be able to make members comfortable with the technology and help them understand it, select the right technological system for the group, and have it prepared properly.[81] Skilled facilitation was a factor in the success of the school board meeting we described earlier.

In particular, facilitators need to understand the difference between *faithful* use of GSS procedures—using them as they were intended—and *ironic* use of GSS—using GSS contrary to their purpose or spirit. Generally speaking, GSS are designed to promote anonymity, equalize participation, and balance member influence; but some groups use GSS in a way not faithful to those intentions. Scott et al. note that it can be very hard to predict how particular GSS will *actually* be used because GSS implementation is a dynamic adaptation between the user and the GSS technology.[82] For example, GSS users exhibit a strong need to figure out who is sending particular messages. Over time, members can figure out the styles of different users. At times, members play games with the technology; they may agree with their own comments to emphasize them, play with the rankings to try to manipulate the outcome of votes, and repeat themselves to assert their opinions. Some users feel powerless when others don't read their messages. And although GSS promote more equal participation than face-to-face meetings, they can also permit social loafing. In addition, sometimes users show little commitment to the group's decision with GSS, so the GSS benefits can decline over time.

Men and women in continuing task groups use different strategies to handle the anonymity feature of GSS.[83] Males try to make the computer-mediated communication more like face-to-face communication (i.e., less anonymous), whereas females try to preserve the anonymity. Sex is a status characteristic; males, who have somewhat higher status in the general society and are motivated to preserve that higher status, circumvent the anonymity feature of GSS by offering social cues that reveal their sex. In contrast, women offer fewer social cues, which serves to preserve their anonymity and helps them acquire greater influence in the group. Flanagin et al. suggest that people use GSS in ways they think will benefit themselves, either by reducing or preserving the anonymity.[84]

To summarize, GSS are generally good for groups, although not useful in every circumstance.[85] Remember the lessons of adaptive structuration theory: The features of GSS by themselves do not determine their effectiveness. Members interact with the technology, sometimes seriously violating its intention or spirit.

On the plus side, GSS-supported groups generate more alternatives in the idea generation phase of problem solving, usually make better decisions, and have more even member participation. On the minus side, GSS groups have difficulty with negotiation and complex, cognitive tasks; they take more time; consensus can be hard to achieve; and member satisfaction is usually lower. GSS are designed to *support*, not *replace*, traditional group problem-solving and decision-making procedures. When they are used consistently with their intended use, they can be very effective, but they don't eliminate the need for members knowledgeable about group processes and skilled in communication.

Recap: A Quick Review

Groups have many tools at their disposal and should use common sense in determining which tools to use.

1. The P-MOPS procedure is flexible; group members should tailor it by emphasizing some steps or eliminating others, depending on the type of problem facing the group.

2. Seven characteristics of problems help members decide which steps are essential and which are not. Task-related characteristics include task difficulty (how complex the task is) and solution multiplicity (how many possible solutions there are, potentially), and cooperative requirements (whether the task is a conjunctive one that requires substantial coordination among members).

3. Member characteristics include intrinsic interest (how genuinely interested members are in the issue) and population familiarity (whether the members have faced similar tasks in the past and are knowledgeable about how to approach the task).

4. Output characteristics include the acceptance requirements (whether the solution requires acceptance by those affected in order to succeed) and technical requirements (whether there are technical standards that must be met for the solution to be acceptable).

5. Several technologies are available to help groups, including telephones, e-mail, electronic bulletin boards, and interactive relay chat rooms.

6. When these technologies are used, it is important that members know how to use them and that the moderators encourage and motivate members to contribute and to use appropriate communication behaviors.

7. Teleconferences can include audio, video, and computer conferences. The effectiveness of these technologies is enhanced when members can meet face-to-face first to create a sense of "groupness."

(continued)

(continued)

8. Group support systems (or group decision support systems) are computer programs designed to help improve group problem solving. They may focus on one particular problem-solving step, such as idea generation, or may be designed to help the entire problem-solving process.

9. GSS groups generate more alternatives, make better decisions, and have more even member participation.

10. GSS groups also have difficulty with negotiation and complex tasks, take more time, have a harder time achieving consensus, and generally have lower member satisfaction.

11. How well a GSS works depends in part on how faithfully members use a system the way it was designed to be used, rather than ironically, in a unique way not intended by the system design.

QUESTIONS FOR REVIEW

 Go to self-quizzes on the Online Learning Center at mhhe.com/galanes12 to test your knowledge of the chapter concepts

This chapter began with a description of a bad decision made by a university's Registration Staff regarding imposing fees for dropped and added classes; it also included a detailed description of a school board that used GSS to help decide two issues.

1. What do you see as the biggest problems with the way the decision was made by the Registration Staff? Which step or steps of P-MOPS seemed to have been handled most poorly?

2. In what ways could group polarization or groupthink have influenced the decision?

3. What individuals or groups, in addition to the Registration Staff, could have participated in a

RISK session before the drop-add decision was implemented? If you were in charge, whom would you have asked about possible risks?

4. What do you see as the characteristics of the problem regarding too many student drop-adds? How could the Registration Staff have modified P-MOPS to fit their problem?

5. Which procedure—P-MOPS, Single Question, or Ideal Solution—would you have used to discuss that issue?

6. Exactly how did the GSS process help the school board? Which features of GSS helped the board overcome its previous problems of not being able actually to decide anything?

KEY TERMS

 Test your knowledge of these key terms by visiting the Online Learning Center Web site at mhhe.com/galanes12

Acceptance requirements
Consensus decision
Cooperative requirements
Group polarization
Group Support Systems (GSS)
   (Group Decision Support
   Systems (GDSS))

Groupthink
Intrinsic interest
Majority decision
Population familiarity
Program Evaluation and Review
   Technique (PERT)

Phasic progression
RISK technique
Solution multiplicity
Task difficulty
Technical requirements
Teleconferences

BIBLIOGRAPHY

Adams, Tyrone, and Norman Clark. *The Internet: Effective Online Communication*. Ft. Worth, TX: Harcourt, 2001.

Cathcart, Robert S., Larry A. Samovar, and Linda D. Henman, eds. *Small Group Communication: Theory and Practice*. 7th ed. Madison, WI: Brown & Benchmark, 1996, Section 3.

Hirokawa, Randy Y., and Marshall S. Poole, eds. *Communication and Group Decision Making*. Beverly Hills, CA: Sage, 1986, 81–111.

Jessup, Leonard M., and Joseph S. Valacich, eds. *Group Support Systems: New Perspectives*. New York: Macmillan, 1993.

Larson, Carl E., and Frank M. J. LaFasto. *TeamWork: What Must Go Right/What Can Go Wrong*. Newbury Park, CA: Sage, 1989.

McGrath, Joseph E., and Andrea Hollingshead. *Groups Interacting with Technology*. Thousand Oaks, CA: Sage, 1994.

Shaw, Marvin E. *Group Dynamics*. 3rd ed. New York: McGraw-Hill, 1981, Chapter 10.

NOTES

1. Michael J. Beatty, "Group Members' Decision Rule Orientations and Consensus," *Human Communication Research* 16 (1989): 79–96.

2. Jay Hall, "Decisions, Decisions, Decisions," *Psychology Today* (November 1971): 51–54; 86–87.

3. Robert F. Bales and Fred L. Strodtbeck, "Phases in Group Problem-Solving," *Journal of Abnormal and Social Psychology* 46 (1951): 485–95.

4. For a complete summary of Fisher's work on decision-making phases, see B. Aubrey Fisher and Donald G. Ellis, *Small Group Decision Making: Communication and the Group Process,* 3rd ed. (New York: McGraw-Hill, 1990), especially Chapter 6.

5. Marshall Scott Poole, "Decision Development in Small Groups I: A Comparison of Two Models," *Communication Monographs* 48 (1981): 1–24; "Decision Development in Small Groups II: A Study of Multiple Sequences in Decision Making, *Communication Monographs* 50 (1983): 206–32; and "Decision Development in Small Groups III: A Multiple Sequence Model of Group Decision Development," *Communication Monographs* 50 (1983): 321–41; M. Scott Poole and Jonelle Roth, "Decision Development in Small Groups IV: A Typology of Group Decision Paths," *Human Communication Research* 15 (1989): 322–56; and "Decision Development in Small Groups V: Test of a Contingency Model," *Human Communication Research* 15 (1989): 549–89.

6. Poole, "Decision Development II" and "Decision Development III."

7. Poole and Roth, "Decision Development V."

8. Thomas M. Scheidel and Laura Crowell, "Idea Development in Small Discussion Groups," *Quarterly Journal of Speech* 50 (1964): 140–45.

9. Teresa C. Sabourin and Patricia Geist, "Collaborative Production of Proposals in Group Decision Making," *Small Group Research* 21 (1990): 404–27.

10. B. Aubrey Fisher and Randall K. Stutman, "An Assessment of Group Trajectories: Analyzing Developmental Breakpoints," *Communication Quarterly* 35 (1987): 105–24.

11. Charles Pavitt and Kelly Kline Johnson, "Scheidel and Crowell Revisited: A Descriptive Study of Group Proposals Sequencing," *Communication Monographs* 69 (March 2002): 19–32.

12. Brant R. Burleson, Barbara J. Levine, and Wendy Samter, "Decision-Making Procedure and Decision Quality," *Human Communication Research* 10 (1984): 557–74.

13. Alan R. Dennis, "Information Exchange and Use in Small Group Decision Making," *Small Group Research* 27 (November 1996): 532–50; Michael G. Cruz, Franklin J. Boster, and Jose I. Rodriquez, "The Impact of Group Size and Proportion of Shared

Information on the Exchange and Integration of Information in Groups," *Communication Research* 24 (June 1997): 291–313.

14. Cruz, Boster, and Rodriquez, "The Impact of Group Size."

15. Carolyn J. Wood, "Challenging the Assumption Underlying the Use of Participatory Decision-Making Strategies: A Longitudinal Case Study," *Small Group Behavior* 20 (1989): 428–48.

16. Paul Miesing and John F. Preble, "Group Processes and Performance in Complex Business Simulation," *Small Group Behavior* 16 (1985): 325–38.

17. Randy Y. Hirokawa, "Consensus Group Decision Making, Quality of Decision and Group Satisfaction: An Attempt to 'Sort Fact from Fiction,'" *Central States Speech Journal* 33 (1982): 407–15.

18. Dennis S. Gouran, "Inferential Errors, Interaction, and Group Decision Making," in *Communication and Group Decision Making,* eds. R.Y. Hirokawa and M. S. Poole (Beverly Hills, CA: Sage, 1986): 93–111.

19. Marvin E. Shaw, *Group Dynamics,* 2nd ed. (New York: McGraw-Hill, 1976): 70–77.

20. Daniel J. Isenberg, "Group Polarization: A Critical Review and Meta-Analysis," *Journal of Personality and Social Psychology* 10 (1986): 1141–51.

21. Jerold Hale and Franklin J. Boster, "Comparing Effects-Coded Models of Choice Shifts," *Communication Research Reports* 5 (1988): 180–86.

22. Martin F. Kaplan and Charles E. Miller, "Group Decision Making and Normative versus Informational Influence: Effects of Type of Issue and Assigned Decision Rule," *Journal of Personality and Social Psychology* 53 (1987): 306–13.

23. Paul F. Cromwell, Alan Marks, James N. Olson, and D'Aunn W. Avary, "Group Effects on Decision-Making by Burglars," *Psychological Reports* 69 (1991): 579–88.

24. Irving L. Janis, *Groupthink: Psychological Studies of Policy Decisions and Fiascoes,* 2nd ed. rev. (Boston: Houghton Mifflin, 1983).

25. Gregory Moorhead, Richard Ference, and Chris P. Neck, "Group Decision Fiascoes Continue: Space Shuttle *Challenger* and a Revised Groupthink Framework," *Human Relations* 44 (1991): 539–50.

26. Rebecca J. Welsh Cline, "Detecting Groupthink: Methods for Observing the Illusion of Unanimity," *Communication Quarterly* 38 (1990): 112–26.

27. Dennis S. Gouran, Randy Y. Hirokawa, and Amy E. Martz, "A Critical Analysis of Factors Related to Decisional Processes Involved in the *Challenger* Disaster," *Central States Speech Journal* 37 (1986): 119–35.

28. Ronald R. Sims, "Linking Groupthink to Unethical Behavior in Organizations," *Journal of Business Ethics* 11 (1992): 651–62.

29. Michael G. Cruz, David Dryden Henningsen, and Mary Lynn Miller Williams," The Presence of Norms in the Absence of Groups? The Impact of Normative Influence under Hidden-Profile Conditions," *Human Communication Research* 26 (January 2000): 104–24.

30. Ronald J. Aldag and Sally Riggs Fuller, "Beyond Fiasco: A Reappraisal of the Groupthink Phenomenon and a New Model of Group Decision Processes," *Psychological Bulletin* 113, no. 3 (1993): 533–52.

31. Paul R. Bernthal and Chester A. Insko, "Cohesiveness without Groupthink: The Interactive Effects of Social and Task Cohesion," *Group and Organization Management* 18 (March 1992): 66–87.

32. Brian Mullen, Tara Anthony, Eduardo Salas, and James E. Driskell, "Group Cohesiveness and Quality of Decision Making: An Integration of the Groupthink Hypothesis," *Small Group Research* 25 (May 1994): 189–204.

33. Tatsuya Kameda and Shinkichi Sudimori, "Psychological Entrapment in Group Decision Making: An Assigned Decision Rule and a Groupthink Phenomenon: *Journal of Personality and Social Psychology* 65 (August 1993): 282–92.

34. Christopher P. Neck and Gregory Moorhead, "Groupthink Remodeled: The Importance of Leadership, Time Pressure, and Methodical Decision-Making Procedures," *Human Relations* 48 (May 1995): 537–57.

35. Cline, "Detecting Groupthink."

36. Wood, "Challenging the Assumptions."

37. Ibid.

38. Anne Gero, "Conflict Avoidance in Consensus Decision Processes," *Small Group Behavior* 16 (1985): 487–99.

39. Shaila M. Miranda, "Avoidance of Groupthink: Meeting Management Using Group Support

Systems," *Small Group Research* 25 (February 1994): 105–36.

40. Randy Y. Hirokawa, "Discussion Procedures and Decision-Making Performance: A Test of the Functional Perspective," *Human Communication Research* 12 (1985): 203–24.

41. Randy Y. Hirokawa, "Group Decision-Making Performance: A Continued Test of the Functional Perspective," *Human Communication Research* 14 (1988): 487–515.

42. Normal R. F. Maier, *Problem-Solving Discussions and Conferences: Leadership Methods and Skills* (New York: McGraw-Hill, 1963): 171–77.

43. David R. Siebold, "Making Meetings More Successful: Plans, Formats, and Procedures for Group Problem Solving," in *Small Group Communication: A Reader,* 6th ed., eds. Robert S. Cathcart and Larry A. Samovar (Dubuque, IA: Wm. C. Brown, 1992): 187.

44. Marvin E. Shaw, *Group Dynamics,* 3rd ed. (New York: McGraw-Hill, 1981): 364.

45. See, for example, John K. Brilhart and Lurene M. Jochem, "Effects of Different Patterns on Outcomes of Problem-Solving Procedures," *Journal of Applied Psychology* 48 (1964): 175–79; Ovid L. Bayless, "An Alternative Model for Problem-Solving Discussion," *Journal of Communication* 17 (1967): 188–97; and Sidney J. Parnes and Arnold Meadow, "Effects of 'Brainstorming' Instruction on Creative Problem Solving by Trained and Untrained Subjects," *Journal of Educational Psychology* 50 (1959): 171–76.

46. Shaw, *Group Dynamics,* 364.

47. Leonard Berkowitz, "Sharing Leadership in Small Decision-Making Groups," *Journal of Abnormal and Social Psychology* 48 (1953): 231–38.

48. James H. Davis, *Group Performance* (Reading, MA: Addison-Wesley 1969).

49. Sue Barnes and Leonore M. Greller, "Computer-Mediated Communication in the Organization," *Communication Education* 43 (April 1994): 129–42.

50. Annette C. Easton, Nancy S. Eickelmann, and Marie E. Flatley, "Effects of an Electronic Meeting System Group Writing Tool on the Quality of Written Documents," *Journal of Business Communication* 31, no. 1 (1994): 27–40.

51. Mathew Schwartz, "The Instant Messaging Debate," *Computerworld* 36 (January 7, 2002): 40.

52. Judith Pena-Shaff, Wendy Martin, and Geraldine Gay, "An Epistemological Framework for Analyzing Student Interactions in Computer-Mediated Communication Environments," *Journal of Interactive Learning Research* 12 (Spring 2001): 41–62.

53. Ibid.

54. Ibid.

55. Ibid.

56. Tyrone Adams and Norman Clark, *The Internet: Effective Online Communication* (Fort Worth, TX: Harcourt, 2001): 105–7.

57. Start Roxanne Hiltz, Kenneth Johnson, and Murray Turoff, "Experiments in Group Decision Making: Communication Process and Outcome in Face-to-Face versus Computerized Conferences," *Human Communication Research* 13 (1986): 225–52.

58. Sharon L. Murrell, "The Impact of Communicating through Computers" (Unpublished doctoral dissertation, State University of New York at Stony Brook, 1983).

59. Vitaly J. Dubrovsky, Sara Kiesler, and Beheruz N. Sethna, "The Equalization Phenomenon: Status Effects in Computer-Mediated and Face-to-Face Decision-Making Groups, "*Human Computer Interaction* 6 (1991): 119–46.

60. Start Roxanne Hiltz, Kenneth Johnson, and Murray Turoff, "Experiments in Group Decision Making, 3: Disinhibition, Deindividuation, and Group Process in Pen Name and Real Name Computer Conferences," *Decision Support Systems* 5 (June 1989): 217–32.

61. Sara Keisler and Lee Sproull, "Group Decision Making and Computer Technology," *Organizational Behavior and Human Decision Processes* 52 (June 1992): 96–123.

62. Robert Johansen, Jacques Vallee, and Kathleen Spangler, *Electronic Meetings: Technical Alternatives and Social Choices* (Reading, MA: Addison-Wesley, 1979): 2.

63. John A. Short, Ederyn Williams, and Bruce Christie, *The Social Psychology of Telecommunications* (London: Wiley, 1976).

64. Johansen et al., *Electronic Meetings,* 113–15.

65. Larry L. Barker, Kathy J. Wahlers, Kittie W. Watson, and Robert J. Kibler, *Groups in Process: An Introduction to Small Group Communication,* 3rd ed. (Englewood Cliffs, NJ: Prentice Hall, 1987): 208.

66. Read, for example, Adams and Clark, *The Internet: Effective Online Communication,* 105–7.

67. Noshir S. Contractor and David R. Siebold, "Theoretical Frameworks for the Study of Structuring Processes in Group Decision Support Systems: Adaptive Structuration Theory and Self-Organizing Systems Theory," *Human Communication Research* 19 (June 1993): 528–63.

68. Marshall S. Poole, Michael Holmes, and Gerardine DeSanctis, "Conflict Management in a Computer-Supported Meeting Environment,"*Management Science* 37 (August 1991): 926–53; Leonard M. Jessup, Terry Connolly, and David A.Tansik, "Toward a Theory of Automated Group Work: The Deindividuation Effects of Anonymity," *Small Group Research* 21 (August 1990): 333–48; Hiltz et al., "Experiments in Group Decision Making."

69. For a more detailed description of these support systems, see Joseph E. McGrath and Andrea B. Hollingshead, *Groups Interaction with Technology* (Thousand Oaks, CA: Sage, 1994).

70. Bolanle A. Olaniran, "Group Process Satisfaction and Decision Quality in Computer-Mediated Communication: An Examination of Contingent Relations," in *Small Group Communication:Theory and Practice,* 7th ed., eds. Robert S. Cathcart, Larry A Samovar, and Linda D. Henman (Madison, WI: Brown & Benchmark, 1996): 134–46.

71. Craig R. Scott, "The Impact of Physical and Discursive Anonymity on Group Members' Multiple Identifications during Computer-Supported Decision Making," *Western Journal of Communication* 63 (Fall 1999): 456–87.

72. S. Opper and H. Fresko-Weiss, *Technology for Teams: Enhancing Productivity in Networked Organizations* (New York:Van Nostrand Reinhold, 1992).

73. Bolanle A. Olaniran, "Group Performance in Computer-Mediated and Face-to-Face Communication Media," *Management Communication Quarterly* 7 (February 1994): 256–81.

74. Marshall Scott Poole and Michael E. Holmes, "Decision Development in Computer-Assisted Group Decision Making," *Human Communication Research* 22 (September 1995): 90–127; Marshall Scott Poole, Michael Holmes, Richard Watson, and Gerardine DeSanctis, "Group Decision Support Systems and Group Communication:A Comparison of Decision Making in Computer-Supported and Nonsupported

Groups," *Communication Research* 20 (April 1993): 176–213.

75. Leonard M. Jessup and Joseph S.Valacich, eds., *Group Support Systems: New Perspectives* (New York: Macmillan, 1993).

76. Izak Benbasat and Lai-Huat Lim, "The Effects of Group,Task, Contest, and Technology Variables on the Usefulness of Group Support Systems: A Meta-Analysis of Experimental Studies," *Small Group Research* 24 (November 1993): 430–62.

77. V. Sambamurthy, Marshall Scott Poole, and Janet Kelly, "The Effects of Variations in GDSS Capabilities on Decision-Making Processes in Groups," *Small Group Research* 24 (November 1993): 523–46.

78. Steven M. Farmer and Charles W. Hyatt, "The Effects of Task Language Demands and Task Complexity on Computer-Mediated Work Groups," *Small Group Research* 25 (August 1994): 331–66.

79. Andrea B. Hollingshead, Joseph E. McGrath, and Kathleen M. O'Connor, "Group Task Performance and Communication Technology: A Longitudinal Study of Computer-Mediated versus Face-to-Face Work Groups," *Small Group Research* 24 (August 1993): 307–33.

80. Poole, Holmes,Watson, and DeSanctis, "Group Decision Support Systems and Group Communication."

81. Victoria K. Clawson, Robert P. Bostrom, and Rob Anson, "The Role of the Facilitator in Computer-Supported Meetings," *Small Group Research* 24 (November 1993): 547–74.

82. Craig R. Scott, Laura Quinn, C. Erik Timmerman, and Diana M. G. Barrett, "Ironic Uses of Group Communication Technology: Evidence from Meeting Transcripts and Interviews with Group Decision Support Users," *Communication Quarterly* 46 Summer 1998): 353–74.

83. Andrew Flanagin,Vanessa Tiyaamornwong, Joan O'Connor, and David Seibold, "Computer-Mediated Group Work: The Interaction of Member Sex and Anonymity," *Communication Research* 29 (February 2002): 66–93.

84. Ibid.

85. Poppy McLeod, "New Communication Technologies for Group Decision Making: Toward an Integrative Framework," in *Communication and Group Decision Making,* 2nd ed., eds. Randy Y. Hirokawa and Marshall Scott Poole (Thousand Oaks, CA: Sage, 1996): 426–61.

Managing Conflict in the Small Group

CENTRAL MESSAGE

If properly managed, the inevitable conflict during a small group's deliberations can improve problem solving and decision making by providing a variety of perspectives that promote critical thinking.

STUDY OBJECTIVES

As a result of studying Chapter 12 you should be able to:

1. Define conflict and explain both the positive and negative effects it can have on a group.

2. Describe a member who is an *innovative* or *opinion deviate* and explain how such a person can help a group improve its decision making.

3. Describe the four types of conflict that typically occur in small group interactions.

4. Describe the distributive (win–lose) and integrative (win–win) orientations and five specific conflict management styles and their tactics typically used to manage small group conflict.

5. Describe the ethical standards needed for dealing with conflict.

6. Explain the *principled negotiation procedure* for helping a group resolve conflict.

7. Explain three alternative methods for breaking a deadlock when negotiation fails, and describe a mediation procedure a group can use if it is deadlocked.

8. Explain the goals of the Common Ground approach to managing conflict and describe its basic rules for dialogue.

Student groups are a staple of university and college campuses. They are central to the student government processes on campuses across the country and also are found in almost every aspect of campus life, including the classroom. Most campuses bring in outside speakers to complement the learning that takes place in the classroom. A university's lecture series might sponsor talks by a variety of regional, national, and international experts. Student groups often are responsible for the yearly programming of these speaker series. On the surface, this kind of planning may appear straightforward and free of conflict, but often it is not. Lori, Kevin, Chris, Diedre, and Tony are members of a university Speaker Committee charged with planning their campus's speaker series. Kevin, Chris, Diedre, and Tony have volunteered for this group. Lori, as the elected student senator from the College of Arts and Humanities, chairs this committee.

Lori and Tony have been friends since high school. She encouraged Tony to join the group because his interest in politics gave him access to numerous contacts locally and nationally. Tony talked her into encouraging his friend Kevin to volunteer after Chris and Diedre had volunteered. The group needed a fifth person and Kevin was eager to join. Lori hesitated because she questioned Kevin's commitment, but ultimately trusted Tony's judgment. Their first meeting did not begin well at all. Kevin, as Lori predicted, did not show up or contact anyone about his absence. Tony was quiet because he did not want to upset Lori any more than she already was and did not want to hurt his friendship with Kevin. When Lori asked for ideas for next year's speakers, she quickly learned that the rest of the members had different ideas about speakers than she did. Tony gently suggested that he and other students were tired of the same old "political" and education topics of national defense, terrorism, and issues. He thought it was time for some fun and hoped they could schedule entertaining speakers. Diedre, on the other hand, confronted Tony directly she expressed a strong opinion that the speakers had to have educational value. Chris remained silent and could not be drawn out by Lori. Lori adjourned the meeting and called for everyone to bring more ideas to the next meeting. As she was leaving, she sarcastically remarked, "This is going to be fun!" Tony promised to get Kevin to the next meeting, after which Lori replied, "Good luck."

Small groups with different member qualities, affiliations, and viewpoints are ideally suited to produce the best decisions. However, the very characteristics that give the group diversity also provide the seeds of conflict. How to get along in this rapidly changing and diverse world is a topic on just about every one's agenda. Pick up any popular general interest magazine and you will probably see an article about how to get along at work, at home, with friends. Sometimes, what you read may give you the impression that conflict should be avoided at all costs! The truth is that whenever individuals come together in any sort of social context, disagreement and conflict are inevitable. Trying to avoid conflict is futile and unwise.

Your cultural lens contributes to how you value, approach, and manage conflict.[1] Americans are ambivalent about conflict. Along with values that stress agreement and getting along, we say, "Stick to your guns." We have trouble reconciling the benefits of *both* harmony and conflict. Our more individualistic approach to conflict tends to emphasize the productive value of conflict and to directly confronting the issue at hand. Individuals are encouraged to work it out in an open climate while sustaining individual dignity. Other cultures do not experience this tension to the same degree. For example, the same Chinese word means both *crisis* and *opportunity*. Eastern cultures, in particular, see such apparently opposing concepts as harmony and conflict as yin and yang, sides of the same coin. Yet more collectivist cultures like Japan and the Amish tend to see conflict as a threat to relational and community dignity; thus, they lean more toward pacifist responses to conflict, such as avoidance and silence. As you will see, different factors come into play and influence how group members choose to reconcile the tension between harmony and conflict so that agreement *and* disagreement can contribute positively to a group's interaction.

In small groups, conflict is an integral part of problem solving and decision making. It is a natural by-product of trying to come to some agreement about an issue or problem. Each member will perceive the situation in a slightly different way and have different values, priorities, and preferences. These variations in perceptions and beliefs are brought out into the open during discussion. If a group's goal is simply for members to understand each other, these differences can remain unresolved. But if a group's goal is to solve a problem or make a choice, divergent opinions must somehow be reconciled.

Conflict is necessary to effective decision making and problem solving. By involving a group, you tacitly acknowledge the value of diversity, the same diversity that guarantees conflict. Conflict *should* occur during group problem solving; if it doesn't, the group members aren't taking advantage of their diversity. Failure to express disagreement and avoiding discussion of conflict-producing issues leads directly to ineffective problem solving and poor decision making.[2] For the group to receive the full benefit of the collective judgment of its members, the members *must* be willing to disagree, point out errors, and even argue.

Although too much conflict can hurt a group or even destroy it, our experience has been that groups of students err in the direction of too little rather than too much conflict. Most of our students are afraid of disagreement and prefer groups with little or no conflict.[3] The more conflict members experience, the more negatively they view the group experience.[4] For that reason, this chapter stresses the benefits of conflict. We explain how to distinguish beneficial from detrimental conflict and how to manage conflicts to produce the best possible decision or solution.

A Definition of Conflict

A variety of definitions exist for **conflict,** ranging from something that occurs when individuals have reached an impasse[5] to a state of genuine difference.[6] We choose Hocker and Wilmot's definition:

> *Conflict* is an expressed struggle between at least two interdependent parties who perceive incompatible goals, scarce resources, and interference from the other party in achieving their goals.[7]

Conflict

The expressed struggle that occurs when interdependent parties, such as group members, perceive incompatible goals or scarce resources and interference in achieving their goals.

This definition embodies several implications consistent with our emphasis on the central role that communication processes play in small group dynamics.

First, the notion of conflict as an *expressed struggle* indicates that conflict involves communicating. Although a group member may *feel* internal distress, this distress becomes interpersonal conflict *only when it is expressed,* whether verbally or in such subtle ways as not making eye contact or shifting nervously in one's chair.

Second, parties to a conflict must have an *interdependent* goal such that it is impossible for one person to attain the goal and not the others. Some groups have understanding of diverse points of view as their goal. In such groups, members do not have to coordinate their beliefs and efforts to agree on a solution. However, many secondary groups must produce something—a report, a proposal, a set of recommendations—that *all* group members must agree to. Such group members are interdependent; one cannot achieve the goal without the others. Therefore, they must find ways of reconciling diverse perspectives and beliefs affecting the decision. For example, Edd may detest Desha's views about what is appropriate treatment of laboratory animals, but that won't matter much unless both are in a group that is charged with recommending a university policy regarding treatment of laboratory animals; for the group to succeed fully, Edd and Desha must reconcile their views enough to collaborate on a policy each can support. Thus, the interdependence group members experience is accompanied by interference. Edd's disagreement with Desha interferes with Desha's having her way, and vice versa. This interference may take the form of Desha's trying to persuade the other group members to accept her view, Edd's trying to undercut Desha's credibility within the group, or Desha's sabotaging Edd's car so that he misses an important meeting.

Third, this definition suggests a number of things over which people conflict, such as *goals* and *scarce resources,* to which we add values, beliefs, and ways of achieving goals. We have observed numerous student groups whose members disagree on group goals. Maria's goal is to earn an A for a group presentation to the class, but Garry's goal is to do just enough to earn a C. Their divergent goals will cause a problem for the group. In contrast, assume that both Maria and Garry want to receive an A for the presentation, but Maria prefers to involve the class in an exercise followed by discussion, whereas Garry prefers to show and discuss a movie. In this instance, they agree on the goal, but differ on the best course of action to reach the goal. Suppose, instead, that Edd believes humans are superior to all other forms of life, which makes it appropriate for laboratory animals to serve human needs, but Desha values all animal life forms equally. This fundamental difference in values may make it impossible for their group to reach consensus on a policy regarding laboratory animals.

Fourth, parties to a conflict must *perceive* that they are in conflict. This perceptual dimension is a very important one. There is nothing that automatically labels a situation as *conflict;* instead, conflict depends on how people perceive the situation. For instance, if Thomas disagrees with a proposal you have made, you have a *choice* about how to perceive Thomas's disagreement. You

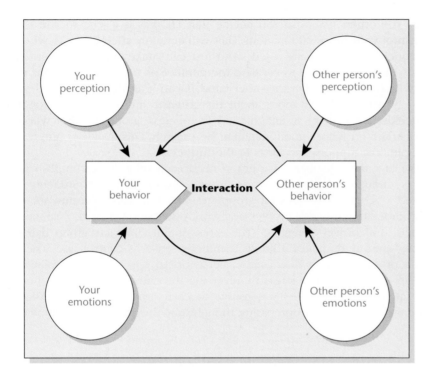

can say, "What a jerk! What makes him think he can do any better!" In this case, you have framed his disagreement as a conflict. However, you could also have said, "I wonder why Thomas disagrees? Maybe there's something in my proposal that I forgot to consider." In this latter case, you have framed his statement of disagreement as a possible attempt on Thomas's part to improve and strengthen your proposal. Thus, perception defines a situation as a conflict.

Perception of a situation is closely associated with emotions and behavior. To illustrate, your feelings can range from mild distress to out-of-control rage, depending on how you perceive the situation. If you think Thomas is a jerk for disagreeing with you or believe he disagreed just to make you look bad in some way, you will feel furious. Furthermore, you may be tempted to seek revenge or escalate the intensity of the conflict. On the other hand, if you perceive Thomas's disagreement to be motivated by a desire to strengthen your idea, then you may be only mildly hurt at his criticism, or even pleased that he cared enough to give your idea such a careful reading. In this latter case, you will behave cooperatively toward Thomas and collaborate to improve the proposal, not try to escalate the conflict. Thus, no perception of conflict, no conflict.

Your perceptions, emotions, and behavior merge with the other person's perceptions, emotions, and behavior to form a feedback loop (see Figure 12.1). Remember, you can't be in a conflict situation alone; your behaviors affect other people, as theirs affect you. Changing one of the elements will automatically change the others. Suppose you decide that Thomas is a jerk, so you rip his criticism of your proposal to shreds. That will certainly affect Thomas, who may now conclude that *you* are a jerk who just can't take constructive criticism. Thomas may now decide to escalate the conflict or try to destroy your credibility within the group. On the other hand, if you indicate to Thomas that you genuinely want to know more about his criticism and the reasons for it, he may decide that you are an enlightened, cooperative group member whom he can trust and on whose good judgment he can rely. This may lead him to seek your opinions, support, and ideas in the future.

The fact that members in a group need each other to accomplish group goals is enough to produce stress among group members. Students have reported a variety of sources for group stress such as lack of teamwork, problems coordinating the task, problematic work distribution, dissent among the members, and power struggles.[8] This stress in turn impacts group dynamics because stress undermines a group member's sense of control, and when we feel out of control we, will engage in behaviors to regain that control. Groups can help reduce member stress by reversing the causes of the stress, perhaps by equalizing the work, being sensitive to each other, completing tasks and rewarding each other, and preparing thoughtfully the work to be completed.

Positive and Negative Outcomes of Conflict

Communication scholars concur that conflict has both beneficial and harmful outcomes.[9] We mentioned earlier that without the kind of conflict that comes from a critical examination of an issue, a group is unlikely to make a good decision, but we also have pointed out that conflict can be harmful. We will now examine some of these positive and negative effects.

Benefits of Conflict   Conflict can affect group decision making, teamwork, and satisfaction. Here are several potential benefits of conflict:

1. **Conflict can produce better understanding of both issues and people.**

   We often assume that most people see things as we do and feel as we do, and are often surprised to discover otherwise. When students discover others holding differing opinions on an issue, Smith et al. found that they become uncertain about their own positions, seek actively to get more information about the issue, are able to take the perspective of the other students, and are better able to retain information, both about their own position and those of other people.[10] Franz and Jin discovered that, during the first half of a meeting, disagreement fosters learning about the issues.[11] Without this disagreement and kicking issues around, creativity and problem analysis and understanding are shortchanged. Although Diedre's direct confrontation of Tony's hope to use the Speaker's Committee to bring more entertaining speakers to campus was unexpected for an initial meeting, it did help the group attend immediately to some procedural issues that might have been ignored.

2. **Conflict can increase member motivation.**
   People who do not care will not expend any energy disagreeing about an issue. However, when group members participate in a conflict episode, they are actively involved with the issue. They are interested and excited and pay close attention, so they learn more about the issue. A student in one of our classes could not accept a statement by a fellow group member that nonverbal signals were more potent than words in conveying meaning. Unable to resolve the issue to his own satisfaction, he investigated the issue by using library and personal resources and discovered the validity of the statement. His search provided some excellent examples that the group was able to use in its class presentation—all because he got into an intellectual argument.

3. **Conflict can produce better decisions.**
   This outcome is the goal of good *group* problem solving. Through conflict, you discover first that others disagree, then *why* they disagree. You find flaws in reasoning, holes in arguments, factors that other members failed to consider, or implications that were ignored. Thus, you help the group prevent mistakes. One of us belonged to a campus staff charged with developing a plan for cutting costs at a commuter campus. The developer of the plan recommended closing the snack bar at 5 PM. Another member of the staff pointed out that closing at 5 PM would leave many evening students who came to the campus directly from work without food service and might eventually lead to a drop in enrollment. After considerable debate, the committee decided to provide expanded vending machine service, which would accomplish the goal of cutting personnel and utility costs, but not leave the evening students without food.

4. **Conflict can produce greater cohesiveness among group members.**
   When a group experiences and resolves conflict successfully, the members learn that the ties holding the group together are strong enough to withstand disagreement. Most of us who have had serious arguments with significant others can recall the closeness we feel after we have "made up." Instead of driving us apart, the conflict serves as a catalyst to strengthen the bonds between us. So it is with groups. The early disagreement that Franz and Jin observed produced eventual understanding and consensus later.[12] The twin outcomes of task success and interpersonal tolerance can increase group cohesiveness. For example, in the food service example, staff members felt so good about the final outcome and so positive about each other's willingness to listen to opposing arguments that they adjourned for lunch together in a spirit of camaraderie.

Negative Effects of Conflict   Although conflict can be beneficial, we all have seen how harmful it can be. If you have ever said to yourself after a group meeting, "I'll be glad when this project is finished; I hope I never have to work with these people again," you have experienced some of the harmful effects of conflict. These include hurt feelings, lowered cohesiveness, and even group dissolution. One of your coauthors had a recent group discussion course end with one group very disappointed in their group experience and each other. Group members were so upset that some of them told friends not to take a group discussion class because people will just end up hating each other. You will note, in the three negative effects of conflicts that we discuss below, a similarity to our previous points about defensive climates (Chapter 8) and unethical group behaviors.

1. **Conflict can cause bad feelings among group members.**
   Most of us do not like to have others disagree with us. This is particularly true when others not only disagree with an idea or proposal we give, but appear to devalue us as people. Their remarks appear caustic, even hostile. This type of perceived attack causes hard feelings. Members may be silent for fear of an attack, thereby depriving the group of valuable information and opinions. (We discuss later how you can deal with such an attack.) Moreover, even a conflict over issues and ideas can be carried on so long that it increases tension and wears group members down to the point where they dread coming to meetings.

2. **Conflict, especially if it involves personal attacks or is carried on too long, can lower group cohesiveness.**
   If you believe that others in a group do not value your contributions, you will not be eager to spend time with that group. If you have a choice, you will spend your time with other groups that seem to value you more. Prolonged conflict and attacks on one's self-concept loosen the bonds of attraction and cohesiveness, which can cause members to reduce the effort they put forth to achieve the group's objectives.

3. **Conflict can split a group apart.**
   A member who believes that a group dislikes his or her ideas, but finds support in other groups, will usually leave the group in which the conflict occurs. Conflict that goes on too long and too intensely tears members apart. One of us once observed a friendship group split up over a political issue. One side believed that busing was an appropriate way to achieve racial equality; the other side disagreed. The two sides did not simply have an intellectual disagreement; they began to impugn each other's goodwill, ability to reason, and commitment to democratic values. Unkind things were said, a rift occurred, and the group died.

Expressing Disagreement in a Group

Many people are reluctant to express opinions that differ from a group's majority opinion because expressing such disagreement may cause such a person to be seen as a deviant member by the rest of the group. (This is especially true in other cultures, such as in Asian ones.) A **deviate** is a member who is viewed by the other members as substantially different in some *important* way from the others. Two common types of group deviates are members who do not participate and members who express incompatible views about the issues and test opinions of the group.[13] You can see them immediately in our Speaker's Committee with Kevin, Chris, and Diedre, respectively. The second type is more likely to be involved in overt disagreement or conflict in a group. Although the deviate's role may be uncomfortable, it is a potentially valuable one for a group. Reluctant as you may be to express a deviant opinion, ethically you should do it for the good of the group. However, you do not want to rebelliously block or withdraw. Instead, you want to be an *innovative* or *opinion deviate,* someone who disagrees with a proposed action or decision of the group but who is strongly committed to the group and its goals. It remains to be seen whether Diedre will be perceived as an opinion deviate or someone who blocks the group from its goals.

Sometimes it is very hard for an opinion deviate to influence a group. Lindskold and Han found that it was nearly impossible for a single conciliatory member to influence a nonconciliatory group.[14] Thameling and Andrews also found that opinion deviates exerted little influence.[15] Other group members responded more emotionally to deviates than to conforming group members. A sex bias has been observed: Members responded more cooperatively to male than to female deviates. Group members appeared to *perceive* male deviates as bright and well informed, and showed a willingness to work with them by asking for evidence, questions, additional information, and so forth; however, they were more likely to *perceive* female deviates as arrogant or overly confident. These researchers suggest that an individual who wants to express a deviant opinion do so cautiously and carefully. If you first develop solid group credentials of loyalty and commitment, other members will trust your motives when you deviate from a majority opinion.

However, even with all these caveats about the difficulty of being an opinion deviate, this kind of disagreement is valuable to the group, particularly for groups in the United States and other Western cultures. Valentine and Fisher found that innovative deviance accounted for one-fourth of group interaction, serving a critical thinking function.[16] What task roles from Chapter 6 might be associated with opinion deviance? Innovative deviance in the form of contradiction, challenging statements by other members, continuing a disagreement started by others, or agreeing with an assertion someone else had attacked was particularly helpful in the group's conflict and decision emergence phases. Furthermore, most innovative deviance occurred immediately prior to consensus, supporting the notion that conflicts can contribute to consensus. Social skill is important, too. Diedre takes a risk in confronting Tony so directly in their first meeting. Her opinion deviance might be perceived more negatively than if she states her strong opinion after some cohesiveness has built in the group, when members are more likely to expect direct expressions of opinion. Her remarks effectively point out potential problems with

Deviate

A group member who differs in some important way from the rest of the group members; opinion or innovative deviates can help groups examine alternatives more thoroughly by forcing the group to take a closer look at something.

focusing on one kind of speaker, but the timing of her remarks may be questioned.

Covey found a high correlation between social skill and the use of verbal reasoning in conflict resolution, as well as a negative correlation of social skill with verbal aggression and physical violence.[17] As we noted in Chapter 6, aggressive members are dominant and try to force ideas and practices on others compared to assertive communication reflected in behavior that attempts to respect self as well as others. It is easy to see how assertive innovative deviance is more beneficial to a group compared to aggressive innovative deviance.

The quality of the argument matters, also. Garlick and Mongeau discovered that argument quality was the only factor that allowed a minority subgroup to influence majority attitudes.[18] Argument quality during group disagreement, not the number of members who support a position, seems to be a better predictor of group influence.[19] To elaborate, successful majority subgroups tend to have critical arguers who use challenges and objections that either provide a context for the argument or put off refutations to the argument. Compared to all other subgroups, losing or not, successful minority subgroups are the most consistent in their arguments. This consistency allows them to maintain their initial stance and resist the arguments from the majority, especially if the majority presents an inconsistent line of reasoning. Deviant opinions, skillfully and sensitively expressed, *can* help a group make better decisions.

Recap: A Quick Review

Groups should not avoid or suppress conflict. Conflict and harmony in groups are both beneficial and necessary aspects of group life. Conflict becomes an issue only when it is managed in anything but a constructive manner.

1. Cultural values offer a lens through which to experience conflict and explain conflict differences. Individualistic cultures tend to have a hard time seeing both the benefits and disadvantages to conflict. They also prefer more directness in confronting conflict. Collectivist cultures have an easier time seeing the interdependence between harmony and conflict and prefer pacifist responses to conflict in an effort to preserve relationships.

2. Conflict is an expressed struggle between at least two interdependent parties who see incompatible goals, scarce resources, and interference from the other in reaching those goals.

3. Individuals or groups in conflict with each other are not independent of each other but interdependent; the goal cannot be reached without the other.

4. Conflict is a communicative phenomenon emerging out of the perceptions of the parties. Group members can see and hear the conflict.

(continued)

(continued)

5. Constructively, conflict can help the group understand its members and issues better, improve member motivation, produce better decisions, and increase cohesiveness.

6. Destructive conflict can produce ill will between members, lower cohesiveness and eventually split the group apart.

7. Any member seen as significantly different from others in the group can emerge as a deviate. This can occur when disagreement is expressed.

8. Opinion deviates disagree significantly with one or more members, but also show commitment to the group goals.

9. Opinion deviancy should be done cautiously, in a climate of cohesiveness and trust. If opinion deviance is expressed assertively rather than aggressively, it can lead to effective decision making and management of conflict.

10. Group influence appears to be a matter more of the quality of the arguments than the number of people expressing the arguments. In addition, minority coalitions who successfully influence the majority display the most consistency in their arguments.

Types of Conflict

As we have already shown, conflict in and of itself is neither necessarily helpful nor harmful to a group. What matters is what the conflict is about, how it is initiated, and how it is managed. Before we examine several types of conflict that can occur within a group and discuss the potential effects of each, we revisit a description of the conflict in our Speaker Committee. Every major type of conflict occurred in this group.

The Speaker Committee—Kevin, Lori, Chris, Diedre, and Tony—met several times, and still made little progress. Kevin either missed meetings or came late; the others were angry with him. The committee couldn't agree on anything. They continued to argue about whether they should select entertaining or educational speakers, whether they should book one major speaker or several lesser-known ones, whether they should decide by consensus or majority vote, and, most of all, what they should do about Kevin. Occasionally, one of the members would ask a question that encouraged the others to examine their decision and the criteria by which to make their decision, and occasionally a member would make a suggestion that received widespread support. In general, though, they exhibited problems in managing their conflicts. The conflicts in this group of students illustrate the four types of conflict described as follows.

Substantive Conflict

Conflict resulting from disagreements over ideas, information, reasoning, or evidence.

Substantive Conflict **Substantive conflict,** also called *intrinsic* conflict, is task-related conflict such as disagreement over ideas, meanings, issues, and other matters pertinent (intrinsic) to the task of the group.[20] Substantive conflict is the basis for effective decision making and problem solving in a discussion group. This secondary tension is the vehicle by which ideas, proposals, evidence, and reasoning are challenged and critically examined, doubts are brought into the open, and the group works together to find the best solution. Opinion and innovative deviance described earlier are usually substantive in nature. In our example, the Speaker Committee debated whether an entertaining or educational speaker would be a better choice. The ensuing argument helped members clarify the purpose of the Speaker Series and presented good reasons for considering each type of speaker.

Affective Conflict

Conflict resulting from personality clashes, likes, dislikes, and competition for power.

Affective Conflict   **Affective conflict,** also called *extrinsic* conflict, is conflict that originates from interpersonal power clashes, likes and dislikes unrelated to the group's task.[21] It represents the *who* in small group conflict and is generally detrimental to the efficient functioning of any group. For example, Speaker Series committee members Lori and Kevin did not like each other and missed no opportunity to disagree or belittle each other. When Kevin agreed with Tony and said he preferred to schedule an entertaining rather than an educational speaker, Lori said, "I could have expected that from you. Let's not learn—let's party!" This statement revealed that Lori personalized the conflict with Kevin. Her dislike compounded the effects of disagreement over work procedures and ideas. She rarely failed to make sarcastic comments to Kevin throughout the meeting. Such conflict is both difficult to resolve and exceedingly harmful to the group.

Although the origin of this type of conflict is difficult to pin down, your coauthors' observations of numerous groups suggest that much of it is rooted in one person's acting as if he or she is superior, and another member's refusal to accept this difference in status or power. Most of this "I am superior, more important, more knowledgeable" signaling is nonverbal, projected by subtle patterns of vocal tones, postures, and head/body angles. Much of what is called interpersonal conflict emerges from a struggle for position and power. Recent research has indicated that group members are able to differentiate between personalized (affective) and depersonalized (substantive) conflict, and that the type of conflict affects group consensus.[22] Because affective conflict can impede resolution of substantive issues, Fisher and Brown recommend disentangling relationship and substantive goals and pursuing them independently.[23] Doing so gives the parties a chance to resolve their substantive differences, even though they may never change their feelings about each other. We talk later about how you might do that.

Procedural Conflict

Conflict resulting from disagreement about how to do something.

Procedural Conflict   **Procedural conflict** is a type of substantive conflict over the procedures a group should follow in working toward its goals. Disagreement is about the *how* of group interaction. For instance, members of a group may disagree about whether they should make decisions by consensus or whether majority rule will suffice. In our Speaker Series Committee, Lori proposed splitting up the money available to the committee and letting each person select whatever speaker he or she wanted with his/her share of the money as the most efficient way of deciding the issue. But Diedre pointed out that if every person chose the same type of speaker, the series would be boring. The group then realized the value of consensus decision making. This disagreement over *how* the group made its major decisions is a clear example of procedural conflict. The difference of opinion expressed by Diedre and Lori helped clarify the issue.

Procedural conflict is sometimes used to mask affective or substantive conflict. Putnam notes that it can occur because members genuinely disagree over procedures, but it also can be used to withdraw from another substantive conflict by forcing a vote or otherwise regulating the group's work.[24] Although procedural conflict may seem to be a straightforward difference over how the group should accomplish something, it may be rooted in differing member needs for structure versus freedom. Members high in needs for procedural order are more comfortable with linear procedures than members who prefer less structured procedural order.

Our discussion of conflict thus far has focused on issues of conflict in face-to-face (FTF) groups, not computer-mediated communication (CMC) in groups. As you recall, groups can use computers to e-mail members, talk to each other online, and some may use group support systems to help them problem-solve. Early research comparing CMC to FTF groups and conflict expression produced inconsistent results.[25] CMC groups engaged in more inflammatory, profane, and negative interactions compared to FTF groups. However, research into the use of group support systems or GSS, discussed in Chapters 3 and 11, was found to exhibit less substantive and affective conflict if members effectively adapted the GSS. Inconsistency in the results suggests that if computer groups were given the time to become familiar with each other and if they adapted effectively to the GSS, then CMC groups may exhibit less damaging conflict expression than FTF groups. However, previous research had not considered the types of conflict.

In a rare study comparing three types of conflict (affective, substantive, and procedural) in both CMC groups and FTF groups, differences were found.[26] Hobman et al. recently found that CMC groups displayed initially more affective and procedural conflict than FTF groups.[27] However, these differences disappeared over time. Both CMC and FTF groups displayed similar amounts of substantive conflict. CMC groups initially, because of the anonymity of CMC, exhibit fewer of the social norms that people use to support and maintain positive self-images. Given time, however, substantive conflict in CMC groups declines as members take the time to get to know each other. The early procedural conflict in CMC groups can be explained by members' initial focus on how to use the computer medium.

Essentially, CMC groups do not follow the same conflict patterns as FTF groups, but they do go on to reach comparable levels over time. Groups that use any type of computer technology need to give themselves the time for social development. They should even consider meeting face-to-face, initially, giving themselves the opportunity to establish social and procedural norms acceptable to their group.[28]

Inequity Conflict

Conflict about perceived unequal workloads or contributions to the group effort.

Conflict over Inequity   One of the most prevalent sources of conflict in the groups we have observed is perceived **inequity** in the group: Group members do not seem to have equal workloads and/or do not make equal contributions to the group. Inequity reduces satisfaction with the group and is associated with high levels of conflict.[29] In our Speaker Series Committee, Kevin's work and contributions to the group were perceived as inadequate. Although Lori rode Kevin the hardest about his lack of commitment to the group, Chris, Diedre, and even his friend Tony mentioned Kevin's lack of follow-through and failure to complete assignments for the group. When Kevin was late again, Chris said, "I'm tired of waiting for the jerk. Let's get started," and later Diedre directly confronted Kevin by listing his behaviors that indicated lack of commitment to the group ("You've missed two of the last four meetings and were late to the ones you did come to."). Kevin's perceived inequity of effort within the group had created serious conflict between him and the other members. Kevin's continued lack of commitment to the group also contributed to Lori's strong feelings of dislike and her constant needling. She scrutinized his contributions more closely than those of the other members and criticized Kevin for statements that she accepted from other people. For example, both Tony and Kevin wanted an entertaining speaker, but Lori singled Kevin out for ridicule about wanting to party more than learn. Because of his inequity of performance, he was being required to measure up more perfectly to the group's performance norms than the others.

Note how easily the stress of inequity can lead to very obvious coalitions that in turn impact the management of group conflict.[30] *Coalitions* emerge in groups when members with access to few resources, minimal power, or little bargaining leverage seek out other members in an attempt to level the playing field. Group members have also been known to form coalitions when some member comes to identify more with his or her own subgroup than with the group as a whole and when conflict styles tend to be accommodative— those who do more of the accommodating over time may align themselves with others to get the upper hand. Coalitions, although sometimes functional, can also be detrimental. Members may become willing to hurt their own goals in an effort to defeat the most popular member. Groups experiencing a great deal of coalition conflict may leave themselves vulnerable to external threats because their attention is on the conflict. In addition, communication among members may decrease. When members can perceive a common ground of interest, many coalitions will disappear.

Although we describe these four types of conflict as though they are distinct, they are not mutually exclusive. One type can easily lead to another. Frequently two or more types blend. In our example this was most clearly seen with Lori, whose dislike of Kevin combined with Kevin's inadequate contribution to the group and his disagreements with Lori. All these conflicts united to intensify Lori's dislike. Lori looked for things over which to be angry with Kevin. She was probably the most relieved member when Kevin eventually left the group.

Managing Conflict

We hope we have convinced you of the value of innovative, opinion deviance and substantive conflict during small group problem solving. Conflict is inevitable when people meet in groups. Avoiding it *circumvents the very reason for engaging in group discussion*—that the thinking of several people is likely to be more valid and thorough than the thinking of one person acting alone. Both the attitudes of group members involved in a conflict and the procedures they use to manage the conflict affect the outcomes. Using further examples of the Speaker Committee, we discuss both attitudes and procedures that facilitate productive conflict.

Basic Approaches toward Conflict Management

Most people have a basic attitude or approach toward managing conflict, either *distributive* or *integrative*. The **distributive approach,** also called a *win-lose* attitude, assumes that what one person gains is at another's expense. Thus, there can be only one winning side; the other or others are losers. In the Speaker Committee, Tony and Kevin wanted to choose an entertaining speaker and Diedre and Lori wanted an educational one. The distributive orientation assumes that only one faction can win. *Either* Tony and Kevin get their entertaining speaker, *or* Lori and Diedre get their educational one. Whichever wins, the other side loses.

The **integrative approach** assumes that there is some way to manage the conflict so that all parties can end up winners; in other words, the main concerns of all parties can be integrated into a solution in which all involved receive what is most important to them. Someone with an integrative orientation would assume that a speaker could be found who is *both* entertaining *and* educational; thus, both factions can win. This approach has also been called a *win-win* attitude. A group may not be able to integrate the concerns of *all* members into its final solution or decision. Perhaps members' values are so divergent that they cannot be merged, or maybe resources are so scarce that needs cannot be fully met. In such cases, perhaps partial integration— *compromise*—is the best that can be achieved. However, even if a group does not develop a fully integrative solution, it *certainly* will not develop one if members begin with the premise that integration is impossible. Without an integrative orientation, members will not expend their energies to develop creative solutions, but will spend time quarreling about the merits of one proposal over another in an attempt to win rather than find the best solution possible.

Distributive Approach

The conflict management approach that assumes fixed resources must be distributed among parties to the conflict; thus, whatever someone wins, someone else loses.

Integrative Approach

The conflict management approach that assumes that solutions can be created to satisfy every party to the conflict.

In a longitudinal study of 11 work groups in large American organizations, Kuhn and Poole discovered that the work groups that took the time and energy to create more integrative solutions to their problems, compared to those that merely confronted or avoided them, produced more effective decisions.[31] In addition, the work groups that used a more integrated conflict style also managed to fulfill other communicative functions effectively. They met the issues head on, worked through obstacles to their problem, and recognized that often they needed collective attention to the problem. These work groups used the difficult task of integration to develop group norms and rules that effectively guided them in future interaction.

The key to Kuhn and Poole's study is found in their observations that integrative solutions do not just happen, but rather they take hard work and time. Schie and Rognes's exploration of member motivational orientations helps explain why.[32] Member characteristics are critical input variables to a group system. Such characteristics affect group processes, including conflict. For example, some members display individualistic orientations toward conflict by pursuing *their* goals, not group ones, and typically use distributive behaviors that are often defensive. In contrast, members with cooperative orientations pursue goals that integrate their personal goals with the group ones; they use integrative behaviors that are supportive. These member orientations influence what members perceive as fair and how they negotiate disagreement. Differing member orientations can harm or help a group's assembly effect and subsequent group outputs.

Schie and Rognes found that these different member orientations influenced how members managed resources during disagreement and members' judgments of fairness. Surprisingly, whether individualists were in the majority or minority, they showed a willingness to exploit resources and use distributive behaviors to get their goals met. Groups composed of all cooperatively oriented members had the highest ratings of fairness compared to mixed groups. This suggests that using distributive behaviors may be effective on one level but may hurt perceptions about how fair the process was. Group members need to be prepared to deal with distributive approaches or suffer from the exploitive and harmful consequences of such approaches. Integrative and distributive approaches to conflict help us begin to see that how any one member perceives and deals with conflict is complicated. We now turn to a discussion of more global conflict management styles.

Recap: A Quick Review

Small group conflict comes in many forms and is managed in a variety of styles, all of which differ in their effectiveness and appropriateness.

1. When groups engage in task-related conflict, they are engaged in substantive conflict. This intrinsic conflict is beneficial to the group if managed well.

(continued)

(continued)

2. Affective conflict emerges over interpersonal clashes between members and is extrinsic to the task. This kind of conflict is rooted in power and status struggles between group members.

3. When group members engage in conflict over how to proceed, they are involved in procedural conflict. Procedural conflict can mask affective conflict.

4. Groups using computer-mediated communication should take time to get to know each other and the computer technology; this helps reduce the amount of affective and procedural conflict that can occur early in these groups compared to face-to-face groups.

5. The unequal distribution of work and member contributions to the task is fertile ground for small group conflict. The stress from the inequality often leads to the formation of coalitions that often battle each other and move the group away from its central task.

6. Conflict styles can be divided into two broad approaches: distributive and integrative.

7. Distributive approaches are grounded in win–lose criteria for managing the conflict and integrative ones are grounded in win–win criteria. Both affect the task and the socioemotional dimensions of group dynamics.

8. Members with individualistic orientations use distributive approaches and can exploit members with cooperative orientations, especially if cooperative members are not ready to deal with the distributive tactics of individualistic members.

Conflict Management Styles and Tactics

Your perception of the conflict situation is a major determinant of how you are likely to deal with the conflict.[33] Elements of the situation include your perceptions about whether the conflict is repetitive, the degree to which you and the other party have mutual goals, how certain you are about how to solve the problem, whether you believe the other party is the source of the conflict, and the degree of negative feelings you have for the other. These combine to influence your desire to cooperate. The specific management style you choose is likely to be a product both of how cooperative and how assertive you are, as illustrated in Figure 12.2.[34]

As you can see, each *style* represents a general pattern of behavior developed over time. Specific choices that people make in particular situations as they manage conflict will be referred to as conflict *tactics*. The key difference between a style and a tactic is the degree to which a person is aware of his or her behavior.[35] Generally we are less aware of our styles than our tactics. Regardless, competent group members exhibit an awareness of not only their own preferred style and tactics but also those of other group members. This awareness is a key factor in changing unproductive patterns of conflict in a group. As we discuss each of the general conflict styles, we will also introduce you to common tactics that group members may use relevant

FIGURE 12.2 Your conflict management style depends in part on how assertive and cooperative you are

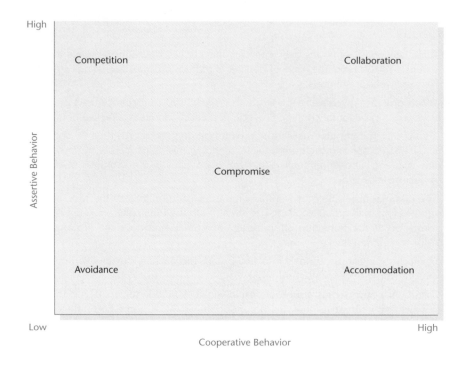

to each style. These styles and representative tactics are summarized in Figure 12.3.

Although no conflict style is always best, some conflict styles are perceived as more appropriate in certain circumstances. Canary and Spitzberg found, for example, that the topic of the conflict interacted with the gender of the participants to influence perceptions of both effectiveness and appropriateness.[36] We recommend a contingency view in which the most productive way for settling a conflict depends on time pressures, distribution of information and skills, group member values and needs, and other input variables. For example, two input variables influencing conflict style are the nature of the relationship between the individuals and the type of conflict.[37] Although more collectivist cultures such as Japan may prefer an integrative style that values harmony, preserving the esteem of the others, and relying less on direct confrontation, they may change the style depending on whom the conflict involves and what it concerns. Japanese in conflict over values and opinions tend to be more avoidant with acquaintances than with close friends; they are more integrative with close friends. And if engaged in a conflict of interest, they have no problem being confrontive and dominant with acquaintances compared to close friends.

Each conflict style is appropriate under certain circumstances, but having an integrative orientation is preferred in most problem-solving discussions.

FIGURE 12.3
Conflict styles and tactics

Avoidance

Denial
Topic changes
Noncommittal remarks
Irreverent remarks

Accommodation

Giving up/giving in
Disengagement
Denial of needs
Expression of desire for harmony

Competition

Personal criticism
Rejection
Hostile imperatives
Hostile jokes
Hostile questions
Presumptive remarks
Denial of responsibility

Collaboration

Analytic remarks
    Descriptive statements
    Qualifying statements
    Solicitation of disclosure
    Solicitation of criticism
Conciliatory remarks
    Support
    Concessions
    Acceptance of responsibility

Compromise

Appeal to fairness
Suggest a trade-off
Offer a quick, short-term solution

Why do we say *most* problem-solving discussions? Because our discussions of conflict and problem solving focus mostly on task groups that have had time to develop a history and thus must attend to both the task and social dimensions of their interactions. In practice, however, we sometimes find ourselves in temporary task groups with strangers who are asked to make relatively quick decisions that will have more of an impact on individuals outside the group than on the group itself.[38] For example, one of your coauthors chairs an academic department that recently underwent a self-study. As part of this study, an *ad hoc* committee was formed of members who did not know each other; they had three days to complete their task, after which they disbanded to go their separate ways. They did not have the usual time to build a strong cohesive climate; their decisions affected others (the department), but not themselves. How do you think this group's composition and task influenced how appropriate and effective it was to use integrative, solution-oriented styles?[39]

In such temporary, highly task-focused groups, members generally perceive integrative styles as more competent. However, sometimes task contingencies may leave the group little room for collaborative decision making, especially if the group is directed to choose quickly among fixed alternatives. Nonconfrontational behaviors (e.g., giving in, avoiding the subject) are particularly problematic because, although they could be appropriate and even effective in response to certain primary tensions, they are *not* helpful when time is at a premium. In comparison, more confrontational, controlling tactics can be highly effective in such short-term task groups, but group members perceive them as inappropriate. Simply stated, more controlling tactics risk harming the relationships between group members, even when time is short. Such tactics are typically viewed as inappropriate, even if they are judged effective under certain contingencies. When you are in a temporary short-term task group, steer clear of avoidance tactics and balance confrontational tactics—as effective as they may seem—with integrative tactics whenever possible. The integrative, solution-oriented, and less confrontational styles tend to be associated with group member satisfaction, improved productivity, increased decision quality, and judgments of effectiveness and appropriateness.[40]

Avoidance

The passive conflict management style that ignores a conflict.

Avoidance   The **avoidance** style is a passive approach in which a person expends no energy discussing or exploring options. The member who disagrees but says nothing is avoiding conflict. Sometimes called *nonconfrontation,* conflict avoidance reduces satisfaction in groups.[41] As we stated earlier, using them is particularly detrimental to task groups that have a relatively short time to solve a problem. Such passive behavior is appropriate only when the problem is unimportant and the risks of making a poor decision are slight. For example, a committee to which one of us belonged was asked to develop a decorating plan for a student lounge/study area. The art instructor on the committee recommended a color scheme not particularly appealing to the chemistry professor on the committee. The students liked the colors, so the chemistry professor kept his objections to himself. He reasoned that because he spent so little time in the lounge, color did not matter much to him.

Individuals avoid conflict by denying, managing the topic, and making noncommittal or irreverent remarks.[42] A group member expresses to you that another member, Kevin, is not doing his fair share of the work and something needs to be done. A response such as "I do not see that as a problem" can be construed as *denial*. Or you might respond with "We are winding down our meeting and need to get to the next agenda item," effectively *shifting the topic* away from the potential issue. A *noncommittal remark* might be, "You know that is Kevin being Kevin." Replying with laughter to the concern is considered an *irreverent remark* that also tries to avoid conflict.

Accommodation **Accommodation,** also called *appeasement,* is a highly cooperative but passive approach that occurs when you give in to someone else. It may occur when the issue is not important to you, or when the relationship is more important to you than the outcome. For instance, in the Speaker Series Committee, after a brief discussion about educational versus entertaining speakers, Tony said, "I can go along with an educational speaker. I just want to avoid this arguing." Tony wanted to accommodate in order to end the arguments. Accommodation is appropriate only when the issue is relatively unimportant to you or the other person's needs are genuinely more important to you. Don't accommodate just to end a fight, because the resentment you carry around with you may eventually poison the relationship anyway.

> **Accommodation**
> The conflict management style in which one person appeases or gives in to the other.

Tony's accommodating tactic is referred as an *expression of desire for harmony* tactic. Tony goes along with an educational speaker in a personal effort to curtail the arguing. Three other accommodating tactics include variations of *giving up/giving in, disengagement,* and *denial of needs.*[43] Had Tony responded with "Have it your way; let's bring in the educational speaker!" he would have given up the conflict. Disengagement would be characterized with a remark such as "You know, I will not even be here for the speaker, so do what you want." Denial of his needs can be found in "It's OK; go ahead with the speaker you want."

Competition **Competition** is a highly aggressive, uncooperative style in which one person tries to win over another. Sometimes called *dominating* or *forcing,* competition is appropriate when you have strong beliefs about something and you perceive that other approaches will not allow your needs to be acknowledged or accommodated. However, competitive approaches can damage relationships and may end up doing more harm than good. In the Speaker Series Committee, Lori and Kevin competed. Lori threatened to quit the group if only entertaining speakers were chosen, and Kevin told Tony not to accommodate so readily because he, Kevin, had plenty of good arguments left in support of entertaining speakers. Both statements imply that the speaker will do whatever is necessary to get his or her way.

> **Competition**
> The uncooperative, aggressive conflict management style in which one person attempts to dominate or force the outcome to his or her advantage.

Competitive style tactics include such actions as personal criticism, hostile joking, rejection, and hostile questions.[44] These obviously denote a win–lose orientation and involve one-upping the other party. Lori's *hostile imperative* served as a threat to leave the group if Kevin got his way. Kevin, on the other hand, created a coalition with Tony to gang up on Lori. Competitiveness between Lori and Kevin can be expressed in other ways. Both may have *personally criticized* the other with remarks such as, "Lori, you are so selfish and unconcerned about the rest of us." Kevin could show *rejection* of Lori's hostile imperative by responding to her with, "Go ahead and quit— we don't need you," effectively dismissing her threat and attacking her personally. A *hostile question* that demeans another person could come in the form of a remark from Lori such as "Kevin, who does most of the work for this group?" Kevin, on the other hand, could attribute feelings to Lori that she has not acknowledged in a *presumptive remark* such as "Lori, you're just making yourself miserable threatening to quit." Parties in competition also have at their disposal tactics that are designed to *deny personal responsibility* for the conflict. How could Lori deny any personal responsibility for the conflict between her and Kevin?

Collaboration

The assertive, cooperative conflict management style that assumes a solution can be found that fully meets the needs of all parties to a conflict.

Collaboration **Collaboration,** also called *negotiating* or *problem solving,* is a cooperative and assertive style that stems from an integrative attitude. It encourages all parties to a conflict to work together in searching for a solution that meets everyone's needs. In the Speaker Series Committee, Diedre eventually suggested that the committee look for a speaker who was both entertaining and educational. In doing this, she assumed that both important needs of the factions could be met without either faction having to give up anything, that each faction's "must have" point could be accommodated. Collaborative solutions can be ideal because all members of groups that arrive at collaborative solutions believe they have won without the others' having lost. However, collaboration often takes more time than other approaches and certainly takes more energy.

Compared to competitive tactics, collaborative ones focus on mutual rather than individual concerns and attempt to facilitate gains for all parties involved in the conflict.[45] They are often referred to as integrative because they recognize the interdependence between parties. The first major category of collaborative tactics is *analytical remarks.* These facilitate collaboration by describing and disclosing important information as the parties try to maximize their gains. These kinds of statements are most like the kind you would expect in a supportive versus defensive group climate. Descriptive statements are nonevaluative remarks about events such as "We have confirmed the availability of individual speakers that fit both categories and some that could be both educational and entertaining." Qualifying remarks from group members would define the nature of the conflict between members. For instance, Chris could say, "Lori and Kevin appear to disagree over the kind of speaker we could get, but I sense that both would entertain the idea of a speaker who could be both entertaining and educational." Group members can also *solicit both disclosure and criticism* in a nonhostile fashion. Tony could add to the discussion by soliciting from Lori what she meant by saying she would quit. Diedre could also solicit criticism of herself by asking for feedback from the group about her behaviors in the conflict between Lori and Kevin.

The second category of collaborative tactics involves those that are conciliatory; they demonstrate one's role in the conflict and display a willingness to work toward mutual gain.[46] For example, Kevin could back off his attacks of Lori and show *support* for her feelings: "I can see why you would want to quit, Lori." Lori, on the other hand, can reconcile with Kevin by showing a willingness to be flexible, offering a *concession,* rather than threatening to quit if she does not get her way. Important to collaboration is recognizing your role in the conflict and thus being accountable for the nature of the conflict. Kevin could show this *acceptance of responsibility* by acknowledging how he ganged up on Lori in order to win or how he had let the group down by not doing his fair share.

Compromise   A **compromise,** also called a *shared outcome,* assumes that each party to the conflict will have to give up something in order to gain something more important. In the Speaker Series Committee, Chris suggested a compromise when he said: "Maybe we can get two speakers, less expensive—one educational and one entertaining." Each faction would have to agree to give up the idea of bringing in one very well-known speaker. Thus, compromises entail some losses for both parties. For this reason, we recommend attempting to find a collaborative, fully integrative solution when the decision is important to all group members, one in which each member will be responsible for implementing the outcome and the group is not pressed for time.

However, we think that compromise should *not* be considered a dirty word! When collaborative resolution is impossible or takes more time than is available, a compromise is a desirable and ethical outcome, especially if each group member feels that what he or she had to give up is fair in comparison with what others had to give up.

Chris's suggestion that they get two speakers by compromising their desires for one well-paid speaker is an example of a *suggested trade-off* tactic common to compromise.[47] He could have also *appealed to fairness* by remarking, "Lori and Kevin, you both got what you wanted last time, so this time let's go with two speakers." *Offering a quick short-term solution,* "We do not have time to complain about this; let's ask the educational speaker because we can get her immediately," is also an option for the group.

Sidebar:
Compromise
The conflict management style that assumes each party must give up something to get something.

Expressing Disagreement Ethically

Ethical behaviors in conflict situations are those that promote the beneficial outcomes of conflict (e.g., greater understanding of issues, increased cohesiveness) while minimizing the destructive outcomes (e.g., hurt feelings, personal attacks). The following suggestions will help members behave with integrity and sensitivity during conflicts:

1. **Do express your disagreement.**
   We have already noted that not confronting disagreements can reduce satisfaction with the group, and failure to express honest disagreement circumvents the decision-making and problem-solving process in a group. By not speaking up when you disagree, you deprive the group of

potentially valuable information. In a sense you deceive, because your silence suggests that you agree.

2. **Stick with the issue at hand.**

   When you disagree, you should deal directly with the issue under discussion. Do not bring up side issues or allow hidden agenda items to motivate you.[48] To do so is as unethical as to use irrelevant emotional stories to arouse support.

3. **Use rhetorical sensitivity in expressing your disagreement.**

   Be sensitive and perceptive enough to select words that will not connote negative images. Especially do not try to push others' emotional buttons. Recall from Chapter 6 that this personality trait involves monitoring the effects of your statements on others and adjusting as appropriate. Use persuasion, not threats, to make your points.[49] Being rhetorically sensitive during conflict also means you'll follow the next ethical guideline.

4. **Disagree with the idea but do not ever criticize the person.**

   Express disagreement so that it does not devalue the person with whom you disagree. Members of groups with norms for expressing conflict cooperatively and integratively are more satisfied with the group's process and outcome than members of groups with norms for competitive and distributive (win–lose) expression of conflict.[50] The highest ratings of fairness are found in groups composed of members with cooperative orientations. Thus, "One flaw in your proposal to shut down the snack bar is that it does not consider the food service needs of evening students" is far superior to "You inconsiderate bozo! What are the evening students supposed to do?" Above all, no name-calling or personal attacks!

5. **Base your disagreement on evidence and reasoning.**

   Disagreements should be reasonable and substantive, based on evidence and reasoning.[51] They should not be based on rumor, innuendo, unsubstantiated information, or emotionalism. If you have no evidence or your reasoning is shown to be potentially faulty, *agree* instead of quarreling. As much as possible, keep the conflict issue based. This has the added advantage of being more likely to be persuasive.

6. **React to disagreement in a spirit of inquiry, not defensiveness.**

   Group members' reactions to argument are more important than the arguments themselves in creating group polarization.[52] We mentioned in Chapter 6 that your willingness to communicate must be greater than your need to protect yourself from disagreement or embarrassment. If someone disagrees with you, do not react defensively as though you had been attacked personally. Keep your mind open to others' ideas, evaluations, and suggestions. Listen actively to your fellow member's remarks. Be certain that the person disagreeing has understood your position correctly, then clarify any misunderstandings, and work together to search for the most effective solutions. In this way you can make conflict work *for* rather than *against* the group. This may not be easy! But it will benefit the group and you will have a clear conscience.

7. **If someone persists in attacking *you*, stay calm and speak reasonably.**

   One of the biggest challenges that a group member has is to respond to a personal attack by another. The worst thing you can do is to let another's attacks intimidate you into being silent! Instead, confront the attacking member calmly and reasonably, explaining how you feel and what you want the other to do: "I resent your personal attacks, and I think they are inappropriate. I am willing to listen to your objections, but I want you to stop your attacks now." If the attacker was caught up in the heat of the moment, he or she may apologize and calm down. If your initial confrontation doesn't succeed, ask for the *group's* intervention: "Do we all think personal attacks are unacceptable behavior?" The other members, who probably are as uncomfortable as you, will now be encouraged to support you in confronting the attacker.

8. **Use an integrative rather than a distributive approach to solving the conflict.**

   Assume that there is a way to satisfy, at least partially, the important needs of all parties to the conflict. Use your energy to search for alternatives that integrate all parties' needs, not to destroy the other party. Act in ways that improve, not damage, the relationship. Remember that a solution satisfying all parties will be more lasting than one leaving one party feeling disgruntled or mistreated. Also, consider the ethics of a person who gains pleasure from beating another in a way that damages the *group!*

No matter how skilled at expressing disagreement and how ethical, group members can still crash on the rocks of conflict if their procedures for handling it are poor. We have selected six procedures for managing stubborn conflicts: *Principled Negotiation, Mediation, Voting, Forcing, Arbitration,* and *Common Ground approaches.*

Recap: A Quick Review

General patterns of integrative and distributive behaviors used to manage conflict can be categorized into five conflict styles, with their related tactics. Effective conflict management can emerge out of the ethical expression of disagreement.

1. These conflict styles vary in their perceived effectiveness and appropriateness. Members are more aware of their specific tactics and less of their overall style.

2. Situational contingencies such as the nature of the topic, gender, culture, time, and nature of the relationship between group members influence these perceptions.

(continued)

(continued)

3. The integrative, solution-centered, and less confrontational styles are generally viewed as the most effective and appropriate; however, the more confrontational styles can be effective given certain contingencies.

4. The avoidance style is passive and nonconfrontational. The tactics of denial, topic changes, and irreverent remarks are especially detrimental to a task group with little time to solve the problem, but may be useful in long-standing groups.

5. The accommodation style is another passive style that is highly appeasing. Captured in tactics such as giving in and disengagement, it can be effective and even appropriate when dealing with certain affective conflicts or when the relationship is more important than fighting over a task issue.

6. Competition is highly confrontational and uncooperative and involves tactics such as hostile remarks and rejection. It may be effective in short-term task groups or when a member feels strongly about his or her positions; however, it rarely is judged appropriate because it harms the socioemotional dimensions of groups.

7. Collaboration is highly integrative, cooperative, and solution centered. It involves a win–win ethic and is expressed in analytical and conciliatory tactics. It is most consistently perceived as effective and appropriate by members, but takes time and effort.

8. Compromise is a moderate style also called *shared outcome*. It is captured in trade-off tactics that are more appropriate when integrative approaches are not possible.

9. Greater understanding of the issues facing groups and increased cohesiveness can be facilitated if members ethically manage their disagreement.

10. Disagreement should be expressed. Follow an integrative path; stay focused; consider your own needs and those of others; use evidence and reasoning; refute the idea, not the person offering the idea; and in the face of distributive tactics stay calm and do not reciprocate in kind.

Negotiating Principled Agreement

Principled Negotiation

A general strategy that enables parties in a conflict to express their needs openly and search for alternatives to meet the needs of all parties without damaging their relationships.

A task-oriented group experiencing a conflict must move toward resolution for the group's goals to be accomplished. There are a variety of techniques designed to help groups manage conflict. We especially like the *principled negotiation* procedure because it is consistent with all the ethical principles we have outlined earlier and is an extremely effective procedure that helps a group negotiate consensus from initially divergent points of view. As described by Fisher and Ury, **principled negotiation** is an all-purpose strategy that encourages all participants in a conflict situation to collaborate by expressing their needs and searching for alternatives that meet those needs.[53] It is called "principled" because it is based on ethical principles that encourage users to remain decent individuals and not act in ways that will damage the relationship among them. It puts the integrative approach into action.

Principled negotiation is an efficient and fair way to develop a solution meeting the legitimate needs of all parties; therefore, it is likely to produce lasting solutions. Tutzauer and Roloff say the guidelines in the principled negotiation procedure are consistent with their discoveries about communication behaviors that produce integrative outcomes.[54] They found that exchanging information, asking questions instead of making demands, and foregoing rigid, inflated positions helped bargainers attain integrative outcomes. *Appropriate communication techniques alone* helped bargainers attain integrative outcomes regardless of their initial orientations. In addition, this type of negotiation will not harm the relationship among participants and frequently improves it. We particularly like it because it recognizes the major elements that enter into conflict—perceptions, emotions, behaviors, and interaction among individuals—and acknowledges that each must be considered. The following description of principled negotiation shows how a group can incorporate the communication principles presented throughout this book, including such concepts as rhetorical sensitivity, active listening, and integrative conflict management, into a practical, effective technique for managing conflict. The group leader, an outside consultant, or members themselves can use the procedure. Here are the four steps:

1. **Separate the people from the problem.**
   In most conflicts, the content of the disagreement becomes tangled with the relationship among the participants. Each should be dealt with directly and separately. All parties should be given the opportunity to explain, without interference, how they perceive the conflict and how they feel about it. Parties should share perceptions as they try to put themselves into each other's shoes. If emotions run high, allow them to be vented. Do not overreact to emotional outbursts, but listen actively and show by your actions as well as your words that you care about the needs of the other members with whom your interests conflict. The goal is not to become bosom buddies with the other party to a conflict (although that may happen), but to develop a good working relationship characterized by mutual respect.[55]

2. **Focus on interests, not positions.**
   When group members stake out certain positions ("I insist that we have an educational speaker!"), they become attached to those *positions* rather than the original *needs* the positions were designed to meet. For example, we discussed earlier the committee that debated closing the food service facility at 5 PM. One side's position was that the snack bar must be closed, but the other side's position was that the snack bar must be kept open. These two positions are incompatible, and there is no way to reconcile them—in their present form, one must win and one must lose. However, when group members started to explore the *interests* behind the positions (the desire to save money and the desire to meet needs of evening students), then an avenue opened whereby both parties could have their desires met by finding a way to do *both simultaneously*—provide the

students with food without raising costs by expanding the vending service. Rigidly adhering to the initial positions would have precluded the discovery of this solution. Support for this comes from Innami, who discovered that when members stick to their positions, decision quality is impaired, but when they exchange facts and reasons, decision quality improves.[56] Moreover, high-quality arguments are more persuasive and overcome the influence of such factors as status differences.[57]

3. **Invent options for mutual gain.**
   The previous example illustrates how a new option, expanded vending service, was created that had not been apparent when the conflict started. We earlier have suggested separating the invention process from the decision process and employing techniques like brainstorming. Negotiators should assume that the interests of all parties can be integrated into the group's final solution. The same committee that debated food service options for evening students also discussed how evening students could be served by the bookstore.[58] The evening student adviser on the committee noted that the campus bookstore was open in the evenings only during the first week of the quarter. Many evening students who drove directly to campus from work could not arrive early enough for the bookstore's regular hours, and so were unable to exchange books, purchase supplies, or even browse. The adviser proposed that the bookstore hours be extended to 8 PM every evening. The campus budget officer objected strongly, noting that the proposal would result in cost increases for personnel salaries unlikely to be recovered by purchases made by evening students.

   The positions adopted by each person represented attempts to meet the legitimate needs of two important groups: the evening students and the budget watchdogs. However, through open discussion focused on the interests (not the positions) of each, a solution was invented that incorporated both sets of needs. The bookstore would remain open two evenings per week throughout the quarter, and would start business later in the morning the rest of the week. The total number of hours of bookstore operation was the same, so costs were not increased, but the distribution of the hours changed to meet the needs of more students.

4. **Use objective criteria.**
   Negotiations will be perceived as fairer if objective criteria *agreed upon by all parties* are established as the standard for judging alternatives. Group members will profit from establishing such criteria at the beginning of any problem-solving session, but they should *insist* on it in prolonged conflicts because such criteria make negotiation less likely to be a contest of wills and more likely to be settled upon principle instead of pressure. This is an egalitarian approach in that much of the battle for dominance is removed from the negotiation process. For example, many people use the *Bluebook* to determine a fair price for used cars. You may want $5,000 for

your 10-year-old Nissan Sentra, and your buyer may want to pay only $100. However, if both of you agree that the *Bluebook* is an appropriate standard and it indicates that a fair price is $1,500 to $2,000, depending on model and condition, this narrows the negotiating range between you and makes reaching agreement more likely.

In another example, the United Way organization of a major midwestern city nearly disintegrated as a result of arguments over which agencies should receive money. Finally, the *ad hoc* committee established a set of cost accounting procedures enabling each agency to determine how many people could be served for what amount. These procedures then served as relatively objective criteria for United Way to use in determining which agencies to fund.

Sometimes, despite a group's best intentions, even principled negotiation fails to bring about consensus, or a group is operating under a time deadline that forces members to use other methods.

When Negotiation Fails: Alternative Procedures

Settlements derived through negotiation by the group itself are preferable to solutions imposed by someone else because they tend to be more acceptable to all members. The first two of the four alternatives presented in the following section involve the group in breaking a deadlock. However, sometimes a group simply is not able to break a deadlock. In that case, when a decision *must* be made, the leader has the two remaining options.

Mediation by the Leader If a seemingly irreconcilable conflict emerges over goals or alternatives, the leader might suggest the following procedure, which is an abbreviated form of that used by professional mediators for apparently deadlocked negotiations between a union and management. The procedure represents a last-chance group attempt to arrive at an acceptable decision without resorting to third-party arbitration. If this procedure fails, other alternative procedures can be taken to resolve the conflict issue without producing consensus. Two-sided conflict is assumed for simplicity.

1. Presentation of alternatives.
   a. A proponent of side 1 presents exactly what the subgroup wants or believes and why. Other members supporting the position may add clarifying statements, arguments, evidence, and claims; but proponents of side 2 can say nothing.
   b. Side 2 can now ask for clarification, restatements, explanations, or supporting evidence, but may not disagree, argue, or propose any other alternative.
   c. A spokesperson for side 2 is now required to explain side 1's position to the complete satisfaction of all other group members, both

FIGURE 12.4
Example of a chart
of pros and cons

How might accidents be reduced on National Ave?
Construct an overpass

Pro	Con
Would eliminate accidents, if used	Would be expensive
Would not impede traffic flow	Students might not use it (inconvenience)
Would not take long to complete (compared to underground tunnel)	People might throw things at cars below

FIGURE 12.4
Example of a chart of pros and cons

side 1 and side 2. (Note the similarity to active listening presented in Chapter 2.) Only when this person has restated side 1's proposal and supporting arguments to everyone's satisfaction is the group ready to advance to the next step.

　　d. Side 2's position is now presented by a spokesperson. Exactly the same procedural rules apply as were used during presentation and clarification of side 1's position.

2. Charting alternatives.

　　a. The group leader now writes both positions on a chalkboard or large poster and underneath lists pros (benefits, advantages) claimed by its proponents and evidence advanced in its support. Under the heading "cons" the leader should list any disadvantages, possible harmful effects, or evidence advanced against the alternative. An example of such a chart is shown in Figure 12.4.

　　b. When all positions have been charted, the group may want to see whether there is unanimity about any of the statements on the chart. What, if anything, do members agree upon?

3. Search for creative alternatives.

　　a. The leader reviews all elements of common ground shared by all group members, such as shared interest in solving the problem, shared history of the group, and so forth, then urges group members to seek a win–win resolution, an alternative that all could accept. The leader may propose such a solution, or

　　b. The leader asks members to compromise and create an alternative that meets the minimum requirements of both sides.

4. Resolution occurs when and if a consensus or compromise alternative is adopted.

　　If this procedure is successful, some time should be spent by group members discussing the procedure itself, how they feel about the group and each of the other members, and how the group can manage future conflicts. Generally, when the previously described procedure is followed out of a sincere desire to resolve the conflict, the group will find at least a compromise and will develop increased cohesiveness and team spirit. Lacking a consensus or compromise, other procedures will be needed to reach a decision.

Voting   *Voting* is one such alternative procedure. Naturally, some members are bound to dislike the outcome, but voting may be a necessary step in overcoming an impasse. You may recall the example presented earlier of a faculty subcommittee's presenting a sweeping proposal to the full faculty committee, only to be met with dismay instead of enthusiasm. After repeated attempts to develop an integrative solution failed, the committee took a vote to decide the issue. One danger with voting is that the group may arrive at premature closure on an issue. Be especially careful, if this is the option you select, that the group really is deadlocked.

Forcing   Another option is *forcing*. Here, the leader breaks the deadlock and decides on behalf of the group. For example, in the U.S. Senate the presiding officer can break a tie. As with voting, several members are likely to be disappointed, but in instances in which an outside group, parent organization, or legitimate authority demands a report or when the group faces a deadline, a leader may have little choice.

Third-Party Arbitration   *Third-party arbitration* occurs when the group brings in an outside negotiator to resolve its differences. This typically happens with joint labor–management disputes and some court-related cases. Arbitrators often have the power to resolve issues any way they please, from deciding entirely in favor of one party to splitting the difference between them. Sometimes, just the threat of bringing in a third-party arbitrator is enough to force conflict participants to negotiate with each other in good faith. Usually, all parties to the conflict end up feeling dissatisfied. Thus, third-party arbitration should be proposed only when the leader believes the group has reached an impasse and the cost of continuing the conflict, including resentment and the possibility of destroying the group, will exceed the cost of arbitration. Of course, group members must agree to such a resolution procedure.

Sometimes, no resolution about a group's issue is possible, but that does not automatically create a hopeless situation. Even when members cannot agree on basic values or goals, they often can find some areas in which they do agree, as with the *Common Ground approaches* we now discuss.

Common Ground Approaches

Common Ground projects have sprung up all over the country.[59] Their purpose is to seek alternative ways to ease tensions surrounding highly contentious and divisive public issues (e.g., abortion, affirmative action, animal testing, bio-genetics, bilingual education, immigration). A unique characteristic of these efforts is their common goal: They do not seek to solve the issue or mediate a compromise. Rather, they attempt to create a safe place for dialogue to occur between deeply divided individuals in the hope of finding common ground, thereby easing tensions and perhaps reducing violence. In addition, they attempt to discover and use areas of genuinely shared values between these individuals constructively, something often hidden in contentious debate. **Common Ground dialogue** is a process of constructively managing socially divisive conflict.[60] The principles guiding Common Ground dialogue are similar to the ones for Public Dialogue (see Chapter 5).

You will notice that Common Ground small groups, in their attempt to manage their conflict, are different from those we have focused on in this chapter. We have dealt with groups whose members must manage conflict in their attempts to select an effective solution to their problem. Common Ground groups offer an interesting way to step back and look at a couple of different kinds of group dynamics. First, they are an example of how socially divisive conflict between groups can be managed. Second, they offer a look at special kinds of small groups—ones whose members, representing larger groups and constituencies, are placed in guided conversations with each other. Third, the process used to facilitate dialogue between these small groups shows how stalemates can be broken.

Common Ground groups are created with the sole purpose of finding a way to bridge highly divisive viewpoints that can result in violence. So these group members enter their groups already knowing they do not agree and their purpose is not to solve their differences or mediate a compromise. All the above procedures for managing failed negotiation assume a goal of resolution; Common Ground dialogue does not. Yet you will see some, if not all, of the same ethical principles in the rules guiding Common Ground dialogue.

Chasin and Herzig have described several behavioral patterns that occur when individuals get caught up in chronic conflict or stalemated controversy.[61] Often those on one side will not listen to those on the other side; individuals become entrenched in their positions. Questions that one side asks the other side clearly have ulterior motives. Members of either side tend to see the members of the other side as all alike. This happens in part because, when confronted, people do minimize their internal differences to appear "together" on the issue. Members of both sides tend to blame the other side for the problem, refuse to see their role in the problem, mind-read the other side, and remain closed-minded about the other side. Attempts by either side to begin a process of conciliation are perceived as propaganda ploys. Finally, members of both sides believe there is value in sticking with the struggle in spite of outsider efforts to break the deadlock. You will see in the following rules of Common Ground dialogue attempts to overcome these behavioral patterns in the pursuit of common ground.

The following is one kind of Common Ground dialogue model applied to the topic of abortion. You will see that the process is far more involved than

---

Common Ground Dialogue

A process of constructively managing divisive conflict, in which the participants are unlikely ever to agree, by focusing on the goals and values they can share and agree to.

you might have expected. This model is comprised of a total of nine steps.[62] Facilitators ensure that both sides of the issue are equally represented and that the sessions are held on neutral ground.

Recruitment of Participants

1. Potential participants are identified through informal networks and activist publications, after which Common Ground coordinators make telephone invitations. During these conversations, potential participants are filled in on the Common Ground procedures and answer questions.

2. Follow-up letters are sent to those wishing to participate. The letter details the kind of dialogue that will be facilitated and includes a chart of the dialogue rules. This chart explains the difference between dialogue and debate. Recruits are also given questions to think about before the meeting.

Premeeting Activity

3. Prior to the actual Common Ground dialogue session, participants get acquainted at an informal dinner. They may *not* talk about abortion and may share whatever they wish about themselves as long as they do not reveal which side of the abortion issue they are on. You can see here that the purpose of this step is to help these individuals see each other as *people,* not positions. Sometimes they are also asked to fill out questionnaires the way they think someone from the other side would complete them.

Establishing the Ground Rules for the Dialogue

4. Participants are assigned seats next to someone on the other side of the issue. They are then reintroduced to the dialogue rules and they are asked verbally to agree to them. They must maintain confidentiality, avoid interrupting each other, use respectful speech (e.g., "pro-choice" not "antilife"), and give each member the right to "pass" if they do not want to respond to a question or comment.

5. The facilitators share with the group their observations of the informal dinner interaction. They point out how much members of each side are in fact more different from each other than the other side assumed.

Rules during the Dialogue

6. Three questions are asked of each member. After a question is read, each member responds in order while everyone else remains attentive and silent. The questions invite members to share a personal experience related to abortion, give what they believe to be the heart of the matter, and identify any gray areas in the abortion issue.

7. Once all three questions are processed, participants are encouraged to ask questions of each other. Participants are encouraged to ask genuine questions of curiosity, not rhetorical ones with hidden agendas. They are

reminded not to attempt to persuade, but to focus on the member present. "They" and "them" are discouraged so that they do not act as representatives of one side. Active listening is facilitated during discussion.

8. When the dialogue begins to wind down, the facilitators move to end the session. They ask two questions in the same format as the three in step 6. Each member is asked to reflect on what she or he did or didn't do to make the dialogue go as it did. And members are asked to share parting thoughts.

Follow-Up

9. A couple of weeks later, participants are telephoned. They are asked to offer any suggestions for improving the model and how they have taken and will take their experience into their daily lives.

Common Ground dialogue models such as this one are another way to manage failed negotiations and, in this case, chronic conflict between groups. This model outlines only the general procedures and does not begin to touch on the many rules that guide the actual dialogue. Each step, when applied in actual dialogue, involves extensive mediation by facilitators so that participants can "hear" each other and safely learn where they have common ground. Then, this discovery is used to promote more positive outcomes and possible joint projects by the participants (e.g., reducing teen pregnancy, funding and supporting adoption as a choice) while allowing them to "agree to disagree."

Recap: A Quick Review

Sometimes resolution of conflict within a group or between groups simply does not occur. When negotiation fails, there are alternatives.

1. The group leader can step in and with structured mediation try to show group members how they can select an alternative through compromise. If a stalemate still ensues, members are left with other alternatives.

2. When integrative solutions are not found after repeated attempts, then members can vote. Although not the best way to break a stalemate, it may be the only way to move on.

3. The group leader can step in and force an alternative by making the decision for the group.

4. Third-party arbitrators can be brought in to select an alternative. These individuals are brought in when the leader and the group believe that all else has failed.

5. Common Ground approaches are a unique way to manage socially divisive conflict between groups. Small groups drawn from members of the larger ones are created and then brought together. Facilitators direct dialogue between the smaller groups in an effort not to resolve the conflict but to promote a conversation between them in the hope of discovering a common ground.

QUESTIONS FOR REVIEW

 *Go to self-quizzes on the Online Learning Center at **mbhe.com/galanes12** to test your knowledge of the chapter concepts*

Lori, Tony, Kevin, Diedre, and Chris worked through a lot of conflict to reach their goal of selecting their university's speaker series.

1. How can you apply the definition of conflict to their case? How was it expressed? How were they interdependent with each other? What were the scarce rewards and incompatible goals? Who is interfering with whom?

2. Who appear to be the innovative deviants? How could their conversation change to show better innovative deviance?

3. What are the substantive and affective conflicts between them? How are they interrelated?

4. How do their conflict styles clash? What are the patterns of their tactics? What kinds of consequences occur in light of these patterns?

5. How could each member better follow the ethical principles for disagreement?

6. How could you advise them to redirect their confrontational efforts along more principled negotiation?

7. If their negotiation failed to produce a speaker list, which alternative would be best to select in an effort to break their stalemate? Why?

KEY TERMS

 *Test your knowledge of these key terms by visiting the Online Learning Center Web site at **mbhe.com/galanes12***

Accommodation	Competition	Inequity conflict
Affective conflict	Compromise	Integrative approach
Avoidance	Conflict	Principled negotiation
Collaboration	Deviate	Procedural conflict
Common Ground dialogue	Distributive approach	Substantive conflict

BIBLIOGRAPHY

Cathcart, Robert S., Larry A. Samovar, and Linda D. Henman. *Small Group Communication: Theory and Practice.* 7th ed. Dubuque, IA: Brown & Benchmark, 1996, Section 4.

Fisher, Roger, and William Ury. *Getting to Yes: Negotiating Agreement Without Giving In.* New York: Penguin Books, 1983.

Hocker, Joyce L., and William W. Wilmot. *Interpersonal Conflict.* 3rd ed. Dubuque, IA: Wm. C. Brown, 1991.

Pearce, W. Barnett, and Kimberly A. Pearce. "Extending the Theory of the Coordinated Management of Meaning (CMM) through a Community Dialogue Process," *Communication Theory,* 10 (2000): 405–23.

Putnam, Linda L. "Conflict in Group Decision Making." In *Communication and Group Decision Making.* Randy Y. Hirokawa and Marshall Scott Poole, eds. Beverly Hills, CA: Sage 1986, 175–97.

NOTES

1. Judith Martin and Thomas K. Nakayama, *Experiencing Intercultural Communication: An Introduction* (Boston: McGraw Hill, 2001): 171.

2. Carolyn J. Wood, "Challenging the Assumptions Underlying the Use of Participatory Decision-Making Strategies: A Longitudinal Case Study," *Small Group Behavior* 20 (1989): 428–48.

3. Victor D. Wall, Jr., Gloria J. Galanes, and Susan B. Love, "Small, Task-Oriented Groups: Conflict, Conflict Management, Satisfaction, and Decision Quality," *Small Group Behavior* 18 (1987): 31–55.

4. Kathleen M. O'Connor, Deborah H. Gruenfeld, and Joseph E. McGrath, "The Experience and Effects of Conflict in Continuing Work Groups," *Small Group Research* 24 (August 1993): 362–82.

5. M. R. Shakun, "Formalizing Conflict Resolution in Policy-Making," *International Journal of General Systems* 7 (1981): 207–15.

6. Gordon L. Lippett, "Managing Conflict in Today's Organization," *Training and Development Journal* 36 (1982): 67–75.

7. Joyce L. Hocker and William W. Wilmot, *Interpersonal Conflict,* 3rd ed. (Dubuque, IA: Wm. C. Brown, 1991): 12.

8. Sally M. Vogl-Bauer, "Examining Stress in Small Groups," in *Small Group Communication: Theory and Practice,* 7th ed., eds. Robert Cathcart, Larry Samovar, and Linda Henman (Madison, WI: Brown & Benchmark, 1996): 195–97.

9. Morton Deutsch, "Conflicts: Productive and Destructive," *Journal of Social Issues* 25 (1969): 7–41; Kenneth W. Thomas, "Conflict and Conflict Management," in *Handbook of Industrial and Organizational Psychology,* ed. M. Dunnette (Chicago: Rand McNally, 1976): 890–934; Louis B. Pondy, "Organizational Conflict: Concepts and Models," *Administrative Science Quarterly* 12 (1976): 296–320; Brent D. Ruben, "Communication and Conflict: A System-Theoretic Perspective," *Quarterly Journal of Speech* 64 (1978): 202–12; J. Guetzkow and J. Gyr, "An Analysis of Conflict in Decision-Making Groups," *Human Relations* 7 (1954): 367–82;

and E. P. Torrance, "Group Decision-Making and Disagreement," *Social Forces* 35 (1957): 314–18.

10. Karl Smith, David W. Johnson, and Roger T. Johnson, "Can Conflict Be Constructive? Controversy versus Concurrence Seeking in Learning Groups," *Journal of Educational Psychology* 73 (1981): 654–63.

11. Charles R. Franz and K. Gregory Jin, "The Structure of Group Conflict in a Collaborative Work Group during Information Systems Development," *Journal of Applied Communication Research* 23 (May 1995): 108–27.

12. Ibid.

13. Sue D. Pendell, "Deviance and Conflict in Small Group Decision Making: An Exploratory Study," *Small Group Behavior* 21 (1990): 393–403.

14. Svenn Lindskold and Gyuseog Han, "Group Resistance to Influence by a Conciliatory Member," *Small Group Behavior* 19 (1988): 19–34.

15. Carl L. Thameling and Patricia H. Andrews, "Majority Responses to Opinion Deviates: A Communicative Analysis," *Small Group Research* 23 (1992): 475–502.

16. Kristin B. Valentine and B. Aubrey Fisher, "An Interaction Analysis of Verbal Innovative Deviance in Small Groups," *Speech Monographs* 41 (1974): 413–20.

17. Mark K. Covey, "The Relationship between Social Skill and Conflict Resolution Tactics" (Paper presented at the annual convention of the Rocky Mountain Psychological Association, Snowbird, Utah, 1983).

18. Rick Garlick and Paul A. Mongeau, "Argument Quality and Group Member Status as Determinants of Attitudinal Minority Influence," *Western Journal of Communication* 57 (Summer 1993): 289–308.

19. Renee Meyers, Dale Brashers, and Jennifer Hanner, "Majority-Minority Influence: Identifying Argumentative Patterns and Predicting Argument-Outcome Links," *Journal of Communication* 50 (2000): 3–30.

20. Guetzkow and Gyr, "An Analysis of Conflict," 367–82.

21. Ibid.

22. Roger C. Pace, "Personalized and Depersonalized Conflict in Small Group Discussions: An Examination of Differentiation," *Small Group Research* 21 (1990): 79–96.

23. Roger Fisher and Scott Brown, *Getting Together: Building a Relationship That Gets to Yes* (Boston: Houghton-Mifflin, 1988): 16–23.

24. Linda L. Putnam, "Conflict in Group Decision Making," in *Communication and Group Decision Making,* eds. Randy Y. Hirokawa and Marshall Scott Poole (Beverly Hills, CA: Sage, 1986): 175–96.

25. Elizabeth Hobman, Prashant Bordia, Bernd Irmer, and Artemis Chang, "The Expression of Conflict in Computer-Mediated and Face-to-Face Groups," *Small Group Research* 33 (2002): 439–65.

26. Ibid.

27. Ibid.

28. Ibid.

29. Victor D. Wall, Jr., and Linda L. Nolan, "Small Group Conflict: A Look at Equity, Satisfaction, and Styles of Conflict Management," *Small Group Behavior* 18 (1987): 188–211.

30. Renee Meyers and Dale Brashers, "Influence Processes in Group Interaction," in *The Handbook of Group Communication Theory & Research,* ed. Lawrence Frey (Thousand Oaks: CA, 1999): 298.

31. Tim Kuhn and Marshall Scott Poole, "Do Conflict Management Styles Affect Group Decision Making?: Evidence from a Longitudinal Field Study," *Human Communication Research* 26 (2000): 558–90.

32. Vidar Schie and Jorn K. Rognes, "Small Group Negotiation: When Members Differ in Motivational Orientation," *Small Group Research* 36 (June 2005): 289–320.

33. R. H. Kilmann and K. Thomas, "Developing a Forced-Choice Measure of Conflict-Handling Behavior: The MODE Instrument," *Educational and Psychological Measurement* 37 (1977): 309–25.

34. Hal Witteman, "Analyzing Interpersonal Conflict: Nature of Awareness, Type of Initiating Event, Situational Perceptions, and Management Styles," *Western Journal of Communication* 56 (Summer 1992): 248–80.

35. Larry Erbert, "Conflict Management: Styles, Strategies, and Tactics," in *Small Group Communication: Theory and Practice,* 7th ed., eds. Robert Cathcart, Larry Samovar, and Linda Henman (Madison, WI: Brown & Benchmark, 1996): 213.

36. Daniel J. Canary and Brian H. Spitzberg, "Appropriateness and Effectiveness Perceptions of Conflict Strategies," *Human Communication Research* 14 (1987): 93–118.

37. Martin and Nakayama, *Experiencing Intercultural Communication,* 173–74.

38. Michael A. Gross, Laura K. Guerrero, and Jess K. Alberts, "Perceptions of Conflict Strategies and Communication Competence in Task-Oriented Dyads," *Journal of Applied Communication Research* 32 (August 2004): 249–270.

39. Ibid.

40. Meyers and Brashers, "Influence Processes in Group Interaction," 297.

41. Hal Witteman, "Group Member Satisfaction: A Conflict-Related Account," *Small Group Behavior* 22 (1991): 24–58.

42. William Wilmot and Joyce Hocker, *Interpersonal Conflict,* 5th ed. (Boston: McGraw Hill, 1998): 118.

43. Ibid., 136.

44. Ibid., 123.

45. Ibid., 139.

46. Ibid., 139.

47. Ibid., 134.

48. Gary L. Kreps, *Organizational Communication,* 2nd ed. (New York: Longman, 1990): 193.

49. Fisher and Brown, *Getting Together.*

50. Gloria J. Galanes, "The Effect of Conflict Expression Styles on Quality of Outcome and Satisfaction in Small, Task-Oriented Groups" (Unpublished doctoral dissertation, Ohio State University, 1985).

51. Kreps, *Organizational Communication.*

52. Steven M. Alderton and Lawrence R. Frey, "Argumentation in Small Group Decision-Making," in *Communication and Group Decision Making,* eds. Randy Y. Hirokawa and Marshall Scott Poole (Beverly Hills, CA: Sage, 1986): 157–73.

53. Roger Fisher and William Ury, *Getting to Yes: Negotiating Agreement Without Giving In* (Boston: Houghton-Mifflin, 1981; Penguin Books, 1983).

54. Frank Tutzauer and Michael E. Roloff, "Communicative Processes Leading to Integrative Agreements," *Communication Research* 15 (1988): 360–80.

55. Fisher and Ury, *Getting to Yes.*

56. Ichiro Innami, "The Quality of Group Decisions, Group Verbal Behavior, and Intervention," *Organizational Behavior and Human Decision Processes* 60 (December 1994): 409–30.

57. Garlick and Mongeau, "Argument Quality and Group Member Status."

58. A version of the discussion about this issue is depicted on the ancillary videotape, *Communicating Effectively in Small Groups* (Dubuque, IA: Wm. C. Brown, 1991). Segment 3 depicts an ineffective discussion, and segment 4 shows an effective discussion where this major issue of bookstore hours is resolved.

59. The information in this section is taken from Trophy R. Olson, "'Common Ground' Discourse as a Way to Mediate in the Abortion Issue: An Interpretive Analysis" (Unpublished master's thesis, California State University, Fresno, 1997).

60. S. Roth, L. Chasin, R. Chasin, C. Becker, and M. Herzig, "From Debate to Dialogue: A Facilitating Role for Family Therapists in the Public Forum," *Dulwich Centre Newsletter* 2 (1992): 41–48.

61. R. Chasin and M. Herzig, "Creating Systematic Interventions for the Sociopolitical Arena," in *The Global Family Therapist: Integrating the Personal, Professional and Political*, eds. B. Bernina-Gould and D. Hillboe DeMuth (Needham, MA: Allyn & Bacon, 1993): 32–69.

62. This is the Public Conversations Project model. See Olson, "'Common Ground' Discourse," 47–52.

Serving as Designated Leader

CENTRAL MESSAGE

A designated leader must perform several administrative, structuring, and developmental activities for the group. Democratic designated leaders encourage members to perform leadership functions for their groups while they serve as completers for functions not supplied by the members.

STUDY OBJECTIVES

As a result of studying chapter 13 you should be able to:

1. Describe the "leader as completer" concept that group-centered, democratic leaders employ and explain its relationship to the philosophy of distributed leadership.

2. Name the three major types of services expected of designated small group leaders and describe specific ways of providing them.

3. Produce written messages essential to the work of small secondary groups, including meeting notices and agendas, minutes, and reports to other groups and organizations.

4. Describe the ethical principles that guide group leaders.

Maureen, an active community volunteer in Springfield, Missouri, was asked by the local Community Foundation to chair a task force charged with producing a community report card. Twenty-seven committee members, who represented numerous community agencies and organizations such as the local health department, the public schools, the city's transportation department, and so forth, had already been selected. Maureen's task was to organize the work of this large group so that, at the end of the eight months of the task force's work, she would have the relevant information to evaluate how the community stacked up in 11 different areas, including business, transportation, housing, economic conditions, education, and recreation. The final professionally designed and printed report would be widely distributed throughout the community by the local organizations that sponsored it: Community Foundation, Chamber of Commerce, United Way, Library System, and Junior League. This high-visibility, high-stakes project had to satisfy a lot of individuals and agencies.

The large group decided to split into 11 subcommittees, each focusing on a different area of the report. The subcommittees were encouraged to add community members with relevant expertise to their ranks; for example, the education committee added the school district's statistician, who supplied (and explained) up-to-date figures about the district's performance. The entire group met monthly and the subcommittees met more frequently to gather information, compare Springfield's performance with other cities, explain the data so that normal people could understand it, and meet the writing deadlines. Maureen faced several leadership challenges: managing the discussion of a group of 27 people, keeping track of the work of the subcommittees and making sure each subcommittee knew what the others were doing, ensuring that the information the subcommittees supplied was understandable and could be defended, and promoting buy-in, so that each committee member accepted the format of the report and the information it contained. Her know-how as a group leader made this a positive experience; each member contributed to the final product and the Community Report Card was released on time, to widespread praise.

Throughout this text, you have been presented with theories, concepts, and advice regarding various elements of the group discussion process. In this chapter, we pull together information to help you become the best group leader you can be:

> [T]he right person in a leadership role can add tremendous value to any collective effort, even to the point of sparking the outcome with an intangible kind of magic.[1]

We intend this chapter to be a type of "leader's manual" for the time when you find yourself in the leader's role or are asked to evaluate a group's leadership. We first discuss general principles guiding the leader's relationship to the group as a whole, then describe the three major types of duties that leaders are expected to perform for small groups in the United States, and conclude with ethical principles leaders should follow. Remember our theme: It is appropriate for *all* group members, not just the leader, to perform leadership services for the group, but the leader has the unique responsibility to make sure the group receives the services it needs.

Group-Centered, Democratic Leadership

To reiterate a major theme from Chapter 9, we believe that leadership should be tailored to fit the specific situation facing the group. In some situations, such as with members who are inexperienced or unwilling, more controlling forms of leadership are appropriate, at least initially. In other situations, with highly experienced and capable members, a designated leader may not even be necessary. However, most situations will fall between those two extremes.

Even so, according to the standards and values of American culture and our political foundations, democratic leadership is ideal; it recognizes the equality of all members and encourages member participation in group decisions. We stress that this is the *ideal*. In group situations that do not seem to call for democratic leadership, we believe the leader should exert the *least* amount of control necessary to help the group achieve its goal.

It may appear that we contradict ourselves when we say, "Be the type of leader a group needs, but be democratic." What we mean is that a leader should first recognize the group's current reality and serve the group as needed, but work to move the group toward the ideal. In an ideal group, members are committed, responsible, and mature; and leadership services are distributed among all members so that any person could serve well as the designated leader.

Leader as Completer

Where does the leader fit when group members assume leadership duties for the group? The metaphor we suggest is that the members are the bricks and the leader is the mortar that binds them together, as shown in Figure 13.1. The bricks provide the support and substance of the group, but the mortar allows the whole group to hold its shape—completes the structure, so to speak. For example, as leader of the Community Report Card task force, Maureen linked the subcommittees together by typing up summaries of task force discussions and decisions and distributing them right away so that everyone could be on the same page. This concept of the **leader as completer,** as articulated by Schutz, suggests that "the best a leader can do is to observe what functions are not being performed by a segment of the group and enable this part to accomplish them" or, if necessary, perform them.[2] Ellis's study of leadership patterns confirmed this notion of stewardship.[3] His work suggests that leaders are not distinguished from other members by their performance of a set of specific behaviors. Instead, leaders vary their communication to each member, whereas the other members' communication behavior is consistent no matter whom they address.

Leader as Completer

A leader who determines which functions or behaviors a group most needs to perform best, then supplies them or encourages others to do so.

FIGURE 13.1
The leader as
"completer" of
the group

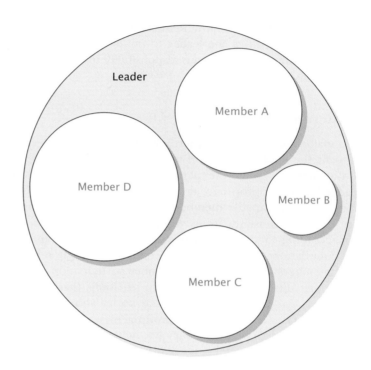

The model we propose promotes *distributed leadership,* in which every member of the group is ultimately responsible for the group. This model makes several demands on *both* the leader and the members. Members should be competent enough both to know what the group needs at any given time and to meet that need by saying and doing the right thing. For example, if the group has digressed too long, a member can, and *should,* jump in with something like: "I think we've gotten offtrack. Can we get back to the topic?" The leader, too, should be competent enough to recognize the need and be able to jump in *if someone else in the group has not already provided the needed leadership behavior.* This means that the leader primarily monitors the group's *process,* with the principal responsibility for maintaining a long-range perspective on the group's progress.

Responsibilities and Techniques of Discussion Leaders and Chairs

Being leader of a group can be time consuming, but if the group has developed along the democratic lines suggested, the tasks will be shared. For example, several members volunteered to pick up tasks that Maureen was ultimately responsible for. One member took care of room arrangements, making sure that the room was booked, the tables were arranged in a large rectangle, and that coffee and water were ready when members came in. Another member made copies of materials to be distributed at the meeting. Still another member served as liaison between the group and one of its major sponsors, the Community Foundation. Ideally, every member can assume responsibility to supply whatever leadership services appear to be needed at any given time—the essence of distributed leadership.

Recap: A Quick Guide

Group leaders fulfill a unique role, but the leader and members are jointly responsible for how well their groups perform.

1. The ideal form of leadership for groups in the United States is group-centered democratic leadership that recognizes all members as equals and encourages member participation in group decisions. Although a given group may initially need more control by the leader, we encourage group leaders to provide the least amount of control needed so that members can eventually assume group leadership functions.

2. Distributed leadership explicitly acknowledges that members should use their particular abilities and interests to help the group succeed; leadership duties and functions are *appropriately* distributed throughout the group.

3. Even though all members can and should provide leadership services to the group, the leader is uniquely a "completer," filling in the functions not being performed by others.

4. Effective leaders are able to adjust their behavior depending on what the group needs, and they consider such things as the group's purpose and goals, expectations of members, skills and maturity of members, and member commitment to the group's task in deciding how to adjust their own behavior.

In Chapter 9 we presented information about contingencies that may affect the degree of control appropriately assumed by the designated leader. Contingency theory, which we support, requires astute leaders to analyze the group's situation and members' needs. Leaders, to function well as completers, must be flexible enough to adjust their behavior to the needs of the group. How does the leader know what to adjust? Attending to the following contingencies can help you optimize your leadership style:

1. **Group purpose and goals.**
   Learning, personal growth, and value-sharing groups need far less structure and control than secondary groups charged with recommending solutions to complex problems. In addition, specific procedures (brainstorming, buzz group procedures, problem census, nominal group technique, etc.) require considerable procedural control.

2. **Member expectations.**

   A designated leader should initially conform to what members expect of the role, but this can later be changed through explicit discussion of the leader's job and through development of the members' own leadership skills. As mentioned in Chapter 5, expectations are largely determined by culture.

3. **Member skills and maturity.**

   As Hersey and Blanchard reported, members who are used to working together, who understand the task, and who are effective communicators need less leader control than inexperienced members or newly formed groups.[4]

4. **Member involvement in the group's task.**

   When the task is important to members personally, they may resist tight procedural control by a leader. For example, at the first Community Report Card meeting, Maureen came with a well-thought-out agenda for the meeting and offered a logical plan for structuring the group's work on the project. However, within about two minutes, it became clear that the members were unhappy about how a previous, similar report had been handled, and they needed to vent. They felt they hadn't been given the chance for enough input in shaping that prior report. Maureen was experienced enough to ditch her agenda and work plan so that the group could develop its own.

5. **The leader's skill and experience.**

   Democratic leadership calls for skills in listening, organizing, summarizing, and timing that take a long time to develop. Don't forget that the other group members can—and should—be invited to serve as resources.

6. **The time factor.**

   If a decision must be made in a hurry, a group will welcome strict control of its procedures. When time is not limited, less leader control is needed.

What makes a good group leader? Two recent studies have addressed that question. LaFasto and Larson used data collected for over 20 years to identify what team members say excellent leaders do,[5] and Galanes interviewed outstanding team leaders to discover what they thought was important.[6] Their findings were highly consistent and are synthesized here.

- **First,** good leaders define the group's goal clearly and keep it alive.
- **Second,** they build the team by fostering a collaborative climate in which members feel safe to share and to disagree.
- **Third,** they build confidence in their members by making sure the group experiences success, assigning important responsibilities to members, and ensuring that the team is well educated about the team's issues.

- **Fourth,** they monitor and manage the team's interaction by checking participation levels, building consensus, and supporting critical thinking.

- **Fifth,** they structure the group's task in several ways. They keep in mind the overall picture of where the group needs to go and communicate this and the group's progress to the members. They keep members focused on the task, remove roadblocks that interfere, use members' time well, and don't let the group become boged down with too many priorities.

- **Sixth,** they manage the group's performance so that expectations are clear and members receive constructive feedback in meeting them.

- **Finally,** they exhibit a number of personal characteristics that inspire confidence and loyalty. For instance, they demonstrate credibility by being knowledgeable about the group's task; use an open, inviting communication style; and are good listeners.

These functions fall into three broad categories of service that you'll be expected to perform as designated leader: administrative duties, discussion coordination, and group development. The advice we give about how to supply these services is based on research findings and the democratic philosophy we espouse. Ideally, each organization has a leader's manual describing the specific duties and responsibilities, so that leaders don't have to guess what they are supposed to do.

Administrative Duties

Leaders handle numerous administrative duties; the most important ones are assembling the team, planning for meetings, following up on meetings, maintaining liaison with other groups, and managing the group's written communication.

Assembling the Group   Even before the group has its first meeting, the leader (or organizational member to whom the group reports) has spent time thinking about who will be in the group and what the group will do.[7]

1. **Select group members carefully.**
   Group leaders, including Maureen, don't always have the luxury of picking the group members, but when they do, effective leaders carefully consider who should be part of the group. Think through what skills, expertise, and personal characteristics are needed for the group's particular task; then select just the people you need and no more! You want motivated, positive people who will contribute. If others need to know what's happening with the group, you can make sure they receive information from the group, but they don't necessarily need to be part of

the group itself. For example, Maureen's group of 27 people would have been double that size if every person added to the subcommittees had been invited to attend the overall group meetings; these members' inclusion on the large committee wasn't necessary to the group's overall work.

2. **Develop a group charter.**

   A **group charter** is a written document that describes the purpose of the group, its specific charge, its area of freedom, its membership, what output the group must produce, and other key information such as deadlines. This may be a formal document approved by the parent organization or an informal memo circulated at the first meeting, but having a group charter helps keep all members on the same page. Maureen's committee spent the first four meetings developing the committee's structure, procedures, and work plan. Once that was done, the subcommittees were able to meet on their own with clarity about their tasks.

3. **Make sure members commit to the group's goals.**

   You may have to recruit group members by personally explaining the purpose of the group and why you want them to be part of it. It's all right to have members who are skeptical and may need to be convinced, but you are better off without a potential member who cannot commit to the group's goals.

Planning for Meetings   Once you've selected the group, you will start to hold meetings. To use everyone's time well, make sure that you have your pre-work finished prior to each meeting. The following checklist can guide your planning:

1. **Define the purpose of the meeting.**

   First, decide whether you need a meeting. Do *not* call a meeting if you can get the job done using other communication avenues (telephone, fax, e-mail, memo), when there isn't time for participants to prepare adequately, when one or more essential people cannot participate, or when the issues are personal and better handled privately.[8]

   Define the purpose of the meeting clearly and formulate *specific* outcomes to be achieved. "To talk about our report" is *not* adequately defined, but "To review the Transportation Subcommittee's draft and make recommendations for change" is defined.

2. **Establish starting and ending times for the meeting.**

   People are busy; respect their time by starting and ending a meeting on time. Running overtime will kill member involvement and attendance and is a barrier to operating democratically.[9] Setting an ending time encourages the group to use its time well. If the work cannot be finished, plan additional meetings. The Community Report Card committee had to add three extra meetings to its schedule.

3. **If special resource people are needed for the meeting, advise and prepare them.**

   Small groups frequently need to question specialists with unique knowledge and skills or experience. Such invited resource persons need to know in advance what information to prepare and what to expect. For example, the Mayor's Commission for Children invited the head of the regional Division of Children and Families to present current information about child abuse and neglect rates in Springfield.

4. **Think through the tools you may need for the meeting.**

   There are countless tools you can use to help you accomplish what you want to do in a particular group meeting. We have described several of these throughout this book. For instance, if you need creative solutions, there are several brainstorming variations that are designed just for that purpose. If you need to plan implementation of a complex project, a PERT chart can help you.

5. **Make all necessary physical arrangements.**

   Has the meeting room been reserved? Are handouts, notepads, chalk, charts, and possibly beverages ready? Leaders should *think about* the selection and use of their meeting space. The room should be comfortable, allow members to see and hear one another and any audiovisual materials presented, and be big enough to hold everyone. It also shouldn't be too big, since that can create psychological distance between members.[10]

6. **Have all the appropriate technology you need and make sure it works.**

   How many times have you waited for someone to fix a computer so that a PowerPoint presentation can proceed? If you are leading a virtual team, make sure that members have the technology necessary and also have been trained in how to use it.

7. **Prepare a procedure for evaluating the meeting.**

   Groups should regularly evaluate their meetings, even if the evaluation is brief. This may take the form of an oral postmortem at the end of the meeting or a written evaluation. We described several such instruments in Chapter 7.

8. **Notify members of the purpose or agenda, necessary preparation, and time and place of the meeting.**

   The chair is responsible for seeing that members are notified and given ample opportunity to prepare for a meeting. In large organizations, this duty may be delegated to a staff person, such as professional secretary, but it is still the *responsibility* of the leader. Maureen delegated this duty to the professional secretary at the Community Foundation, who took care of sending meeting reminders and distributing minutes, although Maureen called her to ensure that these would be done.

Following Up on Meetings   Two kinds of follow-up are needed: touching base with group members and making sure the group's reports are getting to the right groups or individuals. Leaders often call or e-mail group members between meetings for a variety of reasons. One important reason is to make sure members are working on their assignments and have all the information and resources they need to complete their individual tasks. For instance, Maureen discovered that the Housing Subcommittee had made almost no progress on its section. She scheduled a meeting with the subcommittee and invited two individuals from an area social service agency who knew the housing situation. Maureen chaired this meeting and tactfully got the group moving forward. She also continued to monitor that subcommittee's work because its members seemed to need more guidance and help than the other people. But leaders also help maintain good social relationships by interacting with members between meetings. You may want to know what a quiet member really felt about a meeting, or whether a member involved in a disagreement needs to vent to someone. Don't underestimate the value of keeping in regular touch with your group.

In addition, a chair often prepares and sends letters, memoranda, formal reports, notices of group decisions, advice prepared by the committee, and so forth, to appropriate people. This includes getting copies of minutes prepared and distributed, but also involves writing formal resolutions, sending updates to key outside groups, or carrying out whatever decisions for action the group has made. Although the group decides *what* to do, *who* does it is often the group's designated leader.

Liaison

Communication between or among groups; interfacing; a person who performs the liaison function.

Liaison   A **liaison** serves as spokesperson for the group to other groups or to the parent organization; usually this is the designated leader's job. In most organizations, the chairs of standing committees in an organization coordinate with each other. For instance, many organizations have regular meetings of division managers. Whenever you act as liaison, keep in mind that you represent *your group* rather than yourself.

Occasionally, committee chairs will be interviewed by public media. Try to anticipate this happening so that you can be prepared to answer reporters' questions. The chair's statements should accurately reflect the group's work, findings, and beliefs. If internal controversies arise during discussion, the chair normally does not share these outside the group. As one of our friends put it, "Family business is family business, and the group is a family."

Managing Written Communication for a Group   Written messages and records provide continuity from meeting to meeting; remind members of their assignments; confirm agreements and accomplishments; provide legal documentation of attendance, decisions, and actions; bring absentees up to date; and inform the parent organization and others about what the group is doing. Most committees are required to keep minutes of all meetings and to submit written reports to specified personnel. Even a single-meeting group needs a written record. For example, one of us belonged to a community theater for which the written record of an *ad hoc* personnel review committee provided evidence used in a lawsuit to defend the theater from a former employee's assertion that he was fired arbitrarily. Lacking this record, the theater probably would have lost the suit.

Four categories of written messages that contribute to small group leadership are personal notes, meeting records, meeting notices and agendas, and reports and resolutions. All these written messages (except personal notes) can be circulated to members electronically and made available to the group via the e-mail or virtual space when documents can be stored and accessed on the World Wide Web. In fact, the Web provides an easy, convenient way to make up-to-date documents available instantly to all group members. It is up to the leader to set aside the virtual space where such documents can be stored (or to recruit a techno-savvy volunteer).

Personal Notes.   The typical conference room is pictured with notepads and pencils at each seat because taking notes focuses group members' listening so that they aren't likely to lose sight of the group goal or switch subjects. When you take notes, don't try to record a transcript of the whole discussion. Instead, keep track of the thrust of the discussion by jotting down just a key word or two. Personal notes help you, as leader, summarize discussion when needed, double-check the minutes, and follow up between meetings to ensure that assignments are being completed. Examples of personal notes are provided in Figure 13.2.

Group Records.   All ongoing committees should maintain accurate and comprehensive **minutes** that serve as official summary records of the important content of meetings, especially of decisions made. The leader is responsible for seeing that minutes are recorded, that they are accurate, and that they are distributed to members before the next meeting. That task is often delegated to a secretary or a volunteer from the group. An original copy of all minutes should be kept in a safe place as a permanent record of the group's work.

Minutes help a group function efficiently because they prevent wasted time and unnecessary tension. Without such a written record, members often forget important information, fail to complete assignments, or argue about what was decided. For instance, at one meeting of the Community Report Card group, a member questioned why a particular topic was to be included in one section; he thought it should be included in a different section. Maureen referred to the minutes of the meeting (which he had missed) where this topic was discussed and decided. That satisfied the member (and also reminded him to read the minutes more carefully in the future).

Minutes focus on the content, not the process of discussion. They record all task-oriented information shared during the meeting, all ideas proposed as solutions, all decisions and how they were made (majority, consensus, consent), all assignments, and any plans or procedures for future action. Any handouts distributed at a meeting are attached to the official set of minutes.

Minutes

A written record of every relevant item dealt with during a group meeting, including a record of all decisions.

FIGURE 13.2   A discussion leader's personal notes

February 8, 2006 --- Everyone present

Discussion topic: what topics should we include in our class presentation on group polarization?

Main criteria:

    Judy & Bill --- to get an "A" info must be accurate
    Bart --- has to have practical application
    Bev --- Dr. Brilhart wants innovative presentation
    Everybody should have a part in presenting the topic to the class.

Topics

* *Definition of group polarization (all agreed)*
    Risky shift (Hal says can become a cautious shift w/ cautious members --- this term is outdated)

* *Exercises to demonstrate when group takes risks & when it becomes cautious --- Judy says there's a bunch of these in a book she has*

* *Need to show how this applies in real life.*

* *Decisions Made*
Assignments: Me (applications); Judy & Bill (library research); Hal & Bev (exercises -- w/ Judy's book)

Next meeting --- Wed., February 15

The format and formality of minutes vary widely, depending on the nature of the group and the type of organization. At the formal end, meetings whose work is subject to public scrutiny (e.g., school boards, city councils and other government bodies, task forces, and so forth) have a required format that they must follow. In addition, once members have had a chance to review the minutes of a particular meeting, they must vote to approve them as is or to correct any inaccurate information. Figure 13.3 shows a formal set of minutes from the church board, described in Chapter 4, which was legally required to keep minutes. This particular format makes it easy to see what items were discussed and what actions were taken without combing through a lot of narrative. Figure 13.4 shows an informal set of minutes of a student group organizing a project; its main purpose was to remind members of their assignments and the next meeting. Midway between these two, in terms of formality, are the minutes in Figure 13.5, from another student group preparing to make a formal presentation to its parent organization, the Student Government Association. Whatever form minutes take, they should be distributed to members as soon as possible after the meeting. E-mail makes it easy to do this.

FIGURE 13.3   Example of formal minutes of the church board

Board of Directors Meeting Minutes
April 12, 2006

Present: Bill Prior, Norm Kerris, Gary Sloane, Don Bowles, Sally Schultz (directors): Sunni Prior, Marina Kerris (invited guests); Jane Simmons, church secretary.

Call to order: Opening prayer was given by Sally. Minutes of the April 5 meeting were approved as presented.

Topic	Discussion	Actions/Recommendations
Attendance/ offering	120—Sunday, April 9 Total deposit—$1,552.52 Building fund—$5,858.00	
Founders Sun., May 18	Marina will attempt to get the SMSU Gospel Choir to sing for a 30-minute program. Covered dish supper to follow service. Jody (Hospitality Committee) in charge of setup.	
Adult Sun. School	Roy Hackman will be teaching from "Spiritual Economics" starting April 27.	
Rental of facilities	Ada Cole asked cost of renting sanctuary for a workshop. Discussion centered on cost of utilities/wear and tear.	Norm moved, Don seconded, that we establish a policy of charging $30 per half day for all rentals. Passed.
Circle Suppers	Bill shared information about Circle Supper program; it has been very successful at the Columbia church. Discussion followed, and several names suggested to organize.	Sally moved, Gary seconded, that we ask Jean Ames to coordinate; that we hold them monthly on second Saturday. Passed.
Search Committee	Marina reported we have 10 applications; search committee will telephone interview and ask 3 to come for a full interview.	

Meeting adjourned at 8:30 PM Don gave the closing prayer.

Respectfully submitted,

Sally Schultz

FIGURE 13.4
Example of typical informal minutes from a student group

Thursday, April 6

Assignments for project (by April 14)

    Shawna: Research library theft on Internet

    Tyson and Marie: Interview head librarian

    Nate: Reserve a room and computer for PowerPoint presentation on May 4

Next meeting: Friday, April 14, 7 PM, Nate's house

FIGURE 13.5   **Much more detailed than the previous example, this student group wants to ensure that nothing falls through the cracks.**

Report of Third Meeting of Polarization Instruction Group

Date of Meeting: Tuesday, March 14, 2006
Time and Place: 7:30–9:00 PM in Room 8, Craig Hall
Attendance: Bev Halliday, Inez Salinas, Terrell Washington, Bill Miklas, Judy Hartlieb

Report of Second Meeting
    Judy distributed copies of the report of the second meeting to all members. It was approved. It was decided that Judy would be responsible for recording and distributing reports of each group meeting.

Goals
    A suggested outline for problem solving presented by Terrell was followed. This led to a discussion of group polarization and to determining the actions to be taken involving the group's "problem."
    The group goals were identified as 1) understanding group polarization, 2) conducting a presentation with a class exercise on polarization for the class, and 3) each member being able to write a personal essay about the group experience.

Exercise Portion of Presentation
    After some discussion of the type of exercise to be used in the presentation, it was decided that Inez would be responsible for trying to locate a book with sample exercises that could be considered by the group at the next meeting. Bill will also have primary responsibility for this portion of the presentation and will see that copies of the test are produced and ready for the class. The other group members will individually brainstorm for exercise ideas, and further discussion of these will take place during our class meeting of Tuesday, March 21.
    Criteria for class exercises were discussed. It was concluded that the purpose of the exercise would be to demonstrate the phenomenon of group polarization at work. The exercise would be divided in such a way that each individual in the class would first take it alone and then with a small group, and see what shifts occurred.

Leader and Role
    The group determined that the leader would be responsible for developing agendas and outlines for future meetings and should serve as an overall controller and fill-in or backup person for other group members. Bev was selected by unanimous vote to fill this role as group leader.

Structure of Presentation
    A structure and time schedule of the presentation was decided on:
    5 minutes—Each member of the class takes the exercise individually.
    10 minutes—The class is divided into four groups, with four of our small group members serving as observers. Each group will determine how to solve the exercise problem.
    5 minutes—One member of our group will present a short report on group polarization research to the class. At the same time, the four observers will be finishing their notes regarding what happened in their respective groups.

FIGURE 13.5   contiuned...

> 5 minutes—The four groups will each discuss what occurred in the group. The observer may start the discussion or serve as a guide/reference person, answering questions and giving insight into what happened with polarization in the group.
> 5 minutes—The class as a whole will have the opportunity to share what was observed and experienced within the groups. The observers may again start the discussion and open the floor to any class member's contribution.
>
> *Additional Member Roles*
> Bill agreed to present the five-minute oral report on polarization to the class.
> Terrell will be responsible for arranging meeting places and will serve as a backup to any member who might be absent.
>
> *Adjournment and Next Meeting*
> The meeting adjourned at approximately 9:00 PM Further planning will take place on Tuesday, March 21, during class time.

Meeting Notices and Agendas.   A notice of each meeting should be sent to all members in time to allow them to prepare for the meeting. A **meeting notice** normally includes the who, what, when, where, and why of a meeting prior to the meeting. It should include the purpose of the meeting; specific outcomes to be achieved; the agenda listing all items of business to be taken up; and any relevant facts, reading sources, or other preparation members should make prior to meeting. For the first meeting of any group, the notice should also include a list of all group members.

An **agenda** is a list of the items of business, topics, and other matters in the sequence they will be considered in the meeting. For a continuing group, approval or correction of the previous meeting's minutes is usually the first item of business. Figure 13.6 is an example of a combined meeting notice and agenda.

Meeting Notice

A written message providing the time, place, purpose, and other information relevant to an upcoming meeting.

Agenda

A list of items to be discussed at a group meeting.

Date:	February 14, 2006
To:	Curriculum Committee (Berquist, Bourhis, Galanes, Stovall, Sisco)
From:	Kelly McNeilis, chair
Re:	Next meeting of the Curriculum Committee

The next meeting of the Curriculum Committee will be on Friday, February 24, from 1:00 to 3:00 PM in Craig 320.

AGENDA (by the end of the meeting we must have an answer for each of the following questions):

1. What will be the focus of our departmental assessment (student outcomes, student perceptions, alumni perceptions, or something else)?
2. What areas of the department should be assessed?
3. Whom will we recommend as members of subcommittees to plan assessment procedures for each area decided under #2?

FIGURE 13.6
An example of combined meeting notice and agenda

Ideally, reports to be distributed to members should be meeting notice and agenda. The report might include tables, graphs, duplicated copies of text, lists, and drawings. Likewise, prior to the meeting the report maker needs to prepare visual aids such as charts, diagrams, and graphs. Such a report is mentioned in the minutes by citing it ("see attached") and a copy stapled to the official set of minutes.

Formal Reports and Resolutions.   Many small groups must submit written reports of their work to a parent organization or administrator. Such reports are often the end product of a committe's work and may include findings, criteria, and recommendations. Usually, the liason person submitting the written report also gives a brief oral summary.

The leader submits the report, but the actual writing may be done by one or two members. A draft is circulated to all members, inviting their suggestions for revisions and additions. The group then meets to discuss, amend, and eventually approve the draft report. The final version is signed by all members, copied, and submitted.

If the final written report involves a resolution or main motion for the parent organization to consider, the committee chair presents copies to all members of the organization and formally moves its adoption during the section of the assembly's agenda called *Reports of Committees*. The chair makes a brief persuasive speech and answers questions about the motion. Other members of the committee help in answering questions and may make further supportive speeches. Formats for such motions can be found in any comprehensive manual of parliamentary procedure, such as *Robert's Rules of Order,* Newly Revised, or the organization may have its own special format for motions.

Administrative Duties for Virtual Groups

Leaders of virtual teams are responsible for the same administrative functions as leaders of face-to-face (FTF) teams, but the duties are carried out electronically. Whereas members of FTF teams use technology to enhance their FTF work, the technology is the only way a team exists. All the administrative duties described here can be accomplished electronically, including "discussion" among members and joint work. For instance, most word processing programs provide for document sharing, by which several individuals can work on a single document. Virtual meeting programs have a whiteboard on which group members can simultaneously or at different times sketch out their ideas graphically. Even voting can be handled via e-mail.

The leader of a virtual team will likely set up a Web site for the team and virtual chat space for members to interact. Members can interact in real time or whenever it is convenient for them individually. The leader should ensure that all documents relevant to the group—minutes, reports, information— are stored electronically for easy access by team members. Virtual teams lack the full complement of nonverbal signals, so text can easily be misinterpreted;

leaders of virtual teams must be explicit about the rules for communicating and the expectations regarding the team.

Leading Discussions

Administrative duties of designated leaders precede and follow small group meetings. Now we consider what leaders are expected to do *during* actual meetings. In general, leaders must tend to both relational and task goals. The following guidelines will help you balance these broad goals.

Opening Remarks   Opening remarks set the stage for the meeting by creating a positive atmosphere and helping focus the group on its task. They should be brief. Here are several guidelines:

1. **Make sure that members and guests have been introduced.**
   This may seem obvious, but sometimes leaders can become so task focused that they forget this step. Getting acquainted helps members

feel comfortable with each other, which makes it easier for them to contribute. Sometimes you may want to provide name tags. If you are in a group whose leader forgets introductions, you should jump in with something like: "I'm not sure I know everyone. Could we take a moment to get introduced?" The leader will likely thank you for fixing the oversight.

2. **Review the group charter at a group's first meeting, and review or explain the specific purpose of the present meeting including what outcomes should be accomplished.**

   Basically, you are like a band director getting everyone to start on the same page. You may need to allow for discussion of the charter and the meeting agenda, and it's better to do that early rather than late, to prevent misunderstandings.

3. **See that any special roles are established.**

   Will the group need a recorder in addition to the designated leader? Will the group have a member acting as a special observer? The group may choose to rotate such jobs so that various members receive practice performing them.

4. **Distribute any handouts.**

   Handouts may include written materials from the parent organization or administrator, copies of findings, case problems, outlines to structure the problem-solving procedure of the group, or explanations of special discussion techniques.

5. **Establish initial ground rules.**

   Make sure that everyone knows the rules for the group! For instance, you may want to affirm that confidentiality regarding the group's discussions must be maintained. Or, if your meeting involves discussion about a controversial issue, you may want to remind members of the principles for effective listening and respectful disagreement. The leader of a virtual group may want to reinforce the rules for effective online communication, including refraining from flaming others.

6. **Suggest procedures to follow.**

   If you think the group will benefit from using a particular procedure or technique, such as one of the techniques mentioned in this text, present it to the group as a suggestion. Explain the procedure, give members a copy of the procedure, and make sure the group agrees before you proceed. Members should know in advance whether decisions will be by consensus or majority vote.

7. **Focus initial discussion on the first substantive agenda issue with a clear question.**

   Your focus question may require a simple answer: "Tyrone, will you give us last week's sales figures?" Or it may need considerable discussion: "What do we think are the reasons for the drop-off in attendance?"

In either case, the right question helps launch the group into the substantive portion of the agenda. Questions are discussed in more detail in Chapter 11.

Regulating and Structuring Discussions   Once group members are oriented to each other and the task, the leader helps the group function efficiently by adding structure to the group's deliberations. Before presenting specific suggestions for structuring the group's discussion, you need to consider the degree of formality to use. Group discussion should be orderly so that each person has an equal opportunity to speak, but it should not be *over*regulated so that members feel constrained. Generally, the larger the group, the more formal your procedures should be.

Deciding How Formal You Should Be.   Many large groups and assemblies use *Robert's Rules of Order,* Newly Revised as their parliamentary code.[11] When an organization has adopted *Robert's Rules of Order,* the committees of that organization are bound to use Robert's rules for committees. But what many people do *not* know is that these rules for committees are much less formal and detailed than the parliamentary rules you may have encountered. These rules make it unnecessary (and undesirable) for members to utter "question," "point of order," or "We can't discuss this topic because it hasn't been moved and seconded." *Robert's Rules* suggests using parliamentary procedure in groups with over a dozen or so members, but we believe that groups as large as 30 can operate less formally. In Maureen's committee of 27, members raised their hands when they wanted to speak and voted when a particular decision needed to be recorded; but they did not use motions, questions, points of order, and so forth, during their meetings. Discussions in this group were less formal than *Robert's Rules* calls for, but more formal than the typical all-channel, free-flowing discussion of most truly small groups. *Robert's Rules* for committees are summarized in Table 13.1.

In actual practice, Weitzel and Geist found that even members of community groups who thought they were experts on parliamentary procedure made many mistakes in its use.[12] Furthermore, their problem-solving communication did not seem to suffer from their selective use of the rules. What does this mean to you? Don't memorize *Robert's Rules of Order.* Use common sense to determine how formal or informal your discussion will be, and talk about it within the group so that everyone knows how the group will operate. Now that you have thought about the degree of formality to use, we present our guidelines for structuring discussions.

1. **Keep the discussion goal-oriented.**
    You have already focused the group with presentation of the team charter or the meeting agenda. This helps the group stay on track and uses members' time well. Some digression, such as fantasy, helps establish a group's culture; but if a digression lasts too long, bring the discussion

Administrative Matters

- The committee chair can be appointed or elected or is the first person named on the list of members.
- The chair or any two committee members can call a meeting.
- A quorum (the number needed to do official business) is a simple majority of members.
- If a committee cannot reach consensus, the minority can make a report to the parent organization that differs from the majority report.

Chair's Responsibilities

- The chair is responsible for the committee's records, but can delegate that duty.
- The chair can take stands on issues and vote.

Discussing, Making Motions, and Voting

- Members can speak without being "recognized" by the chair, as long as they don't interrupt others.
- Members can discuss anything without having to make a motion.
- Motions, if made, do not need a second.
- Members can speak as often as they want; motions to limit discussion are not allowed.
- Informal discussion without a motion is appropriate; members may want to make a motion for an official vote when a consensus or majority decision seems to be emerging, but motions aren't required to record a vote.
- "Straw" (nonbonding) votes can be taken at any time.
- The chair can ask if members consent or agree, and if no one objects, the decision is made.
- A motion to reconsider a previous vote or decision can be made at any time by any member, even one who voted with the losing side or was absent during the original vote.
- Motions can be amended informally, using consensus rather than voting.

back on track: "How will this help us achieve our goal?" or "What does that have to do with what we were discussing?"

2. **Temporarily "park" off-topic items in the "parking lot," to be taken up later.**

   When a member brings up something that he or she thinks is worth discussing, but is off the current topic, place that new topic or item on a separate flip chart, board, or piece of notepaper (sometimes referred to as the "parking lot") for consideration later. This accomplishes several things. It acknowledges the member's idea, which is supportive. It helps ensure that potentially important topics are actually considered by the group and aren't dismissed just because they are off the current topic. Finally, it helps keep the group on track by encouraging members to complete one topic before embarking on a new one. After the group works its way through the agenda, it can then discuss the items in the parking lot.

3. **Use summaries to make clear transitions between items.**
   Help the group make a smooth transition from one topic or agenda item to the next by achieving closure on the current issue. You can do this by summarizing what the group has decided or concluded, asking whether the summary is adequate, and then checking to see whether the group is ready to move on: "So, we've decided to add two sections to the Community Report Card, one on Housing and one on Early Childhood, right?" [Maureen paused to make sure she understood correctly.] "Now, are we ready to go on to the next topic, which is how we should address the issue of poverty in our community?" [She paused again to give people time to respond and shift gears.] Explicit transitions help keep the group on track.

4. **Help the group manage its time.**
   Ideally, the group will address all or most items on the agenda, but members can get so involved in the discussion that they lose track of time. Nothing is more frustrating than running out of time before you have a chance to discuss an issue important to you! It's up to the designated leader to keep track of time and monitor progress on the agenda: "We are only on our third agenda item, with 15 minutes left. Are we ready to wrap this topic up, or would you rather deal with the remaining agenda items at a special meeting next week?" (But also remember the pitfalls of being a time-oriented listener, which we discussed in Chapter 2; balance is the key.)

5. **Bring the discussion to a definite close.**
   This should be done no later than the scheduled ending time for the meeting, unless all members consent to extending the time. Briefly summarize the progress the group has made and the assignments given to members. Many leaders thank the group, ask for a brief evaluation of the meeting ("How well did this meeting accomplish what you wanted to accomplish today?"), and remind members of the next meeting.

Equalizing Opportunity to Participate   Each member needs a fair share of "air time" in the group. It's up to you to ensure that everyone has an equal opportunity to speak, with no member stage hogging or withdrawing. There are several things you can do to encourage such equality:

1. **Address your comments and questions to the group rather than to individuals.**
   Unless you want to elicit a specific item of information or respond directly to what a member has said, speak to the group as a whole.

Make regular eye contact with everyone when you ask questions, especially with less talkative members.

2. **Make sure all members have an equal opportunity to speak.**

You may have to act as **gatekeeper,** regulating who will speak next so that everyone has a fair, equal chance. Eye contact with less talkative members shows them you expect them to speak, whereas looking at talkative members encourages them to talk more. We suggest you make a visual survey of the entire group every minute or so. If you see a nonverbal sign that a silent member has something to say, you can help that person get the floor: "Pieta, did you want to comment on John's proposal?" or "Pieta, you seem concerned about John's proposal. Would you share your concerns with us?" That opens the gate to Pieta without putting her on the spot if she has nothing to say. Sometimes reticent members can be assigned roles that *require* their participation. For instance, someone might be asked to investigate an issue and report to the group. If you know a member is well informed but has not spoken out, try encouraging participation without forcing: "Selim, I think you studied that issue. Could you give us any information about it?"

Controlling long-winded members is often harder than encouraging quiet members, but it *must* be done for the sake of the group. The following techniques range from the most subtle to the most direct:

a. When feasible, seat talkative members where you can seem to overlook them naturally, and try not to make eye contact when you ask a question of the group.

b. When a windbag has finished one point, cut in with a tactful comment, such as "How do the *rest* of you feel about that issue?" to suggest that someone else speak.

c. Suggest a group rule that each person make one point only, then give up the floor to others, or that each person's comments be held to one minute. You can be lighthearted about this—some groups have used squirt guns, timers, or nerf balls to remind members when it's time to yield the floor.

d. In private, tactfully ask the excessive talker to help you encourage quiet members to speak: "Your ideas have been very helpful to the group, but because you are so articulate, I'm concerned that others feel intimidated about participating. How can you help me get Susan and Juan to contribute to the discussions more often?"

e. Have an observer keep a count of how often or how long each member speaks, and report the findings to the group. If a serious imbalance is apparent, the group can decide what to do.

f. As a last resort, ask the person to control talking or leave the group: "While your ideas are excellent, your constant talking prevents other members, whose ideas are equally good, from contributing. This hurts both group morale and decision making. For the sake of the group, if you will not control your talking, I think you should leave the group."

3. **Listen with real interest to what an infrequent speaker says, and encourage others to do the same.**

Nothing discourages a speaker more than a lack of listening. Yet the evidence is clear that most people ignore comments from a member who previously has said little. Leader intervention can help an infrequent speaker get a fair hearing.

4. **Avoid commenting after each member's remark.**

Some leaders fall into this pattern unaware, producing a wheel network of verbal interaction. Other leaders do this to overcontrol the group. Listen, then speak when you are really needed, but don't become the constant interpreter or repeater of what others say.

5. **Bounce requests for your opinions on substantive issues back to the group.**

Some people have a tendency to accept uncritically what a leader says. Under most circumstances, you encourage independent thinking by members if you withhold your opinions until others have expressed theirs. You might reply, "Let's see what other members think first. What do the rest of you think about . . . ?" When you do offer an opinion, give it as only one point of view to be considered, not as the *right* interpretation.

6. **Remain neutral during arguments.**

When you get heavily involved in an argument, you lose the perspective needed to be a completer and mediator, to summarize, and to perform all the other communicative behaviors of a good leader. If you realize that evaluation is needed, point that out and ask others to provide it. At most, act as a devil's advocate for a point of view that otherwise would not be considered, and tell the group that you're playing the devil's advocate role. Of course, you are always free to support decisions as they emerge.

Stimulating Creative Thinking Groups are potentially more creative than individuals, but often group outputs are mediocre or worse. Sometimes creativity must be stimulated deliberately. Leaders can do several things to encourage creativity:

1. **Defer evaluation and ask group members to do the same.**

The main idea behind brainstorming, described in Chapter 10, is to defer evaluation of ideas until members have no more ideas to suggest. Evaluation stifles creativity; who wants to suggest an idea that will get shot down? To stimulate creativity, the group must establish a safe climate in which people feel safe to propose innovative suggestions. When a group member criticizes a suggestion, gently remind that person of the "defer evaluation" rule.

2. **Try brainstorming and other creativity-enhancing techniques.**
   Brainstorming not only requires deferred judgment, but it also encourages members to be playful with ideas. Brainstorming and other techniques temporarily disable the logical part of the mind so that the creative mind can emerge.

3. **Encourage the group to search for more alternatives.**
   When no one seems to be able to think of any more ideas, you can ask an idea-spurring question: "What *else* can we think of to . . . ?" or "I wonder if we can think of five more ways to . . . ?" Often, the most creative ideas are ones that pop up after the group thinks it has exhausted its possibilities.

4. **One at a time, ask how each component of a solution or item might be improved.**
   For instance, you might ask, "How could we improve the appearance of . . . ?" or "How could we add to the strength of . . . ?"

5. **Be alert to suggestions that open up new areas of thinking; then pose a general question about the new area.**
   For example, if someone suggests putting up posters in the library that show users how much theft costs them, you might ask, "How *else* could we publicize the costs of theft to the library?"

Stimulating Critical Thinking   After a group has done its creative thinking, it must then subject the various options to rigorous evaluation before it reaches a final position. Sometimes groups develop norms of politeness that make this impossible. Here are ways to encourage good critical evaluation:

1. **If the group gets solution-minded too quickly, suggest more analysis of the problem.**
   This is a common problem and a major source of faulty decision making. Chapters 10 and 11 present a systematic method for helping a group focus on problem analysis.

2. **Encourage members to evaluate information.**
   For example:
   a. To check the relevance of evidence, ask: "How does this apply to our problem?" or "How is that like the situation we are discussing?"
   b. To evaluate the source of evidence, ask: "What is the source of that information?" "How well is Dr. So-and-so recognized in the field?" or "Is this consistent with other information on the subject?"
   c. To check on the credibility of information, ask: "Do we have any information that is contradictory?"

d. To encourage thorough assessment of a group member's suggestion, ask: "How will implementing that solve our problem?" or "How will the students (union members, secretaries, neighborhood residents, etc.) react to that suggestion?"

e. To test a statistic, ask how it was derived, who conducted the study, or how an average was computed.

f. Bring in outside experts to challenge the views of the group.

3. Make sure all group members understand and accept the standards, criteria, or assumptions used in making judgments.
For example, you might ask: "Is that criterion clear to us all?" "Does everyone agree that using our professional association's guidelines is a good idea?" or "Do we all accept that as an assumption?"

4. See that all proposed solutions are thoroughly tested before they are accepted as final group decisions.
Encourage the group to apply the available facts and all criteria. Be especially careful to consider possible harmful effects of all proposed solutions.

a. Ask questions such as the following to encourage thorough evaluation:

- Do we have any evidence to indicate that this solution would be satisfactory? Unsatisfactory?

- Are there any facts to support this proposal?

- How well would that idea meet our criteria?

- Would that proposal solve the basic problem?

- Is there any way we can test this idea before we decide whether or not to adopt it?

- What negative consequences might this proposal produce?

b. Ask members to discuss tentative solutions or policies with trusted people outside the group.

c. One or more members can be asked to take the role of critical evaluator or devil's advocate so that all ideas are challenged and everyone has a chance to air doubts.

d. Divide the group into two subgroups under different leaders to evaluate all alternatives; then rejoin to iron out differences.

e. Before reaching a binding solution with far-reaching consequences, hold a "second chance" meeting at which all doubts, ethical concerns, or untested assumptions can be explored.

5. Help prevent groupthink.
Groupthink, described in detail in Chapter 11, can send a group along a path to disaster. Follow the suggestions for preventing groupthink in Chapter 11.

Fostering Meeting-to-Meeting Improvement   A group doesn't achieve its ultimate goal by chance. After each meeting, the designated leader should assess how well the meeting's goals were accomplished and how the meeting could have been improved. That, then, suggests a road map for improving future meetings:

1. **Determine how the meeting could have been improved.**
   After a meeting, take a few minutes to reflect on it. Did the group receive the leadership services it needed at the right time? Were the meeting's purposes clearly communicated? Did members agree on the goals? Was the entire agenda covered in a timely fashion? Was the meeting well structured? Did members stay on the topic, for the most part? Take a few moments to consider the members. Did everyone participate? Did anyone talk too much? Not enough? Did you talk too much? Too little? Were the members allowed to digress too often? Not enough? Did the members seem to enjoy the discussion? After answering these and other questions, you can plan your strategy for the next meeting.

2. **Determine the most important changes to be made at the next meeting and adjust behavior accordingly.**
   After examining all the areas in which you could improve the group meeting, concentrate on improving the two or three that are most potentially harmful to the group. If one or two members monopolized the floor, plan ways to curtail their participation. If someone seemed upset, you may want to touch base by calling or e-mailing that member. If the agenda was half completed, keep better track of time and allow fewer digressions at the next meeting. Feel free to share the plan with the members. Maureen said: "Last week, we got through only half the items on our agenda. This week, I'm going to pay more attention to our time, and I'll be stepping in more often to help us stick to one issue at a time. I'd appreciate your help with this, too."

Regulating and Structuring Discussions in Virtual Groups   Virtual groups often "meet" asynchronously, or not all at the same time. Although the same suggestions apply, the leader doesn't usually try to structure an actual meeting or conversation. However, because of the increased potential for misunderstanding when members don't interact face to face, it is particularly important that expectations be made clear at the beginning. First, once you have made the task demands and the rules for interacting known, monitor the conversation to make sure people aren't flaming or insulting one another. Step in quickly if they are. Second, encourage regular task meetings and electronic "check-ins." Depending on the nature of the task, you may ask members to check in daily or weekly. If someone isn't checking as often as required, call or e-mail to find out why. Third, encourage nontask communication so that members can develop a sense of team connection. That may mean setting aside a chat room just for social interaction. Finally, be familiar with the technological tools that work well for virtual groups and don't hesitate to use them. For instance, some online meeting programs use structured procedures to help ensure systematic problem solving. In addition, several programs help guide electronic brainstorming to enhance creativity.

Recap: A Quick Review

Leaders are expected to lead the group's discussions. To do so effectively, they should attend to the following:

1. In their opening remarks, leaders should make sure that members are introduced to one another; review the group's and the specific meeting's purpose and goals; make sure people have been identified to perform special functions, such as taking minutes; have handouts distributed; make sure that ground rules and specific procedures, such as specialized techniques, have been explained and are followed; and start the group off with a focused, substantive question.

2. In regulating and structuring discussions, the leader must decide how formally or informally the group's discussion should be, including whether parliamentary rules or special rules for committees should apply; must keep the discussion moving toward the goal, including by encouraging members to "park" off-topic items in a "parking lot" for later discussion; provide internal summaries to help keep the group together and provide smooth transitions; keep discussion moving along; and bring the discussion to a definite close.

3. Leaders must equalize members' opportunity to contribute by controlling long-winded members and encouraging quieter members to speak up; by addressing questions to the group as a whole; by not commenting after each member's remarks, so that they don't create a wheel network; by listening with genuine interest; by asking the group for its opinions; and by staying neutral during arguments.

4. Leaders stimulate creative thinking by asking members to refrain from evaluating items right away; using creativity-enhancing techniques, such as brainstorming; and prodding the members to keep thinking about more alternatives and new areas of thinking.

5. Leaders stimulate critical thinking by stopping the group from becoming solution-minded too early, encouraging the critical evaluation of information, making sure that factors such as criteria and assumptions have been discussed and accepted, testing solutions before they are finally adopted, and working to prevent groupthink.

6. Effective leaders evaluate their own and the group's performance to determine how the meeting could have been improved and what adjustments need to be made at the next meeting.

7. In virtual groups, because of the increased possibility of misunderstanding, leaders pay particular attention to whether members are following good communication practices, such as not flaming others; they also set aside virtual space for nontask talk and chit-chat.

Developing the Group

Developing the group involves two fundamental processes: helping the group evolve into an effective team, and helping the individual members grow to their potentials so that distributed leadership can work effectively. Few people start out knowing how to be effective team members or leaders. Developing the communication skills needed takes practice. As leader, you can help develop the talent on your team.

Helping Individuals Grow   An important job for the leader is to develop the members' leadership skills, including the members' abilities to assess the group's throughput processes and suggest appropriate changes. Here are several suggestions:

1. **Encourage members to assess the group's processes and make suggestions.**

   Sometimes the impetus for group growth can be supplied just by asking the group to examine itself and ask, "How are we doing?" Periodic self-assessment is a characteristic of outstanding teams.[13] You can build self-assessment into the group's processes. For instance, a short period of evaluation can end each meeting: "How well do you think our meeting went today?" and "How might we make our next meeting more productive?" The answer to the second question led the church board in Chapter 4 to rearrange its agenda so that "new business" would be discussed early in the meeting before group members became tired and uncreative.

   Another suggestion might be to designate someone as a process observer to watch the interactions and share observations with the group as a whole. The job of process observer may rotate among members so that everyone gets practice observing and assessing. The group may also bring outside consultants in to evaluate the group and offer suggestions for improvement, as Celinda did for the health agency executive committee. Suggestions for what to observe and how to provide feedback were provided in Chapter 7.

2. **Model the behavior that you want others to adopt.**

   As designated leader, you can model group-centered, thoughtful, responsible behavior. Your own behavior does a lot to promote teamwork and develop the trust needed for collaboration. Encourage others to evaluate your suggestions, and react open-mindedly and nondefensively to others' criticisms.

3. **Give members practice at performing needed group duties.**

   Suggest ways in which group members can serve the needs of the group. For instance, rotate the job of recorder so that several members get practice. Give members the chance to report on their areas of expertise to the group and to perform special tasks for the group. Let members substitute for you as discussion leader or liaison to other groups. Don't jump in right away when you see that the group needs something; give the other members a chance to respond before you do.

A particularly striking example of this occurred during a Community Report Card group meeting. The Recreation and Leisure Subcommittee resubmitted its section without fixing the problems that the rest of the committee identified. Instead of expecting Maureen to play bad cop, several members of the committee called the subcommittee members to task and explained why their revision was still unacceptable. The message was more compelling to the subcommittee because it had come from their peers rather than the group leader.

Establishing and Maintaining Trust   True collaboration (literally, "working together") is possible only when members trust each other. Larson and LaFasto found that interviewees from outstanding teams almost always mentioned trust when asked about their group's climate: "Trust is one of those mainstay virtues in the commerce of mankind. It is the bond that allows any kind of significant relationship to exist between people. Once broken, it is not easily— if ever—recovered."[14] Analysis of their data shows four components of trust: honesty (no lies, no exaggerations); openness (a combination of openmindedness and willingness to share); consistency (predictability, dependability); and respect (treating others with fairness and dignity).

The following suggestions can help you establish and retain a climate of trust:

1. **Establish norms, based on ethical principles, that build trust.**
    Communication that builds trust is based on three important ethical principles: working to understand others, communicating to enhance others' identities and self-concepts, and behaving like a responsible group member. Specific behaviors that promote trust are listening actively, encouraging others to explain themselves, helping others with assignments or tasks, maintaining confidentiality, getting assignments done when promised, making sure you understand someone's position before disagreeing, and making others feel free to disagree without being treated as weird or politically incorrect.

2. **Confront trust violators and other problem members.**
    Two of the most common complaints are that groups tolerate members who put self over group and that leaders fail "to confront and resolve issues associated with inadequate performance by team members."[15] If repeated efforts by you and other members to improve things are unsuccessful, it is far better to remove offenders from the group than to allow trust to erode and group energy to be deflected into destructive avenues.

3. **Encourage members to understand and embrace their diversity.**
    As we have said, diversity can be a group's greatest strength, but not if members can't capitalize on that diversity. The leader can help the team recognize one another's differences and the unique strengths provided by those differences. Whether the group's diversity is based on personality characteristics, differences in stage of life, or varying cultural or co-cultural

backgrounds, encouraging members to get to know each other at more than a superficial level can help produce understanding and appreciation. A first step can be not making negative judgments about people just because they are different from you!

It may help to invite an outside trainer in to conduct a workshop about differences and their value. A library staff we know participated in a trainer-led workshop on personality differences revealed by color preference. The staff had fun learning about how different people preferred to approach work. That helped them see that others weren't being contrary; they were just trying to work in the way they felt most comfortable. The staff began to use color vocabulary in a teasing, but friendly, way: "Oh, you're being so green! We blues will never understand you!" The workshop helped improve staff relationships and work efficiency.

4. **Be a principled leader.**
    Principled leaders put the needs of the group ahead of their individual needs and behave in ethical ways consistent with the group's norms.[16] For instance, they do not say they want group participation, then squash members' attempts to participate. Good group leaders have a vision of the group's future, which they convey clearly; they inspire members to work toward that vision. They show personal commitment to the team's goals. Moreover, they work to expose the talents of the other members. Leaders create leaders by giving members the experience and latitude they need to act with self-confidence.

Promoting Teamwork and Cooperation   Establishing a climate of trust will do more than anything else to develop cooperation and teamwork among members. Chapter 8 provided several suggestions for promoting cohesiveness and teamwork in a group, which we won't repeat here. Instead, we provide suggestions that a leader is in the best position to do:

1. **Plan some fun for the group.**
    Fun could be a party, snacks before a meeting, a celebration when a major task is completed, happy hour after work, and so forth. Good task leaders sometimes have trouble with humor. Lee observed, for instance, that many of the most efficient leaders lacked human warmth, but groups need *both* efficiency *and* satisfying interactions.[17] He suggested that taskmasters relax and allow digressions, which can relieve secondary tension. Let the group chain out fantasies that enrich its life and contribute to establishing shared beliefs and values. If this is hard for you, enlist the help of members who are good at it. This builds relationships and ultimately helps work go more smoothly. When the Community Report Card was released to the public, Maureen planned a brunch for committee members prior to the press conference as a tangible "thank you" for their hard work.

2. **Promote the group.**

As one of our friends said, "If the team leader isn't the team's biggest fan, who is?" It's the leader's unique responsibility to make sure that the group is known within the organization for its good work. Let people in the organization, particularly higher-ups, know when the team has accomplished something valuable for the organization, make team members' accomplishments visible to others, and talk about the successes of the group. Members will know that you support them with your loyalty and backing and will work hard for the team.

3. **Share all rewards with the group.**

Leaders often receive praise from authority figures for work the group has done. Wise leaders give credit to the group.

4. **Get group input and buy-in about promoting teamwork.**

Ask team members to recall the best group they've ever been part of, and to identify the behaviors that contributed to that team feeling. Ask them to suggest how that can be recreated in the present group. Their suggestions will provide the guidelines and norms for the group, with the added advantage that they came from the members themselves.

5. **Confront members whose behavior is hurting the team.**

One of the worst things you can do is ignore individualistic, selfish behavior that hurts the team. It will not go away on its own, and you must address it constructively. Talk to the member privately first, focusing on the behavior that you believe is problematic. Say, "Roger, when you type on your laptop while others are talking, we interpret your behavior as lack of interest in the team," not "You jerk! What do you think you're doing ignoring what people are saying?" If you suspect a hidden agenda item is interfering with group functioning or goal achievement, you may want to bring this up in the group: "Alicia, you have rejected every suggestion the group has proposed without examining it fully. We're all becoming frustrated and angry. Is there something going on that we should know about?"

Sometimes, two members just don't like each other and let their personal feelings erupt in team meetings. In such cases, you may have to have what a friend of ours calls a "Come to Jesus" meeting with them. This friend told two warring women on her team that she wanted them to act with respect and friendliness toward each other in the team meetings, even if they had to fake it. She thought they ended up becoming good friends, but found out years later that they had, indeed, faked it because they wanted to stay on her team. Nevertheless, they stopped the offending, harmful behavior. You do not have to like someone to work well with him or her.

6. **Keep arguments focused on facts and issues, not personalities.**

Step in at once if any member starts an attack on another's personality, ethnicity, or character. However, recognize also that members may have strong feelings about some issues, so don't squelch expressions of feeling, as long as those expressions do not denigrate others.

7. **When a group seems to be deadlocked, look for a basis on which to compromise.**

    Perhaps you can synthesize parts of several ideas into a consensus solution or suggest a mediation procedure, such as the *principled negotiation procedure* described in Chapter 12.

Developing Virtual Groups   Virtual group leaders face particular challenges in developing the group, but creating an online community is possible. As we have said previously, insist on etiquette among members and enforce the rules. Encourage nontask communication. Support members in taking specialized training pertinent to the group's task. More and more, such training may be available online through a university or corporate distance learning program. But perhaps the most valuable thing you can do, if at all possible, is get the group together for a face-to-face meeting at the beginning of their work together. This really helps solidify the connections. And if you can provide for additional face-to-face meetings throughout the team's life, so much the better.

Ethical Principles for Group Leaders

As we have suggested, the leader's behavior should serve as a model for members to follow. As Hackman and Johnson said, "Responsible leaders maintain the highest possible standards of ethics."[18] These authors suggest several principles for leaders that we believe are relevant for small groups:

1. **Do not intentionally send deceptive or harmful messages.**

    Not only should leaders tell members the truth; they should hold *truth* to be an appropriate standard for the group's decision making. To us, this means ensuring that *all* relevant information, whether it supports the leader's position or not, is presented to the group and that the group evaluates all information in an unbiased, fair way.

2. **Place concern for others above concern for personal gain.**

    A leader should not take advantage of the power of the leader position for personal gain or advantage. Hidden agendas, whether belonging to the leader or members, should not be allowed to interfere with the needs of the group. Moreover, as we have mentioned previously, leaders should refrain from actions that might harm the self-esteem of members.

3. **Establish clear policies that all group members are expected to follow.**

    Group procedures and rules are clearly understood, and ethical leaders follow the same rules and norms that members are expected to follow.

4. **Respect the opinions and attitudes of members and allow members the freedom to consider the consequences of their actions.**
   This principle supports democratic, group-centered leadership that encourages equal opportunity for all to participate. It also supports our preference for distributed leadership and acknowledges how important it is for leaders to develop the capabilities of members.

5. **Stand behind members when they carry out policies and actions approved by the group.**
   Ethical leaders support members who carry out the plans of the group. They do not save their own skins by leaving group members hanging.

6. **Treat members consistently, regardless of sex, ethnicity, or social background.**
   Ethical leaders minimize external status differences to encourage participation by all. They value members for their contributions to the group.

As with other desirable behaviors, the leader should model ethical behavior that will serve as a standard for members to follow. By doing so, the leader will help create a climate of trust and a spirit of cohesiveness.

Recap: A Quick Review

Good leaders develop their members' own leadership capabilities and skills and act ethically.

1. They help individuals grow by modeling the behavior they want others to adopt, encouraging members' contributions to the group's process, and giving members the opportunity to perform important functions for the group.

2. Leaders help establish and maintain trust by promoting norms that build trust, confronting members who violate group norms and create problems, embracing the group's diversity, and being highly principled.

3. In promoting teamwork and cooperation, leaders plan fun activities and celebrations for the group; serve as advocates and cheerleaders for the group to outsiders; share rewards, including praise, with the group as a whole; seek group buy-in about how to promote teamwork; confront members who are hurting the team; keep arguments evidence-based, not personal; and look for ways to harmonize and compromise divergent views.

4. For virtual groups, leaders try to create online community by doing such things as scheduling face-to-face meetings for the members.

5. Ethical leaders tell the truth, put concern for others ahead of individual gain, establish clear policies that everyone is expected to follow, respect others' opinions and attitudes, stand behind members, and do not discriminate or show favoritism.

QUESTIONS FOR REVIEW

 Go to self-quizzes on the Online Learning Center at mhhe.com/galanes12 to test your knowledge of the chapter concepts

This chapter used the example of Maureen, an experienced community volunteer, and the Community Report Card task force to illustrate a variety of concepts.

1. How did Maureen demonstrate the philosophy of democratic, group-centered leadership? In what ways did she show that she was able to adjust to the needs of the individual members and the group?

2. What administrative duties did she perform? What functions did these serve for the group?

3. How well did she seem to lead the group? What specifics in the story and in other examples throughout the chapter lead you to your conclusion?

4. Did Maureen show evidence of helping develop the skills and leadership abilities of the other members? How so?

5. Do you think Maureen was an ethical group member? Why or why not?

KEY TERMS

 Test your knowledge of these key terms by visiting the Online Learning Center Web site at mhhe.com/galanes12

Agenda	Leader as completer	Meeting notice
Gatekeeper	Liaison	Minutes
Group charter		

BIBLIOGRAPHY

Cathcart, Robert S., and Larry A. Samovar, eds. *Small Group Communication: A Reader.* 6th ed. Dubuque, IA: Wm. C. Brown, 1992, especially Section 8.

Fisher, B. Aubrey. "Leadership: When Does the Difference Make a Difference?" In *Communication and Group Decision-Making.* Randy Y. Hirokawa and Marshall S. Poole, eds. Beverly Hills, CA: Sage, 1986, 197–215.

LaFasto, Frank, and Carl Larson. *When Teams Work Best: 6,000 Team Members and Leaders Tell What It Takes to Succeed.* Thousand Oaks, CA: Sage, 2001, especially Chapter 4.

Robert, Henry M., III, William J. Evans, Daniel H. Honemann, and Thomas L. Balch. *Robert's Rules of Order,* Newly Revised in Brief. Cambridge, MA: Da Capo Press, 2004.

Schwarz, Roger M. *The Skilled Facilitator: Practical Wisdom for Developing Effective Groups.* San Francisco: Jossey-Bass, 1994.

Tropman, John E. *Making Meetings Work: Achieving High Quality Group Decisions.* Thousand Oaks, CA: Sage, 1996, part 2.

NOTES

1. Carl E. Larson and Frank M. J. LaFasto, *TeamWork: What Must Go Right/What Can Go Wrong* (Newbury Park, CA: Sage, 1989): 118.

2. William C. Schutz, "The Leader as Completer," in *Small Group Communication: A Reader,* 3rd ed., eds. Robert S. Cathcart and Larry A. Samovar (Dubuque, IA: Wm. C. Brown, 1979): 400.

3. Donald G. Ellis, "Relational Control in Two Group Systems," *Communication Monographs* 36 (1979): 153–66.

4. Paul Hersey and Kenneth Blanchard, *Management of Organizational Behavior,* 7th ed (New York: PrenticeHall, 1996).

5. Frank LaFasto and Carl Larson, *When Teams Work Best: 6,000 Team Members and Leaders Tell What It Takes to Succeed* (Thousand Oaks, CA: Sage, 2001): 97–156.

6. Gloria J. Galanes, "In Their Own Words: An Exploratory Study of Bona Fide Group Leaders," *Small Group Research* 34 (December, 2003): 741–770.

7. Ibid.

8. Michael Z. Hackman and Craig E. Johnson, *Leadership: A Communication Perspective* (Prospect Heights, IL: Waveland Press, 1991): 129.

9. John Gastil, "Identifying Obstacles to Small Group Democracy," *Small Group Research* 24 (February 1993): 5–27.

10. Roger M. Schwarz, *The Skilled Facilitator: Practical Wisdom for Developing Effective Groups* (San Francisco: Jossey-Bass, 1994).

11. Henry M. Robert, III, William J. Evans, Daniel H. Honemann, and Thomas J. Balch, *Robert's Rules of Order,* Newly Revised, 10th ed. (Cambridge, MA: Perseus Publishing, 2000): 464–525.

12. Al Weitzel and Patricia Geist, "Parliamentary Procedure in a Community Group: Communication and Vigilant Decision Making," *Communication Monographs* 65 (September 1998): 244–59.

13. Larson and LaFasto, *TeamWork,* 130–31.

14. Ibid., 85.

15. Ibid., 136.

16. Ibid., 118–29.

17. Irving J. Lee, *How to Talk with People* (New York: Harper & Row, 1952): 158–60.

18. Hackman and Johnson, *Leadership:* 205.

Making Public Presentations of the Group's Output

A

Often groups must make public presentations of their output, which may take the form of a report, a set of findings or recommendations, and so forth. The group's leader or selected representatives may present a report from the group to the parent organization, a political body, an open meeting of interested community representatives, or another type of public gathering. The members of the audience at such public gatherings may themselves become participants who will discuss the report of the group. These public presentations involve three stages: planning, organizing, and presenting. In the discussion to follow, we will highlight the various decisions that your group will have to make at each stage. We follow this with information about a typical occasion for group presentations: the public meeting.

The Planning Stage

The moment your group knows that a presentation is needed, planning begins. Speaking to an audience requires advanced assessment of the upcoming speaking occasion. Some of the most important areas of assessment that you need to consider are your group's audience, the occasion, your purpose, your topic, group member strengths and limitations, and logistics. Having an effective presentation and a satisfied audience rides on how well you initially assess what your presentation needs and how carefully you follow through as you prepare.

Your Audience

Public presentations are not simply about what a group has to say to an audience. Successful presentations show audience members that *they* matter and are not just window dressing. After all, you will present your group's final product to someone with a vested interest in hearing what you have to say. Good audience analysis helps to create a comfortable speaking environment for both your group and the audience.

Audience analysis is a systematic approach to gathering as much information as possible about the audience. The more you know about the audience, the better you can tailor your presentation to its interests, needs, motives, viewpoints, and so forth. In addition, audience analysis helps you assess what audience members may or may not already know about your

428

topic, which helps you figure out what to say and how to present the information. You do not want to bore them or talk over their heads. Some audience members may not be there by choice. Whether they are required to attend or attend voluntarily affects how you present information and the level of enthusiasm that you may have to muster for the event. The more background you have about your audience, the more you can include them in the presentation.

Your Occasion

Why have you been asked to present your group's final product? Who has asked you? Often, this person can help you understand both the audience and the specifics of the occasion. If this is not a class presentation, find out whether you can visit the place where you will speak to become comfortable with the setting. Ask about the number of people expected to attend. Will there be other speakers? How much control will you have over your setting? Clarify why you have been asked to speak and whether there are specific goals you will be expected to meet.

Later, we discuss public hearings or meetings. These are common occasions for group presentations and present their own set of special challenges.

Your Purpose

Knowing clearly what you are trying to accomplish is an essential step in any effective presentation. If you do not know what you are doing and why, how can your audience figure out what they are supposed to do with the information you present? Many public group presentations are intended to educate and distribute information. For example, if your university's president has convened a student task force to investigate how best to improve student-community relations, then you may be asked to report your findings to the president and the city council. Your purpose is primarily informational. On the other hand, if you are charged with implementing a solution or presenting a recommendation, then your purpose becomes persuasive. Persuasive presentations involve explicit calls to action on the audience's part.

Your Subject or Topic

Sometimes the most difficult part of this stage is figuring out how to begin. The audience, the occasion, and your purpose help identify your specific subject and relevant subtopics. Often, you cannot present all the information you have gathered over the course of a project's life. Sometimes the person or agency that invited you to speak has an agenda that will guide your subject selection. Undoubtedly, there will be a time limit for your presentation. You may be given a particular structure and time limit to follow or simply be told to "fill us in." Make the best of your parameters; novice presenters often present too much information and run out of time, which causes them to lose credibility with the audience or lose the audience altogether!

Member Strengths and Limitations

Knowing and appreciating the difficulties that your group members may have with oral presentations will help you organize and develop your presentation. Which members are knowledgeable about particular topics? What contacts and research did your group develop? What attitudes or feelings do members have about the topic and the presentation? Who are your better speakers? After assessing the strengths of group members, deciding who will present which topics is easier. In addition, if the presentation will be followed by a question and answer period, you can decide who is the best qualified to answer questions that are asked.

Your group also needs to talk about group member concerns and limitations about making oral presentations. The best writer in the group may not be the best oral presenter. Someone who is quiet within the group may actually prefer to speak before larger audiences. On the other hand, a group member who is comfortable in smaller groups may feel threatened in larger settings. Leaders may not necessarily be the best ones to take the lead for the presentation. Anxiety is normal; group members experience it in different ways. Knowing and understanding a group member's difficulty with public communication can allow your group to plan presentation strategies that take the focus off one person by having pairs present together. Oral public presentations also require a considerable behind-the-scenes work that can be done by members less inclined to speak.

Logistics

Near the end of the planning stage, your group knows what you need for your presentation. What kind of supplies do you need to bring with you? Are you using visual aids? Will you need equipment to use these visual aids properly (e.g., TV, VCR, laptop computer, slide or overhead projector, audio player, etc.)? Speakers often forget simple items such as tape and end up worrying more about the poster that keeps falling over than the text of their presentation. Do not expect your teacher, audience members, or a contact person to supply your needs. You need to find out what supplies you need and who will bring them. And it never hurts to be prepared.

Suppose your group were a community group that had investigated ways to create more community spaces for youth to gather safely, and you are now preparing to present your recommendations to the mayor and the city council. You will hurt your presentation if your group has not gone the extra mile to find current pamphlets, booklets, handouts, buttons, balloons, fact sheets, or any other items relevant to your presentation. Very likely, other community organizations mentioned in your recommendations will be happy to supply professional, updated information about your topic.

TABLE A.1   Types of group presentations

Panel: Conversation among Experts	Symposium: Individual Uninterrupted Presentations	Forum: Questions and Comments from Audience
Topics outlined in advance.	Panelists discuss different aspects of topic.	Different viewpoints encouraged.
Controversy encouraged.	No interaction among panelists.	Questions directed at individuals or at entire group.
Moderator as traffic cop.	Moderator introduces topic and panelists.	Moderator selects audience participants.

Types of Group Oral Presentations

Once you have completed your presentation assessment, as a group you must decide which presentation format best fits the purpose and occasion of your presentation. A variety of formats allow for differing viewpoints to be expressed; these are often followed by comments and questions from the audience (see Table A.1).

Panel Discussion

A **panel discussion** is a public presentation in which a small group of people representing varying perspectives informally discusses issues relevant to an important question in front of a listening audience. For example, a panel might discuss abortion laws, solutions to congested parking on campus, what might be done to solve a community's solid waste problem, or the responsibility of society to the victims of crimes. A panel format is sometimes used with a group of aspirants for political office. Panel formats are often the format of choice for classroom presentations when your teacher asks you to present your group's final report to the class.

Groups may participate in panel discussions in a variety of ways. A group may be asked to plan and conduct an entire panel discussion, in which case the entire group must research and present fairly all relevant points of view about the issue. More typically, a group known to support a particular point of view will be asked to supply a representative to serve as a panelist with other panelists who represent different viewpoints. The **moderator** of a panel coordinates the discussion so that it does not ramble and so that all viewpoints are represented. Participants need to be both knowledgeable about the question under discussion and articulate in expressing their, or the group's, opinions. Panelists generally have an outline of questions to follow, but their speaking is relatively impromptu. Panelists need not agree on anything except which issues to discuss; the lively argument that often ensues can make for an intellectually stimulating program. The panel format is excellent for presenting

Panel Discussion

A small group whose members interact informally for the benefit of a listening audience.

Moderator

A person who controls the flow of communication during a public presentation such as a panel or forum discussion.

an overview of different points of view on an issue of public concern. CNN and C-SPAN often include such discussions in their programming.

Preparing for Panel Discussions   Panel and other public discussions call for special physical arrangements and other preparations. First, all discussants should be able to see each other and the audience at all times to facilitate direct interaction. Seat panelists in a semicircle in front of the audience with the moderator either at one end or in the center; thus, panelists have eye contact with each other and the audience. Second, panelists should be seated behind a table, preferably with some sort of cover on the front. Two small tables in an open V make an excellent arrangement. Third, a large name card should be placed in front of each panelist. Fourth, microphones, if needed, should be plentiful enough and unobtrusive. In a large assembly, if a floor mike is required for questions from the audience, it should be placed strategically and audience members instructed in its use. Finally, visual displays of the topic or question under consideration help keep the discussion organized. A chalkboard or easel can be used for this purpose.

The discussion outline for a panel discussion can follow one of several formats. The one described here is common. The moderator should ask panelists in advance to suggest questions and subquestions for the discussion. After these are compiled into a rough outline that the moderator intends to use, panelists should receive a copy in advance so that they have a chance to investigate and think of possible responses to each question.

The moderator prepares a special outline and uses it during the panel discussion. The outline has an introduction, sequence of questions to be raised, and a planned conclusion format. The moderator acts as a conversational traffic officer directing the flow of the discussion. Moderators ask questions of the group of panelists, see that each panelist has an equal opportunity to speak, and clarify ambiguous remarks or ask panelists to do so. They do not participate directly in the arguments. They summarize each major topic or have the panelists do so and keep the discussion moving along the major points of the outline. A moderator's outline might look like this:

Introduction   "What should be the law governing abortions in the United States?"

I. Ladies and gentlemen, the question of what the law should be governing abortions in the United States has been a subject of heated argument, physical confrontation, intensive lobbying, court cases, sermons, and pamphlets—and far too little calm, thoughtful discussion.

II. Today we are fortunate to have a panel of thoughtful experts who represent all major points of view on this subject.

   A. Father Jon McClarety has made an intensive study of the Catholic theology and arguments underlying the church's stand against legalized abortions. He is a member of the Department of Philosophy and Theology of Holy Name Academy.

B. Robert Byron is an attorney for the Legal Aid Society who has served his society in appeals to the Supreme Court that led to the current legal status of abortions.

C. Ms. Martine Giles, founder and director of the Adoption Alternatives Agency, has helped arrange more than 300 private adoptions nationally.

D. Ms. Dorothy Mankewicz, a social worker and volunteer lecturer for Zero Population Growth, has assisted many women who wanted abortions.

E. Professor Maya Kasakrim is historian of ethical and social values at Western State University and author of two books dealing with the abortion law controversy.

III. Our panelists have agreed to discuss four specific issues that are part of the question you see on the poster before you. "What should be the law governing abortions in the United States?"

A. When does a human life begin?

B. Who has the right to decide whether or not a woman should be allowed to have an abortion?

C. What would be the effects of greater restriction on the right of choice to have an abortion?

D. Under what conditions, if any, should abortions be legal?

IV. Each panelist will give a brief statement of his or her position on each issue and the reasoning behind it; then the panelists will question and debate their positions informally. After 50 minutes, the floor will be opened for questions from you, our listening audience. While discussion is proceeding, you may want to jot down questions as they occur to you so that you can remember them for the forum period (described later).

Body of the Discussion

I. "When does a human life begin?"

A. Father McClarety: _____

B. Ms. Mankewicz: _____

C. Professor Kasakrim: _____
and so on.

(All four issues are discussed, with the moderator summarizing; seeing that each panelist gets an opportunity to present a position on each issue, and question, support, or argue with the others; and moving the group to the next major question at a prearranged time.)

Conclusion

I. Let's see if we can summarize what we have learned about each other's positions. I'd like each of you to summarize in a minute or less your position and arguments. (Often the moderator does the summing up, with panelists being free to correct or supplement.)

II. I believe all of us in this room are now better prepared to cope with this vital issue. We now understand each other's positions as well as possible, and the values and beliefs supporting them.

III. Now I wonder what questions our listeners have for the panel? Please raise your hand if you want to ask a question, and wait for me to recognize you by pointing. I will give each person a chance to ask one question before allowing anyone to ask a second question. Your questions can be directed to a particular panel member to answer or to the entire group. If you want a particular panel member to answer, state that person's name. OK, what's our first question? The lady to my right wearing the maroon blazer—please state your question loudly enough for all present to hear. (Suggestions for conducting a successful forum discussion are provided later in this appendix.)

Symposium

Symposium

One of three kinds of group public discussions in which participants deliver uninterrupted speeches on a selected topic.

A **symposium** is more structured than a panel discussion. In place of a relatively free interchange of ideas, the topic is divided into segments, with each discussant presenting an uninterrupted speech on a portion of the topic. The purpose of a symposium is similar to that of panel: to enlighten an audience about an important subject. On September 11, 2001, after the attacks on the World Trade Center in New York City, Governor George Pataki, Mayor Rudolf Giuliani, and other New York dignitaries held a news conference in a symposium format to disseminate information to the public about the recent terrorist attacks. New York and the rest of the world needed information in a quick, controlled format. This symposium allowed each presenter to deliver information without interruption. Most symposiums and panels are usually followed by a forum, which allows the audience to question the symposium presenters or panelists and permits the discussants to answer these questions and comment on each other's presentations. After the press conference in New York City, reporters were allowed to ask questions of each presenter, who was given time to respond from his or her own area of expertise.

Typical procedures for a symposium involve three main steps. First, select a moderator to introduce the speakers and the topic and to offer a conclusion at the end of the symposium. Second, select a small group of experts to present different aspects of the issue. Because each individual presentation is uninterrupted, make sure there will not be much repetition among the speakers. Third, make appropriate physical arrangements as you would for a panel.

Forum Discussions

Sometimes when a group presents a report to a large gathering, members of the audience are permitted to ask questions or express opinions about the group's work. **Forum discussion** refers to this period of verbal interaction during which audience members interact in an organized way with the presenters. The term *forum* also refers to a discussion held by a large gathering of people, such as a university faculty meeting or a town meeting. Frequently a forum follows a panel or symposium presentation. Audience members should be told in advance that a forum will follow the public presentation so that they can think of questions or comments. Microphones often are set up at strategic places for audience members to use. Sometimes, audience members are asked to supply their questions or comments in written form to a moderator, who reads them aloud for the entire gathering, followed by responses from panelists or interviewees.

Forum Discussion

A large audience interacting orally, usually following some public presentation.

Strict procedural control is needed for a successful forum. The moderator should control the forum so that the discussion is interesting and fair to all participants. The following are guidelines to ensure fairness without letting the discussion bog down on one issue:

1. During the introduction to the panel or other program, announce that there will be a forum or question and answer period. This allows listeners to be thinking of questions and remarks.

2. State whether only questions or both questions and comments will be permitted.

3. Just before the audience participation segment, announce definite rules to assure equal opportunity for all to speak, such as:

   a. Raise your hand and wait to be recognized before speaking.

   b. No one may speak a second time until each person who wants the floor has had it once.

   c. Comments or questions should be addressed either to a specific panelist by name or to the entire panel.

   d. Remarks must be limited to not more than _____ seconds.

   e. Speak loudly enough to be heard by everyone or go to the floor microphone.

4. Tell the audience whether there will be a definite length of time for the forum and stick to the time.

5. If the audience is large, recognize people from various parts of the room in a systematic pattern.

6. Encourage different points of view by asking for them: "Does anyone want to present a *different* point of view from that we have just heard?"

7. If a question cannot be heard by all, restate it.

8. If a question is unclear or long, paraphrase it to the originator's satisfaction.

9. When the allotted time is nearly up, state that there is just enough time for one or two more questions or comments.

10. If no one seeks the floor, wait a few seconds, then go on to the next item on the agenda.

11. Following the last question or comment, offer a brief summary and thank everyone for their participation.

The Organizing Stage

The success of this stage depends on how well group members interact and listen to each other. If you lean too much on one person to take the lead, you could be headed for disaster if you expect him or her to plan and organize your entire presentation. In every stage, you should discuss preparation and logistics *as a group*. During the organizing state, you should focus on delegating duties, selecting appropriate verbal and visual materials, and organizing the presentation.

Delegate Duties

After assessing group member strengths and limitations, the group as a whole should be responsible for figuring out how each member's abilities fit the needs of the presentation. If you do not speak up during this critical time, you may be assigned to do something you are not prepared for or do not enjoy. Match subtopics of the presentation with member background and expertise. If you are organizing a presentation on campus parking problems, how might you select who speaks about what? For example, a math major can talk about funding issues and car-space ratios. A history major can provide a detailed history of the ongoing problem. A design major can prepare compelling visual aids, and a communication major might survey students and administrators for their feedback about your analysis.

Once you have decided speaker responsibilities, then you will need to discuss who will be responsible for obtaining verbal and visual aids. Who will set up the TV/VCR or laptop projector? Who will control the lights and sound? Who will make sure the speaking environment is set up in a way that matches the needs of your presentation's format? Who will be responsible for contacting outside speakers if they are required? Who will be your moderator and will this person have other duties? If follow-up is required, who will be the contact person in the group? Every duty needs to be listed, with a group member identified as responsible for the duty.

Gather Verbal and Visual Materials

Verbal Materials   Once duties are delegated, you are ready to work thoroughly on each area of discussion. If you have spent time researching and analyzing a problem, you now must select how much of that information to present. You should *not* simply read your report or material—that is insulting to the audience. You must organize the material into a clear, logical oral presentation. You must decide what information the audience needs to hear and how it is best presented. If you still have information gaps, you must figure out how to fill those. Listed below are common types of verbal supporting material often used during effective presentations.

- **Examples:** Examples can range from detailed factual ones (the story of a real victim of abuse complete with dialogue, names, and dates) to undeveloped factual examples (a list of the countries in the world with child labor laws) to hypothetical ones (how much the dollar would be worth in 10 years given a certain rate of inflation). You must decide the number and type of examples needed to make your case believable to your particular audience.

- **Statistics.** Statistics are numbers or quantification used to explain or support your claims. Audience members can be easily confused by statistics, so make your statistics clear and meaningful. It is hard to imagine how large a country is if the speaker only tells us that it is 200,000 square miles. More helpful is a comparison: about the size of California and Oregon combined.

- **Testimony.** Some people are recognized authorities on certain issues. To support your position, you may want to quote directly or paraphrase what these experts have said or written. Select the ones you believe will have the most impact on your audience. If your audience analysis has shown you that audience members believe in particular opinion leaders, make sure you incorporate quotes from these leaders in your presentation. You might also arrange to invite them as special guests.

  Three common types of testimony are lay, expert, and celebrity. Lay testimony comes from ordinary citizens. Expert testimony comes from someone recognized as an authority on an issue. Celebrity testimony comes from someone famous. If your presentation is on tips for a long-lasting marriage, you may use several different types of testimony. Maybe a group member's parents who have been married for 50 years will be willing to speak. Perhaps your campus has marriage and family communication experts who have written books with material you could use. Remember that celebrities are famous for all sorts of reasons. A quote from former President Clinton on his marriage could be tainted by his relationship with Monica Lewinsky.

Regardless of the number and kind of verbal materials that you choose, make sure they match the needs of the audience.

Visual Materials   What visual materials should you use to help clarify your verbal messages and facilitate audience interest? Visual aids help your audience remember your main points and must be used carefully (see Figure A.1). Lawyers are well aware that juries pay closer attention, understand technical

FIGURE A.1
Simple rules for
using visual aids

- Personally make sure that any equipment your group is using is in operating order before the presentation.
- Be prepared to give the presentation even if the audio and visual aids fail.
- Make sure the visual aid is large enough for all audience members to see.
- Make sure the visual aid is shown long enough to make your point.
- Practice using the visuals and know when you plan to use them.
- Do not pass anything out during your presentation. Materials are passed out before and after the presentation with specific instructions on how the audience is to use them.
- Do not get carried away with the bells and whistles of PowerPoint software. Keep it simple and do not let the slides do the presentation for you—they only complement your presentation.

points better, and remember more when oral testimony is coupled with a visual prop. The image of Johnnie Cochran slipping the leather glove onto the hand of O. J. Simpson while repeating, "If it doesn't fit, you must acquit" during his defense of O. J. Simpson is still talked about today. It was a powerful moment in the trial and probably influenced the jury's verdict. Imagine listening to your favorite TV show and not being able to see it. Visual imagery is important and your group has several options.

Objects: If what you are talking about is small enough, bring it with you. One of our students brought her two small dachshunds to demonstrate a typical veterinary exam. The dogs were well-behaved and effective visual aids. If what you are talking about is too large, bring in a model or a picture.

Model: A model of what you are talking about can show the audience precisely what you are referring to. For example, one student used a small model of a skeleton to illustrate how bones are related to one another.

Picture or video: A photograph, slide, or videotape can focus the audience's attention on your topic. Doppler radar images can effectively show air pollution over California's highway 99 by using time-delayed images that let the audience actually observe the pollution's movement. Slide shows, whether by projector or PowerPoint presentation, must be rehearsed to ensure they appear right side up in the order you want.

Map: Do not assume that just because your small group knows where a city is your audience also knows. Maps are quick references and can show comparative location. Make sure your audience can see them.

Transparency: Placing an outline of your presentation on a transparency or PowerPoint slide allows you to talk to the audience while showing the image. Keep your images simple; do not overload them with information, fancy fonts, or special effects. Reveal the information as needed. Use these only as cues for your presentation—do NOT read material off them because you will bore the audience.

Chart: Charts are useful for showing statistics. Your report may have all kinds of statistical evidence that needs to be summarized for the oral presentation. Charts provide a concise way to present this kind of information. When you show a chart, make sure that you also explain how to interpret the chart images. Different kinds of charts, such as pie or bar charts, can show comparisons.

Handout: Many visual aids can be placed on handouts. Often speakers give the audience a hard copy of slides in their PowerPoint presentation so that audience members can take notes during the presentation. Be careful, though—if you don't manage handouts well, the audience will focus on the handout instead of your presentation.

Chalkboards: These are still used in presentations, especially ones in classrooms without the technology for video and PowerPoint presentations. Use them to illustrate something that you are saying at the same time. Audiences should not have to wait while you place information on the board. Also remember that writing on a chalkboard turns you away from the audience, whereas transparencies and PowerPoint slides let you show the information while you still face the audience.

Multimedia: Many different kinds of computer presentation software are available, such as Microsoft PowerPoint and Adobe Persuasion. These can make your presentation polished and professional. You can present verbal and visual material in any number of ways. In addition, you can access the Internet and even show video clips. If you use this technology, make sure that your speaking environment has the materials you need (television monitor, computer-project table, or an LCD panel).

Organize Materials and Your Presentation

Your verbal and visual information can be a valuable asset as you organize and write your group's presentation. This task is like mapping out how you want the audience to follow your presentation. As with any road map, directions should be clear so that the audience understands how and why you are taking them through the chosen topic. Every speech in the panel or symposium should have an introduction, body, and conclusion (see Table A.2). If your presentation is based on a written group report, you can probably use the same organization used in the written report as a guide for your oral presentation.

Introduction   An introduction has three essential elements: an attention step, a need step, and a thesis statement. First, motivate your audience to listen. You can get their attention in any number of ways, including using humor,

TABLE A.2 Outline of options for an organized presentation

I. Introduction
   A. Attention Material
      1. Striking statement
      2. Striking quotation
      3. Real question
      4. Rhetorical question
      5. Humor
      6. Story
   B. Need Step
      1. Direct
      2. Indirect
   C. Preview
II. Body
   A. Chronological
   B. Spatial
   C. Cause-effect
   D. Problem-solution
   E. Topical
III. Conclusion
   A. Summary
   B. Appeal

asking questions, making a striking statement, offering a striking quotation, or telling a short story (see Figure A.2).

The second essential part of an introduction is the need step. Follow your attention step with a short statement that shows the audience why they need or can benefit from the information your group is about to give them. A direct statement shows them how the presentation is relevant to their lives and how they can benefit from listening. For example, if your topic is the outrageous prices in the campus bookstore, tell them how they can save money. An indirect need step implies that, because the topic is so significant, everyone should

FIGURE A.2 Ways to capture the audience's attention

Humor	Tell a tasteful, relevant joke to get the audience to laugh.
Ask a Question	"How many of you have been late to class because you could not find a place to park?"
Striking Statement	"I can guarantee you an A in this course and in every other course you take this semester."
Striking Quotation	I have heard it said that "A theory is a thing of beauty, until it gets run over by a fact."
Tell a story	People enjoy and can relate to stories about other people; such stories help capture an audience's attention.

know something about it: "What happens to social security will affect all of us no matter how young or old we are today."

The third element of a good introduction is the thesis statement and preview. Tell the audience what you specifically will be talking about. Like a road map, the thesis shows your audience where you are going, making it easier for them to follow your points. Use numbers (i.e., "first, second, third") so that they know how many points to expect.

Body   The main portion of your speech is the body, in which you actually discuss your main ideas. Present your ideas in an easily recognized pattern so that your audience hears the relationship among them. Use transition statements that help move your speech smoothly from point to point.

- **Problem-Solution:** This format follows the same kind of logic you used to analyze your group's problem. This kind of speech pattern is used most often when trying to persuade an audience to accept a recommendation. The problem is described, history discussed, and solution justified. You can also use this pattern to inform an audience about a problem that has already been solved.

- **Chronological:** This kind of pattern follows a time pattern. Talking about how something is made, explaining a historical event, or listing the steps to a process is best matched to this kind of pattern.

- **Spatial:** This kind of pattern best describes locations in space. Showing an audience the best ski areas in California could be done by using a map and moving north to south.

- **Cause and effect or effect to cause:** This kind of pattern is useful for explaining why something has occurred. For example, explaining how the Asian bird flu can move from bird to humans and then affect millions of people can be shown with this kind of pattern. You could also reverse the pattern by talking about effects first, then explaining their causes.

- **Topical:** A topical organization uses the inherent parts of the topic or its essential parts. The American system of government has three parts: executive, legislative, and judicial. You then discuss each component, in order.

No one organizational style is correct and styles may be combined. Be careful, though; use styles to clarify, not confuse. In addition, remember that your audience may not think the way you do. Selecting the most effective pattern is a matter of matching the characteristics of your topic with those of the audience.

Conclusion   If your purpose was to inform, summarize your main points if your purpose was to inform. What do you want the audience to remember? Your summary is similar to your introduction, but should be more concrete.

If your purpose was to persuade, this is your last chance to get the audience emotionally involved in your topic. Use this opportunity to reconnect with your audience, offer a challenge, or help them to see how things could change for better or worse if action is or is not taken.

The Presenting Stage

Surveys show that many Americans fear public speaking more than they fear spiders, snakes, and even death.[1] You may be enrolled in a group communication class because you were trying to avoid the "dreaded speech." However, as a group member, you may be faced with giving a public presentation. Many times in your professional career you may need to speak to a committee or larger audience, so it is wise to work through this fear now. We offer the following advice to help you do just that.

Check Your Language

Speakers often forget that writing the speech is only half the battle; the delivery is just as important. Trying to make your audience feel compelled to listen, participate, and take action requires an effective use of language. Speak to your audience in a conversational style, just as if you were giving the speech to good friends. Avoid a dry monotone or reading manner. Generally, speakers should strive for a style that is clear, vivid, and appropriate.

Clarity requires language that is concrete rather than vague and abstract. Note the difference between explaining that last night you saw Ed "coming down the street" and saying you saw Ed "staggering" or "crawling" or "stumbling" or "skipping down the street." Clarity also is found in the use of terms that the audience understands and in avoiding jargon.

Vivid language attracts attention. Using figurative language, repetition, and amplification will add vividness to your presentation and help your audience pay attention. Listen to Martin Luther King's "I Have a Dream" speech for effective use of repetition and figurative language.

Make sure your language choices are appropriate to the audience and the occasion. A formal classroom presentation probably should not be filled with expletives or street language unless they are being used to illustrate a point in your presentation.

Practice Aloud

There are four ways of delivering an oral presentation: manuscript, memorization, impromptu, and extemporaneous. Each has its own delivery style.

If you write out everything you want to say, word for word in a manuscript, you are less likely to leave something out when you present. Unfortunately, you can become too dependent on your manuscript and pay too little attention to the audience. You may not notice how your presentation resonates (or does not) with the audience. If you decide on a manuscript delivery, you must work with the material enough so that you can connect to the audience in a natural manner.

You can also memorize your presentation. This way you may not leave anything out and can maintain eye contact with the audience. However, you still must practice enough with the material so that you won't panic if you forget something. Also, you want your delivery to appear spontaneous and not robot-like. Remember that eye contact alone does not guarantee that you will come across as interested in your material. You have to be comfortable enough with what you want to say that your delivery sounds conversational.

If you deliver material off-the-cuff, then you are using an impromptu style. You speak from your knowledge and expertise with minimal notes or specific preparation. Forum discussions often involve impromptu responses from group members as they answer questions from the audience. In addition, panel presentations may also be impromptu because the panelists are responding to moderator questions and may or may not have notes. Panelists are there because of their expertise, which is the basis for their responses. However, impromptu deliveries can sound incoherent if the speaker meanders from point-to-point. Even though there is no specific preparation for impromptu speeches, you can review for the presentation. In addition, good impromptu speakers have experience with this kind of speaking.

One of the most common kinds of speeches is one delivered extemporaneously. This is the kind of speech your instructor probably has in mind for classroom presentations. Instead of writing out a manuscript, you make an outline of the points you want to cover and use as few notes as possible. From the outline's main points, you deliver a different presentation each time. Experienced speakers can engage in a conversation with the audience, be flexible enough to alter the presentation, and yet deliver an effective presentation.

Once you have selected the method of delivery, practice your speech out loud. Going over the speech only in your head takes less time than actually saying it out loud. You also need to hear what the speech sounds like—something said easily in your head may be a tongue twister when you try to say it out loud. A colleague of ours was rather embarrassed when he wanted to say "needy student" but instead said, "nudey student." After three attempts to say "needy," he was forced to say "impecunious." Practice with group members so that they get a feel for how every member speaks. This way they can give feedback and during the presentation help each other out.

Be a Good Listener

Public speaking events are not only about speaking—they are also about listening. Being respectful and engaged audience members when other presenters or groups are giving their presentations helps create a comfortable environment for everyone. Perhaps so many of us are fearful of speaking because we know how poorly we have acted when someone else was speaking!

Inviting Public Input Using a Buzz Group Session

Often, people who organize public presentations of a group's work decide to incorporate procedures that allow audience members to discuss what they have heard. A **buzz group session** allows a large audience to be divided into many small groups that discuss the same question or issue, thereby permitting all participants in the large group to become actively involved in the discussion. Sometimes a buzz group session is used to generate a list of questions for panelists or symposium speakers to address; at other times, the audience members are asked to respond to what they have already heard as part of a public presentation. A colleague of ours participated with 500 educational leaders in Kentucky who met to work out techniques for promoting a Minimum Foundation Program for public education in that state. Organizers hoped the large group would identify ways to get the support of taxpayers for approving a state-wide tax to help local schools based on need. This meant higher taxes and money flowing from richer to poorer districts. Several times, after audience members heard initial panel presentations, their work in buzz groups produced arguments in support of the program and inexpensive advertising and promotional techniques to be used. The buzz group procedure is as follows.

1. The chair presents a focused, concise target question to the entire audience. The following are examples of such questions:

   What techniques could be used to publicize the Minimum Foundation Program to citizens of each county or city?
   What new projects might our sorority undertake to help improve poor children's access to dental care?
   What are the arguments for (or against) charging different levels of tuition depending on a student's particular major?

2. The large audience is divided into groups of five or six. If they are in a large auditorium with fixed seating, they can count off by threes in each row, then alternate rows can turn to face each other for the discussion. Each group should be given a copy of the target question, which can also be posted on a blackboard at the front of the room.

3. A recorder is chosen based on seating (for example, "The person sitting in the forward left hand seat will be the recorder.")

4. The group is asked to write down as many answers to the target question as possible in a 5- or 10-minute period. The recorder writes down *all* the ideas presented.

5. Warn the groups when one minute remains. If audience members seem involved, feel free to allow an extra minute or two.

6. The group spends its last minute evaluating the list to decide whether any items should be eliminated and to rank-order the rest of the remaining ideas.

7. At this point, organizers may do any of several things, depending on group size and overall meeting goals.

   a. Ask each recorder to report orally from his or her seat, in round-robin fashion, one new item from the list. An overall secretary can record all items on a chart as they are being presented. This list can be given to a special subcommittee for processing or can be copied and distributed to the entire group.

   b. Each recorder can present the entire list orally to the speaker or panel.

   c. Collect the lists, edit them to eliminate duplication, tally the number of times a particular item was listed, and distribute the total list to the entire group at a later meeting or give it to a special subcommittee to handle.

This versatile technique has many variations. For example, groups may have more than 10 minutes and may even follow a brief outline provided by the event organizers.

Public Meetings

One aspect of preparing for group presentations is understanding the occasion for the presentation. Public meetings are pervasive in our society and involve all the kinds of group presentations that we have discussed thus far. They come with their own challenges, both to the officials who call these meetings and to the public who attend them. Let's take a look at these special occasions for group presentations.

Public meetings or hearings are designed to allow the public or citizens to be a part of public policy making.[2] Public agencies are typically responsible for calling and managing these meetings. They occur at the local, state, or federal level and involve three or more people called for several reasons: to discuss issues, evaluate options, provide and obtain information, create recommendations, review projects, and make decisions. They often have several different interested audiences, including citizen groups, planning committees, school boards, neighborhood associations, and zoning commissions. You have no doubt heard of such meetings. Perhaps your local city council has recently called a public meeting to discuss how citizens feel about new zoning laws or local school board decisions. For example, a local school board in California held public meetings to discuss whether it should end the tradition of using Indian tribe names to refer to school athletic teams. On another occasion, a city council held public meetings to discuss whether it should open city council meetings with a prayer.

These kinds of meetings are part of our American tradition of participatory government. They are intended to encourage the participation of local individuals in government decision making in an effort to share the authority with the public and facilitate face-to-face contact between local, state, and national officials and the public. But do they? Interestingly, not only is there little research on these public meetings, there is also a strong sense that they do not meet their ideal goal. The public often thinks that such meetings are held only because public agencies are legally obligated to hold them, but that such agencies are not interested in the public's opinions.

Public meetings are often conducted using the "DAD" model.[3] The agency in question makes its decision or creates policy (**decides**), advances a campaign to win support for the policy (**advocates**), and only then asks the citizens to comment and approve the policy (**defends**). The public is invited to a meeting, given a forum to comment for a short time limit, and then asked to support the decision that has already been made. No wonder many citizen groups think that these meetings are held only as a formality.

These kinds of meetings are held at every level every day and are an important part of political problem solving. They involve a large group meeting that must be conducted well to be considered satisfactory. In addition, at these meetings smaller groups are sometimes asked to conduct panels, forums, and symposiums. You can improve such public meetings if you know how to make them more effective public problem-solving events.

When agency officials are asked to describe the attributes of a successful public meeting, their responses mirror many of the principles that we outlined in the three stages to an effective public presentation.[4]

- **Planning the public meeting.** Good planning entails selecting the right time and place to encourage participation and providing ample publicity in advance. Since the meetings are open to the public, officials may not always know who will be there and why. Knowing much about the audience is essential. The meeting must have a clear purpose and format. Visual aids must be prepared and scheduled. Any outside agencies need to be contacted and scheduled. Rehearsals have to be held and potential questions must be prepared for.

- **During the meeting.** A strong facilitator must keep the meeting focused and ensure that all sides of the issues are heard. The meeting must be run tightly but with enough flexibility to adapt to any contingencies during the meeting (a change in topic, larger than anticipated audiences, organized protests). Dialogue with those attending is necessary and should be encouraged even after the meeting. Agency officials have to try to encourage a representative number of citizens to attend the meeting.

- **Post meeting.** It is essential to show the citizens how their comments were heard and incorporated into future decisions. Officials should demonstrate a continued interest in keeping in contact with the citizens (setting up future meetings, getting phone lists, etc.). Audience members must be thanked for attending.

Generally, agency officials report more satisfaction with public meetings than the public does. Why is that? Earlier we told you that these meetings often seem to be held because the agency has a legal obligation to hold them. In addition, the public gets the very real sense that a decision has already been made. It is no surprise that many citizens think their comments make no difference to the agency that called the meeting. In addition, audience members may not feel comfortable expressing their thoughts and feelings about the issue. They also may be there for multiple reasons.[5] Some come to see what their neighbors think about an issue and to offer support. Sometimes, just attending such a meeting may help the audience member feel that he or she has actually done something about an issue. Often, the issue is so controversial (e.g., police brutality and local crime) that going to such a meeting provides members of the public with information they desperately seek.

SHEDD is a model of public dialogue developed by communication scholars W. Barnett Pearce and Vernon Cronen to meet the public criticisms of public meetings.[6] This model uses a strong facilitator who helps members of the public to be heard and treats the public's comments as an important and an integral part of the total problem-solving process—it honors the public involvement in its own governance.

- **Getting Started.** Agency leaders commit to hearing all sides of the issue even if they do not want to. Trained facilitators actively listen and summarize participant comments so that divergent comments are validated.

- **Hearing all viewpoints.** The topic of the meeting should be compelling and of interest to a many different factions of the community. The agency leaders need to work to make sure that those constituencies are invited and encouraged to attend the meeting(s).

- **Enriching the conversation.** Neither free-for-alls at open microphones nor strictly controlled events contribute to open discussion. Trained facilitators encourage open dialogue and help participants achieve that end. They may adhere to rules that very much look like the common ground discussions that we detailed in Chapter 12.

- **Deliberating the options.** Agency leaders recognize and use the comments they heard at the public meeting. They do not commit to solutions prior to meetings. Public meeting comments are summarized and provided to decision makers so that more informed decisions can occur.

- **Deciding and moving forward.** A public whose opinions and insight are used by decision makers tends to be more committed to those decisions than a public whose members believe they have been ignored or dismissed.

Public meetings occur every day at all levels of government. As a future professional, you may attend one or more such meeting as an audience member or agency official. The skills you develop as a group member and your insight into group dynamics can help you organize and facilitate public presentations of all kinds. Poor meetings do not have to occur. Meetings can be some of the most rewarding experiences of our lives and an integral part of public policy.

NOTES

1. George Kennedy (trans.), Aristotle, *On Rhetoric* (New York: Oxford, 1991), p. 181.
2. Katherine A. McComas, "Theory and Practice of Public Meetings," *Communication Theory* 11 (February 2001): 36–55.
3. Randy K. Dillon and Gloria J. Galanes, "Public Dialogue: Communication Theory as Public Praxis," *The Journal of Public Affairs* Volume VI, Issue 1, 2002: 79–89.
4. McComas, "Theory and Practice of Public Meetings."
5. Katherine A. McComas, "Trivial Pursuits: Participant Views of Public Meetings," *Journal of Public Relations Research* 15 (2003): 91–115.
6. Dillon and Galanes, "Public Dialogue: Communication Theory as Public Praxis."

Glossary

A

Acceptance requirements: The degree to which the solution for a given problem must be accepted by the people it will affect.

Accommodation: The conflict management style, high in cooperativeness and low in assertiveness, in which one person appeases or gives in to the other.

Action-oriented listener: A listener who focuses on the task, remembers details, and prefers an organized presentation.

Active listening: Listening with the intent of understanding a speaker the way the speaker wishes to be understood and paraphrasing your understanding so that the speaker can confirm or correct the paraphrase.

Activity group: A group formed primarily for members to participate in an activity such as bridge, bowling, hunting, and so forth.

Activity orientation: The extent to which a culture emphasizes doing or being, taking charge or going with the flow.

***Ad hominem* attack:** An attack on a person rather than his or her argument, often involving name-calling; distracts a group from careful examination of an issue or argument.

Adaptive structuration: The version of structuration theory that examines how the structures of computer technology get used during group decision making.

Affective conflict: Conflict resulting from personality clashes, likes, dislikes, and competition for power.

Agenda: A list of items to be discussed at a group meeting.

Aggressiveness: Behavior designed to win or dominate that fails to respect the rights or beliefs of others.

Ambiguous: A characteristic of any word or statement that can reasonably be understood in more than one way.

Antecedent phase: The preliminary phase in group socialization in which individual member characteristics influence member readiness and ability to engage in effective group socialization.

Anticipatory phase: The phase in group socialization in which members form initial expectations about each other and the socialization process.

Area of freedom: The scope of authority and responsibility of a group, including limits on the group's authority.

Assembly effect: A type of group synergy or nonsummativity whereby the decision of group members collectively is superior to adding together (summing) the wisdom, knowledge, experience, and skills of the members individually.

Assertiveness: Behavior that manifests respect both for your own and others' rights as opposed to aggressiveness and nonassertiveness.

Assimilation phase: The phase in group socialization in which the member and the group have worked out a comfortable fit.

Attitude: A network of beliefs and values, not directly measurable, that a person holds toward an object, person, or concept; produces a tendency to react in specific ways toward the object, person, or concept.

Authoritarianism: Tendency to accept uncritically the information, ideas, and proposals of authority figures such as a high-status group member or leader; produces preference for strong leaders and subservience as a follower.

Autocratic leader: A leader who tries to dominate and control a group.

Avoidance: The passive conflict management style that ignores a conflict.

B

Backchannel: Nonverbal vocalizations such as mmhmm and uh-huh that are uttered while another is speaking; partly determined by one's culture; can indicate interest and active listening.

Behavior: Any observable action by a group member.

Behavioral function: The effect or function that a member's behavior has on the group as a whole.

Bona fide group perspective: The perspective that focuses on naturally occurring groups that, in contrast to artificially created groups, are interdependent with their environments and have stable, although permeable, and boundaries and borders.

Boomer generation: Individuals born from 1946 to 1964; key experiences include the Vietnam war, the civil rights movement, and Watergate.

Boundary spanner: A group member who monitors the group's environment to import and export information relevant to the group's success.

Brainstorming: A small group technique for stimulating creative thinking by temporarily suspending evaluation.

Brainwriting: Individual brainstorming producing a written list.

Builder generation: Individuals born before 1945; key experiences include the Great Depression and World War II.

Buzz group session: Method whereby attendees at a large group meeting can participate actively; the large meeting is divided into groups of about six persons each who discuss a target question for a specified time, then report their answers to the entire large assembly.

Bypassing: A misunderstanding that results from two people's not realizing they are referring to different things by the same words, or who have the same referent for different words.

C

Charge: The assignment or goal given to a group, usually by a parent organization or administrator of the parent organization.

Closed system: A system, such as a small group, with relatively impermeable boundaries, resulting in little interchange between the system and its environment.

Co-culture: A grouping that sees itself as distinct but is also part of a larger grouping.

Cognitive complexity: The personal trait that refers to the level of development of a group member's construct system for interpreting signals; cognitively complex individuals are able to synthesize more information and think in more abstract and organized terms than are cognitively simple individuals.

Cohesiveness: The degree of attraction members feel for the group; unity.

Collaborating group: A group whose members come from different organizations to form a temporary alliance for a specific purpose.

Collaboration: The assertive, cooperative conflict management style that assumes a solution can be found that fully meets the needs of all parties to a conflict; a problem-solving conflict management style.

Collectivist culture: A culture in which the needs and wishes of the group predominate over the needs of any one individual; the idea of an individual following a path separate from the group is inconceivable.

Committee: A small group of people given an assigned task or responsibility by a larger group (parent organization) or person with authority.

Ad hoc or special committee: A group that goes out of existence after its specific task has been completed.

Conference Committee: A group composed of representatives from two or more groups; members' responsibilities are to represent the interests of their constituents.

Standing Committee: A group given an area of responsibility that includes many tasks and continues indefinitely.

Common Ground dialogue: A process of constructively managing divisive conflict in which the participants are unlikely ever to agree, by focusing on the goals and values they can share and agree to.

Communication: A process in which signals produced by people are received, interpreted, and responded to by other people.

Communication apprehension (CA): Anxiety or fear of speaking in a variety of social situations; reticence; shyness.

Communication network: The interpersonal channels open for interaction; collectively, who talks to whom.

Communicative competencies: The communication-related skills and abilities of members that help groups achieve their goals.

Competition: The uncooperative, aggressive conflict management style in which one person attempts to dominate or force the outcome to his or her advantage.

Compromise: The conflict management style that assumes that each party must give up something to get something; a shared solution to a conflict situation.

Computer-mediated communication (CMC): Using computers to interact with others.

Concrete words: Low-level abstractions referring to specific objects, experiences, and relationships.

Conflict: The expressed struggle that occurs when interdependent parties (including group members) perceive incompatible goals or scarce resources and interference in achieving their goals.

Conformity: Following group norms and not deviating from them.

Conjunctive task: A type of group task in which each member possesses information relevant to the decision, but no one member alone has all the needed information, thus requiring a high level of coordination among members.

Consensus decision: A choice that all group members agree is the best one that they all can accept.

Consultant: A nonparticipant observer who works with a group to determine what it needs, then attempts to help by providing inputs, such as special techniques, procedures, and information.

Content analysis: An analysis of the content (topics, behaviors, specific words or ideas, fantasy themes, etc.) of a group's discussion.

Content-oriented listener: A listener who enjoys analyzing information, dissecting others' arguments; can be seen as overly critical.

Contingency approaches: The study of leadership that assumes the appropriate leadership style in a given situation depends on factors such as members' skills and knowledge, time available, the type of task, and so forth.

Control touches: Gentle, positive touching of another person in an effort to get that person's attention or request compliance.

Cooperative requirements: The degree to which members' efforts need to be coordinated for a group to complete its task successfully (see also Conjunctive task).

Criteria: Standards for judging among alternatives; may be absolute (must) or relative.

Critical thinking: The systematic examination of information and ideas on the basis of evidence and logic rather than intuition, hunch, or prejudgment.

Critique: Analysis and criticism of something, such as identification of strengths and weaknesses in a small group's process and interaction.

Cultural identity: The identification with and acceptance of a particular group's shared symbols, meanings, norms, and rules for conduct.

Culture: The patterns of values, beliefs, symbols, norms, procedures, and behaviors that have been historically transmitted to and are shared by a given group of persons.

D

Decision making: Choosing from among a set of alternatives.

Defensive listening: Thinking of how to defend some aspect of one's self-image while appearing to listen to what another is saying.

Democratic leader: An egalitarian leader who coordinates and facilitates discussion in a small group, encouraging participation of all members.

Designated leader: A person appointed or elected to a position as leader of a small group.

Deviate: A group member who differs in some important way, such as degree of participation, values, or opinions, from the rest of the group members; opinion or innovative deviates help groups examine alternatives more thoroughly by expressing opinions different from those held by the majority, thus forcing the group to take a closer look.

Dialect: A regional variation in the pronunciation, vocabulary, and/or grammar of a language.

Discussion (small group discussion): A small group of people communicating with each other to achieve some interdependent goal, such as increased understanding, coordination of activity, or solution to a shared problem.

Disjunctive task: A type of group task in which members work on parts of the group problem independently, with little or no coordination of effort through discussion needed.

Distributed leadership: The concept that group leadership is the responsibility of the group as a whole, not just the designated leader; assumes that all members can and should provide needed leadership services to the group.

Distributive approach: The approach to managing conflict that assumes there are fixed resources to distribute among parties to the conflict; thus, whatever someone wins, someone else loses.

Dogmatism: A tendency to hold rigidly to personal beliefs; closed-mindedness to evidence and reasoning contrary to one's beliefs.

E

Egalitarianism: Belief in the equality of all people, resulting in the preference for participation in problem solving by all group members rather than by just a few high-status members.

Electronic brainstorming (EBS): Brainstorming on computers linked to a large screen that display all responses, but no one know who contributed which items.

Emergent leader: Member of an initially leaderless group who, by virtue of information and communication competencies, rises from within the group to enact leadership functions and is viewed as the leader by all or most members.

Emoticon: Typographical symbols used in computer-mediated communication to convey emotions in regular text, such as the smiley face :-) .

Emotive words: Words that evoke specific emotions, connote more than they denote, and serve as triggers for recalling pleasant or unpleasant experiences.

Encounter phase: The phase in group socialization in which members' expectations meet with the actual behaviors and member and group goals become negotiated.

Environment: The context or setting in which a small group system exists; the larger systems of which a small group is a component.

Equifinality: The principle that different systems can reach the same outcome even if they have different starting places.

Ethics: The rules or standards that a person or group uses to determine whether conduct or behavior is right and appropriate.

Ethnocentrism: The belief that one's own culture is inherently superior to all others; tendency to view other cultures through the viewpoint of one's own culture.

Exit phase: The phase in group socialization in which the group disbands or a member leaves and the group must adapt.

F

Fact: A verifiable observed event; a descriptive statement that is true.

Fallacy: A reasoning error.

False dilemma: Either-or thinking that assumes, incorrectly, that only two choices or courses of action are possible.

Fantasy: A statement not pertaining to the here and now of the group that offers a creative and meaningful interpretation of events meeting a group's psychological or rhetorical need.

Fantasy chain: A series of statements by several or all group members in which a story is dramatized to help create a group's view of reality.

Fantasy theme: What the content of the dramatization of a fantasy or fantasy chain is about; the manifest theme is the overt, surface content, and the latent theme is the hidden, underlying meaning.

Faulty analogy: An incomplete comparison that stretches a similarity too far; assuming that because two things are similar in some respects, they are alike in others.

Feedback: A response to a system's output; it may come in the form of information or tangible resources and helps the system determine whether or not it needs to make adjustments in moving toward its goal.

Femininity (as applied to culture): The quality of cultures that value nurturing and caring for others.

Focus group: A special group procedure that encourages freewheeling discussion focusing on a specific topic or issue, often used to analyze people's interests and values for market research.

Formal Role: Refers to a specific position within the group that carries a set of expectations for fulfilling that position, such as a group's chair or secretary.

Formation phase: The stage in the development of a group during which relationship issues predominate as members work out their relationships with each other.

Forum discussion: A large audience interacting orally, usually following some public presentation.

Functional perspective: The approach to group problem solving that focuses on the necessary communicative functions group members must perform for the group to do an effective job of problem solving and decision making.

Functions approach: The study of functions performed by leaders; the theory that leadership is defined by the functions a group needs and can be supplied by any member.

G

Gatekeeper: Any member of a small group controlling who speaks during a discussion; any controller of the flow of messages among members.

Gender: Learned and culturally transmitted sex-role behavior of an individual.

Group: Three or more people with an interdependent goal who interact and influence each other.

Group charter: A written document that describes the purpose of the group, its specific charge, area of freedom, membership, deadlines, and required output.

Group climate: A group's emotional and relational atmosphere.

    Defensive climate: An atmosphere characterized by mistrust, in which members tear each other down.

    Supportive climate: An atmosphere of respect, in which members feel valued and appreciated.

Group culture: The pattern of values, beliefs, and norms shared by group members, developed through interaction and incorporating members' shared experiences in the group, patterns of interaction, and status relationships.

Group Decision Support Systems (GDSS) or group support systems (GSS): Computer-based software and hardware systems designed to help groups improve a variety of group outcomes, such as creativity, problem solving, and decision making.

Grouphate: The feeling of antipathy and hostility that many people have against working in a group, fostered by the many ineffective, time-wasting groups that exist.

Group polarization: The tendency for group members to make decisions that are more extreme (more risky or cautious) than they would make individually.

Group socialization: The process of learning to become part of a group, which involves reciprocal influence among members and between members and the group.

Groupthink: The tendency of some cohesive groups to fail to subject information, reasoning, and proposals to thorough critical analysis leading to faulty decisions.

H

Haptics: The study of the use of and perceptions of touch.

Hidden antagonizer: An unintentional trigger word, not intended to offend, that does in fact provoke an emotional reaction.

High-context communication: Communication wherein the primary meaning of a message is conveyed by features of the situation or context instead of the verbal, explicit part of the message.

High-level abstraction: A word, phrase, or statement commonly used to refer to a broad category of objects, relationships, or concepts; typically refers to intangibles such as love, democracy, etc.

I

Ideal Solution Format: A problem-solving format that takes individual perspectives into account by asking a group to focus on what the ideal solution would do.

Idiosyncrasy credit: Additional leeway in adhering to group norms, given to a member for valuable contributions to the group.

Individualistic culture: A culture in which the needs and wishes of the individual predominate over the needs of the group.

Inequity conflict: Conflict about perceived unequal workloads or contributions to the group effort.

Inference: A statement that includes more than a description of some event, thus going beyond fact; an inference involves some degree of uncertainty or probability and cannot be checked for accuracy by direct observation.

Informal role: Refers to a unique role that evolves through a member's behaviors and others' responses to those behaviors; reflects the traits, personality characteristics, habits and preferences of the member.

Input variables: The energy, information, and raw material used by an open system, which is transformed into output by throughput processes.

Integrative approach: The approach to managing conflict that assumes that solutions can be found to satisfy every party to the conflict.

Intercultural communication: Interaction between and among individuals from different cultures or subcultures.

Interdependence: The property of a system such that all parts are interrelated and affect each other as well as the whole system.

Interdependent goal: An objective shared by members of a small group in such a way that one member cannot achieve the goal without the other members also achieving it.

Intracultural communication: Interaction between and among individuals from the same culture or subculture.

Intrinsic interest: Extent to which the task itself is attractive and interesting to the participants.

Intuitive problem solvers: People who size up a situation, then arrive at a solution without consciously following any perceptible procedure.

K

Kinesics: Study of communication through movements.

L

Laissez-faire leader: A do-nothing designated leader who provides minimal services to the group.

Leader: A person who uses communication to influence others to meet group goals and needs; any person identified by members of a group as leader; a person designated as leader by election or appointment.

Leader as completer: A leader who determines which functions or behaviors are most needed for a group to perform optimally, then supplies them or encourages others to do so.

Leader-Member Exchange (LMX) model: The leadership model based on the finding that supervisors develop different kinds of leadership relationships with their subordinates, depending on characteristics of both the leader and members.

Leadership: Influence exerted through communication that helps a group achieve goals; performance of a leadership function by any member.

Leadership emergence: The process by which someone emerges as the leader of an initially leaderless group in which all members start out as equals.

Learning group (study group): A group conducting a learning discussion.

Least-sized group: The principle that the ideal group contains as few members as possible as long as all necessary perspectives and skills are represented.

Liaison: Communication between or among groups; interfacing; a person who performs the liaison function.

Listening: Receiving and interpreting oral and other signals from another person or source.

Low-context communication: Communication wherein the primary meaning of a message is carried by the verbal or explicit part of the message.

M

Maintenance functions: Relationship-oriented member behaviors that reduce tensions, increase solidarity, and facilitate teamwork.

Majority decision: Decision made by vote, with the winning alternative receiving more than half the members' votes.

Masculinity (as applied to culture): The quality of cultures that value assertiveness and dominance.

Meeting notice: A written message providing the time, place, purpose, and other information relevant to an upcoming meeting.

Message: Any action, sound, or word used in interactions.

Minutes: A written record of every relevant item dealt with during a group meeting, including a record of all decisions.

Moderator: A person who controls the flow of communication during a public presentation such as a panel or forum discussion.

Multifinality: The principle that systems starting out at the same place may reach different end points or outcomes.

Multiple causation: The principle that each change in a system is caused by numerous factors.

N

Net conference: A meeting that is electronically mediated by networked computers.

Net generation: Individual born from 1977 to 1997; the first truly "wired" generation, comfortable with technology in all forms.

Noise: Interference in the communication process; can occur at any step in the process, from the sender's original encoding of the message to the receiver's decoding of it.

Nominal Group Technique: A special procedure in which group members brainwrite to generate ideas, then interact to pool, clarify, and evaluate these ideas until a solution has been accepted by weighted voting.

Nonsummativity: The property of a system that the whole is not the sum of its parts, but may be greater or lesser than the sum.

Nonverbal behavior: Messages other than words to which listeners react.

Norm: An unstated informal rule, enforced by peer pressure, that governs the behavior of members of a small group.

O

Open system: A system with relatively permeable boundaries, producing a high degree of interchange between the system and its environment.

Output variables: Anything that is produced by the throughput processes of a system, such as a tangible product or a change in components of the system; in a small group, outputs are such things as reports, resolutions, changes in cohesiveness, and attitude changes in members.

Overgeneralizing: Assuming that because something is true about one or a few items, it is true of all or most items of the same type.

P

Panel discussion: A small group whose members interact informally and in impromptu manner for the benefit of a listening audience.

Paralanguage: Nonverbal characteristics of voice and utterance, such as pitch, rate, tone of voice, fluency, pauses, and variations in dialect.

Paraphrase: Restatement in one's own words of what one understood a speaker to mean.

Participant-observer: An active participant in a small group who is at the same time observing and evaluating its processes and procedures.

Passive-aggressive behavior: Behavior that outwardly seems helpful but actually sabotages a group's work.

Passiveness: Nonassertive behavior that allows one's own rights and beliefs to be ignored or dominated, often to avoid conflict, even at the expense of good decision making.

People-oriented listener: A listener who is sensitive to others, nonjudgmental, and concerned about how his/her behavior affects others; can become distracted from task by others' problems.

Personal growth group: A group of people who come together to develop personal insights, overcome personality problems, and grow personally through feedback and support of others.

Phasic progression: The movement of a group through fairly predictable phases or stages, each of which is characterized by specific kinds of statements.

Population familiarity: The degree to which members of a group are familiar with the nature of a problem and experienced in solving similar problems or performing similar tasks.

Postmeeting reaction (PMR) form: A form, completed after a discussion, on which group members evaluate the discussion, the group, and/or the leader; PMR responses are usually tabulated and reported back to the group.

Power: The potential to influence behavior of others, derived from such bases as the ability to reward and punish, expertise, legitimate title or position, and personal attraction or charisma.

Power distance: The degree to which a culture emphasizes status and power differences among members of the culture; in low power-distance cultures, status differences are minimized, but in high power-distance cultures, they are highly emphasized.

Preference for procedural order: A trait characterized by need or desire to follow a clear, linear structure during problem solving and decision making.

Premature replying: Responding before one fully understands the speaker's comment or question.

Primary group: A group whose main purpose is to meet members' needs for inclusion and affection.

Primary tension: Tension and discomfort in members that stems from interpersonal (i.e., primary) sources, including the social unease that occurs when members of a new group first meet or during competition for power among members.

Principled negotiation: A general strategy that enables parties in a conflict to express their needs openly and search for alternatives that will meet the needs of all parties without damaging the relationship among parties.

Problem: The difference between what actually happens and what should be happening; components include an existing but undesired state of affairs, a goal, and obstacles to achieving the goal.

Problem census: A technique in which members of a small group are polled for topics and problems that are then posted, ranked by voting, and used to create agendas for future meetings.

Problem question: A question calling the attention of a group to a problem without suggesting any particular type of solution in the question.

Problem solving: A multistage procedure for moving from some unsatisfactory state to a more satisfactory one, or developing a plan for doing so.

Problem-solving group: A group that discusses to devise a course of action to solve a problem.

Procedural conflict: Conflict resulting from disagreement about how to do something.

Procedural Model of Problem Solving (P-MOPS): A five-step general procedure, based on the scientific method, for structuring problem-solving discussions; P-MOPS is adaptable to any type of problem.

Production phase: The stage in the development of a group during which task concerns predominate after a group has reached some socioemotional maturity.

Program Evaluation and Review Technique (PERT): A procedure for planning the details to implement a complex solution that involves many people and resources.

Proxemics: The study of uses of space and territory between and among people.

Pseudolistening: Responding overtly as if listening attentively, but thinking about something other than what the speaker is saying.

Public interview: One or more interviewers asking questions of one or more respondents for the benefit of a listening audience.

Q

Quality circle (quality control circle): A group of employees meeting on company time to investigate work-related problems and to make recommendations for solving these problems.

Question of conjecture: A question that asks a group to speculate or make an educated guess about something.

Question of fact: A question that asks whether something is true or not, or actually happened or not.

Question of policy: A question that asks what course of action a group will take.

Question of value: A question that asks whether something is right, good, preferable or acceptable.

R

Referent: Whatever is denoted by a symbol or statement.

Regulator: Nonverbal signal used to control who speaks during a discussion.

Rhetorical sensitivity: Speaking and phrasing statements in such a way that the feelings and beliefs of the listener are considered; phrasing statements in order not to offend others or trigger emotional overreactions.

RISK technique: A small group procedure for communicating and dealing with all risks, fears, doubts, and worries that members have about a new policy or plan before it is implemented.

Role: A pattern of behavior displayed by and expected of a member of a small group; a composite of a group member's frequently performed behavioral functions.

Rule: A statement prescribing how members of a small group may, should, or must behave, which may be stated formally in writing, or informally as in the case of norms.

S

Search engine: Software that lets you search the Internet using key words.

Secondary group: A group whose major purpose is to complete a task, such as making a decision, solving a problem, writing a report, or providing recommendations to a parent organization.

Secondary tension: Tension and discomfort experienced by group members that stem from task-related (i.e., secondary) sources, including conflicts over values, points of view, or alternative solutions.

Secondary Tension: Work related tension found in the differences of opinion among members as they seek to accomplish their task.

Self-centered functions: Actions of a small group member, motivated by personal needs, that serve the individual at the expense of the group.

Self-managed work group: A small group of peers who determine within prescribed limits their own work schedules and procedures.

Self-monitoring: The extent to which someone pays attention to and controls his or her self-presentation in social situations; high self-monitors are able to assess how others perceive them and adapt their behavior to elicit a desired response.

Sex: Biologically determined femaleness or maleness.

Sidetracking: A poor listening habit whereby one group member spins off on a private reverie unrelated to what another group member has said, or whereby one group member moves the conversation in a direction completely different from what was being discussed.

Single Question format: A special procedure for structuring problem-solving discussions that facilitates critical thinking and systematic problem solving, but is more suitable for members low in preference for procedural order than more highly structured linear procedures.

Small group: A group of at least three, but few enough members for each to perceive all others as individuals, who meet face-to-face, share some identity or common purpose, and share standards for governing their activities as members.

Small group discussion: (see Discussion)

Social loafer: A person who makes a minimal contribution to the group and assumes the other members will take up the slack.

Social presence: The extent to which participants perceive that a communication medium is like face-to-face communication emotionally and socially.

Solution multiplicity: Extent to which there are many different possible alternatives for solving a particular problem.

Solution question: A question directed to a group in which the solution to a problem is suggested or implied.

Status: The position of a member in the hierarchy of power, influence, and prestige within a small group.

Ascribed status: Status due to characteristics external to the group, such as wealth, level of education, position, physical attractiveness, and so forth; status given on the basis of a member's input characteristics.

Earned status: Status earned by a member's valued contributions to the group, such as working hard for the group, providing needed expertise, being especially communicatively competent, and so forth; status that comes from performance during a group's throughput processes.

Structuration: The concept that a group creates and continuously re-creates itself through members' communicative behaviors; the group's communication both establishes and limits how the group develops.

Structure: Organization; arrangement of parts of a system; steps in a procedure.

Styles approach: The leadership approach that studies the interrelationship between leader style and member behaviors.

Substantive conflict: Conflict resulting from disagreements over ideas, information, reasoning, or evidence.

Symbol: An arbitrary, human-created signal used to represent something with which it has no inherent relationship; all words are symbols.

Symbolic convergence: The theory that humans create and share meaning through talk and storytelling, producing an overlapping (convergence) of private symbolic worlds of individuals during interaction.

SYMLOG: System for the Multiple-Level Observation of Groups, both a theory about member characteristics and effects on group interaction, and a methodology that produces a three-dimensional "snapshot" of a group at a given point in time.

Symposium: One of three kinds of group public discussions in which participants deliver uninterrupted speeches on a selected topic.

System: An entity made up of components patterned in interdependent relationship to each other, requiring constant adaptation among its parts to maintain organic wholeness and balance.

T

Task difficulty: Degree of problem complexity and effort required.

Task functions: Task-oriented member behaviors that contribute primarily to accomplishing the goals of a group.

Teambuilding: A set of planned activities designed to increase teamwork, cohesiveness, or other aspects of group performance.

Technical requirements: The degree to which the solution for a given problem is technically feasible or must meet standards of technical excellence.

Teleconference: A meeting of participants who communicate via mediated channels such as television, telephone, or computer rather than face-to-face.

Throughput variables: The actual functioning of a system, or how the system transforms inputs into outputs.

Time-oriented listener: A listener sensitive to time; may be impatient or try to move group prematurely to closure.

Top management teams: Teams composed of upper-level executives responsible for strategic planning and leading an organization.

Trait: Relatively enduring, consistent pattern of behavior or other observable characteristic.

Traits approach: The approach to leadership that assumes leaders have certain traits that distinguish them from followers or members of a group.

Transactional interactants: Mutually and simultaneously define both themselves and others during communication.

Transformational leadership: Leadership that empowers group members to exceed expectations by rhetorically creating an inspiring and motivating vision.

U

Uncertainty avoidance: The degree to which members of a culture avoid or embrace uncertainty and ambiguity; cultures high in uncertainty avoidance prefer clear rules for interaction, whereas cultures low in uncertainty avoidance are comfortable without guidelines.

V

Variable: An observable characteristic that can change in magnitude or quality from time to time.

Verbal interaction analysis: An analysis of who talks to whom and how often during a discussion.

Virtual team: A group in which the members' interactions take place primarily through some combination of electronic systems, such as computers, telephones, and videoconferences, instead of face-to-face.

W

Worldview: One's beliefs about the nature of life, the purpose of life, and one's relation to the cosmos.

X

X generation: Individuals born from 1965 to 1976; key experience includes divorce on a massive scale.

Author Index

Subject Index